STRATEGIES FOR writers

Teacher Edition 7

Senior Author

Rebecca Bowers Sipe, Ed.D.
Eastern Michigan University

Consulting Authors

Julie Coiro, Ph.D.
University of Rhode Island

Amy Humphreys, Ed.M., NBCT
Educational Consultant

Sara B. Kajder, Ph.D.
University of Pittsburgh

Mark Overmeyer, M.A.
Cherry Creek School District, Colorado

Senior Consultant

James Scott Miller, M.Ed.
National Writing Consultant

 Zaner-Bloser

Program Reviewers

Zaner-Bloser wishes to thank these educators who reviewed portions of this program and provided comments prior to publication.

ISBN 978-0-7367-7275-4

Credits
Photo credits: Cover and title page: © McPhoto/Blickwinkel/age fotostock; Z4: © iStockphoto.com/Sean Locke; Z7: © Jamie Grill/Iconica/Getty Images; Z8: author supplied; Z10: author supplied; Z12: author supplied; Z16: © George C. Anderson; Z18: author supplied; Z19: author supplied

Copyright © 2013 Zaner-Bloser, Inc.

Zaner-Bloser, Inc.
1-800-421-3018
www.zaner-bloser.com

Printed in the United States of America   12 13 14 15 16 19840 6 5 4 3 2

SUSTAINABLE FORESTRY INITIATIVE

Certified Chain of Custody
Promoting Sustainable Forestry
www.sfiprogram.org
SFICOC-0130

This SFI label applies to the text paper.

Z2

21st Century Writing Instruction for 21st Century Students

Strategies for Writers is a complete writing and grammar program that prepares all students to be confident, proficient, and effective 21st century writers, ready for college and/or career.

With this program's cutting-edge technology tools, students' digital literacy and engagement in writing increases.

CCSS
Meets 100% of the Common Core State Standards for Writing and Language

Ease of Use

- **Clear, concise lessons** simplify instruction to enhance students' writing skills and produce the results they need for success in college and career.

- *Strategies for Writers* **Online Writing Center** provides a comprehensive digital writing and grammar classroom experience, allowing students to complete and submit their assignments online.

- **Consistent, Common Core State Standards terminology** facilitates improved peer-to-peer, peer-group, and teacher-led conferences. **CCSS**

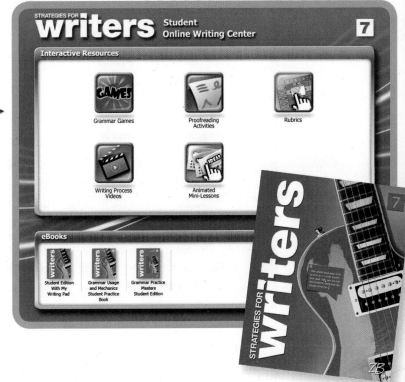

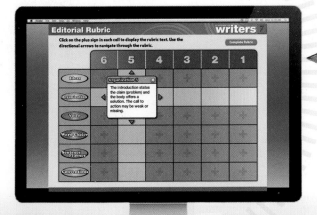

Genre-Specific and Interactive Rubrics

- **Genre-specific rubrics** give students a clear understanding of the expectations for each writing form as they deconstruct models and interactive anchor papers and as they write.

- **Online interactive rubrics** allow students to explore the point-by-point qualities of genre-specific characteristics for the six traits of writing on a four-, five-, or six-point scale.

Table of Contents

Introduction to Strategies for Writers

For a complete program Scope and Sequence, go to **www.sfw.z-b.com.**

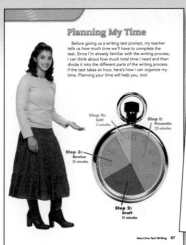

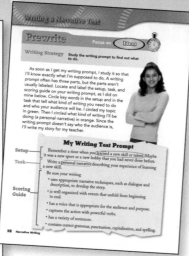

Test Preparation and Assessment

- **A dedicated test-writing chapter** in each unit improves students' confidence and performance on high-stakes writing tests.

- **Online interactive Grammar Assessments** include automatic scoring to provide immediate student feedback and formative assessment data for teachers.

Complete Grammar Instruction ▷ and Practice

- **100% coverage of the CCSS for Language** in the Student Edition ensures students learn the grammar skills they need for success in college and career.

- **Online games and interactive whiteboard activities** get students excited about grammar, usage, and mechanics.

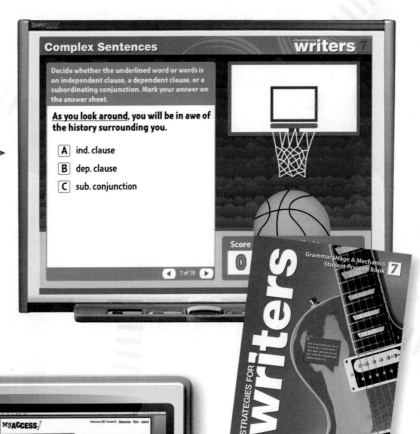

Online Essay Grader and Writing Tutor

Powered by Vantage Learning's MY Access!®, this tool gives students

- **immediate, ongoing, sentence-by-sentence feedback.**

- **helpful suggestions** to improve their draft.

- **a holistic score and a trait-specific score** on their final draft.

- **unlimited response submissions** to the prompts.

21st Century Writing Instruction for 21st Century Teachers

With *Strategies for Writers'* dynamic, versatile mix of print and digital resources, teachers can easily accommodate students' varying learning styles and abilities and customize writing instruction to be fully digital, completely print-based, or a blend of digital and print resources.

This program gives all teachers—from novice to expert—the tools they need to confidently deliver effective, rigorous instruction that meets 100% of the CCSS for Writing and Language.

Complete Online Writing Instruction

- **Online Writing Center** allows teachers to make differentiated assignments and review students' work digitally.
- **Student and Teacher Dashboards** house all of the program's technology tools in one easy-to-manage location.

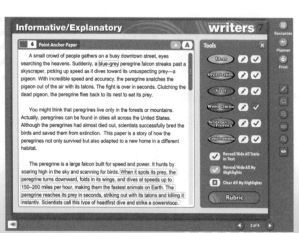

Flexible Instruction

- **Narrative, Informative/Explanatory, Opinion or Argument, and Descriptive Writing units** can be taught in any order to suit any teacher's needs.
- **Choice of four-, five-, and six-point rubrics** is integrated into all aspects of instruction.

Common Core State Standards **CCSS**

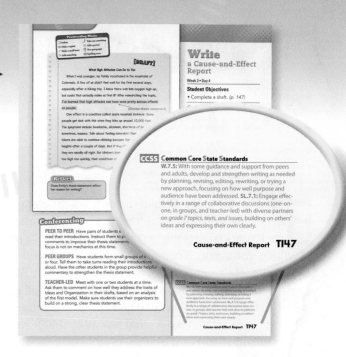

- ***Strategies for Writers* covers 100% of the CCSS for Writing and Language,** so teachers can be confident that their students are prepared to be effective writers in every mode: Narrative, Informative/Explanatory, and Opinion or Argument, and Descriptive.

- **Only *Strategies for Writers* references the CCSS at point-of-use** in the Teacher Edition (print and eBook) to make planning easier.

72 additional Writing Across the Curriculum prompts per grade!

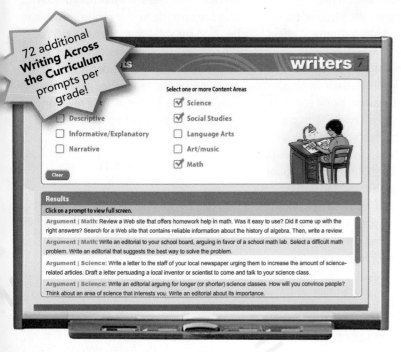

Differentiation and English Language Learner Support ▽

- **Enrichment and Reinforcement activities and tips for four levels of English Language Learners** allow teachers to meet the needs of each student.

- **The program's abundance of grammar, usage, and mechanics resources and activities** provide differentiated skill instruction and practice.

  ‣ Interactive whiteboard grammar games and proofreading activities
  ‣ Online grammar games and proofreading activities
  ‣ Grammar lessons embedded in the Student Edition
  ‣ Additional Grammar Practice in Appendix A of the Student Edition
  ‣ Grammar, Usage & Mechanics Student Practice Book
  ‣ Grammar Practice Masters

◁ Interactive Whiteboard Resources

- **Provide interactive presentation resources and activities** for whole- and small-group interactive whiteboard instruction:

  ‣ interactive anchor papers
  ‣ proofreading practice and grammar games
  ‣ writing process videos
  ‣ interactive graphic organizers and more
  ‣ cross-curricular writing prompts and more

Free Online Resources ▽

The *Strategies for Writers* Online free resources website includes

- customizable presentations.
- four-, five-, and six-point rubrics.
- graphic organizers.
- minilesson videos
- and more!

www.sfw.z-b.com

Foundational Research

by Rebecca Bowers Sipe, Ed.D.

Based on 30 years of solid research in writing development, *Strategies for Writers* reflects the best practices of writing instruction: It combines a writing process approach with a focus on strategy and skills development. Rubrics based on the six traits of writing give students guidance on each writing task as well as provide them with a concrete tool for self-assessment for all four modes of writing. *Strategies for Writers* balances a skills-based and process approach and contains the key elements of successful instruction identified by the national *Writing Next* report (Graham & Perin, 2007).

Strategies for Writers is based on best practices and the Common Core State Standards.

Process Writing and Writing Strategies

Since the 1970s, the process approach to writing has been used increasingly as the base instructional model in language arts (Pritchard & Honeycutt, 2006). With this approach, teachers identify and model the stages of writing (prewriting, drafting, editing, revising, proofreading, and publishing) and engage students in collaborative activities. The process approach is also embedded in the Common Core State Standards (CCSS) for English Language Arts (Common Core State Standards Initiative, 2010; see especially standards under "Production and Distribution of Writing").

Strategy instruction explicitly and systematically teaches the steps of the writing process and has a dramatic effect on writing quality (Graham & Perin, 2007). Strategy instruction seems to help all students improve their writing, regardless of their starting point (Graham, 2008). Key strategic behaviors within the writing process, for example, planning and revising, are important ingredients in writing development. Skilled writers plan and revise better than unskilled writers do, and planning and revising behavior predicts writing performance. Research has thus demonstrated conclusively that "teaching developing writers how to plan or revise has a strong and positive impact on their writing" (Graham & Harris, 2009, 61).

Rubrics and Assessment in Writing

Researchers find that the process approach to generating writing should be coupled with an additional focus on the product of writing to attain greater student improvement (Honeycutt & Pritchard, 2005). Rubrics based on the six traits of writing help students to identify their writing goals during the process as well as to assess their writing products. In addition, as some researchers suggest (NWREL, n.d.; De La Paz, 2009), rubrics can be turned into heuristics that help students prepare for standardized testing, in which they are most often asked to write on demand (Gregg, Coleman, Davis, & Chalk, 2007; Mayer, 2010).

Because it addresses each of the modes in each grade, at grade-appropriate levels of sophistication, *Strategies for Writers* also correlates to the CCSS focus on the range of text types and purposes in writing.

Mode-based lessons incorporate rubrics that are specific to that mode, which can be used for self-assessment as part of the revising process. Recent research suggests that giving students clear goals and expectations for a writing product helps improve their revision process and result in better writing (Butler & Britt, 2011).

Butler, J. A., & Britt, M. A. (2011). Investigating instruction for improving revision of argumentative essays. *Written Communication, 28* (1), 70–96.

Common Core State Standards Initiative. (2010). *Common core state standard for English language arts & literacy in history/social studies, science, and technical subjects.* Retrieved from www.corestandards.org.

De La Paz, S. (2009). Heuristics for developing writing strategies. *Assessment for Effective Intervention, 34*(3), 134–146.

Graham, S., & Perin, D. (2007). *Writing next: Effective strategies to improve writing of adolescents in middle and high schools—A report to Carnegie Corporation of New York.* Alliance for Excellent Education.

Graham, S. (2008). Strategy instruction and the teaching of writing. In C. A. MacArthur, S. Graham, J. Fitzgerald (Eds.), *Handbook of Writing Research.* Guilford, 187–207.

Graham, S., & Harris, K. R. (2009). Almost 30 years of writing research: Making sense of it all with *The Wrath of Khan. Learning Disabilities Research & Practice, 24* (2), 58–68.

Gregg, N., Coleman, C., Davis, M., & Chalk, J. C. (2007). Timed essay writing: Implications for high-stakes tests. *Journal of Learning Disabilities, 40,* 306–318.

Honeycutt, R. L., & Pritchard, R. J. (2005). Using a structured writing workshop to help good readers who are poor writers. In G. Rijlaarrsdan, H. van den Bergh, & M. Couzijin (Eds.), *Studies in Writing* (2nd ed., vol. 4). Kluwer, pp. 141–150.

Mayer, M. (2010). *Two roads diverged and I took both: Meaningful writing instruction in an age of testing.* AuthorHouse (self-published).

Northwest Regional Educational Laboratory. (n.d.) *About 6+1 trait writing.* Retrieved February 18, 2011, from http://educationnorthwest.org/resource/949.

Pritchard, R. J., & Honeycutt, R. L. (2006).The process approach to writing instruction: Examining its effectiveness. In C.A. MacArthur, S. Graham, J. Fitzgerald (Eds.), *Handbook of Writing Research.* Guilford, 275–290.

Please visit **www.sfw.z-b.com** for the complete research report and cited references.

Traits and the Writing Process

by Rebecca Bowers Sipe, Ed.D.

The six traits of writing and the writing process are essential elements of effective writing instruction. While they may be taught and understood separately, they should be viewed as parts of a coherent and complete instructional whole. The traits define and support the writing process, simplify instruction, and facilitate a clear understanding among students of what makes writing work. To demonstrate the relationship between traits and process, let's discuss and define each separately.

Steps of the Writing Process

The writing process is cyclical, recursive, and composed of five steps: **Prewriting, Drafting, Revising, Editing,** and **Publishing.** Instructionally, we must take care to recognize that these steps are not necessarily sequential. During the development of a composition, a proficient writer will certainly employ each of these steps, but the organic evolution of the writing itself will determine the sequence and manner in which the steps are negotiated. In teaching the steps of the writing process explicitly, we help students to understand how good writers go about crafting their work.

Writing Traits

If the writing process is the "how" of excellent writing, then the traits of writing represent the "what." The traits are the specific elements that writers focus upon in each step of the process. They are the six observable, assessable, revisable, and editable features that characterize all writing. The traits comprise a comprehensive way of looking at writing. This model also simplifies our understanding of writing because it allows us to focus our attention upon the

Writing Traits

Ideas represents the concepts, thoughts, insights, assertions, and details that the author wishes to express to the reader.

Organization relates to the effectiveness of the "blueprint" that the author uses to sequence and arrange ideas for the reader.

Voice is closely related to the tone established by the author and the affective mood that results from the way the writing is crafted. Voice also reflects the personality, attitude, and enthusiasm of the author.

Word Choice influences Voice. Excellent Word Choice results when a writer uses exactly the right words to carry the message. Typically, this means that nouns and verbs are clear and precise, carrying the author's message with support from a few carefully chosen modifiers.

Sentence Fluency may be described as the rhythm or flow of sentences that results from variations in length, structure, and beginnings.

Conventions includes grammar, usage, and mechanics. A talented writer may even control Conventions in creative or unique ways to convey or underscore meaning with extreme effectiveness.

individually manageable traits themselves: **Ideas, Organization, Voice, Word Choice, Sentence Fluency,** and **Conventions.**

Traits and Process

In the final analysis, traits and process may be taught and understood separately, but their true partnership and power comes from their interplay during authentic writing. For example, in **Prewriting,** a writer selects ideas and organizes them according to the needs of a specific audience; envisioning one's audience helps the writer establish a stronger voice. In **Drafting,** a writer supports ideas with good word choice, writing these words into sentences that flow, contributing to good sentence fluency. A writer may **Revise**

for ideas, organization, voice, word choice, or sentence fluency, then **Edit** for conventions. During **Publishing,** a writer might pay special attention to the conventions that make the work correct and neat.

Ultimately, the relationship between traits and process is clear: In every step of the writing process, a good writer skillfully and purposefully manages some combination of traits. *Strategies for Writers* fully incorporates the traits of writing within each step of the writing process. Students who use *Strategies for Writers* will learn, practice, and apply writing strategies that support this model in every step of every lesson.

Rubric-Based Instruction

by James Scott Miller, M.Ed.

What is good writing? More specifically, what qualities of writing cause readers to be entertained, persuaded, enlightened, or informed?

Excellent rubrics answer these questions by capturing the essence of a reader's expectations. Rubrics clearly articulate these expectations and provide a scale to measure the extent to which they are accomplished in a piece of writing. The best rubrics speak clearly from reader to writer, almost as if to say, "Here's exactly what I'm looking for in your writing." In fact, the words of a well-crafted and familiar rubric may almost sound to a writer like advice from a trusted friend.

Rubrics Drive Revision and Editing

Since authors write to a variety of audiences and for a variety of purposes, the most common rubrics are specific to either a writing mode (Narrative, Descriptive, Informative/Explanatory, Opinion or Argument), or to a writing genre (like a cause-and-effect essay or a book report). In either case, the greatest value of the instrument lies in its formative properties i.e., its ability to drive effective revision and editing within the writing process. Rubrics may also be used in a summative manner when the writing process is completed. When objective scores and defensible grades are required (as they are in most classrooms), excellent rubrics render scores that are trustworthy.

Effective Rubrics

To be effective, a rubric must have a sufficient number of levels (or "points") to be sensitive to incremental improvements in the writing. Six-point rubrics are perhaps the most common among

formative rubrics. Thoughtfully crafted four- and five-point rubrics may also be used effectively where fewer score points are desired. For very young writers in kindergarten and first grade, it may be appropriate to further reduce the number of levels to three.

Trait-Specific Rubrics

The usefulness of a rubric is based upon the characteristics of writing it seeks to assess. So what exactly should rubrics seek to measure? There are essentially six characteristics, or "traits", evident in all writing: Ideas, Organization, Voice, Word Choice, Sentence Fluency, and Conventions. Presentation is an outgrowth of the trait Conventions, but is often identified separately to emphasize the importance of neatness and appearance. Taken together, these traits constitute the observable, assessable, and revisable features of all writing, so they make an ideal foundation for the development of quality rubrics.

Benefits of Rubrics

The benefits of using trait-specific rubrics are many. To begin with, these rubrics provide a common writing language that helps define clear composition goals. This keeps us focused and honest, challenging our preconceived notions of proficiency and keeping us "balanced" in our analysis of writing. It's important to understand that the goal of rubrics is not to remove all subjectivity from assessment, but to hold us accountable to defensible criteria that reflect the overall quality of the written message (rather than more arbitrary criteria, such as length, ink color, or neatness).

Trait-specific rubrics also clarify, simplify, and accelerate scoring. Like

interchangeable lenses, these instruments allow teachers to assess any number of traits within a given composition. By scoring multiple traits, teachers are able to identify comparative strengths and weaknesses in students' writing and deliver targeted feedback and instruction. Through explicit instruction and consistent modeling of trait-based assessment, teachers accomplish perhaps the most important goal, which is to transfer assessment proficiency to the students themselves. While all six traits should be explicitly instructed and assessed repeatedly throughout the year, rarely is it necessary or recommended to assess all six at once. Over time, as teachers and students use a common set of trait-specific rubrics, a kind of automaticity develops, leading to faster assessment and more consistent and meaningful scores.

Rubrics Support Writers and Teachers

To summarize, quality, trait-specific rubrics help students and teachers to go far beyond simply evaluating the "correctness" (Conventions) of text. These indispensible tools enable writers to focus on the most impactful elements of composition as they prewrite, draft, revise, edit, and publish excellent writing. Trait-specific rubrics also support rapid, precise scoring, making formative and summative assessment easier and more meaningful. For these reasons and many more, *Strategies for Writers* incorporates exemplary trait-based, mode-and-genre-specific rubrics to support the development and assessment of student writing in every lesson.

Multifaceted Assessment

In order to help students progress, teachers must be able to gauge each student's progress. And in order to improve, each student must understand his or her unique strengths and challenges. Without assessment, there can be no progress. That is why *Strategies for Writers* provides a variety of ways to measure progress and guide instruction.

Rubrics Guide Self-Assessment

In *Strategies for Writers,* assessment begins with the rubric.

Each chapter in *Strategies for Writers* presents a genre-specific six-point rubric. This rubric—based on the writing traits of Ideas, Organization, Voice, Word Choice, Sentence Fluency, and Conventions—guides instruction throughout the chapter. That guidance begins as the Student Writing Partner walks the student through using the rubric to assess a successful piece of writing. In this way, the Student Writing Partner models how to assess good writing as he or she explains what good writing looks like in this particular genre.

Throughout each chapter, the genre-specific rubric guides instruction as the Student Writing Partner uses the rubric to model how to create writing that excels in each of the six traits. At the same time, the Student Writing Partner is modeling good self-assessment.

At the end of the chapter, the student is invited to use the genre-specific rubric to assess the Student Writing Partner's final product as well as the student's own writing.

Rubrics to Match a Variety of Needs

The genre-specific rubric in each chapter provides six levels of accomplishment in each trait. A six-point rubric is utilized in many states and allows for more focused assessment in each area.

In addition to the rubrics focused on specific genres, more global rubrics are provided in the back of each Student and Teacher Edition. Based on a single writing mode (i.e., Narrative, Informative/Expository, Opinion or Argument, and Descriptive), these rubrics can be used to assess any type of writing within the targeted mode. For additional flexibility, each mode-specific rubric is available in a four-, five-, or six-point version.

Writing to Take a Test

The real "test" of writing instruction takes place when students must complete writing on demand in test-taking situations. Writing in a testing situation places unique demands upon students, demands that they may not encounter when completing a writing assignment in class over a number of days or weeks. When they write on demand, students must not only be mindful of their writing. They must be mindful of:

- Understanding the writing prompt *(What am I being asked to write?)*

- The unique requirements of the writing prompt *(Am I writing what I am being asked to write?)*

- The limitations of time *(How much time should I spend drafting? How much time should I spend revising?)*

- Staying calm *(What will happen to me if I do poorly on this test?)*

In order to prepare students for these potentially stressful situations, *Strategies for Writers* includes four Test Writing chapters in each grade level (Grades 2 through 8). Each Test Writing chapter focuses on one writing mode (Narrative, Informative/Expository, Opinion or Argument, Descriptive) and provides instruction in how to succeed in a writing-on-demand situation. In addition, these chapters serve as a review of writing strategies that have been presented in previous chapters.

Digital Resources

Strategies for Writers also provides assessment vehicles through its digital resources. A variety of anchor papers are available for projection via an interactive white board, and an online essay grader for specific writing prompts is also available.

Differentiating Instruction
With Strategies for Writers Extensions Online

by Amy Humphreys, Ed.M., National Board Certified Teacher

Our Goal

Maximize student achievement. As classroom educators, our job is to teach in ways that fit learners, rather than forcing students to adjust to our instructional preferences. So how do we do that? It's called Differentiated Instruction (DI). Through DI we deliberately offer multiple avenues through which students can master essential skills and knowledge. This strategic way of planning for student success challenges both regular division and gifted learners. And it is exactly the kind of prescriptive instruction necessary to support at-risk learners under Response to Intervention (RTI).

The Basics of DI

In a differentiated classroom, the learning standards provide the foundation and the teacher, students, and their parents must share a clear understanding of those targets. Add to that

- a research-based curriculum,
- effective formative assessment practices that guide instructional decisions,
- flexible and strategic use of time, resources, and instructional groupings, and
- a commitment to growth for all learners,

and you have the essential ingredients for a differentiated learning environment that maximizes achievement.

Strategies for Writers Extensions Online

While many teachers recognize the value of DI, it is demanding to meet a wide range of learner needs on a daily basis. Help is here. Evidence-based understandings about writing and ways in which students learn best have been translated into each *Strategies for Writers* Extensions Online making them appropriate for varied readiness levels and learning profiles. Every activity uses a combination of visual, written, oral, and kinesthetic elements and deliberately leverages the power of collaboration and conversation so students learn to think like writers in fun and engaging ways. By strategically using the core lessons and extensions, you are providing consistently differentiated learning opportunities that encourage deeper understanding of essential writing skills among all the learners you teach. It is a perfect recipe for student success.

Using the Extensions

Each of the *Strategies for Writers* Extensions Online activities addresses multiple writing traits and can be revisited several different times throughout the year. In fact, you can even incorporate authentic writing, vocabulary, and skills you want to target with your students into many of the activities. That means you provide greater instructional precision for individual students and thereby achieve better results overall.

Although the directions for the Extensions are simple, it is important to briefly discuss them with students and to do some modeling to insure essential learning targets are clear, to maximize time-on-task, and to facilitate smooth transitions into and out of the activities.

Teaching tips are provided for each extension so you can easily adapt many of the games and activities for either whole or small group settings. Suggestions for providing additional support or challenge are also given regularly to insure you have other easy-to-implement ideas to extend your DI efforts and boost students' achievement.

And since we know you're busy, we've designed each Extension so it requires little or no advanced preparation other than copying and perhaps cutting apart task cards and placing items in zip bags for easy use and storage.

Ready, Set, Differentiate

Please take a few minutes to preview the different *Strategies for Writers* Extensions Online available as PDFs at **www.sfw.z-b.com**. By printing and keeping the Extension Overview Chart next to your plan book and Teacher Edition, you can see at a glance the games that correspond to the skills and concepts you are currently addressing. Use assessment results to determine the learning needs of your students, choose an appropriate extension, print, and play. With *Strategies for Writers* Extensions Online, the engaging differentiated learning options your students deserve are just a mouse click away.

Reinforcement and Enrichment

You'll find additional suggestions for differentiating instruction in the *Strategies for Writers* Teacher Edition. Every unit contains a number of Reinforcement activities to help students better understand the targeted skills and concepts, and Enrichment activities that provide additional challenges for your more proficient students.

Working With English Language Learners

Writing Process and ELLs

The process approach to writing instruction helps English Language Learners refine their reading and oral language skills as well as their writing skills, and enables them to explore a variety of forms and functions of academic or "school" language.

Activities for ELLs

Look for tips for English Language Learners throughout each unit of the *Strategies for Writers* Teacher Edition. These tips focus on writing vocabulary and include individual, partner, and whole-group activities that illustrate various writing concepts taught in the unit. Examples include using graphic organizers, using transition words, understanding fact and opinion, using varied sentence lengths, identifying more vivid words, and so on.

ELL Levels to Differentiate Instruction

Strategies for Writers provides suggestions to differentiate instruction based on four levels of English Language Learners. See the box at right for a description of the characteristics of each ELL level.

General Guidelines for Working with ELLs

When introducing a vocabulary word or writing concept, use the following routine as much as possible:

- Introduce the word or concept.
- Model pronunciation or demonstrate meaning.
- Have students repeat.
- Check students' understanding by asking questions, first to the group and then to each student.
- Have each student say the word or demonstrate the concept one more time.

Provide multiple opportunities for repetition as each word or concept is introduced.

If a student makes a mistake, do not ignore it, but do not criticize it. Model the correct pronunciation or wording, and have the student repeat it correctly.

Maximize time for practicing English, both spoken and written, by having students work in pairs in small groups. You might also provide opportunities for higher-level ELLs to work with lower-level ELLs in a "peer teaching" situation.

Levels of English Language Learners

ELL LEVEL	CHARACTERISTICS
Beginning ELLs	• Can draw, point, say *yes* and *no*, and use a few key words • May use only present tense • Will need frequent repetition, visual cues, and other assistance • May not ask for help and may remain silent as they wait for more clues to context and meaning
Intermediate ELLs	• Have a limited vocabulary, which they tend to overuse • Frequently misunderstand • Are beginning to produce simple sentences
Advanced ELLs	• Usually understand English • Are beginning to extend the language beyond the simple present tense and can speak and write some complex sentences • Make mistakes that are often repeated
Advanced High ELLs	• Are beginning to blend in with their English-speaking peers • Are synthesizing information with minimal support • Are growing their social and academic vocabulary, and it may now be comparable to that of their peers

Writer's Workshop

What Is a Writer's Workshop?

Writer's Workshop is a highly effective format for process writing instruction that incorporates authentic practices within a consistent structure. As students write within the Workshop model, they have an array of choices that may include (but are not limited to) topic, genre, ideas, organization, and tone. Students then move freely and at a comfortable pace through the writing process. Some students might move through the steps sequentially. Others might forge their own path, skipping or repeating steps in a unique progression. In the Writer's Workshop classroom, this is normal, natural, and encouraged.

In such an environment, it is common for one student to be prewriting while another is drafting (and yet another may be revising). The Writer's Workshop helps teachers oversee and support each student's writing process while also facilitating sharing and feedback in a variety of groups, such as peer-to-peer, peer-groups, and teacher-led conferences. How is this extraordinary combination of authenticity, flexibility, and oversight possible? The secret to Writer's Workshop lies in its unique structure and routines.

Common Elements of a Writer's Workshop

Time

The craft of writing takes time, so students should be allowed to work at predictable times and for predictable durations so that they can practice and internalize the steps of the writing process. A successful Writer's Workshop is far more process-oriented than product-oriented, so it is expected that students will take varying amounts of time to complete writing projects. When students can't complete an assignment by a deadline, they typically put their unfinished work into a folder to revisit and complete at a later time. Students who finish early may return to previously unfinished pieces from their writing folders, or they may choose to begin the writing process anew with a fresh topic. The Writer's Workshop provides ample time for all writers.

Space

Effective arrangement of space within the Workshop classroom is essential. Desks, chairs, and other furniture should be arranged for comfort, safety, and access to materials (paper, pencils, and writing folders). It's also important to plan for students' frequent movement around the classroom as they group for sharing and conferencing. In a Writer's Workshop, even wall-space is carefully planned, featuring a variety of student work samples, and helpful reference materials (like charts and signs featuring workshop routines, the writing process, the six traits, or writing strategies).

Mini-lessons and Focus Lessons

Mini-lessons are short (about 10 minutes) and focus upon a specific writing skill. In a typical mini-lesson, the teacher will:

- Activate students' prior knowledge

- Directly instruct a skill

- Model the skill

- Engage students in discussing or practicing the skill

- Connect the skill to other learned writing skills

Focus lessons are similar but are used to introduce larger, more complex topics. For example, a focus lesson may be used to introduce students to a new mode, genre, or trait of writing.

Models

As students learn to write, it is critical that they view, analyze, discuss, and emulate a variety of writing models. One type of modeling occurs as the teacher *becomes* a writer in full view of the class by composing and thinking aloud. This is perhaps the most important and indispensible form of modeling. Other kinds of models include mentor text—quality literature and student writing models—which may be used to teach how specific traits, genres, strategies, or steps of the writing process function in published text.

Choice

In a Writer's Workshop, teachers may gently guide students' choices, but topics are not "assigned." Depending upon the nature of the task and the mini-lessons provided, students may also choose how to manage a wide range of writing variables such as genre, main idea, supporting details, theme, organizational structure, and tone. Choice is encouraged and supported in the Writer's Workshop model.

Conferences

In a Writer's Workshop, students will confer frequently with a variety of readers. Conferencing supports the writer with authentic responses that may help shape and develop the composition. When writers conference, they learn to listen to the wants and needs of the reader—an important skill that leads to excellent ideation, precise word choice, and appropriate organization and voice. A few common types of conferences that take place during a Writer's Workshop include:

Teacher-led conferences typically occur during independent writing time. During this conference, the teacher meets individually with students for approximately two-to-three minutes each. One main goal of teacher-led conferences is to help students reflect upon their work and consider revisions to make the writing more effective.

Peer-group conferences take place throughout the writing process. While groups may vary in size, three-to-five students is considered ideal.

Peer-to-peer conferences may also occur throughout the writing process. During these conferences, students share their work with individual classmates and receive authentic feedback.

Whole-Group Sharing

While conferencing certainly incorporates an element of sharing, it is important to also provide an opportunity for writing to be celebrated. (Some teachers use an "Author's Chair" for whole-class sharing.) While it is perfectly acceptable for members of the student audience to comment and ask questions, the main purpose of this type of sharing is to validate and praise the author's accomplishments.

A Typical Schedule

A Writer's Workshop lesson unfolds in three parts:

Mini-lesson and Status of the Class (10–15 minutes)

Following the mini-lesson (described above), the teacher and students take a moment to note where students are in their individual writing processes and to determine what students will work on.

Independent Writing Time (30–40 minutes)

Students work independently. Teacher conferences also take place during this time.

Sharing (5–10 minutes)

Students participate in peer-to-peer or peer-group conferences. Whole-group sharing may also take place.

Strategies for Writers Supports Writer's Workshop

Time

Students can work at their own pace in *Strategies for Writers.* Student Writing Partners are introduced at the beginning of each unit and speak directly to your students in a friendly, first-person voice, guiding them through the steps of the writing process.

Space

***Strategies for Writers* digital resources and posters** include useful reference material to display in your Writer's Workshop classroom.

Mini-lessons and Focus Lessons

Each lesson features:

- **Explicit instruction** for all steps of the writing process and for each of the six traits

- **A clear, trait-specific writing goal** supported by a clearly explained writing strategy

- Trait-specific revising and editing strategies for **targeted mini-lessons**, including multiple mini-lessons for conventions

Models

Accessible student writing models are provided and annotated for genre-specific composition strategies. Each lesson rubric helps student identify the trait-specific strengths in the writing models. **Mentor text exemplars** for each mode and genre are listed in the Teacher Edition.

Choice

Flexible lesson prompts allow students to choose their own topics. Authentic purposes for writing are established to increase student engagement with the writing task. "Apply" sections encourage students to use what they've learned as they continue to work on their own compositions.

Conferences

Students develop a common writing language for conferences as they work with the student-friendly rubrics before they start writing. "Reflect" sections provide questions that students can ask and answer during peer-to-peer and peer-group conferences. Suggestions for peer-to-peer, peer-group, and teacher-led conferences are included in the Teacher Edition.

Whole Group

A variety of **publishing and presentation suggestions** promote creative options for students to share their work with the class or other audiences.

Test Prep in a Writer's Workshop

In *Strategies for Writers*, even test preparation writing lessons support the Writer's Workshop model. Test writing lessons use the same workshop-supporting features described above. They also contain direct instruction to help students analyze writing prompts and scoring guides like the ones on high-stake assessments. **Each test-writing lesson contains full writing process instruction and results in an authentic composition.**

Mentor Texts

Strategies for Writers Senior Author Becky Sipe points out that students cannot produce good writing in the various modes and genres if they do not have the appropriate "mental models." A mental model is a good example of a finished product. Whether it's a personal narrative, a letter to the editor, or a report on a science experiment, students need examples to show them the way.

Strategies for Writers integrates these mental models in four ways.

Exemplar Texts

Each chapter begins with an exemplar text in the targeted mode. The chapter's Student Writing Partner expands upon that piece of writing by explaining in detail why this model is a good model. This explanation is based on the six traits of writing, so students have a clear understanding of how each trait should be represented in this writing genre.

Student Writing Partner's Text

After examining the exemplar text, the Student Writing Partner begins his or her own piece of writing. As the Student Writing Partner moves through the chapter, he or she provides a step-by-step model of what to do and what not to do to create successful writing in this genre. In addition to writing the text and referring to the six traits as exemplified in the chapter's genre-specific rubric, the Student Writing Partner thinks out loud about what he or she is doing. By example and explanation, the Student Writing Partner provides a road map for the student writer to create his or her own piece of writing.

Examples From Literature

The Teacher Edition provides a list of related texts from literature. These text exemplars, many recommended by the Common Core State Standards, can be shared with students to provide additional models of good writing in the targeted genre and examples of the use of specific traits in literature.

Writing Across the Curriculum

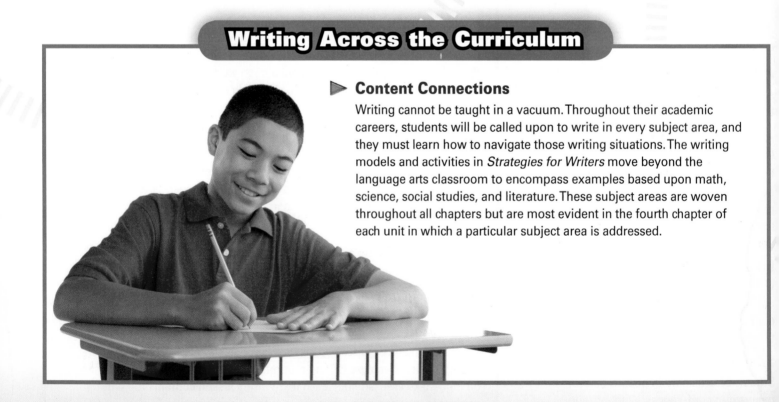

▷ **Content Connections**

Writing cannot be taught in a vacuum. Throughout their academic careers, students will be called upon to write in every subject area, and they must learn how to navigate those writing situations. The writing models and activities in *Strategies for Writers* move beyond the language arts classroom to encompass examples based upon math, science, social studies, and literature. These subject areas are woven throughout all chapters but are most evident in the fourth chapter of each unit in which a particular subject area is addressed.

Integrated Grammar Instruction
Relevant and Related Skills...Paired With Right Practice

Relevant Skills

Grammar instruction is not an end but a means to successful writing. Clear writing demands a keen understanding of important conventions.

Strategies for Writers includes instruction in key grammar, usage, and mechanics (GUM) skills as part of the editing instruction, tied to the Conventions trait, in every chapter. The Student Writing Partner ties the skill to a writing strategy statement and explains he or she used the skill in his or her writing. In addition, a clear explanation of the skill is provided in a Writer's Term box. The Student Writing Partner puts the skill immediately into practice, and an optional page of practice on that skill follows.

Related Skills

Targeting GUM in Conventions instruction is only one facet of grammar instruction in *Strategies for Writers*. Instruction and practice in an additional skill is also included in the body of each chapter. This skill relates to and expands upon the targeted skill. For example, in Grade 4, the targeted GUM skill in Writing a Play is commas in a series. The related skill is commas after introductory phrases. In Grade 7, for example, the targeted GUM skill in Writing a Personal Narrative is avoiding sentence fragments and run-on sentences. The related skill is coordinating conjunctions.

Additional practice in both the targeted and the related skill appears in the back of the Student Edition in Appendix A: Grammar Practice.

Grade 7
Student Edition pages shown

The Right Practice

Two additional resources build upon this foundation. The *Strategies for Writers Grammar, Usage, and Mechanics Student Practice Book* and the *Strategies for Writers Grammar Practice Masters* each provides additional practice pages in a variety of skills related to sentence structure, parts of speech, usage, grammar, and mechanics.

These resources combine to make instruction in grammar, usage, and mechanics skills relevant to the writing task while expanding students' overall knowledge of important writing conventions. Tied to the right practice, *Strategies for Writers* will put your students on the right grammar track!

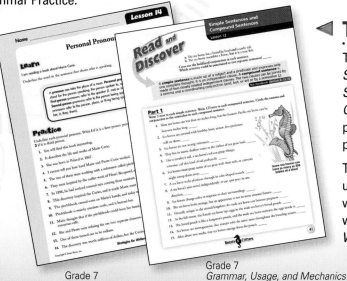

Grade 7
Grammar Practice Masters

Grade 7
Grammar, Usage, and Mechanics
Student Practice Book

21st Century Literacies
Technology, Digital Media, and Writing

by Julie Coiro, Ph.D., and Sara Kajder, Ph.D.

Teaching readers and writers situates us deeply in the texts that our students navigate, compose, and share with others. In addition to journal prompts, written drafts, and polished pieces of writing, the landscape of digital media expands our thinking about authentic writing to include practices such as creating digital stories, listening to podcasts, and interacting with screen casts of peer reviews. Surrounded by these rapidly evolving digital literacy practices, teaching writing requires us to know both how to write an effective thesis statement and how to publish students' work for an engaged, networked, even global audience.

New Technologies

While the writing technology of ink on paper remains, the reality is that the landscape of tools for writers has changed. The changes have come faster than we can possibly learn each tool, and the creation of new tools is changing moment to moment. As a result, writing teachers must sit alongside student writers and learn together.

In addition, teachers of 21st century writers need to be thoughtful. We need strategies for how to navigate what's new and how to best equip our writers to be flexible, purposeful, and effective. We also need to remember that we come to these moments for learning with a great deal of expertise in knowing what it means to be a writer. We aren't starting over. We're just thinking in newer, more open ways.

Digital Literacy Practices

This isn't about learning the "hottest" new technology tool (though you'll find several discussed throughout this Teacher Edition).

The goal is to think about the literacy practices that emerging tools, writing spaces, and digital media make possible, and then to consider how these sit comfortably within your current practices or demand new thinking.

A core document that has led our thinking as teachers navigating digital media right alongside you is the "NCTE Definition of 21st Century Literacies (2008)." (See **www.ncte.org/positions/statements/21stcentdefinition**.) We have tinkered with the framework, aligned the literacy practices it mentions with the genres in each chapter of *Strategies for Writers*, and anchored each section of the text with a "21st Century Literacy Practice."

Effective Technology Use

Each of these practices allows us to look across the range of tools available and make very specific, intentional selections in where we pay attention and why. The goal is to think less about the tool and more about what we want writers to do. Simply put, the practices live significantly beyond the shelf life of a tool, and they value and affirm the knowledge that each of us brings to this work as writing teachers (more than techies).

Technology Support for Teachers

To support your thinking about digital media and writing, you'll find two features in this Teacher Edition. First, each unit begins with a full page that provides core ideas about how to use a range of digital tools, websites, and instructional strategies to foster online inquiry about new topics or inspire creative writing ideas in a particular mode of writing. The second support appears in each chapter as specific teaching tips. Imagine that we're sitting next to you as you read and plan your classes. When opportunities appear, we will use this space to share an idea, a suggestion, or a little "nudge" meant to open your thinking (and teaching) to what we're calling "21st Century Literacies."

Mode/Genre	21st Century Literacy Practice
Narrative	Creating and responding to multimodal texts
Informative/Explanatory	Organizing, evaluating, analyzing, and using online information
Argument/Opinion	Engaging effectively with a connected audience
Descriptive	Designing and creating content for purposeful use

Common Core State Standards
for Writing and Language

by Mark Overmeyer, M.A.

A Unique Opportunity

The advent of the Common Core State Standards provides a unique opportunity for educators in America: the chance to work together to create a meaningful, world-class curriculum for our students. We have not had national standards before. Although organizations such as the National Council of Teachers of English and the International Reading Association have published guidelines for best practices when designing curriculum, this is the first time national standards have been proposed on a grade level basis.

When I first heard of the initiative, I will admit I was worried. At the time, I was volunteering to rewrite the Colorado State standards, and I was concerned that no national standards could truly represent the thinking that goes on in each state. I also worried about some of the unintended consequences of the standards movement itself: long lists of skills and sub-skills students must master at each grade level. The standards movement has encouraged some districts to develop checklists of skills that can be routinely marked as "finished" once they are taught. Without care, standards can create an assembly-line atmosphere in the classroom and the feeling that we need to just cover certain material rather than think deeply about student learning.

Strong, Meaningful Verbs

Upon examination, I have found that the Common Core can easily lead us beyond checklists in a meaningful direction, particularly when we examine the verbs in the Writing and Language Standards documents. In the Writing Standards,

students in grade K–12 are asked to *compose* opinion pieces, *defend* their reasoning, *research* topics, and *develop* narratives. In the Language Standards, students are asked to *apply* their knowledge of grammar and mechanics when they *speak* and *write*. These strong verbs create an image of students actually generating texts, researching ideas, and revising and editing for clarity. As a result, students will be thinking critically, writing, and reflecting instead of completing a series of worksheets to demonstrate they have "mastered" a particular standard.

Apply Knowledge

When we actually ask students to apply their knowledge of grammar and mechanics, we are finally following the research about grammar instruction. The standards do not ask students to "know and understand" the conventions of English, but instead to "form and use" correctly written and spoken English. This is an important distinction. The 2007 Carnegie Report *Writing Next* by Graham and Perin, a document that describes research-based writing practices, states: "Grammar instruction in the studies reviewed involved the explicit and systematic teaching of the parts of speech and structure of sentences... but surprisingly, the effect was negative. Teaching students to focus on *the function and application of grammar within the context of writing* (versus teaching grammar as an independent activity) *produced strong and positive effects on students' writing*" (emphasis added mine). The Common Core follows this research directly: Students write and apply their knowledge of grammar to improve their writing.

Becoming Writers and Teachers

The message in the Common Core is clear across all grade levels: Students must write to become better writers. Students must use and apply their knowledge of grammar to demonstrate their skill as writers and thinkers.

Of course even the Common Core State Standards, as strong as they are, appear in a list. All standards do. But because the Core Standards require students to compose and edit their own work, the standards can only be met by asking students to think and write authentically. Such standards cannot just be "covered," but can be met through meaningful practice, especially if teachers require students to write in increasingly more volume as they progress through grade levels.

Beyond Skills

As teachers, we have always known about the importance of practice. We know our students are apprentices on their writing journeys, but if standards are reductive and become a list of knowledge-level skills, it is easy to get lost in the mire of just covering by teaching skills. Because of its high standards, the Common Core will not create a reductive classroom environment, but rather a place where students think, draft, revise, and edit frequently. Because of this, we should welcome the Common Core. It provides much-needed guidance and expectation for all of us who care about the education of our students.

STANDARD	CORRELATION

WRITING Text Types and Purposes

Anchor Standard 1: Write arguments to support claims in an analysis of substantive topics or texts, using valid reasoning and relevant and sufficient evidence.

Standard 1: Write arguments to support claims with clear reasons and relevant evidence.

1a: Introduce claim(s), acknowledge alternate or opposing claims, and organize the reasons and evidence logically.	**Student Edition:** 266, 268, 269, 270, 271, 275, 276, 277, 288, 290, 291, 292, 296, 297, 298, 299, 312, 316, 317, 318, 323, 338, 340, 341, 342, 343, 347, 362, 364, 369, 370, 372, 373, 375 **Teacher Edition:** T266, T268, T269, T270, T271, T275, T276, T277, T288, T290, T291, T292, T296, T297, T298, T299, T312, T316, T317, T318, T323, T338, T340, T341, T342, T343, T347, T362, T364, T369, T370, T372, T373, T375 **Optional Revising Lessons:** Argument 23, 29 **Grammar, Usage, and Mechanics:** *Student Practice Book:* 97, 194, 217; *Teacher Edition:* T41, T67, T74
1b: Support claim(s) with logical reasoning and relevant evidence, using accurate, credible sources and demonstrating an understanding of the topic or text.	**Student Edition:** 266, 268, 269, 270, 271, 275, 276, 277, 288, 290, 291, 292, 293, 297, 298, 299, 312, 316, 317, 318, 323, 326, 338, 340, 341, 342, 343, 350, 362, 369, 370, 371, 372, 373, 375, 376 **Teacher Edition:** T266, T268, T269, T270, T271, T275, T276, T277, T288, T290, T291, T292, T293, T297, T298, T299, T312, T316, T317, T318, T323, T326, T338, T340, T341, T342, T343, T350, T362, T369, T370, T371, T372, T373, T375, T376 **Optional Revising Lessons:** Argument 21, 23, 29 **Grammar, Usage, and Mechanics:** *Student Practice Book:* 97, 194, 217; *Teacher Edition:* T41, T67, T74
1c: Use words, phrases, and clauses to create cohesion and clarify the relationships among claim(s), reasons, and evidence.	**Student Edition:** 266, 268, 269, 270, 271, 272, 278, 280, 288, 289, 290, 291, 294, 301, 312, 316, 317, 320, 327, 338, 340, 341, 344, 348, 362, 364, 365, 369, 373, 378 **Teacher Edition:** T266, T267, T268, T269, T270, T271, T272, T278, T280, T288, T289, T290, T291, T294, T301, T312, T313, T316, T317, T320, T327, T338, T339, T340, T341, T344, T348, T362, T364, T365, T369, T373, T378 **Optional Revising Lessons:** Argument 22, 24, 25, 28, 30 **Grammar, Usage, and Mechanics:** *Student Practice Book:* 97, 194, 217; *Teacher Edition:* T41, T67, T74
1d: Establish and maintain a formal style.	**Student Edition:** 266, 268, 269, 271, 279, 288, 290, 291, 293, 300, 312, 316, 317, 319, 324, 338, 340, 341, 343, 362, 365, 369, 373, 377 **Teacher Edition:** T266, T268, T269, T271, T279, T288, T290, T291, T293, T300, T312, T316, T317, T319, T324, T338, T340, T341, T343, T362, T365, T369, T373, T377 **Optional Revising Lessons:** Argument 26, 27, 30 **Grammar, Usage, and Mechanics:** *Student Practice Book:* 97
1e: Provide a concluding statement or section that follows from and supports the argument presented.	**Student Edition:** 266, 268, 269, 288, 290, 291, 312, 316, 317, 319, 338, 340, 341, 343, 347, 351, 362, 364, 369, 373 **Teacher Edition:** T266, T268, T269, T288, T290, T291, T312, T316, T317, T319, T338, T340, T341, T343, T347, T351, T362, T364, T369, T373 **Optional Revising Lessons:** Argument 25 **Grammar, Usage, and Mechanics:** *Student Practice Book:* 97

Anchor Standard 2: Write informative/explanatory texts to examine and convey complex ideas and information clearly and accurately through the effective selection, organization, and analysis of content.

Standard 2: Write informative/explanatory texts to examine a topic and convey ideas, concepts, and information through the selection, organization, and analysis of relevant content.

2a: Introduce a topic clearly, previewing what is to follow; organize ideas, concepts, and information, using strategies such as definition, classification, comparison/contrast, and cause/effect; include formatting (e.g., headings), graphics (e.g., charts, tables), and multimedia when useful to aiding comprehension.	**Student Edition:** 134, 136, 138, 139, 140, 145, 146, 147, 148, 156, 158, 162, 163, 164, 165, 170, 171, 188, 190, 194, 195, 196, 197, 203, 214, 216, 220, 221, 222, 223, 227, 242, 244, 249, 251, 252, 253, 254, 255, 408, 410, 411, 417, 430, 432, 433, 435, 441, 482, 489, 490 **Teacher Edition:** T134, T136, T138, T139, T140, T145, T146, T147, T148, T156, T158, T162, T163, T164, T165, T170, T171, T188, T190, T194, T195, T196, T197, T203, T214, T216, T220, T221, T222, T223, T227, T242, T244, T249, T251, T252, T253, T254, T255, T408, T410, T411, T417, T430, T432, T433, T435, T441, T482, T489, T490 **Optional Revising Lessons:** Informative/Explanatory 14, 17, 18, 20; Descriptive 33, 34, 35, 36 **Grammar, Usage, and Mechanics:** *Student Practice Book:* 20, 31, 32, 37, 38, 67, 92, 98, 106, 121, 122, 127, 136, 151, 152, 181, 182, 208, 216, 324; *Teacher Edition:* T21, T24, T25, T33, T40, T44, T48, T49, T52, T56, T64, T71, T74
2b: Develop the topic with relevant facts, definitions, concrete details, quotations, or other information and examples.	**Student Edition:** 134, 136, 138, 139, 140, 145, 148, 156, 158, 162, 163, 164, 165, 170, 171, 176, 178, 188, 190, 194, 195, 196, 197, 202, 203, 206, 214, 216, 220, 221, 222, 223, 227, 230, 242, 244, 249, 251, 252, 253, 408, 410, 411, 412, 430, 432, 433, 434, 446, 480, 482, 492, 493 **Teacher Edition:** T134, T136, T138, T139, T140, T145, T146, T148, T156, T158, T162, T163, T164, T165, T170, T171, T176, T178, T188, T190, T194, T195, T196, T197, T202, T203, T206, T214, T216, T220, T221, T222, T223, T227, T230, T242, T244, T249, T251, T252, T253, T408, T410, T411, T412, T430, T432, T433, T434, T446, T480, T482, T492, T493 **Optional Revising Lessons:** Informative/Explanatory 11, 12, 13, 14, 15, 19, 20; Descriptive 31, 32, 39 **Grammar, Usage, and Mechanics:** *Student Practice Book:* 20, 31, 32, 37, 38, 67, 92, 98, 106, 121, 122, 127, 136, 151, 152, 181, 182, 208, 216, 324; *Teacher Edition:* T21, T24, T25, T33, T40, T44, T48, T49, T52, T56, T64, T71, T74

STANDARD	CORRELATION
2c: Use appropriate transitions to create cohesion and clarify the relationships among ideas and concepts.	**Student Edition:** 134, 136, 138, 139, 142, 158, 190, 216, 220, 221, 223, 231, 242, 249, 256, 245, 408, 410, 411, 413, 418, 419, 430, 480, 494 **Teacher Edition:** T134, T136, T138, T139, T142, T158, T190, T216, T220, T221, T223, T231, T242, T249, T256, T245, T408, T410, T411, T413, T418, T419, T430, T480, T494 **Optional Revising Lessons:** Informative/Explanatory 12, 14, 19; Descriptive 34, 35 **Grammar, Usage, and Mechanics:** *Student Practice Book:* 31, 32, 121, 122; *Teacher Edition:* T24, T28
2d: Use precise language and domain-specific vocabulary to inform about or explain the topic.	**Student Edition:** 136, 138, 139, 142, 150, 158, 162, 163, 166, 190, 194, 195, 198, 207, 216, 220, 221, 224, 228, 229, 241, 245, 249, 258, 408, 410, 411, 414, 417, 421, 430, 432, 433, 436, 480, 482, 483, 489, 496 **Teacher Edition:** T136, T137, T138, T139, T142, T150, T158, T162, T163, T166, T190, T191, T194, T195, T198, T207, T216, T217, T220, T221, T224, T228, T229, T241, T245, T249, T258, T408, T409, T410, T411, T414, T417, T421, T430, T431, T432, T433, T436, T480, T482, T483, T489, T496 **Optional Revising Lessons:** Informative/Explanatory 11, 12, 13, 16, 18, 19, 20; Descriptive 34 **Grammar, Usage, and Mechanics:** *Student Practice Book:* 20, 37, 67, 92, 98, 106, 121, 122, 181, 182, 208, 216, 324 *Teacher Edition:* T21, T25, T33, T40, T44, T48, T64, T71, T74
2e: Establish and maintain a formal style.	**Student Edition:** 136, 138, 139, 141, 149, 158, 188, 190, 194, 195, 197, 204, 205, 214, 216, 220, 221, 223, 242, 249, 257, 410, 411, 413, 420, 430, 432, 433, 443, 444, 445, 482, 495 **Teacher Edition:** T136, T138, T139, T141, T149, T158, T167, T188, T190, T194, T195, T197, T204, T205, T214, T216, T220, T221, T223, T242, T249, T257, T410, T411, T413, T420, T430, T432, T433, T443, T444, T445, T482, T495 **Optional Revising Lessons:** Informative/Explanatory 16, 17, 18, 19, 20; Descriptive 36 **Grammar, Usage, and Mechanics:** *Student Practice Book:* 31, 32, 92, 98, 121, 122, 151, 152, 181, 182, 208, 216, 324 *Teacher Edition:* T24, T40, T48, T56, T64, T71, T74
2f: Provide a concluding statement or section that follows from and supports the information or explanation presented.	**Student Edition:** 136, 138, 139, 158, 162, 163, 165, 172, 190, 214, 216, 220, 221, 223, 242, 432, 433, 435 **Teacher Edition:** T136, T138, T139, T158, T162, T163, T165, T172, T190, T214, T216, T220, T221, T223, T242, T432, T433, T435 **Grammar, Usage, and Mechanics:** *Student Practice Book:* 20, 31, 32, 37, 67, 92, 121, 122, 151, 152, 181, 182, 208, 216, 324 *Teacher Edition:* T20, T24, T25, T33, T40, T48, T56, T64, T71, T74

Anchor Standard 3: Write narratives to develop real or imagined experiences or events using effective technique, well-chosen details, and well-structured event sequences.

Standard 3: Write narratives to develop real or imagined experiences or events using effective technique, relevant descriptive details, and well-structured event sequences.

STANDARD	CORRELATION
3a: Engage and orient the reader by establishing a context and point of view and introducing a narrator and/or characters; organize an event sequence that unfolds naturally and logically.	**Student Edition:** 6, 10, 11, 12, 13, 17, 18, 21, 34, 35, 36, 40, 41, 42, 43, 52, 54, 58, 59, 60, 64, 65, 66, 67, 68, 69, 70, 82, 84, 88, 89, 90, 91, 94, 95, 96, 98, 99, 114, 120, 121, 122, 123, 127, 386, 388, 389, 391, 394, 395, 398, 458, 460, 461, 463, 467 **Teacher Edition:** T6, T10, T11, T12, T13, T17, T18, T21, T34, T35, T36, T40, T41, T42, T43, T52, T54, T58, T59, T60, T64, T65, T66, T67, T68, T69, T70, T82, T84, T88, T89, T90, T91, T94, T95, T96, T98, T99, T114, T120, T121, T122, T123, T127, T386, T388, T389, T391, T394, T395, T398, T458, T460, T461, T463, T467 **Optional Revising Lessons:** Narrative 6; Descriptive 37, 38 **Grammar, Usage, and Mechanics:** *Student Practice Book:* 10, 26, 40, 62, 78, 116, 132, 187, 211, 212, 324 *Teacher Edition:* T22, T26, T32, T36, T41, T46, T51, T65, T73
3b: Use narrative techniques, such as dialogue, pacing, and description, to develop experiences, events, and/or characters.	**Student Edition:** 4, 6, 10, 11, 17, 52, 54, 58, 59, 61, 68, 69, 70, 71, 84, 88, 89, 91, 95, 96, 98, 99, 100, 114, 115, 120, 121, 124, 125, 386, 388, 389, 391, 395, 399, 458, 460, 461, 462, 470 **Teacher Edition:** T4, T6, T10, T11, T17, T52, T54, T58, T59, T61, T68, T69, T70, T71, T84, T88, T89, T91, T95, T96, T98, T99, T100, T114, T115, T120, T121, T124, T125, T386, T388, T389, T391, T395, T399, T458, T460, T461, T462, T470 **Optional Revising Lessons:** Narrative 6, 7, 9, 10 **Grammar, Usage, and Mechanics:** *Student Practice Book:* 10, 26, 40, 62, 78, 116, 132, 187, 211, 212, 306, 324 *Teacher Edition:* T22, T26, T32, T36, T41, T46, T51, T65, T73
3c: Use a variety of transition words, phrases, and clauses to convey sequence and signal shifts from one time frame or setting to another.	**Student Edition:** 4, 6, 20, 32, 34, 35, 37, 42, 43, 52, 54, 58, 59, 61, 66, 126, 386, 388, 389, 458, 471 **Teacher Edition:** T4, T6, T20, T32, T34, T35, T37, T42, T43, T52, T54, T58, T59, T61, T66, T126, T386, T388, T389, T458, T471 **Optional Revising Lessons:** Narrative 4, 5; Descriptive 38 **Grammar, Usage, and Mechanics:** *Student Practice Book:* 116; *Teacher Edition:* T46
3d: Use precise words and phrases, relevant descriptive details, and sensory language to capture the action and convey experiences and events.	**Student Edition:** 4, 6, 10, 12, 18, 22, 32, 34, 35, 38, 45, 52, 54, 58, 59, 62, 73, 84, 88, 89, 92, 96, 97, 115, 123, 124, 125, 128, 386, 388, 389, 392, 396, 397, 400, 458, 460, 461, 464, 468, 469 **Teacher Edition:** T4, T6, T10, T12, T18, T22, T32, T33, T34, T35, T38, T39, T45, T52, T54, T55, T58, T59, T62, T73, T84, T85, T88, T89, T92, T96, T97, T115, T123, T124, T125, T128, T386, T387, T388, T389, T392, T393, T396, T397, T400, T458, T459, T460, T461, T464, T468, T469 **Optional Revising Lessons:** Narrative 1, 2, 3, 4, 5, 6, 7, 8, 9, 10; Descriptive 37, 38 **Grammar, Usage, and Mechanics:** *Student Practice Book:* 10, 26, 40, 62, 78, 116, 187, 211, 212, 324 *Teacher Edition:* T18, T22, T26, T32, T36, T41, T46, T65, T73
3e: Provide a conclusion that follows from and reflects on the narrated experiences or events.	**Student Edition:** 6, 54, 58, 59, 62, 66, 67, 84, 88, 89, 95, 99 **Teacher Edition:** T6, T54, T58, T59, T62, T66, T67, T84, T88, T89, T95, T99 **Optional Revising Lessons:** Informative/Explanatory 12, 14, 19; Descriptive 34, 35 **Grammar, Usage, and Mechanics:** *Student Practice Book:* 211, 212, 324; *Teacher Edition:* T51, T73

STANDARD	CORRELATION

WRITING Production and Distribution of Writing

Anchor Standard 4: Produce clear and coherent writing in which the development, organization, and style are appropriate to task, purpose, and audience.

Standard 4: Produce clear and coherent writing in which the development, organization, and style are appropriate to task, purpose, and audience.

Student Edition: 4, 5, 6, 17, 18, 19, 20, 21, 22, 23, 24, 25, 26, 27, 40, 41, 42, 43, 44, 45, 46, 47, 48, 49, 50, 64, 65, 66, 67, 68, 69, 70, 71, 72, 73, 74, 75, 76, 77, 78, 94, 95, 96, 97, 98, 99, 100, 101, 102, 103, 104, 118, 119, 120, 121, 122, 123, 124, 125, 126, 127, 128, 129, 144, 145, 146, 147, 148, 149, 150, 151, 152, 153, 154, 155, 168, 169, 170, 171, 172, 173, 174, 175, 176, 177, 178, 179, 180, 181, 182, 183, 184, 185, 186, 187, 200, 201, 202, 203, 204, 205, 206, 207, 208, 209, 210, 211, 212, 213, 226, 227, 228, 229, 230, 231, 232, 233, 234, 235, 236, 237, 238, 239, 248, 249, 250, 251, 252, 253, 254, 255, 256, 257, 258, 259, 274, 275, 276, 277, 278, 279, 280, 281, 282, 283, 284, 285, 296, 297, 298, 299, 300, 301, 302, 303, 304, 305, 306, 307, 308, 309, 322, 323, 324, 325, 326, 327, 328, 329, 330, 331, 332, 333, 334, 335, 346, 347, 348, 349, 350, 351, 352, 353, 354, 355, 356, 357, 358, 359, 368, 369, 370, 371, 372, 373, 374, 375, 376, 377, 378, 379, 380, 381, 394, 395, 396, 397, 398, 399, 400, 401, 402, 403, 404, 405, 416, 417, 418, 419, 420, 421, 422, 423, 424, 425, 426, 427, 438, 439, 440, 441, 442, 443, 444, 445, 446, 447, 448, 449, 450, 451, 452, 453, 454, 455, 466, 467, 468, 469, 470, 471, 472, 473, 474, 475, 476, 477, 486, 487, 488, 489, 490, 491, 492, 493, 494, 495, 496, 497, 498, 499

Teacher Edition: T4, T5, T6, T17, T18, T19, T20, T21, T22, T23, T24, T25, T26, T27, T40, T41, T42, T43, T44, T45, T46, T47, T48, T49, T50, T64, T65, T66, T67, T68, T69, T70, T71, T72, T73, T74, T75, T76, T77, T78, T94, T95, T96, T97, T98, T99, T100, T101, T102, T103, T104, T118, T119, T120, T121, T122, T123, T124, T125, T126, T127, T128, T129, T144, T145, T146, T147, T148, T149, T150, T151, T152, T153, T154, T155, T168, T169, T170, T171, T172, T173, T174, T175, T176, T177, T178, T179, T180, T181, T182, T183, T184, T185, T186, T187, T200, T201, T202, T203, T204, T205, T206, T207, T208, T209, T210, T211, T212, T213, T226, T227, T228, T229, T230, T231, T232, T233, T234, T235, T236, T237, T238, T239, T248, T249, T250, T251, T252, T253, T254, T255, T256, T257, T258, T259, T274, T275, T276, T277, T278, T279, T280, T281, T282, T283, T284, T285, T296, T297, T298, T299, T300, T301, T302, T303, T304, T305, T306, T307, T308, T309, T322, T323, T324, T325, T326, T327, T328, T329, T330, T331, T332, T333, T334, T335, T346, T347, T348, T349, T350, T351, T352, T353, T354, T355, T356, T357, T358, T359, T368, T369, T370, T371, T372, T373, T374, T375, T376, T377, T378, T379, T380, T381, T394, T395, T396, T397, T398, T399, T400, T401, T402, T403, T404, T405, T416, T417, T418, T419, T420, T421, T422, T423, T424, T425, T426, T427, T438, T439, T440, T441, T442, T443, T444, T445, T446, T447, T448, T449, T450, T451, T452, T453, T454, T455, T466, T467, T468, T469, T470, T471, T472, T473, T474, T475, T476, T477, T486, T487, T488, T489, T490, T491, T492, T493, T494, T495, T496, T497, T498, T499

Optional Revising Lessons: Narrative 1–10; Informative/Explanatory 11–20; Argument 21–30; Descriptive 31–40

Grammar, Usage, and Mechanics: *Student Practice Book:* 10, 12, 20, 26, 31, 32, 37, 38, 40, 42, 44, 46, 52, 56, 58, 62, 67, 72, 74, 76, 78, 80, 82, 86, 91, 92, 97, 98, 102, 104, 106, 112, 114, 116, 121, 122, 127, 130, 132, 136, 138, 140, 144, 151, 152, 157, 166, 172, 174, 178, 181, 182, 187, 188, 194, 198, 202, 204, 208, 211, 212, 216, 324

Teacher Edition: T18, T19, T21, T22, T24, T25, T26, T27, T28, T29, T30, T31, T32, T33, T35, T36, T37, T38, T40, T41, T43, T44, T45, T46, T48, T49, T50, T51, T52, T53, T54, T56, T57, T60, T61, T62, T63, T64, T65, T67, T68, T69, T70, T71, T73, T74

Anchor Standard 5: Develop and strengthen writing as needed by planning, revising, editing, rewriting, or trying a new approach.

Standard 5: With some guidance and support from peers and adults, develop and strengthen writing as needed by planning, revising, editing, rewriting, or trying a new approach, focusing on how well purpose and audience have been addressed.

Student Edition: 4, 5, 6, 17, 18, 19, 20, 21, 22, 23, 24, 25, 26, 27, 40, 41, 42, 43, 44, 45, 46, 47, 48, 49, 50, 64, 65, 66, 67, 68, 69, 70, 71, 72, 73, 74, 75, 76, 77, 78, 94, 95, 96, 97, 98, 99, 100, 101, 102, 103, 104, 118, 119, 120, 121, 122, 123, 124, 125, 126, 127, 128, 129, 144, 145, 146, 147, 148, 149, 150, 151, 152, 153, 154, 155, 168, 169, 170, 171, 172, 173, 174, 175, 176, 177, 178, 179, 180, 181, 182, 183, 184, 185, 186, 187, 200, 201, 202, 203, 204, 205, 206, 207, 208, 209, 210, 211, 212, 213, 226, 227, 228, 229, 230, 231, 232, 233, 234, 235, 236, 237, 238, 239, 248, 249, 250, 251, 252, 253, 254, 255, 256, 257, 258, 259, 274, 275, 276, 277, 278, 279, 280, 281, 282, 283, 284, 285, 296, 297, 298, 299, 300, 301, 302, 303, 304, 305, 306, 307, 308, 309, 322, 323, 324, 325, 326, 327, 328, 329, 330, 331, 332, 333, 334, 335, 346, 347, 348, 349, 350, 351, 352, 353, 354, 355, 356, 357, 358, 359, 368, 369, 370, 371, 372, 373, 374, 375, 376, 377, 378, 379, 380, 381, 394, 395, 396, 397, 398, 399, 400, 401, 402, 403, 404, 405, 416, 417, 418, 419, 420, 421, 422, 423, 424, 425, 426, 427, 438, 439, 440, 441, 442, 443, 444, 445, 446, 447, 448, 449, 450, 451, 452, 453, 454, 455, 466, 467, 468, 469, 470, 471, 472, 473, 474, 475, 476, 477, 486, 487, 488, 489, 490, 491, 492, 493, 494, 495, 496, 497, 498, 499

Teacher Edition: T4, T5, T6, T17, T18, T19, T20, T21, T22, T23, T24, T25, T26, T27, T40, T41, T42, T43, T44, T45, T46, T47, T48, T49, T50, T64, T65, T66, T67, T68, T69, T70, T71, T72, T73, T74, T75, T76, T77, T78, T94, T95, T96, T97, T98, T99, T100, T101, T102, T103, T104, T118, T119, T120, T121, T122, T123, T124, T125, T126, T127, T128, T129, T144, T145, T146, T147, T148, T149, T150, T151, T152, T153, T154, T155, T168, T169, T170, T171, T172, T173, T174, T175, T176, T177, T178, T179, T180, T181, T182, T183, T184, T185, T186, T187, T200, T201, T202, T203, T204, T205, T206, T207, T208, T209, T210, T211, T212, T213, T226, T227, T228, T229, T230, T231, T232, T233, T234, T235, T236, T237, T238, T239, T248, T249, T250, T251, T252, T253, T254, T255, T256, T257, T258, T259, T274, T275, T276, T277, T278, T279, T280, T281, T282, T283, T284, T285, T296, T297, T298, T299, T300, T301, T302, T303, T304, T305, T306, T307, T308, T309, T322, T323, T324, T325, T326, T327, T328, T329, T330, T331, T332, T333, T334, T335, T346, T347, T348, T349, T350, T351, T352, T353, T354, T355, T356, T357, T358, T359, T368, T369, T370, T371, T372, T373, T374, T375, T376, T377, T378, T379, T380, T381, T394, T395, T396, T397, T398, T399, T400, T401, T402, T403, T404, T405, T416, T417, T418, T419, T420, T421, T422, T423, T424, T425, T426, T427, T438, T439, T440, T441, T442, T443, T444, T445, T446, T447, T448, T449, T450, T451, T452, T453, T454, T455, T466, T467, T468, T469, T470, T471, T472, T473, T474, T475, T476, T477, T486, T487, T488, T489, T490, T491, T492, T493, T494, T495, T496, T497, T498, T499

Optional Revising Lessons: Narrative 1–10; Informative/Explanatory 11–20; Argument 21–30; Descriptive 31–40

Grammar, Usage, and Mechanics: *Student Practice Book:* 10, 31, 32, 33, 34, 58, 62, 63, 64, 82, 91, 92, 93, 94, 104, 112, 121, 122, 123, 124, 132, 134, 151, 152, 153, 154, 181, 182, 183, 184, 190, 211, 212, 213, 214

Teacher Edition: T18, T24, T31, T32, T37, T40, T43, T45, T48, T51, T56, T64, T66, T73

STANDARD	CORRELATION
Anchor Standard 6: Use technology, including the Internet, to produce and publish writing and to interact and collaborate with others.	
Standard 6: Use technology, including the Internet, to produce and publish writing and link to and cite sources as well as to interact and collaborate with others, including linking to and citing sources.	

Student Edition: 26, 45, 50, 51, 64, 65, 78, 79, 104, 105, 144, 154, 155, 184, 185, 212, 213, 225, 236, 237, 276, 284, 285, 306, 307, 321, 324, 332, 333, 356, 357, 393, 404, 405, 426, 427, 452, 453, 476, 477

Teacher Edition: T2C, T26, T27, T39, T45, T50, T51, T63, T64, T65, T75, T78, T79, T93, T104, T105, T132C, T143, T144, T154, T155, T167, T184, T185, T199, T212, T213, T225, T236, T237, T276, T262C, T284, T285, T306, T307, T321, T324, T332, T333, T356, T357, T382C, T393, T404, T405, T426, T427, T452, T453, T476, T477

Optional Revising Lessons: Informative/Explanatory 13; Argument 21; Descriptive 33

Grammar, Usage, and Mechanics: *Student Practice Book:* 136, 212, 218, 325, 326; *Teacher Edition:* T52, T73, T74

WRITING Research to Build and Present Knowledge

STANDARD	CORRELATION
Anchor Standard 7: Conduct short as well as more sustained research projects based on focused questions, demonstrating understanding of the subject under investigation.	
Standard 7: Conduct short research projects to answer a question, drawing on several sources and generating additional related, focused questions for further research and investigation.	

Student Edition: 64, 65, 75, 94, 144, 156, 157, 158, 159, 160, 161, 162, 163, 164, 165, 166, 167, 168, 169, 170, 171, 172, 173, 174, 175, 176, 177, 178, 179, 180, 181, 182, 183, 184, 185, 186, 187, 438, 439, 440

Teacher Edition: T64, T65, T75, T94, T144, T156, T157, T158, T159, T160, T161, T162, T163, T164, T165, T166, T167, T168, T169, T170, T171, T172, T173, T174, T175, T176, T177, T178, T179, T180, T181, T182, T183, T184, T185, T186, T187, T228, T418, T438, T439, T440, T476

Grammar, Usage, and Mechanics: *Student Practice Book:* 67, 97, 98, 127, 136, 157, 217, 218, 326
Teacher Edition: T33, T41, T49, T52, T57, T74

STANDARD	CORRELATION
Anchor Standard 8: Gather relevant information from multiple print and digital sources, assess the credibility and accuracy of each source, and integrate the information while avoiding plagiarism.	
Standard 8: Gather relevant information from multiple print and digital sources, using search terms effectively; assess the credibility and accuracy of each source; and quote or paraphrase the data and conclusions of others while avoiding plagiarism and following a standard format for citation.	

Student Edition: 64, 65, 75, 94, 144, 168, 169, 170, 171, 176, 177, 178, 179, 202, 226, 276, 394, 416, 417, 438, 439, 440, 441

Teacher Edition: T64, T65, T75, T94, T144, T168, T169, T170, T171, T172, T176, T177, T178, T179, T202, T226, T276, T394, T416, T417, T438, T439, T440, T441

Optional Revising Lessons: Narrative 8; Argument 21; Descriptive 33

Grammar, Usage, and Mechanics: *Student Practice Book:* 67, 127, 217; *Teacher Edition:* T33, T49, T74

STANDARD	CORRELATION
Anchor Standard 9: Draw evidence from literary or informational texts to support analysis, reflection, and research.	
Standard 9: Draw evidence from literary or informational texts to support analysis, reflection, and research.	
9a: Apply grade 7 Reading standards to literature (e.g., "Compare and contrast a fictional portrayal of a time, place, or character and a historical account of the same period as a means of understanding how authors of fiction use or alter history").	**Student Edition:** 52, 53, 55, 63, 64, 72, 90, 91 **Teacher Edition:** T52, T53, T55, T63, T64, T72, T80, T90, T91 **Grammar, Usage, and Mechanics:** *Student Practice Book:* 10, 26, 40, 46, 56, 104, 108, 134, 164, 170, 174, 181, 182, 190 *Teacher Edition:* T18, T22, T26, T28, T30, T43, T44, T51, T59, T61, T62, T64, T66
9b: Apply grade 7 Reading standards to literary nonfiction (e.g. "Trace and evaluate the argument and specific claims in a text, assessing whether the reasoning is sound and the evidence is relevant and sufficient to support the claims").	**Student Edition:** 168, 169, 170, 171, 172, 173, 174, 175, 176, 177, 178, 179, 180, 181, 182, 183, 184, 185, 186, 187, 188, 189, 190, 191, 192, 193, 194, 195, 196, 197, 198, 199, 200, 201, 202, 203, 204, 205, 206, 207, 208, 209, 210, 211, 212, 213, 214, 215, 216, 217, 218, 219, 220, 221, 222, 223, 224, 225, 226, 227, 228, 229, 230, 231, 232, 233, 234, 235, 236, 237, 238, 239, 240, 241, 242, 243, 244, 245, 246, 247, 248, 249, 250, 251, 252, 253, 254, 255, 256, 257, 258, 259, 260, 261 **Teacher Edition:** T155, T168, T169, T170, T171, T172, T173, T174, T175, T176, T177, T178, T179, T180, T181, T182, T183, T184, T185, T186, T187, T188, T189, T190, T191, T192, T193, T194, T195, T196, T197, T198, T199, T200, T201, T202, T203, T204, T205, T206, T207, T208, T209, T210, T211, T212, T213, T214, T215, T216, T217, T218, T219, T220, T221, T222, T223, T224, T225, T226, T227, T228, T229, T230, T231, T232, T233, T234, T235, T236, T237, T238, T239, T240, T241, T242, T243, T244, T245, T246, T247, T248, T249, T250, T251, T252, T253, T254, T255, T256, T257, T258, T259, T260, T261 **Grammar, Usage, and Mechanics:** *Student Practice Book:* 24, 46, 52, 88, 166, 168, 198; *Teacher Edition:* T22, T28, T29, T39, T60, T68

STANDARD	CORRELATION

WRITING Range of Writing

Anchor Standard 10: Write routinely over extended time frames (time for research, reflection, and revision) and shorter time frames (a single sitting or a day or two) for a range of tasks, purposes, and audiences.

Standard 10: Write routinely over extended time frames (time for research, reflection, and revision) and shorter time frames (a single sitting or a day or two) for a range of discipline-specific tasks, purposes, and audiences.

Student Edition: 4, 5, 6, 17, 18, 19, 20, 21, 22, 23, 24, 25, 26, 27, 40, 41, 42, 43, 44, 45, 46, 47, 48, 49, 50, 64, 65, 66, 67, 68, 69, 70, 71, 72, 73, 74, 75, 76, 77, 78, 94, 95, 96, 97, 98, 99, 100, 101, 102, 103, 104, 118, 119, 120, 121, 122, 123, 124, 125, 126, 127, 128, 129, 144, 145, 146, 147, 148, 149, 150, 151, 152, 153, 154, 155, 168, 169, 170, 171, 172, 173, 174, 175, 176, 177, 178, 179, 180, 181, 182, 183, 184, 185, 186, 187, 200, 201, 202, 203, 204, 205, 206, 207, 208, 209, 210, 211, 212, 213, 226, 227, 228, 229, 230, 231, 232, 233, 234, 235, 236, 237, 238, 239, 248, 249, 250, 251, 252, 253, 254, 255, 256, 257, 258, 259, 274, 275, 276, 277, 278, 279, 280, 281, 282, 283, 284, 285, 296, 297, 298, 299, 300, 301, 302, 303, 304, 305, 306, 307, 308, 309, 322, 323, 324, 325, 326, 327, 328, 329, 330, 331, 332, 333, 334, 335, 346, 347, 348, 349, 350, 351, 352, 353, 354, 355, 356, 357, 358, 359, 368, 369, 370, 371, 372, 373, 374, 375, 376, 377, 378, 379, 380, 381, 394, 395, 396, 397, 398, 399, 400, 401, 402, 403, 404, 405, 416, 417, 418, 419, 420, 421, 422, 423, 424, 425, 426, 427, 438, 439, 440, 441, 442, 443, 444, 445, 446, 447, 448, 449, 450, 451, 452, 453, 454, 455, 466, 467, 468, 469, 470, 471, 472, 473, 474, 475, 476, 477, 486, 487, 488, 489, 490, 491, 492, 493, 494, 495, 496, 497, 498, 499

Teacher Edition: T4, T5, T6, T17, T18, T19, T20, T21, T22, T23, T24, T25, T26, T27, T40, T41, T42, T43, T44, T45, T46, T47, T48, T49, T50, T64, T65, T66, T67, T68, T69, T70, T71, T72, T73, T74, T75, T76, T77, T78, T94, T95, T96, T97, T98, T99, T100, T101, T102, T103, T104, T118, T119, T120, T121, T122, T123, T124, T125, T126, T127, T128, T129, T144, T145, T146, T147, T148, T149, T150, T151, T152, T153, T154, T155, T168, T169, T170, T171, T172, T173, T174, T175, T176, T177, T178, T179, T180, T181, T182, T183, T184, T185, T186, T187, T200, T201, T202, T203, T204, T205, T206, T207, T208, T209, T210, T211, T212, T213, T226, T227, T228, T229, T230, T231, T232, T233, T234, T235, T236, T237, T238, T239, T248, T249, T250, T251, T252, T253, T254, T255, T256, T257, T258, T259, T274, T275, T276, T277, T278, T279, T280, T281, T282, T283, T284, T285, T296, T297, T298, T299, T300, T301, T302, T303, T304, T305, T306, T307, T308, T309, T322, T323, T324, T325, T326, T327, T328, T329, T330, T331, T332, T333, T334, T335, T346, T347, T348, T349, T350, T351, T352, T353, T354, T355, T356, T357, T358, T359, T368, T369, T370, T371, T372, T373, T374, T375, T376, T377, T378, T379, T380, T381, T394, T395, T396, T397, T398, T399, T400, T401, T402, T403, T404, T405, T416, T417, T418, T419, T420, T421, T422, T423, T424, T425, T426, T427, T438, T439, T440, T441, T442, T443, T444, T445, T446, T447, T448, T449, T450, T451, T452, T453, T454, T455, T466, T467, T468, T469, T470, T471, T472, T473, T474, T475, T476, T477, T486, T487, T488, T489, T490, T491, T492, T493, T494, T495, T496, T497, T498, T499

Optional Revising Lessons: Narrative 1–10; Informative/Explanatory 11–20; Argument 21–30; Descriptive 31–40

Grammar, Usage, and Mechanics: *Student Practice Book:* 10, 12, 20, 26, 31, 32, 37, 38, 40, 42, 44, 46, 52, 56, 58, 62, 67, 72, 74, 76, 78, 80, 82, 86, 91, 92, 97, 98, 102, 104, 106, 112, 114, 116, 121, 122, 127, 130, 132, 136, 138, 140, 144, 151, 152, 157, 166, 172, 174, 178, 181, 182, 187, 188, 194, 198, 202, 204, 208, 211, 212, 216, 324
Teacher Edition: T18, T19, T21, T22, T24, T25, T26, T27, T28, T29, T30, T31, T32, T33, T35, T36, T37, T38, T40, T41, T43, T44, T45, T46, T48, T49, T50, T51, T52, T53, T54, T56, T57, T60, T61, T62, T63, T64, T65, T67, T68, T69, T70, T71, T73, T74

LANGUAGE Conventions of Standard English

Anchor Standard 1: Demonstrate command of the conventions of standard English grammar and usage when writing or speaking.

Standard 1: Demonstrate command of the conventions of standard English grammar and usage when writing or speaking.

1a: Explain the function of phrases and clauses in general and their function in specific sentences.	**Student Edition:** 77, 101, 102, 103, 281, 282, 305, 392, 401, 402, 403, 473, 474, 475, 505, 506, 507, 514, 517, 522, 528, 530 **Teacher Edition:** T77, T101, T102, T103, T281, T282, T283, T305, T392, T401, T402, T403, T473, T474, T475, T505, T506, T507, T514, T517, T522, T528, T530 **Optional Revising Lessons:** Narrative 4, 5, 7, 9, 10; Informative/Explanatory 12, 20; Argument 22, 24, 30; Descriptive 31, 32, 34, 39, 40 **Grammar, Usage, and Mechanics:** *Student Practice Book:* 21, 22, 23, 24, 25, 26, 41, 42, 43, 44, 45, 46, 47, 48, 49, 50, 57, 58, 103, 113, 114, 199, 200, 201, 202, 309, 310, 311, 316; *Teacher Edition:* T21, T22, T27, T28, T29, T31, T43, T46, T69 **Grammar Practice Masters:** 15, 16, 17, 18, 19, 20, 21, 22, 23, 24, 43, 44, 97, 98, 99, 100
1b: Choose among simple, compound, complex, and compound-complex sentences to signal differing relationships among ideas.	**Student Edition:** 6, 10, 11, 14, 15, 23, 24, 25, 32, 34, 35, 38, 46, 54, 56, 57, 62, 63, 74, 75, 84, 88, 89, 92, 93, 100, 101, 102, 103, 112, 116, 119, 136, 138, 139, 142, 158, 162, 163, 166, 180, 190, 194, 195, 198, 208, 216, 220, 221, 224, 232, 242, 246, 249, 253, 266, 268, 269, 272, 282, 288, 290, 291, 294, 302, 312, 316, 317, 320, 338, 339, 340, 341, 344, 352, 362, 366, 369, 373, 386, 388, 389, 392, 408, 410, 411, 414, 422, 424, 425, 430, 432, 433, 436, 448, 458, 460, 461, 464, 472, 480, 484, 487, 491, 505, 506, 507, 514, 522, 528, 530 **Teacher Edition:** T6, T7, T10, T11, T14, T15, T23, T24, T25, T32, T33, T34, T35, T38, T46, T54, T55, T56, T57, T62, T63, T74, T75, T84, T85, T88, T89, T92, T93, T100, T101, T102, T103, T112, T116, T119, T136, T137, T138, T139, T142, T158, T159, T162, T163, T166, T180, T190, T191, T194, T195, T198, T208, T216, T217, T220, T221, T224, T232, T242, T246, T249, T253, T266, T267, T268, T269, T272, T282, T288, T289, T290, T291, T294, T302, T312, T313, T316, T317, T320, T338, T339, T340, T341, T344, T352, T362, T366, T369, T373, T386, T387, T388, T389, T392, T408, T309, T410, T411, T414, T415, T422, T424, T425, T430, T431, T432, T433, T436, T448, T458, T459, T460, T461, T464, T472, T480, T484, T487, T491, T505, T506, T507, T514, T522, T528, T530 **Optional Revising Lessons:** Narrative 10; Descriptive 34, 40 **Grammar, Usage, and Mechanics:** *Student Practice Book:* 41, 42, 45, 46, 199, 200, 201, 202, 310 *Teacher Edition:* T27, T28, T69 **Grammar Practice Masters:** 8, 10, 12, 14, 16, 18, 19, 20, 21, 22, 23, 24, 25, 26, 28, 30, 32, 36, 40, 42, 44, 46, 48, 50, 52, 54, 56, 58, 60, 64, 66, 68, 70, 72, 74, 76, 78, 80, 81, 82, 84, 86, 88, 92, 94, 96, 98, 100, 102, 104, 106
1c: Place phrases and clauses within a sentence, recognizing and correcting misplaced and dangling modifiers.	**Student Edition:** 75, 77, 102, 103, 281, 282, 290, 291, 295, 303, 305, 393, 401, 402, 403, 432, 433, 437, 449, 450, 451, 460, 461, 465, 473, 474, 475, 505, 506, 507, 514, 522, 528, 530 **Teacher Edition:** T75, T77, T101, T102, T103, T281, T282, T283, T290, T291, T295, T303, T305, T393, T401, T402, T403, T432, T433, T437, T449, T450, T451, T460, T461, T465, T473, T474, T475, T505, T506, T507, T514, T522, T528, T530 **Optional Revising Lessons:** Narrative 1, 4, 6, 10; Informative/Explanatory 12; Descriptive 31

STANDARD	CORRELATION
Standard 1c continued	**Grammar, Usage, and Mechanics:** *Student Practice Book:* 21, 22, 23, 24, 25, 26, 41, 42, 43, 44, 45, 46, 47, 48, 49, 50, 57, 58, 103, 113, 114, 173, 174, 199, 200, 201, 202, 309, 310, 311, 316; *Teacher Edition:* T21, T22, T27, T28, T29, T31, T43, T46, T62, T69 **Grammar Practice Masters:** 15, 16, 17, 18,43, 44, 81, 82, 83, 84

Anchor Standard 2: Demonstrate command of the conventions of standard English capitalization, punctuation, and spelling when writing.

Standard 2: Demonstrate command of the conventions of standard English capitalization, punctuation, and spelling when writing.

2a: Use a comma to separate coordinate adjectives (e.g., *It was a fascinating, enjoyable movie* but not *He wore an old[,] green shirt*).	**Student Edition:** 529 **Grammar, Usage, and Mechanics:** *Student Practice Book:* 197, 198, 307; *Teacher Edition:* T68 **Grammar Practice Masters:** 95, 96
2b: Spell correctly.	**Student Edition:** 6, 23, 32, 45, 47, 50, 54, 84, 101, 112, 116, 119, 129, 136, 151, 158, 181, 190, 199, 216, 225, 233, 242, 246, 249, 253, 259, 266, 288, 303, 312, 338, 340, 341, 345, 353, 354, 355, 362, 367, 369, 373, 379, 387, 388, 389, 401, 408, 430, 449, 458, 460, 461, 480, 484, 487, 491 **Teacher Edition:** T6, T7, T23, T32, T45, T47, T50, T54, T84, T101, T112, T116, T119, T129, T136, T151, T158, T159, T181, T190, T191, T199, T216, T225, T233, T242, T246, T249, T253, T259, T266, T267, T284, T288, T289, T303, T312, T313, T338, T339, T340, T341, T345, T353, T354, T355, T362, T367, T369, T373, T379, T380, T386, T387, T388, T389, T401, T408, T409, T423, T430, T449, T458, T460, T461, T480, T484, T487, T491 **Grammar, Usage, and Mechanics:** *Student Practice Book:* 33, 63, 93, 123, 153, 183, 213; *Teacher Edition:* T24, T32, T40, T48, T56, T64 **Grammar Practice Masters:** 29, 30, 31, 32, 41, 42, 47, 48, 49, 50, 51, 52, 53, 54, 55, 56, 57, 58, 59, 60, 75, 76, 93, 94

LANGUAGE Knowledge of Language

Anchor Standard 3: Apply knowledge of language to understand how language functions in different contexts, to make effective choices for meaning or style, and to comprehend more fully when reading or listening.

Standard 3: Use knowledge of language and its conventions when writing, speaking, reading, or listening.

3a: Choose language that expresses ideas precisely and concisely, recognizing and eliminating wordiness and redundancy.	**Student Edition:** 6, 10, 11, 14, 22, 32, 34, 35, 38, 45, 54, 56, 57, 62, 73, 84, 88, 89, 92, 112, 115, 119, 128, 136, 138, 139, 142, 150, 158, 162, 163, 166, 181, 190, 194, 195, 198, 207, 216, 220, 221, 224, 228, 229, 242, 245, 249, 253, 258, 266, 268, 269, 272, 280, 288, 290, 291, 294, 312, 316, 317, 320, 327, 328, 338, 340, 341, 344, 362, 365, 369, 373, 378, 386, 388, 389, 392, 397, 400, 408, 410, 411, 414, 421, 430, 432, 433, 436, 458, 460, 461, 464, 480, 483, 487, 491, 496 **Teacher Edition:** T6, T7, T10, T11, T14, T22, T32, T33, T34, T35, T38, T45, T54, T55, T56, T57, T62, T73, T84, T85, T88, T89, T92, T112, T115, T119, T128, T136, T137, T138, T139, T142, T150, T158, T162, T163, T166, T181, T190, T191, T194, T195, T198, T207, T216, T217, T220, T221, T224, T228, T229, T242, T245, T249, T253, T258, T266, T267, T268, T269, T272, T280, T288, T289, T290, T291, T294, T312, T313, T316, T317, T320, T327, T328, T338, T339, T340, T341, T344, T362, T364, T365, T369, T373, T378, T386, T387, T388, T389, T392, T397, T400, T408, T409, T410, T411, T414, T421, T430, T431, T432, T433, T436, T458, T460, T461, T464, T480, T482, T483, T487, T491, T496 **Optional Revising Lessons:** Narrative 1–10; Informative/Explanatory 11–20; Argument 21–30; Descriptive 31–40 **Grammar, Usage, and Mechanics:** *Student Practice Book:* 57, 58, 61, 63, 64, 310, 311; *Teacher Edition:* T31, T32 **Grammar Practice Masters:** 63, 64, 73, 74

LANGUAGE Vocabulary Acquisition and Use

Anchor Standard 4: Determine or clarify the meaning of unknown and multiple-meaning words and phrases by using context clues, analyzing meaningful word parts, and consulting general and specialized reference materials, as appropriate.

Standard 4: Determine or clarify the meaning of unknown and multiple-meaning words and phrases based on *grade 7 reading and content*, choosing flexibly from a range of strategies.

4a: Use context (e.g., the overall meaning of a sentence or paragraph; a word's position or function in a sentence) as a clue to the meaning of a word or phrase.	**Grammar, Usage, and Mechanics:** *Student Practice Book:* 9, 11, 13, 15, 19, 21, 23, 25, 27, 41, 43, 53, 55, 69, 71, 73, 79, 85, 87, 103, 105, 113, 117, 129, 130, 131, 132, 133, 134, 135, 136, 137, 138, 139, 140, 145, 146, 147, 155, 159, 165, 167, 175, 177, 189, 195, 201, 203, 205; *Teacher Edition:* T18, T19, T20, T21, T22, T23, T27, T30, T34, T35, T37, T38, T39, T43, T44, T45, T46, T47, T50, T51, T52, T53, T54, T55, T58, T60, T61, T62, T63, T66, T67, T68, T69, T70 **Grammar Practice Masters:** 47, 48, 49, 50, 51, 52, 53, 54, 55, 56, 57, 58, 59, 60
4b: Use common, grade-appropriate Greek or Latin affixes and roots as clues to the meaning of a word (e.g., *belligerent, bellicose, rebel*).	**Grammar, Usage, and Mechanics:** *Student Practice Book:* 164; *Teacher Edition:* T59
4c: Consult general and specialized reference materials (e.g., dictionaries, glossaries, thesauruses), both print and digital, to find the pronunciation of a word or determine or clarify its precise meaning or its part of speech.	**Student Edition:** 400 **Teacher Edition:** T273, T327, T348, T378, T400 **Grammar, Usage, and Mechanics:** *Student Practice Book:* 37, 325, 326; *Teacher Edition:* T25

STANDARD	CORRELATION
4d: Verify the preliminary determination of the meaning of a word or phrase (e.g., by checking the inferred meaning in context or in a dictionary).	**Grammar, Usage, and Mechanics:** *Student Practice Book:* 9, 11, 13, 15, 19, 21, 23, 25, 27, 41, 43, 53, 55, 69, 71, 73, 79, 85, 87, 103, 105, 113, 117, 129, 130, 131, 132, 133, 134, 135, 136, 137, 138, 139, 140, 145, 146, 147, 155, 159, 165, 167, 175, 177, 189, 195, 201, 203, 205 *Teacher Edition:* T18, T19, T20, T21, T22, T23, T27, T30, T34, T35, T37, T38, T39, T43, T44, T45, T46, T47, T50, T51, T52, T53, T54, T55, T58, T60, T61, T62, T63, T66, T67, T68, T69, T70

Anchor Standard 5: Demonstrate understanding of figurative language, word relationships, and nuances in word meanings.

Standard 5: Demonstrate understanding of figurative language, word relationships, and nuances in word meanings.

5a: Interpret figures of speech(e.g., literary, biblical, and mythological allusions) in context.	**Student Edition:** 348, 386, 408, 436, 447, 456, 458, 460, 461, 464, 468 **Teacher Edition:** T348, T386, T396, T408, T436, T447, T456, T458, T459, T460, T461, T464, T468, T469 **Optional Revising Lessons:** Narrative 4
5b: Use the relationship between particular words (e.g., synonym/antonym, analogy) to better understand each of the words.	**Optional Revising Lessons:** Descriptive 8
5c: Distinguish among the connotations (associations) of words with similar denotations (definitions) (e.g., *refined, respectful, polite, diplomatic, condescending*).	**Student Edition:** 327, 378 **Teacher Edition:** T327, T378 **Optional Revising Lessons:** Narrative 6, 7, 8; Argument 27

Anchor Standard 6: Acquire and use accurately a range of general academic and domain-specific words and phrases sufficient for reading, writing, speaking, and listening at the college and career readiness level; demonstrate independence in gathering vocabulary knowledge when encountering an unknown term important to comprehension or expression.

Standard 6: Acquire and use accurately grade-appropriate general academic and domain-specific words and phrases; gather vocabulary knowledge when considering a word or phrase important to comprehension or expression.

	Student Edition: 17, 23, 41, 42, 44, 45, 47, 64, 65, 68, 72, 75, 95, 99, 101, 145, 146, 150, 151, 169, 170, 177, 178, 190, 209, 216, 233, 242, 246, 249, 253, 259, 275, 276, 281, 297, 301, 303, 324, 328, 329, 347, 350, 353, 395, 396, 400, 401, 420, 422, 425, 438, 439, 441, 442, 447, 449, 468, 473 **Teacher Edition:** T17, T23, T41, T42, T44, T45, T47, T64, T65, T68, T69, T72, T75, T95, T99, T101, T145, T146, T150, T151, T169, T170, T177, T178, T179, T190, T209, T216, T233, T242, T246, T249, T253, T259, T275, T276, T281, T297, T301, T303, T324, T328, T329, T347, T350, T353, T395, T396, T400, T401, T420, T422, T425, T438, T439, T441, T442, T443, T447, T449, T468, T469, T473 **Optional Revising Lessons:** Narrative 1–10; Informative/Explanatory 11–20; Argument 21–30; Descriptive 31–40 **Grammar, Usage, and Mechanics:** *Student Practice Book:* 9, 11, 13, 15, 19, 21, 23, 25, 27, 41, 43, 53, 55, 69, 71, 73, 79, 85, 87, 103, 105, 113, 117, 129, 130, 131, 132, 133, 134, 135, 136, 137, 138, 139, 140, 145, 146, 147, 155, 159, 165, 167, 175, 177, 189, 195, 201, 203, 205; *Teacher Edition:* T18, T19, T20, T21, T22, T23, T27, T30, T34, T35, T37, T38, T39, T43, T44, T45, T46, T47, T50, T51, T52, T53, T54, T55, T58, T60, T61, T62, T63, T66, T67, T68, T69, T70

SPEAKING AND LISTENING Comprehension and Collaboration

Anchor Standard 1: Prepare for and participate effectively in a range of conversations and collaborations with diverse partners, building on others' ideas and expressing their own clearly and persuasively.

Standard 1: Engage effectively in a range of collaborative discussions (one-on-one, in groups, and teacher led) with diverse partners on *grade 7 topics, texts, and issues,* building on others' ideas and expressing their own clearly.

1a: Come to discussions prepared, having read or researched material under study; explicitly draw on that preparation by referring to evidence on the topic, text, or issue to probe and reflect on ideas under discussion.	**Student Edition:** 3, 4, 5, 6, 7, 10, 11, 12, 13, 14, 15, 28, 30, 31, 32, 33, 34, 35, 36, 37, 38, 39, 51, 52, 53, 54, 55, 56, 57, 58, 59, 60, 61, 62, 63, 80, 82, 83, 84, 85, 86, 87, 88, 89, 90, 91, 92, 93, 106, 110, 111, 112, 113, 114, 115, 116, 117, 130, 131, 134, 135, 136, 137, 138, 139, 140, 141, 142, 143, 155, 156, 157, 158, 159, 160, 161, 162, 163, 164, 165, 166, 167, 186, 187, 188, 189, 190, 191, 192, 193, 194, 195, 196, 197, 198, 199, 213, 214, 215, 216, 217, 218, 219, 220, 221, 222, 223, 224, 225, 238, 240, 241, 242, 243, 244, 245, 246, 247, 260, 261, 264, 265, 266, 267, 268, 269, 270, 271, 272, 273, 285, 286, 287, 288, 289, 290, 291, 292, 293, 294, 295, 308, 310, 321, 333, 336, 337, 338, 339, 340, 341, 342, 343, 344, 345, 358, 360, 361, 362, 363, 364, 365, 366, 367, 380, 381, 384, 385, 386, 387, 388, 389, 390, 391, 392, 393, 405, 406, 407, 408, 409, 410, 411, 412, 413, 414, 415, 428, 429, 430, 431, 432, 433, 434, 435, 436, 437, 454, 456, 457, 458, 459, 460, 461, 462, 463, 464, 465, 477, 478, 479, 480, 481, 482, 483, 484, 485, 498, 499 **Teacher Edition:** T3, T4, T5, T6, T7, T10, T11, T12, T13, T14, T15, T28, T30, T31, T32, T33, T34, T35, T36, T37, T38, T39, T51, T52, T53, T54, T55, T56, T57, T58, T59, T60, T61, T62, T63, T80, T82, T83, T84, T85, T86, T87, T88, T89, T90, T91, T92, T93, T106, T110, T111, T112, T113, T114, T115, T116, T117, T130, T131, T134, T135, T136, T137, T138, T139, T140, T141, T142, T143, T155, T156, T157, T158, T159, T160, T161, T162, T163, T164, T165, T166, T167, T186, T187, T188, T189, T190, T191, T192, T193, T194, T195, T196, T197, T198, T199, T213, T214, T215, T216, T217, T218, T219, T220, T221, T222, T223, T224, T225, T238, T240, T241, T242, T243, T244, T245, T246, T247, T260, T261, T264, T265, T266, T267, T268, T269, T270, T271, T272, T273, T285, T286, T287, T288, T289, T290, T291, T292, T293, T294, T295, T308, T310, T321, T333, T336, T337, T338, T339, T340, T341, T342, T343, T344, T345, T358, T360, T361, T362, T363, T364, T365, T366, T367, T380, T381, T384, T385, T386, T387, T388, T389, T390, T391, T392, T393, T405, T406, T407, T408, T409, T410, T411, T412, T413, T414, T415, T428, T429, T430, T431, T432, T433, T434, T435, T436, T437, T454, T456, T457, T458, T459, T460, T461, T462, T463, T464, T465, T477, T478, T479, T480, T481, T482, T483, T484, T485, T498, T499 **Grammar, Usage, and Mechanics:** *Student Practice Book:* 12, 13, 28, 40, 42, 45, 47, 49, 50, 52, 56, 58, 72, 76, 77, 78, 82, 83, 88, 99, 101, 103, 105, 108, 109, 112, 116, 117, 129, 130, 132, 136, 138, 140, 142, 144, 148, 160, 16, 170, 172, 174, 194, 196, 200, 207, 208; *Teacher Edition:* T18, T19, T20, T21, T22, T23, T26, T27, T28, T29, T30, T31, T34, T35, T36, T37, T38, T39, T42, T43, T44, T45, T46, T47, T48, T49, T50, T51, T52, T53, T54, T55, T56, T57, T58, T59, T60, T61, T62, T63, T64, T65, T66, T67, T68, T69, T70, T71

STANDARD	CORRELATION
1b: Follow rules for collegial discussions, track progress toward specific goals and deadlines, and define individual roles as needed.	**Student Edition:** 3, 4, 5, 6, 7, 10, 11, 12, 13, 14, 15, 28, 30, 31, 32, 33, 34, 35, 36, 37, 38, 39, 51, 52, 53, 54, 55, 56, 57, 58, 59,60, 61, 62, 63, 80, 82, 83, 84, 85, 86, 87, 88, 89, 90, 91, 92, 93, 106, 110, 111, 112, 113, 114, 115, 116, 117, 130, 131, 134, 135, 136, 137, 138, 139, 140, 141, 142, 143, 155, 156, 157, 158, 159, 160, 161, 162, 163, 164, 165, 166, 167, 186, 187, 188, 189, 190, 191, 192, 193, 194, 195, 196, 197, 198, 199, 213, 214, 215, 216, 217, 218, 219, 220, 221, 222, 223, 224, 225, 238, 240, 241, 242, 243, 244, 245, 246, 247, 260, 261, 264, 265, 266, 267, 268, 269, 270, 271, 272, 273, 285, 286, 287, 288, 289, 290, 291, 292, 293, 294, 295, 308, 310, 321, 333, 336, 337, 338, 339, 340, 341, 342, 343, 344, 345, 358, 360, 361, 362, 363, 364, 365, 366, 367, 380, 381, 384, 385, 386, 387, 388, 389, 390, 391, 392, 393, 405, 406, 407, 408, 409, 410, 411, 412, 413, 414, 415, 428, 429, 430, 431, 432, 433, 434, 435, 436, 437, 454, 456, 457, 458, 459, 460, 461, 462, 463, 464, 465, 477, 478, 479, 480, 481, 482, 483, 484, 485, 498, 499 **Teacher Edition:** T3, T4, T5, T6, T7, T10, T11, T12, T13, T14, T15, T28, T30, T31, T32, T33, T34, T35, T36, T37, T38, T39, T51, T52, T53, T54, T55, T56, T57, T58, T59, T60, T61, T62, T63, T80, T82, T83, T84, T85, T86, T87, T88, T89, T90, T91, T92, T93, T106, T110, T111, T112, T113, T114, T115, T116, T117, T130, T131, T134, T135, T136, T137, T138, T139, T140, T141, T142, T143, T155, T156, T157, T158, T159, T160, T161, T162, T163, T164, T165, T166, T167, T186, T187, T188, T189, T190, T191, T192, T193, T194, T195, T196, T197, T198, T199, T213, T214, T215, T216, T217, T218, T219, T220, T221, T222, T223, T224, T225, T238, T240, T241, T242, T243, T244, T245, T246, T247, T260, T261, T264, T265, T266, T267, T268, T269, T270, T271, T272, T273, T285, T286, T287, T288, T289, T290, T291, T292, T293, T294, T295, T308, T310, T321, T333, T336, T337, T338, T339, T340, T341, T342, T343, T344, T345, T358, T360, T361, T362, T363, T364, T365, T366, T367, T380, T381, T384, T385, T386, T387, T388, T389, T390, T391, T392, T393, T405, T406, T407, T408, T409, T410, T411, T412, T413, T414, T415, T428, T429, T430, T431, T432, T433, T434, T435, T436, T437, T454, T456, T457, T458, T459, T460, T461, T462, T463, T464, T465, T477, T478, T479, T480, T481, T482, T483, T484, T485, T498, T499 **Grammar, Usage, and Mechanics:** *Student Practice Book:* 138; *Teacher Edition:* T18, T19, T28, T31, T35, T47, T50, T51, T52, T58, T60, T68, T69
1c: Pose questions that elicit elaboration and respond to others' questions and comments with relevant observations and ideas that bring the discussion back on topic as needed.	**Student Edition:** 3, 4, 5, 6, 7, 10, 11, 12, 13, 14, 15, 28, 30, 31, 32, 33, 34, 35, 36, 37, 38, 39, 51, 52, 53, 54, 55, 56, 57, 58, 59, 60, 61, 62, 63, 80, 82, 83, 84, 85, 86, 87, 88, 89, 90, 91, 92, 93, 106, 110, 111, 112, 113, 114, 115, 116, 117, 130, 131, 134, 135, 136, 137, 138, 139, 140, 141, 142, 143, 155, 156, 157, 158, 159, 160, 161, 162, 163, 164, 165, 166, 167, 186, 187, 188, 189, 190, 191, 192, 193, 194, 195, 196, 197, 198, 199, 213, 214, 215, 216, 217, 218, 219, 220, 221, 222, 223, 224, 225, 238, 240, 241, 242, 243, 244, 245, 246, 247, 260, 261, 264, 265, 266, 267, 268, 269, 270, 271, 272, 273, 285, 286, 287, 288, 289, 290, 291, 292, 293, 294, 295, 308, 310, 321, 333, 336, 337, 338, 339, 340, 341, 342, 343, 344, 345, 358, 360, 361, 362, 363, 364, 365, 366, 367, 380, 381, 384, 385, 386, 387, 388, 389, 390, 391, 392, 393, 405, 406, 407, 408, 409, 410, 411, 412, 413, 414, 415, 428, 429, 430, 431, 432, 433, 434, 435, 436, 437, 454, 456, 457, 458, 459, 460, 461, 462, 463, 464, 465, 477, 478, 479, 480, 481, 482, 483, 484, 485, 498, 499 **Teacher Edition:** T3, T4, T5, T6, T7, T10, T11, T12, T13, T14, T15, T28, T30, T31, T32, T33, T34, T35, T36, T37, T38, T39, T51, T52, T53, T54, T55, T56, T57, T58, T59, T60, T61, T62, T63, T80, T82, T83, T84, T85, T86, T87, T88, T89, T90, T91, T92, T93, T106, T110, T111, T112, T113, T114, T115, T116, T117, T130, T131, T134, T135, T136, T137, T138, T139, T140, T141, T142, T143, T155, T156, T157, T158, T159, T160, T161, T162, T163, T164, T165, T166, T167, T186, T187, T188, T189, T190, T191, T192, T193, T194, T195, T196, T197, T198, T199, T213, T214, T215, T216, T217, T218, T219, T220, T221, T222, T223, T224, T225, T238, T240, T241, T242, T243, T244, T245, T246, T247, T260, T261, T264, T265, T266, T267, T268, T269, T270, T271, T272, T273, T285, T286, T287, T288, T289, T290, T291, T292, T293, T294, T295, T308, T310, T321, T333, T336, T337, T338, T339, T340, T341, T342, T343, T344, T345, T358, T360, T361, T362, T363, T364, T365, T366, T367, T380, T381, T384, T385, T386, T387, T388, T389, T390, T391, T392, T393, T405, T406, T407, T408, T409, T410, T411, T412, T413, T414, T415, T428, T429, T430, T431, T432, T433, T434, T435, T436, T437, T454, T456, T457, T458, T459, T460, T461, T462, T463, T464, T465, T477, T478, T479, T480, T481, T482, T483, T484, T485, T498, T499 **Grammar, Usage, and Mechanics:** *Student Practice Book:* 42, 45, 47, 49, 50, 56, 57, 58, 72, 77, 82, 84, 99, 100, 101, 103, 112, 118, 130, 136, 142, 170; *Teacher Edition:* T18, T19, T28, T31, T35, T47, T50, T51, T52, T58, T60, T68, T69
1d: Acknowledge new information expressed by others and, when warranted, modify their own views.	**Student Edition:** 4, 5, 10, 11, 12, 13, 14, 15, 30, 31, 32, 33, 34, 35, 36, 37, 38, 39, 52, 53, 54, 55, 56, 57, 58, 59, 60, 61, 62, 63, 82, 83, 84, 85, 86, 87, 88, 89, 90, 91, 92, 93, 110, 111, 112, 113, 114, 115, 116, 117, 130, 131, 134, 135, 136, 137, 138, 139, 140, 141, 142, 143, 156, 157, 158, 159, 160, 161, 162, 163, 164, 165, 166, 167, 188, 189, 190, 191, 192, 193, 194, 195, 196, 197, 198, 199, 214, 215, 216, 217, 218, 219, 220, 221, 222, 223, 224, 225, 240, 241, 242, 243, 244, 245, 246, 247, 260, 261, 264, 265, 266, 267, 268, 269, 270, 271, 272, 273, 286, 287, 288, 289, 290, 291, 292, 293, 294, 295, 310, 311, 312, 313, 314, 315, 316, 317, 318, 319, 320, 321, 336, 337, 338, 339, 340, 341, 342, 343, 344, 345, 360, 361, 362, 363, 364, 365, 366, 367, 380, 381, 384, 385, 386, 387, 388, 389, 390, 391, 392, 393, 406, 407, 408, 409, 410, 411, 412, 413, 414, 415, 428, 429, 430, 431, 432, 433, 434, 435, 436, 437, 456, 457, 458, 459, 460, 461, 462, 463, 464, 465, 478, 479, 480, 481, 482, 483, 484, 485, 498, 499 **Teacher Edition:** T4, T5, T10, T11, T12, T13, T14, T15, T30, T31, T32, T33, T34, T35, T36, T37, T38, T39, T52, T53, T54, T55, T56, T57, T58, T59, T60, T61, T62, T63, T82, T83, T84, T85, T86, T87, T88, T89, T90, T91, T92, T93, T110, T111, T112, T113, T114, T115, T116, T117, T130, T131, T134, T135, T136, T137, T138, T139, T140, T141, T142, T143, T156, T157, T158, T159, T160, T161, T162, T163, T164, T165, T166, T167, T188, T189, T190, T191, T192, T193, T194, T195, T196, T197, T198, T199, T214, T215, T216, T217, T218, T219, T220, T221, T222, T223, T224, T225, T240, T241, T242, T243, T244, T245, T246, T247, T260, T261, T264, T265, T266, T267, T268, T269, T270, T271, T272, T273, T286, T287, T288, T289, T290, T291, T292, T293, T294, T295, T310, T311, T312, T313, T314, T315, T316, T317, T318, T319, T320, T321, T336, T337, T338, T339, T340, T341, T342, T343, T344, T345, T360, T361, T362, T363, T364, T365, T366, T367, T380, T381, T384, T385, T386, T387, T388, T389, T390, T391, T392, T393, T406, T407, T408, T409, T410, T411, T412, T413, T414, T415, T428, T429, T430, T431, T432, T433, T434, T435, T436, T437, T456, T457, T458, T459, T460, T461, T462, T463, T464, T465, T478, T479, T480, T481, T482, T483, T484, T485, T498, T499 **Grammar, Usage, and Mechanics:** *Student Practice Book:* 10, 45, 72, 78, 160, 166, 174, 196; *Teacher Edition:* T18, T27, T28, T35, T36, T51, T58, T60, T62, T68, T69

STANDARD	CORRELATION

Anchor Standard 2: Integrate and evaluate information presented in diverse media and formats, including visually, quantitatively, and orally.

Standard 2: Analyze the main ideas and supporting details presented in diverse media and formats (e.g., visually, quantitatively, orally) and explain how the ideas clarify a topic, text, or issue under study.

Student Edition: 10, 11, 12, 13, 14, 15, 30, 31, 32, 33, 34, 35, 36, 37, 38, 39, 52, 53, 54, 55, 56, 57, 58, 59, 60, 61, 62, 63,82, 83, 84, 85, 86, 87, 88, 89, 90, 91, 92, 93, 110, 111, 112, 113, 114, 115, 116, 117, 130, 131, 134, 135, 136, 137, 138, 139, 140, 141, 142, 143, 156, 157, 158, 159, 160, 161, 162, 163, 164, 165, 166, 167, 188, 189, 190, 191, 192, 193, 194, 195, 196, 197, 198, 199, 214, 215, 216, 217, 218, 219, 220, 221, 222, 223, 224, 225, 240, 241, 242, 243, 244, 245, 246, 247, 260, 261, 264, 265, 266, 267, 268, 269, 270, 271, 272, 273, 286, 287, 288, 289, 290, 291, 292, 293, 294, 295, 310, 311, 312, 313, 314, 315, 316, 317, 318, 319, 320, 321, 336, 337, 338, 339, 340, 341, 342, 343, 344, 345, 360, 361, 362, 363, 364, 365, 366, 367, 380, 381, 384, 385, 386, 387, 388, 389, 390, 391, 392, 393, 406, 407, 408, 409, 410, 411, 412, 413, 414, 415, 428, 429, 430, 431, 432, 433, 434, 435, 436, 437, 456, 457, 458, 459, 460, 461, 462, 463, 464, 465, 478, 479, 480, 481, 482, 483, 484, 485, 498, 499

Teacher Edition: T10, T11, T12, T13, T14, T15, T30, T31, T32, T33, T34, T35, T36, T37, T38, T39, T52, T53, T54, T55, T56, T57, T58, T59, T60, T61, T62, T63, T82, T83, T84, T85, T86, T87, T88, T89, T90, T91, T92, T93, T110, T111, T112, T113, T114, T115, T116, T117, T130, T131, T134, T135, T136, T137, T138, T139, T140, T141, T142, T143, T156, T157, T158, T159, T160,T 161, T162, T163, T164, T165, T166, T167, T188, T189, T190, T191, T192, T193, T194, T195, T196, T197, T198, T199, T214, T215, T216, T217, T218, T219, T220, T221, T222, T223, T224, T225, T240, T241, T242, T243, T244, T245, T246, T247, T260, T261, T264, T265, T266, T267, T268, T269, T270, T271, T272, T273, T286, T287, T288, T289, T290, T291, T292, T293, T294, T295, T310, T311, T312, T313, T314, T315, T316, T317, T318, T319, T320, T321, T336, T337, T338, T339, T340, T341, T342, T343, T344, T345, T360, T361, T362, T363, T364, T365, T366, T367, T380, T381, T384, T385, T386, T387, T388, T389, T390, T391, T392, T393, T406, T407, T408, T409, T410, T411, T412, T413, T414, T415, T428, T429, T430, T431, T432, T433, T434, T435, T436, T437, T456, T457, T458, T459, T460, T461, T462, T463, T464, T465, T478, T479, T480, T481, T482, T483, T484, T485, T498, T499

Grammar, Usage, and Mechanics: *Student Practice Book:* 72, 78, 136, 160, 166, 174; *Teacher Edition:* T35, T36, T52, T58, T60, T62

Anchor Standard 3: Evaluate a speakers' point of view, reasoning, and use of evidence and rhetoric.

Standard 3: Delineate a speaker's argument and specific claims, evaluating the soundness of the reasoning and the relevance and sufficiency of the evidence.

Grammar, Usage, and Mechanics: *Student Practice Book:* 52; *Teacher Edition:* T18, T29, T51, T54

SPEAKING AND LISTENING Presentation of Knowledge and Ideas

Anchor Standard 4: Present information, findings, and supporting evidence such that listeners can follow the line of reasoning and the organization, development, and style are appropriate to task, purpose, and audience.

Standard 4: Present claims and findings, emphasizing salient points in a focused, coherent manner with pertinent descriptions, facts, details, and examples; use appropriate eye contact, adequate volume, and clear pronunciation.

Teacher Edition: T204

Grammar, Usage, and Mechanics: *Student Practice Book:* 52, 56, 88, 136; *Teacher Edition:* T22, T29, T30, T39, T43, T44, T45, T46, T52, T53, T55, T61, T70

Anchor Standard 5: Make strategic use of digital media and visual displays of data to express information and enhance understanding of presentations.

Standard 5: Include multimedia components and visual displays in presentations to clarify claims and findings and emphasize salient points.

Teacher Edition: T27, T51, T79, T105, T155, T185, T213, T237, T285, T332, T333, T404, T437, T452, T453, T477

Grammar, Usage, and Mechanics: *Student Practice Book:* 205; *Teacher Edition:* T18, T19, T20, T21, T22, T28, T30, T37, T39, T42, T46, T67, T71

Anchor Standard 6: Adapt speech to a variety of contexts and communicative tasks, demonstrating command of formal English when indicated or appropriate.

Standard 6: Adapt speech to a variety of contexts and tasks, demonstrating command of formal English when indicated or appropriate.

Teacher Edition: T104, T465, T476, T483

Grammar, Usage, and Mechanics: *Student Practice Book:* 198; *Teacher Edition:* T26, T68

STRATEGIES FOR writers

7

Senior Author
Rebecca Bowers Sipe, Ed.D.
Eastern Michigan University

Consulting Authors
Julie Coiro, Ph.D.
University of Rhode Island

Amy Humphreys, Ed.M., NBCT
Educational Consultant

Sara B. Kajder, Ph.D.
University of Pittsburgh

Mark Overmeyer, M.A.
Cherry Creek School District, Colorado

Senior Consultant
James Scott Miller

ZB **Zaner-Bloser**

Photography: Cover ©McPhoto/Blickwinkel/age fotostock; Interior models, Tom Dubanowich; Stopwatch image © Royalty-Free/Corbis; p. 3 © Richard Cumins/Corbis; p. 9 © Michael St. Mauer Sheil/Corbis; pp. 28, 29 © Mystery Spot postcards; p. 133, © Phil Schermeister/Corbis; p. 191 © Free Agents Limited/Corbis; p. 213 © Lois Ellen Frank/Corbis, © Carlos Hernandez/cultura/Corbis; p. 237 © Michael Springer/Getty Images; p. 238 © Jake Wyman/Photographer's Choice/Getty Images; p. 263 © Walter Bibikow/JAI/Corbis; pp. 313, 315 © U.S. Space & Rocket Center. Space Camp® is a registered trademark of Alabama. pp. 333, 334 © Stone Mountain Park. Used with permission. All rights reserved. p. 383 © Michael DeYoung/Corbis; p. 409 © Gary W. Carter/Corbis; p. 427 © Sanford/Agliolo/Corbis; p. 455 © Galen Rowell/Corbis

Art Credits: pp. 4, 30, 52, 134, 156, 188, 264, 286, 310, 384, 406, 428 Illustrated Alaskan Moose Studio; pp. 55, 56, 57, 70, 80, 81 Charles Shaw; pp. 82, 214, 336, 456, 477 Chris Vallo; pp. 267, 444, 453, 454 Marilyn Rodgers Bahney Paselsky

Literature Credits: pp. 192–193 *The Structure That Never Sleeps* by Kim Williams © 2000 by Highlights for Children, Inc., Columbus, Ohio; p. 200–201 *What's So Hot About Spices?* by Gail Jarrow and Paul Sherman © 2000 by Highlights for Children, Inc., Columbus, Ohio

ISBN 978-0-7367-7282-2

Zaner-Bloser, Inc.
1-800-421-3018
www.zaner-bloser.com
Printed in the United States of America   12 13 14 15 19840 6 5 4 3 2

SUSTAINABLE FORESTRY INITIATIVE
Certified Chain of Custody
Promoting Sustainable Forestry
www.sfiprogram.org
SFICOC-0130

Hi, there!

We're your *Strategies for Writers* Writing Partners!

We're here to guide you step-by-step through the stages of the writing process: Prewrite, Draft, Revise, Edit, and Publish.

In each unit, we'll focus on one mode of writing: **narrative, informative/ explanatory, argument,** or **descriptive.**

Have you ever wondered what makes a good personal narrative? Or what the elements of a cause-and-effect report are? How about some reasons for writing a summary or an observation report? We'll answer those questions and more.

We'll focus on these six traits of effective writing: **Ideas, Organization, Voice, Word Choice, Sentence Fluency,** and **Conventions.** We'll explain how to apply the traits to each genre of writing, and we'll show you how the traits work together.

In each chapter, we'll first review a model writing sample. Then we'll use a rubric to score the model. Rubrics are a great way to know exactly what is expected as you plan and evaluate your writing. After that, it's your turn to write!

iii

Narrative writing

Table of Contents

Informative/Explanatory writing

Table of Contents

Tvii

Argument writing

Table of Contents

Descriptive writing

Table of Contents

Appendices

Appendix A: Grammar Practice

Table of Contents

Narrative writing

Personal Narrative

This genre introduces students to narrative writing by encouraging students to connect writing to their own lives by drawing on personal experience.

Prewrite List things the audience should know about the topic.
Make a 5 W's Chart.

Draft Use the 5 W's chart to stay focused and answer the audience's questions.

Revise Reorder sentences that seem out of place.
Use personal pronouns (*I, me*) to connect with the readers.
Choose precise and interesting words and phrases for effect.

Edit Make sure all sentences are complete.

Publish Publish the narrative in a class diary.

E-Mail
Pages T30A–T51

This genre teaches students about using the technology that permeates their lives in an effective and polite way—skills also used in writing letters.

Prewrite List the main idea or purpose for writing. Then list relevant details that support it.
Make a Main Idea Table.

Draft Use transition words to help the reader follow along.

Revise Make sure the tone is appropriate for the topic and the reader.
Avoid the use of slang. Use spell check as well as a dictionary to check spelling.
Check every sentence.

Edit Check for and fix any incorrect shifts in verb tense.

Publish Send the e-mail to the appropriate person.

Historical Episode
Pages T52A–T81

This genre gives students a chance to explore an episode from the past using the techniques of narrative fiction.

Prewrite Gather historical information from several references, including primary sources.
Make a Story Map.

Draft Maintain consistency in style and tone.

Revise Add historical details to make the story authentic.
Replace weak verbs with strong ones.
Use different kinds of sentences.

Edit Check to see that punctuation is correct.

Publish Include the historical episode in the hallway display case.

Play

Pages T82A–T109

Students will express their understanding of a scientific concept or event in the creative form of a play.

Prewrite	Plan the plot and research details. Use a Story Map to logically and effectively sequence events.
Draft	Use specific nouns and powerful verbs.
Revise	Write dialogue and stage directions that inform the reader. Follow the Story Map. Vary sentence patterns for meaning, reader or listener interest, and style.
Edit	Check the use of conjunctions to join sentences.
Publish	Perform the play.

Narrative Test Writing

Pages T110A–T131

Students will learn and practice how to read and respond to a narrative test prompt, plan their time appropriately, and compose a piece of writing.

Prewrite	Study the writing prompt to find out what to do. Respond to the task. Choose a graphic organizer. Check the graphic organizer against the scoring guide.
Draft	Entertain the reader with lively, descriptive details and dialogue.
Revise	Use transition words to clarify sequence. Connect with the readers. Use powerful verbs to give the writing energy.
Edit	Check grammar, punctuation, capitalization, and spelling.

Online Writing Center

Interactive Whiteboard Ready

Complete Digital Writing Instruction!

- My Writing Pad
- Interactive Rubrics
- Anchor Papers
- Graphic Organizers

- Content Area Writing Prompts
- Grammar Games
- Proofreading Activities
- Instructional Videos

- Virtual File Cabinet
- eBooks
- Assessments

For information, go to www.sfw.z-b.com

Also available: **Online Essay Grader and Writing Tutor,** powered by Vantage Learning's MY Access®.

21ˢᵗ Century Literacies
Technology, Digital Media & Writing

by **Julie Coiro, Ph.D.,** University of Rhode Island & **Sara Kajder, Ph.D.,** University of Pittsburgh

 **INSPIRE** ## Websites to Spark Ideas

Writing Historical Episodes

The following websites prompt opportunities for students to experience history through images, photographs, and audio and video clips.

- **American Memory (http://memory.loc.gov/ammem/index.html)** provides open access to written and spoken words, sound recordings, still and moving images, prints, maps, and sheet music that document the American experience. Students can browse the archive by topic, time period, or geographical location.

- **CNN Student News (www.cnn.com/studentnews)** is a ten-minute, commercial-free, daily news program for middle and high school students. Teacher materials—including transcripts for each show, Daily Discussion questions, the Media Literacy Question of the Day, in-depth Learning Activities, downloadable maps, and additional support materials—help students understand the news and enhance students' research, writing, and verbal communication skills.

- **EASE History (www.easehistory.org/index2.html)** provides access to hundreds of historical videos and photographs searchable by theme, keyword, or classroom topic in an Experience Accelerated Supportive Environment (EASE). A Teacher's Learning Guide includes lessons that help students place an event in a broader historical context or analyze the reliability of a source.

Linking Narrative Writing to Science

Many websites offer students the opportunity to link their writing to topics such as math, social studies, science, and art. Here are a few websites to spark ideas for linking narrative writing to science.

How Stuff Works (www.howstuffworks.com) is an award-winning website with a treasure trove of easy-to-understand explanations of how the world actually works. Articles, helpful graphics, and informative podcasts and videos will surely inspire writing ideas for your students.

The Engineer Girl (www.engineergirl.org) website includes profiles of women engineers; a list of engineering careers, including the education requirements, work environments, and job descriptions for specific types of engineering jobs; a Fun Facts link; and a yearly Engineer Girl essay contest.

The Science Museum of Minnesota (http://www.smm.org/explore) links to a variety of websites and learning activities. For example, the *Playful Invention and Exploration (PIE) network* was made to inspire people to create and explore, using a combination of traditional craft materials and new digital technologies. The Tissues of Life website allows students to meet tissue researchers and test their knowledge of viruses, bacteria, and how the human body works to defend itself.

The Why Files (www.whyfiles.org), founded by the National Institute for Science Education, offers written investigations of current topics in science in accessible language. The Why Files publishes a new story each week, a series of *Teacher Activity Pages* linked to the national science teaching standards, and features such as "The Weather Guys" and "Curiosities."

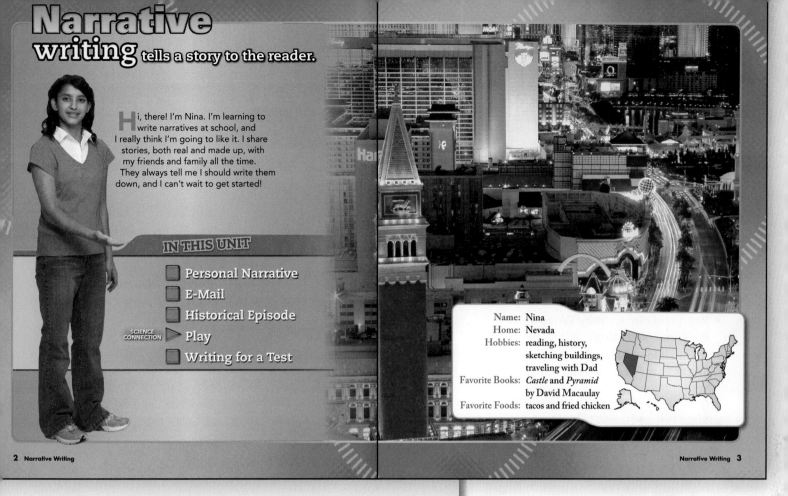

Narrative writing tells a story to the reader.

Hi, there! I'm Nina. I'm learning to write narratives at school, and I really think I'm going to like it. I share stories, both real and made up, with my friends and family all the time. They always tell me I should write them down, and I can't wait to get started!

IN THIS UNIT

- [ ] Personal Narrative
- [ ] E-Mail
- [ ] Historical Episode

SCIENCE CONNECTION ▶ Play

- [ ] Writing for a Test

Name: Nina
Home: Nevada
Hobbies: reading, history, sketching buildings, traveling with Dad
Favorite Books: *Castle* and *Pyramid* by David Macaulay
Favorite Foods: tacos and fried chicken

To differentiate instruction and maximize student achievement, use the Extensions Online activities available at **www.sfw.z-b.com.**

Created by Amy Humphreys, Ed.M., these engaging activities can be used to meet a wide range of learner needs. Each activity uses a combination of visual, written, oral, and kinesthetic elements, and deliberately leverages the power of collaboration and conversation so students learn to think like writers in fun and engaging ways. For more information on Differentiated Instruction, see page Z12.

Meet Your Writing Partner, Nina

The writing partner for this chapter is Nina, a girl from Nevada. Invite students to discuss what they may or may not have in common with Nina, based on the information given about her. Also discuss how Nina's interests might influence what she chooses to write about. Elicit from students that Nina will use what she knows to make decisions about her topic and that this helps to make her writing special and real. Encourage students to use their own background knowledge, interests, and personalities as they write in the same way that Nina does. Narrative writing tells stories, and your students will have many interesting, unique, and authentic stories to tell.

Personal Narrative Planner

WEEK 1

Day 1
Introduce
a Personal Narrative

Student Objectives
- Review the elements of a personal narrative.
- Consider purpose and audience.
- Learn the traits of narrative writing.

Student Activities
- Read and discuss **What's in a Personal Narrative?** (p. 4)
- Read and discuss **Why Write a Personal Narrative?** (p. 5)
- Read **Linking Narrative Writing Traits to a Personal Narrative.** (p. 6)

Day 2
Analyze
Read a Personal Narrative

Student Objectives
- Read a model personal narrative.

Student Activities
- Read **"A Journey Back in Time."** (pp. 7–9)

Day 3
Analyze
Introduce the Rubric

Student Objectives
- Learn to read a rubric.

Student Activities
- Review **"A Journey Back in Time."** (pp. 7–9)
- Read and discuss the **Personal Narrative Rubric.** (pp. 10–11)

WEEK 2

Day 1
Write
Prewrite: Ideas

Student Objectives
- Read and understand a prewriting strategy.

Student Activities
- Read and discuss **Prewrite: Focus on Ideas.** (p. 16)
- Apply the prewriting strategy.

Day 2
Write
Prewrite: Organization

Student Objectives
- Make a 5 W's Chart to answer *Who, What, Where, When,* and *Why.*

Student Activities
- Read and discuss **Prewrite: Focus on Organization.** (p. 17)
- Reflect on the model 5 W's Chart.
- Apply the prewriting strategy to create a 5 W's Chart.
- Participate in a peer conference.

Day 3
Write
Draft: Ideas

Student Objectives
- Use a 5 W's Chart to begin writing.

Student Activities
- Read and discuss **Draft: Focus on Ideas.** (p. 18)
- Reflect on the model draft. (p. 19)
- Apply the drafting strategy by using a 5 W's Chart to write a draft.
- Participate in a peer conference.

WEEK 3

Day 1
Write
Revise: Voice

Student Objectives
- Revise for first-person point of view.

Student Activities
- Read and discuss **Revise: Focus on Voice.** (p. 21)
- Reflect on a model draft.
- Apply the revising strategy.
- Participate in a peer conference.

Day 2
Write
Revise: Word Choice

Student Objectives
- Revise for precise language.

Student Activities
- Read and discuss **Revise: Focus on Word Choice.** (p. 22)
- Reflect on the model draft.
- Apply the revising strategy.

Note: Optional Revising Lessons appear on the *Strategies for Writers* CD-ROM.

Day 3
Write
Edit: Conventions

Student Objectives
- Edit for complete sentences.

Student Activities
- Read and discuss **Edit: Focus on Conventions.** (p. 23)
- Reflect on the model draft.
- Apply the editing strategy.

Note: Teach the Conventions mini-lessons (pp. 24–25) if needed.

Day 4

Analyze
Ideas, Organization, and Voice

Student Objectives
- Read a model personal narrative.
- Use the personal narrative rubric.
- Use the model personal narrative to study Ideas, Organization, and Voice.

Student Activities
- Review **"A Journey Back in Time."** (pp. 7–9)
- Read and discuss **Using the Rubric to Study the Model.** (pp. 12–13)

Day 5

Analyze
Word Choice, Sentence Fluency, and Conventions

Student Objectives
- Read a model personal narrative.
- Use the personal narrative rubric.
- Use the model personal narrative to study Word Choice, Sentence Fluency, and Conventions.

Student Activities
- Review **"A Journey Back in Time."** (pp. 7–9)
- Read and discuss **Using the Rubric to Study the Model.** (pp. 14–15)

Day 4

Write
Draft

Student Objectives
- Complete a draft.

Student Activities
- Finish the draft. (p. 19)

Day 5

Write
Revise: Organization

Student Objectives
- Revise sentence order to keep event sequence logical.

Student Activities
- Read and discuss **Revise: Focus on Organization.** (p. 20)
- Reflect on a model draft.
- Apply the revising strategy.

Day 4

Write
Publish: +Presentation

Student Objectives
- Discuss preparation for publishing and presentation.
- Use a final editing checklist to publish their work.

Student Activities
- Read and discuss **Publish: +Presentation.** (p. 26)
- Apply the publishing strategy.

Day 5

Write
Publish: +Presentation

Student Objectives
- Use a personal narrative rubric.
- Share a published personal narrative.

Student Activities
- Share their work.
- Use the rubric to reflect upon and evaluate the model and their own writing. (pp. 10–11, 27–29)

Grammar, U... Mechanics

Differentiating Instruction

For additional Differentiating Instruction activities, see Strategies for Writers *Extensions Online at* **www.sfw.z-b.com.**

English Language Learners

Conferencing

Technology Tip

 Connection Letter
Reproducible letter (in English and Spanish) appears on the *Strategies for Writers* CD-ROM and at **www.sfw.z-b.com.**

Online Writing Center

Provides IWB resources, interactive games and practice activities, videos, eBooks, and a virtual file cabinet.

 Strategies for Writers Online
Go to **www.sfw.z-b.com** for free online resources for students and teachers.

To complete the chapter in fewer days, combine the learning objectives and activities in a way that supports students as they write.

Int[ro]duce
a Personal Narrative

Student Objectives

- Review the elements of a personal narrative. *(p. 4)*
- Consider purpose and audience. *(p. 5)*
- Learn the traits of narrative writing. *(p. 6)*

What's a Personal Narrative?

Ask for volunteers to share brief, memorable stories. It might be helpful to use a prompt, such as: *I'll never forget the day I (we) ____.*

Explain that students are telling a specific type of narrative, or story, called the *personal narrative.* In this type of writing, an author writes about an event that occurred in his or her own life. Emphasize that personal narratives are written in first person (*I, me*).

What's in a Personal Narrative?

Reflect as a class on the narratives just shared by volunteers. Ask students to identify these elements of a personal narrative:

- Narrator
- Sequence
- Tone
- The 5 W's

Confirm students' understanding of these elements by reading aloud the definitions on page 4.

 Strategies for Writers Online
Go to **www.sfw.z-b.com** for additional online resources for students and teachers.

What's a **Personal Narrative?**

It's a true story about an event that really happened to me. I think this kind of writing is fun because I get to write about something interesting, exciting, or even sad from my own life.

What's in a **Personal Narrative?**

Narrator
That's me! The narrator is the person who is telling the story. I've experienced many things that I'd like to tell people. Now I'll be able to share one of my stories with an audience!

Sequence
This is the order in which things happened. I'll describe the events of my story as they happened because I want my reader to understand the big picture, from beginning to end.

Tone
Tone is how I want my story to sound and how I want my readers to feel. I can change the tone depending on what I'm writing about. It sounds tricky, but it isn't. I might use short sentence patterns to build suspense, powerful verbs to create drama, or descriptive language to create a mysterious, sad, or funny tone.

The 5 W's
These are the details that tell the **who, what, when, where,** and **why** of my story. I'll use all of these in my story, but I have to remember to keep each detail vivid and true!

Narrative Text Exemplars (Personal Narrative)

Alcott, Louisa May. *Little Women.* Penguin, 1989. CCSS
Little Women is a story of the four March sisters as they grow up in 19th century New England. The sisters struggle to help their family while holding true to their own dreams.

Cisneros, Sandra. "Eleven." *Woman Hollering Creek and Other Stories.* Random House, 1991. CCSS
"Eleven" is a short story about a young girl who has an awful experience on her eleventh birthday. However, as she fights to be understood, she shows a maturity well beyond her years.

Why write a Personal Narrative?

There are plenty of reasons to write a personal narrative. I listed some here. I hope they will help me as I think about what I want to write.

Entertainment
Entertaining the reader is one good reason to write a personal narrative. Sometimes something happens to me that is so funny, exciting, or sad that I just want to share it with someone else.

Personal Reflection
Writing helps me reflect, or make sense out of the things I remember. Reflecting can help me understand how I've been affected by something I've experienced.

Information
Sometimes I might experience something that would be useful for others to read about. I can write my account in order to educate, instruct, or inform my reader.

Summary
Some things I've experienced would make long and complicated stories. Often there are many smaller details that lead up to one main event, so it's important for me to summarize only the details my reader really needs to know. It's also good to practice using my summarization skills, especially since I'll use them a lot in school.

Personal Narrative **5**

Why write a Personal Narrative?

Explain that good writers always understand their purpose for writing and the audience that will be reading their work. Both the purpose and audience influence how the writer crafts his or her writing.

Read page 5 aloud. Ask students how the writing might differ according to the purpose and audience. For example, a writer might use a humorous tone, colorful descriptions, and clever anecdotes to entertain. However, a writer might use a more somber tone with a focus on personal feelings if he or she is writing for personal reflection. When writing to inform, a writer is more likely to include some facts and explain how and why events took place.

Conclude by explaining to students that they are going to study and practice strategies for writing a personal narrative.

Greenwald, Lisa. *My Life in Pink & Green.* Amulet Books, 2010. Lucy is a 12-year-old girl living in small-town Conneticut. When she finds out that the pharmacy run by her mom and grandmother is in danger of foreclosure, Lucy tries to drum up business by offering makeup tips and applications. This idea evolves into creating an eco-spa once Lucy joins her school's Earth Club. *My Life in Pink & Green* is an inspiring story that tackles large issues in an uplifting manner.

Taylor, Mildred D. *Roll of Thunder, Hear My Cry.* Puffin Books, 2004. **CCSS** *Roll of Thunder, Hear My Cry* is the story of an African American family's struggle to keep their honor and pride intact as they face racism in Mississippi during the Depression. As the family fights to stay together, the children harden against social injustice and bigotry.

CCSS **C**ommon **C**ore **S**tate **S**tandards

SL.7.1: Engage effectively in a range of collaborative discussions (one-on-one, in groups, and teacher-led) with diverse partners on *grade 7 topics, texts, and issues,* building on each others' ideas and expressing their own clearly.

Personal Narrative **T5**

Introduce
a Personal Narrative

Linking Narrative Writing Traits to a Personal Narrative

Read page 6 aloud to help students understand that they will follow Nina as she models how to use the writing process and the narrative writing traits together. A good personal narrative will focus on one event, provide vivid sensory details, describe events in chronological order, and be told in a voice appropriate for the subject. Tell students they will read a model personal narrative as an example of how one writer used narrative writing traits.

In this chapter, you will write a story about an experience you want to share. This type of narrative writing is called a personal narrative. Nina will guide you through the stages of the writing process: Prewrite, Draft, Revise, Edit, and Publish. In each stage, Nina will show you important writing strategies that are linked to the Narrative Writing Traits below.

Narrative Writing Traits

Ideas	• a single, focused topic with relevant, engaging details that develop the experiences or events • a narrator or characters that bring the story to life
Organization	• well-structured and logical event sequences, often in chronological order, that guide the reader through the story • an engaging beginning and a satisfying conclusion that reflects on the story's events • a variety of transition words that signal time or setting changes
Voice	• a voice that is appropriate for the audience and purpose • dialogue that, if used, is realistic and helps develop the characters and story
Word Choice	• precise, descriptive words and phrases
Sentence Fluency	• a variety of sentences that flow and are a pleasure to read aloud
Conventions	• no or few errors in grammar, usage, mechanics, and spelling

Before you write, read Melanie Van der Hoff's personal narrative on the next three pages. Then use the personal narrative rubric on pages 10–11 to decide how well she did. (You might want to look back at What's in a Personal Narrative? on page 4, too!)

Narrative Writing Traits in a Personal Narrative

 **Ideas** Details that answer the 5 W's will acquaint the reader with the narrator or characters and make the reader feel like part of the experience.

 **Organization** Transition words organize events into a logical sequence. A strong introduction engages the reader, and a satisfying conclusion wraps up the events.

 **Voice** Using first-person point of view and an energetic voice is appropriate in a personal narrative.

Online Writing Center

 Provides six **interactive anchor papers** for each mode of writing.

T6 Narrative Writing

A JOURNEY BACK IN TIME

by Melanie Van der Hoff

Narrator

The older people in our family used to talk often about World War II. The years were passing, but the men's memories of fighting to free Europe remained strong. Then the movie *Saving Private Ryan* came out in 1998, and Uncle Harry knew he had to go back to see France again. I was lucky enough to be one of the family members who went with him that year. The area that our visit would primarily focus on was the Normandy Beaches. About 150 miles to the west of Paris, these beaches were the landing spot in June 1944 for 175,000 British, American, and Canadian forces. They had crossed the English Channel from Britain in boats and planes. Their goal was to retake Europe from Nazi Germany. Uncle Harry was one of the soldiers who made the landing.

Who
What
Why
Where
When
Sequence

The journey back in time began when our plane landed in Paris. This beautiful city became the headquarters for our trip. From a small hotel in the district called the Latin Quarter, it was an easy Metro, or subway, ride to the city's main attractions. We strolled along the Seine River, stood in line for the elevators to the top of the Eiffel Tower, and saw the *Mona Lisa* at the Louvre Museum. But these sights, though impressive, were not the real reason for our trip.

Great Britain
English Channel
Normandy
Paris
France
Spain

Personal Narrative **7**

Word Choice Good writers use precise words and phrases to bring their stories to life. Original choice and use of words will make a writer's work stand out.

Sentence Fluency A variety of sentence types and structures are used in a good narrative to give the writing energy and flow. The writing is a pleasure to listen to or to read aloud.

Conventions A good writer carefully edits his or her work prior to publishing. Mistakes in spelling, punctuation, capitalization, and grammar will confuse the reader and obscure the author's purpose.

Analyze
the Model

Week 1 • Day 2

Student Objectives

- Read a model personal narrative. *(pp. 7–9)*

Read the Model

Read aloud "A Journey Back in Time." Post on the board some questions for students to think about as they read so they will be ready to discuss the personal narrative later on.

- How does the setting (where, when) affect the story told by the author?

- What details do you find most memorable? Why?

- How are the events organized? How do you know?

- How does the first-person point of view affect how you connect with the story?

Elements of a Personal Narrative

Have students refer to What's in a Personal Narrative? on page 4 as you refer to the model. Discuss the notes on the model to enhance students' understanding of the terms, such as *narrator* and *5 W's.*

CCSS Common Core State Standards
R/Lit.7.3: Analyze how particular elements of a story or drama interact (e.g., how setting shapes the characters or plot).

On the fourth day, we rented a car and set out for our true destination. Meandering north through the French countryside, we saw ancient, sleepy villages as well as some with a more modern appearance. Uncle Harry explained that these newer-looking towns had probably been bombed out during the war and then rebuilt. Within a few hours, we were approaching the invasion area.

Sequence

Our guidebooks and maps traced out a quiet route along the coast. From our car, we saw the remains of German artillery in two different areas. The ancient, rusting hulks, once so threatening to the Allied invaders, sat placidly in the sun. We joined the few tourists walking around one site, touching the artillery, and looking out to the sea. Uncle Harry did not want to get out of the car, though. He was saving his strength for the two things he had really come to see.

The first of these was the area called Omaha Beach. A long, open stretch of land, this was the main invasion area for the American forces. I recalled the chaotic scenes from *Saving Private Ryan,* the soldiers shouting and dying everywhere, the boats and artillery all around. What a contrast with the quiet scene on the day we visited! Few, if any, signs of the great struggle remained. There was a family camping area nearby, and on the beach lay groups of teenagers sunbathing. I wondered if anyone in their families had ever shared wartime recollections with them. Uncle Harry shook his head almost sorrowfully. "It's all so different now," he whispered.

I wondered if Uncle Harry was ready for the other site he had wanted to visit: the American cemetery overlooking Omaha Beach. One look at his determined face, though, gave us our answer.

Books for Professional Development

Heitman, Jane. *Teach Writing to Older Readers Using Picture Books: Every Picture Tells a Story.* 2nd ed. Santa Barbara, CA: Linworth Publishing, 2005. This resource explains how to use the unique style of picture books to teach the basic literary elements of character, point of view, setting, plot, style, and theme and to improve students' writing and literacy skills.

Peregoy, Suzanne F., and Owen F. Boyle. *Reading, Writing and Learning in ESL: A Resource Book for K–12 Teachers.* 4th ed. Boston: Allyn & Bacon, 2004. This is an outstanding resource book for elementary and secondary teachers who work with ESL students.

Tompkins, Gail E. *Teaching Writing: Balancing Process and Product.* 4th ed. Upper Saddle River: Prentice Hall, 2003. This book contains information on teaching

Strategies for Writers Online
Go to **www.sfw.z-b.com** for additional online resources for students and teachers.

The American cemetery is one of the most impressive sites you will ever see. More than 9,000 soldiers killed on invasion day or soon after are buried there. The white crosses, interrupted now and then by Stars of David, are lined up in rows as far as one can see. The simple birth and death dates engraved on the grave markers tell nothing of the agony those soldiers endured. And some graves are not even identified. Engraved on these headstones are the words "HERE RESTS IN HONORED GLORY A COMRADE IN ARMS KNOWN BUT TO GOD."

Tone → Uncle Harry had never given us the particulars, but we knew that several of his close buddies had died on Omaha Beach. Now we asked him if he wanted to look for any of their graves. Too choked up with emotion to speak, Uncle Harry stood at the memorial in the center of the cemetery and shook his head no. He had done his duty just by going there. And it felt as if, by accompanying him and bearing witness to what he had endured, we had done our duty, too.

writing strategies and processes for grades K–8 through writing workshop, literature focus units, and thematic units. Numerous authentic children's writing samples are interspersed throughout the material, along with the author's well-respected mini-lessons and thoughtful discussion of performance-based tools for assessment.

Wood, Karen D., and Janis M. Harmon. *Strategies for Integrating Reading and Writing in Middle and High School Classrooms.* **Westerville, OH: NMSA, 2001.** These easy-to-use, research-based strategies are designed to improve students' performance and interest in course content by increasing the time they spend reading and writing. Each chapter addresses a topic relevant to middle school and high school literacy and offers sample lessons to illustrate the application to various subject areas.

CCSS **Common Core State Standards**

R/Lit.7.1: Cite several pieces of textual evidence to support analysis of what the text says explicitly as well as inferences drawn from the text.

Analyze
the Model

Week 1 • Day 3

Student Objectives

- Learn to read a rubric.
  (pp. 10–11)

Use the Rubric

Explain the Rubric Explain that a rubric is a tool for planning, improving, and assessing a piece of writing. Tell students that a rubric helps a writer focus on key elements, or traits, in writing (**Ideas, Organization, Voice, Word Choice, Sentence Fluency, Conventions,** and **Presentation**).

Explain the 6-point system. Point out that column 6 on page 10 represents a good personal narrative, one that received the highest score in all categories. The other columns represent writing that needs improvement.

Discuss the Rubric Guide students in a discussion of the rubric. Read the descriptors that go with each trait. Discuss the difference between columns to be sure students fully understand the point system.

Remind students to keep the rubric in mind when they write their own personal narrative and again when they revise it.

Rubric

Use this 6-point rubric to plan and evaluate a personal narrative.

	6	5	4
Ideas	The narrative orients the reader to and focuses on one event. Memorable description of the 5 W's develops the experience and answers the audience's questions.	The narrative focuses on one event. Many interesting details mention the 5 W's and answer the reader's questions.	The narrative focuses on one event and is clear more often than not. Some quality details include some of the 5 W's.
Organization	Ideas are organized to unfold naturally and logically. The lead engages the reader.	Ideas are organized logically. The lead is strong.	The overall organization works. The lead is functional.
Voice	The writer makes a strong connection with the reader by using first-person point of view and a personal tone.	The writer connects with the reader by using first-person point of view and a personal tone.	The writer fails to connect with the reader in the beginning. The voice is distant or too formal.
Word Choice	Precise words and phrases convey the experience and bring the story to life.	Vivid words and phrases help the reader form mental images of the story.	Some catchy words or phrases are used. Some descriptions are vague, but the overall meaning is still clear.
Sentence Fluency	Variety in sentence length and beginnings is striking. The narrative flows smoothly.	There is noticeable variety in sentence length and beginnings. The writing has a rhythm when read out loud.	There is some variety in sentence length and beginnings. The writing is easy to read.
Conventions	Conjunctions are used correctly in compound sentences, and all sentences are complete.	Minor errors with conjunctions and sentence construction do not interfere with the meaning.	There are noticeable errors with conjunctions and sentence construction, but they don't distract the reader.
✛ Presentation	Visuals (photographs or illustrations) are used effectively.		

CCSS Common Core State Standards

Personal Narrative

The Common Core State Standards are woven throughout the instruction in *Strategies for Writers*. Writing in the Narrative mode can engage the Common Core State Standards for all forms of Narrative writing. In this chapter, the Ideas rubric descriptors reflect standards **W.7.3.a** and **W.7.3.b** in their emphasis on orienting the reader to the narrative and using the narrative technique of description to develop the writer's experience. The Organization rubric is drawn directly from standard **W.7.3.a** where the standard specifies that events should unfold naturally and logically.

Online Writing Center

Provides a variety of **interactive rubrics,** including 4-, 5-, and 6-point models.

3	2	1	
The narrative is often not focused. The details are general or vague and do not answer the 5 W's.	The narrative is not clear. Broad details do little to enhance the writing.	The writing lacks details. The focus is missing.	**Ideas**
The organization is confusing in places. The lead is not designed to catch the reader's interest.	The organization is difficult to follow throughout. The lead may be missing or confusing.	The reader feels lost. The lead is missing.	**Organization**
The writer's voice is often hard to relate to. The voice is rarely personal.	There is just a hint of the writer's voice. The voice isn't a good match for the audience or purpose.	The writer's voice is absent. The reader does not know who is writing the story.	**Voice**
Many words are too general and don't create clear descriptions.	The writing contains very few descriptions. Descriptive words that are used are tired and unclear.	Most of the words are dull and general. The reader cannot form clear mental images. The words simply fill the page and don't speak to the reader.	**Word Choice**
Sentence beginnings are repetitive, and there is little variety in length.	Little variety in the sentences makes the story hard to read aloud.	The story is difficult to read even with practice. Sentences are repetitive or incomplete.	**Sentence Fluency**
Noticeable errors with conjunctions and sentence construction cause the reader to reread parts of the story.	Many mistakes with conjunctions and sentence construction make the writing hard to read.	Frequent, serious mistakes with conjunctions and sentence construction make the writing almost impossible to read.	**Conventions**

See Appendix B for 4-, 5-, and 6-point narrative rubrics.

The focus on precise language to convey experiences found in standard **W.7.3.d** is reflected in the Word Choice rubric. As in all chapters, standards **L.7.1** and **L.7.2** are represented in the Conventions rubric.

Apply the Rubric

Assign Groups Assign a small group of students to check the model for the traits. One person in each group should be responsible for recording one or two strong examples of each trait as described by the rubric. Ask students to score the model for each trait. They should be able to support the score given with concrete examples from the model. Note that although the models were written to score high against the rubric, students should not assume that each trait should receive a 6.

Reassemble Class Bring the class back together and ask one person from each group to report their findings to the class. Do all students agree on score values? At the end of the discussion, take a vote on the score for each trait to see whether the class comes to a consensus. Remember, though, that the focus of this exercise is not so much to score the model but to practice identifying the traits within a piece of writing.

Additional Rubrics Appendix B includes 4-, 5-, and 6-point rubrics that can be used with any piece of narrative writing. The rubrics are also available as blackline masters, beginning on page T543.

CCSS Common Core State Standards

SL.7.1.a: Come to discussions prepared, having read or researched material under study, explicitly draw on that preparation by referring to evidence on the topic, text, or issue to probe and reflect on ideas under discussion.

Analyze
the Model

Week 1 • Day 4

Student Objectives

- Read a model personal narrative. *(pp. 7–9)*
- Use the personal narrative rubric. *(pp. 10–11)*
- Use the model personal narrative to study Ideas, Organization, and Voice. *(pp. 12–13)*

Study the Model

Assess the Model Have volunteers read aloud each section on pages 12–13. As a class, discuss whether students agree or disagree with each of Nina's assessments of the model. Use questions such as the following to initiate the conversation. Be sure students can back up their answers with clear examples from the narrative.

- Which description of one of the 5 W's do you find most memorable? Why? (Possible response: The description of Uncle Harry at the graveyard answers *why* in a very memorable way. It is moving to see how Uncle Harry reacts, and it helps provide an understanding of why he needed to come to this place.)

Strategies for Writers Online
Go to **www.sfw.z-b.com** for additional online resources for students and teachers.

T12 Narrative Writing

Using the Rubric to Study the Model
Personal Narrative

Did you notice that the model on pages 7–9 points out some key elements of a personal narrative? As she wrote "A Journey Back in Time," Melanie Van der Hoff used these elements to help her describe a personal experience. She also used the 6-point rubric on pages 10–11 to plan, draft, revise, and edit the writing. A rubric is a great tool to evaluate writing during the writing process.

Now let's use the same rubric to score the model. To do this, we'll focus on each trait separately, starting with Ideas. We'll use the top descriptor for each trait (column 6), along with examples from the model, to help us understand how the traits work together. How would you score Melanie on each trait?

Ideas

- The narrative orients the reader to and focuses on one event.
- Memorable description of the 5 W's develops the experience and answers the audience's questions.

Melanie's narrative focuses on one event—a family trip to France. She answers many of the 5 W's in the very first paragraph, such as *who* (Uncle Henry and family), *where* (France), *what* (a trip to France), and even *why* (for Uncle Harry to revisit where he once fought in WWII).

[from the writing model]

Then the movie *Saving Private Ryan* came out in 1998, and Uncle Harry knew he had to go back to see France again. I was lucky enough to be one of the family members who went with him that year.

English Language Learners

BEGINNING

The 5 W's Locate a photograph of a birthday party invitation. You may choose to draw an invitation on the board with the *who, what, when, where,* and *why* information filled in. Point to the picture and ask, *What is this?* When a student gives an answer, say, *It is a party.* Have students repeat. On the board, write *What: a party.* Repeat for *who, when, where,* and *why.* After you finish, review the list on the board. Ask, *What is it? Who is it for?* and so on. If time and students' abilities allow, review the questions and have students ask each other.

INTERMEDIATE

The 5 W's Tell students, *Let's plan a party!* Draw a blank party invitation on the board with *Party!* at the top. Ask students, *What kind of party will we have?* If students say, for example, *a birthday party,* write *What: birthday* on the invite. Repeat for the remaining 5 W's.

Organization

- Ideas are organized to unfold naturally and logically.
- The lead engages the reader.

Melanie's opening made me feel as though I was sitting around a table with her family, about to hear stories from long ago. The lead grabbed my attention and I was excited to read on. Melanie also organizes each part of her narrative in a logical order, which makes it easy to read and understand.

[from the writing model]

> The older people in our family used to talk often about World War II. The years were passing, but the men's memories of fighting to free Europe remained strong.

Voice

- The writer makes a strong connection with the reader by using first-person point of view and a personal tone.

It was easy to connect with Melanie's narrative because she uses first-person point of view (*I, we*) and a personal tone. However, she keeps her voice respectful and serious, which is appropriate when considering her narrative's theme.

[from the writing model]

> Uncle Harry had never given us the particulars, but we knew that several of his close buddies had died on Omaha Beach. Now we asked him if he wanted to look for any of their graves.

- How has Melanie organized the events in her narrative? (Possible response: Melanie presented the events in chronological order, which made it easy to follow along.)

- How would you describe the tone Melanie uses? (Possible response: Melanie uses a somber, respectful voice throughout the narrative, which reflects how she feels about Uncle Harry and his experience in the war.)

ADVANCED

Identifying the 5 W's Read a short story to students. The story should clearly answer the 5 W's. After you read the story the first time, give students 3 minutes to work quietly with a partner to fill out the 5 W's chart. After 3 minutes, read the story again. Have partners revise their charts as necessary. Have students review their charts as a group.

ADVANCED HIGH

Identifying the 5 W's Give each student a language-level-appropriate narrative to read. It can be a newspaper article, a decodable book, or a leveled reader from a reading program. After students have read their piece, have them fill in a 5 W's chart. Tell them that they may have to use other clues, such as pictures, to gather the information. Then have them trade selections and 5 W's charts with a partner. The partner should read the selection and review the chart for mistakes.

CCSS **Common Core State Standards**
SL.7.1.b: Follow rules for collegial discussions, track progress toward specific goals and deadlines, and define individual roles as needed. **SL.7.1.c:** Pose questions that elicit elaboration and respond to others' questions and comments with relevant observations and ideas that bring the discussion back on topic as needed.

Analyze
the Model

Week 1 • Day 5

Student Objectives

- Read a model personal narrative. (pp. 7–9)
- Use the personal narrative rubric. (pp. 10–11)
- Use the model personal narrative to study Word Choice, Sentence Fluency, and Conventions. (pp. 14–15)

Continue the Discussion Use questions such as the following to discuss the traits analyzed on pages 14–15:

- How does Melanie's choice of words and phrases affect how you experience the story? (Possible response: Melanie uses accurate, vivid words that really brought the scene to life for me.)

- Choose one other example of a sentence with an interesting beginning that helps the writing flow. (Possible response: *The white crosses, interrupted now and then by Stars of David, are lined up in rows as far as one can see.*)

- Has Melanie effectively used conjunctions to vary her sentence length and structure? (Possible response: Melanie uses both long and short sentences to keep things flowing. In addition, she uses conjunctions well to avoid too many short sentences.)

Strategies for Writers Online
Go to **www.sfw.z-b.com** for additional online resources for students and teachers.

Word Choice

- Precise words and phrases convey the experience and bring the story to life.

Melanie uses so many precise and colorful descriptions of her family trip that I can picture each scene in my mind like a movie. She uses adjectives that are specific, creative, and appropriate for her subject. They make her narrative really come alive for me.

[from the writing model]

> From our car, we saw the remains of German artillery in two different areas. The ancient, rusting hulks, once so threatening to the Allied invaders, sat placidly in the sun. We joined the few tourists walking around one site, touching the artillery, and looking out to the sea.

Sentence Fluency

- Variety in sentence length and beginnings is striking.
- The narrative flows smoothly.

At first I wondered why Melanie's narrative flows so smoothly, why it is so easy to read and understand. But then I realized that she uses well-constructed sentences of varying lengths and with different types of beginnings, and this makes all the difference.

[from the writing model]

> We strolled along the Seine River, stood in line for the elevators to the top of the Eiffel Tower, and saw the *Mona Lisa* at the Louvre Museum. But these sights, though impressive, were not the real reason for our trip.

14 Narrative Writing

Technology Tip — for 21st Century Literacies

Asking students to prewrite while using a storyboard allows us to engage student writers' thinking across modes. Consider differentiating across storyboards so that some students work simply from a sequence of images while those who need more textual support (or a challenge) add portions of writing beneath and around corresponding images. Storyboarding tools such as DigiDif Storyboard are available online, but the goal here isn't to engage with technology. The goal is to think visually in order to evoke and write a richer, more detailed story that follows an intentional—though not necessarily chronological—path. Digital tools can help with this.

See **www.sfw.z-b.com** for further information about and links to these websites and tools.

Conventions

- Conjunctions are used correctly in compound sentences, and all sentences are complete.

Melanie obviously proofread her work carefully—I did not find any incomplete sentences. She also uses conjunctions such as *and* and *but* correctly in each of her compound sentences. I get distracted when reading narratives full of mistakes, so I really appreciate her hard work before publishing.

[from the writing model]

Uncle Harry had never given us the particulars, but we knew that several of his close buddies had died on Omaha Beach. Now we asked him if he wanted to look for any of their graves.

+ Presentation

Visuals (photographs or illustrations) are used effectively.

My Turn!

I'm going to write a personal narrative, too. Follow along to see how I use good writing strategies. I'm going to use the rubric to help me write.

Personal Narrative **15**

Differentiating Instruction

ENRICHMENT

Augment the Visuals Encourage students who seem comfortable with the process of writing a personal narrative to take their work to the next level, specifically regarding visuals. Challenge them to think of new and creative ways to publish their work. Perhaps they can utilize a computer program to publish a mini-book or use a computer program to create slides to show as they read their narratives to the class.

REINFORCEMENT

Use the Computer Lab Schedule computer lab sessions during which students can work with and learn how to use the various word-processing functions of the computer. Determine the level of students' ability to use the computer and match instruction to their needs.

Presentation Students should always apply the basics of good presentation:

- neat handwriting or word processing
- adequate margins
- clear paragraphs (indent or add extra space before block paragraphs)

Photographs or illustrations make a great addition to a personal narrative. Help students understand that they should avoid using copyrighted photographs.

Think About the Traits Ask students which traits they think are the most important in a personal narrative. Remind them that all of the traits are important in every piece of writing; however, some traits play a more important role in specific types of writing. For example, some students may feel that **Organization** is very important in a narrative because if events are not presented in a logical order, the story falls apart or simply cannot be followed. Others may feel **Word Choice** is a more important trait as powerful and precise language helps the reader envision the story's events vividly.

CCSS **Common Core State Standards**
SL.7.1.c: Pose questions that elicit elaboration and respond to others' questions and comments with relevant observations and ideas that bring the discussion back on topic as needed. **SL.7.1.d:** Acknowledge new information expressed by others and, when warranted, modify their own views.

Write
a Personal Narrative

Week 2 • Day 1

Student Objectives

- Read and understand a prewriting strategy. *(p. 16)*

Prewrite

Focus on Ideas

Collect Details Read page 16 aloud. Point out that prior to drafting her story, Nina collected notes on the Mystery Spot, writing down every important detail she could remember. Explain that, although she focused on visual details, she also included several observations or reflections regarding her visit to the Mystery Spot. Encourage students to collect as many details as possible so they will be able to select the best details. They should understand that the more details they collect about their event, the easier it will be to write a strong and engaging story.

T16 Narrative Writing

Prewrite   Focus on Ideas

The Rubric Says   The narrative orients the reader to and focuses on one event.

Writing Strategy   List things the audience should know about the topic.

My dad took me to see the Mystery Spot in California. Right away, I knew I wanted to design buildings as cool as this. When my teacher asked us to write a personal narrative, I chose the Mystery Spot. There is so much I could say, but I wanted to focus on things my audience would want and need to know. I made notes listing important points. That was my strategy. Here are my notes.

Notes About the Mystery Spot

- ✔ first visited Mystery Spot two years ago with Dad
- ✔ a couple of miles from downtown Santa Cruz, California
- ✔ Mystery Spot is on a hill, in the redwoods
- ✔ stand on 2 x 4s, smaller person looks taller (Dad and a kid)
- ✔ board sticking out of window—does the ball roll up?
- ✔ floor at 30-degree angle; pendulum easier to push one way than the other
- ✔ not really gravity—Dad got the answers
- ✔ psychologist from U. of California checked out Mystery Spot
- ✔ angles, tilts, and hill create optical illusions (define)
- ✔ loved the Mystery Spot, and loved the explanation
- ✔ made me want to be a creative builder, too

Apply

Pick an event that you want to tell others about. Gather information by making notes on what you saw.

16 Narrative Writing

English Language Learners

BEGINNING/INTERMEDIATE

What is a personal narrative? Tell a very brief story using simple words that students know. Try to include all of the 5 W's. Have volunteers retell the story, one event at a time. Tell students, *A story is a narrative.* Have students repeat the sentence. Write it on the board. Have students say the sentence again, first as a group and then individually. Repeat the process for the sentence *A story about you is a personal narrative.* Review usage of the pronouns *I* and *me*.

ADVANCED/ADVANCED HIGH

Making Notes Ask students to think of a fun story about themselves. As each student tells the story to a partner, the partner should make notes on a piece of paper. After the story is completed, have students review the notes that their partners wrote. Have students switch roles and repeat the activity. Finally students should add further details to their notes.

Prewrite
Focus on **Organization**

The Rubric Says	Ideas are organized to unfold naturally and logically.
Writing Strategy	Make a 5 W's Chart.

Before I write, I'll fill out a 5 W's chart. With all my information organized, it will be easy to keep all the events in a logical order as I write. I want the narration to flow naturally from one idea or event to the next.

Writer's Term

5 W's Chart
A **5 W's Chart** organizes information by asking and answering the questions *What* happened? *Who* was there? *Why* did it happen? *When* did it happen? *Where* did it happen?

5 W's Chart

W hat happened?
- visited Mystery Spot
- stood on 2 x 4s
- smaller person looks taller; board sticking out of window
- floor at 30-degree angle; pendulum
- Mystery Spot made me want to design buildings

W ho was there?
- Dad and I

W hy did it happen?
- not really gravity—Dad got the answers
- psychologist from U. of Cal. checked out Mystery Spot
- angles, tilts, and hill create optical illusions (define)

W hen did it happen?
- first visited two years ago

W here did it happen?
- on a hill, a couple of miles outside of Santa Cruz, in the redwoods

Reflect
Why does including all of the 5 W's make a good narrative?

Apply
Organize your ideas by using your own notes to make a 5 W's Chart.

Personal Narrative **17**

Conferencing

PEER TO PEER Once students' 5 W's charts are complete, have pairs exchange charts. Instruct students to review each other's charts and comment on which of the 5 W's needs more details.

PEER GROUPS Assemble students in groups of three or four. Have students pass their 5 W's charts to the left around the group. Students should read each chart and write a question they would like the narrative to answer on an adhesive note that they affix to the chart.

TEACHER-LED Hold conferences with pairs of students. Have students read each other's charts. Then have them point out one detail that they found interesting and ask one question they would like to see answered in the narrative. Coach students on giving constructive feedback by prompting them with questions and ideas.

Write
a Personal Narrative

Student Objectives

- Make a 5 W's Chart to answer *Who, What, Where, When,* and *Why. (p. 17)*

Prewrite

Focus on **Organization**

Organize Ideas Explain that writers use different types of organizers to put their ideas in order. Nina used a 5 W's Chart to help her organize the details she had already written down. Have students study the organizer and then ask how a 5 W's Chart can be an effective tool when writing a personal narrative. (Possible response: A 5 W's Chart helps keep track of the important information needed to write a good narrative.)

Writer's Term _____

5 W's Chart A 5 W's Chart organizes the answers to the questions *Who, What, Where, When,* and *Why.* Organizing this information helps writers include the details necessary to convey an experience. The chart will also help organize the details in a logical order and alert the writer when vital information is missing.

CCSS Common Core State Standards
W.7.3.a: Engage and orient the reader by establishing a context and point of view and introducing a narrator and/or characters; organize an event sequence that unfolds naturally and logically. **W.7.3.b:** Use narrative techniques, such as dialogue, pacing, and description, to develop experiences, events, and/or characters.

Personal Narrative **T17**

Write a Personal Narrative

Week 2 • Day 3

Student Objectives

• Use a 5 W's Chart to begin writing. *(p. 18)*

Draft

Focus on Ideas

Draft a Personal Narrative Read page 18 aloud. Ask students to explain what it means to draft a personal narrative. Be sure students understand that they will use their 5 W's Chart to guide them through the drafting process.

Point out that, like Nina, students should not be overly concerned with correctness at this point. The main goal is to get their ideas down on paper or into a computer; they will have plenty of time to correct spelling, grammar, and punctuation later. If they are writing their drafts in class, plan and facilitate time for writing, conferences, and reflection.

Explain that students will go through each step of the writing process to create their final copy. Editing is only part of the process.

Note: To help facilitate editing when the time comes, proofreader's marks are provided as a reference on page 19.

Online Writing Center

Provides student eBooks with an **interactive writing pad** for drafting, revising, editing, and publishing.

Draft

Focus on Ideas

The Rubric Says	The narrative orients the reader to and focuses on one event. Memorable description of the 5 W's develops the experience and answers the audience's questions.
Writing Strategy	Use the 5 W's chart to stay focused and answer the audience's questions.

I'm going to use my 5 W's Chart to write my draft. The rubric says to focus on one event, and to use memorable details to answer the 5 W's. Well, my chart is already complete, so now I'll use it as a guide while writing to keep me focused on the main topic.

I'll open my narrative by describing where I went (Santa Cruz, California) and what I did there (visited the Mystery Spot). I'll use loads of interesting and vivid details to help the reader visualize my trip. The rest of the 5 W's will be answered throughout my narrative. I'll worry about spelling and grammar later. Right now I just need to get started!

Differentiating Instruction

ENRICHMENT

Write a Longer Story Have students write a longer, more in-depth personal narrative. Challenge them to include as many details as possible in their 5 W's charts and to write a story that exceeds a minimum length you assign (say, three pages). Explain that one way to add length and depth to the story is to share personal reflections on what the experience meant to the writer.

REINFORCEMENT

Support the 5 W's To help your students understand what an audience needs to know to thoroughly enjoy a narrative, facilitate a discussion about a movie most of them have seen. As students provide details, stop them and ask: *Was the detail just given important? Would someone who has not seen the movie need to know that detail? Which of the 5 W's does that detail answer, if any?*

[DRAFT]

[starts with something to think about]

A Visit That Inspired Me

[where, when, who, what]

I've heard the saying that you can't learn everything you need to know in your own backyard. I'm not sure that's exactly true. I do think you can lern a lot of things on trips to interesting places, though. When I first visited the Mystery Spot two years ago with my dad, we were traveling to California. I learned two important things. One is that buildings can be designed in very interesting ways. The other is that I might want to desing some interesting buildings myself.

The Mystery Spot is just a few miles from downtown Santa Cruz, in the middle of some redwoods. Dad and I had noticed it on our way into the city. Then the desk clerk at our motel told us that we should stop there, that it was really worth seeing. So the next day we decided to make a special trip to the Spot. The signs along the road made it easy to find the place.

Reflect

What do you think? Do the introductory details grab and hold your interest?

Apply

Write a draft using interesting details from your 5 W's Chart to grab your audience's attention.

Write
a Personal Narrative

Week 2 • Day 4

Student Objectives

• Complete a draft.

Continue Drafting It is important that students are given ample time to draft their personal narratives. As conferencing is important throughout the writing process, be sure to also plan time for peer-to-peer, peer group, or teacher-led conferences. Remind students that this is the time to get their ideas down on paper in a creative and engaging way. Assure them that they will have plenty of time to fix any mistakes later.

Conferencing

PEER TO PEER Have partners exchange drafts. Ask students to comment on their partner's use of the 5 W's and tell which of the W's he or she would like to know more about. Remind students to speak respectfully to one another.

PEER GROUPS Have students work in groups of three. Tell students to take turns reading their draft aloud. The other students should comment by telling their favorite part of the draft and pointing out one place where they thought information was missing.

TEACHER-LED Hold individual conferences with students. Ask students to explain to you how their drafts are organized and where they answered the 5 W's. Give suggestions about how students can improve the organization of their narratives.

CCSS Common Core State Standards

W.7.5: With some guidance and support from peers and adults, develop and strengthen writing as needed by planning, revising, editing, rewriting, or trying a new approach, focusing on how well purpose and audience have been addressed. **SL.7.6:** Adapt speech to a variety of contexts and tasks, demonstrating command of formal English when indicated or appropriate.

Write
a Personal Narrative

Week 2 • Day 5

Student Objectives

- Revise sentence order to keep event sequence logical. *(p. 20)*

Revise

Focus on Organization

Reorder Sentences Read page 20 aloud. Discuss the importance of logical sentence order. Have one volunteer read aloud the draft excerpt without the revisions and then have another volunteer read the revised excerpt. Point out how much clearer Nina's writing is after her revisions.

Remind students that when revising their own drafts, they should pay close attention to sentence order. If they find that some of their ideas are confusing or unclear, simply rearranging some sentences could be helpful. If students are writing their drafts by hand, suggest ways for them to indicate revisions:

- Write on every other line in order to leave space for revisions.

- Use a colored pencil to draw lines and arrows to move sentences.

- If a sentence needs to be moved, mark that sentence with a letter in a circle; then place the same letter at the spot to where the sentence should move.

 Strategies for Writers Online
Go to **www.sfw.z-b.com** for additional online resources for students and teachers.

Revise

Focus on **Organization**

The Rubric Says   Ideas are organized to unfold naturally and logically.

Writing Strategy   Reorder sentences that seem out of place.

I thought the sentences in my narrative were organized well when I read it over. They take the reader through the story in a logical order. However, in the paragraph about the ball rolling up the board, I can see that if I change the order of the sentences just a little, this scene would make a lot more sense.

[DRAFT]

The area where things began to get really bazaar was the cabin. This structure looked old and wore down. Filled with

[reordered sentences]

surprises. When we walked up to the cabin, ~~the guide rolled a ball down the long board.~~ We saw a long board sticking out a front window. It was pretty obvious that the end sticking out was higher than the end resting inside. Then the guide rolled a ball down the board. The ball went a little way it stopped and rolled right back up! What was going on here?

Apply

Are your sentences in a logical order? If not, rearrange them to make sure they make sense to the audience.

English Language Learners

BEGINNING/INTERMEDIATE

Personal Pronouns Review usage of the first-person pronouns *I, me,* and *my.* Give several simple examples, such as *I live in Texas, Mom loves me,* and *My name is Ana.* Write other examples on the board, but do not include the pronouns. Have Beginning ELLs fill in the appropriate pronouns, and ask Intermediate ELLs to check for mistakes.

ADVANCED/ADVANCED HIGH

Using Precise Words Write a generic word, such as *good,* on the board. Use the Web or Continuum Scale graphic organizer to brainstorm other words that have the same meaning as *good* or have stronger meanings. For example, on a Continuum Scale, you could write *good, all right, fine, fantastic, incredible, amazing, awesome, magnificent, stellar,* and so on. Tell students to use this idea when choosing words for their personal narratives.

Revise

Focus on **Voice**

The Rubric Says	The writer makes a strong connection with the reader by using first-person point of view and a personal tone.
Writing Strategy	Use personal pronouns (*I, me*) to connect with the readers.

My job as a narrator is to help my reader fully connect with and understand my story. I use first-person pronouns throughout my narrative, but I did find an area where my voice is a bit too formal. I will make some revisions now to create a more casual tone.

[DRAFT]

[used casual tone]

         → pretty

The Mystery Spot is a small area, only about 150 feet in

diameter. You have to climb a hill to reach it, and the tour guides

      → strange things

promise that ~~puzzling events~~ will start happening the minute you

         → lying

step into it. These guides are not ~~misleading~~.

Reflect

What do you think about Nina's revisions? Is her tone more casual and easier to connect with now?

Apply

Use first person and a casual tone to connect with the reader.

Personal Narrative **21**

Conferencing

PEER TO PEER Have pairs of students exchange drafts. Have students lightly circle in pencil words or phrases that are not consistent with the writer's voice.

PEER GROUPS Have students work in groups of four and pass their drafts around the group. Tell each student to point out one place in each draft where the writer could include a first-person comment or use language that is less formal.

TEACHER-LED Hold conferences with groups of three students. Have students read each other's drafts, then facilitate a discussion about either organization or voice. Encourage students to offer examples of where the trait is particularly strong and point out places where revisions could be made.

Write
a Personal Narrative

Week 3 • Day 1

Student Objectives

- Revise for first-person point of view. (*p. 21*)

Revise

Focus on Voice

Connect With Readers Explain to students the importance of connecting with the audience, adding that voice is one tool writers use to accomplish this. The choice of language, tone, point of view, and style all affect a writer's voice.

A good writer will keep the purpose and the audience in mind when determining the voice he or she wants to use. Remind students that their purpose is to tell a story, and their audience consists of their peers. Explain that when writing a personal narrative, first-person point of view is most appropriate. Using the pronouns *I* and *me* tells the reader who the narrator is (the author) and helps the audience engage with the author's point of view.

Remind students that the tone and language a writer uses also affect his or her voice. Using language that is too formal will make it hard for readers to identify with the events and emotions within a personal narrative.

CCSS **C**ommon **C**ore **S**tate **S**tandards

W.7.3.a: Engage and orient the reader by establishing a context and point of view and introducing a narrator and/or characters; organize an event sequence that unfolds naturally and logically. **SL.7.6:** Adapt speech to a variety of contexts and tasks, demonstrating command of formal English when indicated or appropriate.

Personal Narrative **T21**

Write
a Personal Narrative

Week 3 • Day 2

Student Objectives

• Revise for precise language. *(p. 22)*

Revise

Focus on

Use Precise Language Read page 22 aloud. Remind students that a narrative writer's goal is to connect with the reader and share an experience. Overused and boring words will not accomplish this. However, when a writer uses precise, descriptive language, it is easy for the reader to engage with the story and share the writer's experience.

Nina was intrigued and excited by the strange things she experienced at the Mystery Spot. She wants her readers to feel the same way but knows some of her language is too vague or boring. Nina's revisions paint a more precise and vivid picture for the reader and add energy to her writing. Encourage students to review their narratives and replace vague or overused words with precise and interesting words and phrases.

Revise — Focus on **Word Choice**

The Rubric Says	Precise words and phrases convey the experience and bring the story to life.
Writing Strategy	Choose precise and interesting words and phrases for effect.

I want my reader to feel as excited as I felt when I visited the Mystery Spot. But some sections of my draft are boring. I'll add some precise and interesting words to liven things up, just as the rubric says.

[DRAFT]

[added specific phrases] → from work
A few days later, Dad come home with some answers. One of his coworkers told him that a psychologist from the University of California had checked out the place. He discovered that all the strange things we had experienced are based on optical illusions., or sights that appear different from what they really are

Remember that the Mystery Spot was built on a hill. That, along with the angles and walls, confuses people into thinking things is not level—when they actually are.
→ crazy   → tilted
[added interesting words]

Apply
Add specific and interesting words to your draft to bring your story to life.

22 Narrative Writing

Optional Revising Lessons

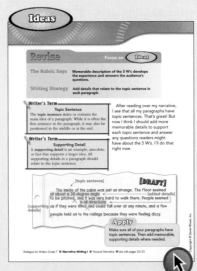
Narrative 1

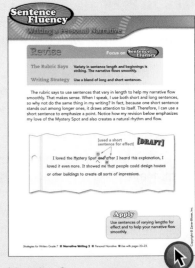
Narrative 2

Go to ➡ Strategies for Writers Grade 7 CD-ROM

Edit

Focus on Conventions

The Rubric Says	Conjunctions are used correctly in compound sentences, and all sentences are complete.
Writing Strategy	Make sure all sentences are complete.

✎ Writer's Term
Sentence Fragment
A **sentence fragment** is a group of words that begins with a capital letter and ends with a period or other end punctuation but does not state a complete thought.

✎ Writer's Term
Run-on Sentence
A **run-on sentence** is two simple sentences that are run together and not joined correctly.

I'm almost done! Now I just have to check my spelling, punctuation, and capitalization. The rubric says all sentences should be complete, and conjunctions should be used properly. I'll keep my eyes open for these things, too.

[DRAFT]

[corrected sentence fragment]

The area where things began to get really ~~bazaar~~ bizarre was the cabin. This structure looked old and wor~~e down~~n, but it was filled with surprises.

Reflect
What do you think? How did Nina do with her grammar, spelling, and punctuation? Can you find any incomplete sentences?

Apply — Conventions
Your turn! Check your draft for spelling, punctuation, and capitalization. Make sure all sentences are complete and conjunctions are used properly.

For more practice fixing incomplete sentences and using conjunctions correctly, use the exercises on the next two pages.

Personal Narrative 23

Related Grammar Practice

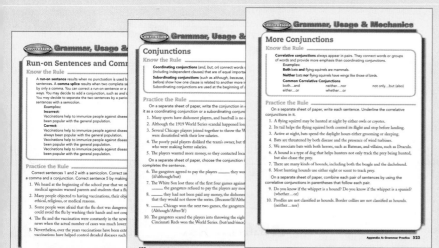

Student Edition pages 508, 522, 523

Go to ➡ Appendix A: Grammar Practice

Write
a Personal Narrative

Week 3 • Day 3

Student Objectives
- Edit for complete sentences. (p. 23)

Edit

Focus on Conventions

Edit for Accuracy Remind students to go back and correct any mistakes in punctuation and capitalization. Explain that computers have a spell-check option that can be very helpful; however, this function will not catch commonly misused words, such as *to*, *too*, and *two*.

Use the mini-lessons on pages T24 and T25 for students having trouble with sentence fragments or run-on sentences; then have students complete pages 24 and 25.

✎ Writer's Term
Sentence Fragment Remind students to ask themselves *who* is doing *what*. If either question cannot be answered, they have a sentence fragment.

✎ Writer's Term
Run-on Sentence Review that a comma indicates a small pause and a period indicates a longer pause.

CCSS Common Core State Standards
L.7.2: Demonstrate command of the conventions of standard English capitalization, punctuation, and spelling when writing. **L.7.3.a:** Choose language that expresses ideas precisely and concisely, recognizing and eliminating wordiness and redundancy. **W.7.3.d:** Use precise words and phrases, relevant descriptive details, and sensory language to capture the action and convey experiences and events.

Personal Narrative T23

Conventions

Mini-Lesson

Student Objectives

- Identify and correct sentence fragments, run-ons, and comma splices. *(p. 24)*

Sentence Fragments, Run-ons, and Comma Splices

Review the definition of each sentence problem. Call on students to create and write their own examples of each type of faulty sentence on the board. Ask other students to come to the board, identify which of the three errors each sentence represents, and then correct the sentence. Leave plenty of time for several students to take a turn at the board to ensure the entire class understands the lesson.

Before students work independently, ask them to identify the sentence problem in each sentence on page 24.

Sentence Fragments, Run-ons, and Comma Splices

Know the Rule

Correct a **sentence fragment** in one of these ways:
- Add a subject, a predicate, or both.
  Example: Dad and I made a visit to the Mystery Spot.
- Attach the fragment to a related sentence.
  Example: Dad and I planned a special trip, a visit to the Mystery Spot.

Correct a **run-on sentence** or a **comma splice** (when two independent clauses are joined by only a comma) in one of these ways:
- Combine the sentences with both a comma and a conjunction such as *and, but, or,* or *for*.
  Example: I loved the Mystery Spot, **and** I wanted to go back soon.
- Combine the sentences with a semicolon.
  Example: I loved the Mystery Spot; I wanted to go back soon.
- Write two separate sentences.
  Example: I loved the Mystery Spot. I wanted to go back soon.

Practice the Rule

Number a sheet of paper from 1–10. Write **F** for each sentence fragment. Write **RO** for each run-on sentence. Write **CS** for each comma splice. For each fragment, write **S** if the subject is missing or **P** if the predicate is missing.

1. Architecture, a topic of interest to many people. F, P
2. Very high structures particularly interesting. F, P
3. The very earliest skyscrapers in the 1880s. F, P
4. City real estate was very expensive, it was cheaper to build up than to build out. CS
5. Some call Chicago the home of the skyscraper others say New York. RO
6. Famous skyscrapers in both Chicago and New York. F, P
7. The Sears Tower in Chicago has a new name it is called the Willis Tower. RO
8. The Empire State Building has 102 stories the Willis Tower has 110 stories. RO
9. The invention of elevators meant that buildings could become taller, taller buildings were built. CS
10. The tallest building in the world. F, P

Related Grammar Practice

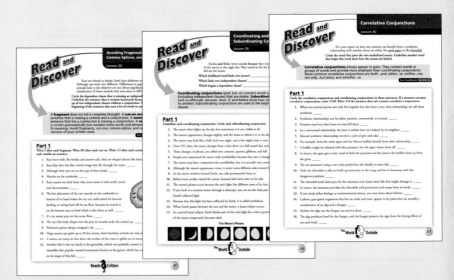

Pages 57, 115, 117

Go to ➡ **G.U.M. Student Practice Book**

Online Writing Center

Provides **interactive grammar games** and **practice activities** in student eBook.

Coordinating Conjunctions

Know the Rule

Coordinating conjunctions (*and, but, or*) connect words or groups of words (including independent clauses) that are closely related. They can be used to fix run-on sentences, sentence fragments, and comma splices.

> **Example:** This morning I made strawberry pancakes, **and** then I went for a long walk.

> **Example:** Father told us we could go to the movies, **but** there are no movies playing that we would like to see.

Practice the Rule

Read each incomplete sentence below. Then on a separate piece of paper, rewrite each one using the correct coordinating conjunction.

1. It doesn't matter if your favorite music is classical, _____ if you prefer listening to hip hop. **or**

2. It's a simple, everyday thing, _____ music has the power to stir your imagination. **but**

3. For example, listen closely to this piano music, _____ then tell me what you envision in your mind. **and**

4. The music might sound to you like a storm approaching, _____ it might sound like the raging ocean crashing against barren cliffs. **or**

5. One hundred people might all envision one hundred different scenes, _____ remember, there are no wrong answers in this kind of an exercise. **but**

6. I like to listen to music when I work, _____ some people find music too distracting. **but**

7. They start paying too much attention to the music, _____ then their imagination takes over. **and**

8. They get lost in the images in their mind, _____ they lose track of their work. **and**

9. Music is as old as humankind, _____ it constantly renews itself with each generation. **and**

10. Some people don't believe it, _____ having music in your life is beneficial in many ways. **but**

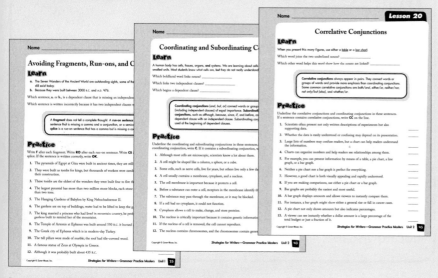

Pages 25, 43, 45

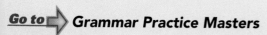

Go to ➡ **Grammar Practice Masters**

Mini-Lesson

Student Objectives

- Identify and correctly use coordinating conjunctions. *(p. 25)*

Coordinating Conjunctions

Coordinating conjunctions connect words or groups or words of equal importance. Display these sentences on the board. Discuss with students how the meanings differ, depending on which coordinating conjunction is used:

- I could do my homework now, or I could do it later.

- I could do my homework now, and then I could go to a movie later.

- I could do my homework now, but I would rather do it later.

Ask students which conjunction they would use to do the following:

- add one thing to another (and)
- offer a choice (or)
- show contrast (but)

CCSS Common Core State Standards

L.7.2: Demonstrate command of the conventions of standard English capitalization, punctuation, and spelling when writing.

Write
a Personal Narrative

Week 3 • Day 4

Student Objectives

- Discuss preparation for publishing and presentation. (*p. 26*)
- Use a final editing checklist to publish their work. (*p. 26*)

Publish ✛Presentation

Publishing Strategy Explain to students that publishing her personal narrative in the class's diary is an excellent way for Nina to share her story with a wider audience. She feels confident that most classmates (her audience) will share in her excitement about the Mystery Spot, and her publishing choice suits her purpose.

As an alternative to a class diary, ask students to make a list of different ways they could collectively publish their personal narratives. The class may wish to create a magazine that documents personal narratives or a "true story" journal of collected stories. Provide students with examples of magazines to allow them to study layouts and magazine features. After publishing, be sure to place the narratives in a location where students can access them easily during free time.

Strategies for Writers Online

Go to **www.sfw.z-b.com** for additional online resources for students and teachers.

Publish ✛Presentation

Publishing Strategy	Publish the narrative in a class diary.
Presentation Strategy	Use photographs or illustrations to help tell the story.

That was fun to write, and it will be even more fun to share. I think I'll publish my personal narrative in our class diary so my classmates can share in the mystery of the Mystery Spot. I'll use some photographs from my trip to give even more details of my adventure. I'll be sure to place the photos near the appropriate text to avoid confusion. I'll be sure my work is neat and readable, whether I write it by hand or use a computer. I'll also need to read it one last time to make sure it includes all the items on my checklist.

My Final Checklist

Did I—

- ✓ fix any incomplete sentences?
- ✓ correctly use coordinating conjunctions?
- ✓ use helpful and properly placed photographs or illustrations?
- ✓ neatly handwrite or type my paper?
- ✓ put my name on each page of my narrative?

Apply

Make a checklist to check your personal narrative. Then make a final draft to publish.

26 Narrative Writing

Differentiating Instruction

ENRICHMENT

Add Captions Have students conduct research to find photos and illustrations of real places or events that relate to their personal narratives. Have them write short captions identifying each illustration. Tell students their captions should be accurate and interesting.

REINFORCEMENT

Help with Visuals Conference with individual students to help them brainstorm ideas for visuals to accompany their personal narratives. Allow students to include just one photo or illustration if they are struggling to find ideas or locate visuals.

A VISIT THAT INSPIRED ME
by Nina

I've heard the saying that you can't learn everything you need to know in your own backyard. I'm not sure that's exactly true. I do think you can learn a lot of things on trips to interesting places, though. When I first visited the Mystery Spot two years ago with my dad, we were traveling in California. I learned two important things. One is that buildings can be designed in very interesting ways. The other is that I might want to design some interesting buildings myself.

The Mystery Spot is just a few miles from downtown Santa Cruz, in the middle of some redwoods. Dad and I had noticed it on our way into the city. Then the desk clerk at our motel told us that we should stop there, that it was really worth seeing. So the next day we decided to make a special trip to the Spot. The signs along the road made it easy to find the place.

The Mystery Spot is a pretty small area, only about 150 feet in diameter. You have to climb a hill to reach it, and the tour guides promise that strange things will start happening the minute you step into it. These guides are not lying. For example, one of the first things you see is 2 × 4s that stretch across two pieces of concrete. Our guide asked for volunteers to stand at each end of a 2 × 4. My dad and a kid several inches shorter volunteered, and then they traded places. It looked like the kid was taller than my dad! I could tell right away that I was going to like this place.

The area where things began to get really bizarre was the cabin. This structure looked old and worn down, but it was filled with surprises.

Technology Tip for 21st Century Literacies

Consider leading students to examine how working from an image or a sound early in their writing impacted the emotion within their personal narrative. Did they dig deeper into a memory or use stronger language? How did the sequencing of images lead—or constrain—the stories they meant to tell? As important as it is for students to think with images or other media as they prewrite and draft, reflecting on how they used those as writers to create a smarter narrative should be part of the process. Reflection can be written, expressed during a discussion, recorded in a writer's notebook or blog, and so on.

Write
a Personal Narrative

Week 3 • Day 5

Student Objectives

- Use a personal narrative rubric. (pp. 10–11)
- Share a published personal narrative. (pp. 27–29)

Presentation Strategy Explain to students that adding photographs or illustrations is an excellent way to enhance the story and help the reader make an even deeper connection with the details. However, students may not have photos from their experience, or they may prefer not to share personal photos. Tell students that they may search for photos and images on the Internet or in magazines that relate to the theme or the locations in their narrative. Remind students that it is important to insert their chosen visuals near the appropriate text or they risk confusing their readers. There are many computer programs that make it easy to insert photographs or computer-generated drawings into text. Encourage students to explore different possibilities before they make their decision.

Explain to students how important neatness is when creating a final copy of their work. Messy or illegible work will turn readers away, while a neat and interesting format draws readers in.

CCSS Common Core State Standards
W.7.4: Produce clear and coherent writing in which the development, organization, and style are appropriate to task, purpose, and audience.

Reflecting on a Personal Narrative

Instruct students to refer to the rubric on pages 10–11 as they reread Nina's final copy on pages 27–29. As they read, remind them to pay close attention to how Nina's revisions and edits have shaped her final copy. After students have finished reading, ask them what they think of Nina's changes. Did those revisions and edits strengthen or weaken her narrative? What score would they give Nina for each writing trait? Take a poll to see how close the scores are. Be sure students can support their scores with examples from Nina's writing.

Now have students think back on this assignment as a whole.

You might ask questions such as these to prompt students' thinking:

- What did you like about this assignment?

- What surprised you about writing a personal narrative?

- Compare writing a personal narrative to the last writing assignment you completed. What is one thing that you did better in this assignment?

- What is one thing you will do differently the next time you write a personal narrative?

Have students write their answers to these questions in a journal or have them discuss their reflections as a class or in small groups.

Strategies for Writers Online

Go to **www.sfw.z-b.com** for additional online resources for students and teachers.

When we walked up to the cabin, we saw a long board sticking out a front window. It was pretty obvious that the end sticking out was higher than the end resting inside. Then the guide rolled a ball down the board. The ball went a little way, but it stopped and rolled right back up! What was going on here? Could it be that the laws of gravity didn't work in this place?

The inside of the cabin was just as strange. The floor seemed to be pitched at about a 30-degree angle, and it was very hard to walk there. People seemed as if they were tilted in all directions and could fall over at any minute, and a few people held on to the railings because they were feeling dizzy. Another weird thing was the pendulum, which hung from the ceiling. You could push it in both directions, but it was much easier to push it to one side of the cabin than to the other.

I was finding the Mystery Spot totally fascinating, but I was also wondering what was going on. Our guide kept talking about strange gravitational forces, but my logical mind was telling me that this didn't quite make sense.

A few days later, Dad came home from work with some answers. One of his coworkers told him that a psychologist from the University of California had checked out the place. He discovered that all the strange things we had experienced are based on optical illusions, or sights that appear different from what they really are. Remember that the Mystery Spot was built on a hill. That, along with the crazy angles and tilted walls, confuses people into thinking things are not level—when they actually are.

I loved the Mystery Spot. After I heard this explanation, I loved it even more. It showed me that people could design houses or other buildings to create all sorts of impressions. They aren't exactly optical illusions, but there must be ways to make small rooms seem bigger and tall buildings seem even higher. I thought about some of the drawings I've done in industrial arts class. Maybe I could learn to combine my ideas into plans for some really neat buildings.

Reflect

What do you think? Did Nina use all the traits of a good personal narrative? Check her writing against the rubric. Then use the rubric to check the personal narrative you wrote!

CCSS Common Core State Standards

W.7.6: Use technology, including the Internet, to produce and publish writing and link to and cite sources as well as to interact and collaborate with others, including linking to and citing sources.

E-Mail Planner

WEEK 1

Day 1
Introduce
an E-Mail

Student Objectives
- Review the elements of an e-mail.
- Consider purpose and audience.
- Learn the traits of narrative writing.

Student Activities
- Read and discuss **What's in an E-Mail?** (p. 30)
- Read and discuss **Why Write an E-Mail?** (p. 31)
- Read **Linking Narrative Writing Traits to an E-Mail.** (p. 32)

Day 2
Analyze
Read an E-Mail

Student Objectives
- Read a model e-mail.

Student Activities
- Read Mary Kubik's e-mail. (p. 33)

Day 3
Analyze
Introduce the Rubric

Student Objectives
- Study an e-mail rubric.

Student Activities
- Review Mary Kubik's e-mail. (p. 33)
- Read and discuss the **E-Mail Rubric.** (pp. 34–35)

WEEK 2

Day 1
Write
Prewrite: Ideas

Student Objectives
- Read and understand a prewriting strategy.

Student Activities
- Read and discuss **Prewrite: Focus on Ideas.** (p. 40)
- Apply the prewriting strategy.

Day 2
Write
Prewrite: Organization

Student Objectives
- Make a Main Idea Table to organize main idea and supporting details.

Student Activities
- Read and discuss **Prewrite: Focus on Organization.** (p. 41)
- Reflect on the model Main Idea Table.
- Apply the prewriting strategy to create a Main Idea Table.
- Participate in a peer conference.

Day 3
Write
Draft: Organization

Student Objectives
- Use a Main Idea Table to begin writing
- Use transitions.

Student Activities
- Read and discuss **Draft: Focus on Organization.** (p. 42)
- Reflect on a model draft. (p. 43)
- Apply the drafting strategy by using a Main Idea Table to write a draft.
- Participate in a peer conference.

WEEK 3

Day 1
Write
Revise: Word Choice

Student Objectives
- Revise to avoid slang.

Student Activities
- Read and discuss **Revise: Focus on Choice.** (p. 45)
- Reflect on the model draft.
- Apply the revising strategy.
- Participate in a peer conference.

Day 2
Write
Revise: Sentence Fluency

Student Objectives
- Revise for accuracy and flow.

Student Activities
- Read and discuss **Revise: Focus on Sentence Fluency.** (p. 46)
- Reflect on the model draft.
- Apply the revising strategy.

Note: Optional Revising Lessons appear on the *Strategies for Writers* CD-ROM.

Day 3
Write
Edit: Conventions

Student Objectives
- Edit for correct use of verb tenses.

Student Activities
- Read and discuss **Edit: Focus on Conventions.** (p. 47)
- Reflect on a model draft.
- Apply the revising strategy.

Note: Teach the Conventions mini-lessons (pp. 48–49) if needed.

Day 4	Day 5
Analyze Ideas, Organization, and Voice	**Analyze** Word Choice, Sentence Fluency, and Conventions

Student Objectives
- Read a model e-mail.
- Use the e-mail rubric.
- Use the model e-mail to study Ideas, Organization, and Voice.

Student Activities
- Review Mary Kubik's e-mail. *(p. 33)*
- Read and discuss **Using the Rubric to Study the Model.** *(pp. 36–39)*

Student Objectives
- Read a model e-mail.
- Use the e-mail rubric.
- Use the model e-mail to study Word Choice, Sentence Fluency, and Conventions.

Student Activities
- Review Mary Kubik's e-mail. *(p. 33)*
- Read and discuss **Using the Rubric to Study the Model.** *(pp. 36–39)*

Day 4	Day 5
Write Draft	**Write** Revise: Voice

Student Objectives
- Complete a draft.

Student Activities
- Finish the draft. *(p. 43)*
- Participate in a peer conference.

Student Objectives
- Revise for tone.

Student Activities
- Read and discuss **Revise: Focus on Voice.** *(p. 44)*
- Reflect on a model draft.
- Apply the revising strategy.

Day 4	Day 5
Write Publish: +Presentation	**Write** Publish: +Presentation

Student Objectives
- Discuss preparation for publishing and presentation.
- Use a final editing checklist to publish their work.

Student Activities
- Read and discuss **Publish: +Presentation.** *(p. 50)*
- Apply the publishing strategy.

Student Objectives
- Use an e-mail rubric.
- Share a published e-mail.

Student Activities
- Share their work.
- Use the rubric to reflect upon and evaluate the model and their own writing. *(pp. 34–35, 51)*

To complete the chapter in fewer days, combine the learning objectives and activities in a way that supports students as they write.

Resources at-a-Glance

Grammar, Usage & Mechanics

Differentiating Instruction

For additional Differentiating Instruction activities, see Strategies for Writers *Extensions Online at* **www.sfw.z-b.com.**

English Language Learners

Conferencing

Technology Tip

 Connection Letter
Reproducible letter (in English and Spanish) appears on the *Strategies for Writers* CD-ROM and at **www.sfw.z-b.com.**

Online Writing Center

Provides IWB resources, interactive games and practice activities, videos, eBooks, and a virtual file cabinet.

 Strategies for Writers Online
Go to **www.sfw.z-b.com** for free online resources for students and teachers.

Introduce
an E-Mail

Week 1 • Day 1

Student Objectives

- Review the elements of an e-mail. *(p. 30)*
- Consider purpose and audience. *(p. 31)*
- Learn the traits of narrative writing. *(p. 32)*

What's an E-Mail?

Ask volunteers to share experiences with writing or receiving e-mails. Make sure students understand the difference between instant messages (IMs) and e-mails. IMs use abbreviations and symbols to save space and increase the speed at which the message is typed. E-mails can be more formal, especially when they are used for business communication.

Ask students to discuss how these elements of an e-mail affect the recipient's impression of the e-mail:

- E-mail Etiquette (Possible response: Disrespect for the reader might cause the e-mail to be disregarded.)
- Tone (Possible response: An inappropriate tone might offend or distract the reader.)
- Organization (Possible response: If the organization doesn't make sense, the recipient won't understand the message.)

▶ Strategies for Writers Online

Go to **www.sfw.z-b.com** for additional online resources for students and teachers.

What's an E-Mail?

It's an electronic message I send to someone I know. I like to send e-mail because I can just click the send button and the message is delivered right away!

What's in an E-Mail?

Sender
I'm the sender, the person who is writing the message. Instead of talking to someone on the phone, I can write an e-mail they can read when they're ready!

"E-Mail Etiquette"
E-mail etiquette is using the most polite, most accepted, or clearest way to write an e-mail. For example, I include a subject line and make sure my spelling and grammar are correct—even in a friendly e-mail.

Tone
I use a friendly and lively tone when I'm writing an e-mail. That doesn't mean I get sloppy! Nor does it mean that I'm not serious. After a friendly greeting, I get right to the point, and I avoid using slang words.

Organization
I make sure to use multiple paragraphs in my e-mail, and I give information in an order that makes sense. E-mail is a quick, friendly way to share information, but if it's not in any kind of order, the person who receives it will have no idea what I'm talking about!

Narrative Text Exemplars (E-Mail)

Katz, Jon. *Geeks: How Two Lost Boys Rode the Internet Out of Idaho.* Broadway Books, 2001. CCSS
Geeks is the true story about Jesse and Eric, two outsiders living in Idaho who have a love for technology. The two friends use the Internet to leave Idaho and shape a new future for themselves in a new community they could belong to in Chicago.

Peck, Richard. *A Long Way From Chicago.* Penguin Books, 2004. A young boy describes his annual trips to Illinois with his sister to visit their larger-than-life grandmother during the Great Depression. The stories are funny tales about small-town life.

Why write an E-Mail?

There are lots of reasons to write an e-mail. Here are some of the most common reasons. I have sent e-mail for all of them.

Give Information

Sometimes an e-mail is the best way to give information. I can send an e-mail to educate, instruct, or inform my reader.

Stay in Touch

Sometimes I write e-mails to let people know how and what I'm doing. I send e-mails to friends, family members, and even to my teacher, who always writes back.

Make Plans

Often e-mails are used to set up social events and meetings. For example, our band director can send e-mails to every member of the marching band if he needs to change practice times. He can e-mail all of us at once! I like to send e-mail invitations to weekend sleepovers. I can invite six friends by pressing just one button!

Lustig, Susan J. *E-mails From Shilo.* Barkley Publishing, LLC, 2008. A woman comes across a folder on her computer that she doesn't recognize, and discovers dozens of e-mails written by her golden retriever, Shilo, to another dog. This book is about how a dog makes sense of the human world around him and his relationship with his human family.

Stead, Rebecca. *When You Reach Me.* Yearling, 2009. Miranda is a twelve-year-old girl living in New York City. Her life is turned upside down when a series of mysterious notes arrive that seem to ignore the laws of space and time.

Why write an E-Mail?

Review that a good writer always keeps both purpose and audience in mind when writing, even when writing an e-mail. If either purpose or audience is not carefully considered, the writing will be weak or ineffective.

Read page 31 aloud. Ask students how e-mails will differ, depending on the purpose and audience. For example, a person writing an e-mail to share information may use a friendly tone but still have well-developed paragraphs. Someone writing to stay in touch may use a less formal tone and include short updates regarding recent events. A writer trying to make plans with a friend will need to carefully organize the plan's details and clearly state how the receiver should respond to the invitation. Clear communication is the key in all these examples.

Conclude by explaining to students that they are going to study and practice strategies for writing an e-mail.

CCSS **Common Core State Standards**

SL.7.1: Engage effectively in a range of collaborative discussions (one-on-one, in groups, and teacher-led) with diverse partners on *grade 7 topics, texts, and issues,* building on each others' ideas and expressing their own clearly.

Introduce
an E-Mail

Linking Narrative Writing Traits to an E-Mail

Read page 32 aloud to help students understand that they will follow Nina as she models using the writing process and the narrative writing traits together. A good e-mail will do the following:

- focus on one topic
- provide descriptive details in a logical order
- have a tone appropriate for purpose and audience
- follow proper e-mail format and etiquette

If possible, project a sample e-mail from your computer screen. Otherwise, make an e-mail frame on an overhead transparency and ask the class to identify and fill in each part of the e-mail, from the subject line to the closing. Review proper e-mail etiquette. Ask students why etiquette is important when writing an e-mail. (Possible response: The recipient may not take the e-mail seriously if it seems too casual or does not respect the reader.)

Online Writing Center

Provides six **interactive anchor papers** for each mode of writing.

T32 Narrative Writing

Linking Narrative Writing Traits to an E-Mail

In this chapter, you will send a message electronically. This type of writing is called an e-mail. Nina will guide you through the stages of the writing process: Prewrite, Draft, Revise, Edit, and Publish. In each stage, Nina will show you important writing strategies that are linked to the Narrative Writing Traits below.

Narrative Writing Traits

- a single, focused topic with relevant, engaging details that develop the experiences or events
- a narrator or characters that bring the story to life

- well-structured and logical event sequences, often in chronological order, that guide the reader through the story
- an engaging beginning and a satisfying conclusion that reflects on the story's events
- a variety of transition words that signal time or setting changes

- a voice that is appropriate for the audience and purpose
- dialogue that, if used, is realistic and helps develop the characters and story

- precise, descriptive words and phrases

- a variety of sentences that flow and are a pleasure to read aloud

- no or few errors in grammar, usage, mechanics, and spelling

Before you write, read Mary Kubik's e-mail on the next page. Then use the e-mail rubric on pages 34–35 to decide how well she did. (You might want to look back at What's in an E-Mail? on page 30, too!)

Narrative Writing Traits in an E-Mail

Ideas The writer focuses on one, clearly defined topic. Descriptive, informative details are included to fully inform the reader of the subject and purpose of the e-mail.

Organization Details are provided in a well-organized, logical order. If a story is being told, events are given in chronological order. Transition words and phrases guide the reader through the writing.

Voice As always, the audience and purpose dictate what kind of voice is appropriate. When the recipient is someone the writer knows, a friendly yet formal tone will keep the reader engaged and convey the message.

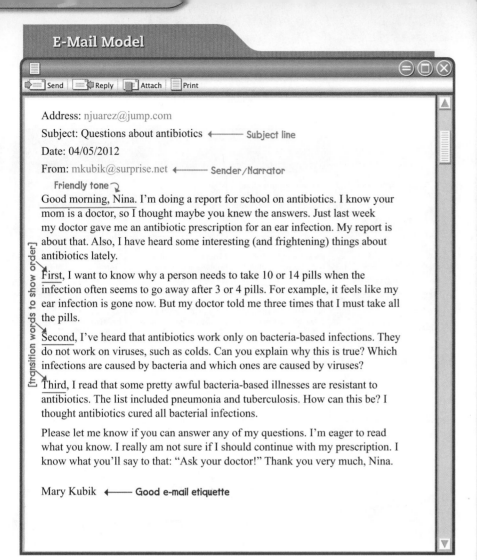

Address: njuarez@jump.com

Subject: Questions about antibiotics ←——— Subject line

Date: 04/05/2012

From: mkubik@surprise.net ←——— Sender/Narrator

Friendly tone ⤸

Good morning, Nina. I'm doing a report for school on antibiotics. I know your mom is a doctor, so I thought maybe you knew the answers. Just last week my doctor gave me an antibiotic prescription for an ear infection. My report is about that. Also, I have heard some interesting (and frightening) things about antibiotics lately.

[transition words to show order]

First, I want to know why a person needs to take 10 or 14 pills when the infection often seems to go away after 3 or 4 pills. For example, it feels like my ear infection is gone now. But my doctor told me three times that I must take all the pills.

Second, I've heard that antibiotics work only on bacteria-based infections. They do not work on viruses, such as colds. Can you explain why this is true? Which infections are caused by bacteria and which ones are caused by viruses?

Third, I read that some pretty awful bacteria-based illnesses are resistant to antibiotics. The list included pneumonia and tuberculosis. How can this be? I thought antibiotics cured all bacterial infections.

Please let me know if you can answer any of my questions. I'm eager to read what you know. I really am not sure if I should continue with my prescription. I know what you'll say to that: "Ask your doctor!" Thank you very much, Nina.

Mary Kubik ←——— Good e-mail etiquette

E-Mail **33**

Word Choice A good writer uses precise, descriptive words and phrases to communicate with the reader as clearly and effectively as possible. Slang and abbreviations are avoided.

Sentence Fluency A variety of sentence types and structures in an e-mail give the writing energy and flow. All sentences are accurate.

Conventions A good writer carefully edits his or her work prior to sending an e-mail. If the e-mail is for business purposes, the writer should avoid emoticons and unconventional uses of punctuation.

Analyze
the Model

Week 1 • Day 2

Student Objectives

• Read a model e-mail. (p. 33)

Read the Model

Read Mary Kubik's model e-mail aloud. Ask students to listen for tone and to note her use of transitions to organize information and guide readers along. Also ask students to think about how Mary's use of proper e-mail etiquette affects the overall quality of her writing.

Elements of an E-Mail

Have students refer to What's in an E-Mail? on page 30 as you refer to the model. Discuss the notes on the model to enhance students' understanding of the terms. Ask students what they think about Mary's e-mail. Was her tone engaging? Was her information organized in a way that makes sense? Did she forget any parts of an e-mail?

CCSS **Common Core State Standards**

SL.7.1: Engage effectively in a range of collaborative discussions (one-on-one, in groups, and teacher-led) with diverse partners on *grade 7 topics, texts, and issues,* building on each others' ideas and expressing their own clearly.

E-Mail **T33**

Analyze
the Model

Week 1 • Day 3

Student Objectives

- Study an e-mail rubric.
  (pp. 34–35)

Use the Rubric

Explain the Rubric Explain that a rubric is a tool for planning, improving, and assessing a piece of writing. Tell students that a rubric helps a writer focus on key elements, or traits, in writing (**Ideas, Organization, Voice, Word Choice, Sentence Fluency, Conventions,** and **Presentation**).

Explain the 6-point system. Point out that column 6 describes a very good e-mail, one that has received the highest score in all categories. This is what students should strive for when they write their own e-mails.

Discuss the Rubric Suggest that, when students evaluate a piece of writing, they first consider whether it falls on the right-hand side of the rubric (a score of 1–3) or the left-hand side of the rubric (a score of 4–6). Then they can refine their scoring to a specific score.

Remind students to keep the rubric in mind when they write their own e-mail and again when they revise it.

Online Writing Center

Provides a variety of **interactive rubrics,** including 4-, 5-, and 6-point models.

Rubric

Use this 6-point rubric to plan and evaluate an e-mail.

	6	5	4	
Ideas	The writer's main idea is clear and focused. The details are relevant and striking.	The main idea is clear. The details are relevant and clear.	The main idea is clear. Some of the details are interesting, but a few may be irrelevant.	
Organization	Details are presented in an order that makes sense. A variety of transitions smoothly connect the details and guide the reader.	Details are presented in a logical order. Transitions connect details and guide the reader.	The organization of details makes the writing easy to follow. Transitions are present.	
Voice	The writer's voice enhances the writing and connects with the reader. The tone is respectful and friendly.	The writer's voice connects with the reader most of the time. It may sound too informal in places.	The writer's voice sounds too casual. Exclamations and words in capital letters "scream" at the reader.	
Word Choice	The writing is precise and free of informal or slang words.	The writing is precise in most places and does not use slang. One or two informal words may be present.	Some vague or general words are used. Some overly informal or slang words are used.	
Sentence Fluency	All sentences are complete and correct. They flow well and are enjoyable to read.	There may be a sentence fragment or run-on sentence. The writing flows well.	Some sentence fragments or other problems are present. They are distracting in places.	
Conventions	All verb tenses are correct. The writing is easy to understand.	The writing contains a few verb tense errors, but the reader must hunt for them.	Verb tense errors are noticeable but don't confuse the reader.	
+ Presentation	The e-mail is accurately typed and has extra space between paragraphs.			

CCSS Common Core State Standards

E-Mail

The Common Core State Standards are woven throughout the instruction in *Strategies for Writers*. The rubrics and strategies for writing an e-mail are based principally on Narrative Standards. In this chapter, the Ideas rubric reflects standard **W.7.3.a** in its focus on description through the use of striking details. The Organization rubric descriptors are drawn directly from standard **W.7.3.c,** which emphasizes the use of transitions, and standard **W.7.3.a,** which highlights logical sequence.

3	2	1	
The main idea is somewhat clear. The details are very general.	The main idea is unclear. Details are sketchy.	The writing is too sketchy to have a main idea.	**Ideas**
Many details are out of order. Transitions may or may not be present.	The writing is hard to follow because there is no logical order. Transitions are unclear or missing.	The writing is confusing. Transitions are missing.	**Organization**
The writer's voice lacks character and fades in and out.	The writer's voice is difficult to find at times. The voice may not be a good match for the audience or purpose.	The writer's voice is missing.	**Voice**
The language is unclear and/or too informal in many places. Some slang words are used.	Most of the language is vague, unclear, and too informal, and many slang expressions are used.	The language is so vague that it's hard to follow; the tone is too informal and filled with slang.	**Word Choice**
Several sentence fragments, run-ons, or other problems are confusing for the reader at times.	Many sentence fragments, run-ons, and other problems make the writing difficult to read.	So many sentences are incorrect that the writing is nearly impossible to understand.	**Sentence Fluency**
Noticeable errors in verb tense confuse the reader.	The writing contains many errors in verb tenses and is difficult to read.	The writing is filled with serious errors in verb tenses that impede reading.	**Conventions**

See Appendix B for 4-, 5-, and 6-point narrative rubrics.

Apply the Rubric

Take a Poll Ask students to raise their hands to indicate what score they would give the e-mail on one or more of the traits. Record the results. Ask students to offer examples from the e-mail to support their scores. If there are students who seem to disagree with most of their classmates by a difference of more than two points, gently probe as to why they think so. If students score the e-mail 5 or below on any trait, ask what the writer could do to raise the score.

Additional Rubrics Appendix B includes 4-, 5-, and 6-point rubrics that can be used with any piece of narrative writing. The rubrics are also available as blackline masters, beginning on page T543.

The focus on precise language to convey experiences found in standard **W.7.3.d** is reflected in the Word Choice rubric. As in all chapters, standards **L.7.1** and **L.7.2** are represented in the Conventions rubric.

CCSS **C**ommon **C**ore **S**tate **S**tandards

SL.7.1.a: Come to discussions prepared, having read or researched material under study, explicitly draw on that preparation by referring to evidence on the topic, text, or issue to probe and reflect on ideas under discussion.

Analyze
the Model

Student Objectives

- Read a model e-mail. *(p. 33)*
- Use the e-mail rubric. *(pp. 34–35)*
- Use the model e-mail to study Ideas, Organization, and Voice. *(pp. 36–37)*

Study the Model

Assess the Model Use questions such as the following to guide a conversation about the model e-mail. Be sure students back up their answers with solid examples from the e-mail.

- Does Mary provide enough helpful, supportive details for her reader to fully understand the purpose of her e-mail? (Possible response: Yes, Mary clearly explains her questions and concerns about antibiotics. It was easy to understand the subject.)

- How has Mary organized her e-mail? Is it effective? (Possible response: Mary organizes her e-mail by writing one paragraph for each question. It is effective, because the reader can easily understand what Mary wants to know.)

- Why does it makes sense for Mary to maintain a friendly tone in her e-mail? (Possible response: Mary is writing to a classmate, not somebody she needs to impress.)

▶ Strategies for Writers Online
Go to **www.sfw.z-b.com** for additional online resources for students and teachers.

E-Mail

Using the E-Mail Rubric to Study the Model

Did you notice that the model on page 33 points out some key elements of an e-mail? As she wrote her e-mail, Mary Kubik used these elements to help her. She also used the 6-point rubric on pages 34–35 to plan, draft, revise, and edit the writing. A rubric is a great tool to evaluate writing during the writing process.

Now let's use the same rubric to score the model. To do this, we'll focus on each trait separately, starting with Ideas. We'll use the top descriptor for each trait (column 6), along with examples from the model, to help us understand how the traits work together. How would you score Mary on each trait?

Ideas
- The writer's main idea is clear and focused.
- The details are relevant and striking.

I like how Mary gets right to the point. She states her purpose almost immediately, and then provides helpful, relevant supporting details to explain further.

[from the writing model]

Good morning, Nina. I'm doing a report for school on antibiotics. I know your mom is a doctor, so I thought maybe you knew the answers. Just last week my doctor gave me an antibiotic prescription for an ear infection. My report is about that. Also, I have heard some interesting (and frightening) things about antibiotics lately.

English Language Learners

BEGINNING

What is an e-mail? Show students a handwritten letter and the envelope it came in. Say, *This is a letter.* Have students repeat the word. Then point to a computer. Say, *A letter sent from a computer is an e-mail.* Have students repeat the word. Bring up an e-mail account. Project it on a whiteboard, if possible. Review meanings for simple terms related to e-mails, such as *new, inbox, attach, drafts,* and *send.*

INTERMEDIATE

Tone of Voice Write the greetings *Hey* and *Dear Miss Kay* on the board. Ask, *If you are sending an e-mail to your friend, do you use* Hey *or* Dear Miss Kay? *If you are sending an e-mail to your teacher, do you use* Hey *or* Dear Miss Kay? Help students see that they should use different (more or less formal) words depending on to whom the e-mail will be sent. Repeat for other greetings and different possible e-mail recipients.

**Organization**

- Details are presented in an order that makes sense for the topic.
- A variety of transitions smoothly connect the details and guide the reader.

Mary asks several questions, but because she uses transition words (such as *first*, *second*, and *third*), I was able to follow along without feeling lost. The order of the questions makes sense to me and helps me follow details about a topic I don't know much about.

[from the writing model]

First, I want to know why a person needs to take 10 or 14 pills when the infection often seems to go away after 3 or 4 pills. For example, it feels like my ear infection is gone now.

Voice

- The writer's voice enhances the writing and connects with the reader.
- The tone is respectful and friendly.

Mary's voice is serious, which suits her topic, yet friendly and respectful. She uses words like *please* and *thank you*, which everyone loves to hear. Who wouldn't want to respond when asked like that?

[from the writing model]

Please let me know if you can answer any of my questions. I'm eager to read what you know. I really am not sure if I should continue with my prescription. I know what you'll say to that: "Ask your doctor!" Thank you very much, Nina.

ADVANCED

Main Ideas and Details Write the following paragraph on the board: *Many birds live in our yard. They like our bird feeder. They can build their nests in our trees.* Ask students to tell the most important information in the paragraph. Underline the first sentence and tell students that it is the main idea. Write *main idea* under it. Tell students that the other two sentences give more information about the main idea. They are the supporting details.

ADVANCED HIGH

Transition Words Create a story that is a few sentences long. Write it on the board, but mix up the order of the sentences. Have students put the story in order. Then introduce transition words and phrases that can be used to help the story flow better, such as *first, then,* and *after that*. Add them to the story, and have a volunteer reread it.

CCSS **Common Core State Standards**
SL.7.1.b: Follow rules for collegial discussions, track progress toward specific goals and deadlines, and define individual roles as needed. **SL.7.1.c:** Pose questions that elicit elaboration and respond to others' questions and comments with relevant observations and ideas that bring the discussion back on topic as needed.

Analyze the Model

Week 1 • Day 5

Student Objectives

- Read a model e-mail. *(p. 33)*
- Use the e-mail rubric. *(pp. 34–35)*
- Use the model e-mail to study Word Choice, Sentence Fluency, and Conventions. *(pp. 38–39)*

Think About the Traits Remind students that all the traits are important in every piece of writing; however, some traits play a more important role in specific types of writing. For example, some students may feel that **Ideas** are very important in an e-mail because if ideas and details are not conveyed clearly, or if vital information is left out, the reader will feel confused and the writing cannot achieve its purpose. Others may think **Organization** is a more important trait.

Use questions such as these to discuss the model:

- How do you think Nina would have responded if Mary had used slang or abbreviations throughout her e-mail? (Possible response: The use of slang or abbreviations would have weakened Mary's writing, and Nina might have been confused or offended.)

Strategies for Writers Online

Go to **www.sfw.z-b.com** for additional online resources for students and teachers.

 **Word Choice**
- The writing is precise and free of informal or slang words.

Mary uses words accurately. She doesn't waste time with slang or informal speech, which only weakens her purpose and distances the reader. Reading her e-mail was fun, and responding will be, too!

[from the writing model]

> Second, I've heard that antibiotics work only on bacteria-based infections. They do not work on viruses, such as colds. Can you explain why this is true? Which infections are caused by bacteria and which ones are caused by viruses?

 **Sentence Fluency**
- All sentences are complete and correct.
- They flow well and are enjoyable to read.

Mary uses sentences that are complete and properly constructed. She uses both short and long sentences, which helps her writing flow naturally. I enjoyed reading her e-mail.

[from the writing model]

> Third, I read that some pretty awful bacteria-based illnesses are resistant to antibiotics. The list included pneumonia and tuberculosis. How can this be?

Technology Tip for 21st Century Literacies

Storytellers often play with different genres and modes in order to aid in communicating their intended meaning. Walk students through a discussion of what e-mail does that makes it a distinct form of communication. Then create a series of e-mails that offer a story through their contents (what is said) *and* the way they play with what makes e-mail unique (e.g., e-mail addresses, cc and bc lines, attachments). Doing this as a class will lower the stakes, as you'll be asking students to create a "layered" and complex story.

Conventions
- All verb tenses are correct.
- The writing is easy to understand.

Mary's spelling is great—and so is her punctuation and grammar. I couldn't find any errors in her e-mail! She also uses past and past participle verb forms correctly.

[from the writing model]

> Just last week my doctor gave me an antibiotic prescription for an ear infection. . . . Also, I have heard some interesting (and frightening) things about antibiotics lately.

⁺Presentation The e-mail is accurately typed and has extra space between paragraphs.

My Turn!

I'm going to write an e-mail about something I want to know more about. I'm going to use the rubric and good writing strategies. Read on to see what I do!

Differentiating Instruction

ENRICHMENT
Create an E-mail Exchange Have students work in pairs to create an e-mail exchange that includes at least four e-mails. One writer initiates the exchange, the other writer responds to the questions and asks one or two questions of his or her own, and so on. Students will have to cooperate while drafting so that they know what questions to respond to.

REINFORCEMENT
Support Word Choice To demonstrate why avoiding slang is important, rewrite the model e-mail using slang. Ask students to listen as you read an e-mail like this one: *Like, second, what's the deal with those antibiotics? How come they don't cure EVERYTHING? They're kind of sketchy. It's totally annoying. Whatever.* Then read the model. Encourage students to discuss how the slang affected the e-mail's purpose and how it might affect the audience.

- Find another example of a place where Mary uses long and short sentences to make her writing flow. (Possible response: *Just last week my doctor gave me an antibiotic prescription for an ear infection. My report is about that.*)

- Why is it important to use verb tenses correctly? (Possible response: The reader will not be able to follow what you are talking about if he or she cannot tell whether you are talking about the present, future, or past.)

Presentation Remind students that Presentation is just as important as any of the other traits. The presentation of a piece of writing is like the wrapping on a gift or the icing on a cake. If it is not neatly and thoughtfully done, the overall effect of the finished product is weakened.

E-mails should be neatly and accurately typed. Remind students to use white space—for example, between paragraphs—to help organize the text and make it easier on the reader's eyes. Finally the font should be easily readable—nothing too fancy, too small, or too light in color.

Remind students to take advantage of the spell-check features offered by every computer. They should note, however, that spell checkers will not catch mistakes made with homophones. Students need to be aware of commonly misused words, such as *there, their,* and *they're.*

CCSS Common Core State Standards
SL.7.1.c: Pose questions that elicit elaboration and respond to others' questions and comments with relevant observations and ideas that bring the discussion back on topic as needed. **SL.7.1.d:** Acknowledge new information expressed by others and, when warranted, modify their own views.

Write an E-Mail

Week 2 • Day 1

Student Objectives

• Read and understand a prewriting strategy. (p. 40)

Prewrite

Focus on Ideas

Collect Details Read page 40 aloud. Point out that prior to drafting her e-mail, Nina jotted down several details about her chosen topic—different dialects. Explain that in addition to recording her observations and questions, she wrote down whom she would send her e-mail to, as well as a reminder to get the correct e-mail address at home. Remind students that Nina's organization will not only help her remember to include all the important information in her e-mail, but also ensure she sends it to the proper e-mail address. Because e-mail addresses are usually case-sensitive, accurately recording an address is vital if the writer wants the intended reader to receive it.

Prewrite

Focus on Ideas

The Rubric Says	The writer's main idea is clear and focused. The details are relevant and striking.
Writing Strategy	List the main idea or purpose for writing. Then list relevant details that support it.

Hmmm...who am I going to send an e-mail to? And what will I write about? I know! I've been wondering why people from different places use different words for things, even when they all speak English. That will be my main idea. I'll e-mail my fourth grade teacher, Ms. Jackson. She knows a lot about words and languages. But first I'll list all of the important supporting details to make sure my purpose is crystal clear.

> **E-Mail Assignment**
>
> Main Idea: People from different places speak different dialects of English.
>
> Details:
> ✔ new kids at school from different places use unfamiliar words
> ✔ Abby is from the South
> ✔ Jill is from Maine
> ✔ where did *wicked* come from
> ✔ also, *tote* and *I'm fixing to*
> ✔ announcers on TV sound perfect—why?
> ✔ English is not the same everywhere, I guess
> ✔ send to Ms. Jackson, my fourth-grade teacher
> ✔ get Ms. Jackson's e-mail address from home

Apply

Write down the main idea for an e-mail you want to write. Then make a list of details to cover in the e-mail.

English Language Learners

BEGINNING/INTERMEDIATE

Main Idea Table Draw a Main Idea Table on the board. In the Main Idea section, write *How Animals Move*. Ask students to give examples of the different ways that animals move, such as *fly, swim, walk*. Then write their answers in the Supporting Details section.

ADVANCED/ADVANCED HIGH

Main Idea Table Have students think of an event that happened recently that they would like to share with a friend. Introduce the Main Idea Table. Ask them to write the main idea and supporting details in the appropriate part of the table. Then have them trade tables with a partner. The partner should follow along in the table as the first student tells the story.

Online Writing Center

Provides **interactive graphic organizers** as well as a variety of graphic organizers in PDF format.

Prewrite
Focus on **Organization**

The Rubric Says	Details are presented in an order that makes sense for the topic.
Writing Strategy	Make a Main Idea Table.

✏ Writer's Term_____
Main Idea Table
A **Main Idea Table** shows how a main idea is supported by details.

OK, I've got my main idea and lots of supporting details. Now I need to organize those details in a way that makes the most sense for my purpose. I'll use a Main Idea Table. This will help me organize my information into good paragraphs, too.

MAIN IDEA TABLE

Main Idea: People from different places speak different dialects of English.

Supporting Detail	Supporting Detail	Supporting Detail	Supporting Detail	Supporting Detail
Dialect is words and phrases that are used in specific places.	Jill from Maine says, "Those pancakes were wicked good."	Abby from the South says, "I'm fixing to" and "tote."	Evening starts right after lunch.	TV announcers don't even have accents.

Reflect
Did Nina organize her details well? Do her details support her main idea?

Apply
Make a Main Idea Table to organize your supporting details.

E-Mail **41**

Conferencing

PEER TO PEER Have pairs of students exchange Main Idea Tables. Tell students to look at each detail and determine how it relates to the main idea. If they are unclear on how any detail connects to the main idea, have them write their questions and give them to their partner.

PEER GROUPS Divide students into small groups. Have students pass their Main Idea tables around the group. For each table they review, students should write a statement that begins *If I were receiving this e-mail, I would want to know _____.* on a sticky note and attach it to the table.

TEACHER-LED Conference with individual students. Discuss their topics to make sure they are suitable for an e-mail. Review their tables and ask which detail they think is the most interesting and important. Help students decide if they have included irrelevant details they should delete.

Student Objectives

• Make a Main Idea Table to organize main idea and supporting details. *(p. 41)*

Prewrite

Focus on **Organization**

Organize Ideas Explain that writers use different types of graphic organizers to organize their ideas. Nina used a Main Idea Table to help her organize the main idea of her e-mail and all the related supporting details. After students have had enough time to review the organizer, ask them how they think a Main Idea Table will help them write an e-mail. (Possible response: A Main Idea Table will help me keep track of and properly organize each of my supporting details in order of importance.)

✏ Writer's Term_____
Main Idea Table A Main Idea Table clearly defines the main idea and then shows how each of the related details supports this main idea. Once students have created a Main Idea Table, they can determine a logical order in which to present their supporting details.

CCSS **Common Core State Standards**
W.7.3.a: Engage and orient the reader by establishing a context and point of view and introducing a narrator and/or characters; organize an event sequence that unfolds naturally and logically.

E-Mail **T41**

Write
an E-Mail

Week 2 • Day 3

Student Objectives

• Use a Main Idea Table to begin writing. *(p. 42)*

Draft

Focus on Organization

Draft an E-Mail Read page 42 aloud. Ask students to explain what it means to draft an e-mail. Be sure that students understand that they will use their Main Idea Table to guide them through the drafting process.

If students are writing their drafts in class, plan and facilitate time for writing, conferences, and reflection. Explain that students will go through each step of the writing process to create their final copy. Editing is only part of the process.

Note: To help facilitate editing, proofreader's marks are provided as a reference on page 43.

 Writer's Term _____

E-Mail Etiquette is a written form of good manners. Using good e-mail etiquette not only shows consideration for the reader, it also strengthens the writing as a whole.

Online Writing Center

Provides student eBooks with an **interactive writing pad** for drafting, revising, editing, and publishing.

Draft

Focus on **Organization**

The Rubric Says Details are presented in an order that makes sense for the topic. A variety of transitions smoothly connect the details and guide the reader.

Writing Strategy Use transition words to help your reader follow along.

> **Writer's Term**
>
> **E-Mail Etiquette**
>
> **E-mail etiquette** is the polite or accepted way to write an e-mail message. For good e-mail etiquette, do the following:
> 1. Write a clear subject line.
> 2. Include a salutation.
> 3. Do not use emoticons (such as ☺ or ☹) unless you are writing to a really good friend.
> 4. Do not use all capital letters.

Well, it's time to start writing. I need to present my questions and details the right way, or things might get confusing. The rubric says to present the details in a logical way, and to use a variety of transitions to guide the reader. If I write, "I have several questions about dialect," then Ms. Jackson will know to expect more than one question. Then phrases like *First of all* and *My second question is* will help her follow along. Transitions help the reader move from paragraph to paragraph without feeling lost.

E-mail etiquette is also very important. Ms. Jackson was my teacher, but she is not a friend my own age. I won't use emoticons and abbreviations in this e-mail; that would seem disrespectful, and she wouldn't take my questions seriously. I'll write my draft first and then worry about grammar and spelling later.

42 Narrative Writing

Differentiating Instruction

ENRICHMENT

Explore E-mail Applications Allow students time to explore the different options a computer has to offer when writing an e-mail. For example, in the cases where several people should receive the same e-mail, it's possible to "string" several e-mail addresses in a row. Also discuss when it is appropriate to use Reply All as opposed to Reply to Sender.

REINFORCEMENT

Practice Finding Main Ideas and Details Select paragraphs from a textbook for students to diagram in a Main Idea Table.

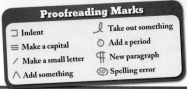

Proofreading Marks

⌐ Indent   ℓ Take out something
≡ Make a capital   ⊙ Add a period
/ Make a small letter   ⊕ New paragraph
∧ Add something   ⑤ℙ Spelling error

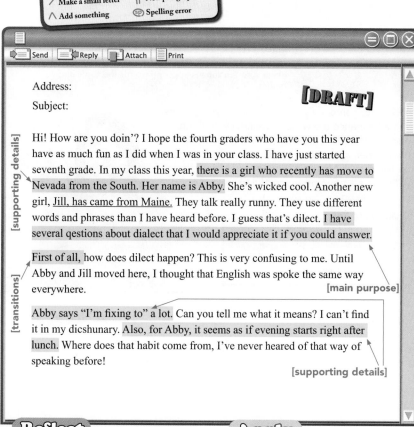

Send   Reply   Attach   Print

Address:

Subject:

[DRAFT]

[supporting details]

Hi! How are you doin'? I hope the fourth graders who have you this year have as much fun as I did when I was in your class. I have just started seventh grade. In my class this year, there is a girl who recently has move to Nevada from the South. Her name is Abby. She's wicked cool. Another new girl, Jill, has came from Maine. They talk really runny. They use different words and phrases than I have heard before. I guess that's dilect. I have several qestions about dialect that I would appreciate it if you could answer.

[main purpose]

[transitions]

First of all, how does dilect happen? This is very confusing to me. Until Abby and Jill moved here, I thought that English was spoke the same way everywhere.

Abby says "I'm fixing to" a lot. Can you tell me what it means? I can't find it in my dicshunary. Also, for Abby, it seems as if evening starts right after lunch. Where does that habit come from, I've never heared of that way of speaking before!

[supporting details]

Reflect

Has Nina explained her main purpose clearly? Are her details in a logical order?

Apply

List your details in a logical order and connect them with a variety of transitions.

E-Mail **43**

Write
an E-Mail

Week 2 • Day 4

Student Objectives

• Complete a draft. *(p. 43)*

Continue the Draft Point out the writing strategy and discuss with students why transitions are important. Tell them to include transitions where appropriate as they draft. Explain that they will have time to add more transitions or change their transitions later when they revise their work. At this point, they should think about how to link the ideas they are writing down and plan on checking their transitions when they revise.

It is important that students are given ample time to draft their e-mails. As conferencing is important throughout the writing process, be sure to also plan time for peer-to-peer, peer group, or teacher-led conferences. Remind students that this is the time to get their ideas down on paper in a well-organized and engaging way. Assure them that they will have plenty of time to fix any mistakes later.

Conferencing

PEER TO PEER Have pairs exchange drafts. Tell students to check their partner's draft for e-mail etiquette and point out any lapses. Also have students tell their partner what they like best about his or her e-mail.

PEER GROUPS Organize students into small groups. Have students take turns reading their e-mail aloud. Tell group members to make suggestions for transitions the writer could include.

TEACHER-LED Conference with pairs of students. Have students read their e-mails aloud. Comment on an aspect of each e-mail that you feel was well done. Help students make suggestions for improving e-mail etiquette and transitions in each other's e-mails.

CCSS **C**ommon **C**ore **S**tate **S**tandards

W.7.3: Write narratives to develop real or imagined experiences or events using effective technique, relevant descriptive details, and well-structured event sequences. **W.7.3.c:** Use a variety of transition words, phrases, and clauses to convey sequence and signal shifts from one time frame or setting to another.

Write
an E-Mail

Week 2 • Day 5

Student Objectives

• Revise for tone. (p. 44)

Revise

Focus on Voice

Use Proper Tone Direct students to page 44. Read the text aloud. Discuss the importance of using the proper tone to suit both purpose and audience. Now direct students' attention to Nina's excerpt and revision. Explain that although the deleted sentence is not offensive, it is very casual language and is not appropriate in this setting.

Writer's Term

Tone is the way an author's writing sounds. Good writers will adjust their tone for their purpose, and they will maintain that tone throughout the writing. For example, if a writer's purpose is to entertain, a humorous and light tone will be used. However, if a serious or negative tone is used, the purpose—to entertain—will not shine through and the reader will not understand the message.

 Strategies for Writers Online

Go to **www.sfw.z-b.com** for additional online resources for students and teachers.

Revise

Focus on **Voice**

The Rubric Says	The writer's voice enhances the writing and connects with the reader. The tone is respectful and friendly.
Writing Strategy	Make sure the tone is appropriate for the topic and reader.

Now for some revision. The rubric says my voice should enhance the writing, connect with the reader, and remain respectful and friendly. Ms. Jackson was my teacher, not a close friend. I think my tone might be too casual. My topic is not overly serious, but I need to sound more respectful to make a good impression on my reader.

Writer's Term

Tone

Tone is how the writing sounds. A writer's tone can be serious, funny, sarcastic, or objective.

[DRAFT]

In my class this year, there is a girl who recently has move to Nevada from the South. Her name is Abby. ~~She's wicked cool.~~

[kept appropriate tone]

Apply

Keep your voice friendly, but appropriate for your topic and intended reader.

44 Narrative Writing

English Language Learners

BEGINNING/INTERMEDIATE

Alphabetical Order In order to use a dictionary, students must know how to alphabetize. Write *ABC* on the board. Write *dust* and *club* on the board. Point to the words and ask, *Which is first?* If necessary, prompt the answer by reciting *A, B, C* and then make the connection between *C* and the *c* in *club*. Do a few more examples. Have students look up 5 words from their e-mail drafts in a dictionary.

ADVANCED/ADVANCED HIGH

Spell Check Point out the spell-check feature of the e-mail program students are using. Demonstrate how to run the spellchecker and then show students how to select the correct spelling from the offered choices. Remind students to be careful. The spellchecker may not suggest the word that students actually meant to use, and it will not notice if a homophone was used incorrectly.

Revise

Focus on Word Choice

The Rubric Says	The writing is precise and free of informal or slang words.
Writing Strategy	Avoid the use of slang.

✎ Writer's Term

Spell Check

Spell check is a function on your computer. It checks the spelling of every word in the document. Be careful, though, because sometimes it suggests words different from the one you're trying to write. If you can't tell which way is correct, look the word up in a dictionary.

I'm going to look at the rubric again. I see that I need to make sure I didn't use any informal or slang words. I can see some spelling errors already. I will fix those right away. Do you see any slang or informal words? Check out my draft and see if I caught the same things you did.

[replaced slang]

[DRAFT]

~~Hi! How are you doin'?~~ Hello, Ms. Jackson. I hope the fourth graders who have you this year have as much fun as I did when I was in your class. I have just started seventh grade. In my class this year, there is a girl who recently has move to Nevada from the South. Her name is Abby. ~~She's wicked cool~~.

Reflect

Is Nina's draft better now? Did she get rid of slang? Do you think Ms. Jackson will enjoy reading Nina's e-mail?

Apply

Check your draft for slang. Then fix all the spelling errors you can find. Spell check really helps with that.

E-Mail 45

Conferencing

PEER TO PEER Have pairs of students exchange drafts. Tell students to choose one word they thought was well-chosen in their partner's draft and one or two words they feel could be replaced with something either more precise or less casual.

PEER GROUPS Have students work in groups of three or four. Have students take turns reading their drafts aloud with expression. Have the students comment on the tone of voice used by each writer and whether it sounds too casual, too formal, or just right.

TEACHER-LED Hold conferences with individual students. Ask students what they like best about their draft and what they want to improve. Make suggestions to help students revise the areas they feel are weak.

Write
an E-Mail

Student Objectives

• Revise to avoid slang. *(p. 45)*

Revise

Focus on Word Choice

Avoid Slang Ask students to imagine how Ms. Jackson might react to the unrevised e-mail, with its casual opening and misspelled words.

Draw students' attention to the rubric descriptor at the top of page 45 and point out that it mentions precise writing. Have students look at the draft excerpt to decide whether there is any other language that should be made more formal.

✎ Writer's Term

Spell Check Caution students that the spell check feature does not catch words that are spelled correctly but misused, such as homophones (*plain, plane*); nor will it catch words that are spelled correctly but wrong (*how* instead of *who*). Students will need to pay close attention to find these errors.

CCSS Common Core State Standards

W.7.3.d: Use precise words and phrases, relevant descriptive details, and sensory language to capture the action and convey experiences and events. **W.7.4:** Produce clear and coherent writing in which the development, organization, and style are appropriate to task, purpose, and audience. **L.7.3.a:** Choose language that expresses ideas precisely and concisely, recognizing and eliminating wordiness and redundancy.

Write
an E-Mail

Week 3 • Day 2

Student Objectives

- Revise for accuracy and flow. (p. 46)

Revise

Focus on  Sentence Fluency

Write Smooth, Clear Sentences
Read page 46 aloud. Explain to students that a good writer will make sure to write every sentence so that it reads smoothly and clearly. Eliminating inappropriate fragments, run-ons, or comma splices from the writing will help ensure smooth, clear sentences.

Direct students' attention to Nina's draft excerpt at the bottom of the page. Have one volunteer read the excerpt without the revisions; then have another read it with the revisions made. Ask the class how Nina's changes clarified her ideas and strengthened her writing. Encourage students to take their time reviewing for each and every sentence in their e-mails for accuracy.

Revise — Focus on Sentence Fluency

The Rubric Says	All sentences are complete and correct. They flow well and are enjoyable to read.
Writing Strategy	Check every sentence.

To make sure my writing flows smoothly, I'll check that each sentence is complete and accurate. I'll also make sure I've followed proper e-mail etiquette. For instance, I see some SHOUTING. I'll also delete all emoticons, which are just for casual e-mails to friends.

[DRAFT]

[fixed sentence fragment]

I've also noticed that announcers on TV don't talk like Southerners, People from Maine, OR people from Nevada. Why does their speech sound so perfect?

[took out SHOUTING]   [delete emoticons]

I'm beginning to think that English is VERY complicated. Please answer me my e-mail and help me figure it out.

Nina Juarez

[inserted full name]

Apply
Fix any incomplete sentences.
Be sure to use good e-mail etiquette.

46   Narrative Writing

Optional Revising Lessons

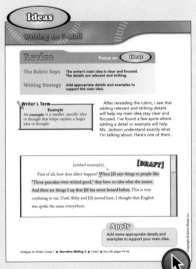

Narrative 3   Narrative 4

Go to ➡ Strategies for Writers Grade 7 CD-ROM

Online Writing Center

Provides **interactive proofreading activities** for each genre.

Edit — Conventions

The Rubric Says   All verb tenses are correct. The writing is easy to understand.

Writing Strategy   Check for and fix any incorrect shifts in verb tense.

Writer's Term

Past and Past Participle Forms of Verbs
The **past tense form of a verb** tells about something that happened in the past. The past tense form does not have a helping verb. The **past participle form of a verb** needs a helping verb, such as *have, has, had, is,* or *was.* Many verbs, called irregular verbs, have different past and past participle forms.

The last step is to proofread my e-mail to check my grammar, spelling, and punctuation. The rubric also says to make sure all verb tenses are correct. I will carefully proofread my e-mail one last time.

[DRAFT]

First of all, how does dialect happen? When Jill says things to people like "Those pancakes were wicked good," they have no idea what she means. And there are things I say that Jill has never ~~heared~~ heard before. This is very confusing to me. Until Abby and Jill moved here, I thought that English was spoken the same way everywhere.

[corrected past participle form of verb]

Reflect

Did Nina catch all her errors in punctuation and grammar? How did she do with her verb forms?

Apply — Conventions

Review your draft for punctuation, grammar, and spelling errors. Check that all verb tenses are used correctly.

For more practice with past, past participle, and perfect verb forms, see the next two pages.

E-Mail **47**

Related Grammar Practice

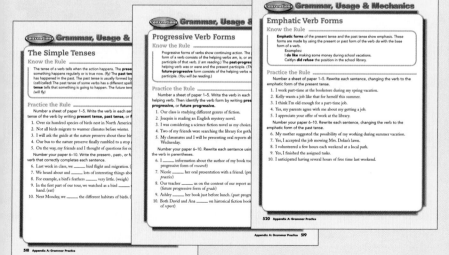

Student Edition pages 518, 519, 520

Go to   Appendix A: Grammar Practice

Write an E-Mail

Week 3 • Day 3

Student Objectives

• Edit for correct use of verb tenses. (*p. 47*)

Edit

Focus on Conventions

Edit for Verb Tenses Remind students that now is the time to correct any mistakes in spelling, grammar, punctuation, and capitalization. Suggest that students carefully read each sentence in their e-mail starting with the last sentence and working their way backward. That way, their attention is on mechanics rather than content.

Remind students to pay close attention to shifts in verb tense, as this is a common area where mistakes are sometimes overlooked.

Use the mini-lessons on pages T48 and T49 for students having trouble with verb tenses. Then have students complete pages 48 and 49.

Writer's Term

Past and Past Participle Forms of Verbs Keeping the tense consistent throughout a piece of writing is key to making the meaning clear.

CCSS Common Core State Standards
W.7.3.d: Use precise words and phrases, relevant descriptive details, and sensory language to capture the action and convey experiences and events. **L.7.1:** Demonstrate command of the conventions of standard English grammar and usage when writing or speaking.

Conventions

Mini-Lesson

Student Objectives

• Understand the difference between past and past participle verb forms. *(p. 48)*

Past and Past Participle Verb Forms

Before class, prepare for the activity by doing the following: On separate slips of paper, write each form of the verbs shown on page 48. Put the slips of paper into an open-topped container or a bag.

In class, pass the container to students who then draw out a slip of paper and use the word in a sentence. Ask students to confirm that the word was used correctly.

Past and Past Participle Verb Forms

Know the Rule

A past tense verb tells about an action that happened in the past. The past participle tells about an action that was completed in the past but may have continued over a period of time.

Past tense form of a verb: I **gave** my teacher a printout from the dialect website.

Past participle form of a verb: She **has given** me a lot of support for my dialect project.

Incorrect: She **has gave** me a lot of support for my dialect project.

This table gives the **present, past,** and **past participle forms** of a few common verbs. If you are not sure of the correct form of a verb, check a dictionary.

Forms of Verbs		
Present	**Past**	**Past Participle**
go	went	(has, have) gone
write	wrote	(has, have) written
speak	spoke	(has, have) spoken

Practice the Rule

Read each sentence. If the verb is incorrect, rewrite the verb correctly on a separate sheet of paper. If the verb is correct, write **Correct**.

1. English is spoke different ways in different countries. **spoken**
2. My pen pal in Britain may have wrote you a letter about his family's car. **written**
3. He may have chosen to use some words that are unfamiliar to you. **Correct**
4. He wrote that the boot had been damaged in an accident. **Correct**
5. Would you have knew which part of the car was the boot? **known**
6. Then he wrote that he have visited his aunt in her flat. **has**
7. Who knew that a flat is an apartment? **Correct**
8. I has spoken with my pen pal on the phone only once. **have**
9. He has promised to make a list of fun British dialect for me to learn. **Correct**
10. I have agree to do the same for him and include it in my next letter. **agreed**

Online Writing Center

Provides **interactive grammar games** and **practice activities** in student eBook.

Related Grammar Practice

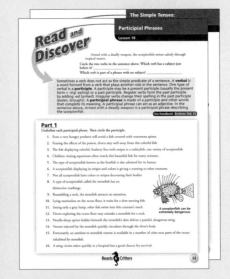

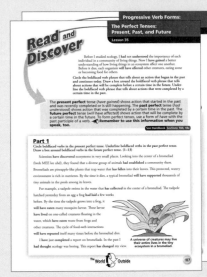

Pages 53, 105

Pages 107, 109

Go to ➡ **G.U.M. Student Practice Book**

The Perfect Tenses

Know the Rule

> The **present perfect tense** (*have eaten*) shows action that started in the past and was recently completed or is still happening. The **past perfect tense** (*had eaten*) shows action that was completed by a certain time in the past. The **future perfect tense** (*will have eaten*) shows action that will be complete by a certain time in the future. To form **perfect tenses**, use a form of *have* with the **past participle** of a verb.

Practice the Rule

Read each sentence. If the verb is incorrect, rewrite the verb correctly on a separate sheet of paper. If the verb is correct, write **Correct**.

1. I ~~had wrote~~ to my cousin, Tess, several times over the school year about our upcoming summer vacation together. **have written**
2. Tess had responded within an hour each and every time! **Correct**
3. These days, I am so busy with the holidays, I have forgotten to stay in touch. **Correct**
4. But just now, I ~~have sended~~ a long e-mail, explaining why I have been so busy. **sent**
5. Tess is such a great pen pal, I am sure she will have written back by bedtime tonight. **Correct**
6. Tess and I have spent three summer vacations together. **Correct**
7. I ~~has~~ always enjoyed her company when we have gotten together. **have**
8. Before our first vacation together, Tess ~~has~~ spent her summers going to camp. **had**
9. She ~~has~~ told me that she did not enjoy camp at all.
10. By the time next school year rolls around, I ~~had~~ enjoyed a great summer with Tess. **will have**

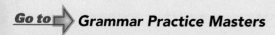

Go to ➡ Grammar Practice Masters

Mini-Lesson

Student Objectives

- Identify and understand the use of the perfect tenses. *(p. 49)*

The Perfect Tenses

Write the following sentences on the board:

- *Jamie will have run in two marathons by this spring.*
- *Jack had entered the race at the last minute.*
- *James has forgotten his running shoes.*

Ask a volunteer to point out the sentence showing past perfect tense. (the second sentence) Explain that the action of entering the race ended in the past.

Ask another volunteer to point out the sentence showing future perfect tense. (the first sentence) Explain that the verb *will have run* shows action that will be completed by spring.

Explain that the remaining sentence (the third sentence) shows a verb in present perfect tense. The verb *has forgotten* shows action that began in the past and is still occurring—James still has no running shoes!

Allow time to discuss as a class the difference between the tenses and how to determine which tense is which.

CCSS Common Core State Standards
L.7.2: Demonstrate command of the conventions of standard English capitalization, punctuation, and spelling when writing.

Write
an E-Mail

Week 3 • Day 4

Student Objectives

- Discuss preparation for publishing and presentation. (p. 50)
- Use a final editing checklist to publish their work. (p. 50)

Publish +Presentation

Publishing Strategy Explain to students that although it makes sense for Nina to publish her e-mail by sending it to Ms. Jackson, students have other options when it comes to publishing their e-mail. For example, students could use the class computer to project their e-mails on the board. Another idea is to print out all the e-mails, collect them, and randomly "send" them to students' classmates or perhaps a different class. If you have not already discussed a specific publishing strategy, ask students for their suggestions. Encourage them to use their creativity, write down the most popular ideas, and then take a vote on which strategy the class will use.

Direct students to review Nina's final checklist. Ask students what other items they think should be on the checklist. Encourage the class to use the checklist as they type their final copies.

 Strategies for Writers Online
Go to **www.sfw.z-b.com** for additional online resources for students and teachers.

Publish +Presentation

Publishing Strategy	Send my e-mail to the appropriate person.
Presentation Strategy	Check my typing and add spaces between paragraphs.

I'm finished! I not only neatly typed my e-mail using block-style paragraphs, but I also left extra space between paragraphs to make reading easier on the eyes. Now I could share my e-mail with a friend or my language arts class, but I think sending it to Ms. Jackson is the most important thing to do. I hope she will write back with some information about dialect soon. But before I hit the Send button, I will read through my e-mail one last time to make sure it includes all the items on my final checklist.

My Final Checklist

Did I—
- ✔ fix all of my spelling, grammar, and punctuation errors?
- ✔ properly use all past and past participle verb forms?
- ✔ properly use all perfect tense verb forms?
- ✔ leave extra space between each paragraph?

Apply
Make a checklist to go over your e-mail. Then make the corrections you need and publish a final copy. Then it's time to hit that send button!

50 Narrative Writing

Differentiating Instruction

ENRICHMENT
Real-Life E-Mailing Provide students with the opportunity to practice writing e-mails by setting up a Correspondence Club. Students choose from a variety of subjects (a school event, a subject being studied in class, or a recent holiday) and then write and send the e-mail to another group of students in another class. The recipients could then respond to the e-mail, sticking with the chosen topic. This will give students plenty of practice with both writing and properly responding to e-mails in a real-life setting.

REINFORCEMENT
Practice E-Mail Form Write several poorly written e-mails to demonstrate what *not* to do when writing an e-mail. Use your computer to project the e-mail onto the board for discussion.

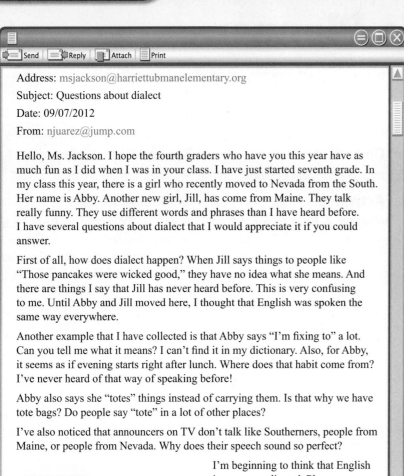

Address: msjackson@harriettubmanelementary.org

Subject: Questions about dialect

Date: 09/07/2012

From: njuarez@jump.com

Hello, Ms. Jackson. I hope the fourth graders who have you this year have as much fun as I did when I was in your class. I have just started seventh grade. In my class this year, there is a girl who recently moved to Nevada from the South. Her name is Abby. Another new girl, Jill, has come from Maine. They talk really funny. They use different words and phrases than I have heard before. I have several questions about dialect that I would appreciate it if you could answer.

First of all, how does dialect happen? When Jill says things to people like "Those pancakes were wicked good," they have no idea what she means. And there are things I say that Jill has never heard before. This is very confusing to me. Until Abby and Jill moved here, I thought that English was spoken the same way everywhere.

Another example that I have collected is that Abby says "I'm fixing to" a lot. Can you tell me what it means? I can't find it in my dictionary. Also, for Abby, it seems as if evening starts right after lunch. Where does that habit come from? I've never heard of that way of speaking before!

Abby also says she "totes" things instead of carrying them. Is that why we have tote bags? Do people say "tote" in a lot of other places?

I've also noticed that announcers on TV don't talk like Southerners, people from Maine, or people from Nevada. Why does their speech sound so perfect?

I'm beginning to think that English is very complicated. Please answer my e-mail and help me figure it out.

Nina Juarez

Reflect

How do you like it? Did Nina use all the traits of a good e-mail? Check it against the rubric to find out. Then use the rubric to check your own e-mail.

E-Mail **51**

Technology Tip   for 21st Century Literacies

While much of what we write is made up of print text, we can use a variety of technologies to recast or represent that content. Ask students to copy the content of a series of e-mails (either from the first tip on page T38 or a different sequence) to create a word-cloud using an online tool like Wordle. By transforming their print text into a visual image (in which repeated words are larger, and the writer can adjust color, layout, and font), students can examine what they said and how they said it, and set goals for later work.

See **www.sfw.z-b.com** for further information about and links to these websites and tools.

Write
an E-Mail

Week 3 • Day 5

Student Objectives

• Use an e-mail rubric. *(pp. 34–35)*

• Share a published e-mail. *(p. 51)*

Presentation Strategy Explain to students how important neatness is when creating a final copy of their work. Messy or inaccurate typing detracts from the purpose and frustrates or confuses readers. Details to pay attention to include: neat margins, using one or two legible fonts, and indented paragraphs or space between block-style paragraphs. Remind students to use a friendly closing, as well as their full names (unless writing to a good friend).

Reflecting on an E-Mail

Ask students to reflect on the experience of writing an e-mail using questions such as the following:

• How was writing this e-mail similar to or different from other experiences you've had with e-mail?

• How will writing this e-mail affect the ways you write e-mails or other messages in the future?

• What did you enjoy the most and the least about writing an e-mail?

CCSS Common Core State Standards

W.7.4: Produce clear and coherent writing in which the development, organization, and style are appropriate to task, purpose, and audience.

Historical Episode Planner

WEEK 1

Day 1
Introduce
a Historical Episode

Student Objectives
- Review the elements of a historical episode.
- Consider purpose and audience.
- Learn the traits of narrative writing.

Student Activities
- Read and discuss **What's in a Historical Episode?** (p. 52)
- Read and discuss **Why Write a Historical Episode?** (p. 53)
- Read **Linking Narrative Writing Traits to a Historical Episode.** (p. 54)

Day 2
Analyze
Read a Historical Episode

Student Objectives
- Read a model historical episode.

Student Activities
- Read **"Wanted: A Boat to India."** (pp. 55–57)

Day 3
Analyze
Introduce the Rubric

Student Objectives
- Learn to read a rubric.

Student Activities
- Review **"Wanted: A Boat to India."** (pp. 55–57)
- Read and discuss the **Historical Episode Rubric.** (pp. 58–59)

WEEK 2

Day 1
Write
Prewrite: Ideas

Student Objectives
- Read and understand a prewriting strategy.

Student Activities
- Read and discuss **Prewrite: Focus on Ideas.** (pp. 64–65)
- Apply the prewriting strategy.

Day 2
Write
Prewrite: Organization

Student Objectives
- Make a Story Map to organize the parts of the story.

Student Activities
- Read and discuss **Prewrite: Focus on Organization.** (pp. 66–67)
- Reflect on the model Story Map.
- Apply the prewriting strategy to create a Story Map.
- Participate in a peer conference.

Day 3
Write
Draft: Voice

Student Objectives
- Use a Story Map to begin writing.

Student Activities
- Read and discuss **Draft: Focus on Voice.** (p. 68)
- Reflect on the model draft. (pp. 69–71)
- Apply the drafting strategy by using a Story Map to write a draft.

WEEK 3

Day 1
Write
Revise: Word Choice

Student Objectives
- Revise to replace weak verbs with strong ones.

Student Activities
- Read and discuss **Revise: Focus on Word Choice.** (p. 73)
- Reflect on the model draft.
- Apply the revising strategy.
- Participate in a peer conference.

Day 2
Write
Revise: Sentence Fluency

Student Objectives
- Revise to use different kinds of sentences.

Student Activities
- Read and discuss **Revise: Focus on Sentence Fluency.** (p. 74)
- Apply the revising strategy.

Note: Optional Revising Lessons appear on the *Strategies for Writers* CD-ROM.

Day 3
Write
Edit: Conventions

Student Objectives
- Edit for correct punctuation.

Student Activities
- Read and discuss **Edit: Focus on Conventions.** (p. 75)
- Reflect on the model draft.
- Apply the revising strategy.

Note: Teach the Conventions mini-lessons (pp. 76–77) if needed.

Analyze
Ideas, Organization, and Voice

Student Objectives
- Read a model historical episode.
- Use the historical episode rubric.
- Use the model historical episode to study Ideas, Organization, and Voice.

Student Activities
- Review **"Wanted: A Boat to India."** *(pp. 55–57)*
- Read and discuss **Using the Rubric to Study the Model.** *(pp. 60–63)*

Analyze
Word Choice, Sentence Fluency, and Conventions

Student Objectives
- Read a model historical episode.
- Use the historical episode rubric.
- Use the model historical episode to study Word Choice, Sentence Fluency, and Conventions.

Student Activities
- Review **"Wanted: A Boat to India."** *(pp. 55–57)*
- Read and discuss **Using the Rubric to Study the Model.** *(pp. 60–63)*

Day 4	Day 5

Write
Draft

Student Objectives
- Complete a draft.

Student Activities
- Finish the draft. *(pp. 69–71)*
- Participate in a peer conference.

Write
Revise: Ideas

Student Objectives
- Revise to include historical details.

Student Activities
- Read and discuss **Revise: Focus on Ideas.** *(p. 72)*
- Reflect on a model draft.
- Apply the revising strategy.

Day 4	Day 5

Write
Publish: +Presentation

Student Objectives
- Discuss preparation for publishing and presentation.
- Use a final editing checklist to publish their work.

Student Activities
- Read and discuss **Publish: +Presentation.** *(p. 78)*
- Apply the publishing strategy.

Write
Publish: +Presentation

Student Objectives
- Use a historical episode rubric.
- Share a published historical episode.

Student Activities
- Share their work.
- Use the rubric to reflect upon and evaluate the model and their own writing. *(pp. 58–59, 79–81)*

To complete the chapter in fewer days, combine the learning objectives and activities in a way that supports students as they write.

Resources at-a-Glance

Grammar, Usage & Mechanics

Differentiating Instruction

For additional Differentiating Instruction activities, see Strategies for Writers Extensions Online at **www.sfw.z-b.com.**

English Language Learners

Conferencing

Technology Tip

 Connection Letter
Reproducible letter (in English and Spanish) appears on the *Strategies for Writers* CD-ROM and at **www.sfw.z-b.com.**

Online Writing Center

Provides IWB resources, interactive games and practice activities, videos, eBooks, and a virtual file cabinet.

 Strategies for Writers Online

Go to **www.sfw.z-b.com** for free online resources for students and teachers.

Introduce
a Historical Episode

Student Objectives

- Review the elements of a historical episode. (*p. 52*)
- Consider purpose and audience. (*p. 53*)
- Learn the traits of narrative writing. (*p. 54*)

What's a Historical Episode?

Discuss the definition of a historical episode with students. Explain that a historical episode is a particular type of narrative writing that is based on a real person, real events, or a time period in history. Ask volunteers to mention periods in history they find especially interesting. Point out that with some research, they can write historical episodes of their own.

What's in a Historical Episode?

Remind students that although their historical episodes will be fictional, specific elements are necessary to make the writing strong and the story believable.

Explain that research during the prewriting stage will be necessary to help them write believable dialogue, include factual details, and capture the overall essence of their chosen time period.

 Strategies for Writers Online
Go to **www.sfw.z-b.com** for additional online resources for students and teachers.

What's a **Historical Episode?**

It's a story about something that happened in the past. It can make the reader feel as if he or she were right there when the episode was happening. I'm excited about trying this kind of writing because I can pretend that I'm there!

What's in a **Historical Episode?**

Historical Details
These are the parts of the story that come from history. I'll have to read up on the setting and gather information—and keep track of where my facts come from, too.

Sequence
This is the order in which events happen. I'll need to tell the story so that it has a beginning and middle that lead naturally to the conclusion.

Dialogue
This is conversation between characters in the episode. It will be fun to make up what the people in my story are saying to each other. I'll have to make the dialogue sound realistic to help develop a believable and engaging story.

Third-Person Point of View
This is when the narrator of the story is not a character. I won't use the words *I, me, my, you, your, we, us,* or *our*. Instead, I'll use *he, she, they,* and *them*. I'll be an all-knowing, invisible narrator!

Narrative Text Exemplars (Historical Episode)

Fradin, Dennis Brindell and Judith Bloom. *The Power of One: Daisy Bates and the Little Rock Nine.* Clarion Books, 2004. Get to know Daisy Bates through her involvement in one of the most memorable events in civil rights history, the integration of nine African American students into Central High School in Little Rock in 1957. This book not only highlights this important turning point, but also provides background on Daisy Bates' life growing up and becoming a part of the civil rights movement.

Forbes, Esther. *Johnny Tremain.* Yearling, 1987. In this classic, Newberry Award winning novel, Forbes tells the story of Jonny Tremian, a young silversmith who was caught up in the American Revolution. It is an insightful story full of adventure, excitement, sadness, and inspiration.

Why write a Historical Episode?

I can think of a whole bunch of reasons to write a historical episode. Here's a list of a few. I hope it will help me decide what I want to write about.

Information
Writing about history is a fun way to give people knowledge of the past. It can be more fun to read a historical episode with characters and dialogue than to read history from a textbook.

Personal Exploration
I like to find out how people in the past solved their problems. Did they have problems that were similar to mine? I also like to imagine what I would experience if I traveled to another place and time.

Lessons From the Past
Some events in the past teach important lessons about today. By including relevant, factual details, I can show what we have in common with the past so maybe we can avoid struggles they had back then.

Entertainment
Historical episodes can be very entertaining. They can be exciting, sad, or funny. They can also introduce characters who are larger than life, with interesting personalities.

Hopkinson, Deborah. *Shutting Out the Sky: Life in the Tenements of New York, 1880-1924.* **Orchard, 2003.** Hopkinson takes the reader into the lives of five families in New York City around the turn of the century. She recounts stories of triumph and struggle and highlights the fighting spirit of early immigrants trying to capture the American dream.

Miller, Lee. *Roanoke: The Mystery of the Lost Colony.* **Scholastic, 2007.** Travel back in time to the late 1500s when the colony of Roanoke, which was made up of 115 men, women, and children, vanished into thin air. Readers of Miller's book become detectives using clues provided from primary sources to try and solve the mystery of what really happened to the lost colony of Roanoke.

Why write a Historical Episode?

Explain to students that there are many reasons why a person would choose to write a historical episode. Read page 53 out loud. Remind students that all writing has a purpose. Writers write for many reasons and for a variety of audiences, and both purpose and audience always help shape the writing.

Discuss the way purpose can influence the form a historical episode will take. For example, someone wishing to share information about a certain period in history, or perhaps help define a lesson learned in the past, would include plenty of facts and explanations to help his or her audience understand. However, someone writing to entertain might use a tone that conveys excitement, humor, or suspense.

Encourage students to think about their reasons for writing a historical episode and how these reasons will affect the tone and focus of their writing.

CCSS **C**ommon **C**ore **S**tate **S**tandards

SL.7.1: Engage effectively in a range of collaborative discussions (one-on-one, in groups, and teacher-led) with diverse partners on *grade 7 topics, texts, and issues,* building on each others' ideas and expressing their own clearly.

Introduce
a Historical Episode

Linking Narrative Writing Traits to a Historical Episode

Read page 54 aloud to help students understand that they will follow Nina as she models using the writing process and the narrative writing traits together. A good historical episode will focus on one event; provide descriptive, accurate historical details; describe events in chronological order; and be told in a voice appropriate for the subject (typically third-person point of view). Tell students they will read a model historical episode as an example of how one writer used narrative writing traits.

Online Writing Center

Provides six **interactive anchor papers** for each mode of writing.

T54   Narrative Writing

Linking Narrative Writing Traits to a Historical Episode

In this chapter, you will write a story about something that happened in the past. This type of narrative writing is called a historical episode. Nina will guide you through the stages of the writing process: Prewrite, Draft, Revise, Edit, and Publish. In each stage, Nina will show you important writing strategies that are linked to the Narrative Writing Traits below.

Narrative Writing Traits

	• a single, focused topic with relevant, engaging details that develop the experiences or events • a narrator or characters that bring the story to life
	• well-structured and logical event sequences, often in chronological order, that guide the reader through the story • an engaging beginning and a satisfying conclusion that reflects on the story's events • a variety of transition words that signal time or setting changes
	• a voice that is appropriate for the audience and purpose • dialogue that, if used, is realistic and helps develop the characters and story
	• precise, descriptive words and phrases
	• a variety of sentences that flow and are a pleasure to read aloud
	• no or few errors in grammar, usage, mechanics, and spelling

Before you write, read Art Foley's historical episode on the next three pages. Then use the historical episode rubric on pages 58–59 to decide how well he did. (You might want to look back at What's in a Historical Episode? on page 52, too!)

Narrative Writing Traits in a Historical Episode

 Ideas Interesting historical details are included to engage the reader and to help the reader best imagine the events being described and bring the characters to life.

 **Organization** A historical episode is usually told in chronological order. A variety of transition words signal changes of time and the relationship of events.

 **Voice** An objective third-person point of view is appropriate for a historical episode. Dialogue can help move the plot along.

Wanted: A Boat to India

by Art Foley

Beginning

Third-person narrator

Marco Polo was beginning to wonder if he was ever going to get to Cathay. His father and uncle had returned to Venice from that country in the Far East, laden with spices, gold, and other rich treasures. Marco had been excited when the men said he could accompany them on this next trip, but so far things had not gone smoothly. They had traveled far out of their way to avoid a war in Armenia. They had struggled across a vast, hot desert in Persia, where packs of bandits roamed around terrorizing travelers. Then the other day their own party had been attacked by one of these bandit hordes, and they had been lucky to escape alive.

Historical details

Now, though, they were finally at Hormuz, at the edge of the sea.

"It's as hot here as it was in the desert," Marco said to himself. "But maybe our luck will change. Maybe we will be able to hire a boat that will get us at least as far as India."

Marco accompanied Niccolò and Maffeo, his father and uncle, when they went down to the harbor. Along with them went Omar, a trader from Hormuz who had recently done business with them. Omar, a tall man with a broad face and easy smile, assured them that they would have no trouble getting a boat.

Historical Episode **55**

 **Word Choice** A good writer uses precise and descriptive words and phrases to bring a historical episode to life.

 **Sentence Fluency** A variety of sentence types and structures in a good narrative give the writing energy and flow. The writing is a pleasure to listen to or to read aloud.

 **Conventions** A good writer carefully edits his or her work prior to publishing. Mistakes in spelling, punctuation, capitalization, and grammar will confuse the reader and obscure the author's purpose. When dialogue is used, special attention is paid to punctuation.

Analyze
the Model

Week 1 • Day 2

Student Objectives

• Read a model historical episode. (pp. 55–57)

Read the Model

Have volunteers read aloud "Wanted: A Boat to India." As they listen to the story, ask them to listen for historical details, authentic-sounding dialogue, and how events in the plot are organized. When the narrative is over, ask students how these elements affected their understanding and connection with the writing.

Elements of a Historical Episode

Have students refer to What's in a Historical Episode? on page 52 as you talk about the model. Discuss the notes on the model to enhance students' understanding of the elements. Point out that the main character, Marco Polo, is introduced immediately in an engaging way. Have a volunteer read just the dialogue again. How has Art Foley crafted authentic-sounding dialogue?

CCSS **C**ommon **C**ore **S**tate **S**tandards
R/Lit.7.3: Analyze how particular elements of a story or drama interact (e.g., how setting shapes the characters or plot).

Historical Episode **T55**

Middle

"Look at all the ships in this harbor," he insisted. "These captains and their crews cross back and forth to India every week. They will fall all over themselves trying to get your business."

The Polos looked around a little doubtfully. The harbor was indeed filled with boats. Their crooked triangular sails swayed slightly as a hot breeze rippled through them. All but two or three of the boats, though, looked far too small to make the crossing.

"Talk to that captain over there," Niccolò told Omar, "and ask if we can see his boat."

 Dialogue

"An excellent choice," Omar praised him. "This man has been a captain for over twenty years with never a mishap."

Even as they approached the boat, however, the Polos began to get apprehensive. Like all the others, it had only one mast, one rudder, and one sail.

"Ask the captain how his ship can be seaworthy," Maffeo told Omar. "What happens if that single mast snaps in the wind? And what holds the boards together? I don't see any iron nails."

"Of course there aren't any nails," Omar responded. "Shipbuilders around here use wooden pegs, which work quite well. They stitch the planks together with strong threads made of coconut fibers. And the masts are lightweight and very flexible. I think perhaps you are worrying too much."

Books for Professional Development

Benjamin, Amy. *Writing in the Content Areas.* **New York: Eye On Education, 2005.** This book—for teachers of social studies, science, and the humanities—provides strategies and techniques to help improve the quality of students' essays, term papers, observation reports, and other writing tasks. This second edition also offers activities and strategies that involve technology (word processing, presentation programming, the Internet, and e-communications), differentiated instruction, and brain-based learning.

Nickelsen, Leann. *Teaching Elaboration and Word Choice.* **New York: Scholastic, 2001.** This book includes creative lessons on using lively verbs, colorful adjectives, specific nouns, and easy and effective mini-lessons and activities that help students enrich and enliven their writing.

 Strategies for Writers Online
Go to **www.sfw.z-b.com** for additional online resources for students and teachers.

Maffeo reminded Omar that Venice, the city where the Polos lived, was known for its merchants sailing to distant ports. He and his brother had seen a good ship or two in their day.

"These ships are lightweight and flexible," Omar continued, almost as if he hadn't heard them. "They are well suited to ride the storms of the Indian Ocean."

Marco was getting a little tired of listening to this haggling. "These boats don't look so bad to me," he thought. "Isn't it important for us to try to move along?"

Marco looked up at the boat owner, who was gesturing to him to climb aboard. As soon as he did, a foul odor assailed his nose. "Could you ask the captain what causes that terrible smell?" he called down to Omar.

"It's the fish oil," Omar explained. "Shipbuilders in this region use the oil instead of tar to caulk the seams of the boat. And really, the oil, despite the bad smell, does its job quite well. These ships are lightweight and flexible, and. . ."

Historical details

By this time, all the Polos, even Marco, had had enough. They just could not believe that small, flimsy boats like these, held together with wooden pegs and fish oil, could get them safely to their destination. They thanked their friend Omar for his help, nodded politely to the captain, and walked away.

I guess we haven't gotten rid of our bad luck yet, thought Marco. We will have to find another way to continue eastward.

Conclusion

Kashatus, William C. *Past, Present and Personal: Teaching Writing in U.S. History.* **Portsmouth, NH: Heinemann, 2002.** In this book, Kashatus offers methods to move teenage students from basic descriptive writing to more complex expository essays and term papers on U.S. History. Reflecting his title, Kashatus divides his book into three parts: "Past History" explores interpretation and assessment of historic documents. "Present History" examines research-based writing. "Personal History" offers experiential techniques to create a "living history classroom."

Anderson, Jeff. *Mechanically Inclined: Building Grammar, Usage, and Style Into Writer's Workshop.* **Portland, ME: Stenhouse, 2005.** This user-friendly book provides strategies to help teachers merge grammar and mechanics with craft in the context of meaningful writing.

CCSS Common Core State Standards

R/Lit.7.3: Analyze how particular elements of a story or drama interact (e.g., how setting shapes the characters or plot).

Analyze the Model

Week 1 • Day 3

Student Objectives

• Learn to read a rubric. (pp. 58–59)

Use the Rubric

Explain the Rubric Explain that a rubric is a tool for planning, improving, and assessing a piece of writing. Tell students that a rubric helps a writer focus on key elements, or traits, in writing (**Ideas, Organization, Voice, Word Choice, Sentence Fluency, Conventions,** and **Presentation**).

Explain the 6-point system. Point out that column 6 describes a very good historical episode, one that has received the highest score in all categories. This is what students should strive for in their own historical episodes.

Discuss the Rubric Guide students in a discussion of the rubric. Read the descriptors that go with each trait. Discuss the difference between columns to be sure students fully understand the point system.

Remind students to keep the rubric in mind when they write their own historical episode and again when they revise it.

Rubric

Use this 6-point rubric to plan and evaluate a historical episode.

	6	5	4
Ideas	Rich, well-researched historical details add authenticity. The details are relevant and striking.	Historical details add authenticity to the writing. The writing makes sense.	The writing contains some interesting details, but more information would help.
Organization	The story is well organized, ending with a conclusion that follows naturally from the story events. A variety of transitions guide the reader through the story.	The story has a clear beginning, middle, and ending. Transitions connect ideas.	The story is organized into a beginning, middle, and ending. Transitions are present.
Voice	Third-person narration is used consistently in an original way. Realistic-sounding dialogue develops the characters.	Third-person narration is used consistently. Dialogue sounds realistic for the most part.	Point of view is inconsistent. Sometimes the reader cannot tell who is speaking. Dialogue is sometimes stiff.
Word Choice	Precise words, such as powerful verbs, capture the action and convey the events clearly.	Strong verbs show the action in the story. Verbs used in speaker tags show action.	Some verbs are strong and others are ordinary or repetitious. Vague words are present.
Sentence Fluency	An exceptional variety of sentences move the story along smoothly. The story is enjoyable to read.	A variety of sentence beginnings and lengths are noticeable. The story is easy to read.	There is some variety in sentence beginnings and length. Some sections may be choppy to read.
Conventions	The writer has used different sentence structure correctly to enhance meaning.	A few errors in sentence structure require a careful look to find them.	The reader will notice a few errors in sentence structure that don't interfere with writing.
+Presentation	Illustrations are thoughtfully integrated with the writing.		

58 Narrative Writing

CCSS Common Core State Standards

Historical Episode

The Common Core State Standards are woven throughout the instruction in *Strategies for Writers*. The rubrics and strategies for the historical episode are based principally on Narrative standards. In this chapter, the Ideas rubric reflects standard **W.7.3.a**. The standard calls for writers to engage and orient the reader; the rubric encourages students to provide historical details to orient their readers. The Organization rubric descriptors are drawn directly from standard **W.7.3.c**, which emphasizes the use of transitions, and standard **W.7.3.e**, which underlines a conclusion that flows naturally from the events in the narrative.

Online Writing Center

Provides a variety of **interactive rubrics,** including 4-, 5-, and 6-point models.

3	2	1	
Some parts of the writing are unclear. Details are present but are very general.	Details are vague. The main idea is unclear.	The writing has no focus. Details are missing, vague, or poorly researched.	**Ideas**
The writing structure doesn't help the reader follow the story. Some transitions are missing.	Lack of organization makes the story difficult to follow. Transitions are missing or are incorrect.	Transitions are missing. The story doesn't have an introduction and just stops without a logical ending.	**Organization**
The writer's voice comes and goes. Dialogue is unrealistic and may be confusing.	The writer's voice is unclear or absent from the writing. Dialogue is missing or confusing.	The writer's voice is absent from the writing. No dialogue is present.	**Voice**
Weak verbs are evident in the writing, along with vague words or more language than is necessary.	Verbs are missing from the writing. The message is not clear.	Words and phrases are vague or unclear. The meaning is also unclear.	**Word Choice**
Some sentences have the same beginnings. Lack of variety in sentence length or structure makes some sections dull.	Many sentences are incomplete, and other problems are evident. The writing may need to be reread for meaning.	Many sentence problems make the writing difficult to read throughout.	**Sentence Fluency**
Many errors in sentence structure require the reader to slow down. The message may not be clear.	Frequent, serious errors in sentence structure make the writing hard to read.	The message is unclear throughout because of serious errors in sentence structure.	**Conventions**

See Appendix B for 4-, 5-, and 6-point narrative rubrics.

The focus on precise language to convey experiences found in standard **W.7.3.d** is reflected in the Word Choice rubric. The Voice rubric emphasizes the narrative technique of dialogue, which is highlighted in standard **W.7.3.b**. As in all chapters, standards **L.7.1** and **L.7.2** are represented in the Conventions rubric.

Apply the Rubric

Assign Groups Separate students into six groups. Assign each group one trait. Each group is responsible for reviewing the model and extracting at least three solid examples that best reflect their assigned trait. A volunteer from each group should record the examples on a piece of paper.

Reassemble Class Starting with the "Ideas" group, have a volunteer from each group read their examples to the class. After each group has revealed their chosen examples, the class as a whole should then take a vote and assign a score to that trait.

Note that although the models were written to score high against the rubric, students should not assume each trait will receive a 6. Encourage students to thoroughly consider and discuss each trait's examples before assigning a score.

Additional Rubrics Appendix B includes 4-, 5-, and 6-point rubrics that can be used with any piece of narrative writing. The rubrics are also available as blackline masters, beginning on page T543.

CCSS **C**ommon **C**ore **S**tate **S**tandards

SL.7.1.a: Come to discussions prepared, having read or researched material under study, explicitly draw on that preparation by referring to evidence on the topic, text, or issue to probe and reflect on ideas under discussion.

Analyze
the Model

Week 1 • Day 4

Student Objectives

- Read a model historical episode. (*pp. 55–57*)
- Use the historical episode rubric. (*pp. 58–59*)
- Use the model historical episode to study Ideas, Organization, and Voice. (*pp. 60–61*)

Study the Model

Assess the Model Have volunteers read aloud each section on pages 60–61. Discuss as a class whether students agree or disagree with each of Nina's assessments of the model. Use questions such as the following to initiate the conversation. Be sure students can back up their answers with clear examples from the narrative.

- Does Art include enough historical details to accurately portray the setting? (Possible response: Yes, there are plenty of details to help the reader clearly envision the story but not so many that the story is lost in the description.)

Strategies for Writers Online
Go to **www.sfw.z-b.com** for additional online resources for students and teachers.

Using the Rubric to Study the Model

Historical Episode

Did you notice that the model on pages 55–57 points out some key elements of a historical episode? As he wrote "Wanted: A Boat to India," Art Foley used these elements to help him describe a historical event. He also used the 6-point rubric on pages 58–59 to plan, draft, revise, and edit the writing. A rubric is a great tool to evaluate writing during the writing process.

Now let's use the same rubric to score the model. To do this, we'll focus on each trait separately, starting with Ideas. We'll use the top descriptor for each trait (column 6), along with examples from the model, to help us understand how the traits work together. How would you score Art on each trait?

Ideas
- The writer's main idea is clear and focused.
- The details are relevant and striking.

I love how Art immediately introduces the historical event he is writing about, and in such a creative way—I can't help but want to continue reading. His details are vivid and authentic, providing me with a clear and accurate vision of the events he is describing.

[from the writing model]

Marco Polo was beginning to wonder if he was ever going to get to Cathay. His father and uncle had returned to Venice from that country in the Far East, laden with spices, gold, and other rich treasures.

English Language Learners

BEGINNING

Parts of a Story On the board, draw three stick people on one side and a house on the other. Read a simple and brief story to students. Make sure the story has characters and an obvious setting. After you finish reading, say the name of the character(s) (for example, Goldilocks) in the story you read. Ask, *Is Goldilocks a person or a place? Is the three bears' house a person or a place?* Introduce the terms *character* and *setting*. Write them on the board and have students repeat.

INTERMEDIATE

Parts of a Story Have a volunteer tell their favorite story, either from childhood or from a book they have recently read. Ask other students to listen carefully and identify the characters, setting, and basic plot of the story. Discuss as a class.

Organization

- The story is well organized, ending with a conclusion that follows naturally from the story events.
- A variety of transitions guide the reader through the story.

Art uses transitions like *Now* and *By this time* to help me understand time passing or a shift in scenes. The entire episode flows naturally and ends with a satisfying conclusion.

[from the writing model]

By this time, all the Polos, even Marco, had had enough. They just could not believe that small, flimsy boats like these, held together with wooden pegs and fish oil, could get them safely to their destination. They thanked their friend Omar for his help, nodded politely to the captain, and walked away.

Voice

- Third-person narration is used consistently in an original way.
- Realistic-sounding dialogue develops the characters.

Art uses third-person point of view (*he, his, they,* and *them*) throughout his writing. The dialogue Art uses is very realistic; he includes words and phrases used during Marco Polo's time. This helped me get a good feel for the characters who are speaking.

[from the writing model]

"Look at all the ships in this harbor," he insisted. "These captains and their crews cross back and forth to India every week. They will fall all over themselves trying to get your business."

Historical Episode 61

- What do you think of Art's conclusion? (Possible response: The conclusion neatly wraps up how the Polos handled the situation and left me feeling this particular story was complete.)

- What does Art's tone tell you about his purpose? (Possible response: Art uses an energetic and sometimes humorous voice, which tells me his main purpose was to entertain.)

ADVANCED

Historical Settings Draw a chart on the board with the last 10 decades as column heads; for example *1910s, 1920s,* and so on. Set the following row heads: *Airplanes, Cars, Telephones, Video Games, Personal Computers, Cell Phones.* Have students work with a partner to determine if the item in each row—cars, for example—was widely used in each decade. They should use print or online encyclopedias to find unknown information. Tell students they will need to use such resources when researching the historical time periods for their historical episodes.

ADVANCED HIGH

Historical Settings Have partners select a historical time period and research the food, clothing, social customs, and technology that were used at the time. Have the partners prepare a short presentation about the time period and deliver it to the class.

CCSS **Common Core State Standards**

SL.7.1.b: Follow rules for collegial discussions, track progress toward specific goals and deadlines, and define individual roles as needed. **SL.7.1.c:** Pose questions that elicit elaboration and respond to others' questions and comments with relevant observations and ideas that bring the discussion back on topic as needed.

Historical Episode T61

Analyze
the Model

Week 1 • Day 5

Student Objectives

- Read a model historical episode. (*pp. 55–57*)
- Use the historical episode rubric. (*pp. 58–59*)
- Use the model historical episode to study Word Choice, Sentence Fluency, and Conventions. (*pp. 62–63*)

Continue the Discussion Use questions such as the following to prompt the discussion:

- How does Art's choice of language affect your experience with the story? (Possible response: I could imagine myself in the scenes Art described)

- What makes the story enjoyable to read? (Possible responses: the variety of sentence types; the clear, interesting images; the catchy dialogue)

- How does the quality of editing affect the reader? (Possible response: If there were lots of mistakes, especially in punctuating the dialogue, the reader would feel confused and maybe stop reading.)

 Strategies for Writers Online
Go to **www.sfw.z-b.com** for additional online resources for students and teachers.

 **Word Choice**
- Precise words, such as powerful verbs, capture the action and convey the events clearly.

Art uses the most creative and precise verbs in his historical episode, which made reading his piece fun. Words like *gesturing* and *assailed* are strong and clear. From the description, the scene that played in my mind as I read was clear and animated.

[from the writing model]

Marco looked up at the boat owner, who was gesturing to him to climb aboard. As soon as he did, a foul odor assailed his nose. "Could you ask the captain what causes that terrible smell?" he called down to Omar.

Sentence Fluency
- An exceptional variety of sentences move the story along smoothly.
- The story is enjoyable to read.

Art uses questions to make the story more interesting and to help us know what is going on in Marco Polo's mind. The questions really made me wonder what was going to happen next!

[from the writing model]

Marco was getting a little tired of listening to this haggling. "These boats don't look so bad to me," he thought. "Isn't it important for us to try to move along?"

62 **Narrative Writing**

Technology Tip **for 21st Century Literacies**

A timeline is a traditional way of creating a visual representation of the order of specific events. Digital tools like Dipity or Capzles offer students a multimodal environment in which to compose a timeline. Challenge students to embed/post historical artifacts or primary sources, audio clips of speeches or other related texts, or other media in a timeline that supplements their writing in this unit. Because some of these tools are collaborative, this task can be expanded to include differing perspectives, participants, and points of view.

See **www.sfw.z-b.com** for further information about and links to these websites and tools.

Conventions

• The writer has used different sentence structures correctly to enhance meaning.

I can't find any spelling, punctuation, or capitalization errors in Art's story. He uses several different sentence structures, including quotations. Each type of sentence is used correctly. Take a look at this example of dialogue.

[from the writing model]

"Talk to that captain over there," Niccolò told Omar, "and ask if we can see his boat."

"An excellent choice," Omar praised him.

+Presentation

Illustrations are thoughtfully integrated with the writing.

My Turn!

I want to do as well as Art Foley did as I write my historical episode. I'm glad I can lean on the rubric as a guide. I can't wait to get started. Follow along and see how I do.

Historical Episode **63**

Differentiating Instruction

ENRICHMENT

Historical Details Have students make lists of the historical details included in "Wanted: A Boat to India." Make sure they can distinguish fact from fiction. Ask them what would happen if the historical details were inaccurate. How would that make them feel about the rest of the story?

REINFORCEMENT

Support Quotations Show students how to make quotation marks. Have them point to the quotation marks in the model. Help them distinguish between the opening quotation marks and the closing quotation marks. Remind them to be especially careful of the punctuation at the end of the quotation. A comma indicates that the sentence does not end with the quoted speech.

Presentation Explain to students that Presentation is just as important as any of the other traits. Explain that the way a piece of writing looks makes an impression on the reader: if the writing is neat and includes engaging details, such as illustrations or photographs, a reader feels pulled in and is excited to read the piece.

Explain that the illustrations should be chosen and placed in such a way that they work well with the text and deepen the reader's understanding of the historical event. Remind students not to use photographs or illustrations for which they do not have permission.

Think About the Traits Remind students that some traits play a more important role in specific types of writing. For example, some students may believe that **Ideas** are more important because without rich, accurate details from the specific time period, a historical episode will be weak and boring. Other students may feel that **Voice** is more important because how the writer tells the story greatly influences how the reader responds.

CCSS **Common Core State Standards**

SL.7.1.c: Pose questions that elicit elaboration and respond to others' questions and comments with relevant observations and ideas that bring the discussion back on topic as needed. **SL.7.1.d:** Acknowledge new information expressed by others and, when warranted, modify their own views.

Write
a Historical Episode

Week 2 • Day 1

Student Objectives

- Read and understand a prewriting strategy. *(pp. 64–65)*

Prewrite

Focus on Ideas

Gather Information Read pages 64–65 aloud. Emphasize that even writers of fiction have to do plenty of research to make their narratives plausible.

Remind students that not every website on the Internet is reliable. To ensure the information is reliable, they should only use trustworthy websites, such as online history magazines or university websites. Be sure to remind students to carefully record where they find their information so that they may properly cite their sources later.

✎ Writer's Term _____

Historical Period A specific time period can be defined by the events, language, attire, inventions, and/or fads that existed then.

✎ Writer's Term _____

Primary Source A primary source offers an inside view of a particular event.

Strategies for Writers Online

Go to **www.sfw.z-b.com** for additional online resources for students and teachers.

Prewrite   Focus on ⟨Ideas⟩

The Rubric Says   Rich, well-researched historical details add authenticity.

Writing Strategy   Gather historical information from several references, including primary sources.

I've thought a lot about what historical period I want to write about. We've been reading in our social studies class about the slave trade in Africa in the 1700s and 1800s. I decided I want to write a story set in that time. I'll use the strategy of getting information about the period from reference sources.

I'll start with an encyclopedia to get an overview. Then I'll go to the Internet. Maybe I'll be lucky to find a great primary source, such as a slave's actual story of being captured and transported across the ocean. (You can't always find a primary source, but I'll try hard to find one.) And I'll keep track of the sources I use.

✎ Writer's Term_____

Historical Period
A **historical period** is a time gone by. Colonial America, the Victorian age, and the 1980s are all historical periods.

✎ Writer's Term_____

Primary Source
A **primary source** is a person or book that provides a firsthand account of the information. For example, a primary source about a war would be the journal, diary, or letter of a person who experienced the war firsthand.

Here are two good ways to find primary sources:

- **Talk to an older person that you know.** The person may have firsthand experiences or letters from older friends or relatives to share.
- **Use the Internet.** Enter your topic idea in a good search engine used in your school. Be sure you use only reliable websites.

64   Narrative Writing

English Language Learners

BEGINNING/INTERMEDIATE

Third-Person Pronouns Review usage of the third-person pronouns *he, she, it, they, him, her,* and *their.* Give several simple examples, such as *They are basketball players* or *She passed the ball to him.* Write other examples on the board, but do not include the pronouns. Have Beginning ELLs fill in the appropriate pronouns, and ask Intermediate ELLs to check for mistakes. Tell students they will write their historical episodes from a third-person point of view.

ADVANCED/ADVANCED HIGH

Conflict and Resolution Ask a student to explain the terms *conflict* and *resolution.* It should be clear that the *conflict* in the story is the problem, and the *resolution* is the solution. Have partners help each other brainstorm possible plots for their historical episodes, including an interesting conflict and its resolution.

As I did my research, I took notes on anything that I thought could be used in a story. Here are a few of my notes from my primary source, the narrative by captured slave Olaudah Equiano.

Slave trade in Africa—1700s and 1800s/Olaudah's capture
- ✔ families lived in fenced compounds, more than one building
- ✔ meals—goat stew, plantains, yams
- ✔ made clothes, rugs, etc., on hand & foot loom
- ✔ when adults working in the fields, children often watching as lookouts from trees
- ✔ kidnapping pretty common
- ✔ Olaudah heard of prisoners shackled in dungeons
- ✔ kidnappers snuck over walls of family compound, kidnapped Olaudah and his sister
- ✔ covered their mouths, carried them off into the woods

Story ideas
- ✔ Africa during slave trade—1760
- ✔ African family living in compound—family life
- ✔ brother and sister at home
- ✔ kidnappers in an African village

Apply

Gather information from references and primary sources, and jot down some story ideas. Keep track of where you found your information.

Direct students to page 65. Explain that as Nina researched her chosen historical period, she took detailed notes about information she thought would be important when drafting her story.

Point out that while researching her time period, Nina still had not determined what the plot of her historical episode would be. At the bottom of her notes, she jotted down several story ideas she thought were interesting. Once her notes were complete, she could read them over and choose the story idea that she found most interesting.

CCSS **C**ommon **C**ore **S**tate **S**tandards

W.7.3.a: Engage and orient the reader by establishing a context and point of view and introducing a narrator and/or characters; organize an event sequence that unfolds naturally and logically. **W.7.8:** Gather relevant information from multiple print and digital sources, using search terms effectively; assess the credibility and accuracy of each source; and quote or paraphrase the data and conclusions of others while avoiding plagiarism and following a standard format for citation.

Write
a Historical Episode

Week 2 • Day 2

Student Objectives

- Make a Story Map to organize the parts of the story. *(pp. 66-67)*

Prewrite

Focus on  Organization

Organize Ideas Nina decided the best organizer to use for her historical episode was a Story Map. She understood that a Story Map would help her organize the important information, like character names and setting, as well as the major events of her plot. Nina could then use her completed Story Map as a guide when she went to write her draft. Remind students that the more organized they are prior to writing, the easier the writing will be.

✎ Writer's Term_____

Story Map A Story Map is designed to organize the important information to be used when crafting a story. Details like setting, characters' names, major events, and obstacles or problems that characters face are organized in the map. The Story Map guides the writer from the story's beginning to its end.

Online Writing Center

 Provides **interactive graphic organizers** as well as a variety of graphic organizers in PDF format.

Prewrite
Focus on **Organization**

The Rubric Says	The story is well organized, ending with a conclusion that follows naturally from the story events.
Writing Strategy	Make a Story Map.

When I finished my research, I had a lot of information! Before I can use it in a story, I have to think of a simple plot I can develop without getting confused with all the details. I think a good, exciting story might be about an African girl who manages to hide from some slave traders.

My strategy is to organize my ideas with a Story Map. Since there's no set order for filling in a Story Map, I can write in the plot/problem and the outcome first because I know what they are. Then I can look through my notes for information about the setting and fill that in. I need names for my major characters and also will write down who the minor characters will be.

Finally I will go back to my notes to get ideas for the major events of my episode. This is actually turning out to be a little easier than I expected.

✎ Writer's Term_____

Story Map
A **Story Map** organizes the setting, major and minor characters, plot and problem, major events, and outcome of the story.

Conferencing

PEER TO PEER Have partners exchange Story Maps. Tell students to focus on the Plot/Problem, Events, and Outcome. Have students give suggestions to fill any logical gaps they see in the way these are linked.

PEER GROUPS Have students work in groups of three or four. Students take turns giving verbal summaries of their Story Maps. Each student in the group is allowed to interrupt once to ask for clarification.

TEACHER-LED Hold conferences with individual students. Read through the Story Maps with students and prompt them with questions such as the following to help them evaluate their work: *Are all your events logically linked together? Have you explained clearly where and when the story takes place?*

STORY MAP

Setting

Where small village, not far from the coast in West Africa

When 1760

↓

Major **C**haracters Binta, a 12-year-old African girl; Diallo, her 10-year-old brother

Minor **C**haracters three slave traders; Binta and Diallo's mother

↓

Plot/**P**roblem

A girl and her brother have to get away from some slave traders.

↓

Event 1	Event 2	Event 3
Binta and Diallo are left alone as their parents go to work in the fields.	Traders come into their village and toward their family compound.	The girl and her brother look for a place to hide.

↓

Outcome

The girl and her brother avoid being captured.

Reflect

What do you think about Nina's Story Map? Did she cover all of the story elements?

Apply

Make a Story Map that organizes the parts of your historical episode.

Historical Episode 67

Writing a Conclusion Remind students that the Story Map will help them include all the elements of their stories. The plot and the events all lead toward the outcome, or conclusion, which should wrap up the story in a satisfying way.

CCSS **C**ommon **C**ore **S**tate **S**tandards

W.7.3.a: Engage and orient the reader by establishing a context and point of view and introducing a narrator and/or characters; organize an event sequence that unfolds naturally and logically. **W.7.3.e:** Provide a conclusion that follows from and reflects on the narrated experiences or events.

Historical Episode T67

Write
a Historical Episode

Week 2 • Day 3

Student Objectives

• Use a Story Map to begin writing. (p. 68)

Draft

Focus on Voice

Draft a Historical Episode Read page 68 aloud. Explain that this is the time for students to get their ideas down on paper without worrying too much about mistakes. Remind them that there will be plenty of time later in the writing process for fixing spelling, grammar, punctuation, and capitalization errors. Reinforce that they should use their Story Maps as guides throughout the drafting process. Note that when the time comes to begin editing, proofreader's marks are provided on page 69.

Have students find words (other than the highlighted ones) that show Nina wrote in the third person. Also discuss whether Nina's draft includes the elements she noted on her Story Map.

T68 Narrative Writing

Draft

Focus on **Voice**

The Rubric Says	Third-person narration is used consistently in an original way.
Writing Strategy	Maintain consistency in style and tone.

Writer's Term

Point of View
Point of view tells the reader who is telling the story. Writers use **first person** to tell about their own experiences and to show that they are part of the story. Writers use **third person** to tell about the experiences of others and to show that they are not part of the story.

As I write my draft, I need to think about who is telling the story. I know from the rubric that my story should be written in the third-person point of view. This means that I should write as if a narrator is telling the story. This is someone who is not part of the story and not one of the characters. So I need to make sure I don't use the word *I*. Instead, I'll use *he*, *she*, or *they* as I write about the characters. To help my reader follow along, it's also important to keep my style and tone consistent throughout my writing.

Right now I just need to get my ideas on paper. Later I can polish my writing when I check for correct spelling, punctuation, and grammar.

68 Narrative Writing

Differentiating Instruction

ENRICHMENT

Emphasize Dialogue Challenge students to use dialogue to advance the plot as they draft. Explain that sometimes dialogue can actually tell the reader what is happening in the story, and not just record characters' reactions to events. Have students find examples in books and stories they have read of dialogue that advances the plot. Challenge them to use dialogue in a similar way.

Proofreading Marks

⏋ Indent	ℓ Take out something
≡ Make a capital	⊙ Add a period
/ Make a small letter	⌗ New paragraph
∧ Add something	⑤℗ Spelling error

A Daring Escape

by Nina

[DRAFT]

[used third-person point of view]

Binta was a twelve-year-old girl. She lived in a small village in West Africa. She loved her parents and her brothers and sisters, and they had many happy times together. But Binta was always afraid.

There were many things that frighten Binta. When she had to light the fire to cook the family's food. She was afraid that she could not do household chores well enough. Most of all, she was afraid to be left alone when the older people left went out to work in the fields. In that year, 1760, everybody knew that there were slave traders around. They kidnaped healthy-looking young people and sold them. A man from the villige had travel down the river. He came back and told everyone about a traders' fort.

One morning, Binta's mother was going out to work in the field as usual. Watch your little brother carefully, she said, and make sure he stays inside our compond walls. Your father has heard that there are traders around."

All at once Binta got very afraid, but she tried hard not to show it. She promised that "she would take good care of her brother."

The morning went by and nothing happened. Every half hour or so, Binta had Diallo, her brother, climb the tall silk-cotton tree in their

Historical Episode **69**

REINFORCEMENT

Review Story Maps Go through the rubric with students. Have them locate every element on Nina's Story Map as you read together. After this exercise, give them the opportunity to go back and revise their Story Maps in small groups before they draft.

Write
a Historical Episode

Week 2 • Day 4

Student Objectives

• Complete a draft. (p. 69)

Finish Drafting Students need ample time to draft their historical episodes. As conferencing is important throughout the writing process, be sure to also plan time for peer-to-peer, peer group, or teacher-led conferences. Remind students that this is the time to get their ideas down in a creative and engaging way. Assure them that they will have plenty of time to fix any mistakes later.

Writer's Term_____

Point of View Point of view signals to the reader who the narrator is, or who is telling the story. Writers use first person (using the pronouns *I*, *me*, and *we*) to show that they are a character in the story. Second person (using the pronoun *you*) is used when the writer wants the reader to be involved with the writing. Second person rarely appears in narrative writing—it is typically used in argument or opinion writing. Writers use third person (using the pronouns *he*, *she*, and *they*) to tell about the experiences of others and to signal that they are not part of the story.

CCSS **Common Core State Standards**

W.7.3: Write narratives to develop real or imagined experiences or events using effective technique, relevant descriptive details, and well-structured event sequences. **W.7.3.b:** Use narrative techniques, such as dialogue, pacing, and description, to develop experiences, events, and/or characters.

Historical Episode **T69**

Focus on Point of View Discuss the use of point of view in the model. Ask:

• What is the point of view of the speakers in the dialogues? (first person)

Help students see that the story is narrated in the third-person point of view but the dialogue quotes are in first-person point of view for the speakers. Ask how first-person dialogue helps the reader engage with the story. (Possible response: It allows the reader to find out how the characters are feeling and what they are thinking in the characters' own words.)

[DRAFT]

yard to look for kidnappers, but except for the birds' screetches, the forest around the village was quiet. Binta was starting to relax in the afternoon when she sent Diallo up the tree one more time.

He had climb about ten feet when he came scrambling back down. He had a terrifyed look on his face. "Sister, there are two men and a woman sneaking up to the village"! he whispered. "What shall we do?"

Binta was as frightened as her brother. For a minute she stood paralyzed. Then she could hear the kidnappers' careless talk.

"It is my impression that there are not any adults in the vicenity," one muttered to the others. "Let us attempt to locate some children."

"That is an excellent plan," said the woman's voice. "We shall examine what is behind that nearby wall. Be silent as we approach."

Binta and Diallo could hear the rustle of dry branches as the kidnappers came closer to the walls around their family compound.

"If they climb over, they're going to get us," said Diallo.

"But if we try to go out through the gate, they'll see us anyway," Binta replied. It seemed as if. There was no escape.

Binta had an idea. She remembered the place behind her mother's quarters where they used to burrow under the fence. "If we can

70 Narrative Writing

Conferencing

PEER TO PEER Have pairs exchange drafts. Tell students to point out what they like best about their partner's draft and ask one *Who, What, Where, When, Why,* or *How* question about the events in the narrative.

PEER GROUPS Have students choose the section of their draft that they found most difficult to write and read it aloud to the group or mark it with brackets for their partners to read silently. Have students explain why they had trouble with that section; ask the other students to offer one suggestion for overcoming the difficulty.

TEACHER-LED Hold conferences with individual students. Offer suggestions for revising for point of view.

 Strategies for Writers Online
Go to **www.sfw.z-b.com** for additional online resources for students and teachers.

get through there now, maybe we can hide in the forest until the kidnappers go away."

The small opening was on the opposite side of the compound from where the kidnappers were approaching. So Binta and Diallo had time to make their escape. Diallo went under first, then helped his sister squeeze through. Their compound was close enough to the forest that it was easy to get there and hide.

From their spot behind some low, thick bushes, Binta and Diallo could hear the kidnappers messing up their family compound.

"I'm sure there were children here a minute ago," said the woman. "Where do you suppose they went?"

"Forget it," one of the men replied. "Let's try somewhere else."

Binta and Diallo stayed in the woods for a long time. Finally, when they heard their parents returning, they went back to the compound.

"Why were you outside?" Binta's mother said to her. "I told you to keep your brother safe from harm."

"That's just what I did, Mother," Binta replied. And as she thought about it, she knew she had reason to be proud. She had been afraid, but she did what she had to do anyway.

Reflect

Read Nina's draft. How well did she use third-person point of view?

Apply

Write a draft using third-person point of view. Double-check to see that you are using it correctly.

Historical Episode 71

CCSS Common Core State Standards

W.7.3: Write narratives to develop real or imagined experiences or events using effective technique, relevant descriptive details, and well-structured event sequences. **W.7.10:** Write routinely over extended time frames (time for research, reflection, and revision) and shorter time frames (a single sitting or a day or two) for a range of discipline-specific tasks, purposes, and audiences.

Write
a Historical Episode

Week 2 • Day 5

Student Objectives

- Revise to include historical details. (p. 72)

Revise

Focus on Ideas

Add Details Write the word *authentic* on the board. Explain that something that is authentic is something that is real. Explain that although students are writing fiction, historical episodes need to contain rich and accurate historical details to sound and feel authentic.

Direct students to page 72. Read the text aloud. Ask students how Nina's revisions affected her story. Encourage students to look for places in their writing where they could revise to add vivid, authentic historical details.

✎ Writer's Term _____

Historical Detail Historical details are used to define and clarify setting, characters' dialogue, period dress, and other details that relate to an era. For example, horse-drawn carriages, cobblestone streets, leatherwork aprons, and pewter drinking mugs are all historical details related to Colonial New England.

▶ Strategies for Writers Online

Go to **www.sfw.z-b.com** for additional online resources for students and teachers.

Revise

Focus on **Ideas**

The Rubric Says   Rich, well-researched historical details add authenticity. The writing is clear, focused, and well-paced.

Writing Strategy   Add historical details to make the story authentic.

Well, I let my writing partner, Brandon, read my finished draft. He really liked the faster pace of my story, which enhances the excitement and drama of the episode. But he thought my story would be more authentic if I used more historical details at the beginning. I went back to my notes, found a little more information, and added it to my paper.

✎ Writer's Term _____

Historical Detail
A **historical detail** is a fact that is correct in its relationship to a certain time or place in history.

[DRAFT]

[historical details]

There were many things that frighten Binta. When she had to light dinner of goat stew, plantains, and yams the fire to cook the family's food. She was afraid that she could not her cloth weaving on the hand-and-foot loom was not done do household chores well enough.

English Language Learners

BEGINNING/INTERMEDIATE

Word Choice Write the following words on the board or on index cards: *travel, yell, reply, head out, whisper, leave, vacation, scream*. Then have students work in pairs to sort the words into "go" words and "talk" words. Encourage them to try to use more interesting words in their writing.

ADVANCED/ADVANCED HIGH

Using Different Kinds of Sentences Write the following sentences on the board: *When Christopher saw land, he was very excited. How excited Christopher must have been to see land!* Ask students which sentence sounds more dramatic. Write other plain sentences on the board, and have students suggest ways to make them more dramatic by using questions, exclamations, or commands.

Revise

Focus on Word Choice

The Rubric Says	Precise words, such as powerful verbs, capture the action and convey the events clearly.
Writing Strategy	Replace weak verbs with strong ones.

The rubric reminds me to use precise and powerful verbs to show action. I went back and reread my writing to see if I could find any verbs that needed strengthening. I want my readers to "see" my story unfold in their minds as if they were watching a movie. The more specific the verb, the more powerful the connection will be between the reader and my story.

I guess *messing up* is not a very strong or accurate description of what is truly happening in the scene below. I will revise that sentence now. What do you think of my new verb?

[DRAFT]

[used powerful verb]

From their spot behind some low, thick bushes, Binta and Diallo
could hear the kidnappers ~~messing up~~ ransacking their family compound.

Reflect

What do you think of Nina's revision? Can you "see" this scene better now?

Apply

Use precise words, including powerful verbs, to clearly describe your episode for your reader.

Historical Episode **73**

Conferencing

PEER TO PEER Have pairs of students exchange drafts. Have students circle one verb in their partner's draft that they think their partner could replace with a more precise one.

PEER GROUPS Have students work in groups of four and pass their drafts around the group. Have students circle two words in each draft that could be replaced with words that are more precise. Students should then work together to think of replacement words.

TEACHER-LED Hold conferences with pairs of students. Have students read each other's drafts and pick out the verbs they think are strongest. Tell students to circle one or two verbs in their partner's draft that could be more precise. Help students discuss possible replacements for these verbs.

Student Objectives

• Revise to replace weak verbs with strong ones. *(p. 73)*

Revise

Focus on Word Choice

Use Precise Language Read page 73 out loud. Explain that using just the right verb can also strengthen the tone of the writing. For example, the word *holler* implies someone is speaking with a raised voice. Children holler in the playground, parents kindly holler to other family members to come to dinner, and so on. On the other hand, *scream* implies something very different; when used it greatly affects the tone.

Ask a volunteer to read Nina's draft excerpt both before and after the revision was made. Ask students how her revision affected her writing, and how it affects the way they envision the events of the story.

CCSS **Common Core State Standards**

W.7.3.a: Engage and orient the reader by establishing a context and point of view and introducing a narrator and/or characters; organize an event sequence that unfolds naturally and logically. **W.7.3.d:** Use precise words and phrases, relevant descriptive details, and sensory language to capture the action and convey experiences and events. **L.7.3.a:** Choose language that expresses ideas precisely and concisely, recognizing and eliminating wordiness and redundancy.

Historical Episode **T73**

Write a Historical Episode

Week 3 • Day 2

Student Objectives

- Revise to use different kinds of sentences. (*p. 74*)

Revise

Focus on  Sentence Fluency

Use a Variety of Sentences Ask students the following questions:

- How would you feel when listening to a teacher just talk and talk without stopping? (Possible responses: bored, ignored)

- What could a teacher do to energize the lesson and engage the students more? (Possible response: Stop every so often to ask a question.)

- What if the teacher stopped periodically and asked questions related to the lecture? (Possible response: Students might be more interested.)

Explain to students that writers can energize their writing and engage their readers in the same way. Questions add drama and invite the reader to think about something. Have one volunteer read Nina's excerpt on page 74 prior to her revisions. Then have another volunteer read the same passage with the revisions in place. Ask the class how Nina's changes affected how they felt about the writing.

Online Writing Center

Provides **interactive proofreading activities** for each genre.

Revise

Focus on Sentence Fluency

The Rubric Says An exceptional variety of sentences move the story along smoothly. The story is enjoyable to read.

Writing Strategy Use different kinds of sentences.

I'm going to look at my sentences. I know using a variety of sentences helps my writing flow smoothly and makes reading more enjoyable for my reader. I will use a question here to mix things up a bit.

[DRAFT]

Binta had an idea. ~~She remembered the place behind her mother's quarters where they used to burrow under the fence.~~ "If we can get through there now, maybe we can hide in the forest until the kidnappers go away."

[added question] "Remember that place behind Mother's quarters where we used to burrow under the fence?

Apply

Do you have any questions in your historical episode? Try putting in a few to add to the drama.

Optional Revising Lessons

Narrative 5

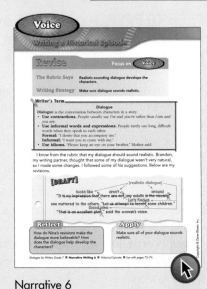

Narrative 6

Go to **Strategies for Writers Grade 7 CD-ROM**

| The Rubric Says | The writer has used different sentence structures correctly to enhance meaning. |
| Writing Strategy | Check to see that punctuation is correct. |

Writer's Term

Quotation

A **quotation** restates the exact words of a speaker or writer. A quotation is placed within quotation marks and is credited to the speaker or writer.

It's time to look for errors in my episode. I've used all kinds of sentence structures to enhance my story, including quotations. But I sometimes forget a comma or a quotation mark, so I need to check for those. Here's a quotation that's missing some punctuation. I'll go and fix it now.

[DRAFT]

One morning, Binta's mother was going out to work in the field as usual. [added quotation marks] "Watch your little brother carefully," she said, "and make sure he compound stays inside our ~~compond~~ walls. Your father has heard that there are traders around."

Reflect

What do you think of the edits? Could you find any punctuation mistakes that Nina did not catch and fix? How do Nina's edits help you better enjoy her historical episode?

Apply   **Conventions**

Edit your draft for spelling, grammar, and punctuation errors. Pay extra attention to quotations.

For more practice with punctuation, use the exercises on the next two pages.

Historical Episode 75

Related Grammar Practice

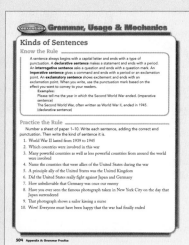

Student Edition page 504

Student Edition page 531

Go to ➡ **Appendix A: Grammar Practice**

Write
a Historical Episode

Week 3 • Day 3

Student Objectives
• Edit for correct punctuation. (p. 75)

Edit

Focus on **Conventions**

Edit for Accuracy Explain to students that now is the time to go back and correct any mistakes in spelling, grammar, punctuation, and capitalization. Suggest that students read their work out loud to themselves, as it is sometimes easier to find errors in this way.

Remind students that computers have a spell-check option that can be very helpful; however, this function will not catch commonly misused words, such as *choose* and *chose*.

Use the mini-lessons on pages T76 and T77 to give students extra practice properly punctuating quotations and using hyphens and parentheses. Then have the class complete pages 76 and 77.

Writer's Term

Quotation Proper punctuation is important. The words being spoken are placed within quotation marks. Other punctuation is placed inside the quotation marks.

CCSS **Common Core State Standards**

W.7.4: Produce clear and coherent writing in which the development, organization, and style are appropriate to task, purpose, and audience. **L.7.1:** Demonstrate command of the conventions of standard English grammar and usage when writing or speaking.

Mini-Lesson

Student Objectives

- Learn to recognize and punctuate quotations. *(p. 76)*

Punctuation of Quotations

Explain to students that every quotation or written dialogue must contain quotation marks and usually an end punctuation of some sort (comma, period, exclamation point, or question mark).

Write the following sentence on the board: *Sarah said I have never seen such rain before.*

Ask students where quotation marks should be placed. (before *I* and after the period) Ask where a comma should be placed. (after *said*)

Create and use several more examples like this, including divided quotes.

Write the following text on the board: *"Oh!" "I miss Mom so much!"*

Ask students if this quotation is punctuated correctly. (no) How would they fix it? (Remove the quotations after *Oh!* and before *I.*) Ask volunteers to come to the board and rewrite the sentence to make it correct. (Possible response: *"Oh!" cried James. "I miss Mom so much!"*)

Online Writing Center

Provides **interactive grammar games** and **practice activities** in student eBook.

T76 Narrative Writing

Punctuation of Quotations

Know the Rule

A **direct quotation** is the exact words of a speaker. It is enclosed in quotation marks. A comma separates the speaker's words from the rest of the sentence.
> **Example:** "I really liked your book," Marion said.

An **indirect quotation** is a retelling of the speaker's words.
> **Example:** Marion said that she enjoyed my book.

Here are some rules for using quotation marks:
- Begin and end a direct quotation with quotation marks.
- If a direct quotation is a sentence, begin it with a capital letter. If it is part of a sentence, do not use a capital letter.
- Place a comma, period, question mark, or exclamation mark that ends a quote inside the quotation marks.
- If a quotation is divided, enclose both parts within quotation marks.
- Do not use quotation marks around an indirect quotation. In an indirect quotation, the speaker's words are often preceded by the word *that*.

Practice the Rule

Find the quotation error in each sentence below. Then write the corrected sentences on a separate sheet of paper.

1. "I really like reading historical fiction, don't you"? Antonio asked his friend Laura.
2. "Yes," said Laura. Some of the stories we read in literature class were really good."
3. "I liked *Number the Stars*, by Lois Lowry, a lot," she said.
4. Isn't that the story about the family that protects their friends from the Nazis during World War II?" Mai Li asked.
5. Laura answered, "Yes, and it certainly made that period of history come alive for me."
6. Antonio responded that he enjoyed reading tales about King Arthur and his knights.
7. Mai Li said, "I'm not sure if those count as historical fiction or fantasy."
8. Laura said that she enjoyed reading fantasy as much as she enjoyed historical fiction.

Related Grammar Practice

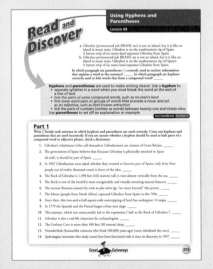

Page 203

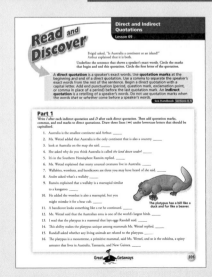

Page 205

Go to ➡ G.U.M. Student Practice Book

Hyphens and Parentheses

Know the Rule

Hyphens and parentheses are used to make writing more clear. Use a hyphen to
- separate syllables in a word when you must break the word at the end of a line of text.
- link the parts of some compound words, such as *twelve-year-old*.
- link some word pairs or groups of words that precede a noun and act as an adjective, such as *well-known actor*.
- link the parts of numbers (written as words) between twenty-one and ninety-nine.

Use parentheses to set off an explanation or example, especially when the information is not essential to the sentence (nonrestrictive).

Example: Sushi (raw fish served in a roll of rice) must be prepared with care.

Practice the Rule

Copy the following sentences on a separate piece of paper. Then add hyphens and parentheses as needed to make each sentence correct. **Possible answers given.**

1. Today is Nana's (my grandmother's) birthday, and we are heading to her favorite restaurant, The Piper's Den.

2. This family-owned business has been located on High Street for over thirty-five years.

3. Nana always orders eggplant parmesan (an Italian dish of eggplant, sauce, and cheese).

4. Some of the world's most delicious food comes from Italy—a country in the Medi-terranean section of Europe.

5. The chef at The Piper's Den has known Nana since he was twenty-one.

6. Nana used to be the editor-in-chief of a famous cooking magazine.

7. The chef brought out cannoli and tiramisu (well known Italian desserts) as a birthday treat for Nana.

8. This was truly the best way to celebrate Nana's eighty-sixth birthday!

Historical Episode 77

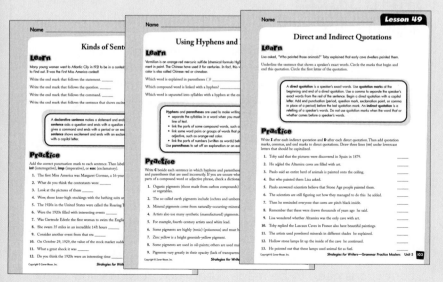

Pages 19, 101, 103

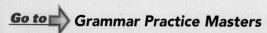

Go to ➡ **Grammar Practice Masters**

Mini-Lesson

Student Objectives
- Practice using hyphens and parentheses. *(p. 77)*

Hyphens and Parentheses

Explain to students that hyphens are visual cues that words are being linked together to function as one idea, and these linked words have a slightly different definition than when the words appear alone. In the case of breaking a word between two lines, explain that without the hyphen, the broken text would be extremely confusing and greatly diminish the quality of the writing.

Parentheses are used to set apart an explanation or an example, particularly when the information is not an essential part of the sentence. In a narrative, parentheses are sometimes used in a humorous way by the narrator to provide certain information on the side. Often times, the information revealed within the parentheses offers some insight into the personality of the narrator, as well. For example: *Frederick apologized for arriving late for afternoon tea (as if he was ever on time for anything), and I graciously assured him that it was no bother at all.*

CCSS Common Core State Standards

L.7.2: Demonstrate command of the conventions of standard English capitalization, punctuation, and spelling when writing.

Write
a Historical Episode

Week 3 • Day 4

Student Objectives

- Discuss preparation for publishing and presentation. (*p. 78*)
- Use a final editing checklist to publish their work. (*p. 78*)

Publish ⁺Presentation

Publishing Strategy Read pages 78–81 with the class. Review Nina's final checklist and direct students to create and use a final checklist of their own when writing their final copies.

Remind students to reflect upon both their purpose for writing and their audience, as a good writer keeps both in mind when deciding how to publish. If you have not already determined your publishing strategy, discuss as a class how students will publish their work. For example, they could compile the stories into one class book with the historical episodes arranged in chronological order. Or perhaps students are excited to display their work in the hallway display case, as Nina did, to showcase their illustrations. Remind students of how hard they have worked on their stories and that publishing is their chance to show off their work.

 Strategies for Writers Online
Go to **www.sfw.z-b.com** for additional online resources for students and teachers.

Publish ⁺Presentation

Publishing Strategy	Include the historical episode in the hallway display case.
Presentation Strategy	Add illustrations that support and enhance the story.

Now it's time to publish my historical episode. I'm so proud of this piece. My teacher wants students to hang their finished work in the class's hallway display, so it needs to be neatly written or typed. I think if I add a few illustrations to enhance my story—just like in a book—that would be perfect. I'll be sure my illustrations do not conflict with the story's details. First I want to read it through one last time and make sure it includes all the items on my final checklist.

My Final Checklist

Did I—

✔ correctly use all punctuation, including quotation marks, hyphens, and parentheses?

✔ correct all my spelling and grammar errors?

✔ add neatly drawn illustrations to support and enhance my story?

✔ neatly handwrite or type my historical episode for presentation?

Apply

Make a final checklist to check your historical episode. Then make a final draft to publish.

78 Narrative Writing

Differentiating Instruction

ENRICHMENT

Submit for Publication Allow students to use the Internet to research both online and printed magazines that publish students' short stories. Encourage them to mail a copy of their finished work to the magazine for possible publication. If their primary source was a person they know, encourage them to make a copy of their story to give to that individual to enjoy.

REINFORCEMENT

Review the Checklist Write Nina's final checklist out on the board. Then direct students back to Nina's draft on pages 69–71. Using the checklist on the board, go through the draft, stopping every few lines and asking students what corrections need to be made. Then look at Nina's final copy to see how she made the corrections.

A Daring Escape

by Nina Juarez

Binta was a twelve-year-old girl. She lived in a small village in West Africa. She loved her parents and her brothers and sisters, and they had many happy times together. But Binta was always afraid.

There were many things that frightened Binta. She was afraid when she had to light the fire to cook the family's dinner of goat stew, plantains, and yams. She was afraid that her cloth weaving on the hand-and-foot loom was not done well enough. Most of all, she was afraid to be left alone when the older people went out to work in the fields. In that year, 1760, everybody knew that there were slave traders around. They kidnapped healthy-looking young people and sold them. A man from the village had traveled down the river. He came back and told everyone about a traders' fort where prisoners were shackled together and led, crying for mercy, into a dark underground dungeon.

One morning, Binta's mother was going out to work in the field as usual. "Watch your little brother carefully," she said, "and make sure he stays inside our compound walls. Your father has heard that there are traders around."

All at once Binta got very afraid, but she tried hard not to show it. She promised her mother that she would take good care of her brother.

The morning went by, and nothing happened. Every half hour or so, Binta had Diallo, her brother, climb the tall silk-cotton tree in their yard to look for kidnappers, but except for the birds' screeches,

Technology Tip for 21st Century Literacies

Student writers are hungry for feedback from peers, teachers, and other writers. Provide an opportunity for students to compose in a different mode by offering audio feedback to students' work. You could do this by using the comment feature in VoiceThread, recording audio and movement using a screencast tool like Jing, or using an audio editor like Audacity or GarageBand. Encourage students to return to the recording as they work on subsequent texts, as it is meant to be a tool and an artifact.

See **www.sfw.z-b.com** for further information about and links to these websites and tools.

Write
a Historical Episode

Week 3 • Day 5

Student Objectives

- Use a historical episode rubric. (pp. 58–59)
- Share a published historical episode. (pp. 79–81)

Presentation Strategy Explain to students how important neatness is when creating a final copy of their work. Messy or illegible work will turn readers away, while a neat and interesting format draws readers in. Remind students of the many word processing features computers have to offer. It's easy to set neat margins, use the tab key to indent paragraphs, double-space text, and select one or two neat fonts. Also remind students to use the header or footer function to label each page with the title, their name, and the page number.

Point out that adding a few thoughtfully placed illustrations can greatly enhance their historical episodes, especially if the illustrations feature something specific to the time period. Students should carefully consider what parts of their story they'd like to illustrate, and then add the drawings near the appropriate text.

CCSS Common Core State Standards
W.7.4: Produce clear and coherent writing in which the development, organization, and style are appropriate to task, purpose, and audience. **SL.7.5:** Include multimedia components and visual displays in presentations to clarify claims and findings and emphasize salient points.

Reflecting on a Historical Episode

Instruct students to refer to the rubric on pages 58–59 as they reread Nina's final copy on pages 79–81. As they read, remind them to note and reflect upon all of Nina's revisions and edits. When they are done reading, ask students to explain how the changes to the writing affected the overall quality of Nina's historical episode. Did the revisions and edits strengthen or weaken her narrative? Were any of her revisions unnecessary? What score would they give Nina for each writing trait? Take a poll to see how close the scores are. Be sure students can support their scores with examples from Nina's writing.

Have students think back on this assignment as a whole. You might ask:

- What part of this assignment did you most enjoy?

- How easy was it to find primary sources?

- Compare writing a historical episode to the last writing assignment you completed. How was writing a historical episode similar or different?

- What is one thing you will do differently the next time you write a historical episode?

Strategies for Writers Online

Go to **www.sfw.z-b.com** for additional online resources for students and teachers.

the forest around the village was quiet. Binta was starting to relax in the afternoon when she sent Diallo up the tree one more time.

He had climbed only about ten feet when he came scrambling back down. He had a terrified look on his face. "Sister, there are two men and a woman sneaking up to the village!" he whispered. "What shall we do?"

Binta was as frightened as her brother. For a minute she stood paralyzed. Then she could hear the kidnappers' careless talk.

"It looks like there aren't any adults around," one muttered to the others. "Let's find us some children."

"Good idea," said the woman's voice. "Let's see what's behind that wall over there. Be quiet now."

Binta and Diallo could hear the rustle of dry branches as the kidnappers came closer to the walls around their family compound.

"If they climb over, they're going to get us," said Diallo.

"But if we try to go out through the gate, they'll see us anyway," Binta replied. It seemed as if there was no escape.

Suddenly, Binta had an idea. "Remember that place behind Mother's quarters where we used to burrow under the fence? If we can get through there now, maybe we can hide in the forest until the kidnappers go away."

The small opening was on the opposite side of the compound from where the kidnappers were approaching. So Binta and Diallo had time to make their escape. Diallo went under first. Then he helped his sister squeeze through. Their compound was close enough to the forest that it was easy to get there and hide.

From their spot behind some low, thick bushes, Binta and Diallo could hear the kidnappers ransacking their family compound.

"I'm sure there were children here a minute ago," said the woman. "Where do you suppose they went?"

"Forget it," one of the men replied. "Let's try somewhere else."

Binta and Diallo stayed in the woods for a long time. Finally, when they heard their parents returning, they went back to the compound.

"Why were you outside?" Binta's mother said to her. "I told you to keep your brother safe from harm."

"That's just what I did, Mother," Binta replied. And as she thought about it, she knew she had reason to be proud. She had been afraid, but she did what she had to do anyway.

Reflect

How did Nina do? Did she use all the traits of a good historical episode in her writing? Check it against the rubric. Don't forget to use the rubric to check your own historical episode.

Allow ample time for students to share their thoughts and opinions. If the class is very large, you may want to write these questions on the board and organize students into smaller discussion groups.

CCSS **C**ommon **C**ore **S**tate **S**tandards

W.7.6: Use technology, including the Internet, to produce and publish writing and link to and cite sources as well as to interact and collaborate with others, including linking to and citing sources.

Play Planner

WEEK 1

Day 1
Introduce
a Play

Student Objectives
- Review the elements of a play.
- Consider purpose and audience.
- Learn the traits of narrative writing.

Student Activities
- Read and discuss **What's in a Play?** (p. 82)
- Read and discuss **Why Write a Play?** (p. 83)
- Read **Linking Narrative Writing Traits to a Play.** (p. 84)

Day 2
Analyze
Read a Play

Student Objectives
- Read a model play.

Student Activities
- Read **"The Birth of Oxygen."** (pp. 85–87)

Day 3
Analyze
Introduce the Rubric

Student Objectives
- Learn to read a rubric.

Student Activities
- Review **"The Birth of Oxygen."** (pp. 85–87)
- Read and discuss the **Play Rubric.** (pp. 88–89)

WEEK 2

Day 1
Write
Prewrite: Ideas

Student Objectives
- Read and understand a prewriting strategy.

Student Activities
- Read and discuss **Prewrite: Focus on Ideas.** (p. 94)
- Apply the prewriting strategy.

Day 2
Write
Prewrite: Organization

Student Objectives
- Make a Story Map to organize events.

Student Activities
- Read and discuss **Prewrite: Focus on Organization.** (p. 95)
- Reflect on the model Story Map.
- Apply the prewriting strategy to create a Story Map.
- Participate in a peer conference.

Day 3
Write
Draft: Word Choice

Student Objectives
- Use a Story Map to begin writing with a focus on using specific nouns and powerful verbs.

Student Activities
- Read and discuss **Draft: Focus on Word Choice.** (p. 96)
- Reflect on the model draft. (p. 97)
- Apply the drafting strategy by using a Story Map to write a draft.

WEEK 3

Day 1
Write
Revise: Organization

Student Objectives
- Revise to follow the Story Map and enhance the play's events.

Student Activities
- Read and discuss **Revise: Focus on Organization.** (p. 99)
- Reflect on the model draft.
- Apply the revising strategy.
- Participate in a peer conference.

Day 2
Write
Revise: Sentence Fluency

Student Objectives
- Revise to vary sentence patterns to enhance meaning and style.

Student Activities
- Read and discuss **Revise: Focus on Sentence Fluency.** (p. 100)
- Reflect on a model draft.
- Apply the revising strategy.

Note: Optional Revising Lessons appear on the *Strategies for Writers* CD-ROM.

Day 3
Write
Edit: Conventions

Student Objectives
- Edit for accurate use of conjunctions to join shorter sentences.

Student Activities
- Read and discuss **Edit: Focus on Conventions.** (p. 101).
- Reflect on a model draft.
- Apply the editing strategy.

Note: Teach the Conventions mini-lessons (pp. 102–103) if needed.

Day 4	Day 5
Analyze Ideas, Organization, and Voice	**Analyze** Word Choice, Sentence Fluency, and Conventions

Student Objectives
- Read a model play.
- Use the play rubric.
- Use the model play to study Ideas, Organization, and Voice.

Student Activities
- Review **"The Birth of Oxygen."** (pp. 85–87)
- Read and discuss **Using the Rubric to Study the Model.** (pp. 90–93)

Student Objectives
- Read a model play.
- Use the play rubric.
- Use the model play to study Word Choice, Sentence Fluency, and Conventions.

Student Activities
- Review **"The Birth of Oxygen."** (pp. 85–87)
- Read and discuss **Using the Rubric to Study the Model.** (pp. 90–93)

Day 4	Day 5
Write Draft	**Write** Revise: Ideas

Student Objectives
- Complete a draft.

Student Activities
- Finish the draft. (p. 97)
- Participate in a peer conference.

Student Objectives
- Revise to add dialogue and stage directions.

Student Activities
- Read and discuss **Revise: Focus on Ideas.** (p. 98)
- Reflect on a model draft.
- Apply the revising strategy.

Day 4	Day 5
Write Publish: +Presentation	**Write** Publish: +Presentation

Student Objectives
- Discuss preparation for publishing and presentation.
- Use a final editing checklist to publish their work.

Student Activities
- Read and discuss **Publish: +Presentation.** (p. 104)
- Apply the publishing strategy.

Student Objectives
- Use a play rubric.
- Share a published play.

Student Activities
- Share their work.
- Use the rubric to reflect upon and evaluate the model and their own writing. (pp. 88–89, 105–109)

To complete the chapter in fewer days, combine the learning objectives and activities in a way that supports students as they write.

Resources at-a-Glance

Grammar, Usage & Mechanics
Simple and Compound
   Sentences T102
Complex Sentences T103
Grammar Practice T101–T103

Differentiating Instruction
Using the Rubric T93
Draft T96
Publish T104
For additional Differentiating Instruction activities, see Strategies for Writers *Extensions Online at* **www.sfw.z-b.com.**

English Language Learners
Using the Rubric T90–T91
Prewrite T94
Revise T98

Conferencing
Peer to Peer T95, T97, T99
Peer Groups T95, T97, T99
Teacher-Led T95, T97, T99

Technology Tip
Using the Rubric T92
Publish T105

 Connection Letter
Reproducible letter (in English and Spanish) appears on the *Strategies for Writers* CD-ROM and at **www.sfw.z-b.com.**

Online Writing Center

Provides IWB resources, interactive games and practice activities, videos, eBooks, and a virtual file cabinet.

 Strategies for Writers Online

Go to **www.sfw.z-b.com** for free online resources for students and teachers.

Introduce
a Play

Student Objectives

- Review the elements of a play. *(p. 82)*
- Consider purpose and audience. *(p. 83)*
- Learn the traits of narrative writing. *(p. 84)*

What's a Play?

Ask the class if anyone has been to see a play. Has anyone performed in a play? What features or details about the experience do they remember the most? How was watching a play different than watching a movie?

Explain that a play is a type of narrative that is performed by actors and actresses on a stage. Many writers choose to write plays as the most effective way to get their message across to the audience.

What's in a Play?

Reflect as a class on the experiences students have had with plays. Ask them to define:

- Plot
- Conflict
- Characters
- Scene
- Stage Directions

Confirm students' understanding of these elements by reading aloud the definitions on page 82.

 Strategies for Writers Online
Go to **www.sfw.z-b.com** for additional online resources for students and teachers.

What's a Play?

It's a story—typically acted out on a stage by actors—told almost entirely through dialogue. I think writing a play and seeing it performed will be exciting!

What's in a Play?

Plot
The plot is made up of all the events arranged by the author to develop the story line or idea. Important parts of the plot are the introduction, rising action, climax, falling action, and resolution.

Conflict
This is the challenge or problem that the main character must somehow overcome. The conflict is the force that drives the plot toward the resolution.

Characters
As there is limited time to develop characters, plays usually focus on a small number of characters. The plot revolves around the main character, or *protagonist*. The character or force that opposes the protagonist is called the *antagonist*.

Scene
Scenes show time and location. Different backgrounds or props can be used to show a change of scene. This helps the audience follow the plot.

Stage Directions
These are written instructions, set apart from the dialogue in parentheses, for each character to follow. Stage directions may tell actors where to walk or how to say their lines.

Narrative Text Exemplars (Play)

Davis, Ossie. *Escape to Freedom: A Play About the Young Frederick Douglass.* Penguin Group: 1990.
Escape to Freedom is the story of Frederick Douglass. Frederick Douglass was a slave who escaped to freedom in the North. This play describes his contributions as writer, orator, and diplomat.

Fletcher, Louise. *Sorry, Wrong Number.* Dramatists Play Service, 1998. CCSS When Leona tries to call her husband at the office, she overhears two men planning a crime. Events take a turn for the worse when Leona learns that she is the target of the crime!

Why write a Play?

There are plenty of reasons to write a play. Below, I've explained some of the most common. I'm sure one will inspire me as I get ready to write my own play.

Personal Enjoyment
There is something magical about creating characters and "watching" how they behave in a story. With a play, you get to literally watch your characters come to life. They speak the lines you've given them, and they move as you've instructed. This is going to be fun!

Entertainment
I love telling stories through writing. But writing a play has an extra benefit—I can watch others act out my story. I get to share a story, message, or information in a different and interesting way. I might even want to play one of the characters!

Share Information
Writing a play is a creative way to share a message or information with an audience. Sure, writing essays or short stories is effective, but using live actors and a stage can get information out there in a powerful and engaging way.

Gibson, William. *The Miracle Worker: A Play.* **Scribner, 2007.** Deaf, blind, and mute twelve-year-old Helen Keller fought against anyone who tried to teach her. When Annie Sullivan arrives to help her, she begins a monumental struggle to help Helen discover the world around her.

Goodrich, Frances, and Albert Hackett. *The Diary of Anne Frank: A Play.* **Dramatists Play Service, 1998.**
CCSS This play is about Anne Frank, a Jewish teenager who hid from the Nazis in an Amsterdam warehouse with her family and friends. In this moving story the audience learns about Anne's dreams, passions, and fears.

Why write a Play?

Explain that good writers always understand their purpose for writing and the audience who will be reading or watching their work. Both the purpose and audience influence not only how the writer crafts his or her writing, but also the form in which the writer presents the work. A writer who wants their story to be performed live in front of an audience deliberately chooses to write a play. There are many possible reasons why a writer wants to share a story, and a writer's purpose will be reflected in how the play is written.

Read page 83 aloud. Discuss with students the different reasons given for writing a play. Can they think of any other reasons? Is it possible for a writer to want to write a play for all three reasons at the same time? Invite students to begin thinking about why they will be writing a play. Remind them that their reasons for writing will inevitably shape different elements of the play, such as plot, tone, and even the props used by characters.

CCSS Common Core State Standards
SL.7.1: Engage effectively in a range of collaborative discussions (one-on-one, in groups, and teacher-led) with diverse partners on *grade 7 topics, texts, and issues,* building on each others' ideas and expressing their own clearly.

Introduce
a Play

Linking Narrative Writing Traits to a Play

Read page 84 aloud to help students understand that they will follow Nina as she models how to use the narrative traits throughout the writing process. A good play will focus on one event, provide descriptive details through dialogue and stage directions, relate events in a chronological order, bring the action to an exciting climax, and wrap the plot up with a satisfying resolution.

Linking Narrative Writing Traits to a Play

In this chapter, you will write a story to be performed. This type of narrative writing is called a play. Nina will guide you through the stages of the writing process: Prewrite, Draft, Revise, Edit, and Publish. In each stage, Nina will show you important writing strategies that are linked to the Narrative Writing Traits below.

Narrative Writing Traits

	• a single, focused topic with relevant, engaging details that develop the experiences or events • a narrator or characters that bring the story to life
	• well-structured and logical event sequences, often in chronological order, that guide the reader through the story • an engaging beginning and a satisfying conclusion that reflects on the story's events • a variety of transition words that signal time or setting changes
	• a voice that is appropriate for the audience and purpose • dialogue that, if used, is realistic and helps develop the characters and story
	• precise, descriptive words and phrases
	• a variety of sentences that flow and are a pleasure to read aloud
	• no or few errors in grammar, usage, mechanics, and spelling

Before you write, read Aleem Martel's play on the next three pages. Then use the play rubric on pages 88–89 to decide how well he did. You might want to look back at What's in a Play? on page 82, too!

Narrative Writing Traits in a Play _____

 **Ideas** Memorable characters, interesting and thoughtful stage directions, and revealing dialogue bring the story to life for the audience.

 **Organization** It is most effective to relate the events of a play in chronological order. The audience can then easily follow the story's events and better connect with the play as a whole experience.

 **Voice** The voice of a play is revealed in the subject, the dialogue written for the characters, and even in the stage directions.

THE BIRTH OF OXYGEN

by Aleem Martel

characters

CHARACTERS

Antoine Lavoisier, a French scientist

Marie-Anne, Antoine Lavoisier's wife and assistant

Pierre-Simon Leplace, Antoine Lavoisier's colleague

stage directions — scene

SCENE 1: *It is the late 1770s. Lavoisier is sitting at a long desk in his personal library at his home in Paris, France. Books and loose papers are scattered all over his desk. Sconces are lit on the walls—it is in the middle of the night.*

Lavoisier: (*bent over his books, quill in his right hand, his left elbow on the desk, his left hand supporting his forehead*) This cannot be! I simply do not accept it! This phantom element—phlogiston—blast it! It does not exist. (*Marie-Anne softly enters the room.*)

Marie-Anne: Love…it is three in the morning. I know you are on the verge of discovery, but when will you rest your weary mind?

Lavoisier: I cannot rest now, Marie-Anne, I'm almost done. Let me be.

Marie-Anne: Why not wait until tomorrow, when Monsieur Leplace and I are at your call in the laboratory?

Lavoisier: You do not understand, good wife. This phlogiston—it taunts me. Yes, I agree with the notion that there is an element present during combustion, an element aiding the process and altering all that burns, but phlogiston? Johann Joachim Becher's theory of a colorless, tasteless, odorless, and weightless substance found in all combustible materials is pure lunacy! (*He slams his fist down on the desk.*) But where does that lost mass go? It *must* go somewhere! It can't just…just disappear. This is unknown territory in the science world. Yet, I am so close….

conflict

plot

Play **85**

Word Choice Precise language will ensure that the audience fully understands characters' intentions, scene elements, and plot.

Sentence Fluency Using a variety of sentences reflects natural speech, and the more realistic characters sound, the better the audience can connect with the play.

Conventions Actors cannot perform a play properly if it is full of errors.

Analyze
the Model

Week 1 • Day 2

Student Objectives

• Read a model play. *(pp. 85–87)*

Read the Model

Turn to "The Birth of Oxygen" on pages 85–87. Read the play out loud or, for a change of pace, assign roles to different students, making sure someone other than a character reads the stage directions and setting descriptions in italics. Ask students to pay attention to how each element serves as an important part of the play. Encourage them to consider how they would feel about the play if, for example, there were no stage directions.

Elements of a Play

Have students refer to What's in a Play? on page 82 as you discuss the model. Point out how characters are listed, the style in which stage directions are written, and how the conflict is revealed. Be sure that students fully understand each of the terms listed.

CCSS **C**ommon **C**ore **S**tate **S**tandards

R.7.3: Analyze how particular elements of a story or drama interact (e.g., how setting shapes the characters or plot).

SCENE 2: *Lavoisier, wearing a long white laboratory coat, is frantically moving about his laboratory, setting up a number of large and strangely shaped vessels.*

Lavoisier: Marie-Anne, when did Pierre-Simon say he would arrive?

Marie-Anne: Monsieur Leplace will be here any moment, my love.

(*A finely-dressed man rushes into the room. Lavoisier remains busy.*)

Lavoisier: Pierre-Simon! You have finally arrived! Not a moment to lose. I've had a breakthrough, and today you and I will make scientific history!

Pierre-Simon Leplace: (*putting on a long white laboratory coat and then standing at the end of the lab table*) I *knew* you were on the verge of discovery! But before we begin—please tell me what you are thinking. Remember—I am forever a student of science.

Lavoisier: (*continues to set up apparatus while talking*) You are familiar with the insane idea of phlogiston. You know that I have never agreed with Becher's theory. And yet, I too believed there was *something* universal that perhaps fueled the act of combustion.

Pierre-Simon: Yes. According to Becher, this stuff, this *phlogiston* (*the word is spoken scornfully*) is released into the air when a substance burns, and it has neither mass, nor odor, nor color. Ridiculous! But *what* allows combustion to occur?

Lavoisier: Well, today we shall burn this substance here (*points to a pile of powder in an enclosed vessel*), but we shall do so within enclosed vessels. This enclosed system will allow us to trap all released gases, which shall enable us to weigh them, evaluate them, and document the results. I believe that although a combusted substance appears to lose mass, this mass is simply *transferred* into something else, my guess—a gas.

Pierre-Simon: (*puts hand to forehead*) Of course! It's so simple, yet revolutionary. To the experiment!

Books for Professional Development

Calkins, Lucy, Amanda Hartman, and Zoe Ryder White. *One to One: The Art of Conferring with Young Writers*. Portsmouth, NH: Heinemann, 2005. After 30 years of studying her students' growth in the writing workshop, Calkins knows that one of the most powerful ways to support good writers is clear, purposeful writing conferences. In *One to One,* Calkins and her colleagues show the practices and principles that create effective conferences using predictable, principled interactions that follow a few simple frameworks.

Anderson, Carl. *How's It Going? A Practical Guide to Conferring With Student Writers*. Portsmouth, NH: Heinemann, 2000. Anderson provides samples that demonstrate various techniques and strategies that will help both teacher and students refine their conferences.

 Strategies for Writers Online
Go to **www.sfw.z-b.com** for additional online resources for students and teachers.

Lavoisier: (*turns to his wife*) Marie-Anne, please document these next critical hours. Should we meet with success, this information shall be then put into a paper to be released to the scientific community. The death of phlogiston is near!

SCENE 3: *Marie-Anne is writing at the desk in the library. Pierre-Simon is standing behind her, while Lavoisier is pacing the length of the room.*

Lavoisier: In conclusion, our experiments have proven the presence of an invisible element that aids the act of combustion. This element is *not* phlogiston, for it has mass. It should be noted that the combusted material did lose mass. However, this loss in mass matched exactly the mass of the gases collected in the second enclosed vessel. This proves that even during a violent reaction such as burning, matter is not created or destroyed—it is simply transformed. I have named the gaseous element aiding the combustion process *oxygen*.

Pierre-Simon: Remarkable! We must tell our scientific peers at once!

Marie-Anne: (*She gathers up the papers and hands them to Lavoisier.*) Your endless nights have served you well. Your restless mind can now find peace.

Lavoisier: Dear wife, this is not the end. It is merely a slight distraction. But make no mistake, this discovery—this birth of oxygen—is but the dawn of a new scientific day. And I plan on leading the way! (*Lavoisier exits the room.*)

Pierre-Simon: How does it feel, Marie-Anne, to be married to the Father of Modern Chemistry? Well, we are off to tell the world! Wish us well, for we will need it. (*Pierre-Simon leaves the room. Marie-Anne watches him leave, then places her hand on her forehead and slowly shakes her head from side to side. The lights dim.*)

THE END

Barbiere, Maureen. *"Change My Life Forever": Giving Voice to English-Language Learners.* **Portsmouth, NH: Heinemann, 2002.** As a public school staff developer in New York's Chinatown, Barbieri realized that the students in her new middle school had stories to tell, questions to ask, and opinions to share. Through daily interactions with literacy immersion in writing, they came to value English as a means of discovery and expression.

Parsons, Les. *Revising and Editing: Using Models and Checklists to Promote Successful Writing Experiences.* **Markham, ON: Pembroke, 2001.** This source provides reproducible pages for eight series of revision models, labeled "junior" or "intermediate." The author covers narratives, essays, projects or extended assignments, poetry, the entire drafting process, and peer conferencing.

CCSS Common Core State Standards
R/Lit.7.1: Cite several pieces of textual evidence to support analysis of what the text says explicitly as well as inferences drawn from the text.

Analyze
the Model

Week 1 • Day 3

Student Objectives

- Learn to read a rubric.
  (pp. 88–89)

Use the Rubric

Explain the Rubric Explain that a rubric is a tool for planning, improving, and assessing a piece of writing. Tell students that a rubric helps a writer focus on key elements, or traits, in writing (**Ideas, Organization, Voice, Word Choice, Sentence Fluency, Conventions,** and **Presentation**).

Explain the 6-point system. Point out that column 6 describes a very good play, one that has received the highest score in all categories. This is what students should strive for when writing their own plays.

Discuss the Rubric Guide students in a discussion of the rubric. Read the descriptors that go with each trait. Discuss the difference between columns to be sure students fully understand the point system.

Remind students to keep the rubric in mind when they write their own play and again when they revise it.

Rubric

Use this 6-point rubric to plan and evaluate a play.

	6	5	4
Ideas	Dialogue and stage directions clearly develop plot, characters, and setting. Details are accurate.	Dialogue and stage directions develop the story. Most details are accurate.	Dialogue develops the story. More stage directions are needed. Most details are accurate.
Organization	The play is organized and well paced. A logical sequence of events builds tension toward the climax and provides a resolution at the end.	The play is organized and well paced. Most of the events build tension toward the climax and provide a resolution at the end.	The play is organized but not well paced. Some of the events build tension toward the climax, and there is an identifiable resolution.
Voice	The dialogue sounds believable and reveals the characters' personalities.	Most of the dialogue sounds believable. One character's voice may need to be stronger.	Some of the dialogue sounds believable. Characters' personalities emerge now and again.
Word Choice	Precise language, such as specific nouns and powerful verbs, energize the play.	Specific nouns and strong verbs are used in the play.	Specific nouns and strong verbs are used most of the time.
Sentence Fluency	A variety of sentences adds interest. Fragments, if used, are effective.	Most of the sentences add interest. Fragments, if used, are effective.	Some of the sentences are varied. Fragments, if used, are effective.
Conventions	Sentences are punctuated correctly. Conjunctions are used correctly.	Most sentences are punctuated correctly. Most conjunctions are used correctly.	Several sentences are not punctuated correctly. One or two conjunctions are used incorrectly.

✛ Presentation   The format makes the play easy to follow.

88   Narrative Writing

CCSS Common Core State Standards

Play

The Common Core State Standards are woven throughout the instruction in *Strategies for Writers*. The rubrics and strategies for writing a play are based principally on Narrative standards. In this chapter, the Ideas rubric reflects standard **W.7.3.a** in its focus on narrative techniques such as dialogue, stage directions, and pacing. The Organization rubric descriptors are drawn from standard **W.7.3.a,** which emphasizes a logical sequence of events, and standard **W.7.3.e,** which focuses on a conclusion that follows from the events in the narrative.

Online Writing Center

Provides a variety of **interactive rubrics,** including 4-, 5-, and 6-point models.

3	2	1	
Dialogue and stage directions do not develop the story enough. Most details are accurate.	Dialogue or stage directions are not clear. Details may not be accurate or relevant.	Dialogue and stage directions are not used to develop the story. Details are vague.	**Ideas**
The play is organized but not well paced. Events simply occur, but they do not lead to a clear climax or resolution.	The play is poorly organized. The climax is vague, and there is no clear resolution.	The writing is not organized. Both the climax and resolution are missing.	**Organization**
The dialogue sounds unrealistic in places. There is little sense of the characters' personalities.	The dialogue is very weak. There is no sense of the characters' personalities.	Dialogue is weak and confusing to follow.	**Voice**
Nouns and verbs are ordinary. They do not bring energy to the play.	Vague or misleading nouns and verbs confuse the reader.	Words are weak or used incorrectly.	**Word Choice**
Most of the sentences are not varied. Fragments, if used, are effective.	Sentences are not varied. Fragments are not used intentionally.	Sentences are written incorrectly, causing the reader to struggle to understand the meaning.	**Sentence Fluency**
Many errors are repeated and cause confusion. Conjunctions may be missing or used incorrectly.	Serious errors interfere with meaning. Most sentences are written incorrectly.	The writing has not been edited.	**Conventions**

See Appendix B for 4-, 5-, and 6-point narrative rubrics.

Apply the Rubric

Assign Groups Divide students up into three groups. Assign one act from the play to each group. Instruct the groups to read their assigned act and then use the rubric to discuss how each trait should be scored. The point of this exercise is not to score the model, but rather to practice identifying and evaluating the traits within a piece of writing.

Reassemble Class After each group has had plenty of time to score their act, reassemble the class and have each group report their scores. Be sure students can support their decisions with examples from the play.

Additional Rubrics Appendix B includes 4-, 5-, and 6-point rubrics that can be used with any piece of narrative writing. The rubrics are also available as blackline masters, beginning on page T543.

The focus on precise language to convey experiences found in standard **W.7.3.d** is reflected in the Word Choice rubric. The Voice rubric emphasizes the narrative technique of dialogue, which is highlighted in standard **W.7.3.b**. The Voice rubric takes up the mention in standard **W.7.3.b** of dialogue as a narrative technique. As in all chapters, standards **L.7.1** and **L.7.2** are represented in the Conventions rubric.

CCSS **C**ommon **C**ore **S**tate **S**tandards

SL.7.1.a: Come to discussions prepared, having read or researched material under study, explicitly draw on that preparation by referring to evidence on the topic, text, or issue to probe and reflect on ideas under discussion.

Analyze
the Model

Week 1 • Day 4

Student Objectives

- Read a model play. (pp. 85–87)
- Use the play rubric. (pp. 88–89)
- Use the model play to study Ideas, Organization, and Voice. (pp. 90–91)

Study the Model

Assess the Model Have volunteers read aloud each section on pages 90–91. Discuss as a class whether students agree or disagree with each of Nina's assessments of the model. Use questions such as the following to initiate the discussion. Be sure students can back up their answers with clear examples from the narrative.

- How do the stage directions help you understand how a character is feeling or what's going on in the play? (Possible response: The information at the beginning of Scene 2 makes it clear Lavoisier is restless and anxious.)

 Strategies for Writers Online
Go to **www.sfw.z-b.com** for additional online resources for students and teachers.

Using the Rubric to Study the Model
(play)

Did you notice that the model on pages 85–87 points out some key elements of a play? As he wrote "The Birth of Oxygen," Aleem Martel used these elements to help him explain a scientific topic in the form of a play. He also used the 6-point rubric on pages 88–89 to plan, draft, revise, and edit the writing. A rubric is a great tool to evaluate writing during the writing process.

Now let's use the same rubric to score the model. To do this, we'll focus on each trait separately, starting with Ideas. We'll use the top descriptor for each trait (column 6), along with examples from the model, to help us understand how the traits work together. How would you score Aleem on each trait?

Ideas
- Dialogue and stage directions clearly develop plot, characters, and setting.
- Details are accurate.

Aleem uses both stage directions and dialogue to paint vivid and powerful scenes. Each character's unique personality becomes clear through both body language and dialogue. I can also envision the rooms in which the action takes place. Aleem was even careful to use props and language appropriate for the time period.

[from the writing model]

Lavoisier: (*bent over his books, quill in his right hand, his left elbow on the desk, his left hand supporting his forehead*) This cannot be! I simply do *not* accept it! This phantom element—phlogiston—blast it! It does not exist.

90 Narrative Writing

English Language Learners

BEGINNING

Types of Performances If available via the Internet or on video, show students part of a play. Say, *This is a play.* Have students repeat. Write *play* on the board. Repeat for *movie, television program,* and *musical.*

INTERMEDIATE

Parts of a Story Introduce a play by showing students a short video or a photograph of a stage production. Teach the terms *play, actors, scene,* and *stage.* Review the elements of a story with students: *characters, setting, plot, conflict,* and *resolution.* Tell students that a play has all the same elements as a story, and it also includes *stage directions,* which tell the actors where to stand and how to interact with each other.

Organization

- The play is organized and well paced.
- A logical sequence of events builds tension toward the climax and provides a resolution at the end.

Aleem opens his play with a bang. I am instantly engaged and can't wait to see if and how Lavoisier succeeds. I like the fast pace of each scene, too. Each event is clear and efficiently moves the reader toward the climax. At the end, the resolution is very satisfying.

[from the writing model]

Lavoisier: Marie-Anne, when did Pierre-Simon say he would arrive?

Marie-Anne: Monsieur Leplace will be here any moment, my love.

(*A finely dressed man rushes into the room. Lavoisier remains busy.*)

Lavoisier: Pierre-Simon! You have finally arrived! Not a moment to lose. I've had a breakthrough, and today you and I will make scientific history!

Voice

- The dialogue sounds believable and reveals the characters' personalities.

As I read the play, I could almost hear the characters' voices inside my head. The dialogue cleverly reveals aspects of their personalities, which helps me feel connected to the plot as a whole. Believable dialogue makes it easy to emotionally connect with the characters.

[from the writing model]

Marie-Anne: Love…it is three in the morning. I know you are on the verge of discovery, but when will you rest your weary mind?

Lavoisier: I cannot rest now, Marie-Anne, I'm almost done. Let me be.

Marie-Anne: Why not wait until tomorrow, when Monsieur Leplace and I are at your call in the laboratory?

Play **91**

- What is the climax of the play? (Possible response: The moment when Lavoisier and Leplace rush off to do the experiment.)

- How does Aleem reveal Lavoisier's personality? (Possible responses: His wife talks about how hard he works; Lavoisier's words show that he is high-strung and disdainful of his colleague; his body language also shows his agitation.)

ADVANCED

Reasons to Write a Play If students are unfamiliar with a stage play, introduce the concept to them. Ask students for reasons to write a play and what types of stories might be a good plot for a play. Have a class discussion about the topic. Introduce sentence frames for students to practice, such as, *One reason to write a play would be to _____. I think/I don't think a good plot for a play would be _____.*

ADVANCED HIGH

Story Map Review the elements of a story. Ask, *What can you find in a story?* Students should be able to answer questions such as *What is a character/setting/plot?* Students should know that the *conflict* in the story is the problem, and the *resolution* is the solution. Have partners brainstorm ideas for a play and complete a Story Map as a prewriting activity.

CCSS **Common Core State Standards**

SL.7.1.b: Follow rules for collegial discussions, track progress toward specific goals and deadlines, and define individual roles as needed. **SL.7.1.c:** Pose questions that elicit elaboration and respond to others' questions and comments with relevant observations and ideas that bring the discussion back on topic as needed.

Analyze
the Model

Week 1 • Day 5

Student Objectives

- Read a model play. *(pp. 85–87)*
- Use the play rubric. *(pp. 88–89)*
- Use the model play to study Word Choice, Sentence Fluency, and Conventions. *(pp. 92–93)*

Discuss the Traits Continue the traits discussion by asking questions such as the following:

- How does Aleem's choice in words and phrases affect the way you experience the play? (Possible response: Aleem weaves accurate scientific references throughout the dialogue.)

- Choose some dialogue that feels natural and flows well. What types of sentences does it include? (Possible response: *I knew you were on the verge of discovery! But before we begin—please tell me what you are thinking. Remember—I am forever a student of science;* a short exclamation followed by a longer sentence and a shorter sentence)

- What has Aleem done to help someone reading his play easily follow along? (Possible response: Aleem did a great job editing, and he used a clear, and easy-to-follow play format.)

Strategies for Writers Online
Go to **www.sfw.z-b.com** for additional online resources for students and teachers.

Word Choice
- Precise language, such as specific nouns and powerful verbs, energize the play.

What powerful nouns and verbs Aleem uses in this play! Words like *taunts, notion, combustion,* and *lunacy* all add power and life to the story. These words add zeal to the plot and keep the audience or reader engaged.

> [from the writing model]
>
> **Lavoisier:** You do not understand, good wife. This phlogiston—it taunts me. Yes, I agree with the notion that there is an element present during combustion, an element aiding the process and altering all that burns, but phlogiston? Johann Joachim Becher's theory of a colorless, tasteless, odorless, and weightless substance found in all combustible materials is pure lunacy!

Sentence Fluency
- A variety of sentences adds interest.
- Fragments, if used, are effective.

I like how Aleem uses a variety of sentence structures. He mixes up short and long sentences to create a sort of rhythm that is easy to both listen to and read. This variety also keeps the dialogue realistic and interesting.

> [from the writing model]
>
> **Pierre-Simon:** Yes. According to Becher, this stuff, this *phlogiston (the word is spoken scornfully)* is released into the air when a substance burns, and it has neither mass, nor odor, nor color. Ridiculous! But *what* allows combustion to occur?

Technology Tip — for 21st Century Literacies

Writers often speak of how they envision their texts as plays or movies that they see in their minds and transfer to writing. To facilitate that work as students compose, consider using storytelling apps like Toontastic or Xtranormal to create two different "castings" and "stagings" of one scene in their work. Bringing their imagined story to life (and motion) puts interesting pressure on their writing, challenging them to be specific, to revise, and to consider how their script comes alive. As an alternative, students could exchange papers and have a peer create the staging based on the directions supplied in the script.

See **www.sfw.z-b.com** for further information about and links to these websites and tools.

Conventions
- Sentences are punctuated correctly.
- Conjunctions are used correctly.

I've read Aleem's play several times and still can't find any spelling, grammar, or punctuation errors. He even uses conjunctions correctly! I want my play to be just as powerful and accurate as Aleem's, so I'll work hard and pay close attention to my conventions.

[from the writing model]

Lavoisier: Well, today we shall burn this substance here (*points to a pile of powder in an enclosed vessel*), but we shall do so within enclosed vessels. This enclosed system will allow us to trap all released gases, which shall enable us to weigh them, evaluate them, and document the results.

✛ Presentation The format makes the play easy to follow.

Now it's my turn to write a play. I'll use the rubric and good writing strategies to help me. Read on to see how I do it.

Play 93

ENRICHMENT

Read and View a Play Have students read part of a play, such as *The Wizard of Oz*, that is also a film. Tell students to pay careful attention to the stage directions as they read. Then show students the film version of the scenes they read. Discuss with students how the stage directions translated to the action in the movie.

REINFORCEMENT

Review Plot Diagram Have students reread the Organization descriptor on page 91. Review the concepts of building tension and climax by displaying a simple plot diagram on the board showing an introduction, rising action, climax, and resolution.

Presentation Explain to students that Presentation is just as important as any of the other traits. In fact, the format is crucial when writing a play, and standard play format should be followed. Encourage students to type their plays on a computer, as the word-processing functions will greatly enhance both neatness and layout. Direct students to look over the model play. Point out specific details in the presentation of a play (the white space between scenes, the use of double-spacing, stage directions set in italics, characters' names set in boldface). Remind them that although a play can be handwritten, using a computer will make their work much easier and neater. Encourage students to refer to the model play's format often while drafting their own plays.

Think About the Traits Ask students which traits are key to writing a play. Some students may feel that **Word Choice** and **Sentence Fluency** are key because of their impact on the dialogue. Other students may say **Presentation** because of the special format for a play.

CCSS Common Core State Standards

SL.7.1.c: Pose questions that elicit elaboration and respond to others' questions and comments with relevant observations and ideas that bring the discussion back on topic as needed. **SL.7.1.d:** Acknowledge new information expressed by others and, when warranted, modify their own views.

Write
a Play

Week 2 • Day 1

Student Objectives

• Read and understand a prewriting strategy. *(p. 94)*

Prewrite

Focus on Ideas

Gather Information Read page 94 aloud. Point out that Nina first had to decide on a topic for her play. Once she settled on Marie Curie, she did some research to gather important information to incorporate into her play. Point out that details and facts such as dates and setting are important to crafting a solid and believable story, and these details can be worked into the play's dialogue.

Online Writing Center

 Provides **interactive graphic organizers** as well as a variety of graphic organizers in PDF format.

Prewrite

Focus on Ideas

The Rubric Says Dialogue and stage directions clearly develop plot, characters, and setting. Details are accurate.

Writing Strategy Plan the plot and research details.

It's Science Week at my school, and this year we've been asked to dramatize a special moment in science. We can choose a specific discovery, a science-related event, or even a conversation between two or more scientists. Of course, all dialogue will be fictional, but the play must be based on scientific facts.

My first task is to decide on a plot, or what my play will be about. Then I'll do some research to gather accurate information. Next I'll decide on my list of characters and where the action will take place, or the setting. I'll take notes on all my ideas as I go.

Notes About the Science Play

✔ topic: Marie Curie

✔ born in Poland—moved to Paris to pursue education

✔ married Pierre Curie; worked together in lab

✔ used Henri Becquerel's work on uranium as background for their work on radiation

✔ discovered and named polonium (1898), radium (1898), radioactivity

✔ won two Nobel Prizes for her work in science (1903 & 1911)

✔ met with great prejudice because she was a woman

✔ characters—Marie, Pierre, maybe Henri?

✔ setting—in the lab. They were always there!

Apply

Research a science-related topic. Take notes and decide on your list of characters and setting.

English Language Learners

BEGINNING/INTERMEDIATE

Create a Story Map Give students a story idea, such as *a monkey in my bedroom*. Have partners use a Story Map to plan a play. Make sure they include characters' names, a description of the setting, a problem (conflict), plot events, and a resolution. They may use just a few words to describe each.

ADVANCED/ADVANCED HIGH

Developing Ideas Ask groups of three to work together to finalize the Story Maps and plot ideas they started during prewriting. Ask a volunteer from each group to describe the play's characters, setting, and plot to the rest of the class. The plot should include several events leading up to the climax of the story.

Prewrite

The Rubric Says	The play is organized and well paced. A logical sequence of events builds tension toward the climax and provides a resolution at the end.
Writing Strategy	Use a Story Map to logically and effectively sequence events.

✎ **Writer's Term**_____

Story Map
A **Story Map** is a graphic organizer that helps you plan the major aspects, such as a list of characters and the conflict, of your story.

Now that I've decided on my plot, characters, and setting, it's time to develop the plot. I'll use a Story Map to help me pace the events from beginning to end.

Story Map

Setting	Inside the Curies' lab and office	
Major Character(s)	Marie Curie, Pierre Curie	
Minor Character(s)	A telegram delivery boy	
Theme	Marie's discoveries and her struggle to be taken seriously in the field of science	
Conflict	To overcome the prejudice against women and get credit for her discoveries	

Plot

Event 1	Event 2	Event 3
April 1898, Marie discovers polonium	December 1989, Marie discovers radium	1903, Marie and Pierre receive the Nobel Prize in Physics (climax)

Resolution Pierre given his own lab; Marie becomes its Director of Research; she breaks down barriers against women in science

Reflect

How will this Story Map help Nina stay on track as she writes her draft?

Apply

Complete a Story Map to help you sequence the events of your play.

Play **95**

Conferencing

PEER TO PEER Have students use their Story Maps to give a short verbal summary of their planned play to their partner. As the partner listens, he or she should jot down questions about any items that need clarification.

PEER GROUPS Organize students in groups of three or four. Students should pass their Story Maps around the group. Have them think of one question they hope will be answered in the play for each Story Map, write it on an adhesive note, and attach it to the Story Map.

TEACHER-LED Hold conferences with individual students about their Story Maps. Discuss whether the events listed in the map lead logically to the resolution. Help students decide how they will fix any gaps in logic you may find together.

Write
a Play

Week 2 • Day 2

Student Objectives

- Make a Story Map to organize events. (p. 95)

Prewrite

Focus on  Organization

Organize Events Direct students to page 95. Explain that writers use different types of organizers to organize their ideas. Nina uses a Story Map to organize her gathered information as well as the events of her play. Have students study the Story Map. Then ask them how they foresee a Story Map helping them as they draft their plays. (Possible response: A Story Map will help me stay on topic because it will include only relevant details for my play.)

✎ **Writer's Term**_____

Story Map A Story Map helps a writer organize and review details, such as characters, theme, and conflict. The map also helps a writer put events into a logical order. A Story Map can also alert a writer if vital information is missing.

CCSS Common Core State Standards

W.7.3.a: Engage and orient the reader by establishing a context and point of view and introducing a narrator and/or characters; organize an event sequence that unfolds naturally and logically. **W.7.3.b:** Use narrative techniques, such as dialogue, pacing, and description, to develop experiences, events, and/or characters.

Write
a Play

Week 2 • Day 3

Student Objectives

- Use a Story Map to begin writing with a focus on using specific nouns and powerful verbs. *(p. 96)*

Draft

Focus on Word Choice

Draft a Play Read page 96 aloud. Discuss with students the featured line, "show me, don't tell me." Ask them how they interpret that line when it comes to writing a play. Remind students how important word choice is when writing. Point out that because a play consists almost entirely of dialogue, using specific nouns and powerful verbs is even more important.

Encourage students to put their energies into getting their ideas down on paper at this point. Using precise language, logically organizing events, and creating effective stage directions is the focus while drafting. Remind students that they will have plenty of time later on to fix errors in spelling, grammar, capitalization, and punctuation.

Note: To help facilitate editing, proofreader's marks are provided as a reference on page 97.

Online Writing Center

Provides student eBooks with an **interactive writing pad** for drafting, revising, editing, and publishing.

T96 Narrative Writing

Draft

Focus on Word Choice

The Rubric Says Precise language, such as specific nouns and powerful verbs, energize the play.

Writing Strategy Use specific nouns and powerful verbs.

We've all heard the phrase "show me, don't tell me." It's a great line to keep in mind while writing a play. I want my audience to connect with my characters on an emotional level. To do so, my characters will really have to *show* how they feel through their dialogue and actions. Using specific nouns and powerful verbs will help.

Using a few well-selected words can be so much more effective than a string of vague, weak words. For example, *He clutched at his empty belly* is so much more powerful than, *The man was very hungry*. As I write, I'll be sure to choose descriptive and specific words.

Now it's time to draft my play. I'll use my Story Map to keep me on track. I won't worry too much about spelling, grammar, or punctuation at first. I know I'll fix any mistakes in my final copy. Right now, I just need to focus on writing my play.

96 Narrative Writing

Differentiating Instruction

ENRICHMENT

Use More Characters Encourage students to write plays with three or more main characters. Tell them to think about using precise language in the dialogue and carefully chosen body language in the stage directions to establish and differentiate the characters' personalities.

REINFORCEMENT

Write with a Partner Have students work in pairs to choose a topic, make a Story Map, and draft a play. Tell the pairs to write a play with just two main characters. Each student can take responsibility for one of the characters, writing that character's lines and stage directions. Students should review each other's work and offer suggestions for more precise language as they draft.

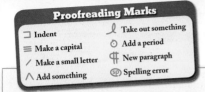

[DRAFT]

What a Woman Can Do

by Nina

Characters

Marie Curie, a scientist

Pierre Curie, Marie's husband and scientific partner

Delivery Boy   [used specific nouns and powerful verbs]

Scene 1 *(Both Marie and Pierre are working in their laboratory. Scientific apparatis is spread out along a long table. Pierre is bent over some equipment. Marie is carefully measuring something and then taking notes.)*

[used specific nouns and powerful verbs]

Marie: *(walks over to Pierre while looking at her notebook)* Pierre, I am getting the same figures again! I've replicated my work for a third time and the results are still the same

Pierre: *(sharply looks up, eyes wide with excitement)* You have discovered an unknown more powerful than Henri Becquerel's uranium?

Reflect

How well has Nina used specific nouns and powerful verbs? Where could she strengthen her language?

Apply

Write a draft of your play using your Story Map as a guide. Remember to include powerful, specific language.

Play 97

Write
a Play

Week 2 • Day 4

Student Objectives

• Complete a draft. *(p. 97)*

Finish a Draft It is important that students are given ample time to draft their plays. As conferencing is important throughout the writing process, be sure to also plan time for peer-to-peer, peer group, or teacher-led conferences. Remind students that this is the time to get their ideas down on paper in a creative and engaging way. Encourage them to refer to the format of the model play for guidance. Assure them that they will have plenty of time to fix any mistakes in conventions later.

Conferencing

PEER TO PEER Have pairs exchange drafts. Tell students to pay particular attention to the dialogue and circle in pencil two words that could be more precise. Have students discuss possible replacements for the circled words in both drafts.

PEER GROUPS Have students work in small groups. Students should take turns performing a section of their draft. Ask group members to describe the personality of one character in the draft. If the group's description does not match the writer's idea of the character's personality, he or she can ask for suggestions for revising the draft so that it more clearly conveys his or her intention.

TEACHER-LED Hold conferences with individual students. Perform the draft play together, with each of you taking one or two roles. Discuss what revisions the student wants to make after having heard the play read aloud.

CCSS **Common Core State Standards**

W.7.3.d: Use precise words and phrases, relevant descriptive details, and sensory language to capture the action and convey experiences and events. L.7.3.a: Choose language that expresses ideas precisely and concisely, recognizing and eliminating wordiness and redundancy.

Write
a Play

Week 2 • Day 5

Student Objectives

- Revise to add dialogue and stage directions. *(p. 98)*

Revise

Focus on Ideas

Enhance Dialogue Direct students to page 98. Remind students that a play consists almost entirely of dialogue; almost all essential details and events are revealed through the words each character speaks and the way each character acts. *How* the words are spoken is equally important. Have one student read Nina's excerpt prior to the revisions. Then have another student read the excerpt including the revisions. Ask students how the changes helped them better understand what Marie was thinking or feeling.

Point out that watching a play is a visual and auditory experience. For an audience to truly connect with the plot, they will need to fully see and hear what the main characters are thinking and feeling, and dialogue alone cannot express this.

Remind students that when revising their own drafts, they should pay close attention to dialogue and stage directions.

 Strategies for Writers Online
Go to **www.sfw.z-b.com** for additional online resources for students and teachers.

Revise

Focus on Ideas

The Rubric Says	Dialogue and stage directions clearly develop plot, characters, and setting.
Writing Strategy	Write dialogue and stage directions that inform the reader.

In a play, it's the dialogue that informs the audience of the plot, conflict, and setting. I worked hard at writing dialogue that is not only realistic but also informative. Of course, stage directions help out, too. I put a lot of thought into my stage directions to make every movement on stage count. As I was reading over my play, I found a spot where Marie's lines don't really reflect her feelings of insecurity. I'll add some stage directions and revise her lines to make things clearer.

[used revealing stage directions and dialogue]

[DRAFT]

(nods) Yes. It's all here in the numbers.

Marie: At first I believed I was just incorrectly duplicating

Becquerel's experiments with uranium. But I've conducted the same
and yet... (shaking her head and closing her notebook)
experiment over and over

Apply

Use stage directions and dialogue to inform your audience of characters' personalities, setting, and plot development.

English Language Learners

BEGINNING/INTERMEDIATE

Dialogue Write the following dialogue on the board:
ACTOR 1: *Where is the monkey?*
ACTOR 2: *The monkey is under my bed!*
After students practice the sentences several times, give them directions for how to say the sentences. For example, use the following emotions: excited, frightened, angry. Demonstrate each emotion.

ADVANCED/ADVANCED HIGH

Dialogue and Stage Directions Conduct the Dialogue activity above. After students have practiced the dialogue with the assigned emotion several times, add stage directions for them to practice. For example, if they are excited, have the actors jump up and down or laugh as they deliver their lines. Demonstrate. Teach the term *stage directions*.

Revise

Focus on Organization

The Rubric Says	The play is organized and well paced. A logical sequence of events builds tension toward the climax and provides a resolution at the end.
Writing Strategy	Follow the Story Map.

It's my job to pace the events of the plot logically and effectively. When more information is being given, the pace should be slower to allow the audience time to process everything. As the action rises, the pace should quicken. The climax is the part of the play in which the audience should be at the edge of their seats. I thought there could be more action to build the excitement around the climax, so I added some stage directions to tighten the pace.

Writer's Term

Rising Action The pace of the story's events quickens. Tension within the plot is building.

Climax The tension between the protagonist and the antagonist has peaked.

Resolution The conflict is resolved and the end of the story is near.

[DRAFT]

(Quickly turning to Pierre.)
Marie: Pierre! It's from the Royal Swedish Academy of Sciences.

What could this mean?

Pierre: Open it and see! It's been five years since our ~~quickly~~ discoveries. Too long for anyone to challenge us now. (He stands

and walks to Marie's side. Marie and Pierre then silently read the
→ The delivery boy strains to secretly read it over their shoulders.
letter together.)
[added action to climax]

Reflect

How has Nina effectively used events to build tension toward the climax?

Apply

Organize the events of your play effectively. Build tension toward the climax and slow things down during the resolution.

Play 99

Conferencing

PEER TO PEER Have pairs of students read each student's draft aloud, taking one or two roles each. Tell students to comment on what they like best about each draft and choose one place in each draft to add stage directions or dialogue to add more information.

PEER GROUPS Organize students into groups of three or four. Students should pass their drafts around the group. Tell students to focus on the stage directions. Have them point out one place in each draft where they would like to see a stage direction added or expanded.

TEACHER-LED Hold conferences with individual students. Work with students to compare their drafts with their Story Maps. Help students think of ways they can revise elements of their draft that depart from their Story Map.

Write
a Play

Student Objectives

- Revise to follow the Story Map and enhance the play's events. *(p. 99)*

Revise

Focus on Organization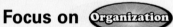

Enhance the Events Explain that when a lot of important facts are being revealed, the pace should slow down to allow the audience time to absorb the information. If the pace is too fast the information won't be noted.

Writer's Term

Rising Action leads from the beginning of a play to its climax. The playwright exposes the conflict and quickens the pace to increase tension for the audience.

Climax The tension reaches its highest point, and the audience anticipates the solution to the conflict.

Resolution At the resolution, the pace slows again. The playwright wraps up by connecting to the beginning of the play, exploring the consequences of the solution, or giving a hint of what might happen next.

CCSS **C**ommon **C**ore **S**tate **S**tandards

W.7.3.a: Engage and orient the reader by establishing a context and point of view and introducing a narrator and/or characters; organize an event sequence that unfolds naturally and logically. **W.7.3.b:** Use narrative techniques, such as dialogue, pacing, and description, to develop experiences, events, and/or characters. **W.7.3.e:** Provide a conclusion that follows from and reflects on the narrated experiences or events.

Write a Play

Week 3 • Day 2

Student Objectives

• Revise to vary sentence patterns to enhance meaning and style. (p. 100)

Revise

Focus on  Sentence Fluency

Vary Sentence Patterns Read page 100 aloud. Explain that because a play is mostly dialogue, it is critical that the dialogue be as natural-sounding and effective as possible. If a writer uses the same sentence structure over and over again, the dialogue will sound stiff and, if the play is performed live, the audience will quickly become bored.

Remind students that when people speak, they naturally use a wide variety of sentence types and structures. They also mix in sentence fragments along with complete sentences. Encourage students to revise their dialogue to do the same. Although fragments are not typically correct in writing, they are acceptable in limited amounts in this genre if they make sense.

Online Writing Center

Provides **interactive proofreading activities** for each genre.

Revise

Focus on **Sentence Fluency**

The Rubric Says	A variety of sentences adds interest. Fragments, if used, are effective.
Writing Strategy	Vary sentence patterns for meaning, reader or listener interest, and style.

Most of the time, complete sentences are the rule when you write. However, in a piece of writing that contains a lot of dialogue, such as a play, effective fragments are fine. After all, people do use sentence fragments when they're speaking naturally. As long as a fragment makes sense and fits the character, it's OK to use. Plus, using all kinds of sentence patterns keeps the dialogue lively and the audience interested.

[DRAFT]

Pierre: (sharply looks up, eyes wide with excitement) ~~You have~~
An
~~discovered an~~ unknown more powerful than Henri Becquerel's
uranium?

[used sentence fragment]

Apply

To keep dialogue realistic and interesting, use a few effective fragments throughout your play. Make sure they are clear, though.

Optional Revising Lessons

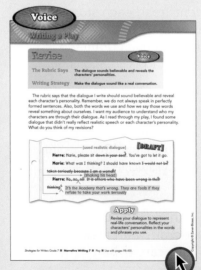

Narrative 7

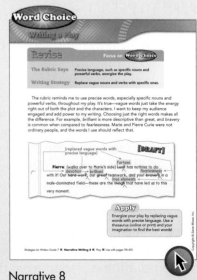

Narrative 8

Go to **Strategies for Writers Grade 7 CD-ROM**

Edit

Focus on Conventions

The Rubric Says	Sentences are punctuated correctly. Conjunctions are used correctly.
Writing Strategy	Check the use of conjunctions to join sentences.

My play's almost done! Now I need to carefully read it over and fix any spelling, punctuation, and capitalization mistakes. I'll also look for places where I can use a conjunction to change two sentences into one compound-complex sentence. A variety of sentences keeps writing interesting.

Writer's Term_____

Types of Sentences
All sentences fall into just four types: simple, compound, complex, and compound-complex. Be sure the punctuation makes the meaning of the sentences clear.

[DRAFT]

Marie: That was *our* work, Pierre! Now you must suffer because your partner is a woman—and your wife as well? I tell you—I'm sick of it all. It's been years since we've published our findings. Although The scientific world seemed to accept it as fact. There is still no , and there is word from the Academy. No funding for further research.

[formed a compound-complex sentence]

Reflect

How is Nina's editing? Can you find any mistakes she might have missed? Has she used all conjunctions correctly?

Apply Conventions

Check your draft for spelling, punctuation, and capitalization. Make sure you've used conjunctions and pronouns correctly.

For more practice identifying complex and compound-complex sentences, use the exercises on the next two pages.

Play 101

Related Grammar Practice _____

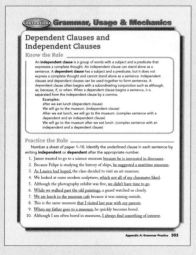

Student Edition page 505

Go to ▷ **Appendix A: Grammar Practice**

Student Objectives

- Edit for accurate use of conjunctions to join shorter sentences. *(p. 101)*

Edit

Focus on Conventions

Edit for Accuracy Suggest that students read their plays out loud to a friend or family member. They should ask the listener to pay special attention to the flow. Are there any spots where several short sentences can be joined with the use of a conjunction?

Use the mini-lessons on pages T102 and T103 for students needing more practice with different types of sentences. Then have students complete pages 102 and 103.

✏ **Writer's Term_____**

Types of Sentences Using different types of sentences will ensure that the dialogue flows naturally and realistically. Correct punctuation will help the reader know how to read the dialogue.

CCSS **C**ommon **C**ore **S**tate **S**tandards

L.7.1: Demonstrate command of the conventions of standard English grammar and usage when writing or speaking. **W.7.3.a:** Engage and orient the reader by establishing a context and point of view and introducing a narrator and/or characters; organize an event sequence that unfolds naturally and logically. **W.7.3.b:** Use narrative techniques, such as dialogue, pacing, and description, to develop experiences, events, and/or characters.

Play T101

Conventions

Mini-Lesson

Student Objectives

- Identify and work with simple and compound sentences. (p. 102)

Simple and Compound Sentences

Prior to class, prepare strips of paper that contain simple sentences. For example: *The bus screeched to a stop. It sent up a cloud of dust./ Hannah hadn't eaten in hours. She was starved./Mother requested veggie wraps for dinner. Father wants pizza.*

In addition, prepare strips of paper that contain a conjunction (*and, but, or*), a comma, or a semicolon.

In class, distribute the strips of paper with the sentences and the punctuation marks to students. Ask students to arrange the paper strips into compound sentences.

When students seem comfortable with the idea of simple and compound sentences, have them complete page 102. Review the answers in class.

▶ Online Writing Center

 Provides **interactive grammar games** and **practice activities** in student eBook.

Simple and Compound Sentences

Know the Rule

A **simple sentence** is made up of a subject and a predicate and expresses only one complete thought. It is an independent clause.
> **Example:** The dog barked loudly.

A **compound sentence** is made of two closely related independent clauses. (The two clauses can be joined by a comma and a coordinating conjunction (*and, but, or, so, for,* or *yet*) or by a semicolon (*;*).
> **Example:** The dog barked loudly, but no one was home to hear.

Practice the Rule

On a separate sheet of paper, write whether each sentence is simple or compound. For compound sentences, write the conjunction or punctuation that joins the clauses.

1. We planned a surprise party for Mother, but she suspected nothing. compound
2. I had to send out invitations. simple
3. Mother is allergic to wheat, so Father ordered a gluten-free birthday cake. compound
4. For dinner we're serving homemade soup, or perhaps some people will prefer the chili. compound
5. Auntie Linda offered to take care of the balloons and streamers. simple
6. Uncle Richard made a beautiful birthday banner; he forgot it at his house, which is over an hour away! compound
7. Everything was set up just in time for the party to begin. simple
8. Mother arrived home from work promptly at 6:30. simple
9. When she entered the room, Father turned on the lights, and everyone else jumped up to shout, "Surprise!" compound
10. Mother let out a cry of surprise and joy. simple

Related Grammar Practice

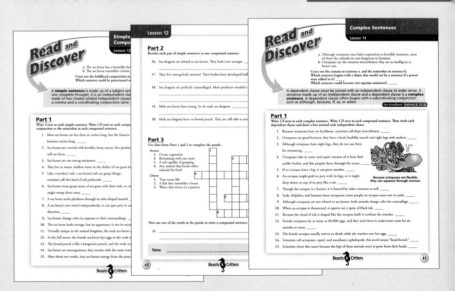

Pages 41, 42, 45

Go to ⇨ **G.U.M. Student Practice Book**

Complex Sentences

Know the Rule

A dependent clause must be joined with an independent clause to make sense. A sentence made up of an independent clause and a dependent clause is a **complex sentence**. A dependent clause often begins with a subordinating conjunction such as *although*, *because*, *if*, *as*, or *when*. If a dependent clause begins a sentence, it is followed by a comma.

>   **Example:** Although they were cold and drenched, the marching band played throughout halftime.

A sentence that has at least two independent clauses and one or more dependent clauses is a compound-complex sentence.

>   **Example:** When you are no longer thirsty, please rinse out your canteen and place it back on the shelf above the water pump.

Practice the Rule

On a separate sheet of paper, write whether each sentence is a complex sentence or a compound-complex sentence.

1. While I'm much younger, my elderly neighbor and I have become great friends. complex
2. Mr. Morrison, although he is almost 90 years old, walks me to my bus stop each morning, and then he walks me back home each afternoon. compound-complex
3. When it gets hot in summer, we often stay inside to play checkers, or he'll sit and tell me stories about his life. compound-complex
4. When he gets tired, he gently tells me it's time for his afternoon nap. complex
5. As we've planned, Mr. Morrison and I are going to a baseball game tomorrow morning. complex
6. Mr. Morrison said he had a surprise for me, and just before the game started, he gave me a team jersey. compound-complex
7. If our team is victorious, we plan on celebrating with a banana split back at my house. complex
8. Sometime while the seventh inning was being played, we knew we'd lost the game, yet we still hoped for the best. compound-complex
9. When I think back on it, I'll know that day spent with Mr. Morrison was one of my favorites. complex
10. Whether it rains or shines, Mr. Morrison and I do fun things together, and I'm so lucky he lives right next door. compound-complex

Play **103**

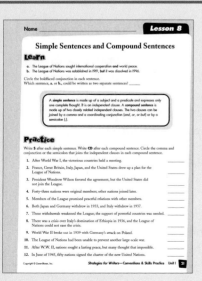

Page 21

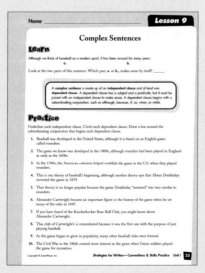

Page 23

Go to ⟹ *Grammar Practice Masters*

Conventions

Mini-Lesson

Student Objectives

• Identify and correctly construct complex sentences. *(p. 103)*

Complex Sentences

Write the following dependent clause on the board: *Although it was snowing.*

Then ask volunteers to think of a related independent clause to join with the example. (**Possible answers:** *we still went for our morning run/ we still had to go to school*) Let students instruct you on how to join the clauses. Encourage them to try different patterns.

Once students understand the concept of complex sentences, explain to them that when a sentence has at least two independent clauses and one or more dependent clauses, it is a compound-complex sentence. Write the following example on the board: *After the car is warmed up, I will drive Gracie to basketball practice and you will take Sebastian to violin practice.* Ask volunteers to locate and name the clauses. Create and use several more examples before students complete page 103.

CCSS Common Core State Standards
L.7.1.b: Choose among simple, compound, complex, and compound-complex sentences to signal differing relationships among ideas. **L.7.2:** Demonstrate command of the conventions of standard English capitalization, punctuation, and spelling when writing.

Play **T103**

Write
a Play

Week 3 • Day 4

Student Objectives

- Discuss preparation for publishing and presentation. *(p. 104)*
- Use a final editing checklist to publish their work. *(p. 104)*

Publish ⁺Presentation

Publishing Strategy Read page 104 out loud. Discuss Nina's excitement about watching her play performed live. Discuss as a class the different possibilities regarding the plays. Do students want to perform their plays for the class? For another class? Does the school or a student have a way of filming the plays so they can be shown to an audience (perhaps to parents on a Parent-Teacher night) at a later date? Encourage students to brainstorm different ideas and then take a vote to implement the most popular ideas.

Review Nina's final checklist with students. Ask students what items they think should be added to the checklist. Remind them to create a final checklist of their own before creating their final copies.

 Strategies for Writers Online
Go to **www.sfw.z-b.com** for additional online resources for students and teachers.

Publish ⁺Presentation

Publishing Strategy	Perform the play.
Presentation Strategy	Prepare the play on the computer.

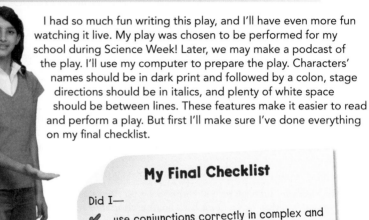

I had so much fun writing this play, and I'll have even more fun watching it live. My play was chosen to be performed for my school during Science Week! Later, we may make a podcast of the play. I'll use my computer to prepare the play. Characters' names should be in dark print and followed by a colon, stage directions should be in italics, and plenty of white space should be between lines. These features make it easier to read and perform a play. But first I'll make sure I've done everything on my final checklist.

My Final Checklist

Did I—
- ✔ use conjunctions correctly in complex and compound-complex sentences?
- ✔ check for spelling, grammar, and punctuation mistakes?
- ✔ type my play neatly?
- ✔ use bold type, italics, and white space to make my play easy to read and perform?

Apply

Make a checklist to check your play. Then make a final copy that's ready to be read and performed!

104   Narrative Writing

Differentiating Instruction

ENRICHMENT

Enhance the Performance Have students work in a group to rehearse and perform one or two of the plays. Allow students to assign responsibilities such as directing, prop master, costumes, and scenery creation within the group. Encourage students to stage their plays with appropriate props, costumes, and other pieces to set the scene, and give them time to rehearse several times before performing.

REINFORCEMENT

Format Review Work with students who are unfamiliar with word processing to format their plays, or have more computer-literate students assist them. Show students the features they can use to choose fonts, make type boldface or italic, set margins, and add space between lines. Create an extra copy of students' drafts and encourage them to use these to experiment with word-processing features.

WHAT A WOMAN CAN DO

by Nina

CHARACTERS

Marie Curie, a scientist

Pierre Curie, Marie's husband and scientific partner

Delivery Boy

SCENE 1: *Both Marie and Pierre are working in their laboratory. Scientific apparatus is spread out along a long table. Pierre is bent over some equipment. Marie is carefully measuring something and then taking notes.*

Marie: (*walks over to Pierre while looking at her notebook*) Pierre, I am getting the same figures again! I've replicated my work for a third time and the results are still the same.

Pierre: (*sharply looks up, eyes wide with excitement*) An unknown more powerful than Henri Becquerel's uranium?

Marie: (*nods*) Yes. It's all here in the numbers. At first I believed I was just incorrectly duplicating Becquerel's experiments with uranium. But I've conducted the same experiment over and over and yet…. (*shaking her head and closing her notebook*)

Pierre: Do not doubt your qualifications as a chemist and physicist, Marie. You are, by far, one of the most brilliant scientific minds at work right now in Paris.

Technology Tip for 21st Century Literacies

Throughout this unit, students have written in a variety of modes and across media. Be sure that you are creating opportunities for students to evaluate that work—and to do so in a way that captures what is different about pairing modes and writing "layered" texts. Create a class "values" list that details what writers do differently in multimodal text, especially when it comes to choice, meaning, revision, pairing, and sharing/publishing.

Write
a Play

Week 3 • Day 5

Student Objectives

- Use a play rubric. *(pp. 88–89)*
- Share a published play. *(pp. 105–109)*

Presentation Strategy Explain to students how important neatness is when creating a final copy of their work. The way the script is presented will help the actors read with appropriate expression, which in turn helps the audience understand and appreciate the play.

Explain that Nina's decision to prepare her play on a computer was an excellent choice, as it suits both her purpose and her audience. She wants her play to be easy to read and perform, and using proper play format is key. The word-processing features on a computer make it easy to set stage directions in italics, put characters' names in boldface, and leave extra space between lines and scenes. Remind students to use only one or two neat, legible fonts. Also remind students to use the header or footer function to label each page with the title, their name, and the page number.

CCSS Common Core State Standards

W.7.4: Produce clear and coherent writing in which the development, organization, and style are appropriate to task, purpose, and audience. **SL.7.4:** Present claims and findings, emphasizing salient points in a focused, coherent manner with pertinent descriptions, facts, details, and examples; use appropriate eye contact, adequate volume, and clear pronunciation. **SL.7.5:** Include multimedia components and visual displays in presentations to clarify claims and findings and emphasize salient points.

Reflecting on a Play

Instruct students to refer to the rubric on pages 88–89 as they reread Nina's final copy on pages 105–109. As they read, remind them to pay close attention to all of Nina's revisions and edits. After students have finished reading, ask them what they think of Nina's changes. Did those revisions and edits strengthen or weaken the play? What score would Nina have received for each writing trait? Take a poll to see how close the scores are. Be sure students can support their scores with examples from Nina's writing.

Now have students think back on this assignment as a whole. What are their impressions of writing a play? Do they have a greater understanding of the writing process and specific format now that the assignment is over? You might ask:

- What did you like about this assignment?

- What surprised you about writing a play?

- What was the most challenging part of writing a play?

- Compare writing a play to the last writing assignment you completed. What is one thing you did better in this assignment?

- What is one thing you will do differently the next time you write a play?

Strategies for Writers Online
Go to **www.sfw.z-b.com** for additional online resources for students and teachers.

Marie: How I wish your support affected the world outside our laboratory walls! I grow weary of having to prove my discoveries over and over again, merely because I am a woman. And then—to have others still insinuate that I am merely repeating what *you* truly discovered. (*sarcastically*) A woman! How could a woman discover anything of scientific value!

Pierre: I know you constantly meet with resistance and indifference in our field of study, but they are fools. Put their doubts far from your mind. Tell me—what have you found?

Marie: (*Sighing deeply, she picks up her notebook, opens it, and calmly reads her notes aloud.*) "April 1898—Today I have recorded the exact numbers yet again. Both substances pitchblende and chalcolite are more powerful, emit more particles, than uranium. Determined to isolate more powerful element. Have done so. Results show a new, unrecorded element." (*hands Pierre her notebook*)

Pierre: What a discovery, Marie! You've done it! Let's isolate this new element one more time together, for prudence's sake. No one will dispute your clean and precise work. What name will you give this new element?

Marie: Polonium—after my motherland, Poland. (*The lights fade with both working at Marie's end of the table.*)

SCENE 2: *Marie and Pierre are both working in the laboratory. Even more equipment is set up along the table. Both are carefully watching their experiments and taking notes.*

Marie: Can you believe our fortune, Pierre? Discovering yet *another* new element only eight months after our first?

Pierre: (*walks over to Marie's side*) Fortune has nothing to do with it! Our devotion, our brilliant teamwork, and your fearlessness in a male-dominated field—these are the true elements that have led us to this very moment.

Marie: I've been thinking. This new element—it's so powerful. It literally *radiates* particles. It should be named *radium*.

Pierre: Brilliant! It's true. As an element—it's so active. It has such an effect on its surroundings. One could say an element as such displays *radioactivity*.

Marie: Let's begin writing our paper to release to our scientific peers. I do not want others to claim this discovery for themselves. Woman or not—I've completed this work with my very heart and hands. I do not wish to be robbed at this point in time.

Pierre: I could not agree more. To our office! (*Both leave the laboratory as lights dim.*)

SCENE 3: *Marie and Pierre are in their office. Two small desks face each other to form one large desk. Pierre is sitting at his desk, watching Marie as she paces back and forth from her desk to a large bookcase on the other side of the office. Piles of books cover both desks and areas of the floor as well.*

Pierre: Marie, please sit. You've got to let it go.

Marie: What was I thinking? I should have known!

Pierre: (*shaking his head*) It's the Academy that's wrong. They are fools if they refuse to take your work seriously.

Allow students to discuss the questions or write their answers in their journals.

CCSS **Common Core State Standards**

W.7.6: Use technology, including the Internet, to produce and publish writing and link to and cite sources as well as to interact and collaborate with others, including linking to and citing sources.

Marie: That was *our* work, Pierre! Now you must suffer because your partner is a woman—and your wife as well? I tell you—I'm sick of it all. It's been years since we've published our findings. Although the scientific world seemed to accept it as fact, there is still no word from the Academy, and no funding for further research!

Pierre: We have always found a way. Still do. I have no desire to be rich and famous.

Marie: Nor do I—you know that, Pierre! But just think of what research could be completed with proper funding. Think of the many struggling scientists we know—all on the verge of their own discoveries. The world may never know, never benefit, if they can't fund their own work.

(*There's a knock at the door. Marie opens the door, and a delivery boy hands her an envelope.*)

Delivery Boy: (*standing straight and speaking officially*) Special telegram for Madame Marie Curie.

Marie: (*quickly turning to Pierre*) Pierre! It's from the Royal Swedish Academy of Sciences. What could this mean?

Pierre: Open it and see! It's been five years since our discoveries. Too long for anyone to challenge us now. (*He quickly stands and walks to Marie's side. Marie and Pierre then silently read the letter together. The delivery boy strains to secretly read it over their shoulders.*)

Strategies for Writers Online

Go to **www.sfw.z-b.com** for additional online resources for students and teachers.

Delivery Boy: (*no longer sounding official*) But what does it mean? What does it say?

Marie: It means we've done it! We—Pierre, myself, and Henri Becquerel—have been awarded the Nobel Prize for Physics! We all are being recognized for our work with radiation. (*Marie and Pierre embrace as the lights dim. The delivery boy moves to front of stage. One spotlight shines on him.*)

Delivery Boy: Marie and Pierre went on to share their award money with other scientists and friends in need. They used some of the money to fund their own research as well. Pierre was then offered a professorship and his own laboratory. Marie was made the Director of Research for Pierre's new lab. In 1911, Marie was awarded the Nobel Prize for Chemistry for her work with polonium and radium. She was not only the first *woman* to receive a Nobel Prize, but she was also the first *person* to be awarded two Nobel Prizes. Marie's research and accomplishments paved the way for women in physics and chemistry.

Reflect

How did Nina do? Did she use all the traits of a good play in her writing? Check it against the rubric. Don't forget to use the rubric to check your own play, too.

CCSS Common Core State Standards
W.7.6: Use technology, including the Internet, to produce and publish writing and link to and cite sources as well as to interact and collaborate with others, including linking to and citing sources.

Narrative Test Planner

WEEK 1

Day 1
Introduce
Narrative Test Writing

Student Objectives
- Learn the components of the writing prompt.

Student Activities
- Read and discuss **Read the Writing Prompt.** (pp. 110–111)

Day 2
Analyze
Introduce the Scoring Guide

Student Objectives
- Recognize the relationship of the scoring guide to the rubric and the six traits of writing.
- Read a model writing test response.

Student Activities
- Read **Writing Traits in the Scoring Guide.** (p. 112)
- Read the writing prompt response model. (p. 113)

Day 3
Analyze
Apply the Scoring Guide

Student Objectives
- Apply the scoring guide to the writing prompt response model.

Student Activities
- Read and discuss **Using the Scoring Guide to Study the Model.** (pp. 114–115)

WEEK 2

Day 1
Write
Prewrite: Ideas

Student Objectives
- Read and understand the writing prompt for narrative writing.
- Apply the six traits of writing to the writing prompt.

Student Activities
- Read and discuss **Prewrite: Focus on Ideas.** (pp. 118–119)

Day 2
Write
Prewrite: Ideas

Student Objectives
- Learn how to respond to the task in the writing prompt.

Student Activities
- Read and discuss **Prewrite: Focus on Ideas.** (p. 120)

Day 3
Write
Prewrite: Organization

Student Objectives
- Learn how to choose a graphic organizer for the writing prompt.

Student Activities
- Read and discuss **Prewrite: Focus on Organization.** (p. 121)

WEEK 3

Day 1
Write
Revise: Organization

Student Objectives
- Revise for transitions.

Student Activities
- Read and discuss **Revise: Focus on Organization.** (p. 126)

Day 2
Write
Revise: Voice

Student Objectives
- Revise to connect with readers.

Student Activities
- Read and discuss **Revise: Focus on Voice.** (p. 127)

Day 3
Write
Revise: Word Choice

Student Objectives
- Revise to add powerful verbs to give the writing energy.

Student Activities
- Read and discuss **Revise: Focus on Word Choice.** (p. 128)

Note: Optional Revising Lessons appear on the *Strategies for Writers* CD-ROM.

Day 4	**Day 5**

Analyze Apply the Scoring Guide	**Analyze** Time Management

Student Objectives

- Continue to apply the scoring guide to the writing prompt response model.

Student Activities

- Read and discuss **Using the Scoring Guide to Study the Model.** *(p. 116)*

Student Objectives

- Learn to budget time during a writing test.

Student Activities

- Read and discuss **Planning My Time.** *(p. 117)*

Day 4	**Day 5**

Write Prewrite: Organization	**Write** Draft: Ideas

Student Objectives

- Learn how to check the graphic organizer against the scoring guide.

Student Activities

- Read and discuss **Prewrite: Focus on Organization.** *(pp. 122–123)*

Student Objectives

- Use the graphic organizer to begin a writing test response that entertains the reader with lively, descriptive details.

Student Activities

- Read and discuss **Draft: Focus on Ideas.** *(pp. 124–125)*

Day 4	**Day 5**

Write Edit: Conventions	**Review** Test Tips

Student Objectives

- Edit the writing test for proper grammar, spelling, capitalization, and punctuation.

Student Activities

- Read and discuss **Edit: Focus on Conventions.** *(pp. 129–130)*

Student Objectives

- Review tips for writing for a test.

Student Activities

- Read and discuss the **Test Tips.** *(p. 131)*

To complete the chapter in fewer days, combine the learning objectives and activities in a way that supports students as they write.

Resources at-a-Glance

Differentiating Instruction

For additional Differentiating Instruction activities, see Strategies for Writers *Extensions Online at* **www.sfw.z-b.com.**

English Language Learners

 Connection Letter

Reproducible letter (in English and Spanish) appears on the *Strategies for Writers* CD-ROM and at **www.sfw.z-b.com.**

Online Essay Grader and Writing Tutor

Powered by Vantage Learning's MY Access!®, includes writing prompts and ongoing feedback for students as they write. Available for Grades 5–8.

Online Writing Center

Provides IWB resources, interactive games and practice activities, videos, eBooks, and a virtual file cabinet.

 Strategies for Writers Online

Go to **www.sfw.z-b.com** for free online resources for students and teachers.

Introduce
Narrative Test Writing

Week 1 • Day 1

Student Objectives

- Learn the components of the writing prompt. (pp. 110–111)

Introduce the Writing Prompt

Narrative Test Writing Explain that the purpose of a writing test is to evaluate how well each student can understand and respond to a writing prompt. Explain that in this chapter, Nina will guide them through the writing test process.

Explain to students how important it is to carefully read through the writing prompt before they begin any aspect of writing. A writing prompt typically consists of three parts: the setup, the task, and the scoring guide. Read pages 110–111 out loud. Point out each part of the writing prompt.

Setup The setup does just what its name says: it sets writers up to do a good job. It gets writers to think about the writing topic in general before they narrow it down to something they can write.

Strategies for Writers Online
Go to **www.sfw.z-b.com** for additional online resources for students and teachers.

Narrative test writing

Read the Writing Prompt

When you take a writing test, you'll be given a writing prompt. Most writing prompts have three parts:

Setup This part of the writing prompt gives you the background information you need to get ready to write.

Task This part of the writing prompt tells you exactly what you are supposed to write: a personal narrative describing your experience of learning a new skill.

Scoring Guide This section tells how your writing will be scored. To do well on the test, you should make sure you do everything on the list.

Remember the rubrics you used earlier in the unit? When you take a writing test, you don't always have all of the information that's on a rubric. However, the scoring guide is a lot like a rubric. It lists everything you need to think about to write a good paper. Like the rubrics you've used in this unit, many scoring guides are based on these six important traits of writing:

Ideas   Organization   Voice

Word Choice   Sentence Fluency   Conventions

Online Essay Grader and Writing Tutor

Powered by Vantage Learning's MY Access!®, this tool gives students

- immediate, ongoing, sentence-by-sentence feedback.
- helpful suggestions to improve their draft.
- a holistic score and a trait-specific score on their final draft.
- unlimited response submissions to the prompts.

Writing MODEL Prompt

Think about a time when you learned a new skill. Maybe it was a new sport or a new hobby that you had never done before.

Write a personal narrative describing your experience of learning a new skill.

Be sure your writing

- uses appropriate narrative techniques, such as dialogue and description, to develop the story.
- is well organized with events that unfold naturally from beginning to end.
- uses a voice that is appropriate for the audience and purpose.
- captures the action with powerful verbs.
- has a variety of sentences.
- contains correct grammar, punctuation, capitalization, and spelling.

Task The task explains what to write about and what kind of writing to do: narrative, descriptive, informative/explanatory, or argument. Explain that even a well-written paper will not receive a strong grade if it misses the topic or uses the wrong form.

Scoring Guide The scoring guide helps students plan and evaluate their writing.

Have students review the model prompt on page 111. Ask:

- What does this prompt make you think of?

Guide their responses to show that the scoring guide is very much like the rubrics they have used in the previous chapters. This scoring guide, just like a rubric, will help them plan their writing.

Then ask these questions:

- Which bullets tell you how to organize your narrative and keep your audience in mind? (the first and second bullets)

- Which bullets help you extend and revise your writing? (the third and fourth bullets)

- Which bullet reminds you about errors to watch for during editing? (the sixth bullet)

CCSS Common Core State Standards

SL.7.1.c: Pose questions that elicit elaboration and respond to others' questions and comments with relevant observations and ideas that bring the discussion back on topic as needed.

Analyze
the Scoring Guide

Week 1 • Day 2

Student Objectives

- Recognize the relationship of the scoring guide to the rubric and the six traits of writing.
- Read a model writing test response. *(pp. 112–113)*

Writing Traits in the Scoring Guide

Scoring Guide as a Rubric
Remind students how they used rubrics to guide, evaluate, and improve their writing of other descriptive pieces. Point out that in a writing test, the scoring guide acts as a rubric. Ask students for definitions and examples of each item in each category. For example, ask the following questions:

- What techniques have you used to organize other narratives?
  (Possible responses: Story Maps, 5 W's Charts, Main Idea Tables)

- Which graphic organizer might help you write this test?
  (Possible response: Story Map)

Tell students that they will sometimes use writing prompts that do not include guidance for each of the six categories in the rubric by name.

Online Writing Center

 Provides six **interactive anchor papers** for each mode of writing.

TII2 Narrative Writing

Writing Traits in the Scoring Guide

The scoring guide in the prompt on page 111 has been made into this chart. Does it remind you of the rubrics you've used? Not all prompts include all the writing traits, but this one does. Use the scoring guide to do your best writing. Remember to write neatly and put your name on each page.

- Be sure your writing uses appropriate narrative techniques, such as dialogue and description, to develop the story.

- Be sure your writing is well organized with events that unfold naturally from beginning to end.

- Be sure your writing uses a voice that is appropriate for the audience and purpose.

- Be sure your writing captures the action with powerful verbs.

- Be sure your writing has a variety of sentences.

- Be sure your writing contains correct grammar, punctuation, capitalization, and spelling.

Look at Nick Vaughan's story on the next page. Did he follow the scoring guide?

English Language Learners

BEGINNING
The Writing Process Review the steps in the writing process using simple words. Use the following words to substitute for *prewrite, draft, revise, edit,* and *publish: about/plan, write, change, fix,* and *show.* Remind students to follow all of these steps during a writing test.

INTERMEDIATE
Sequence of Events To help with organization during a narrative writing test, suggest students use a Sequence Chain graphic organizer. Give partners a brief story to read. Have them complete a graphic organizer to track the events of the story. Then have them trade stories and sequence chains with another pair who will read the story and verify the correct order of events.

Climbing Higher

by Nick Vaughan

The climbers around here call it "Red Rock," a rust-colored boulder near my home that's about two stories high and always seems to have a small crowd of climbers ascending and descending it. Now it was my turn. I'd had fun at indoor climbing gyms, but now I was ready to finally conquer Red Rock. One summer morning, I joined three other students and our instructor, Paul, to learn to rock climb outdoors.

Paul, who was in his twenties, was lean and tan from spending a lot of time rock climbing. He explained to the group that the safest way to start outdoors was top-roping. That's where a rope secured to the top of a boulder is attached to the body harness worn by both the climber and the belayer, who is the person on the ground who helps let out and pull in rope.

With my harness adjusted, Paul gave me some pointers on climbing. "Use your legs and not your arms," Paul said. "Stand straight up with your legs to get higher; don't pull yourself up with your arms." He eased my fears by reminding me that top-roping was safe. "Well, relatively safe," he added.

With my heart pumping fast, I started up the rock. I hugged the wall tightly as my hands clung onto the crevices. Then, as Paul instructed, I lifted my legs up to reach the next level. As I climbed, I could feel beads of sweat starting to form on my forehead.

Once, my foot missed the crevice I was trying to use, and I started to slip. My heart raced. I hung on as hard as I could. My belayer, a college student named Sarah, pulled the rope taut so I wouldn't fall. "Belay!" she yelled. After what seemed like minutes, my foot finally found the crevice. "On belay!" I yelled back, to let her know I was OK and ready to keep going.

Even though Red Rock was only a couple stories high, I was still nervous. I tried not to look down but instead focused on reaching the top. With each step higher, the top of the rock was closer, and my fears were further away.

At last, I made it. My arms and legs were trembling, but I had done it and I was proud. I had finally conquered Red Rock.

Writing Prompt Response Read aloud "Climbing Higher" on page 113 as students follow along in their books. You may wish to photocopy the model and instruct each student to use a pen or highlighter to identify and label the writing traits. As a class, score the model against the Scoring Guide. Take a vote to score each trait. Do most students agree on the scores? Be sure students can support their responses.

ADVANCED

Word Choice Remind students that when they draft, they should use powerful verbs. Write the following verbs on the board or on index cards: *giggle, stumble, hoot, joke, stroll, stagger, skip, howl, wander, race, trudge.* Then have students work in pairs to sort the words into *walk* words and *laugh* words. Ask which words are more descriptive.

ADVANCED HIGH

Using Different Kinds of Sentences Tell students they can make their writing more interesting by varying the types of sentences they write. Write the following sentences on the board: *He said something funny. And what do you think he said? You'll never guess what he said!* Ask students which sentence sounds the most dramatic. Write other plain sentences on the board, and have students suggest ways to make them more dramatic by using questions, exclamations, or commands.

CCSS **C**ommon **C**ore **S**tate **S**tandards

SL.7.1.d: Acknowledge new information expressed by others and, when warranted, modify their own views.

Analyze
the Model

Week 1 • Day 3

Student Objectives

- Apply the scoring guide to the writing prompt response model. (pp. 114–115)

Using the Scoring Guide to Study the Model

Review the Scoring Guide Remind students that the scoring guide is the tool that an evaluator—a teacher or other trained professional—will use to score the writing test. Students are given the scoring guide so they will know the criteria on which the writing will be judged.

Use the Scoring Guide Have students use the Writing Traits in the Scoring Guide chart on page 112 to evaluate the test written in response to the writing prompt on page 110. The chart is based on the scoring guide to the writing prompt.

Find More Examples Explain that pages 114–116 show how the writing model on page 113 meets all six writing traits. Have students read pages 114–115 and look for additional examples of **Ideas, Organization, Voice,** and **Word Choice** in the model.

Strategies for Writers Online
Go to **www.sfw.z-b.com** for additional online resources for students and teachers.

Using the Scoring Guide to Study the Model

Now we'll use the scoring guide to check Nick's writing test, "Climbing Higher." Let's see how well his story meets each of the six writing traits.

Ideas

- The writing uses appropriate narrative techniques, such as dialogue and description, to develop the story.

Nick does a great job helping me envision Red Rock and his first experience climbing it. His vivid descriptions and dramatic dialogue held my interest throughout the story.

> The climbers around here call it "Red Rock," a rust-colored boulder near my home that's about two stories high and always seems to have a small crowd of climbers ascending and descending it.

> My belayer, a college student named Sarah, pulled the rope taut so I wouldn't fall. "Belay!" she yelled.

Organization

- The writing is well organized with events that unfold naturally from beginning to end.

Nick's writing moves smoothly from point to point. When I reached the end, I didn't feel that I had missed any part of the story.

> At last, I made it. My arms and legs were trembling, but I had done it and I was proud. I had finally conquered Red Rock.

Differentiating Instruction

ENRICHMENT

Create a Rubric Have the students design a rubric based on the traits in the scoring guide. Have them write the six levels of assessment for each of the six writing categories. Point out that a well-written test will follow the traits listed in the scoring guide and would receive top marks based on the rubric they create. Have them think about what would constitute a writing test that would receive the middle or low marks. Have them fill in their scoring guides.

Voice

• The voice is appropriate for the audience and purpose.

Nick's purpose is to entertain and inspire other readers his own age. His voice reflects this well. It was easy to connect with his writing, and I felt ready to face my own fears after reading "Climbing Higher."

Even though Red Rock was only a couple stories high, I was still nervous. I tried not to look down but instead focused on reaching the top. With each step higher, the top of the rock was closer, and my fears were further away.

Word Choice

• The writing captures the action with powerful verbs.

Nick uses a lot of powerful verbs that helped create a strong image in my mind as I read. I could really "see" what was happening, and my attention was held from beginning to end.

With my heart pumping fast, I started up the rock. I hugged the wall tightly as my hands clung onto the crevices. Then, as Paul instructed, I lifted my legs up to reach the next level. As I climbed, I could feel beads of sweat starting to form on my forehead.

Narrative Test Writing 115

REINFORCEMENT

Focus on Dialogue Make a copy of the model and replace all the dialogue with narration (For example: *Paul told us to use our legs and not our arms. He also said we should stand straight up with our legs to get higher instead of pulling ourselves up with our arms.*). Read both versions of the model aloud as students follow along. Discuss with students the differences in how they reacted to the two versions. Prompt them with questions such as: Which model was livelier? Which one made you feel more like you were sharing Nick's experience? What does dialogue add to a story?

CCSS **C**ommon **C**ore **S**tate **S**tandards

SL.7.1.b: Follow rules for collegial discussions, track progress toward specific goals and deadlines, and define individual roles as needed. **SL.7.1.d:** Acknowledge new information expressed by others and, when warranted, modify their own views.

Analyze
the Model

Student Objectives

- Continue to apply the scoring guide to the writing prompt response model. *(p. 116)*

Analyze the Model Read page 116 out loud. Continue to use the scoring guide to evaluate how Nick did with the last two traits in "Climbing Higher." Ask a volunteer to read a paragraph of the model out loud. Ask students if Nick's writing flows well. Is it easy to read and a pleasure to listen to? Ask if anyone found an error Nick might have missed. Did he use all punctuation correctly? Encourage students to keep all six traits in mind as they prepare for and write a narrative test.

Think About the Traits Once students have thoroughly discussed the narrative test writing model, ask them which traits they think are the most important in a personal narrative. For example, students might say that **Voice** is very important because readers read personal narratives to get to know something about the writer. Or, they may say that **Organization** is important because a narrative will lose the reader if the reader cannot follow the events as they unfold.

Strategies for Writers Online

Go to **www.sfw.z-b.com** for additional online resources for students and teachers.

Using the Scoring Guide to Study the Model

Sentence Fluency

- A variety of sentences are used.

I like how Nick uses a variety of sentences. Mixing shorter sentences with longer sentences helps the writing flow and makes reading the story more enjoyable.

Once, my foot missed the crevice I was trying to use, and I started to slip. My heart raced. I hung on as hard as I could. My belayer, a college student named Sarah, pulled the rope taut so I wouldn't fall.

Conventions

- The writing contains correct grammar, punctuation, capitalization, and spelling.

From what I could tell, Nick uses correct capitalization, punctuation, spelling, and grammar. Don't forget to check for mistakes in your own work. If you know you often misspell words, for instance, you should pay close attention to spelling. Editing for grammar and mechanics throughout the writing process will help you avoid errors on your final test.

Planning My Time

Before giving us a writing test prompt, my teacher tells us how much time we'll have to complete the test. Since I'm already familiar with the writing process, I can think about how much total time I need and then divide it into the different parts of the writing process. If the test takes an hour, here's how I can organize my time. Planning your time will help you, too!

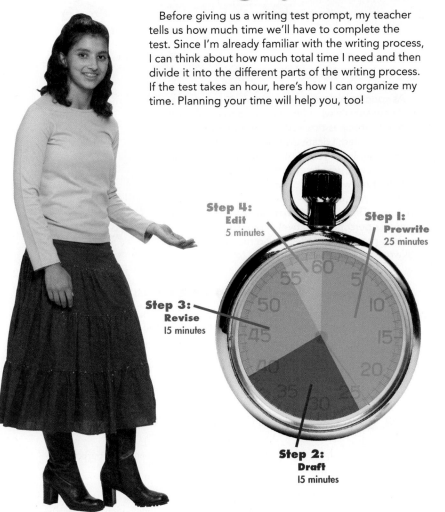

Step 4: Edit — 5 minutes
Step 1: Prewrite — 25 minutes
Step 3: Revise — 15 minutes
Step 2: Draft — 15 minutes

Differentiating Instruction

REINFORCEMENT

Many students have grown up with digital rather than analog clocks. Practice dividing the writing time (60 minutes) using a digital clock. Give students a starting time of 11:00. Have them plan their time by minutes. (11:00–11:25 Prewrite; 11:25–11:40 Draft; 11:40–11:55 Revise; 11:55–12:00 Edit) You may want to repeat the exercise with another start time. Remind students, however, that these times are estimates. Students may use several minutes less or more for a step of the process as long as they stay close to their time plan and leave time for editing.

Analyze
Time Management

Week 1 • Day 5

Student Objectives

- Learn to budget time during a writing test. (p. 117)

Planning My Time

Time Management Explain to students that when they write for a test, they must complete all the steps of the writing process quickly. Students may be surprised that the student guide, Nina, has allotted so much of the writing time—25 minutes out of 60—to prewriting. Ask students why this time is necessary. (Possible response: Without a plan for writing, students may write a draft that does not respond to the task. Then they will not have time to write another draft.)

Remind students also that revising is part of the writing task. Drafting and revising together take about as much time—30 minutes—as prewriting; five minutes remain to edit. Tell students that when they have a shorter or longer time in which to write a test, they can use a similar time plan: about the same amount of time for prewriting as for drafting/revising, with a shorter time for editing.

CCSS **C**ommon **C**ore **S**tate **S**tandards

W.7.10: Write routinely over extended time frames (time for research, reflection, and revision) and shorter time frames (a single sitting or a day or two) for a range of discipline-specific tasks, purposes, and audiences.

Write
a Narrative Test

Week 2 • Day 1

Student Objectives

- Read and understand the writing prompt for narrative writing. *(p. 118)*
- Apply the six traits of writing to the writing prompt. *(p. 119)*

Prewrite

Focus on Ideas

Study the Writing Prompt Read Nina's words on page 118 out loud. Emphasize to students the importance of reading and understanding the writing prompt prior to drafting. Remind them that even students who write an excellent paper will not score well unless they have followed the instructions outlined in the scoring guide.

Ask a volunteer to describe Nina's method for understanding the setup and task. (She circles key words and phrases with colored ink.) Explain to students that, even if they do not have colored pens or pencils, focusing in on key words and phrases in the writing prompt is a helpful method when preparing to write.

Strategies for Writers Online
Go to **www.sfw.z-b.com** for additional online resources for students and teachers.

Prewrite

Focus on ⟨ **Ideas** ⟩

Writing Strategy Study the writing prompt to find out what to do.

As soon as I get my writing prompt, I study it so that I'll know exactly what I'm supposed to do. A writing prompt often has three parts, but the parts aren't usually labeled. Locate and label the setup, task, and scoring guide on your writing prompt, as I did on mine below. Circle key words in the setup and in the task that tell what kind of writing you need to do and who your audience will be. I circled my topic in green. Then I circled what kind of writing I'll be doing (a personal narrative) in orange. Since the writing prompt doesn't say who the audience is, I'll write my story for my teacher.

My Writing Test Prompt

Setup — Remember a time when you learned a new skill or talent. Maybe it was a new sport or a new hobby that you had never done before.

Task — Write a personal narrative describing your experience of learning a new skill.

Scoring Guide — Be sure your writing

- uses appropriate narrative techniques, such as dialogue and description, to develop the story.
- is well organized with events that unfold from beginning to end.
- has a voice that is appropriate for the audience and purpose.
- captures the action with powerful verbs.
- has a variety of sentences.
- contains correct grammar, punctuation, capitalization, and spelling.

118 Narrative Writing

English Language Learners

BEGINNING

Writing Prompt Give students a copy of the standard narrative test writing prompt. Have them look at each word in the prompt and circle the words they do not know. Then teach the most important words, such as *remember, skill, talent, personal narrative, describing, dialogue, organized,* or *voice.* You might have a higher-level ELL work with a lower-level ELL to review the meanings of these words.

INTERMEDIATE

Writing Prompt Have students read the narrative writing prompt and write down words they do not know. Review how to ask for help, such as, *What does* skill *mean? Does* skill *mean "ability"?* Have them practice asking and answering with two other students. Finally, ask students to write their answers; for example, *A skill is being able to do something.* Review as a class.

Think about how the scoring guide relates to the six writing traits you've studied in the rubrics. All of the traits might not be included in every scoring guide, but you need to remember them all to write a good narrative.

Ideas
- Be sure your writing uses appropriate narrative techniques, such as dialogue and description, to develop the story.

I'll need to come up with an entertaining story and use clear, descriptive language to create a vivid picture for my reader.

Organization
- Be sure your writing is well organized with events that unfold naturally from beginning to end.

I'll keep my story well organized and complete, and I'll use transitions to smoothly guide my reader from one event to the next.

Voice
- Be sure your writing uses a voice that is appropriate for the audience and purpose.

I'll use a voice that is not too formal, but not too casual either. I want my reader to connect with my story and also believe it.

Word Choice
- Be sure your writing captures the action with powerful verbs.

I can think of lots of powerful verbs to describe the action in my story and hold my reader's attention. This will be fun!

Sentence Fluency
- Be sure your writing has a variety of sentences.

I can add variety to my writing by using different kinds of sentences. This will help my writing flow better.

Conventions
- Be sure your writing contains correct grammar, punctuation, capitalization, and spelling.

I will pay close attention to my grammar and mechanics as I write.

Walk students through page 119, encouraging them to add their own responses to Nina's. How will they make sure that their voice is appropriate for the audience? How will they organize their narratives so that they unfold logically and naturally?

ADVANCED

Writing Prompt Make a few copies of the narrative writing prompt. Cut apart the sentences in the scoring guide. Have partners work together to assign the sentences to one of the rubric writing traits—Ideas, Organization, Voice, Word Choice, Sentence Fluency, and Conventions.

ADVANCED HIGH

Writing Prompt Have students read the narrative writing prompt and write down no more than three words in each part of the prompt that they think are most important. Then have them compare with a partner and discuss the differences.

CCSS **C**ommon **C**ore **S**tate **S**tandards

W.7.5: With some guidance and support from peers and adults, develop and strengthen writing as needed by planning, revising, editing, rewriting, or trying a new approach, focusing on how well purpose and audience have been addressed. **SL.7.1.c:** Pose questions that elicit elaboration and respond to others' questions and comments with relevant observations and ideas that bring the discussion back on topic as needed.

Write
a Narrative Test

Week 2 • Day 2

Student Objectives

• Learn how to respond to the task in the writing prompt. *(p. 120)*

Prewrite

Focus on Ideas

Gather Information Read page 120 out loud. Ask that students think back for a moment on the previous writing assignments from this unit, focusing specifically on the information-gathering step prior to drafting. Remind them that a good writer always collects details and information before starting to write. This process ensures that every important detail and event is included in the narrative.

Point out how Nina chooses an event to satisfy the task (learning how to in-line skate) and then jots down several details from that event. Tell students that this first step, deciding what you are going to write about and taking a few related notes, must be completed before moving on to the next step, which is organizing the information.

Ask students to take a moment to think of new skills that they have recently learned. What experience did they choose? What related notes would they write down?

➤ Online Writing Center
 Provides **interactive graphic organizers** as well as a variety of graphic organizers in PDF format.

Prewrite Focus on Ideas

Writing Strategy Respond to the task.

Before you begin to write, you should always gather information. When you write to take a test, you can get information from the writing prompt. I'll take another look at the task now, since this is the part of the writing prompt that explains what I'm supposed to write. There isn't much time to rewrite, so it's really important to think about how you'll respond *before* you begin to write!

The writing prompt says to remember a time when I learned a new skill. I wrote down some notes about my idea to help.

Task —— [Write a personal narrative describing your experience of learning a new skill.

Notes

✔ I learned to in-line skate last year.

✔ It was a pretty exciting day!

✔ I fell a few times.

Apply

Before you start writing your story for a test, you should already know how you are going to respond to the task.

120 Narrative Writing

Differentiating Instruction

ENRICHMENT

Add a Category Have students create a 5 W's + H chart, adding a space for *How* in their graphic organizers. Discuss the types of details they might include in the *How* category, such as how to perform the skill they learned or how they learned the skill.

Prewrite

Focus on **Organization**

Writing Strategy   **Choose a graphic organizer.**

I'll begin by organizing my ideas. First I'll choose a useful graphic organizer. I know that a really good graphic organizer for a personal narrative is a 5 W's Chart. It'll help me organize my story by answering the following questions: *What* happened? *Who* was there? *Why* did it happen? *When* did it happen? *Where* did it happen? Take a look at how I filled out this 5 W's Chart.

What happened?
- I learned to in-line skate.
- I fell three times—luckily, I was wearing pads and a helmet.
- Dad held onto me at first; then I was able to skate on my own. He said it was a lot like ice skating, which I know how to do, and he was right.
- I had to learn to stop.

Who was there?
- Just my dad and I

Why did it happen?
- I got in-line skates for my birthday and couldn't wait to try them out.
- I've always wanted to learn how to in-line skate.
- Dad's a good teacher because he used to play Roller Hockey.

When did it happen?
- The day after my 12th birthday; I couldn't wait any longer.

Where did it happen?
- We went to the parking lot at my dad's office on a Saturday—he wanted me to have plenty of room to skate.

Reflect

Did Nina answer all the questions with enough detail in her graphic organizer?

Apply

Use a graphic organizer to help you recall the important details for a personal narrative.

Narrative Test Writing 121

REINFORCEMENT
Review Graphic Organizers To help students recall how graphic organizers can help them organize their notes, ask for volunteers to name the graphic organizers they have used in the past. (Possible responses: 5 W's charts, Story Maps, Main Idea Tables) Ask them when they might use each of the types of graphic organizers they mentioned. Discuss reasons Nina might have had for choosing a 5 W's chart. (Possible response: Answering the 5 W's ensures that Nina includes all the important details about her experience.)

Write
a Narrative Test

Student Objectives
- Learn how to choose a graphic organizer for the writing prompt. *(p. 121)*

Prewrite

Focus on **Organization**

Organize Information Explain to students that once they've decided on their topic and written a few notes describing it, the next step is to organize their information. Choosing the appropriate graphic organizer for this step is crucial.

Remind students that filling out a graphic organizer is prewriting and that prewriting should take up the biggest chunk of their allotted time during a writing test. A filled-out graphic organizer helps a writer the way a map helps a hiker—both items smoothly guide the person toward their chosen goal.

CCSS **Common Core State Standards**

W.7.3.a: Engage and orient the reader by establishing a context and point of view and introducing a narrator and/or characters; organize an event sequence that unfolds naturally and logically. **W.7.3.b:** Use narrative techniques, such as dialogue, pacing, and description, to develop experiences, events, and/or characters.

Narrative Test Writing   **T121**

Write
a Narrative Test

Week 2 • Day 4

Student Objectives

- Learn how to check the graphic organizer against the scoring guide. *(pp. 122–123)*

Prewrite

Focus on  Organization

Check the Graphic Organizer
Direct students to page 122. Explain that even though Nina has completed her 5 W's Chart, she is not yet ready to begin writing. Then ask students if they know why. (Possible response: She needs to first check her chart against the scoring guide.) Remind students that Nina could produce a well-written paper and still not receive a good score if she does not meet the requirements outlined in the Scoring Guide. Only after Nina refers back to the scoring guide to make sure she meets all of the criteria will she truly be ready to start writing. Explain to students that they should always do the same.

Strategies for Writers Online
Go to **www.sfw.z-b.com** for additional online resources for students and teachers.

Prewrite
Focus on **Organization**

Writing Strategy   Check the graphic organizer against the scoring guide.

You won't have much time for revisions during a test. That's why prewriting is a good idea! I'll check my 5 W's Chart against the scoring guide in the writing prompt before I start writing.

What happened?
- I learned to in-line skate.
- I fell three times—luckily, I was wearing pads and a helmet.
- Dad held onto me at first; then I was able to skate on my own. He said it was a lot like ice skating, which I know how to do, and he was right.
- I had to learn to stop.

Who was there?
- Just my dad and I

Why did it happen?
- I got in-line skates for my birthday and couldn't wait to try them out.
- I've always wanted to learn how to in-line skate.
- Dad's a good teacher because he used to play Roller Hockey.

When did it happen?
- The day after my 12th birthday; I couldn't wait any longer.

Where did it happen?
- We went to the parking lot at my dad's office on a Saturday—he wanted me to have plenty of room to skate.

• Be sure your writing uses appropriate narrative techniques, such as dialogue and description, to develop the story.

I'll include lots of details from my 5 W's chart, as well as some dialogue, to "paint" a vivid picture of my story's events.

• Be sure your writing is well organized with events that unfold naturally from beginning to end.

I'll describe events as they happened by using transition words such as *next* and *then*. I won't skip around and confuse my reader.

• Be sure your writing uses a voice that is appropriate for the audience and purpose.

I'll keep my voice casual and use first-person point of view.

• Be sure your writing captures the action with powerful verbs.

I'll need to remember to use powerful verbs to give my writing energy.

• Be sure your writing has a variety of sentences.

I'll keep this in mind as I write my draft.

Conventions

• Be sure your writing contains correct grammar, punctuation, capitalization, and spelling.

When I go back and edit my draft, I'll make sure the grammar and mechanics are correct.

Reflect

Why is it important to check your graphic organizer before you begin writing?

Apply

Reread the scoring guide in the writing prompt before you start to write to be sure you know just what to do.

Prepare to Draft Have students turn to page 123. Ask for volunteers to read the bulleted text and Nina's words after each of the six traits. Once the page is read, ask the class to review Nina's 5 W's Chart. Ask:

• Does Nina's graphic organizer include all the criteria outlined in the scoring guide? If not, then which traits are not represented there? (Voice, Sentence Fluency, Word Choice, and Conventions)

Point out that students will not be able to check these traits until they begin drafting their personal narrative. At this stage, they should use the **Ideas** and **Organization** descriptors to make sure they are on topic and that their organization is logical and sound. Reading the rest of the traits will serve as a reminder of what they should keep in mind as they draft.

CCSS Common Core State Standards

W.7.3.a: Engage and orient the reader by establishing a context and point of view and introducing a narrator and/or characters; organize an event sequence that unfolds naturally and logically.

Write
a Narrative Test

Week 2 • Day 5

Student Objectives

• Use the graphic organizer to begin a writing test response that entertains the reader with lively, descriptive details. (pp. 124–125)

Draft

Focus on Ideas

Draft a Personal Narrative Read Nina's words on page 124 aloud. Explain that Nina is starting her paper in the most efficient way: she is using her 5 W's Chart as a guide while keeping the scoring guide in mind. She understands how important it is to use vivid details and energetic, realistic dialogue to write an engaging and descriptive personal narrative.

Explain that when writing for a test, students should leave space between the lines of text so that they will have room to make changes and additions when it comes time to edit their work. Remind them how important it is, however, that they produce clear and neat work from the very beginning, as there will not be enough time to rewrite their papers at the end of their allotted time.

Online Writing Center

 Provides student eBooks with an **interactive writing pad** for drafting, revising, editing, and publishing.

Draft

Focus on Ideas

Writing Strategy Entertain the reader with lively, descriptive details and dialogue.

As I look back at the scoring guide, I'm reminded that I want to write a story that's interesting and entertaining. I'll use my 5 W's chart as a guide as I write my draft. I'll add lots of vivid details and even some interesting dialogue to liven things up.

[DRAFT]

Time to Roll

by Nina

For my birthday, I got a pair of in-line skates. I couldn't wait to get them on. But I didn't know how to skate. Fortunately, my dad, who used to play Roller Hockey, agreed to teach me. He had a plan: the next day, Saturday, he and I would head out to his office parking lot so that I could finally learn how to in-line skate! ⤹ [entertaining, descriptive detail]

As we headed to his office that Saturday morning, I couldn't wait to get my skates on and go! My dad told me to be patient and gave me some pointers. He told me that in-line skating was a lot like ice skating, which I already knew how to do. He asked me if I was nervous. "I am not nervous at all," I said, "I am ready to skate." [interesting dialogue]

One skate around the parking lot and I knew I wasn't quite ready to skate. Giant oak trees lined the edge of the parking lot. You see,

124 Narrative Writing

English Language Learners

BEGINNING

Word Order On the board, write *summer we California went Last to.* Ask, *Is this a sentence?* Tell students that the words need to be rearranged. Ask partners to fix the order of words in the sentence: *Last summer we went to California.* Underline *we* and circle *went*. Point out that this sentence has a subject and a verb, so it is complete.

INTERMEDIATE

Sentence Order Narrative writing tells a story in the order of events. To practice this, have students write a four-sentence story about the last time they were at a party. They should begin each sentence on a new line. Make sure students use appropriate words to signal order. Then have them cut apart their sentences and trade with another student. The second student should put the sentences in the proper order using order words and context to do so.

Proofreading Marks

⏺ Indent	ℓ Take out something
≡ Make a capital	⊙ Add a period
/ Make a small letter	¶ New paragraph
∧ Add something	SP Spelling error

[DRAFT]

stopping in Ice Skates and stopping in In-line Skates are two different things. I forgot to ask my dad how to stop until it was too late Before I hit his car, I fell to the ground, right on my hands! Fortunately, I was wearing a helmet and pads on my knees, elbows, and wrists.

Dad explained that to stop, I just had to lean back on my heels, where the stoppers were. For the next try, my dad suggested I hold on to him, just to get a feel for things without failing. Slowly, I skated with him.

                    — [more dialogue]

"Try to stop." he instructed me. I lifted my toes and gently pressed. I came to a stop.   [entertaining, descriptive details]

He let me go on my own and had me practice turns. Uh-oh! My legs got a little crisscrossed once and I took another spill, legs tanlged and all. I was a still a little wobbly, but with every turn around the parking lot I began to feel more confident.

I fell once more, but that was because I'd gotten my speed up so much that I panicked when it was time to stop, but I was now an In-line Skater, ready to go out on my own and glide somewhat gracefully with my friends.

Reflect

What do you think? What makes Nina's story entertaining?

Apply

To help enliven your personal narrative, include fun, descriptive details and dialogue that make your story stand out!

Now read Nina's draft excerpt out loud. Point out the highlighted text and notes. Ask:

• What do you think of Nina's details? Are they interesting? Do you feel engaged with her narrative? (Possible response: I like the description *crisscrossed* when she describes her legs while skating. I could envision her legs that way.) Then ask: What do you think of the dialogue? Is it stiff or realistic? (Possible response: Her dialogue sounded realistic and humorous.)

Encourage students to include plenty of vivid details and energetic dialogue when writing their own personal narratives.

ADVANCED

Using Powerful Verbs After students have written their first drafts, have them circle all the verbs they used in the first paragraph. Then have them trade with a partner who will read the paragraph and change each of the circled verbs to a stronger one. Then have the partners discuss why they made each change. Monitor to make sure students make the appropriate changes.

ADVANCED HIGH

Peer Review After students have drafted their personal narratives, have them trade with another student. Partners should review the draft and specifically look for details. Students should point out weak supporting sentences and suggest more vivid words their partners could use. As you monitor, identify two or three examples of weak words or sentences, and discuss ways to strengthen them as a class.

CCSS Common Core State Standards

W.7.3.b: Use narrative techniques, such as dialogue, pacing, and description, to develop experiences, events, and/or characters.

Write
a Narrative Test

Week 3 • Day 1

Student Objectives

• Revise for transitions. *(p. 126)*

Revise

Focus on  Organization

Time Management Point out that students have about fifteen minutes to revise their drafts, and that there are three revision tasks. Students might wish to subdivide their planned revising time into three 5-minute segments and tackle one strategy at a time.

Clarify Sequence Remind students that using transitions is the most effective way to guide readers from one event in a narrative to the next.

Have a volunteer read Nina's draft prior to her revisions, and then after her revisions. Ask students how the newly added transition words will clarify the sequence of events for the reader. Do they agree with Nina's revisions? Be sure students can support their responses.

Encourage students to use a wide variety of transitions to clarify the order in which events occur in their personal narratives. Remind them that readers connect with and enjoy stories that are easy to follow and understand.

Strategies for Writers Online
Go to **www.sfw.z-b.com** for additional online resources for students and teachers.

Revise   Focus on Organization

Writing Strategy   Use transition words to clarify sequence.

I'll read my paper again for organization. The scoring guide says my writing should flow naturally from beginning to end. I know transition words connect ideas and help my writing flow. I found a spot that could be more clear, so I'll use some transitions to help my readers understand the sequence of events.

[added transition words]   **[DRAFT]**

→ Next

He let me go on my own and had me practice turns. Uh-oh! My legs

got a little crisscrossed once and I took another spill, legs tanlged and

→ When I got back up,

all. I was a still a little wobbly, but with every turn around the parking

lot I began to feel more confident.

Reflect
Is Nina's story easier to follow now that she's added some transition words?

Apply
Use transition words to help the reader follow your story.

Differentiating Instruction

ENRICHMENT

Resource List In non-test writing situations, students should have resources at hand to help them improve aspects of their writing. Students who finish their test early can compile a list of transitions to use in their future writing assignments.

Revise

Focus on **Voice**

Writing Strategy Connect with the readers.

The scoring guide says my voice should be appropriate for my audience and purpose. I'm sharing a personal experience, so first person is a great way to connect with my reader. But I found some dialogue that's too formal. What do you think of my revision?

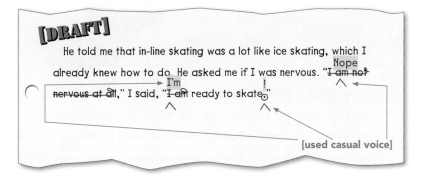

[DRAFT]

He told me that in-line skating was a lot like ice skating, which I
already knew how to do. He asked me if I was nervous. "~~I am not~~
~~nervous at all~~," I said, "~~I am~~ ready to skate~~.~~"

Nope

I'm

!

[used casual voice]

Reflect

Is it easier to connect with this scene now that Nina has revised the voice?

Apply

Use a voice that's appropriate for both your purpose and audience.

Narrative Test Writing 127

REINFORCEMENT

Quiet Reading Remind students that reading their writing aloud helps to hear how the writing sounds. This way, the writer can decide what part of the writing needs to be strengthened. However, during a test, reading aloud is inappropriate. Work with students to think of ways that they can review their writing without disturbing others.

Student Objectives

- Revise to connect with readers. *(p. 127)*

Revise

Focus on **Voice**

Connect With Readers Remind students of the importance of connecting with the reader and that **Voice** is a great tool to use to accomplish this connection. Explain that the language they use, the tone, point of view, and style of their writing all affect their writing voice. Then remind them that a good writer will keep both the purpose and audience in mind when determining how the writing will sound.

Remind students that using first person (*I, me*) allows the writer to show the reader how he or she experienced the event firsthand.

Now direct students' attention to Nina's revisions. As she read over her writing, she noticed the tone of her dialogue was too formal. Keeping her purpose and audience in mind, Nina knew that this formal dialogue was not completely realistic, so she revised to make it sound more casual.

CCSS **C**ommon **C**ore **S**tate **S**tandards

W.7.3.a: Engage and orient the reader by establishing a context and point of view and introducing a narrator and/or characters; organize an event sequence that unfolds naturally and logically. **W.7.3.c:** Use a variety of transition words, phrases, and clauses to convey sequence and signal shifts from one time frame to another.

Narrative Test Writing **T127**

Write
a Narrative Test

Week 3 • Day 3

Student Objectives

- Revise to add powerful verbs to give the writing energy. *(p. 128)*

Revise

Focus on  Word Choice

Use Precise Language Have students turn to page 128. Read Nina's words out loud and then direct students' attention to her draft excerpt at the bottom of the page. Ask: *What do you think of the new words Nina has used? How do these words add energy to her writing?* (Possible response: Both *whirl* and *tumbled* are more descriptive than the original words—I can envision the action much better.)

Encourage students to look back on other sections of Nina's writing to see if there are other verbs that could use strengthening.

Encourage students to look for all kinds of words that could be more precise, not just verbs. Remind them that the more vivid their descriptions are, the more powerful their writing will be as a whole.

Online Writing Center

Provides **interactive proofreading activities** for each genre.

Revise
Focus on **Word Choice**

Writing Strategy Use powerful verbs to give the writing energy.

With my draft written, I'll read it to see if anything is missing. The scoring guide says to use powerful verbs. So I'll go back through and find some areas where I can change the verbs to be more powerful and exciting.

[DRAFT]

One ~~skate~~ *whirl* around the parking lot and I knew I wasn't quite ready to skate. Giant oak trees lined the edge of the parking lot. You see, stopping in Ice Skates and stopping in In-line Skates is a little bit different. I forgot to ask my dad how to stop until it was too late Before I hit his car, I ~~fell~~ *tumbled* to the ground, right on my hands!

[added powerful verbs]

Apply

Sometimes just changing a weaker verb to a more powerful one can add drama to your story.

128 Narrative Writing

Optional Revising Lessons

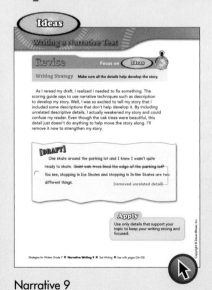

Ideas
Writing a Narrative Test

Revise
Focus on **Ideas**

Writing Strategy Make sure all the details help develop the story.

As I reread my draft, I realized I needed to fix something. The scoring guide says to use narrative techniques such as description to develop my story. Well, I was so excited to tell my story that I included some descriptions that don't help develop it. By including unrelated descriptive details, I actually weakened my story and could confuse my reader. Even though the oak trees were beautiful, this detail just doesn't do anything to help move the story along. I'll remove it now to strengthen my story.

[DRAFT]

One skate around the parking lot and I knew I wasn't quite ready to skate. ~~Giant oak trees lined the edge of the parking lot~~ You see, stopping in Ice Skates and stopping in In-line Skates are two different things.

[removed unrelated detail]

Apply

Use only details that support your topic to keep your writing strong and focused.

Strategies for Writers Grade 7 ■ Narrative Writing 9 ■ Test Writing ■ Use with pages 126–128.

Narrative 9

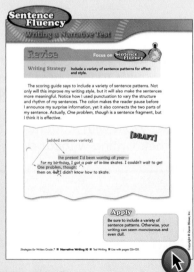

Sentence Fluency
Writing a Narrative Test

Revise
Focus on **Sentence Fluency**

Writing Strategy Include a variety of sentence patterns for effect and style.

The scoring guide says to include a variety of sentence patterns. Not only will this improve my writing style, but it will also make the sentences more meaningful. Notice how I used punctuation to vary the structure and rhythm of my sentences. The colon makes the reader pause before I announce my surprise information, yet it also connects the two parts of my sentence. Actually, *One problem, though* is a sentence fragment, but I think it is effective.

[added sentence variety]

[DRAFT]

the present I'd been wanting all year—
For my birthday, I got a pair of in-line skates. I couldn't wait to get One problem, though:
them on. ~~But~~ I didn't know how to skate.

Apply

Be sure to include a variety of sentence patterns. Otherwise, your writing can seem monotonous and even dull.

Strategies for Writers Grade 7 ■ Narrative Writing 10 ■ Test Writing ■ Use with pages 126–129.

Narrative 10

Go to ➡ *Strategies for Writers Grade 7 CD-ROM*

Edit   Focus on Conventions

Writing Strategy Check the grammar, punctuation, capitalization, and spelling.

The scoring guide says to use correct grammar, punctuation, capitalization, and spelling. I made sure to leave enough time to do that.

[FINAL DRAFT]

Time to Roll
by Nina

the present I'd been wanting all year—
For my birthday, I got a pair of in-line skates. I couldn't wait to get
One problem, though:
them on. ~~But~~ I didn't know how to skate. Fortunately, my dad, who

used to play ~~R~~oller ~~h~~ockey, agreed to teach me. He had a plan. The

next day, Saturday, he and I would head out to his office parking lot

so that I could finally learn how to in-line skate!

As we headed to his office that Saturday morning, I couldn't wait to

get my skates on and go! My dad told me to be patient and gave me

some pointers. He told me that in-line skating was a lot like ice skating,

which I already knew how to do. He asked me if I was nervous. "~~I am~~
Nope
I'm   !
not ~~nervous at all~~," I said, "~~I am~~ ready to skate~~.~~"
whirl
One ~~skate~~ around the parking lot and I knew I wasn't quite ready

to skate. ~~Giant oak trees lined the edge of the parking lot.~~ You see,

Apply

It's important to check your grammar, punctuation, capitalization, and spelling every time you write for a test.

Narrative Test Writing 129

Differentiating Instruction

ENRICHMENT
Early Finishers Remind students that a writing test is never completely "done." If students have revised for writing traits and checked for conventions once, instruct them to reread the writing prompt and then carefully read their narratives one more time while keeping the writing traits and the writing task in mind.

REINFORCEMENT
Review the Rules For students who regularly make the same type of error, review the appropriate grammar mini-lesson and practice pages in Appendix A, beginning on page T500.

Write
a Narrative Test

Week 3 • Day 4

Student Objectives
• Edit the writing test for proper grammar, spelling, capitalization, and punctuation. *(pp. 129–130)*

Edit

Focus on Conventions

Edit the Test Have students turn to pages 129–130. Direct their attention to the proofreading marks on the pages. Point out how each revision and edit has been made neatly so the work is still easy to read. Remind students that they will not have time to rewrite their work, so this process must be accomplished as neatly and clearly as possible. Explain that the goal is to produce a well-written narrative, not a perfect copy of a narrative.

CCSS Common Core State Standards

W.7.3.d: Use precise words and phrases, relevant descriptive details, and sensory language to capture the action and convey experiences and events. **L.7.1:** Demonstrate command of the conventions of standard English grammar and usage when writing or speaking. **L.7.2:** Demonstrate command of the conventions of standard English capitalization, punctuation, and spelling when writing.

Narrative Test Writing T129

Review
Test Tips

Week 3 • Day 5

Student Objectives

• Review tips for writing a test. (p. 131)

Test Tips

Reviewing Test Writing Explain to students that not all writing test prompts will be as clearly divided into parts as the writing prompt used in this chapter. However, students can still find and label the three important sections. Students can even generate a scoring guide if needed. Write this prompt on the board: *Everybody gets surprised sometimes. Write about a time you were surprised by someone or something. Revise and edit your report.*

Now ask:

• What is the setup? (Everyone gets surprised sometimes.) Circle and label the setup, and point out that it is rather brief. Ask students how they might expand on it to get a better sense of the background for this writing prompt. (Possible response: We could think about the kinds of surprises that happen to us—times when someone surprised us on purpose or times when something surprising just happened.)

Strategies for Writers Online
Go to **www.sfw.z-b.com** for additional online resources for students and teachers.

---

stopping in Ice Skates and stopping in In-line Skates are two different things. I forgot to ask my dad how to stop until it was too late. Before
I hit his car, I ~~fell~~ tumbled to the ground, right on my hands! Fortunately, I was wearing a helmet and pads on my knees, elbows, and wrists.

Dad explained that to stop, I just had to lean back on my heels, where the stoppers were. For the next try, my dad suggested I hold onto him, just to get a feel for things without ~~failing~~ falling. Slowly, I skated with him.

"Try to stop," he instructed me. I lifted my toes and gently pressed. I came to a stop.
Next
He let me go on my own and had me practice turns. Uh-oh! My legs got a little crisscrossed once and I took another spill, legs ~~tanlged~~ tangled and
When I got back up,
all. I was ~~a~~ still a little wobbly, but with every turn around the parking lot I began to feel more confident.

I fell once more, but that was because I'd gotten my speed up so much that I panicked when it was time to stop, but I was now an In-line Skater, ready to go out on my own and glide somewhat gracefully with my friends.

Reflect

Did Nina miss anything? Check her story against the scoring guide. Remember to use the scoring guide in your writing prompt to check your own writing anytime you take a test!

Guess what? We're finished! That wasn't bad at all! Here are some important tips to remember when you write for a test.

TEST TIPS

1. **Study the writing prompt before you start to write.** Most writing prompts have three parts: the setup, the task, and the scoring guide. The parts probably won't be labeled. You'll have to figure them out for yourself!

2. **Make sure you understand the task before you start to write.**
   - Read all three parts of the writing prompt carefully.
   - Circle key words in the task part of the writing prompt that tell what kind of writing you need to do. The task might also identify your audience.
   - Make sure you know how you'll be graded.
   - Say the assignment to yourself in your own words.

3. **Keep an eye on the clock.** Decide how much time you will spend on each part of the writing process and try to stick to your schedule. Don't spend so much time on prewriting that you don't have enough time to write.

4. **Reread your writing. Compare it to the scoring guide at least twice.** Remember the rubrics you have used all year? A scoring guide on a writing test is like a rubric. It can help you keep in mind what's important.

5. **Plan, plan, plan!** You don't get much time to revise during a test, so planning is more important than ever.

6. **Write neatly.** Remember: If the people who score your test can't read your writing, it doesn't matter how good your essay is!

Narrative Test Writing 131

Next ask:

- **What is the task?** (Write about a time you were surprised by someone or something.)

Circle and label the task, and point out that it is missing some information. For example, it does not tell specifically what kind of writing is called for. Ask:

- **How can you decide what kind of writing the task requires?** (Possible response: The task says to write about something that happened in the writer's life. A personal narrative tells a story from the writer's own experiences. So we are supposed to write a personal narrative.)

Ask:

- **What can you do to make up a scoring guide when the writing prompt has only general instructions to "revise and edit"?** (Possible response: We know that we can make writing better by using the six traits. We can write a quick list of the traits for a personal narrative to remind ourselves of what we want to do as we write.)

Have students volunteer the names of the traits and how they apply to a personal narrative. Write students' responses on the board in a bulleted list. Show students that they have just figured out a useful scoring guide from their own experience. Students will see that even a brief writing prompt can give them the tools and guidance they need to write a successful test.

CCSS Common Core State Standards
L.7.1: Demonstrate command of the conventions of standard English grammar and usage when writing or speaking. **L.7.2:** Demonstrate command of the conventions of standard English capitalization, punctuation, and spelling when writing.

Narrative Test Writing T131

Informative/Explanatory writing

Cause-and-Effect Report

Pages T134A–T155

This genre opens the door to expository writing by encouraging students to relate writing to reasons (causes) that lead to specific results (effects).

Prewrite   Do research and take notes about a cause-effect relationship in nature. Use a Cause-and-Effect Chain to organize the ideas.

Draft   Include a concise thesis statement that reflects the purpose for writing.

Revise   Make sure the ideas are in order.
Maintain consistency in style and tone.
Clearly explain unfamiliar terms and jargon.

Edit   Check the use of commas and apostrophes.

Publish   Submit the report to the school website.

Research Report

Pages T156A–T187

This genre gives students an opportunity to ask questions, research answers, and explain discoveries.

Prewrite   Choose a topic and make a K-W-S Chart to gather research. Then make note cards. Make an Outline to organize the information from the note cards.

Draft   Include a strong introduction, body, and conclusion that will guide the reader through the report.

Revise   Add quotes and information from experts.
Make sure that borrowed information is paraphrased accurately.
Create sentence variety by breaking up long, wordy sentences.

Edit   Check the capitalization and punctuation of proper nouns, proper adjectives, abbreviations, and initials.

Publish   Present the report as part of a multimedia presentation.

Summary

Pages T188A–T213

This genre gives students a chance to summarize the main points of a piece of writing.

Prewrite   Read an article. Jot down the 5 W's from the article.
Make a Main-Idea Table to organize main ideas and details.

Draft   Maintain consistency in style and tone.

Revise   Delete information that is not relevant or important.
Recognize and eliminate wordiness and redundancy.
Choose punctuation for effect.

Edit   Recognize and correct inappropriate shifts in pronoun number and person.

Publish   Publish the summary in a class news magazine.

Unit Overview

SOCIAL STUDIES CONNECTION

Problem-Solution Essay

Pages T214A–T239

Students will use a social studies topic to explain a problem and recommend a solution.

Prewrite   Choose and narrow a topic that can be explained in a report. Take notes.
Make a Problem-Solution Frame to organize the notes.

Draft   Define words that are unfamiliar to the audience.

Revise   Use details that are concrete and credible.
Use transition words or phrases to connect sentences and paragraphs.
Use parallel sentence structures.

Edit   Recognize and correct inappropriate shifts in verb tense.

Publish   Use text features and illustrations.

Informative/Explanatory Test Writing

Pages T240A–T261

Students will learn and practice how to read an informative/explanatory test prompt and how to plan their time. They will also learn and practice writing strategies for successful test writing in the informative/explanatory mode.

Prewrite   Study the writing prompt to find out what to do. Respond to the task.
Choose a graphic organizer.
Check the graphic organizer against the scoring guide.

Draft   Write a clear, concise thesis statement.

Revise   Use appropriate transition words to show cause and effect.
Connect with the readers.
Choose language that expresses ideas precisely and concisely, recognizing and eliminating wordiness and redundancy.

Edit   Check the grammar, punctuation, capitalization, and spelling.

Online Writing Center

Interactive Whiteboard Ready

Complete Digital Writing Instruction!

- My Writing Pad
- Interactive Rubrics
- Anchor Papers
- Graphic Organizers

- Content Area Writing Prompts
- Grammar Games
- Proofreading Activities
- Instructional Videos

- Virtual File Cabinet
- eBooks
- Assessments

For information, go to
www.sfw.z-b.com

Also available: **Online Essay Grader and Writing Tutor**, powered by Vantage Learning's MY Access®.

TI32B

21st Century Literacies
Technology, Digital Media & Writing

by **Julie Coiro, Ph.D.,** University of Rhode Island & **Sara Kajder, Ph.D.,** University of Pittsburgh

 **INQUIRE** First Locate, Then Evaluate

Online Search Tools

A number of exceptional search engines and Web portals have been designed with the needs and interests of a younger audience in mind. Each has their own unique features. Some include a list of websites, while some contain other types of documents (e.g., blog posts, wiki pages, group discussion threads, PDFs, PowerPoints). Students should be encouraged to search the same topic in different search engines to see which ones might be most helpful. A few of the most popular are listed below.

- **Google (www.google.com)** is a huge database that very quickly scans sites and returns a list of relevant websites with a short annotation and a link. The articles are listed in rank order, with the most popular and relevant at the top. Help your students select the "Google Safe Search" option from the preferences menu to block inappropriate websites.

- **Kids Click! (www.kidsclick.org)** was created by librarians and organizes 5,000 websites into more than 600 categories.

- **Fact Monster (www.factmonster.com)** combines the contents of reference materials for kids with other educational resources. A link to TeacherVision will lead you to 20,000 pages of classroom-ready lesson plans and printable resources.

- **Enchanted Learning (www.enchantedlearning. com)** provides access to a huge database guaranteed to spark writing ideas.

- **TekMom Search Tools for Students (http:// tekmom.com)** links readers to research tools designed with young learners in mind.

Evaluating Accuracy

As your students venture out onto the Internet to locate information for informative/explanatory writing projects, they should be equipped with strategies to verify that what they find is actually true. Here are three tips to model for your students as you explore new informational websites together.

- **Read the website.** Reading for accuracy requires close reading. Ask yourself: *Does the information make sense? When was the information last updated? Does the author list the bibliographic sources for the information?* Answers to these questions may provide clues about whether the information is accurate and up-to-date.

- **Read other websites.** Can the information be verified at another website created by a different author? Use a search engine and refined keyword strategies to search for two or three other websites that contain similar facts by different authors.

- **Read a primary source website.** Students should also expect that different information might appear on different sites. This often happens when the facts from real events are modified over time as they are shared with different people. Discuss the differences between primary sources and secondary sources. Then recommend that students include at least one primary source in their research report. The **Library of Congress' American Memory database (www. loc.gov/teachers/usingprimarysources)** provides excellent lessons on using primary sources.

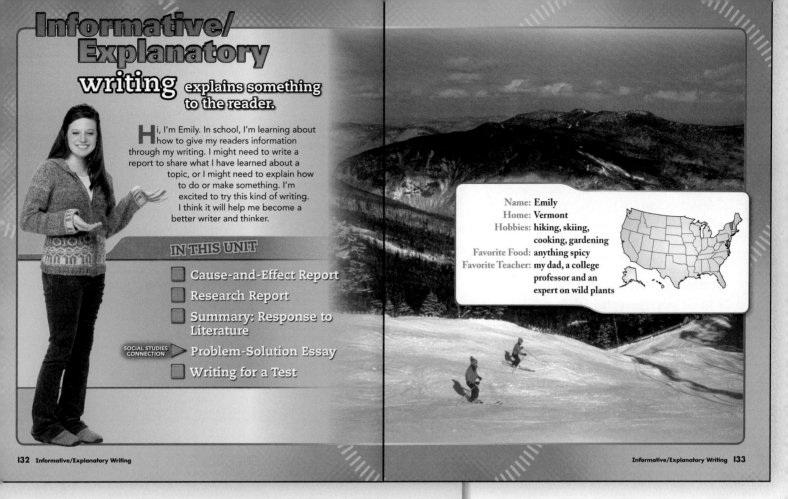

Informative/Explanatory writing explains something to the reader.

Hi, I'm Emily. In school, I'm learning about how to give my readers information through my writing. I might need to write a report to share what I have learned about a topic, or I might need to explain how to do or make something. I'm excited to try this kind of writing. I think it will help me become a better writer and thinker.

IN THIS UNIT

- ☐ Cause-and-Effect Report
- ☐ Research Report
- ☐ Summary: Response to Literature
- SOCIAL STUDIES CONNECTION ▷ Problem-Solution Essay
- ☐ Writing for a Test

Name: **Emily**
Home: **Vermont**
Hobbies: **hiking, skiing, cooking, gardening**
Favorite Food: **anything spicy**
Favorite Teacher: **my dad, a college professor and an expert on wild plants**

To differentiate instruction and maximize student achievement, use the Extensions Online activities available at **www.sfw.z-b.com.**

Created by Amy Humphreys, Ed.M., these engaging activities can be used to meet a wide range of learner needs. Each activity uses a combination of visual, written, oral, and kinesthetic elements, and deliberately leverages the power of collaboration and conversation so students learn to think like writers in fun and engaging ways. For more information on Differentiated Instruction, see page Z12.

Meet Your Writing Partner, Emily

The writing partner for this chapter is Emily, a girl from Vermont who wears a prosthetic leg. You may wish to explore with students how having an artificial limb might affect Emily's interests, hobbies, and decisions, and how these in turn might influence her choice of writing topics. Also encourage students to use their own background knowledge, interests, and personalities as they write. Informative/Explanatory writing explores many real-world topics, and your students will have many interesting, unique, and authentic ideas to explain and inform their readers about.

Cause-and-Effect Report Planner

WEEK 1

Day 1
Introduce
a Cause-and-Effect Report

Student Objectives
- Review the elements of a cause-and-effect report.
- Consider purpose and audience.
- Learn the traits of informative/explanatory writing.

Student Activities
- Read and discuss **What's in a Cause-and-Effect Report?** and **Why Write a Cause-and-Effect Report?** (pp. 134–135)
- Read **Linking Informative/Explanatory Writing Traits to a Cause-and-Effect Report.** (p. 136)

Day 2
Analyze
Read a Cause-and-Effect Report

Student Objectives
- Read a model cause-and-effect report.

Student Activities
- Read **"The Perils of Sleep Deprivation."** (p. 137)

Day 3
Analyze
Introduce the Rubric

Student Objectives
- Learn to read a rubric.

Student Activities
- Review **"The Perils of Sleep Deprivation."** (p. 137)
- Read and discuss the **Cause-and-Effect Report Rubric.** (pp. 138–139)

WEEK 2

Day 1
Write
Prewrite: Ideas

Student Objectives
- Read and understand a prewriting strategy.

Student Activities
- Read and discuss **Prewrite: Focus on Ideas.** (p. 144)
- Apply the prewriting strategy.

Day 2
Write
Prewrite: Organization

Student Objectives
- Make a Cause-and-Effect Chain to organize ideas.

Student Activities
- Read and discuss **Prewrite: Focus on Organization.** (p. 145)
- Apply the prewriting strategy to create a Cause-and-Effect Chain.

Day 3
Write
Draft: Ideas

Student Objectives
- Use a Cause-and-Effect Chain to begin writing.

Student Activities
- Read and discuss **Draft: Focus on Ideas.** (p. 146)
- Apply the drafting strategy by using a Cause-and-Effect Chain to write a draft.

WEEK 3

Day 1
Write
Revise: Voice

Student Objectives
- Revise for a formal style and tone.

Student Activities
- Read and discuss **Revise: Focus on Voice.** (p. 149)
- Reflect on the model draft.
- Apply the revising strategy.
- Participate in a peer conference.

Day 2
Write
Revise: Word Choice

Student Objectives
- Revise for clearly explained terms and jargon.

Student Activities
- Read and discuss **Revise: Focus on Word Choice.** (p. 150)
- Reflect on the model draft.
- Apply the revising strategy.

Note: Optional Revising Lessons appear on the *Strategies for Writers* CD-ROM.

Day 3
Write
Edit: Conventions

Student Objectives
- Edit for correct use of commas and apostrophes.

Student Activities
- Read and discuss **Edit: Focus on Conventions.** (p. 151)
- Reflect on the model draft.
- Apply the editing strategy.

Note: Teach the Conventions mini-lessons (pp. 152–153) if needed.

Day 4	Day 5
Analyze Ideas, Organization, and Voice	**Analyze** Word Choice, Sentence Fluency, and Conventions

Student Objectives
- Read a model cause-and-effect report.
- Use the cause-and-effect report rubric.
- Use the model cause-and-effect report to study Ideas, Organization, and Voice.

Student Activities
- Review **"The Perils of Sleep Deprivation."** (p. 137)
- Use the rubric. (pp. 138–139)
- Read and discuss **Using the Rubric to Study the Model.** (pp. 140–141)

Student Objectives
- Read a model cause-and-effect report.
- Use the cause-and-effect report rubric.
- Use the model cause-and-effect report to study Word Choice, Sentence Fluency, and Conventions.

Student Activities
- Review **"The Perils of Sleep Deprivation."** (p. 137)
- Use the rubric. (pp. 138–139)
- Read and discuss **Using the Rubric to Study the Model.** (pp. 142–143)

Day 4	Day 5
Write Draft	**Write** Revise: Organization

Student Objectives
- Complete a draft.

Student Activities
- Finish the draft. (p. 147)
- Participate in a peer conference.

Student Objectives
- Revise for the logical organization of ideas.

Student Activities
- Read and discuss **Revise: Focus on Organization.** (p. 148)

Day 4	Day 5
Write Publish: +Presentation	**Write** Publish: +Presentation

Student Objectives
- Discuss preparation for publishing and presentation.
- Use a final editing checklist to publish their work.

Student Activities
- Read and discuss **Publish: +Presentation.** (p. 154)
- Apply the publishing strategy.

Student Objectives
- Use a cause-and-effect report rubric.
- Share a published cause-and-effect report.

Student Activities
- Share their work.
- Use the rubric to reflect upon and evaluate the model and their own writing. (pp. 138–139, 155)

To complete the chapter in fewer days, combine the learning objectives and activities in a way that supports students as they write.

Resources at-a-Glance

Grammar, Usage & Mechanics

Differentiating Instruction

For additional Differentiating Instruction activities, see Strategies for Writers *Extensions Online at* **www.sfw.z-b.com.**

English Language Learners

Conferencing

Technology Tip

 Connection Letter
Reproducible letter (in English and Spanish) appears on the *Strategies for Writers* CD-ROM and at **www.sfw.z-b.com.**

Online Writing Center

Provides IWB resources, interactive games and practice activities, videos, eBooks, and a virtual file cabinet.

 Strategies for Writers Online
Go to **www.sfw.z-b.com** for free online resources for students and teachers.

Introduce
a Cause-and-Effect Report

Week 1 • Day 1

Student Objectives

- Review the elements of a cause-and-effect report. *(p. 134)*
- Consider purpose and audience. *(p. 135)*
- Learn the traits of informative/explanatory writing. *(p. 136)*

What's a Cause-and-Effect Report?

Help students understand that a cause-and-effect report deals with reasons (causes) that lead to specific results (effects). Discuss with students reasons they might need to write a cause-and-effect report. Ask whether they are ever curious about how and why certain things happen. Point out that anytime they explain in writing how and why things occur, they are using the cause-and-effect report genre.

What's in a Cause-and-Effect Report?

Read and discuss with students the four elements of a cause-and-effect report listed on page 134: Cause and Effect, Thesis Statement, Supporting Evidence, and Transition Words and Phrases. Then discuss specific reasons that each element may be important.

Strategies for Writers Online
Go to **www.sfw.z-b.com** for additional online resources for students and teachers.

What's a Cause-and-Effect Report?

It's a type of writing that deals with reasons (causes) that lead to specific results (effects). I think this kind of writing will be fun because I can pretend to be a detective who's looking for clues!

What's in a Cause-and-Effect Report?

Cause and Effect
These are the main reasons for the report. Every action, or cause, has a reaction, or effect. A cause-and-effect report focuses on cause-and-effect relationships.

Thesis Statement
This statement explains the main cause-and-effect relationship that the author wants to prove. A clear thesis statement can serve as the writer's starting point.

Supporting Evidence
Plenty of details should support the thesis statement in a cause-and-effect report. Details can include statistics, quotations, or real-life examples.

Transition Words and Phrases
Transition words and phrases connect important ideas in a cause-and-effect report. The writer often uses terms such as *because, if, so,* and *then* to let the reader know that one thing causes or results in another.

Informative/Explanatory Text Exemplars (Cause-and-Effect Report)

Levine, Ellen. *If You Lived with the Iroquois.* Scholastic, 1998. Get to know one of the most powerful and influential Indian nations through a book that explores the culture, daily life, and customs of the Iroquois League.

Tagliaferro, Linda. *How Does An Earthquake Become A Tsunami?* Heinemann-Raintree, 2009. Learn more about the causes of earthquakes, the characteristics of a tsunami, and how the two are related.

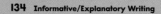

Why write a Cause-and-Effect Report?

There are plenty of reasons to write a cause-and-effect report. I listed some here, since I'm still thinking about why I want to write.

Make Connections
A cause-and-effect report tells readers about a connection they may not have known about. It breaks down an event, showing how it happened and connecting it to a specific cause.

Solve a Problem
A cause-and-effect report often answers the question "Why?" It also helps readers explore a problem and better understand it.

Entertain
A cause-and-effect report can be entertaining. Details can be lively and written in an upbeat tone. Think about some of the science shows you've seen on TV. Many of them explore cause-and-effect relationships in an exciting, interesting way, just like some reports.

Encourage Change
Sometimes it's hard to make a change until the causes and effects are explained. For example, if you want to put an end to a bad habit, you should first try to understand the causes and effects of your habit.

Why write a Cause-and-Effect Report?

Read and discuss with students the reasons for writing a cause-and-effect report listed on page 135. Point out that all writing has a purpose and is aimed at a specific audience. These authentic purposes help authors shape their writing. Someone writing to make connections may break down an event to show how it connects to a specific cause. A writer who is writing to solve a problem may help readers understand the problem better. A person who is writing to entertain may use a light and lively tone. Encourage students to share their own reasons for writing cause-and-effect reports. Are they writing to make connections, solve a problem, entertain, or encourage change? Ask them to discuss how these reasons will affect the tone and focus of their writing.

Bishop, Amanda and Walker, Vanessa. *Avalanche and Landslide Alert!* Crabtree Publishing Compnay, 2004. *Avalanche and Landslide Alert!* explores the causes of these natural disasters and effects they have on our environment and way of life. Vivid photographs help illustrate how devastating these occurrences can be.

Walker, Jane. *Famine, Drought, and Plagues.* Stargazer Books, 2004. Walker outlines the most common causes, effects, and consequences of famine, drought, and plague, as well as the role humans play in these natural disasters.

CCSS Common Core State Standards

SL.7.1: Engage effectively in a range of collaborative discussions (one-on-one, in groups, and teacher-led) with diverse partners on *grade 7 topics, texts, and issues,* building on each others' ideas and expressing their own clearly.

Introduce
a Cause-and-Effect Report

Linking Informative/ Explanatory Writing Traits to a Cause-and-Effect Report

Read page 136 aloud to help students understand that they will follow Emily as she models using the writing process and the informative/explanatory writing traits together. A good cause-and-effect report will be built around a clear, focused thesis with supporting details, appropriate transitions that connect ideas to show relationships, and domain-specific vocabulary. The report will use a voice and tone that are appropriate for the purpose and audience.

Online Writing Center

Provides six **interactive anchor papers** for each mode of writing.

Linking Informative/Explanatory Writing Traits to a **Cause-and-Effect Report**

In this chapter, you will write to explain how one thing causes another. This type of informative/explanatory writing is called a cause-and-effect report. Emily will guide you through the stages of the writing process: Prewrite, Draft, Revise, Edit, and Publish. In each stage, Emily will show you important writing strategies that are linked to the Informative/ Explanatory Writing Traits below.

Informative/Explanatory Writing Traits

 Ideas
- a clear, focused thesis
- relevant facts and concrete details that support and develop the thesis

 Organization
- a strong introduction, body, and conclusion
- paragraphs that have a topic sentence and supporting details
- appropriate and varied transitions that connect ideas and show relationships

 Voice
- appropriate voice and tone for the purpose and audience

 **Word Choice**
- precise language
- domain-specific vocabulary that is used correctly and explained as necessary

 Sentence Fluency
- clear sentences whose structure supports the purpose

 Conventions
- no or few errors in grammar, usage, mechanics, and spelling

Before you write, read Dennis Nilssen's cause-and-effect report on the next page. Then use the cause-and-effect report rubric on pages 138–139 to decide how well he did. (You might want to look back at What's in a Cause-and-Effect Report? on page 134, too!)

Informative/Explanatory Writing Traits in a Cause-and-Effect Report

 **Ideas** The writer builds the report around a clear, focused thesis. The thesis is supported by relevant facts and concrete details that anticipate the reader's questions.

 **Organization** The paragraphs in the report are organized by cause and effect, and the ideas are ordered logically.

 **Voice** To ensure that the reader is engaged throughout the cause-and-effect report, it's important to use the appropriate voice and tone. Using a formal style is the best way to achieve this in such a report.

The Perils of Sleep Deprivation

by Dennis Nilssen

How much sleep is enough? Experts agree that just about everyone needs eight hours a night. And how long do most people sleep? The average is fewer than seven hours. About one third of adults get fewer than six and a half hours per night. People may laugh off their sleep needs, saying that there aren't enough hours in the day to get everything done. But not getting enough sleep can harm a person's health and safety—as well as that of others—in many ways. — *Thesis Statement*

Have you ever heard the saying "A tired worker is only half a worker"? Everyone knows that sleepy workers can be a real problem in the workplace. They often get to work late. They don't contribute at meetings because they are too tired to pay attention. If they work with heavy equipment, they can easily injure themselves. If they are surgeons or pilots, they may botch surgeries or cause plane crashes. Consider the Chernobyl nuclear reactor accident and the Exxon Valdez oil spill. Both of these environmental catastrophes may have been the result of a worker not having enough sleep.

Transition Words and Phrases

Some doctors think that a constant lack of sleep can damage a person's health. There is no conclusive proof yet, but certain tests have shown that sleep deprivation can strongly change a person's metabolism (the biological process by which the body turns food into energy). Lack of sleep can alter the rate at which the body is able to re-energize and replenish itself. Sleep deprivation may even cause diabetes. In young people, it may also trigger conditions related to old age. Tests on sleep deprivation have also been done with laboratory rats. The results have shown that the less sleep an animal gets, the less able it is to ward off infections. The same may be true of humans.

Cause and Effect

Supporting Evidence

The most dangerous sleepy person, however, may be the sleepy driver. This is because nearly 100,000 traffic accidents per year are due, in part, to drowsy drivers. More than 1,500 passengers and drivers lose their lives each year in such accidents.

It is clear that lack of sleep results in all kinds of problems. If you are a six-hours-a-night person, do yourself a favor: Start going to bed and getting up at reasonable times. Your days will be much better!

Cause-and-Effect Report 137

Student Objectives

• Read a model cause-and-effect report. *(p. 137)*

Read the Model

Read "The Perils of Sleep Deprivation" aloud to the class. Ask students to listen for a thesis statement and concrete details and to notice how the details are organized. Also ask students to think about and discuss how a formal, serious style affected how they connected with the story. How were their reactions different from their peers?

Elements of a Cause-and-Effect Report

Have students refer to "What's in a Cause-and-Effect Report?" on page 134 as you refer to the model. Discuss the notes "written" on the model to enhance students' understanding of the terms.

Word Choice A skilled writer uses precise language and domain-specific vocabulary to make a report more believable. Jargon, if used, is correct and explained.

Sentence Fluency Transitions are used effectively in a good cause-and-effect report. Using a variety of transitions adds to a smooth sentence flow and better cohesion among ideas.

Conventions Correct use of punctuation, particularly commas and apostrophes, enhances the clarity of the writing in a cause-and-effect report.

CCSS **Common Core State Standards**

R/Inf.7.6: Determine an author's point of view or purpose in a text and analyze how the author distinguishes his or her position from that of others.

Analyze
the Model

Week 1 • Day 3

Student Objectives

• Learn to read a rubric.
  (pp. 138–139)

Use the Rubric

Explain the Rubric Explain that a rubric is a tool for planning, improving, and assessing a piece of writing. Tell students that a rubric helps a writer focus on key elements, or traits, in writing (**Ideas, Organization, Voice, Word Choice, Sentence Fluency, Conventions,** and **Presentation**).

Point out that column 6 describes a very good cause-and-effect report, one that has received the highest score in all categories. This is what students should strive for in their own writing.

Discuss the Rubric As students measure their own papers against the rubric, they should first decide whether the papers fall on the left of the rubric (use the trait well) or on the right (need improvement in using the trait). By examining their papers more closely, students can refine their scores for each trait to single numbers.

Online Writing Center

Provides a variety of **interactive rubrics,** including 4-, 5-, and 6-point models.

Rubric

Use this 6-point rubric to plan and evaluate a cause-and-effect report.

	6	5	4	
Ideas	The thesis statement is concise and clear. The writing provides relevant facts and concrete details that anticipate the reader's questions.	The thesis statement is clear. Many relevant facts and concrete details satisfy the reader's interest.	The thesis statement can be found easily. Several facts and concrete details help inform the reader.	
Organization	Paragraphs are organized by cause and effect. The ideas in each paragraph are ordered logically.	Paragraphs are organized by cause and effect. Most ideas are ordered logically.	Paragraphs are largely organized by cause and effect. Some ideas are out of logical order within paragraphs.	
Voice	The writer consistently uses a formal style.	The writer uses a formal style with very few breaks in style.	The writer uses a formal style in much of the essay.	
Word Choice	Jargon, if used, is correct and explained.	One or two jargon terms are not clearly explained.	Some jargon terms may be used incorrectly or not clearly explained.	
Sentence Fluency	Transitions are used effectively to vary sentence structure, resulting in smooth sentence flow and cohesion among ideas.	Transitions vary sentence structure, aiding sentence flow and cohesion among ideas in most of the essay.	Transitions are lacking or weak in a few places. Better transitions would improve flow and cohesion.	
Conventions	Correct use of commas and apostrophes enhances the clarity of the writing.	Commas and apostrophes appear in the writing with minor errors that are easily overlooked.	Noticeable errors with commas and apostrophes don't interfere with meaning.	
⁺ Presentation	The fonts are legible and limited in number.			

138   Informative/Explanatory Writing

CCSS **C**ommon **C**ore **S**tate **S**tandards
Cause-and-Effect Report

Strategies for Writers was designed and written to weave the Common Core State Standards throughout every unit. For Informative/Explanatory writing, the standards inform the unit's writing rubrics, objectives, and strategies.

The lessons for the cause-and effect report are based principally on the writing standards for Informative/Explanatory writing. The Ideas and Organization rubrics reflect standards **W.7.2, W.7.2.a,** and **W.7.2.b,** which address choosing, developing, and organizing a topic. In the cause-and-effect genre, the concept of organizing ideas and supporting them with concrete details translates easily to the focus of the report. Additionally, standard **W.7.2.e** addresses establishing a formal style, the central theme of the Voice rubric.

3	2	1	
The thesis statement is not clear. Some facts are unrelated to the thesis, and details are vague or lacking.	The thesis statement is present but hard to understand. The facts and details are vague and mostly unrelated.	No thesis statement is present. The essay reads like a random collection of vague details.	Ideas
Paragraphs are sometimes organized by cause and effect. The order of ideas within paragraphs is sometimes unclear.	Paragraphs are not organized by cause and effect. The order of ideas within paragraphs is hard to follow.	The writing is not organized into paragraphs. The order of ideas is impossible to follow.	Organization
The writer's style wavers between formal and informal.	The writer's style is mostly informal.	The writer's style is impossible to discern.	Voice
Some jargon terms are used incorrectly or not explained at all.	Several jargon terms are used incorrectly. Explanations are missing.	All jargon used in the report is incorrect, unexplained, or both.	Word Choice
Transitions are lacking or weak in several places, resulting in poor sentence flow and lack of cohesion.	Few transitions are used. Sentence flow is choppy, leading to confusion of ideas.	No transitions are used. Sentences are impossible to follow, and ideas are unconnected.	Sentence Fluency
Noticeable errors with commas and apostrophes make the reader slow down to read.	Frequent errors with commas and apostrophes force the reader to reread sections of the report.	Many serious errors with commas and apostrophes interfere with the meaning.	Conventions

See Appendix B for 4-, 5-, and 6-point informative/explanatory rubrics.

Apply the Rubric

Assign Groups Divide the class into six small groups to examine the model. Assign a trait to each group. One person in each group should be responsible for recording one or two strong examples of the assigned trait. Each group should then decide on a score for the trait. Students should not assume that any trait should receive a 6. Instead, encourage the groups to discuss their traits thoroughly before scoring them.

Reassemble Class Bring the class back together and ask one person from each group to report their findings to the class. The point of this exercise is not to score the model, but rather to practice identifying and evaluating the traits within a piece of writing.

Additional Rubrics Appendix B includes 4-, 5-, and 6-point rubrics that can be used with any piece of informative/explanatory writing. The rubrics are also available as blackline masters in the back of this Teacher Edition, beginning on page T543.

The Sentence Fluency and Word Choice rubrics are also drawn from the Informative/Explanatory standards. Standard **W.7.2.c** emphasizes the use of transitions to clarify relationships among ideas, the central theme of the Sentence Fluency rubric. The Word Choice rubric aligns with standard **W.7.2.d,** which focuses on using precise language and domain-specific vocabulary to explain the topic.

The language standards (**L.7.1** and **L.7.2**) are addressed, and there are multiple opportunities to address the speaking and listening standards. Most important, this chapter will help your students produce coherent writing (**W.7.4**), improve their writing (**W.7.5**), and use technologies to publish and present their finished pieces (**W.7.6**).

CCSS **Common Core State Standards**

SL.7.1.a: Come to discussions prepared, having read or researched material under study; explicitly draw on that preparation by referring to evidence on the topic, text, or issue to probe and reflect on ideas under discussion.

Analyze
the Model

Week 1 • Day 4

Student Objectives

- Read a model cause-and-effect report. (p. 137)
- Use the cause-and-effect report rubric. (pp. 138–139)
- Use the model cause-and-effect report to study Ideas, Organization, and Voice. (pp. 140–141)

Study the Model

Assess the Model Read aloud each section on pages 140–141. Discuss as a class whether students agree or disagree with each point in Emily's assessment of the report. Use questions such as the following to discuss the pages with students. Be sure students can back up their answers with concise examples from the report.

- Does Dennis Nilssen have a clear, concise thesis statement near the beginning of his report? (Possible response: Yes, the thesis sentence is clear and introduced in the first paragraph.)

- What organization does Dennis use? How well does it work? (Possible responses: Dennis organized his paragraphs by cause and effect. The ideas in each paragraph are ordered logically. The report is easy to follow.)

Strategies for Writers Online
Go to **www.sfw.z-b.com** for additional online resources for students and teachers.

TI40 *Informative/Explanatory Writing*

Using the Rubric to Study the Model

Cause-and-Effect Report

Did you notice that the model on page 137 points out some key elements of a cause-and-effect report? As he wrote "The Perils of Sleep Deprivation," Dennis Nilssen used these elements to help him describe the effects of a cause. He also used the 6-point rubric on pages 138–139 to plan, draft, revise, and edit the writing. A rubric is a great tool to evaluate writing during the writing process.

Now let's use the same rubric to score the model. To do this, we'll focus on each trait separately, starting with Ideas. We'll use the top descriptor for each trait (column 6), along with examples from the model, to help us understand how the traits work together. How would you score Dennis on each trait?

Ideas
- The thesis statement is concise and clear.
- The writing provides relevant facts and concrete details that anticipate the reader's questions.

Dennis clearly introduces his thesis statement in the very first paragraph. Then, in the following paragraphs, he answers readers' possible questions about why sleep deprivation is a problem. By the end, I had a strong understanding of why sleep is so important.

[from the writing model]

Some doctors think that a constant lack of sleep can damage a person's health. There is no conclusive proof yet, but certain tests have shown that sleep deprivation can strongly change a person's metabolism (the biological process by which the body turns food into energy).

140 *Informative/Explanatory Writing*

English Language Learners

BEGINNING
Cause and Effect Show a photo or a picture card of rain. Say *It is raining*, write the sentence on the board, and have students repeat. Do the same for *I wear a raincoat*. Write *cause* and *effect* next to the appropriate sentences on the board, read the words, and have students repeat. Explain *cause* is why something happens and *effect* is what happens as a result. Repeat for other examples.

INTERMEDIATE
Cause and Effect Write on the board *It is raining so I wear my raincoat*. Underline the cause with one color and the effect with another. Explain *cause* is an action and *effect* is a reaction, or what happens as a result. On strips of paper give students causes such as *I didn't study for my test; My mom makes cookies; My friend is moving*. Have students write an effect to complete the sentences and share with a partner.

Organization

- Paragraphs are organized by cause and effect.
- The ideas in each paragraph are ordered logically.

I like how Dennis introduces a cause and then lists some of the related effects. This method just makes sense to me and really helped me understand the information.

[from the writing model]

Everyone knows that sleepy workers can be a real problem in the workplace. They often get to work late. They don't contribute at meetings because they are too tired to pay attention.

Voice

- The writer consistently uses a formal style.

Dennis understands the possible severe consequences of too little sleep, and he wants his reader to understand, too. His style throughout his writing is formal, which helps get the message across.

[from the writing model]

Consider the Chernobyl nuclear reactor accident and the Exxon Valdez oil spill. Both of these environmental catastrophes may have been the result of a worker not having enough sleep.

- Does Dennis use a style and voice that are appropriate for the purpose and audience? (Possible response: Dennis uses a formal style to make sure he gets his ideas across to the reader.)

ADVANCED

Cause and Effect Write the following sentences on the board: *At night I brush my teeth, and then I go to bed; Lightning struck the tree, and then the tree fell down.* Explain that although one action follows another, it doesn't necessarily make it a cause-and-effect sentence. Read the sentences and ask students to determine which one is a cause-and-effect sentence. Have students write three sentences, two of which show cause and effect. Then have partners determine which are the cause-and-effect sentences.

ADVANCED HIGH

Cause and Effect Write on the board *It's raining so I wear my raincoat. I wear my raincoat because it's raining.* Explain that cause-and-effect sentences can be written in either order—cause/effect or effect/cause. Review other transition words and phrases, such as *as a result, due to,* and *therefore.*

CCSS Common Core State Standards

SL.7.1.b: Follow rules for collegial discussions, track progress toward specific goals and deadlines, and define individual roles as needed. **SL.7.1.c:** Pose questions that elicit elaboration and respond to others' questions and comments with relevant observations and ideas that bring the discussion back on topic as needed.

Analyze
the Model

Week 1 • Day 5

Student Objectives

- Read a model cause-and-effect report. *(p. 137)*
- Use the cause-and-effect report rubric. *(pp. 138–139)*
- Use the model cause-and-effect report to study Word Choice, Sentence Fluency, and Conventions. *(pp. 142–143)*

Continue Discussing the Model

Use questions such as the following to continue analyzing the model:

- Does Dennis clearly explain all jargon? Which terms does he explain? (Possible responses: It is helpful that Dennis explains metabolism right after he uses the term.)

- Which part of the model is especially smooth flowing? What makes the sentences flow? (Possible responses: the next-to-the-last paragraph; Dennis does a good job of using transitions to vary the sentence structures.)

- Does Dennis make correct use of commas and apostrophes? (Possible responses: Yes, Dennis uses commas to help separate several independent clauses in one sentence.)

 **Word Choice**

- Jargon, if used, is correct and explained.

I'm glad Dennis clearly explains all jargon right after using the difficult term. If I didn't know what the word meant, I wouldn't fully understand or enjoy his paper.

> [from the writing model]
>
> There is no conclusive proof yet, but certain tests have shown that sleep deprivation can strongly change a person's metabolism (the biological process by which the body turns food into energy). Lack of sleep can alter the rate at which the body is able to re-energize and replenish itself.

Sentence Fluency

- Transitions are used effectively to vary sentence structure, resulting in smooth sentence flow and cohesion among ideas.

Dennis does a great job of using transitions like *however* and *in part* to create sentence variety. His sentences flow together smoothly, and I can see how his ideas are connected. When ideas have cohesion, they fit together well.

> [from the writing model]
>
> The most dangerous sleepy person, however, may be the sleepy driver. This is because nearly 100,000 traffic accidents per year are due, in part, to drowsy drivers. More than 1,500 passengers and drivers lose their lives each year in such accidents.

Technology Tip
for 21st Century Literacies

When learning more about a topic for a report, keywords are critical to any online search. Divide students into small groups, assigning each a different search engine. Using a common, general keyword that you identify as a class, see what different findings result across the range of search engines. Then work together to narrow the keywords used. Talk with students about the implications of what you've learned and the choices they make when conducting an online search. Together create a bookmark, handout, or classroom poster of search guidelines they can refer to.

Strategies for Writers Online

Go to **www.sfw.z-b.com** for additional online resources for students and teachers.

Conventions

• Correct use of commas and apostrophes enhances the clarity of the writing.

Dennis uses commas and apostrophes correctly throughout his report. All contractions and possessive nouns are written accurately, and commas are used to help separate several independent clauses in one sentence.

[from the writing model]

People may laugh off their sleep needs, saying that there aren't enough hours in the day to get everything done. But not getting enough sleep can harm a person's health and safety—as well as that of others—in many ways.

✚**Presentation** The fonts are legible and limited in number.

My Turn!

I'm going to write a cause-and-effect report of my own. I'll follow the rubric and use good writing strategies. Read on to see how I do it!

Cause-and-Effect Report **143**

Differentiating Instruction

ENRICHMENT

Understand Cause-and-Effect Structures Discuss with students two possible structures for cause-and-effect reports: 1) a cause results in several effects; 2) a cause leads to an effect that becomes another cause. Then ask students to think of topics that fit these patterns.

REINFORCEMENT

Understand Cause-and-Effect Relationships Explain to students that one action preceding another does not necessarily mean it causes the other.

Presentation Point out to students that Presentation is equally as important as the other traits. Ask why Presentation is important. (Possible response: It can make a difference as to whether readers can, or even want, to read a piece of writing. It is also a reader's first impression of the writer.) Stress to students that neatness is always a priority. Text should be clearly handwritten in pen or typed, using only a few readable fonts. Remind students that paragraphs should be indented (use the tab key if typing), or space should be left between block paragraphs. Talk about how white space can be used to organize text. Good margins make the line lengths comfortable to read, and a centered title stands out on a page.

Think About the Traits Ask students which traits they think are most important in a cause-and-effect report. Students might say, for example, that in a cause-and-effect report, the trait of **Organization** is very important because if the causes and effects are not ordered logically, the report will not make sense. Others may think that **Voice** is more important because it establishes a formal style and tone which help get the writer's points across and help the reader understand that the writer is serious about the topic.

CCSS **C**ommon **C**ore **S**tate **S**tandards

SL.7.1.c: Pose questions that elicit elaboration and respond to others' questions and comments with relevant observations and ideas that bring the discussion back on topic as needed. **SL.7.1.d:** Acknowledge new information expressed by others and, when warranted, modify their own views.

Write
a Cause-and-Effect Report

Week 2 • Day 1

Student Objectives

• Read and understand a prewriting strategy. *(p. 144)*

Prewrite

Focus on Ideas

Collect Information Ask students to name things in their local environment that might direct them toward a writing topic. (Possible responses: too much/not enough sun; too much/not enough wooded land) Then point out Emily's notes on page 144. Explain that she will probably need more details about her topic as she starts to write. Encourage students to research their topics for interesting, accurate details. If they use the Internet, remind them to choose reliable, up-to-date websites. Talk about ways that writing can be organized, and tell them they will use a Cause-and-Effect Chain to help them organize the information they collect.

Online Writing Center

Provides **interactive graphic organizers** as well as a variety of graphic organizers in PDF format.

T144 Informative/Explanatory Writing

Prewrite   Focus on Ideas

The Rubric Says	The thesis statement is concise and clear.
Writing Strategy	Do research and take notes about a cause-effect relationship in nature.

Living near mountains can teach you a thing or two about high altitudes. There's less oxygen high up and you need to ascend a mountain gradually to allow your body to adjust. But what, exactly, *can* happen? To find the answer, I looked at science texts and websites that I knew were reliable and appropriate. I found three specific effects of altitude on humans. Here are my notes.

1. high altitude pulmonary edema (fluid in lungs)
- tightness in the chest, feeling of suffocation, cough
- skin may turn colors, thinking becomes unclear, may even die
- go down, seek medical help

2. high altitude cerebral edema (brain tissue swells, fluid leaks)
- loss of coordination, confused mental functions, could lead to death
- could happen after about a week at high altitude
- go down right away, get treatment

3. acute mountain sickness (pretty common)
- generally get it over 10,000 feet
- headaches, dizziness, shortness of breath, sometimes nausea
- usually feel better when adjusted to level of altitude

Apply

Select a natural event and do research on it. Then take notes.

144 Informative/Explanatory Writing

English Language Learners

BEGINNING/INTERMEDIATE

Logical Order Read a simple nonfiction text that shows a clear order of events such as the life cycle of a butterfly or frog. Draw a Flow Chart on the board. Have students tell the steps in order. Write them on the Flow Chart, and have students fill out their own Flow Charts. Have students cut apart the steps of their flow charts and put them in logical order. Check for the correct order.

ADVANCED/ADVANCED HIGH

Thesis Statement Give each student a language-level appropriate nonfiction text to read. Explain that a thesis statement states the main idea. Have students use a Main Idea Table and write the main idea and supporting details in the appropriate parts of their tables. Then have a partner follow along in the table as the first student rereads the article or text.

Prewrite

Focus on Organization

The Rubric Says	Paragraphs are organized by cause and effect.
Writing Strategy	Make a Cause-and-Effect Chain to organize the ideas.

The rubric says my paragraphs should be organized by cause and effect. The better organized my notes are, the easier it will be to write well-organized paragraphs. A Cause-and-Effect Chain is the perfect organizer for this task.

Writer's Term

Cause-and-Effect Chain
Sometimes one cause has several effects. An effect can also become a cause of another effect. When this happens, you can use a **Cause-and-Effect Chain** to show the causes of certain effects.

Cause-and-Effect Chain

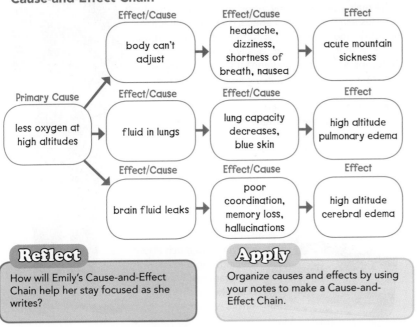

Reflect

How will Emily's Cause-and-Effect Chain help her stay focused as she writes?

Apply

Organize causes and effects by using your notes to make a Cause-and-Effect Chain.

Cause-and-Effect Report 145

Conferencing

PEER TO PEER When students have completed their Cause-and-Effect Chains, have pairs exchange their chains. Ask students to review each other's chains and comment on which areas might need more explanation.

PEER GROUPS Have students work in groups of three or four. Have each student take turns sharing his or her Cause-and-Effect Chain. Then have the other students in the group take turns offering suggestions to improve it by making connections or adding relevant facts and concrete details.

TEACHER-LED To demonstrate the importance of a focused Cause-and-Effect Chain, create your own chart on the board, leaving several areas blank. Discuss how the missing information might affect the writing of an effective report.

Write
a Cause-and-Effect Report

Week 2 • Day 2

Student Objectives

• Make a Cause-and-Effect Chain to organize ideas. *(p. 145)*

Prewrite

Focus on

Organize Ideas Explain that writers use a variety of organizers to get started writing. Emily used a Cause-and-Effect Chain to help her organize her notes. Help students understand that the better organized their notes are, the easier it will be to write well-organized paragraphs. Ask students to study the organizer; then ask how a Cause-and-Effect Chain can be an effective tool when writing a Cause-and-Effect Report. (Possible response: A Cause-and-Effect Chain helps you follow each cause and its corresponding effect.)

Writer's Term

Cause-and-Effect Chain
Sometimes one cause has several effects. An effect can also become a cause of another effect. When this happens, the writer can use a Cause-and-Effect Chain to show the causes of certain effects.

CCSS **Common Core State Standards**
W.7.2: Write informative/explanatory texts to examine a topic and convey ideas, concepts, and information through the selection, organization, and analysis of relevant content.

Write
a Cause-and-Effect Report

Week 2 • Day 3

Student Objectives

• Use a Cause-and-Effect Chain to begin writing. (p. 146)

Draft

Focus on Ideas

Draft a Cause-and-Effect Report
Read page 146 aloud. Reassure students that drafting gives them a chance to get ideas on paper without having to worry about making mistakes. They will have plenty of time to revise and edit their drafts. Then ask them to read Emily's draft on page 147. Have a volunteer read the thesis statement in the first paragraph. Encourage students to include their thesis statement in the first paragraph and to use their Cause-and-Effect Chain to draft the rest of their report.

Writer's Term

Thesis Statement A thesis statement briefly states the purpose or main idea of a report. In order to get an idea across in a cause-and-effect report, the writer should include a clear and concise thesis statement, usually in the first paragraph. This helps the audience understand the point.

Online Writing Center

 Provides student eBooks with an **interactive writing pad** for drafting, revising, editing, and publishing.

Draft

Focus on **Ideas**

The Rubric Says The thesis statement is concise and clear.

Writing Strategy Include a concise thesis statement that reflects the purpose for writing.

Writer's Term

Thesis Statement
The **thesis statement** briefly states the purpose or main idea of an essay or a report.

The main purpose of my report is to explain that high altitudes can have serious effects on health. I'll follow the rubric and write a thesis statement to get that idea across. A thesis statement usually comes in the first paragraph so that the audience understands the point the writer will be making. In a cause-and-effect report, the thesis statement focuses on the cause-and-effect relationship to be discussed.

I have a good thesis statement in mind, so now I'll use my Cause-and-Effect Chain to help me organize the rest of my report. I think it will be easiest to devote one paragraph to each of the three effects on the right-hand side of my graphic organizer. As I draft, I'll concentrate on getting my ideas down without worrying too much about spelling, capitalization, and grammar. I know that I can always check for errors when I edit.

146 Informative/Explanatory Writing

Differentiating Instruction

ENRICHMENT

Use an Organizer Have students discuss the various organizers they have used to help them focus as they write in their classes. (Examples may include: Problem-Solution Frames, K-W-L Charts, Main Idea Tables, etc.) Then invite them to create a prewriting guide of organizers as a resource to share in class.

REINFORCEMENT

Use the Rubric Some students may benefit from direct instruction to draft their cause-and-effect reports. Display the rubric on pages 138–139. Highlight the Organization trait. Point out to students that they should remember to use their Cause-and-Effect Chains to organize each paragraph of their reports.

[DRAFT]

What High Altitudes Can Do to You

When I was younger, my family vacationed in the mountains of Colorado. A few of us didn't feel well for the first several days, especially after a hiking trip. I knew there was less oxygen high up, but could that actually make us feel ill? After researching the topic, I've learned that high altitudes can have some pretty serious effects on people. ⟵ [concise thesis statement]

One effect is a condition called acute mountain sickness. Some people get sick with this when they hike up around 10,000 feet. The symptoms include headache, dizziness, shortness of breath, and sometimes, nausea. Talk about feeling miserable! Most of the time, hikers are able to continue climbing because they get used to the heights after a couple of days. And if they climb at a moderite pace, they are usually all right. But climbers have to be careful. If they climb too high too quickly, their conditions can get worse.

Reflect

Does Emily's thesis statement reflect her reason for writing?

Apply

It's time to start your draft. Be sure to include a brief thesis statement that explains your purpose.

Cause-and-Effect Report 147

Conferencing

PEER TO PEER Have pairs of students exchange and read their introductions. Instruct them to provide helpful comments to improve their thesis statements. Be sure the focus is not on mechanics at this time.

PEER GROUPS Have students form small groups of three or four. Tell them to take turns reading their introductions aloud. Have the other students in the group provide helpful commentary to strengthen the thesis statement.

TEACHER-LED Meet with one or two students at a time. Ask them to comment on how well they address the traits of Ideas and Organization in their drafts, based on an analysis of the first model. Make sure students use their organizers to build on a strong, clear thesis statement.

Write
a Cause-and-Effect Report

Week 2 • Day 4

Student Objectives
• Complete a draft. (p. 147)

Continue Drafting It is important that students are given ample time to draft their reports. As conferencing is important throughout the writing process, be sure to also set aside class time for peer-to-peer, peer group, or teacher-led conferences. Remind students that as they draft, their goal is to use their organizers to get their ideas down on paper. Assure them that they will have plenty of time to make changes and correct errors later. Use conferences to support them during the process.

As students complete their drafts, encourage short conferences between writing partners. The goal is to have readers respond to how well the writer conveys his or her purpose to the audience. Encourage them to list the strengths and the weaknesses on adhesive notes or scraps of paper. The notes should be returned with the drafts for the writers' use.

CCSS **C**ommon **C**ore **S**tate **S**tandards

W.7.5: With some guidance and support from peers and adults, develop and strengthen writing as needed by planning, revising, editing, rewriting, or trying a new approach, focusing on how well purpose and audience have been addressed. **SL.7.1:** Engage effectively in a range of collaborative discussions (one-on-one, in groups, and teacher-led) with diverse partners on *grade 7 topics, texts, and issues,* building on others' ideas and expressing their own clearly.

Write
a Cause-and-Effect Report

Week 2 • Day 5

Student Objectives

- Revise for the logical organization of ideas. *(p. 148)*

Revise

Focus on Organization

Reorder Ideas Direct students to page 148, and read the text aloud. Discuss the importance of making sure ideas are in a logical order. Have one volunteer read the draft excerpt without the revisions and another volunteer read the revised excerpt. Point out how much clearer Emily's writing is after she reordered some of the sentences. Explain to students that if readers cannot clearly understand the causes and effects, it will be difficult for them to follow the report.

Strategies for Writers Online

Go to **www.sfw.z-b.com** for additional online resources for students and teachers.

Revise
Focus on Organization

The Rubric Says	The ideas in each paragraph are ordered logically.
Writing Strategy	Make sure the ideas are in order.

I think I did a great job ordering the ideas in my paragraphs! I wrote a topic sentence for each paragraph, and then wrote several, logically ordered supporting sentences to follow. But now that I reread my draft, I see that the ideas in my conclusion need to be reordered to make more sense.

[DRAFT]

[reordered ideas]

People must be careful and observant when they're at heights that are unusual for them. But altitude sickness does not always cause serious problems.

Apply

Make sure your ideas are logically ordered in each paragraph.

English Language Learners

BEGINNING/INTERMEDIATE

Thesis Statement and Supporting Evidence Write the following paragraph on the board: *Breakfast is the most important meal of the day. It gives your body energy. It also helps you think and do better in school.* Ask students to tell the most important information in the paragraph. Underline the first sentence and tell students that it is the thesis statement. Write *thesis statement* under it. Tell students the other two sentences give more information about the thesis statement. They are the supporting evidence.

ADVANCED/ADVANCED HIGH

Transition Words Write *Breakfast is the most important meal of the day.* Create a cause-and-effect paragraph to support this thesis statement. Write it on the board but mix up the order of the sentences. Have students put the paragraph in order. Then review transition words that can be used to connect important ideas such as *because, so, if,* and *then.*

Revise

Focus on **Voice**

The Rubric Says The writer consistently uses a formal style.

Writing Strategy Maintain consistency in style and tone.

The rubric says I should be consistent in using a formal style. My writing style is created from the choices I make in using words, phrases, and sentence structures. My tone is the attitude I convey to the reader; it shows how I feel about the subject. My style choices set the tone of the essay.

Now that I think about it, using a formal style makes a lot of sense for this essay because I take altitude sickness very seriously. To make sure I'm using a formal style consistently to set the tone, I'll remove casual language and rewrite any sentences that are incomplete or incorrect.

[DRAFT]

The symptoms include headache, dizziness, shortness of breath, and sometimes, nausea. ~~Talk about feeling miserable!~~ Most of the time, hikers are able to continue climbing because they get used to the heights after a couple of days.

[deleted casual style]

Reflect

What do you think? How would the deleted sentence affect Emily's credibility if she had not removed it?

Apply

Use a serious style to keep your writing credible and strong.

Cause-and-Effect Report **149**

Conferencing

PEER TO PEER Have pairs of students exchange drafts. After reading the draft, each partner should offer helpful feedback on whether the writer's style and tone are consistent with the purpose and audience. Encourage students to work together to improve their voice throughout their reports.

PEER GROUPS Separate students into small groups. Have them take turns reading sections of their drafts aloud. Have the other students in each group comment on whether the writer has maintained an appropriate style and tone. Where consistency has not been maintained, have students suggest ways to improve the writer's credibility.

TEACHER-LED Meet with individual students to discuss their revisions for Voice.

Write
a Cause-and-Effect Report

Week 3 • Day 1

Student Objectives

- Revise for a formal style and tone. (p. 149)

Revise

Focus on

Maintain Consistency Explain to students the importance of connecting with the audience. Remind them that the best way to do this in a cause-and-effect report is to use a formal style and tone. Their writing style is created from the types of words and phrases they choose. The tone is the attitude they convey to the reader. It is important to maintain a formal style and tone in a cause-and-effect report because students want their readers to take the topic seriously. Using language that is too casual will make it difficult for readers to think seriously about the topic. The writer should maintain a consistent formal style and use a serious tone throughout the cause-and-effect report. This will keep the report strong and credible.

CCSS **Common Core State Standards**

W.7.2.e: Establish and maintain a formal style. **W.7.2.f:** Provide a concluding statement or section that follows from and supports the information or explanation presented.

Cause-and-Effect Report **T149**

Write
a Cause-and-Effect Report

Week 3 • Day 2

Student Objectives

• Revise for clearly explained terms and jargon. (p. 150)

Revise

Focus on Word Choice

Explain Jargon Read page 150 aloud. Remind students that good writers understand the importance of connecting with the audience. In a cause-and-effect report, some unfamiliar terms or jargon related to the topic may be required. If used, domain-specific vocabulary should be defined and explained. Tell students that they should first ask themselves whether any specialized terms are necessary for understanding the topic. Also, remind them that while jargon can be very helpful in writing, it should not be overused.

✏ Writer's Term_____

Jargon Jargon can be useful, time-saving shorthand for people within groups (profession, trade, sport, or hobby), but it is often meaningless to outsiders. Before using jargon, it is important that students understand their audience and remember to explain each unfamiliar term.

▶ Online Writing Center

Provides **interactive proofreading activities** for each genre.

Revise   Focus on Word Choice

The Rubric Says   Jargon, if used, is correct and explained.

Writing Strategy   Clearly explain unfamiliar terms and jargon.

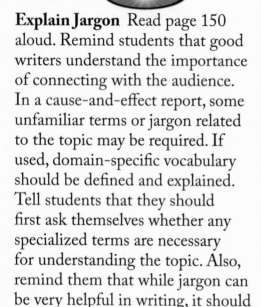

✏ Writer's Term_____

Jargon

Jargon is the language used by a group of people to describe their profession, trade, or hobby. One group (such as nurses or horseback riders) might not understand the jargon used by another group (such as athletes or skydivers). For this reason, whenever jargon is used, it should always be carefully explained.

I'm concerned that the reader will be unfamiliar with some of the words I've used in my report. The rubric says to make sure all jargon is clearly explained, so I'll reread my draft now, looking for words that need further clarification.

[DRAFT]

Finally, high altitude cerebral edema can occur after about a week spent at high altitude. Because the brain is affected, symptoms may include

[explained jargon] ──▶ High altitude cerebral edema is the name of a condition in which the brain's fluid begins to leak out, causing a swelling in brain tissue.

Apply

Make sure to explain all unfamiliar terms and jargon.

150 Informative/Explanatory Writing

Optional Revising Lessons

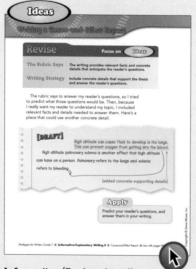

Informative/Explanatory II

Informative/Explanatory I2

Go to ▶ **Strategies for Writers Grade 7 CD-ROM**

Edit

Focus on Conventions

The Rubric Says	Correct use of commas and apostrophes enhances the clarity of the writing.
Writing Strategy	Check the use of commas and apostrophes.

✏️ Writer's Term

Apostrophes
Use an **apostrophe** to form singular and plural possessives. Also use an apostrophe to replace the missing letter(s) in a contraction.

I know that punctuation mistakes will confuse my reader and make reading my work difficult. I'll fix any errors with commas and apostrophes now.

[DRAFT]

[corrected a plural possessive]

decreases

[corrected a singular possessive]

As the lungs' capacity ~~decreeses~~, a persons' skin may turn blue. Other possible effects of lessened lung capacity are coughing and chest tightness, or a feeling of suffocation. If the edema isnt treated, a person can die from it. That's why it's important to descend from high altitude and get medical help at the first signs of edema.

[corrected a contraction]

Reflect

How do Emily's edits help her writing make more sense and flow better?

Apply Conventions

Edit your draft for spelling, punctuation, and capitalization, making sure apostrophes and commas are used correctly.

For more practice with apostrophes and commas, use the exercises on the next two pages.

Cause-and-Effect Report 151

Related Grammar Practice

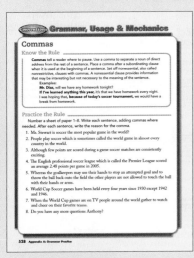

Student Edition page 528

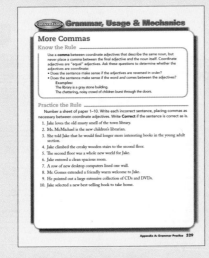

Student Edition page 529

Go to ➡ Appendix A: Grammar Practice

Student Objectives

- Edit for correct use of commas and apostrophes. (p. 151)

Edit

Focus on  Conventions

Edit for Accurate Punctuation
Remind students that this is the time to go back and correct mistakes in spelling, punctuation, grammar, and capitalization. Suggest that students read their drafts again, paying special attention to how they used commas and apostrophes. Remind students that computers have a spell-check option that can be very helpful; however, this function will not catch commonly misused words. Use the mini-lessons on pages T152–T153 for students having problems with using commas and apostrophes correctly. Then have students complete the exercises on pages 152 and 153. Go over their answers in class.

✏️ Writer's Term

Apostrophes Remind students to think carefully about placing the apostrophe in plural nouns. When using an apostrophe to form a contraction, always be sure to place the apostrophe in the exact spot where the letter has been removed.

CCSS Common Core State Standards
L.7.1: Demonstrate command of the conventions of standard English grammar and usage when writing or speaking.

Cause-and-Effect Report T151

Conventions

Mini-Lesson

Student Objectives

• Use apostrophes correctly. (p. 152)

Apostrophes

Have students review the Know the Rule box on page 152. Then write the following sentences on the board:

• *The cat chased its tail.*

• *The cat chased its' tail.*

• *The cat chased it's tail.*

Ask students what questions they need to ask themselves to determine which sentence is correct. (Possible responses: Is this a singular or plural possessive? Is this a contraction?) Then ask students which sentence is correct. (*The cat chased its tail.*)

Write the following on the board: *The boats dont move quickly upstream.* Then ask a volunteer to add the missing apostrophe. (*don't*) Finally ask why the apostrophe is needed. (The apostrophe forms a contraction by replacing the letter *o* in *not*.)

Remind students that it is important to use apostrophes correctly in their cause-and-effect reports. Otherwise, readers might have difficulty understanding the point of the report.

Online Writing Center

Provides **interactive grammar games** and **practice activities** in student eBook.

Apostrophes

Know the Rule

Apostrophes are used to form possessive nouns and contractions.

• Singular nouns and plural nouns not ending in *s* form the possessive by adding **'s**.
   Examples: friend (friend**'s**)   children (children**'s**)

• Singular nouns ending in *s* form the possessive by adding **'s**.
   Examples: James (James**'s**)   bus (bus**'s**)

• Plural nouns ending in *s* form the possessive by adding an apostrophe.
   Examples: trees (trees**'**)   buses (buses**'**)

• An apostrophe replaces the missing letter or letters in a contraction.
   Examples: do + not = don**'**t   I + would = I**'**d

• Use an apostrophe to form the contraction of *it is*, but do not use an apostrophe to form the possessive of *it*.
   Example: The cat hurt **its** paw, but **it's** going to be OK.

Practice the Rule

On a separate sheet of paper, rewrite the sentences using correct punctuation.

1. Its difficult to predict who will suffer from high altitude sickness.
2. Peoples reactions are different at different levels.
3. But youre probably going to get sick if you go too high too soon.
4. As altitude increases, the airs oxygen level decreases.
5. A persons body has to adjust.
6. The bodys response could be headache, nausea, or interrupted sleep.
7. Ive never had altitude sickness myself, but it doesnt sound like much fun at all.
8. Its a risk everyone takes if they want to climb mountains.
9. Its less likely youll get altitude sickness if you take time to let your body get used to higher elevations.
10. Climbers physical condition may also make a difference in whether theyll get sick.

Related Grammar Practice

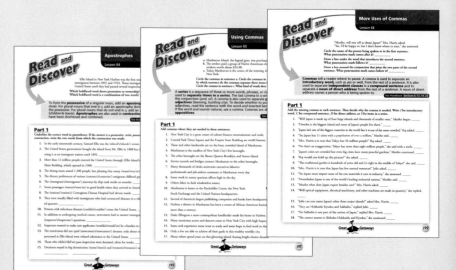

Pages 195, 197, 199

Go to ⟹ **G.U.M. Student Practice Book**

Commas

Know the Rule

Commas tell a reader where to pause. A comma is used to separate an **introductory word**, such as *yes* or *well*, from the rest of the sentence.
  Example: No, I don't think I'll be going out tonight.

A comma is also used to separate **independent clauses** in a compound sentence and to separate a **noun of direct address** from the rest of a sentence. A noun of direct address names a person who is being spoken to.
  Example: Every Tuesday night is pasta night at my house, and this week we've invited the neighbors over to share.

  Example: Jincy, would you like to study together after school?

Practice the Rule

Copy the following sentences onto a separate sheet of paper, adding commas where they are needed.

1. Doris, can you remember where you put your glasses?
2. Well, I certainly haven't seen them for days!
3. I know you need them for reading, but will you be all right driving home?
4. Oh, no, I think I see what happened to your glasses.
5. Yes, I do believe the dog has them and has chewed them quite thoroughly.
6. Oh, dear, I can see they're mostly intact, but can you actually use them?
7. These are your glasses, Doris, and they are in need of some serious repair!
8. It's kind of you to forgive me, but I insist on paying to have them fixed.
9. I know a good optical shop, but it won't be open until tomorrow morning.
10. Indeed, I'll be happy to bring your glasses there as soon as I can.

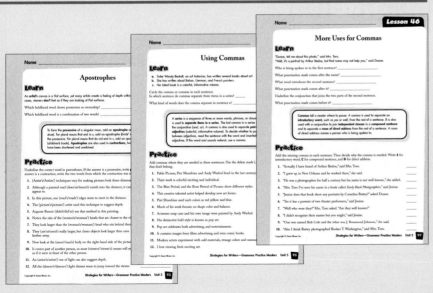

Pages 93, 95, 97

Go to ➡️ *Grammar Practice Masters*

Mini-Lesson

Student Objectives

• Use commas correctly. *(p. 153)*

Commas

Have students review the Know the Rule box on page 153. Then write the following sentences on the board, being sure to leave out the commas:

- *Alex would you please help me with my project?*
- *Yes I'd be happy to help you.*
- *I can help you tomorrow but it will have to be after school.*
- *I am grateful Alex for your willingness to help.*
- *Well I'm happy to do it for a friend!*

Ask volunteers to direct you where to place commas. (After: *Alex, Yes, tomorrow, grateful, Alex, Well*) Then ask students to identify how the commas are used in each sentence. (Direct address, introductory word, independent clause, direct address, introductory word) Remind students that commas tell a reader where to pause. It is important to use commas correctly in writing. Otherwise, readers can get confused and lose interest in the point the writer is trying to make.

CCSS Common Core State Standards
L.7.2: Demonstrate command of the conventions of standard English capitalization, punctuation, and spelling when writing.

Write
a Cause-and-Effect Report

Week 3 • Day 4

Student Objectives

- Discuss preparation for publishing and presentation. (p. 154)
- Use a final editing checklist to publish their work. (p. 154)

Publish +Presentation

Publishing Strategy Point out that Emily's choice is not the only option for publishing her work. Invite students to name other ways they could publish their own cause-and-effect reports. They might choose to compile their reports into a slideshow presentation and share it at a school function for parents and/or other teachers. Provide class time for students to plan and implement their presentation.

Have each student make a checklist and perform a final evaluation of his or her work before publishing it. Remind students that while typing their reports on a computer allows them to choose multiple fonts, they should remember to select only a couple of clear fonts. Otherwise, their report could seem less formal and serious.

Strategies for Writers Online
Go to **www.sfw.z-b.com** for additional online resources for students and teachers.

Publish +Presentation

Publishing Strategy	Submit my report to the school website.
Presentation Strategy	Use a limited number of clear fonts.

I'm finished with my cause-and-effect report, and I can't wait to publish it! I've decided to submit my paper to the school website. That means I'll have to type my paper on a computer. I like using a computer because it lets me keep good margins, and I love choosing cool fonts. But I'll be sure to use only one or two clear fonts to keep things readable. I'll choose one font for the title and one for the body of my paper. Before I submit it, I also need to check it one last time against my final checklist.

My Final Checklist

Did I—

✔ use apostrophes in contractions and possessives correctly?

✔ use commas correctly?

✔ use only a few clear fonts for my paper?

✔ correct all spelling, grammar, and punctuation mistakes?

Apply

Check your cause-and-effect report against this checklist. Then make a final copy to publish.

154 Informative/Explanatory Writing

Differentiating Instruction

ENRICHMENT
Write Across the Content Areas Explain to students that many other school subjects contain topics, issues, and events that students may want to write about. Encourage students to choose a topic and consult with their teachers for more ideas on writing in other content areas.

REINFORCEMENT
Use a Final Checklist Meet with a small group of students to discuss the checklist on page 154. Have students work together to perform a final edit. After editing, assist students in selecting one or two clear fonts to type their reports.

What High Altitudes Can Do to You

by Emily

When I was younger, my family vacationed in the mountains of Colorado. A few of us didn't feel well for the first several days, especially after a hiking trip. I knew there was less oxygen high up, but could that actually make us feel ill? After researching the topic, I've learned that high altitudes can have some pretty serious effects on people.

One effect is a condition called acute mountain sickness. Some people get sick with this when they hike up around 10,000 feet. The symptoms include headache, dizziness, shortness of breath, and sometimes, nausea. Most of the time, hikers are able to continue climbing because they get used to the heights after a couple of days. And if they climb at a moderate pace, they are usually all right. But climbers have to be careful. If they climb too high too quickly, their conditions can get worse.

High altitude pulmonary edema is another effect that high altitude can have on a person. *Pulmonary* refers to the lungs, and *edema* refers to bleeding. High altitude can cause fluid to develop in the lungs. This can prevent oxygen from getting into the blood. As the lungs' capacity decreases, a person's skin may turn blue. Other possible effects of lessened lung capacity are coughing and chest tightness, or a feeling of suffocation. If the edema isn't treated, a person can die from it. That's why it's important to descend from high altitude and get medical help at the first signs of edema.

Finally, high altitude cerebral edema can occur after about a week spent at high altitude. High altitude cerebral edema is the name of a condition in which the brain's fluid begins to leak out, causing a swelling in brain tissue. Because the brain is affected, symptoms may include poor coordination, memory loss, and hallucinations. Once these symptoms are noticed, sufferers should immediately descend and seek medical help. Otherwise, death is possible.

Altitude sickness does not always cause serious problems. But people must be careful and observant when they're at heights that are unusual for them.

Reflect

Did Emily use all the traits of a good cause-and-effect report? Check her writing against the rubric, and don't forget to use the rubric to check your own work, too.

Cause-and-Effect Report **155**

Technology Tip for 21st Century Literacies

Writers often use visual tools to help them develop their writing. As students work on their cause-and-effect reports; ask them to visually represent their argument to aid in creating balance. This also helps them manage the information with which they are working. Consider the merits of using a digital info-graphic tool to organize ideas, like those available on the ReadWriteThink website. Or build a similar mapping/sequencing tool using Google Forms or Docs. This exercise is as much about student writing as it is about using digital information.

See **www.sfw.z-b.com** for further information about and links to these websites and tools.

Write
a Cause-and-Effect Report

Week 3 • Day 5

Student Objectives

- Use a cause-and-effect report rubric. (*pp. 138–139*)
- Share a published cause-and-effect report. (*p. 155*)

Presentation Strategy Remind students of the importance of neatness when creating a final, polished copy of their work. Mention the numerous word processing options available on computers. Computers make it easy to set neat margins, indent paragraphs, and select clear fonts for creativity. Also remind students to use the header or footer function to label each page with the report title, the writer's name, and a page number.

Reflecting on a Cause-and-Effect Report

Have students reflect on the assignment as a whole. How did they feel about writing a cause-and-effect report? Do they understand the writing process better now that they have completed the assignment? Allow time for students to share their thoughts.

CCSS **C**ommon **C**ore **S**tate **S**tandards

W.7.4: Produce clear and coherent writing in which the development, organization, and style are appropriate to task, purpose, and audience. **W.7.6:** Use technology, including the Internet, to produce and publish writing and link to and cite sources as well as to interact and collaborate with others, including linking to and citing sources.

Research Report Planner

WEEK 1

Day 1
Introduce
a Research Report

Student Objectives
- Review the elements of a research report.
- Consider purpose and audience.
- Learn the traits of informative/explanatory writing.

Student Activities
- Read and discuss **What's in a Research Report? and Why Write a Research Report?** (pp. 156–157)
- Read **Linking Informative/Explanatory Writing Traits to a Research Report.** (p. 158)

Day 2
Analyze
Read a Research Report

Student Objectives
- Read a model research report.

Student Activities
- Read **"The Weight Problem in America."** (pp.159–161)

Day 3
Analyze
Introduce the Rubric

Student Objectives
- Learn to read a rubric.

Student Activities
- Review **"The Weight Problem in America."** (pp. 159–161)
- Read and discuss the **Research Report Rubric.** (pp. 162–163)

WEEK 2

Day 1
Write
Prewrite: Ideas

Student Objectives
- Read and understand a prewriting strategy.

Student Activities
- Read and discuss **Prewrite: Focus on Ideas.** (pp. 168–169)
- Apply the prewriting strategy.

Day 2
Write
Prewrite: Organization

Student Objectives
- Make an Outline to organize information.

Student Activities
- Read and discuss **Prewrite: Focus on Organization.** (pp. 170–171)
- Apply the prewriting strategy to create an Outline from note cards.
- Participate in a peer conference.

Day 3
Write
Draft: Organization

Student Objectives
- Use an Outline to begin writing.

Student Activities
- Read and discuss **Draft: Focus on Organization.** (p. 172)
- Apply the drafting strategy by using an Outline to write a draft.

WEEK 3

Day 1
Write
Revise: Word Choice

Student Objectives
- Revise to paraphrase borrowed information accurately.

Student Activities
- Read and discuss **Revise: Focus on Word Choice.** (pp. 178–179)
- Apply the revising strategy.

Day 2
Write
Revise: Sentence Fluency

Student Objectives
- Revise to create sentence variety by breaking up long, wordy sentences.

Student Activities
- Read and discuss **Revise: Focus on Sentence Fluency.** (p. 180)
- Apply the revising strategy.

Note: Optional Revising Lessons appear on the *Strategies for Writers* CD-ROM.

Day 3
Write
Edit: Conventions

Student Objectives
- Edit for correct use of conventions.

Student Activities
- Read and discuss **Edit: Focus on Conventions.** (p. 181)
- Reflect on the model draft.
- Apply the editing strategy.

Note: Teach the Conventions mini-lessons (pp. 182–183) if needed.

Day 4

Analyze
Ideas, Organization, and Voice

Student Objectives
- Read a model research report.
- Use the research report rubric.
- Use the model research report to study Ideas, Organization, and Voice.

Student Activities
- Review **"The Weight Problem in America."** *(pp. 159–161)*
- Read and discuss **Using the Rubric to Study the Model.** *(pp. 164–165)*

Day 5

Analyze
Word Choice, Sentence Fluency, and Conventions

Student Objectives
- Read a model research report.
- Use the research report rubric.
- Use the model research report to study Word Choice, Sentence Fluency, and Conventions.

Student Activities
- Review **"The Weight Problem in America."** *(pp.159–161)*
- Read and discuss **Using the Rubric to Study the Model.** *(pp. 166–167)*

Day 4

Write
Draft

Student Objectives
- Complete a draft.

Student Activities
- Finish the draft. *(pp. 173–175)*
- Participate in a peer conference.

Day 5

Write
Revise: Voice

Student Objectives
- Revise for a knowledgeable voice by adding quotes and information from experts.

Student Activities
- Read and discuss **Revise: Focus on Voice.** *(pp. 176–177)*
- Reflect on the model draft.
- Apply the revising strategy.

Day 4

Write
Publish: +Presentation

Student Objectives
- Discuss preparation for publishing and presentation.
- Use a final editing checklist to publish their work.

Student Activities
- Read and discuss **Publish: +Presentation.** *(p. 184)*
- Apply the publishing strategy.

Day 5

Write
Publish: +Presentation

Student Objectives
- Use a research report rubric.
- Share a published research report as part of a multimedia presentation.

Student Activities
- Share their work.
- Use the rubric to reflect upon and evaluate the model and their own writing. *(pp. 162–163, 185–187)*

To complete the chapter in fewer days, combine the learning objectives and activities in a way that supports students as they write.

Grammar, Usage & Mechanics

Proper Nouns/Adjectives,
  Abbreviations, and Initials . .T182
Titles T183
Grammar Practice T181–T183

Differentiating Instruction

Using the Rubric T167
Draft T172–T173
Revise. T179
Publish T184
For additional Differentiating Instruction activities, see Strategies for Writers Extensions Online at **www.sfw.z-b.com**.

English Language Learners

Using the Rubric T164–T165
Prewrite T168
Revise. T176–T177

Conferencing

Peer to Peer T170, T174, T178
Peer Groups. T170, T174, T178
Teacher-Led T170, T174, T178

Technology Tip

Using the Rubric T166
Publish. T185

 Connection Letter
Reproducible letter (in English and Spanish) appears on the *Strategies for Writers* CD-ROM and at **www.sfw.z-b.com**.

Online Writing Center

Provides IWB resources, interactive games and practice activities, videos, eBooks, and a virtual file cabinet.

 Strategies for Writers Online

Go to **www.sfw.z-b.com** for free online resources for students and teachers.

Introduce
a Research Report

Student Objectives

- Review the elements of a research report. *(p. 156)*
- Consider purpose and audience. *(p. 157)*
- Learn the traits of informative/ explanatory writing. *(p. 158)*

What's a Research Report?

Help students understand that a research report presents information that a writer discovers after asking questions, researching answers, and explaining discoveries about a specific topic. Discuss with students the reasons they might need to write research reports in various classes. Point out that the writer's task in writing a research report is to find answers to questions about a topic.

What's in a Research Report?

Read and discuss with students the four elements of a research report listed on page 156: Topic, Structure, Quotes, and Paraphrased Information. Explain that many of these elements are also common to other forms of writing. Then discuss specific reasons that each element may be important when writing a research report.

 Strategies for Writers Online
Go to **www.sfw.z-b.com** for additional online resources for students and teachers.

What's a **Research Report?**

A research report contains information that a writer discovers after asking questions, researching answers, and explaining discoveries about a specific topic. I like learning about new stuff, so I can't wait to get started!

What's in a **Research Report?**

Topic
A research report focuses on one main topic. When I write my report, I'll choose a topic that's interesting to me. Then, I can have fun while doing my research!

Structure
This is the way the report is organized. A good research report should include a strong introduction, body, and conclusion. It should also include a list of my sources.

Quotes
Concrete details from experts can add credibility to research writing. That's why it's important to include quotations in a research report.

Paraphrased Information
Writers paraphrase information when they use their own words to restate what someone else has said. It's important to paraphrase and give credit to my sources so that I can avoid plagiarism—stealing someone else's ideas or words.

Informative/Explanatory Text Exemplars (Research Report)

Murphy, Jim. *Blizzard! The Storm That Changed America.* Scholastic, 2000. On March 12, 1888, snow began gently falling on New York City. It had been a rather mild winter up until this point. As people went about their normal evening activities, they had little idea of the approximate 21 inches of snow that would come their way. Murphy takes you into the panic and devastation that resulted from the storm that changed America.

Murphy, Jim. *An American Plague.* Clarion, 2003. *An American Plague* is a riveting account of the Yellow Fever Epidemic of 1793. Murphy chronicles this epidemic from its beginning, introducing us to key characters who risked and, in some cases, sacrificed their lives to help bring an end to this devastating disease.

Why write a Research Report?

I don't know yet why I want to write a research report, but here are a few reasons I'm thinking about.

Learning About a Topic
Doing research is a way to find out more about a topic. I bet I'll learn a lot in the process of writing my research report.

Public Service
Sometimes a research report includes public service information that can help people. For example, I once read a report on severe weather conditions, and now I know how to stay safe during a storm.

Entertainment
A research report can be entertaining. For instance, it would be kind of fun to do research on how to join the circus!

Researching Sources
Writing a research report can help me learn how to judge sources. If I see the same information in several different sources, I can probably trust the authors. Then I can look for more sources written by the same authors.

Why write a Research Report?

Read and discuss with students the reasons for writing a research report listed on page 157. Point out that all writing has a purpose and is aimed at a specific audience. These authentic purposes help authors shape their writing. A writer who is writing to learn about a topic may focus on doing in-depth research. A person who is writing as a public service may include information that is helpful to others. Someone writing to entertain may select a fun, appealing topic. A person who is writing to judge sources will verify and present accurate information from many sources. Encourage students to think about their own reasons for writing research reports and how these reasons will affect the tone and focus of their writing.

Greenberg, Jan, and Sandra Jordan. *Vincent Van Gogh: Portrait of an Artist.* Random House, 2001. **CCSS** Vincent van Gogh was a passionate artist who pioneered new painting techniques and style. Although he never received fame or praise in his lifetime, today he is remembered as a brilliant and original artist.

Myers, Jack. *What Happened to the Mammoths? and Other Explorations of Science in Action.* Boyds Mills Press, 2000. Complete with detailed illustrations and a bibliography, *What Happened to the Mammoths?* is an engaging resource for investigating the possible cause of the extinction of the mammoths.

CCSS **C**ommon **C**ore **S**tate **S**tandards
SL.7.1.c: Pose questions that elicit elaboration and respond to others' questions and comments with relevant observations and ideas that bring the discussion back on topic as needed.

Introduce
a Research Report

Linking Informative/ Explanatory Writing Traits to a Research Report

Read page 158 aloud to help students understand that they will follow Emily as she models using the writing process and the informative/explanatory writing traits together. A good research paper will be built around a clearly defined topic with details from reliable sources; a strong introduction, body and conclusion; and borrowed ideas that are accurately paraphrased. It will use quotations and information from experts to create a knowledgeable and credible voice. Tell students they will read a model of how one writer used these traits to write a research report.

Linking Informative/Explanatory Writing Traits to a **Research Report**

In this chapter, you will write to inform your readers about an important topic. This type of informative/explanatory writing is called a research report. Emily will guide you through the stages of the writing process: Prewrite, Draft, Revise, Edit, and Publish. In each stage, Emily will show you important writing strategies that are linked to the Informative/Explanatory Writing Traits below.

Informative/Explanatory Writing Traits

 Ideas
- a clear, focused thesis
- relevant facts and concrete details that support and develop the thesis

 Organization
- a strong introduction, body, and conclusion
- paragraphs that have a topic sentence and supporting details
- appropriate and varied transitions that connect ideas and show relationships

 Voice
- appropriate voice and tone for the purpose and audience

 Word Choice
- precise language
- domain-specific vocabulary that is used correctly and explained as necessary

 Sentence Fluency
- clear sentences whose structure supports the purpose

Conventions
- no or few errors in grammar, usage, mechanics, and spelling

Before you write, read Isabel Sandoval's research report on the next three pages. Then use the research report rubric on pages 162–163 to decide how well she did. (You might want to look back at What's in a Research Report? on page 156, too!)

Informative/Explanatory Writing Traits in a Research Report

 **Ideas** The writer builds the report around a clearly defined topic. Relevant facts and concrete details from reliable sources enhance the ideas for the reader.

 **Organization** A strong introduction presents the topic, the body organizes information, and the concluding section (conclusion) supports the information presented. The information is organized in such a way that the reader can follow along easily.

 **Voice** Using quotations and information from experts is one good way to establish a writer's credibility in a research report.

The Weight Problem in America
by Isabel Sandoval

Structure: Introduction

Topic →

Next time you're in a crowd, take a look around you. If the crowd is typical, many people are probably heavier than they should be. Weight has become a real health concern in America. This paper will present several facts and discuss some of the causes of overweight Americans. It will also suggest possible ways to overcome this epidemic.

Are all overweight Americans unhealthy or unfit? No. Muscular people weigh more than others who look about the same size. This is because muscle is heavier than fat. Also, pregnant women weigh more than they normally do, but this doesn't mean they're unfit. And some people are naturally heavier than others, but again, this doesn't always mean they're unhealthy. However, many people are seriously overweight, and these are the ones at risk for health problems.

Here are some figures to think about: More than 97 million Americans are overweight. According to the American Obesity Association, about 39 million of these are obese, which means they are more than 30 pounds overweight. Obesity is the cause of some 300,000 deaths in this country every year. It is also a risk factor in many ailments, including heart disease, arthritis, diabetes, high cholesterol, and cancer.

Quotes →

Obesity is not unknown in other countries; however, it is a much bigger problem in the United States. Consider Sam Moore, who moved here from Sierra Leone in 1998. His story is fairly common: "When I first came," Sam told writer Lawrence Lindner, "I was around 165 [pounds]. Now I'm looking at close to 200. It creeps up on you" (T11). Sam is 5 foot 9 inches tall. He should definitely be concerned about letting two hundred pounds "creep up" on him.

Other immigrants report similar weight gain. Some of them were asked to think why this has happened. Many pointed out the size of restaurant portions. Over and over, they talked about the size of meals served in American restaurants. One woman commented on a huge salad and an enormous dish of pasta that she was served for dinner. She noted that even her 6-foot 5-inch boyfriend couldn't have eaten it all. Yet the meal is a typical size for a dinner in an American restaurant.

Structure: Body

Word Choice Borrowing ideas from knowledgeable sources is an important aspect of writing a research report. However, it is important that the writer's words are distinct from the ideas of others.

Sentence Fluency A variety of sentence structures are used effectively in a good research report. Using different sentence structures gives the writing rhythm and flow.

Conventions Correct use of punctuation, particularly capitalization, enhances the clarity of the writing in a research report.

Analyze
the Model

Week 1 • Day 2

Student Objectives

• Read a model research report. (pp. 159–161)

Read the Model

Read "The Weight Problem in America" aloud to the class. Ask students to listen for a clear topic supported by concrete details and relevant facts. They should also notice how the details are organized. Also ask students to think about and discuss how a knowledgeable and credible voice affected the way they connected to the report. How were their reactions different from their peers?

Elements of a Research Report

Have students refer to What's in a Research Report? on page 156 as you refer to the model. Discuss the notes "written" on the model to enhance students' understanding.

CCSS Common Core State Standards
R/Inf.7.1: Cite several pieces of textual evidence to support analysis of what the text says explicitly as well as inferences drawn from the text.

The amount that Americans eat is only part of the problem. Another problem is the kind of food eaten. In China, a meal might consist of a low-calorie clear soup containing several vegetables. This would satisfy a person's hunger because of the high fiber and water content. But compare this meal with the all-too-common American dinner consisting of a cheeseburger, French fries, and a soft drink. A large portion of each would total about an 1800-calorie meal. Yet, fast food restaurants now account for about 40 percent of the average American family's food budget.

Besides eating large, unhealthy portions, Americans also like to snack, and it's no surprise that many of these popular snacks are high in fat and calories. For example, a 4-ounce bag of cheese puffs or potato chips contains about 640 calories, and a piece of cheesecake has about 470 calories. By contrast, an apple or a pear has fewer than 90 calories.

Another important part of the American weight problem is Americans' lack of exercise. In 1991, nearly half of our schools had daily physical education classes. By 1997, this number decreased to 27 percent. Also, many students watch TV or play video games after school instead of participating in afterschool sports. In a recent study by the Centers for Disease Control, only 28 percent of overweight adults who tried to exercise actually did so enough to make a difference. And many overweight adults do not exercise at all.

⤷ Paraphrased Information

So what can we do? Well, here's one good piece of advice: Get a better understanding of what is an appropriate portion. In spite of what restaurants serve, the average eater doesn't need a serving-bowl portion of pasta. Nor should he or she return from the salad bar carrying a plate of nachos in addition to (or in place of) a real salad. Some researchers consider portion control the biggest help in losing weight.

Strategies for Writers Online
Go to **www.sfw.z-b.com** for additional online resources for students and teachers.

Also, if you are going to snack, snack sensibly. Read the labels on snack-food packages to see how many calories are in each serving, and beware of packages that don't give this information. Also, remember that unpackaged foods such as fruits and vegetables are the healthiest snacks of all.

Finally, exercise should be an important part of any plan to lose weight. The typical overweight adult should exercise 30 minutes a day, 5 days a week. However, if this schedule is impossible to keep, try to exercise at least three days a week instead.

Obesity is a serious problem in America, and it's not going to disappear anytime soon. However, people can make real progress by following the advice in this report. After all, slimming down and becoming more fit are healthier, happier life choices.

Structure: Conclusion

Works Consulted

Bowser, Betty Ann. "Obese Children." *PBS* 1 May 2001, accessed October 20, 2012, http://www.pbs.org/newshour/bb/health/jan-june01/obesekids_05-01.html.

Goff, Karen Goldberg. "Big, Bigger, SUPERBIG." *Insight on the News* 25 Sept. 2000: 22.

Jibrin, Janis. *The Unofficial Guide to Dieting Safely.* New York: Macmillan, 1998.

Lindner, Lawrence. "It's a Big Country: When People Move to the U.S., They Get Fat. What Does This Tell Us About How We Eat?" *The Washington Post* 27 Mar. 2001: T11.

What Is Obesity? 2 May 2005. American Obesity Association, accessed October 20, 2012, http://www.obesity.org.

Structure: Sources Listed

CCSS **Common Core State Standards**

R/Inf.7.1: Cite several pieces of textual evidence to support analysis of what the text says explicitly as well as inferences drawn from the text.

Analyze
the Model

Student Objectives

- Learn to read a rubric. *(pp. 162–163)*

Use the Rubric

Explain the Rubric Explain that a rubric is a tool for planning, improving, and assessing a piece of writing. Tell students that a rubric helps a writer focus on key elements, or traits, in writing (**Ideas, Organization, Voice, Word Choice, Sentence Fluency, Conventions,** and **Presentation**).

Point out that column 6 describes a very good research report, one that has received the highest score in all categories. This is what students should strive for in their own writing.

Discuss the Rubric As students measure their own papers against the rubric, they should first decide whether the papers fall on the left of the rubric (use the trait well) or on the right (need improvement in using the trait). By examining their papers more closely, students can refine their scores for each trait to single numbers.

Online Writing Center

 Provides a variety of **interactive rubrics,** including 4-, 5-, and 6-point models.

Rubric

Use this 6-point rubric to score and evaluate a research report.

	6	5	4
Ideas	The topic is clearly defined. Relevant facts and concrete details from reliable sources enhance the ideas.	The topic is clear. Support from reliable sources is accurate and relevant.	The topic is clear. More concrete, relevant information would enhance the writing.
Organization	A strong introduction presents the topic, the body organizes information, and the concluding section (conclusion) supports the information presented.	An introduction, body, and conclusion are present and well defined.	The introduction and conclusion are adequate, and the reader can follow the organization of the body.
Voice	Quotations and information from experts help make the voice sound knowledgeable and credible.	The writer's voice is informed and believable. Several quotations enhance the writer's credibility.	The writer's voice is sometimes weak. A few quotations by experts are used.
Word Choice	Borrowed ideas are accurately paraphrased. The writer's words are distinct from the ideas of others.	Borrowed ideas are paraphrased. Ideas from other sources are clearly defined.	Borrowed ideas are sometimes paraphrased incorrectly or are not distinguished from the writer's words.
Sentence Fluency	A variety of sentence structures gives the writing rhythm and flow.	Sufficiently varied sentence structures give the writing rhythm and flow.	Several sentences could be combined, lengthened, or shortened to improve rhythm and flow.
Conventions	Capitalization is used correctly throughout the report.	Minor errors in capitalization are easily overlooked.	Noticeable errors in capitalization do not get in the way of the message.
+ Presentation	Each page of the report is clearly labeled.		

CCSS Common Core State Standards

Research Report

The lessons for research report are based principally on the writing standards for Informative/Explanatory writing. The Organization and Ideas rubrics reflect standards **W.7.2, W.7.2.a,** and **W.7.2.f,** which address defining and introducing the topic as well as providing a concluding statement that follows from the topic. In the research report genre, the concept of organizing ideas and providing a concluding statement translates easily to the focus of the report. Additionally, standard **W.7.2.b** addresses developing the topic with relevant quotations and other examples. This coincides with the Voice rubric, which stresses the use of quotations and information from experts to make the voice sound knowledgeable and credible.

The Sentence Fluency and Word Choice rubrics are also drawn from the Informative/Explanatory standards. Standard

3	2	1	
The topic can be identified. General details fill the writing, and facts are lacking.	The writer's topic is not clear. Few facts are provided, and the sources may not be reliable.	Topic is missing from the writing. No facts are provided.	**Ideas**
The body is poorly organized in places. The introduction and conclusion are present but both need work.	The report is not organized. The introduction or conclusion may be missing.	The writing is a random list of facts. There is no introduction or conclusion.	**Organization**
The writer's voice is inconsistent and lacks confidence. Quotations are few or they are unrelated to the topic.	The voice is weak or absent. Quotations, if used, are unrelated to the topic and do not build credibility.	The voice is difficult to identify. No quotations are used.	**Voice**
Several paraphrases are inaccurate or quote the original too closely. The writer's ideas are hard to tell from those of others.	Paraphrases are not correct or direct quotes from the original. They are not distinguished from the writer's ideas.	The writer does not attempt to paraphrase borrowed ideas.	**Word Choice**
Most sentences share the same structure. The rhythm is predictable.	Sentences are not varied. Several are very long and hard to follow (or very short and choppy).	Many sentences are incomplete. Ideas are hard to grasp.	**Sentence Fluency**
Several noticeable errors in capitalization confuse the reader.	Frequent errors in capitalization get in the way of the message.	Many serious errors in capitalization make the writing difficult to read.	**Conventions**

See Appendix B for 4-, 5-, and 6-point informative/explanatory rubrics.

Apply the Rubric

Assign Groups Divide the class into six small groups to examine the model. Assign a trait to each group. One person in each group should be responsible for recording one or two strong examples of the assigned trait. Each group should then decide on a score for the trait. Students should not assume that any trait should receive a 6. Instead, encourage the groups to discuss their traits thoroughly before scoring them.

Reassemble Class Bring the class back together and ask one person from each group to report the group's findings to the class. The point of this exercise is not to score the model, but rather to practice identifying and evaluating the traits within a piece of writing.

Additional Rubrics Appendix B includes 4-, 5-, and 6-point rubrics that can be used with any piece of informative/explanatory writing. The rubrics are also available as blackline masters in the back of this Teacher's Edition, beginning on page T543.

W.7.8 emphasizes gathering relevant information from multiple sources and paraphrasing to avoid plagiarism. This standard aligns with the Word Choice rubric. The Sentence Fluency rubric emphasizes the use of a variety of sentence structures to give the report rhythm and flow, as addressed by standard **W.7.2.c**.

The language standards (**L.7.1** and **L.7.2**) are addressed during editing and skills practice. In addition, there are multiple opportunities to address the speaking and listening standards during the writing process. Most important, this chapter will help your students produce coherent writing (**W.7.4**), improve their writing (**W.7.5**), and use technologies to publish and present their finished pieces (**W.7.6**).

CCSS **Common Core State Standards**
SL.7.1.b: Follow rules for collegial discussions, track progress toward specific goals and deadlines, and define individual roles as needed.

Analyze
the Model

Week 1 • Day 4

Student Objectives

- Read a model research report. *(pp. 159–161)*
- Use the research report rubric. *(pp. 162–163)*
- Use the model research report to study Ideas, Organization, and Voice. *(pp. 164–165)*

Study the Model

Assess the Model Have volunteers read aloud each section on pages 164–165. Discuss as a class whether students agree or disagree with each point in Emily's assessment of the report. Use questions such as the following to discuss the pages with students. Be sure students can back up their answers with concise examples from the report.

- Does Isabel Sandoval have a clearly defined topic? (Possible response: Yes, the topic is clearly defined in the introduction.)

- What organization does Isabel use? How well does it work? (Possible responses: Isabel organized her paragraphs with a strong introduction, body, and conclusion. The structure works well and supports the information presented.)

 Strategies for Writers Online
Go to **www.sfw.z-b.com** for additional online resources for students and teachers.

Research Report
Using the Rubric to Study the Model

Did you notice that the model on pages 159–161 points out some key elements of a research report? As she wrote "The Weight Problem in America," Isabel Sandoval used these elements to help her inform her readers. She also used the 6-point rubric on pages 162–163 to plan, draft, revise, and edit the writing. A rubric is a great tool to evaluate writing during the writing process.

Now let's use the same rubric to score the model. To do this, we'll focus on each trait separately, starting with Ideas. We'll use the top descriptor for each trait (column 6), along with examples from the model, to help us understand how the traits work together. How would you score Isabel on each trait?

> ### Ideas
> - The topic is clearly defined.
> - Relevant facts and concrete details from reliable sources enhance the ideas.
>
> By clearly stating the topic early on, Isabel helped me focus as I read her report. I learned so much from the many concrete facts she includes. I never knew weight was such a problem here in the United States.
>
> [from the writing model]
> Weight has become a real health concern in America.
>
> [from the writing model]
> More than 97 million Americans are overweight. According to the American Obesity Association, about 39 million of these are obese, which means they are more than 30 pounds overweight.

164   Informative/Explanatory Writing

English Language Learners

BEGINNING

Topic Write the following sentence on the board: *A cat is from the feline family.* Ask, *What is this sentence about?* Tell students that cat is the topic of the sentence. Say *topic*, write it on the board, and have students repeat. Repeat the activity and have students determine the topic of several other sentences.

INTERMEDIATE

Topic Explain that a topic is what a report is about. Write a topic sentence on the board. Give students strips of paper with sentences that may or may not go with this topic sentence. Students read the sentence to the class and tell whether it should be included in the paragraph. Using the correct sentences, write a paragraph on the board that goes with the topic sentence.

- A strong introduction presents the topic, the body organizes information, and the concluding section (conclusion) supports the information presented.

Isabel's report is so well organized. I moved easily from the introduction, through the body, and to the strong ending. I like how she explained, in her opening paragraph, the different areas to be discussed in the report. I think I'll do the same in mine.

[from the writing model]

This paper will present several facts and discuss some of the causes of overweight Americans. It will also suggest possible ways to overcome this epidemic.

- Quotations and information from experts help make the voice sound knowledgeable and credible.

I learned so much from Isabel's report! She included many solid, interesting facts, and she used expert sources to back up her claims. Without those facts and sources her paper would read more like an opinion, and much of the impact would have been lost.

[from the writing model]

In a recent study by the Centers for Disease Control, only 28 percent of overweight adults who tried to exercise actually did so enough to make a difference. And many overweight adults do not exercise at all.

- Does Isabel use a style and voice that are appropriate for the purpose and audience? (Possible response: Isabel uses quotations and information from experts to make the voice sound knowledgeable and credible.)

ADVANCED
Paraphrasing Read a language-level appropriate newspaper article. Cut up the article and give students different sections. Have students write a paraphrase of their portion of the article. Then have a volunteer read the paraphrased article to class.

ADVANCED HIGH
Paraphrasing Have two students read the same short newspaper article. Separately, have them rewrite the article in their own words. Have students compare paraphrases and decide which one was most appropriate. Discuss as a group.

CCSS Common Core State Standards

SL.7.1.b: Follow rules for collegial discussions, track progress toward specific goals and deadlines, and define individual roles as needed. **SL.7.1.c:** Pose questions that elicit elaboration and respond to others' questions and comments with relevant observations and ideas that bring the discussion back on topic as needed.

Analyze
the Model

Week 1 • Day 5

Student Objectives

- Read a model research report. (pp. 159–161)
- Use the research report rubric. (pp. 162–163)
- Use the model research report to study Word Choice, Sentence Fluency, and Conventions. (pp. 166–167)

Continue Discussing the Traits

Use questions such as the following to continue to analyze the model:

- Does Isabel accurately paraphrase borrowed ideas to make her words distinct? (Possible responses: Isabel does a good job of rewording information in her own words. She is careful to document where she gathered her ideas.)

- What helps give Isabel's writing rhythm and flow? (Possible response: Isabel uses a variety of sentence structures and a mixture of sentence lengths and types.)

- Does Isabel make correct use of capitalization? (Possible response: Yes, Isabel capitalizes all proper nouns, proper adjectives, abbreviations, and initials.)

- Borrowed ideas are accurately paraphrased.
- The writer's words are distinct from the ideas of others.

Even though Isabel gathered her information from the American Obesity Association's website, she does a great job reworking that information into her own words. But she's careful to properly document where she gathered her facts.

[from the writing model]

> The amount that Americans eat is only part of the problem. Another problem is the kind of food eaten. In China, a meal might consist of a low-calorie clear soup containing several vegetables. This would satisfy a person's hunger because of the high fiber and water content.

- A variety of sentence structures gives the writing rhythm and flow.

Isabel's writing is energetic and flows well. She uses a mixture of sentence lengths and types to keep things lively and easy to read.

[from the writing model]

> So what can we do? Well, here's one good piece of advice: Get a better understanding of what is an appropriate portion. In spite of what restaurants serve, the average eater doesn't need a serving-bowl portion of pasta.

166 Informative/Explanatory Writing

Technology Tip for 21st Century Literacies

As much as our students might appear to know what they are doing when searching for online information, take time to discuss and evaluate sites together. The RADCAB model moves students through the steps of considering a website's **r**elevance, **a**ppropriateness, **d**etail, **c**urrency, **a**uthority, and **b**ias. Unpack each of these steps over the course of multiple tasks, as each is spelled out in kid-friendly language but requires some smart thinking for readers to internalize and apply. Where the site includes rubrics, you could also work with students to co-construct one appropriate for your class.

See **www.sfw.z-b.com** for further information about and links to these websites and tools.

Strategies for Writers Online

Go to **www.sfw.z-b.com** for additional online resources for students and teachers.

Conventions
- Capitalization is used correctly throughout the report.

I checked Isabel's spelling, grammar, punctuation, and capitalization, and it looks like she didn't make any mistakes in her writing. She does a really good job with capitalizing proper nouns, proper adjectives, abbreviations, and initials. Take a look at the example here.

[from the writing model]

Obesity is not unknown in other countries; however, it is a much bigger problem in the United States. Consider Sam Moore, who moved here from Sierra Leone in 1998. His story is fairly common: "When I first came," Sam told writer Lawrence Lindner, "I was around 165 [pounds]. Now I'm looking at close to 200. It creeps up on you" (T11).

+Presentation Each page of the report is clearly labeled.

My Turn!
I'm going to write my own research report. Follow along to see how I use the rubric to help me practice good writing strategies. Wish me luck!

Differentiating Instruction

ENRICHMENT
Determine Objectivity Versus Subjectivity Discuss with students the importance of being objective rather than subjective when writing a research report. Explain that *subjectivity* refers to personal feelings, beliefs, and opinions. *Objectivity* refers to facts, knowledge, and evidence. In order for writing to be objective, adjectives such as *wonderful, best,* and *incredible* should be avoided. Ask students to brainstorm a list of words that suggest subjectivity and another list of words that suggest objectivity.

REINFORCEMENT
Formatting on the Computer For students with limited experience in using a computer, arrange time in the computer lab or with a mentor who can show them how to access the formatting features.

Presentation Point out to students that Presentation is equally as important as the other traits. Discuss and elicit responses as to why presentation is important. (Possible responses: It can make a difference as to whether readers can or even want to read a piece of writing. It is also a reader's first impression of the writer.) Stress to students that neatness should always be a priority. Also, remind them to clearly label each page of the report with both their name and the page number. Ask them why labeling might be particularly important for a research report. (Possible response: It can help eliminate any chance of confusion, especially when students are planning to insert a video clip with the text.) Show them how to use a computer to create a header or footer to keep the report organized.

Think About the Traits All traits are important, but ask students which ones stand out in a research report. Students might say, for example, that in a research report **Organization** is very important because if the report does not contain a strong introduction, body, and conclusion, the reader may find it difficult or impossible to follow the writer's ideas. Others may think that **Word Choice** is more important because in a research report it is especially important that a writer avoid plagiarism by quoting or paraphrasing borrowed ideas and citing the sources.

CCSS Common Core State Standards
SL.7.1.d: Acknowledge new information expressed by others and, when warranted, modify their own views.

Write
a Research Report

Week 2 • Day 1

Student Objectives

• Read and understand a prewriting strategy. *(pp. 168–169)*

Prewrite

Focus on Ideas

Collect Information Ask students to think about interesting issues that might direct them toward a writing topic. (Possible responses: how to stay safe in storms such as tornadoes or hurricanes; how cell phone and/or computer technology has changed communications; how different forms of energy affect the environment, etc.) Tell students that after choosing topics, they will have to do research to gather information. If they use the Internet, remind them to choose reliable sources with up-to-date information on their topics. Finally, point out that writing can be organized in many ways. One way is to show what you already know, what you want to know, and the sources where you might find your answers. A K-W-S Chart can help writers organize information in this way. Note Cards help writers keep track of questions, answers, and sources to record on a K-W-S Chart.

 Strategies for Writers Online
Go to **www.sfw.z-b.com** for additional online resources for students and teachers.

Prewrite

Focus on ⟨ Ideas ⟩

The Rubric Says	The topic is clearly defined.
Writing Strategy	Choose a topic and make a K-W-S Chart to gather research. Then make note cards.

Writer's Term__

K-W-S Chart
A **K-W-S Chart** organizes the things you already know, the things you want to know, and the sources you used to answer your research questions.

I like to hike in the woods with my dad, so I'm pretty familiar with plants that grow in the wild. But I've always wondered what kinds of medicines come from these plants. So when my teacher said I'd be writing a research report, I already had my topic chosen. Then I made a K-W-S Chart.

K-W-S Chart

What I Know	What I Want to Know	Sources to Answer My Questions
Many medicines are derived from plants.	How many?	Bierer, Carlson, King article
Quinine and digitalis are well-known medicines from plants.	How were these discovered? What are they used for?	Sumner book
Old tribal remedies are sometimes sources of medicines.	What are some examples?	Cox article
Tropical rain forests are home to many medicinal plants.	Why do so many grow there?	Bierer, Carlson, King article

168 Informative/Explanatory Writing

English Language Learners

BEGINNING/INTERMEDIATE

Quotation Marks Explain that we use quotation marks to separate dialogue in text. Ask a student, *What do you like to eat?* On the board, write *The teacher asked What do you like to eat?* Show students the correct placement of the comma and quotation marks. Then write a student's answer in this way: *The student said I like to eat pizza.* Have a student insert quotes and a comma. Have partners create their own correctly punctuated dialogues and read them to the class.

ADVANCED/ADVANCED HIGH

Conclusion Read a short research report without the conclusion. On the board write two concluding sentences—one weak, one strong. Ask students which one they think is stronger. Read another short research report. Write a weak concluding sentence on the board and have students suggest ways to make it stronger.

Note Cards

A **note card** is a place to put information about a topic. It should contain the following:
- a question from your K-W-S Chart that you would like to get answered
- information relating to the topic (either summarized or directly quoted)
- the source of the information

Use one note card for each source of information.

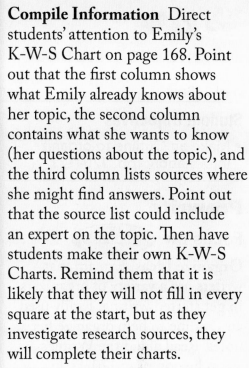

I found three useful sources. As I went through each one, I made note cards to record the information I found. Here is one of the cards I made. I put the information in quotation marks because it is a direct quote.

> Why do so many medicinal plants grow in the rain forest?
> "Plants living in tropical forest habitats have had to develop and survive under intense competition for resources and nutrients. They have also had to develop an extraordinary array of defenses, most of them chemical, to protect themselves from viral diseases, fungal pathogens, insects and mammalian predators."
>
> Bierer, Donald E, Thomas J Carlson, and Steven R King. "Shaman Pharmaceuticals: Integrating Indigenous Knowledge, Tropical Medicinal Plants, Medicine, Modern Science and Reciprocity into a Novel Drug Discovery Approach." NetSci May 1996, accessed November 15, 2012, http://www.netsci.org/Science/Special/feature11.html.

Reflect

It seems Emily's K-W-S Chart helped her focus her research. Did she include enough information on each note card?

Apply

Choose a topic and make a K-W-S Chart. Then make note cards to help you keep track of your sources.

Research Report **169**

Compile Information Direct students' attention to Emily's K-W-S Chart on page 168. Point out that the first column shows what Emily already knows about her topic, the second column contains what she wants to know (her questions about the topic), and the third column lists sources where she might find answers. Point out that the source list could include an expert on the topic. Then have students make their own K-W-S Charts. Remind them that it is likely that they will not fill in every square at the start, but as they investigate research sources, they will complete their charts.

Make sure students have an adequate supply of index cards on which to record notes from their sources. Have them refer to the example note card on page 169 as often as necessary to write their own. Remind students to record detailed information on note cards and keep track of their sources to complete their K-W-S Charts.

Writer's Term

Note Cards Information should be directly quoted or summarized in the writer's own words. The source should be included on the corresponding note card. Students may find it helpful to alphabetize or number their note cards for easy reference.

CCSS **Common Core State Standards**

W.7.8: Gather relevant information from multiple print and digital sources, using search terms effectively; assess the credibility and accuracy of each source; and quote or paraphrase the data and conclusions of others while avoiding plagiarism and following a standard format for citation.

Write
a Research Report

Week 2 • Day 2

Student Objectives

• Make an Outline to organize information. *(pp. 170–171)*

Prewrite

Focus on  Organization

Organize Ideas Explain that writers use a variety of organizers to get started writing. Emily used an Outline to help organize her notes. Read aloud the Writer's Term box on page 170. Help students understand how an Outline categorizes different types of information by explaining that each Roman numeral section moves from a general statement to specific details. In this way, an Outline helps form the paragraphs in the body of a piece of writing.

Ask students to study the organizer; then ask why an Outline is an effective tool when writing a research report. (Possible response: An Outline is an excellent tool for organizing a research report because it breaks down the topic in a very detailed, organized way.) Have a volunteer read aloud Emily's words on page 170. Note that she plans to rely on her Outline as she writes. Remind students to make Outlines from the details listed on their note cards.

Online Writing Center

 Provides **interactive graphic organizers** as well as a variety of graphic organizers in PDF format.

Prewrite
Focus on Organization

The Rubric Says	A strong introduction presents the topic, the body organizes information, and the concluding section (conclusion) supports the information presented.
Writing Strategy	Make an Outline to organize the information from the note cards.

By the time I finished my research, I had a lot of note cards. I had to get my information organized, but I also wanted to do it in a way that would help me structure the introduction, body, and conclusion of my report. So I used a Topic Outline.

Most of the information that I gathered came directly from my research, but I also had some opinions of my own. I marked them on my Outline so that I wouldn't confuse them for facts when I was ready to start drafting.

Writer's Term

Outline

An **Outline** shows the main points and the supporting details of the paragraphs in an essay or report. A **Topic Outline** contains words and phrases to help a writer organize information. A **Sentence Outline** contains complete sentences. Use the same form for both Outlines:
• Use Roman numerals (I, II, III, IV) to indicate major sections or topics.
• Use capital letters (A, B, C, D) to indicate major paragraphs.
• Use Arabic numerals (1, 2, 3, 4) to indicate supporting details within each paragraph.
• Use lowercase letters (a, b, c, d) to indicate less important details in a paragraph.
• Use a period after each symbol.

170 Informative/Explanatory Writing

Conferencing

PEER TO PEER When students have completed their Outlines, have pairs exchange them. Ask partners to review each other's Outlines and comment on which areas might need better organization.

PEER GROUPS Separate students into small groups. Instruct them to exchange ideas for organizing their note cards to write a clear, well-organized Outline.

TEACHER-LED To demonstrate the importance of a Topic Outline, create your own outline on the board, leaving several areas blank. Discuss how the missing information might affect the writing of an effective research report.

Outline

I. Some plant-based medicines around for many years
   A. Quinine
      1. derived from bark of cinchona tree
      2. known about at least since 1600s
      3. treatment for malaria
   B. Digitalis
      1. derived from leaves of foxglove plant
      2. treatment for heart ailments (slows down pulse, regulates heartbeats)
   C. More than 120 plant-based medicines in use now
II. Some plant-based medicines found through new research
   A. Research with native peoples
      1. interview with woman in western Samoa
      2. information on more than 100 traditional remedies
      3. one remedy became basis for prostratin (used with AIDS patients)
III. Rain forest problems must be overcome [OPINION]
   A. Fertile source of medicinal plants
      1. 25 percent of medicines come from there
      2. plants strong and effective because they compete to survive
   B. Ethical problems to overcome
      1. much information comes from native people
      2. need to pay these people [OPINION]
      3. long-term and short-term ways to pay
   C. Problem of disappearing rain forests
      1. about 150 acres per minute lost to development
      2. need to work out compromise with developing countries [OPINION]
         a. pay people for information
         b. pay people to help with research

Reflect
How will Emily's Outline help her draft her report?

Apply
Make an Outline to organize your research information.

Writer's Term
Outline An Outline shows the main points and the supporting details of the paragraphs in a report. It breaks down the topic in an organized way, using a series of indented numbers and letters to show levels of importance. If a writer begins with a well-organized outline, it is more likely that the result will be a clear, effective research report.

CCSS **Common Core State Standards**
R/Inf.7.5: Analyze the structure an author uses to organize a text, including how the major sections contribute to the whole and to the development of ideas.

Write
a Research Report

Week 2 • Day 3

Student Objectives

- Use an Outline to begin writing. (*p. 172*)

Draft

Focus on

Draft a Research Report Remind students that drafting is a chance to get ideas on paper without having to worry about making mistakes. Be sure that students understand that they will use their Outlines to guide them through the drafting process. Read page 172 aloud. Then ask students to silently read Emily's draft on pages 173–175. Discuss whether Emily's draft includes a strong introduction, body, and conclusion. Point out that Emily repeatedly refers to the rubric as she writes. Encourage students to get into the habit of using the rubric to help guide their own writing. Then have students use their Outlines to draft their own research reports. Remind them that they should guide the reader through the writing with a strong introduction, body, and conclusion.

Draft
Focus on Organization

The Rubric Says	A strong introduction presents the topic, the body organizes information, and the concluding section (conclusion) supports the information presented.
Writing Strategy	Include a strong introduction, body, and conclusion that will guide the reader through the report.

According to the rubric, I need a strong introduction, body, and conclusion to guide my reader successfully through my report. My outline contains great information to get me started, but first I want to think things through.

I know a good introduction clearly states the topic and prepares the reader for the areas of discussion covered throughout the report. The body must consist of several strong paragraphs that are full of relevant and accurate facts. Everything in the body must relate back to the topic, and the information must be organized in such a way that the reader can follow along easily. The conclusion should be brief, yet strong, and support the information I presented in the report. I definitely should not introduce any new ideas in the conclusion.

Writing my draft will take a while, so I won't worry too much about spelling or capitalization right now. I know I'll go back and fix any mistakes later on.

172 Informative/Explanatory Writing

Differentiating Instruction

ENRICHMENT
Evaluate Sources Have students evaluate different types of sources and then create a chart explaining the sources' strengths and weaknesses. For example, students might list *personal interview* as a source and then explain when an interview would be effective. Challenge students to include at least six types of sources on their charts. Display these charts in the classroom as references.

Online Writing Center

Provides student eBooks with an **interactive writing pad** for drafting, revising, editing, and publishing.

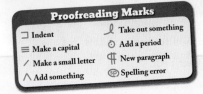

Proofreading Marks

☐ Indent   ℓ Take out something
≡ Make a capital   ⊙ Add a period
╱ Make a small letter   ¶ New paragraph
∧ Add something   ⑤℗ Spelling error

[DRAFT]

Modern Medicines From Ancient Plants   [introduction]

Most Americans know that many of our foods come from plants. It is not so well known, though, that a great number of medicines also come from plants. This paper will give some examples of plant-based medicines. It will also talk about how they are discovered and how scientists learn about them.

Here is a number that might surprise you. More than 30 percent of our medicines. They include treatments for such things as malaria, heart problems, and Parkinson's disease.

One of the best-known plant-based medicines is quinine. It is a standard treatment for malaria. Quinine comes from the bark of the cincho tree. Indians in south America have used the bark for centuries. It was brought to europe in the 1600s. Before that, there was no effective malaria treatment there. As quinine became more commonly used, malaria was all but wiped out in many areas of the world.

Another widely used medicine is digitalis. Digitalis is derived from the leaves of the Foxglove Plant. Some say that it was used as long ago as 1500 B.C. In earlier times, it was used to treat swelling and wounds.

[body]

Research Report   **173**

REINFORCEMENT

Use the Rubric Some students may need direct instruction in beginning to draft their research reports. Make a transparency of the rubric on pages 162–163. Display it in the classroom, and highlight the Organization trait. Point out to students that they should remember to use their Outlines to organize each paragraph of their reports. Work with students to help them draft their introductions.

Write
a Research Report

Week 2 • Day 4

Student Objectives

• Complete a draft. *(pp. 173–175)*

Continue Writing a Draft It is important that students are given ample time to draft their reports. Remind students that this is the time for getting their ideas down on paper. Suggest strategies to prevent writer's block, such as circling initial word choices, underlining grammatical structures, or adding question marks for source information. Doing so will make it easier for them to revisit and revise later. Assure them as often as necessary that they will have plenty of time to make changes and corrections later. Support them during the process by discussing their progress through conferencing.

CCSS **C**ommon **C**ore **S**tate **S**tandards

W.7.5: With some guidance and support from peers and adults, develop and strengthen writing as needed by planning, revising, editing, rewriting, or trying a new approach, focusing on how well purpose and audience have been addressed. **SL.7.1:** Engage effectively in a range of collaborative discussions (one-on-one, in groups, and teacher-led) with diverse partners on *grade 7 topics, texts, and issues,* building on others' ideas and expressing their own clearly.

Now it is used most often as a treatment for heart ailments. It slows down the pulse and regulates the heartbeat.

By talking to native people in remote areas, scientists are constantly learning about more mecidinal plants. For example, Paul Alan Cox is Director of the national tropical botanical gardens in Hawaii and Florida. He interviewed an elderly woman in western Samoa, an island in the pacific. Over several weeks, she gave him instructions on how to prepare more than 100 remedies. These were derived from ferns and flowering plants. The National cancer Institute tested one of her preperations. It became the basis for a new antiviral drug called prostatrin. This drug has been used in treating AIDS.

The tropical rain forests are a fertile source of medicinal plants. About 25 percent of medicines now on the market come from them. Many scientists think the rain forests are home to even more medicinal plants. What is the reason that so many of these plants might be in the rain forests. The answer is simple. Rain forest plants have had to find ways of defending themselves from diseases, funguses, animals, and insects. In doing so, theyve become stronger.

There are at least two problems associated with rain forest research. One is an ethical one. Many plant remedies found in rain forests come from native peoples such as the western Samoan woman. By rights, such people should be payed for sharing their knowledge. It is not always easy to do this, however. Some native medicines may not be proven truly effective for years. Some may never be proven

[body]

Conferencing

PEER TO PEER Have pairs of students exchange drafts. Instruct them to provide helpful comments for their partners regarding the overall organization of their research reports. (Does the report present the topic in the introduction? Does the body organize the information? Does the conclusion support the information that is presented? Are sources cited?) Be sure the focus is not mechanics at this time.

PEER GROUPS Organize students into small groups. Have them take turns reading sections of their research reports aloud. Have listeners take turns providing helpful commentary to strengthen the report.

TEACHER-LED Schedule conferences with pairs of students. Have them read each other's drafts and coach them in giving constructive criticism on using the traits of Ideas and Organization as described in the rubric on page 162.

Strategies for Writers Online
Go to **www.sfw.z-b.com** for additional online resources for students and teachers.

effective. In the meantime, though, people could be payed in other ways. For example, they might recieve health care, educational faculties, or help starting rain-forest-friendly businesses.

The other problem is that the rain forests themselves are disappearing, by, according to some estimates, about 150 acres of rain forest each minute. The reason is development by corporations that clear the forests for timber, grazing lands, mining operations, and roadways. As a result, valuable plants are destroyed. And once a plant species disappears, it is gone forever.

It would be wonderful if a compromise could be worked out. Rain forests are much more valuable than grazing lands or roadways. Maybe local governments could invite more researchers and limit developers. Maybe local people could be paid for pointing out medicinal plants. They could be hired to work with scientists to help discover and study plants.

According to some researchers, less than one percent of plant speecies have been thoroughly examined for mecidinal value. By saving as many of these as we can, who knows what remarkable cures we might find.

[conclusion]

Reflect

How did Emily do? Is her topic clear? Does her writing guide you from one point to the next?

Apply

When you draft your report, make sure to include a strong introduction, body, and conclusion.

CCSS Common Core State Standards

W.7.9: Draw evidence from literary or informational texts to support analysis, reflection, and research.
W.7.10: Write routinely over extended time frames (time for research, reflection, and revision) and shorter time frames (a single sitting or a day or two) for a range of discipline-specific tasks, purposes, and audiences.

Write
a Research Report

Week 2 • Day 5

Student Objectives

- Revise for a knowledgeable voice by adding quotes and information from experts. (pp. 176–177)

Revise

Focus on Voice

Add Quotes and Information from Experts Explain to students that the inclusion of quotes and paraphrased information from experts is an important part of writing a research report. Note that all sources that are quoted or paraphrased must be included in a list of Works Consulted at the end of the report. Point out to students that it is unethical to use the words or ideas of others without giving proper credit.

Then read aloud the Writer's Term box on page 177, and have students pay particular attention to how each type of entry is punctuated and capitalized. Have students work together as they develop their lists of Works Consulted. Tell students to first determine which type of reference they are citing and follow the pattern on page 177. Finally have students look for places in their research reports where they can add quotes and information from experts.

 Strategies for Writers Online
Go to **www.sfw.z-b.com** for additional online resources for students and teachers.

Revise
Focus on Voice

The Rubric Says	Quotations and information from experts help make the voice sound knowledgeable and credible.
Writing Strategy	Add quotes and information from experts.

The rubric says adding quotations and information from experts will add credibility to my voice. When I use quotes, I have to blend the words into my own writing, and, most importantly, I have to make sure they're accurate. I must use the exact words from my source, and I must name my source correctly. Doing this helps me avoid plagiarism, which is a serious offense. *Plagiarism* means stealing someone else's quotations or ideas. I just found the perfect place to insert a great quotation.

[DRAFT]

↙ [added a quote]

According to several research chemists, "over 120 pharmaceutical products currently in use are plant-derived" (Bierer, Carlson, and King). This is

Here is a number that might surprise you. More than 30 percent of our medicines. They include treatments for such things as malaria, heart problems, and Parkinson's disease.

English Language Learners

BEGINNING

Research Tell students they need to listen so they can learn facts. Read a simple nonfiction text. While slowly turning the pages of the book and showing the pictures, ask *What did you learn from this book?* If students are reluctant to answer, ask a simple specific question. Repeat students' answers in a complete sentence and write them on the board. Repeat until two or three facts are written on the board.

INTERMEDIATE

Research Explain to students that the purpose for reading is to learn. Begin a simple nonfiction book. At the end of the first page, ask *What did you learn?* Repeat after the second page. Say, *As you read, think about what you are learning.* Assign a language-level appropriate nonfiction book to each student. Have them write five facts they learned from the book and share the facts with a partner.

Because I included quotes and other information, I needed to cite my sources in a list of Works Consulted at the end of my report. I used the following examples to help me format my list.

Citing Sources: Works Consulted

When **citing sources,** list where you found borrowed information. The examples below show how to present this information in a list of **Works Consulted.** Place the list at the end of your paper, and include each source used, regardless of whether direct quotes were pulled from that source. Pay special attention to the order of the information and the use of punctuation. Entries in a list of Works Consulted are arranged alphabetically according to authors' last names. When there is no author, use the first word in the title. In addition, use the styles shown here.

To cite an article in an online periodical:
Author's last name, author's first name. "Article title." *Online periodical title* Date of publication, date of access, web address (URL).

Example:
Bierer, Donald E., Thomas J. Carlson, and Steven R. King. "Shaman Pharmaceuticals: Integrating Indigenous Knowledge, Tropical Medicinal Plants, Medicine, Modern Science and Reciprocity into a Novel Drug Discovery Approach." *NetSci* May 1996, accessed November 15, 2012, http://www.netsci.org/Science/Special/feature11.html.

To cite a magazine or newspaper article:
Author's last name, author's first name. "Article title." *Magazine/newspaper title* Date of publication: page number(s).

Example:
Cox, Paul Alan. "Will Tribal Knowledge Survive the Millennium?" *Science* 7 Jan. 2000: 44.

To cite a book:
Author's last name, author's first name. *Book title*. City of publication: Publisher, date of publication.

Example:
Sumner, Judith. *The Natural History of Medicinal Plants*. Portland: Timber Press, 2000.

Apply

Add quotes and information from experts to the body of your report. Then include a list of Works Consulted at the end.

Research Report **177**

✏️ **Writer's Term_____**
Citing Sources: Works Consulted

The ethics of research demand that source material belonging to someone else is credited. *Plagiarism* means borrowing ideas without giving credit to the original source, and it is a serious offense. To avoid plagiarism, students need to remember to list *all* of the sources they have consulted during their research. Their lists should appear at the end of their reports. Regardless of whether direct quotes were used or paraphrased, all consulted sources must be cited. The order of the information and the use of punctuation in a Works Consulted list are important. Students need to pay extra attention to these conventions. Entries are arranged in alphabetical order by the authors' last names. If no author is attributed to the source, the first word in the title is used. When the Works Consulted list is complete, it is important to verify that all sources are listed accurately.

ADVANCED

Using Sources Give students several note cards with a question written on each one. Have students use reliable print and online resources to research and write an answer to each question. Ask them to record the source where they found the answer.

ADVANCED/ADVANCED HIGH

Using Sources Print several online articles for a given topic such as global warming. Include articles from a variety of sources .gov, .edu, .org, .com, and .net. Discuss what makes an article reliable or unreliable. Point out that .gov, .edu, and .org are generally considered to be more reliable domains than .com or .net. Have students highlight the characteristics that make it reliable or unreliable and share their findings with a partner.

CCSS **C**ommon **C**ore **S**tate **S**tandards
W.7.2.b: Develop the topic with relevant facts, definitions, concrete details, quotations, or other information and examples. **W.7.8:** Gather relevant information from multiple print and digital sources, using search terms effectively; assess the credibility and accuracy of each source; and quote or paraphrase the data and conclusions of others while avoiding plagiarism and following a standard format for citation.

Research Report **T177**

Write
a Research Report

Week 3 • Day 1

Student Objectives

- Revise to paraphrase borrowed information accurately. (pp. 178–179)

Revise

Focus on  Word Choice

Paraphrase Borrowed Information Accurately Have a volunteer read aloud Emily's words on page 178. Then review the information on paraphrasing and plagiarizing in the Writer's Term box. Emphasize again that information from their sources must be quoted and paraphrased with great care. Have students study Emily's draft on page 179 and identify where and how she gave credit to Dr. Bierer. Finally have students check their drafts to see if they have accurately paraphrased and cited borrowed information.

Strategies for Writers Online

Go to **www.sfw.z-b.com** for additional online resources for students and teachers.

Revise

Focus on **Word Choice**

The Rubric Says Borrowed ideas are accurately paraphrased. The writer's words are distinct from the ideas of others.

Writing Strategy Make sure that borrowed information is accurately paraphrased.

After I added my expert quote, I looked at the rubric again to see if I was missing anything else. It reminded me to make sure that I had accurately paraphrased borrowed information. So I reread my report, looking for places where I had used someone else's words or ideas. I know it's OK to borrow information, but if I don't explain where it comes from, that's not borrowing; that's stealing!

I quickly realized that I had included several of my own opinions in one of my paragraphs. But there was one opinion that was someone else's—and it was mixed in with my own. I wanted to make sure the reader would understand the difference, so I revised the paragraph, adding the true source of the information.

> **Writer's Term**
> **Paraphrase/Plagiarize**
> To **paraphrase** is to restate the meaning of a particular passage in your own words. Don't **plagiarize**! To plagiarize means to present another person's ideas as your own.

178 Informative/Explanatory Writing

Conferencing

PEER TO PEER Have pairs of students exchange drafts. After reading the draft, each student offers helpful feedback with different ways to strengthen Word Choice.

PEER GROUPS Separate students into small groups. Have them take turns reading sections of their drafts aloud. Group members should then suggest areas that seem to need better paraphrasing of borrowed information.

TEACHER-LED Hold conferences with individual students about their drafts. Point out places where quotations might be effectively placed. Then ask students if there is other information they can quote or paraphrase to strengthen their writing. Remind them to cite the borrowed information.

[DRAFT]

It would be wonderful if a compromise could be worked out. Rain forests are much more valuable than grazing lands or roadways. Maybe local governments could invite more researchers and limit developers. Maybe local people could be paid for pointing out medicinal plants. They could be hired to work with scientists to help discover and study plants.

, as Dr. Bierer suggests,

[accurately paraphrased]

Reflect

What do you think of Emily's revisions? How have they made her writing clearer?

Apply

Make sure borrowed information is paraphrased, not plagiarized.

Writer's Term _____

Paraphrase/Plagiarize

Paraphrasing helps writers grasp the full meaning of the original text they are using. It serves as a legitimate way to integrate credible information from a variety of sources into a paper. Paraphrasing helps researchers borrow information without plagiarizing by helping them restate text in their own words. To plagiarize means to use another's ideas as one's own. It is unethical and a serious offense.

Differentiating Instruction

ENRICHMENT

Learn to Paraphrase Separate students into pairs. Cut up a magazine article into equal-sized sections and distribute one section to each pair of students. Have pairs work together to paraphrase their section. Then collect the magazine paraphrases and put the article back together. Discuss with students whether the paraphrasing captured the spirit and meaning of the original.

REINFORCEMENT

Avoid Plagiarism Have students read passages from their drafts where they have used information from another source. Then have students compare their wording to the original source. Together, determine if their paraphrases are accurate.

CCSS Common Core State Standards

W.7.6: Use technology, including the Internet, to produce and publish writing and link to and cite sources as well as to interact and collaborate with others, including linking to and citing sources. **W.7.7:** Conduct short research projects to answer a question, drawing on several sources and generating additional related, focused questions for further research and investigation.

Write
a Research Report

Week 3 • Day 2

Student Objectives

- Revise to create sentence variety by breaking up long, wordy sentences. *(p. 180)*

Revise

Focus on Sentence Fluency

Create Sentence Variety Have students read Emily's words on page 180 and note the changes she made to her draft. Relate to students that writers of research reports have a tendency to write long, wordy sentences, but a string of such sentences can really test a reader's patience. Have students create sentence variety in their drafts by breaking up long, wordy sentences.

Revise

Focus on **Sentence Fluency**

The Rubric Says A variety of sentence structures gives the writing rhythm and flow.

Writing Strategy Create sentence variety by breaking up long, wordy sentences.

Before I finished revising my draft, I looked at the rubric one more time. I was reminded to vary my sentence length throughout my report. When I reread my draft, I noticed a place where I had a bunch of long, wordy sentences. I broke them up into smaller sentences to make the writing flow in a much more lively way.

[DRAFT]

[created sentence variety]

The other problem is that the rain forests themselves are disappearing. by, according to some estimates, about 150 acres of are lost rain forest each minute. The reason is development by corporations that clear the forests for timber, grazing lands, mining operations, and roadways. As a result, valuable plants are destroyed. And once a plant species disappears, it is gone forever.

Apply

Break up long, wordy sentences in your report. Your readers will thank you!

180 Informative/Explanatory Writing

Optional Revising Lessons

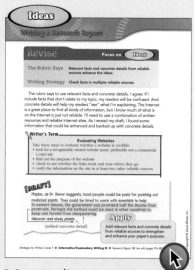

Ideas

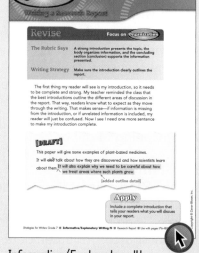

Organization

Informative/Explanatory 13   Informative/Explanatory 14

Go to **Strategies for Writers Grade 7 CD-ROM**

Online Writing Center

 Provides **interactive proofreading activities** for each genre.

T180 Informative/Explanatory Writing

Edit

Focus on Conventions

The Rubric Says	Capitalization is used correctly throughout the report.
Writing Strategy	Check the capitalization and punctuation of proper nouns, proper adjectives, abbreviations, and initials.

✏ Writer's Term_____

Proper Nouns/Adjectives, Abbreviations, and Initials
Proper nouns and **proper adjectives** are always capitalized. **Initials** and **abbreviations** that are part of names are capitalized and followed by periods.

It's time to correct spelling and grammar errors. I'll also be sure proper nouns and adjectives, abbreviations, initials, and titles are all capitalized accurately. I caught a few errors in my Works Consulted list, so I went ahead and corrected them.

[DRAFT] [added correct punctuation]

Bierer, Donald E., Thomas J. Carlson, and Steven R. King. "Shaman Pharmaceuticals: Integrating Indigenous Knowledge, Tropical Medicinal Plants, Medicine, Modern Science and Reciprocity into a Novel Drug Discovery Approach." NetSci May 1996, accessed November 15, 2012, http://www.netsci.org/Science/Special/feature11.html.

Reflect

What do you think? Can you find any capitalization or punctuation errors that Emily missed?

Apply Conventions

Edit for spelling grammar, punctuation, and capitalization. Be sure your title is written properly, too.

For more practice with punctuation and capitalization of proper nouns/adjectives, abbreviations, and initials, use the exercises on the next two pages.

Research Report 181

Related Grammar Practice _____

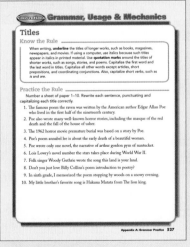

Student Edition page 527

Go to ▷ Appendix A: Grammar Practice

Write
a Research Report

Week 3 • Day 3

Student Objectives

• Edit for correct use of conventions. (p. 181)

Edit

Focus on Conventions

Edit for Accurate Capitalization and Punctuation Talk with students about the unique aspects of writing a research paper. Point out that the frequent use of formal names and citations makes paying attention to capitalization and punctuation especially important. Remind students to check their reports for proper spelling, capitalization, and punctuation. Use the mini-lessons on pages on T182–183 for students having problems with punctuation and capitalization of proper nouns/ adjectives, abbreviations, initials or titles. Have students complete the exercises on pages 182 and 183. Review the answers in class.

✏ Writer's Term_____

Proper Nouns/Adjectives, Abbreviations, and Initials
Omitting capitalization and punctuation can be confusing for the reader and make a research report more difficult to follow.

CCSS Common Core State Standards

L.7.1: Demonstrate command of the conventions of standard English grammar and usage when writing or speaking. **L.7.2:** Demonstrate command of the conventions of standard English capitalization, punctuation, and spelling when writing.

Research Report T181

Mini-Lesson

Student Objectives

- Use proper nouns/adjectives, abbreviations, and initials correctly. (p. 182)

Proper Nouns/ Adjectives, Abbreviations, and Initials

Have students review the Know the Rule box on page 182. Then write the following on the board:

- *Emily's dog was an Irish setter.*

Ask students if the words in this sentence are capitalized correctly. (yes) What proper noun is in the sentence? (Emily) What proper adjective is in the sentence? (Irish)

Write the following on the board:

- *Station wxyz played many of Tom T Hall's hit records.*

Ask students if the words in this sentence are punctuated correctly? (no) What is incorrect? (WXYZ should be capitalized; Hall's middle initial should be followed by a period.)

Ask which words in the sentence are proper nouns. (WXYZ, Tom T. Hall)

Remind students that it is important to use proper nouns/adjectives, abbreviations, and initials correctly in their research reports.

Online Writing Center

Provides **interactive grammar games** and **practice activities** in student eBook.

Proper Nouns/Adjectives, Abbreviations, and Initials

Know the Rule

Proper nouns name particular persons, places, and things. All important words in proper nouns are capitalized. **Initials** and **abbreviations** that are part of names are capitalized and followed by periods.

> Examples: Dr. Luz T. Lopez, M.D.
> *The Call of the Wild* (book title)
> Fell Company

Proper adjectives are formed from proper nouns, and they are always capitalized.

> Examples: Danish cheese
> Latin music

Practice the Rule

Rewrite the sentences with correct capitalization and punctuation on a separate sheet of paper.

1. Dr. Frieda Nannigan, of New york University, has done a number of studies.
2. She was assisted by Louis Franz jr. and other scientists.
3. One of her research papers was called "your health depends on what you eat."
4. Studies have been done by European and canadian researchers as well.
5. A dutch study showed that eating apples might prevent heart attacks.
6. Our science teacher, Mr. nakamura, asked us to read some of the studies on food and health.
7. He says that, here in california, we have access to lots of fresh fruits and vegetables.
8. In fact, california supplies fruits and vegetables to stores across the United states.
9. My doctor, dr. Nameed, told me I should try to eat more fresh vegetables.
10. Here in the city of los angeles, there are lots of places to buy freshly picked vegetables.

Related Grammar Practice

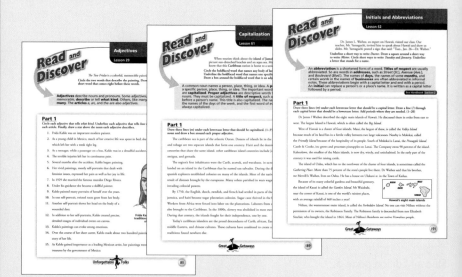

Pages 85, 189, 191

Go to ⇨ **G.U.M. Student Practice Book**

Titles

Know the Rule

Underline the titles of long works, such as **books, magazines, newspapers,** and **movies.** However, these are written in italics in printed text.
> Example: <u>Hatchet</u> by Gary Paulsen (a book)

Use quotation marks around the titles of shorter works, such as **songs, stories,** and **poems.**
> Example: "Jimmy Jet and His TV Set" by Shel Silverstein
> (a poem)

Capitalize the first word and the last word in titles. Capitalize all other words except articles, short prepositions, and coordinating conjunctions. Remember to capitalize short verbs, such as *is* and *are.*
> Example: "Fire and Rain" (a song)

Practice the Rule

If students type their answers, the underlined titles should be in italics.

Rewrite each sentence correctly on a separate sheet of paper.

1. I'm halfway through <u>Pride and Prejudice</u>, and I just can't put the book down!
2. Hurry up! We don't want to be late for the 6:00 showing of <u>How to train your dragon</u>.
3. Every day, Nick would race to the mailbox to see if the next issue of <u>Highlights</u> had arrived.
4. Have you ever read Lewis Carroll's poem "Jabberwocky" out loud? I never knew how fun saying silly words out loud could be.
5. You should stand and place your right hand over your heart every time you sing "The Star-Spangled Banner."
6. My grandpa was listening to an old song called "Where Is the Love?"
7. <u>The New York Times</u> is my mom's favorite newspaper; she reads it every day.
8. We read "Paul Revere's Ride" for our poetry unit last year.
9. When I was little, I thought <u>Charlotte's Web</u> was great both as a book and a movie.
10. My Uncle Ted likes to look for recipe ideas in a magazine called <u>Cuisine</u>.

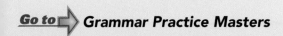
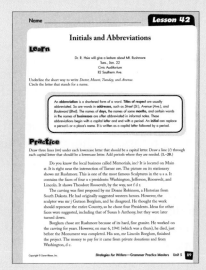

Pages 87, 89

Go to ▶ Grammar Practice Masters

Mini-Lesson

Student Objectives

- Use titles correctly. *(p. 183)*

Titles

Have students review the Know the Rule box on page 183. Then write the following sentences on the board, being sure to leave out correct punctuation of titles. Ask volunteers to correct the example sentences.

- *My grandpa loves to read the sports pages in his favorite newspaper, the boston globe.*
- *Have you ever read adventures of huckleberry finn by Mark Twain?*
- *My favorite poem is the road not taken by Robert Frost.*
- *Washington Irving wrote the legend of sleepy Hollow, one of my favorite short stories.*

CCSS Common Core State Standards
W.7.5: With some guidance and support from peers and adults, develop and strengthen writing as needed by planning, revising, editing, rewriting, or trying a new approach, focusing on how well purpose and audience have been addressed. **L.7.2:** Demonstrate command of the conventions of standard English capitalization, punctuation, and spelling when writing.

Write
a Research Report

Week 3 • Day 4

Student Objectives

- Discuss preparation for publishing and presentation. *(p. 184)*
- Use a final editing checklist to publish their work. *(p. 184)*

Publish +Presentation

Publishing Strategy Ask students if they like Emily's choice for sharing her research report. Tell the class that her choice is not the only option for publishing her work. Invite students to name other ways they could publish their own research reports.

Have each student make a checklist and perform a final evaluation of his or her work before publishing it. As students type their final copies, remind them to use only a few different fonts that are clear and easy to read. Encourage students to make copies and share their finished reports with other students, friends, and family members.

Strategies for Writers Online
Go to **www.sfw.z-b.com** for additional online resources for students and teachers.

Publish +Presentation

Publishing Strategy	Present the report as part of a multimedia presentation.
Presentation Strategy	Label each page.

My class is working hard to combine our reports as one multimedia presentation. My report will be a great addition to the project, and I have the perfect video clip to include with my text. To make sure there's no confusion, though, I'll label each page with both my name and the page number. Creating a header or footer with a computer is easy. But first, I'll use my final checklist to make sure my paper's ready for publication.

My Final Checklist

Did I—

✔ capitalize all proper nouns and adjectives, abbreviations, and initials?

✔ capitalize and punctuate all titles of books, magazines, websites, and newspapers cited in my report?

✔ label each page with my name and the page number?

Apply

Make a checklist to check your research report. Then make a final copy to publish.

184 Informative/Explanatory Writing

Differentiating Instruction

ENRICHMENT

Edit With a Peer Have pairs of students exchange their edited reports to proofread each other's changes. When partners have completed their final edits, have students exchange reports and defend their edits. As they prepare their final copies, invite students with word-processing experience to assist others in adding visuals to their reports.

REINFORCEMENT

Prepare a Final Copy Meet with a small group of students to discuss their editing checklists. Also remind them to follow the model on page 177 for editing their Works Consulted lists. Assist as needed, and remind them to make sure that all proper nouns/adjectives, abbreviations, initials, and titles are punctuated and capitalized correctly throughout the report (see pages 181–183).

Modern Medicines From Ancient Plants

by Emily

Most Americans know that many of our foods come from plants. It is not so well known, though, that a great number of medicines also come from plants. This paper will give some examples of plant-based medicines. It will talk about how they are discovered and how scientists learn about them. It will also explain why we need to be careful about how we treat areas where such plants grow.

Here is a number that might surprise you. According to several research chemists, "over 120 pharmaceutical products currently in use are plant-derived" (Bierer, Carlson, and King). This is more than 30 percent of our medicines. They include treatments for such things as malaria, heart problems, and Parkinson's disease.

One of the best-known plant-based medicines is quinine. It is a standard treatment for malaria. Quinine comes from the bark of the cinchona tree. Indians in South America have used the bark for centuries. It was taken to Europe in the 1600s. Before that, there was no effective malaria treatment there. As quinine became more commonly used, malaria was all but wiped out in many areas of the world.

Another widely used medicine is digitalis. Digitalis is derived from the leaves of the foxglove plant. Some say that it was used as long ago as 1500 B.C. In earlier times, it was used to treat swelling and wounds. Now it is used most often as a treatment for heart ailments. It slows down the pulse and regulates the heartbeat.

By talking to native people in remote areas, scientists are constantly learning about more medicinal plants. For example, Paul Alan Cox is director of the National Tropical Botanical Gardens in

Emily, Page 1

Technology Tip for 21st Century Literacies

Sharing student research can be challenging since few adults are eager to delve into an adolescent's formal written paper. To engage responses from an authentic audience, encourage students to recast their research into a podcast or radio show (suitable for school broadcast or publishing online if possible). Replicate the structure of NPR-like shows with interviews, guests, skits, or other creative presentations of their work. Consider using Skype or similar tools to connect students with experts who can help move their thinking past the current draft of their writing.

See **www.sfw.z-b.com** for further information about and links to these websites and tools.

Write
a Research Report

Week 3 • Day 5

Student Objectives

- Use a research report rubric. (pp. 162–163)
- Share a published research report as part of a multimedia presentation. (pp. 185–187)

Presentation Strategy Remind students of the importance of neatness when creating final, polished copies of their work. Remind students of the numerous word-processing options available on computers. Computers make it easy to set neat margins, indent paragraphs, and select a couple of clear fonts for creativity. Also remind students to use the header or footer function to label each page with the report title, the writer's name, and a page number.

Encourage students to brainstorm different ways they could collectively publish their research reports. They might choose to compile all of their reports into a slide-show presentation and share it at a school function. Provide class time for students to coordinate and implement their presentation plans.

CCSS Common Core State Standards

W.7.4: Produce clear and coherent writing in which the development, organization, and style are appropriate to task, purpose, and audience. **W.7.6:** Use technology, including the Internet, to produce and publish writing and link to and cite sources as well as to interact and collaborate with others, including linking to and citing sources.

Reflecting on a Research Report

Instruct students to refer to the rubric on pages 162–163 as they reread Emily's final copy on pages 185–187. As they read, remind them to pay close attention to all of Emily's changes. After students have finished reading, ask them what they think of Emily's changes. Did her revisions and edits strengthen or weaken her research report? What score would Emily have received for each writing trait? Take a poll to see how close the scores are. Be sure students can support their scores with examples from Emily's writing.

Next have students reflect on the assignment as a whole. How did they feel about writing a research report? Do they understand the writing process better now that they have completed the assignment? You might ask:

- What was your favorite part of this assignment?

- Was there one part that was particularly challenging or easy?

- Name one thing about writing you think you improved.

- Think about all the steps you took to complete your research report. What worked well? What could be improved?

Hawaii and Florida. He interviewed an elderly woman in western Samoa, an island in the Pacific. Over several weeks, she gave him instructions on how to prepare more than 100 remedies. These were derived from ferns and flowering plants. The National Cancer Institute tested one of her preparations. It became the basis for a new antiviral drug called prostratin. This drug has been used in treating AIDS.

The tropical rain forests are a fertile source of medicinal plants. About 25 percent of medicines now on the market come from them. Many scientists think the rain forests are home to even more medicinal plants. What is the reason that so many of these plants might be in the rain forests? The answer is simple. Rain forest plants have had to find ways of defending themselves from diseases, funguses, animals, and insects. In doing so, they've become stronger.

There are at least two problems associated with rain forest research. One is an ethical one. Many plant remedies found in rain forests come from native peoples such as the western Samoan woman. By rights, such people should be paid for sharing their knowledge. It is not always easy to do this, however. Some native medicines may not be truly effective for years. Some may never be proven effective. In the meantime, though, people could be paid in other ways. For example, they might receive health care, educational facilities, or help starting rain-forest-friendly businesses.

The other problem is that the rain forests themselves are disappearing. According to some estimates, about 150 acres of rain forest are lost each minute. The reason is development. Corporations clear the forests for timber, grazing lands, mining operations, and roadways. As a result, valuable plants are destroyed. And once a plant species disappears, it is gone forever.

Emily, Page 2

186 Informative/Explanatory Writing

Strategies for Writers Online

Go to **www.sfw.z-b.com** for additional online resources for students and teachers.

It'd be wonderful if a compromise could be worked out. Rain forests are much more valuable than grazing lands or roadways. Maybe local governments could invite more researchers and limit developers. Maybe, as Dr. Bierer suggests, local people could be paid for pointing out medicinal plants. They could be hired to work with scientists to help discover and study plants. In western Samoa, the government was promised half the income from prostratin. Perhaps this method could be used in other countries to keep rain forests from disappearing.

According to some researchers, less than one percent of plant species have been thoroughly examined for medicinal value. By saving as many of these as we can, who knows what remarkable cures we might find.

Works Consulted

Bierer, Donald E., Thomas J. Carlson, and Steven R. King. "Shaman Pharmaceuticals: Integrating Indigenous Knowledge, Tropical Medicinal Plants, Medicine, Modern Science and Reciprocity into a Novel Drug Discovery Approach." *NetSci* May 1996, accessed November 15, 2012, http://www.netsci.org/Science/Special/index.html.

Cox, Paul Alan. "Will Tribal Knowledge Survive the Millennium?" *Science* 7 Jan. 2000: 44.

Sumner, Judith. *The Natural History of Medicinal Plants.* Portland: Timber Press, 2000.

Reflect

Did Emily use all the traits of a good research report? Check her paper against the rubric, and don't forget to use the rubric to check your own work, too.

Emily, Page 3

Allow time for students to share their thoughts. Depending on class size, you may want to write these questions on the board and organize students into smaller groups to facilitate discussion.

CCSS **Common Core State Standards**

W.7.4: Produce clear and coherent writing in which the development, organization, and style are appropriate to task, purpose, and audience.

Summary Planner

Day 4	**Day 5**
Analyze Ideas, Organization, and Voice	**Analyze** Word Choice, Sentence Fluency, and Conventions
Student Objectives • Read a model summary. • Use the summary rubric. • Use the model summary to study Ideas, Organization, and Voice.	**Student Objectives** • Read a model summary. • Use the summary rubric. • Use the model summary to study Word Choice, Sentence Fluency, and Conventions.
Student Activities • Review **"The Structure That Never Sleeps."** *(pp. 191–193)* • Read and discuss **Using the Rubric to Study the Model.** *(pp. 196–197)*	**Student Activities** • Review **"The Structure That Never Sleeps."** *(pp. 191–193)* • Read and discuss **Using the Rubric to Study the Model.** *(pp. 198–199)*

Day 4	**Day 5**
Write Draft	**Write** Revise: Ideas
Student Objectives • Complete a draft.	**Student Objectives** • Revise to delete information that is not relevant or important.
Student Activities • Finish the draft. *(p. 205)* • Participate in a peer conference.	**Student Activities** • Read and discuss **Revise: Focus on Ideas.** *(p. 206)* • Reflect on a model draft. • Apply the revising strategy.

Day 4	**Day 5**
Write Publish: +Presentation	**Write** Publish: +Presentation
Student Objectives • Discuss preparation for publishing and presentation. • Use a final editing checklist to publish their work.	**Student Objectives** • Use a summary rubric. • Share a published summary.
Student Activities • Read and discuss **Publish +Presentation.** *(p. 212)* • Apply the publishing strategy.	**Student Activities** • Share their work. • Use the rubric to reflect upon and evaluate the model and their own writing. *(pp. 194–195, 213)*

To complete the chapter in fewer days, combine the learning objectives and activities in a way that supports students as they write.

Resources at-a-Glance

Grammar, Usage & Mechanics

Differentiating Instruction

For additional Differentiating Instruction activities, see Strategies for Writers Extensions Online *at* **www.sfw.z-b.com.**

English Language Learners

Conferencing

Technology Tip

 Connection Letter

Reproducible letter (in English and Spanish) appears on the *Strategies for Writers* CD-ROM and at **www.sfw.z-b.com.**

▶ Online Writing Center

Provides IWB resources, interactive games and practice activities, videos, eBooks, and a virtual file cabinet.

 Strategies for Writers Online

Go to **www.sfw.z-b.com** for free online resources for students and teachers.

Introduce
a Summary

Student Objectives

- Review the elements of a summary. *(p. 188)*
- Consider purpose and audience. *(p. 189)*
- Learn the traits of informative/ explanatory writing. *(p. 190)*

What's a Summary?

Discuss with students the definition of a summary. Ask whether any students keep a journal or a blog. Note that students could probably restate the main ideas of a journal or blog entry in just a couple of sentences. Then explain that any time students use their own words to shorten the main ideas of a longer piece of writing which they have read and understand, they are using the summary genre. Also point out that the purpose in writing a summary is to share the main ideas and important details in the original text with the reader.

What's in a Summary?

Read and discuss with students the four elements of a summary listed on page 188: Focus, Short Length, Relevant Details, and Direct Style. Then discuss specific reasons that each element may be important when writing a summary.

 Strategies for Writers Online
Go to **www.sfw.z-b.com** for additional online resources for students and teachers.

What's a **Summary?**

It's a short piece of writing that sums up, or tells the main points of, another piece of writing. It's a way to offer my audience a brief retelling of a piece of writing that they might be interested in reading for themselves.

What's in a **Summary?**

Focus
A summary focuses on one piece of writing. The author reads an article, book, or other piece and then sums up its main points in writing.

Short Length
A summary is brief. It explains the main ideas of a piece of writing, but not in an overly detailed way.

Relevant Details
Every word in a summary should be necessary, or relevant. It's not the time to get creative or use long descriptions. Give just enough relevant details to help other people decide if the summarized piece of writing would be interesting or useful to them.

Direct Style
A summary has a direct, formal style. The author uses declarative sentences and active voice to present information in a small amount of space without getting too casual.

Informative/Explanatory Text Exemplars (Summary)

TIME for Kids BIG book of Why: 1,001 Facts Kids Want to Know. **Time for Kids, 2010.** Curious readers will find answers to everything from why we have eyebrows to why wet fingers stick to frozen metal. With facts grouped into categories such as animals, environment/ nature, technology, and space, information is easy to find.

Becker, Helaine. *What's the Big Idea? Inventions that Changed Life on Earth Forever.* **Maple Tree Press, 2009.** Becker provides a glimpse into the key inventions that helped humans meet their six basic needs in life: food, sleep, security, shelter, companionship, and health.

Why write a Summary?

There are a bunch of reasons for writing a summary. I'm still thinking about why I want to write, so I'll list some reasons here.

Share With Others
If I read something good that I want to share with someone else, I can summarize the piece so that others can decide whether they want to read it.

Save Space
I don't have room to keep copies of everything I read. But I have plenty of space to keep summaries. Also, if the material I'm reading belongs to the library, I can summarize it instead of checking it out.

Practice
Summarizing a piece of writing gives me good practice. The skills I use during reading, writing, and summarizing are some of the same skills I'll need in other classes at school.

Research
Summarizing will help me do research. I can skim through sources and summarize the information as I go. Then I can use my summaries to remind me of the most helpful resources.

Morrison, Taylor. *Wildfire.* **Houghton Mifflin Books for Children, 2006.** This is a fascinating overview of wildfires, their causes, and the techniques and equipment used to control them. The book also describes how firefighters work to stop wildfires, as well as some of the dangers they face.

Gifford, Clive. *1000 Years of Famous People.* **Kingfisher, 2002.** This book is a collection of the most famous, and infamous, figures of the past thousand years. Readers will learn about explorers, leaders, writers, among others, and the achievements and legacies they left behind.

Why write a Summary?

Read and discuss with students the reasons for writing a summary listed on page 189. Point out that all writing has a purpose and is aimed at a specific audience. These authentic purposes help authors shape their writing. Someone writing to share with others will be especially careful to be accurate. A writer who wants to save space will focus only on getting down the main ideas, making sure not to include complex examples or long, descriptive details. A person who is writing for practice will sharpen his or her summarizing skills by reading a variety of texts for various purposes. Someone who is writing for research will often summarize different types of text found in a variety of sources. Encourage students to share their own reasons for writing a summary. You may also wish to point out that when the summary is for the writer's use alone, the summary is usually not polished or published. This chapter focuses on writing a summary for publication.

CCSS **C**ommon **C**ore **S**tate **S**tandards
SL.7.1.c: Pose questions that elicit elaboration and respond to others' questions and comments with relevant observations and ideas that bring the discussion back on topic as needed. **R/Inf.7.2:** Determine two or more central ideas in a text and analyze their development over the course of the text; provide an objective summary of the text.

Introduce
a Summary

Linking Informative/ Explanatory Writing Traits to a Summary

Read page 190 aloud to help students understand that they will follow Emily as she models using the writing process and the informative/explanatory writing traits together. A good summary will be built around a clear, focused thesis with supporting details, appropriate transitions that connect ideas and show relationships, and domain-specific vocabulary. It will use a voice and tone that are appropriate for the purpose and audience.

Online Writing Center

 Provides six **interactive anchor papers** for each mode of writing.

TI90   Informative/Explanatory Writing

Linking Informative/Explanatory Traits to a **Summary**

In this chapter, you will write a brief account of an article you have read. This type of informative/explanatory writing is called a summary. Emily will guide you through the stages of the writing process: Prewrite, Draft, Revise, Edit, and Publish. In each stage, Emily will show you important writing strategies that are linked to the Informative/Explanatory Writing Traits below.

Informative/Explanatory Writing Traits

Ideas	• a clear, focused thesis • relevant facts and concrete details that support and develop the thesis
Organization	• a strong introduction, body, and conclusion • paragraphs that have a topic sentence and supporting details • appropriate and varied transitions that connect ideas and show relationships
Voice	• appropriate voice and tone for the purpose and audience
Word Choice	• precise language • domain-specific vocabulary that is used correctly and explained as necessary
Sentence Fluency	• clear sentences whose structure supports the purpose
 **Conventions**	• no or few errors in grammar, usage, mechanics, and spelling

Before you write, read Lidia Peretsky's summary of an article. Then use the summary rubric on pages 194–195 to decide how well she did. (You might want to look back at What's in a Summary? on page 188, too!)

Informative/Explanatory Writing Traits in a Summary

 **Ideas** The summary contains important main ideas from the source. All details are relevant and important.

 **Organization** The paragraphs in the summary are organized into an introduction, body, and conclusion. There is a strong topic sentence and supporting details.

 **Voice** The voice and tone suit the writer's purpose and audience. Establishing and maintaining a formal style is the best way to achieve objectivity in a summary.

"The Structure That Never Sleeps"

by Kim Williams
Summary by Lidia Peretsky

Focus →

Relevant Details ↘

Short Length

The Romans did not invent the arch. However, they were the first people who really knew how to build it, and they influenced people who came after them. Before the Romans, people built square rather than curved openings.

The Romans often built freestanding arches to celebrate great victories. Such arches were huge and visible from great distances. "Triumphal" arches of this type have been built in many places around the world.

Today, you will find arches in all kinds of modern buildings and structures. They are built with a variety of materials and in a variety of shapes and sizes. Besides being useful to us, arches also capture our imaginations.

Direct Style ↗

Arc de Triomphe in Paris, France

Summary **191**

Word Choice A skilled writer uses precise language and domain-specific vocabulary to make a summary informative and credible. The writing is concise and economical.

Sentence Fluency The writer uses well-written declarative sentences to effectively communicate meaning to the reader.

Conventions A good writer carefully edits his or her work prior to publishing. Correct use of grammar, particularly pronouns with clear antecedents, enhances the clarity of the writing in a summary.

Analyze
the Model

Student Objectives

• Read a model summary. *(pp. 191–193)*

Read the Model

Before students look at the summary on page 191, read aloud or have them read the article on pages 192–193. Make a list of the main ideas and details that students predict Kim Williams will include in her summary. Then have students read the summary and compare it against the list. Did Kim include the information that students said she would? Did she include additional main ideas or details? Did she omit any main ideas or details? Conclude that a well-written summary includes only the most important information.

Elements of a Summary

Have students refer to What's in a Summary? on page 188 as you point out the model. Discuss the notes "written" on the model to enhance students' understanding of the terms.

CCSS **C**ommon **C**ore **S**tate **S**tandards

R/Inf.7.1: Cite several pieces of textual evidence to support analysis of what the text says explicitly as well as inferences drawn from the text. **R/Inf.7.5:** Analyze the structure an author uses to organize a text, including how the major sections contribute to the whole and to the development of the ideas.

Summary **T191**

The Structure That Never Sleeps

by Kim Williams

As tributes to especially important victories or as tributes to the greatness of the emperors themselves, special monumental arches called triumphal arches were erected in Rome. The Arch of Titus was built in A.D. 81 to celebrate Emperor Titus's capture of Jerusalem in A.D. 70, and the Arch of Constantine was built in A.D. 312 and 315 to celebrate Emperor Constantine's victory over his rival and brother-in-law, Emperor Maxentius. These were freestanding arches. That is, they stood alone, without being part of a wall, and were placed in prominent positions so that they could be seen from very far away.

Why did the Romans choose the arch as a symbol of triumph? It may be because the arch represented the triumph of Roman engineering over the most difficult structural problems.

The architects of ancient Egypt and Greece knew about the arch, but their architecture was mostly trabeated, based on vertical columns spanned by horizontal, flat beams. The Romans didn't invent the arch; they adopted the form from the architecture of the Etruscans, the people who ruled Italy before the beginning of the Roman Republic in the sixth century B.C. But to their credit, the Romans perfected the techniques of arch construction, making Roman architecture different from anything that came before it. It was because they understood the techniques of arch construction that Roman architects would later be able to develop even more complicated structures, such as the vault and the dome.

Even though the Roman Empire eventually collapsed in the fifth century A.D., its architecture continued to have a huge influence in later centuries. Triumphal arches were built long after there were no more Roman emperors. Perhaps the most famous triumphal arch of all is the Arc de Triomphe in Paris, commissioned by Napoleon Bonaparte in 1806 to honor the Grand Army and completed in 1836.

In the United States, the Washington Arch was built in New

Strategies for Writers Online

Go to **www.sfw.z-b.com** for additional online resources for students and teachers.

York City's Washington Square to celebrate the one-hundred-year anniversary of the inauguration of George Washington as President of the United States. Actually, there were two Washington arches. The first one, built in 1889, was a temporary arch made of wood and plaster, and was intended to be taken down when the celebration ended. New Yorkers, however, liked the arch so much that it was soon decided to build a permanent one in marble. This one was dedicated in 1895.

Today arches are found everywhere. Small arches can be used as doors, and large ones as bridges. Arches can be built of brick, stone, concrete, or steel. They don't have to be round, either, but can be made in lots of special shapes. In addition to their usefulness, arches still have the power to capture our imaginations.

One such arch stands on the banks of the Mississippi River in St. Louis, Missouri. The "Gateway to the West" was designed in the late 1940s by architect Eero Saarinen to honor Thomas Jefferson and the expansion of the United States to the west. Topped off in 1965 and dedicated in 1968, the Gateway Arch has the form of a catenary curve. (If you hold each end of a chain and let it droop between your hands, you have created a catenary curve.) As high as a sixty-three-story building, the carbon-steel arch is covered in gleaming stainless steel. A special kind of tram carries visitors to the top.

Of all the ways that architects have invented of going from "here" to "there," the sweeping curves of the arch may be the most beautiful. Now that you know about arches, look around you. You're sure to find these lovely shapes in your town or city, too.

Gateway Arch in St. Louis, Missouri

CCSS **Common Core State Standards**
R/Inf.7.2: Determine two or more central ideas in a text and analyze their development over the course of the text; provide an objective summary of the text.

Analyze
the Model

Student Objectives

• Learn to read a rubric. (pp. 194–195)

Use the Rubric

Explain the Rubric Explain that a rubric is a tool for planning, improving, and assessing a piece of writing. Tell students that a rubric helps a writer focus on key elements, or traits, in writing (**Ideas, Organization, Voice, Word Choice, Sentence Fluency, Conventions,** and **Presentation**).

Point out that column 6 describes a very good summary, one that has received the highest score in all categories. This is what students should strive for in their own writing.

Discuss the Rubric Guide students in a discussion of the rubric. Read the descriptors that go with each trait. Discuss the difference between columns to be sure students fully understand the point system. Remind students to keep the rubric in mind when they write their own summary and again when they revise it.

Online Writing Center

Provides a variety of **interactive rubrics,** including 4-, 5-, and 6-point models.

Rubric

Use this 6-point rubric to plan and evaluate a summary.

	6	5	4	
Ideas	The summary contains important main ideas from the source. Details are relevant and important.	The summary contains main ideas from the source. Most details are relevant and important.	The summary may miss one main idea from the source. Some irrelevant or minor details are included.	
Organization	Paragraphs have a strong topic sentence and supporting details.	Paragraphs have a topic sentence and supporting details.	The topic sentence in some paragraphs may be hard to find. A few more supporting details would be helpful.	
Voice	The writer establishes and maintains a formal style.	The writer establishes a formal style and maintains it throughout most of the summary.	The writer sets a formal style at the start, but it becomes more casual as the summary progresses.	
Word Choice	The writing, which uses precise language and domain-specific vocabulary, is concise and economical.	The writing is concise and uses some domain-specific vocabulary. There are few unnecessary words.	The writing is concise most of the time. Some vague or unnecessary words are used, but the message is clear.	
Sentence Fluency	Well-written, declarative sentences effectively communicate meaning to the reader.	Declarative sentences effectively communicate meaning to the reader.	Some declarative sentences are poorly written and hard to follow.	
Conventions	Pronouns are used correctly and have clear antecedents. The summary is easy to read and understand.	Most pronouns are used correctly and have clear antecedents. The errors do not interfere with meaning.	A few pronouns are used incorrectly and do not have clear antecedents. The errors are noticeable but not distracting.	

➕ Presentation Visuals are labeled and thoughtfully integrated with the text.

CCSS Common Core State Standards

Summary

The Common Core State Standards appear throughout every unit. The lessons for summary are based principally on the writing standards for Informative/Explanatory writing. The Organization and Ideas rubrics reflect standards **W.7.2, W.7.2.a,** and **W.7.2.b,** which address defining and introducing the topic as well as providing details that support the topic. In the summary genre, the concept of organizing ideas that support the topic sentence translates easily to the focus of the text. Additionally, standard **W.7.2.b** stresses including only details that are relevant and important to the summary. This coincides with the Voice rubric, which calls for establishing and maintaining a formal style.

3	2	1	
The summary is missing more than one main idea from the source. Several details are irrelevant.	The summary lacks sufficient ideas. The details seem randomly chosen.	The summary lacks a purpose and reads like a random list of thoughts.	**Ideas**
A few paragraphs lack a topic sentence or supporting details.	Most paragraphs lack a topic sentence or supporting details.	The paragraphs contain no structure. They read like a list of random thoughts.	**Organization**
The writer's style wavers between formal and casual throughout the summary.	The writer's style is difficult to find.	There is no style in the writing. Words were just put on paper.	**Voice**
Some of the writing is too wordy, and few domain-specific words are used. Vague language muddies the message.	Wordy, imprecise writing takes away from the meaning. The writer uses domain-specific words incorrectly.	Words are vague and unrelated, and the message is unclear.	**Word Choice**
Several awkward declarative sentences make the summary hard to read aloud.	Many declarative sentences are awkward or incorrect, making the meaning hard to find.	Sentences are incomplete or incorrect. The reader cannot understand the meaning.	**Sentence Fluency**
Noticeable, distracting errors with pronouns and antecedents sometimes confuse the reader.	Basic errors with pronouns and antecedents get in the way of the meaning.	Many serious errors with pronouns and antecedents make the writing difficult to understand.	**Conventions**

See Appendix B for 4-, 5-, and 6-point informative/explanatory rubrics.

Assign Groups Divide the class into small groups to examine the model. Assign a trait to each group. One person in each group should be responsible for recording one or two strong examples of the trait as described by the rubric. Ask students to score each trait accordingly. They should be able to support the score with valid points. Note that although the models were written to score high against the rubric, students should not assume each trait would receive a 6. Encourage each group to thoroughly discuss each trait before assigning a score.

Reassemble Class Bring the class back together and ask one person from each group to report the group's findings to the class. The point of this exercise is not to score the model, but rather to practice identifying and evaluating the traits within a piece of writing.

Additional Rubrics Appendix B includes 4-, 5-, and 6-point rubrics that can be used with any piece of informative/explanatory writing. The rubrics are also available as blackline masters in the back of this Teacher Edition, beginning on page T543.

Standard **W.7.4** emphasizes producing clear and coherent writing in which the development, organization, and style are appropriate to task, purpose, and audience. This standard aligns with the Sentence Fluency rubric, which stresses using well-written, declarative sentences to communicate meaning to the reader. The Word Choice rubric emphasizes the use of precise and domain-specific vocabulary to explain the topic. This skill is addressed by standard **W.7.2.d**.

The language standards for grade 7 students (**L.7.1** and **L.7.2**) are addressed during editing and skills practice. In addition, there are multiple opportunities to address the speaking and listening standards. Most important, this chapter will help your students produce coherent writing (**W.7.4**), improve their writing (**W.7.5**), and use technologies to publish and present their finished pieces (**W.7.6**).

CCSS **C**ommon **C**ore **S**tate **S**tandards
SL.7.1.b: Follow rules for collegial discussions, track progress toward specific goals and deadlines, and define individual roles as needed.

Analyze
the Model

Student Objectives

- Read a model summary.
  (pp. 191–193)
- Use the summary rubric.
  (pp. 194–195)
- Use the model summary to study Ideas, Organization, and Voice.
  (pp. 196–197)

Study the Model

Assess the Model Have volunteers read aloud each section on pages 196–197. Discuss as a class whether students agree or disagree with each point in Emily's assessment of the summary. Use questions such as the following to discuss the pages with students. Be sure students can back up their answers with concise examples from the summary.

- Does Lidia Peretsky include a main idea or focus at the beginning of the summary? (Possible responses: Yes, the main idea, or focus, of the story is arches. The main idea is shown at the very beginning of the summary.)

- Does Lidia include relevant details that support the main idea? (Possible response: Yes, relevant details are introduced in the first paragraph.)

 Strategies for Writers Online
Go to **www.sfw.z-b.com** for additional online resources for students and teachers.

Using the Rubric to Study the Model
Summary

Did you notice that the model on page 191 points out some key elements of a summary? As she wrote her summary, Lidia Peretsky used these elements to help her summarize an article. She also used the 6-point rubric on pages 194–195 to plan, draft, revise, and edit the writing. A rubric is a great tool to evaluate writing during the writing process.

Now let's use the same rubric to score the model. To do this, we'll focus on each trait separately, starting with Ideas. We'll use the top descriptor for each trait (column 6), along with examples from the model, to help us understand how the traits work together. How would you score Lidia on each trait?

Ideas
- The summary contains important main ideas from the source.
- Details are relevant and important.

I like how Lidia's summary gets right to the point. She immediately introduces the main ideas from the article and then provides plenty of relevant, supporting details.

[from the writing model]

The Romans did not invent the arch. However, they were the first people who really knew how to build it, and they influenced people who came after them. Before the Romans, people built square rather than curved openings.

English Language Learners

BEGINNING
The 5 W's Locate an action photograph. On the board write *what, who, when, why,* and *where.* Point to the picture and ask, *What is happening?* When a student gives an answer, repeat it, and write it on the board. Repeat for *who, when, where,* and *why.* Review the list. Ask, *What is happening? Who is there?* and so on. Demonstrate how to answer in a complete sentence.

INTERMEDIATE
The 5 W's Read a short story that clearly answers the 5 W's. Write on the board *what, who, when, why,* and *where.* As volunteers take turns filling out the information on the board, those at their seats fill in a 5 W's chart. Review the 5 W's chart by asking, *What happened? Who was there?* and so on. Have students ask these questions to each other.

Organization

• Paragraphs have a strong topic sentence and supporting details.

Lidia's paragraphs are clear and well written. Each has a strong topic sentence, letting me know what the paragraph is about, and several informative supporting sentences.

[from the writing model]

Today, you will find arches in all kinds of modern buildings and structures. They are built with a variety of materials and in a variety of shapes and sizes. Besides being useful to us, arches also capture our imaginations.

Voice

• The writer establishes and maintains a formal style.

Lidia's purpose is to summarize an informative article, and she uses an appropriately formal style to do it. She gets straight to the point and doesn't use up precious space with personal or casual comments. Her matter-of-fact style is efficient and effective.

[from the writing model]

The Romans often built freestanding arches to celebrate great victories. Such arches were huge and visible from great distances. "Triumphal" arches of this type have been built in many places around the world.

Summary 197

• Does Lidia use a style and voice that are appropriate for the purpose and audience? (Possible responses: Lidia uses a direct, formal style to make sure she gets her message across. Her purpose is to summarize an informative article, and she gets straight to the point. She doesn't waste space with casual comments.)

ADVANCED

Identifying the 5 W's Tell students a short story about a time you were scared. Write on the board *what, who, when, why,* and *where*. Ask *What happened in my story? Who was there?* and so on. Write students' answers. Have partners tell each other about a time they were scared, or have them tell a funny adventure story. Have one student fill in the 5 W's chart for their partner's story.

ADVANCED HIGH

Identifying the 5 W's Ask each student to read an article from the school newspaper. After students have read their piece, have them fill in a 5 W's chart. Then have them trade selections and 5 W's charts with a partner. The partner should read the selection and review the chart for mistakes.

CCSS Common Core State Standards

SL.7.1.b: Follow rules for collegial discussions, track progress toward specific goals and deadlines, and define individual roles as needed. **SL.7.1.c:** Pose questions that elicit elaboration and respond to others' questions and comments with relevant observations and ideas that bring the discussion back on topic as needed.

Analyze
the Model

Week 1 • Day 5

Student Objectives

- Read a model summary. (pp. 191–193)
- Use the summary rubric. (pp. 194–195)
- Use the model summary to study Word Choice, Sentence Fluency, and Conventions. (pp. 198–199)

Continue the Discussion Use questions such as the following to continue analyzing the model:

- Does Lidia use precise language? Is her writing concise and economical? (Possible responses: Lidia uses precise and efficient language. She did not ramble on or repeat herself.)

- Which part of the model does an especially good job of communicating meaning to the reader? What makes the meaning clear? (Possible responses: The first paragraph is especially clear. Lidia does a good job of using well-written, declarative sentences.)

- Does Lidia make correct use of pronouns and antecedents? (Possible responses: Yes, and her spelling, capitalization, and punctuation are also correct.)

Strategies for Writers Online

Go to **www.sfw.z-b.com** for additional online resources for students and teachers.

Word Choice

- The writing, which uses precise language and domain-specific vocabulary, is concise and economical.

Not only does Lidia get right to the point of her summary, but she also uses her "space" wisely. Each word serves a specific purpose. Her language is precise and efficient. She doesn't ramble or repeat herself. She also uses domain-specific words—words that relate to the topic—correctly. Notice how she makes it clear what an arch is.

[from the writing model]

The Romans did not invent the arch. However, they were the first people who really knew how to build it, and they influenced people who came after them. Before the Romans, people built square rather than curved openings.

Sentence Fluency

- Well-written, declarative sentences effectively communicate meaning to the reader.

Lidia's summary consists of well-written, declarative sentences. She doesn't confuse the reader with questions or waste space with exclamations. The reader understands her purpose is to inform, and the facts are easily understood.

[from the writing model]

The Romans often built freestanding arches to celebrate great victories. Such arches were huge and visible from great distances. "Triumphal" arches of this type have been built in many places around the world.

198   Informative/Explanatory Writing

Technology Tip   for 21st Century Literacies

Teachers can use "plagiarism detection" websites to screen their students' work, but these tools come with a price that impacts class community and budgets. Teach the rules behind paraphrasing and summary writing, and share free tools/sites that, while not perfect, can help them take the initiative to make sure their work is original and correctly cited. Our students have grown up in a culture where the boundaries about sharing and ownership have been blurred and we toss around terms like *open* and *remix*. Pay attention to that culture, and look for opportunities to learn together.

See **www.sfw.z-b.com** for further information about and links to these websites and tools.

Conventions • Pronouns are used correctly and have clear antecedents. The summary is easy to read and understand.

There are no spelling, capitalization, or punctuation mistakes in Lidia's summary. Also, every pronoun refers back to its antecedent. In this example, it's easy to tell that *They* refers to *arches*.

[from the writing model]

Today, you will find arches in all kinds of modern buildings and structures. They are built with a variety of materials and in a variety of shapes and sizes.

+Presentation Visuals are labeled and thoughtfully integrated with the text.

My Turn!

I'm excited to write a summary of my own. I already have an article in mind. I'm glad I have the rubric to help me with good writing strategies. Follow along as I get started.

Differentiating Instruction

ENRICHMENT

Practice Summarizing Challenge students to retell a favorite book or movie by summarizing the main story line or theme. Caution students that they should not share long, descriptive details or state their personal opinions. Listeners should feel that they have received essential information about the work.

REINFORCEMENT

Using a Computer Some students may benefit from using a computer to draft their summaries. A computer allows them to capture their ideas and make changes more easily. In addition, the size of the fonts can be adjusted for ease of reading.

Presentation Point out to students that Presentation is equally as important as the other traits. Discuss why presentation is important. (Possible response: It can make a difference as to whether readers can or even want to read a piece of writing.) Text should be clearly handwritten in pen or typed, using a few readable fonts. Remind students that paragraphs should be indented (using the tab key if typed), or space should be left between blocked paragraphs. Talk about the use of white space to organize text. Good margins make the line lengths comfortable to read, and a centered title stands out on a page. Also remind students that other text features such as spacing and a bold font can be used to create headings and highlight information. When visuals are used, they should be placed so as to support the text.

Think About the Traits All the traits are important in every piece of writing, but some of the traits stand out more in some genres than in others. Ask students for their opinions. Students might say, for example, that **Organization** is very important because if the paragraphs do not have a clear topic sentence and supporting details, the summary makes no sense. Others may think that **Word Choice** is more important because precise language helps the writer get right to the point of the summary, which helps get the main ideas across.

CCSS Common Core State Standards

SL.7.1.d: Acknowledge new information expressed by others and, when warranted, modify their own views.

Write
a Summary

Week 2 • Day 1

Student Objectives

- Read and understand a prewriting strategy. *(pp. 200–202)*

Prewrite

Focus on Ideas

Collect Information Direct students' attention to Emily's words on page 200. Remind them that in order to write their summaries, they will first have to select and read articles of interest. Point out that Emily chose to summarize "What's So Hot About Spices?" an article she had just read. Remind students that they can do the same, or they can choose to seek out a new article.

Assist students in selecting an article by suggesting some they have read in class or by working with your school librarian to supply a resource pile of appropriate magazine, newspaper, and/or journal articles. Allow class time for students to skim through this resource pile and find articles of interest. Be sure that students record where they found their articles so that they can give proper credit.

Strategies for Writers Online

Go to **www.sfw.z-b.com** for additional online resources for students and teachers.

Prewrite   Focus on Ideas

The Rubric Says	The summary contains important main ideas from the source.
Writing Strategy	Read an article. Jot down the 5 W's from the article.

When my teacher said to write a summary of an informational article, I got pretty excited. I had just read a really interesting article about spicy food, and I knew I could write a good summary of it. Here is the article I read.

What's So Hot About Spices?
by Gail Jarrow and Paul Sherman

Sour pork curry from India. Spicy shrimp from Vietnam. Hot tamales from Mexico. Spicy foods seem to come from countries with a tropical climate.

Two scientists, Jennifer Billing and Dr. Paul Sherman, wondered why. They thought that healthy eating habits probably helped people survive. But how could eating spicy foods in hot climates make diners healthier?

Spices come from plant parts: leaves, flowers, fruits, seeds, or roots. (Salt isn't a true spice since it doesn't come from a plant.) Chemicals in spice plants have aromas and tastes that people like.

The desire for spices was so great that it affected the course of history. The Arabs, Phoenicians, and Europeans explored the world in search of shortcuts to tropical regions of Asia, where many of the popular spices grew. Christopher Columbus was looking for such a shortcut when he bumped into America.

Without refrigeration, foods spoil quickly and can cause illness. Since ancient times, people have used spices to keep food from spoiling—to preserve it. The Romans used red cumin and coriander. Pirates preserved wild game for sea travel by smoking it and rubbing it with allspice. The Egyptians also knew that spices could prevent decay. They even used them in mummification.

Strong Chemicals

Hundreds of years ago people didn't know how certain spices preserved foods. Since then, scientists have discovered that spices contain powerful chemicals. These chemicals protect the spice plants from bacteria, insects, fungi, and hungry animals. When we use spices, the same chemicals prevent the growth of bacteria that spoil our food and can sometimes make us sick.

200 Informative/Explanatory Writing

English Language Learners

BEGINNING

Declarative Sentences Write on the board *Today is sunny.* Read the sentence and have students repeat. Explain that this sentence tells information; it's a declarative sentence. Erase *sunny* and replace it with *Monday.* Read the sentence and have students repeat. Encourage students to create their own simple declarative sentences. Use picture prompts.

INTERMEDIATE

Pronouns Write the subject and object pronouns from page 210 on the board. Write two related sentences, such as *The girl watched a movie. The girl liked the movie.* Underline *the girl* and *the movie.* Ask, *Which pronoun can replace the girl?* Repeat for *the movie.* Write two new sentences on the board and have students read both sentences. Repeat the activity with other examples.

Scientists have tested thirty spices on dozens of food-spoiling bacteria. Every spice affected at least one type of bacterium. The super bacteria killers were allspice, garlic, onion, and oregano. These spices killed or slowed the growth of all bacteria on which they were tested.

Some spices aren't so appealing—at least until you get used to them. You probably wouldn't cover yourself with the scent of garlic or onion if you were trying to impress your friends. Eating fresh hot peppers and chilies can blister your mouth.

Then why did people start eating foods seasoned with these red-hot spices? Ms. Billings and Dr. Sherman had a clue. The two scientists guessed that people who added the spices to their food would have been healthier than those who didn't.

If that guess was right, recipes from tropical climates (where foods spoil faster and the risk of food poisoning is higher) should contain more bacteria-killing spices than those from cool climates. To test their idea, the scientists studied recipes in nearly one hundred cookbooks from all over the world.

First they picked traditional dishes that used meat, since meat spoils quickly. They chose older recipes that were first used before refrigeration. Collecting more than 4,500 recipes from thirty-six countries, they listed all the spices used.

The bacteria killers were the big winners! Seven of the world's ten most commonly used spices have strong antibacterial power: onion, garlic, hot peppers, bay leaf, cinnamon, cloves, and thyme.

Another finding puzzled the scientists. Pepper and lemon/lime juice ranked second and fifth in the Top Ten. This was surprising because these two spices aren't great at wiping out bacteria. But it turns out that they boost the bacteria-killing power of other spices used with them.

The Spiciest Dishes

What about climate? Did warmer countries have spicier dishes? The scientists compared the average temperature of each country to the number of spices used. They found that dishes from cooler countries had few spices. (In Scandinavia many recipes have no spices at all.)

Foods get spicier as the climate gets hotter. Dishes from tropical countries like Ethiopia, India, and Indonesia used the most spices in the world. They had an average of more than six spices per recipe.

Recipes from hot climates also won the prize for including the most bacteria-killing spices. For example, key ingredients in curry dishes popular in India are cumin, cinnamon, and cloves, all good at killing bacteria or slowing their growth. In the United States, garlic, onion, and hot peppers are used more in the South than they are in the North.

Spices in our food make it more tasty. But as scientists discovered, spices often do an even more important job. People living in hot climates had good reason to get used to strong-tasting spices. These bacteria killers helped preserve foods and kept people healthy.

Today we have other ways to preserve our food, such as refrigerating it and freezing it. But that tasty chili powder might still make your taco a healthier lunch.

ADVANCED

Specific Language Write on the board *My friend came to my house. My friend rode his bike to my house.* Read the sentences, students repeat. Ask *Which sentence gives more detail?* Write several nonspecific sentences. With a partner, students change sentences to use more specific language. Read to the class.

ADVANCED HIGH

Redundancy Explain that words that are unnecessary or repetitive are considered redundant. Write on the board *Every day, Sunday through Saturday, I play soccer outside in the yard. I play with my friends. My friends are Jack, Bill, Jose, Yousef, and Jay. We play until late in the evening. We're out there until maybe 7 or 8 pm.* Have students remove redundancies to create brief, to-the-point sentences. Have partners compare the changes they made.

CCSS **Common Core State Standards**
W.7.8: Gather relevant information from multiple print and digital sources, using search terms effectively; assess the credibility and accuracy of each source; and quote or paraphrase the data and conclusions of others while avoiding plagiarism and following a standard format for citation.

Record Information After students have had time to select articles to summarize, ask them to read Emily's words on page 202. Instruct them to jot down the 5 W's (*who, what, when, where,* and *why*) from the articles they have read. Urge them to note main ideas only, excluding any irrelevant or overly detailed information.

Prewrite

Focus on Ideas

The Rubric Says	The summary contains important main ideas from the source.
Writing Strategy	Read an article. Jot down the 5 W's from the article.

Before writing, I recorded the facts in the article that answer the 5 W's. These are always the most important facts, and I want to be sure to include them in my summary.

The 5 W's for "What's So Hot About Spices?"

What: the value and use of spices

Who: two scientists studying the use of spices

Why: spices important in food preparation and preservation

When: starting in early times and continuing to the present

Where: the hotter the climate, the more spices used

Apply

Find an article that interests you. Then write down the 5 W's from the article.

202 Informative/Explanatory Writing

Online Writing Center

Provides **interactive graphic organizers** as well as a variety of graphic organizers in PDF format.

Prewrite

The Rubric Says	Paragraphs have a strong topic sentence and supporting details.
Writing Strategy	Make a Main-Idea Table to organize main ideas and details.

After answering the 5 W's, I used a Main-Idea Table to organize my information. I soon realized I had two main ideas, each with several supporting details. Now I can use my Main-Idea Table to help me write complete, strong paragraphs.

✎ Writer's Term

Main-Idea Table
A **Main-Idea Table** can help you organize the main idea and supporting details for a piece of writing. Write your main ideas in each of the main blocks. Then fill in the "legs" with supporting facts, details, and examples.

Main-Idea Table

Main Idea
People have always known that spices are important in food preservation.

Detail	Detail	Detail	Detail
Early people traveled to find spices.	Spices keep food from spoiling.	Early people didn't know how spices worked.	Scientists found that chemicals keep bacteria from growing.

Main Idea
Scientists wondered if eating spicy food in hot climates made people healthier.

Detail	Detail	Detail	Detail
Scientists compared climates and number of spices used.	They found that people in hot climates used more spices.	Most bacteria-killing spices were also used in hot climates.	People use spices and stay healthy.

Reflect
How will the Main-Idea Table help Emily stay focused as she writes?

Apply
Make your own Main-Idea Table to help organize your thoughts.

Summary **203**

Conferencing

PEER TO PEER When students have completed their Main-Idea Tables, have pairs exchange them. Ask students to review each other's tables and comment on which areas might need more facts and supporting details.

PEER GROUPS Have students meet in small groups of three or four. Instruct them to take turns sharing how they organized their 5 W's notes into clear, focused Main-Idea Tables. Then have each group share their strategies with the other groups.

TEACHER-LED To demonstrate the importance of a focused summary, create your own Main-Idea Table on the board, leaving several areas blank. Discuss how the missing information might affect the writing of an effective summary.

Write
a Summary

Student Objectives

- Make a Main-Idea Table to organize main ideas and details. (p. 203)

Prewrite

Focus on **Organization**

Organize Ideas Explain that writers use a variety of organizers to begin writing. Help students understand that the better organized their notes are, the easier it will be to write well-organized paragraphs. Ask students to study the organizer; then ask how a Main-Idea Table can be an effective tool when writing a Summary. (Possible response: A Main-Idea Table helps you organize your thoughts and stay focused as you write.) Remind students to use the notes they jotted down about their articles' 5 W's to make their Main-Idea Tables.

✎ Writer's Term

Main-Idea Table A Main-Idea Table helps organize ideas by using visual "blocks" and "legs." The "blocks" are the Main Ideas, and the "legs" are the supporting details and examples. A Main-Idea Table helps writers stay focused as they organize information for a summary.

CCSS **Common Core State Standards**
R/Inf.7.5: Analyze the structure an author uses to organize a text, including how the major sections contribute to the whole and to the development of ideas.

Write
a Summary

Week 2 • Day 3

Student Objectives

• Use a Main-Idea Table to begin writing. (p. 204)

Draft

Focus on Voice

Draft a Summary Remind students that drafting gives them a chance to get their ideas on paper without having to worry about making mistakes. Be sure that students understand that they will use their Main-Idea Tables to guide them through the drafting process. Have students compare Emily's draft to her Main-Idea Table. Ask them how her summary relates to the Table. (Possible response: It contains one paragraph for each main idea in the Main-Idea Table.)

Point out that Emily also refers to the rubric as she writes. Encourage students to use the rubric as a guide for their own writing. Then have students use their Main-Idea Tables to draft their own summaries. Remind them to keep their summaries short and accurate. Explain that there will be time to make changes and corrections later.

Online Writing Center

 Provides student eBooks with an **interactive writing pad** for drafting, revising, editing, and publishing.

Draft

Focus on **Voice**

The Rubric Says	The writer establishes and maintains a formal style.
Writing Strategy	Maintain consistency in style and tone.

The rubric reminds me that I should write with a formal style right from the start and use that style consistently throughout my summary. My purpose is to convey the main points of the article clearly and directly. A casual, chatty style would not be appropriate for this goal. It's easy to lapse into using informal language even after I've started out with a formal style, so I'll need to pay attention and keep my style consistent as I write.

My Main-Idea Table will help me write the topic sentences for each paragraph. I'll look back at the article to make sure I only use information found there. I'll do my best with spelling and grammar, but I know I can fix any mistakes later. Now to get writing!

✏ Writer's Term

Formal Style

Style is made up of the choices you make as you write. The words and phrases you select create your style. When you use a **formal style,** you write as though you are addressing a teacher or other adult whom you want to take your work seriously. You don't have to use long or difficult words to create a formal style. However, you do have to use complete sentences with good grammar and avoid casual or slang expressions.

204 **Informative/Explanatory Writing**

Differentiating Instruction

ENRICHMENT

Connect With Informational Text Inform students that summarizing is a skill that can be useful in all their classes. Summarizing what they have read is a good strategy for making sure that they have understood their reading.

REINFORCEMENT

Summarize Orally Work with students individually or in small groups to summarize an article orally before they write. Talking before writing will help students think through what they want to write.

Proofreading Marks

⌐ Indent	ℓ Take out something
≡ Make a capital	⊙ Add a period
/ Make a small letter	⌗ New paragraph
∧ Add something	⑤℗ Spelling error

[DRAFT]

"What's So Hot About Spices?"

by Gail Jarrow and Paul Sherman

Summary by Emily   [short summary]

People have always known that spices are important in food preservation. Many early explorers actually were looking for routes to Asia, where they could find the spices they wanted. The Phoenicians and Arabs and even Christopher Columbus went [formal style] in search of spices, but did they know how spices worked? Now we know that chemicles in it keep all kinds of living bacteria from growing in food, spoiling it, and making us humans sick.

They studied recipes that were used in different climates before refrigeration. They looked at curry recipes and recipes for meat dishes. Two scienctists tried to figure out if eating spicy food in hot countries made early people healthier. The scientists also listed each recipe's ingreedients. We found that people in hot climates—where foods spoil more quickly—used more spices. They also used the most bacteria-killing spices: onion, garlic, hot peppers, and cloves. For both early people and us, spices could really make us a lot healthier.

Reflect

How does using a formal style strengthen Emily's writing?

Apply

As you write your draft, use a formal style throughout.

Summary **205**

Conferencing

PEER TO PEER Have pairs of students exchange drafts. Ask students to think of two or three questions they would like to ask to clarify information or supply missing details. Instruct them to ask questions and provide helpful comments for each other regarding the overall organization of their summaries. Be sure the focus is not on mechanics at this time.

PEER GROUPS Organize students into small groups. Have them take turns reading sections of their summaries aloud. Other group members should provide helpful commentary to strengthen specific areas of each report.

TEACHER-LED Meet with pairs of students. Go over their organizers and make sure they know how they will use their Main-Idea Tables to write their drafts. Encourage students to keep these comments in mind when writing their drafts.

Write
a Summary

Week 2 • Day 4

Student Objectives

• Complete a draft. *(p. 205)*

Continue Drafting It is important that students are given ample time to draft summaries. Be sure to also plan time for conferencing throughout the process. Remind students that drafting is the time for getting their ideas on paper in a creative and engaging way. Assure them that they will have plenty of time to make changes and corrections later.

Writer's Term

Formal Style A writer's style is a combination of the choices he or she makes while writing. Using a formal style is important when writers want to sound knowledgeable about the topic. When the purpose for writing is to convey accurate information found in another source, it is especially important to use a formal style. To sound confident and credible, the writer uses a formal style that complements the topic and avoids chatty, casual language, and slang expressions.

CCSS Common Core State Standards
W.7.2.e: Establish and maintain a formal style. **W.7.5:** With some guidance and support from peers and adults, develop and strengthen writing as needed by planning, revising, editing, rewriting, or trying a new approach, focusing on how well purpose and audience have been addressed. **SL.7.1:** Engage effectively in a range of collaborative discussions (one-on-one, in groups, and teacher-led) with diverse partners on *grade 7 topics, texts, and issues,* building on others' ideas and expressing their own clearly.

Write
a Summary

Week 2 • Day 5

Student Objectives

- Revise to delete information that is not relevant or important. *(p. 206)*

Revise

Focus on (Ideas)

Omit Irrelevant Information

Write the word *irrelevant* on the board and explain to students that it refers to something that is not needed. To model irrelevancy, write sets of phrases on the board, with one irrelevant phrase in each group. For example, you might write *bathing suit, snowshoes, sun block, beach towel.* Ask which item in the list is not relevant to a trip to the beach. (snowshoes) Invite students to make up their own examples. Explain that irrelevant or unrelated details distract the reader.

Discuss the importance of making sure all information is relevant. Have one volunteer read the Draft excerpt on page 206 without the revisions, and then have another volunteer read the revised excerpt. Point out how much stronger and clearer Emily's writing is after she deleted irrelevant information.

 Strategies for Writers Online
Go to **www.sfw.z-b.com** for additional online resources for students and teachers.

Revise

Focus on (Ideas)

The Rubric Says   Details are relevant and important.

Writing Strategy   Delete information that is not relevant or important.

After I wrote my draft, I checked it against the rubric. I thought I stayed on topic very well, but there was one place that contained information that was too detailed for a summary. I want all my details to be relevant, so I deleted the extra information.

[DRAFT]

[deleted irrelevant details]

They studied recipes that were used in different climates before refrigeration. ~~They looked at curry recipes and recipes for meat dishes.~~ Two scienctists tried to figure out if eating spicy food in hot countries made early people healthier. The scientists also listed each recipe's ingreedients. We found that people in hot

Apply

Delete irrelevant or overly detailed information from your draft.

206   Informative/Explanatory Writing

English Language Learners

BEGINNING/INTERMEDIATE

Main-Idea Table Draw a Main-Idea Table on the board. In the Main Idea section, write *Breakfast Foods*. Ask students to give examples of the different foods they eat for breakfast. Then write their answers, such as *cereal, eggs, rice,* in the Supporting Details section.

ADVANCED/ADVANCED HIGH

Relevant Details Assign a topic to each student. Remind students that details should be relevant and necessary. Using a Web graphic organizer, have students fill in relevant details and a few irrelevant details for their topics. Then have them switch Webs with a partner and identify unnecessary details.

Revise
Focus on Word Choice

The Rubric Says	The writing, which uses precise language and domain-specific vocabulary, is concise and economical.
Writing Strategy	Recognize and eliminate wordiness and redundancy.

Summaries are meant to be brief. The rubric says my writing should be concise and economical—meaning that every word I use is important and I shouldn't waste space with unnecessary words. I need to mention only the most important ideas from the article and use only the necessary words to do so. I'll reread my draft now and either delete unnecessary words or add precise words where more information is required.

[DRAFT]

[deleted unnecessary words]

The Phoenicians and Arabs and even Christopher Columbus went in search of spices, but did they know how spices worked? Now we know that chemicles in it keep ~~all kinds of living~~ bacteria from growing in food, ~~spoiling it, and making us humans sick.~~

Reflect
What do you think? How have Emily's revisions helped make her summary stronger and more precise?

Apply
Delete any unnecessary words, and use only informative and precise words in your summary.

Summary **207**

Conferencing

PEER TO PEER   Have partners exchange drafts. After reading the draft, have students offer helpful feedback, pointing out redundant or unnecessary words that should be deleted to strengthen Word Choice.

PEER GROUPS   Have students form small groups of three or four. Then have them take turns reading sections of their drafts aloud. Ask group members to suggest areas where unnecessary words should be deleted. Advise writers to check word resources to replace overused or redundant words with precise ones.

TEACHER-LED   Conference with pairs of students. Have them read each other's drafts and coach them in giving constructive criticism on Word Choice.

Write
a Summary

Week 3 • Day 1

Student Objectives

- Revise to eliminate wordiness and redundancy. *(p. 207)*

Revise

Focus on  Word Choice

Eliminate Wordiness and Redundancy Read page 207 aloud. Explain to students that effective summaries are brief and to the point. It is important to make sure that the writer uses precise language and domain-specific vocabulary from the source. Because a summary is brief, each word should be concise, economical, and have a purpose. A summary is not the place for rambling or repetitive writing. Explain to students that *redundant words* are unnecessary words that clutter a summary and detract from its meaning. The language throughout should be precise, efficient, and clear. Remind students to keep their summaries brief and to delete any redundant or unnecessary words.

CCSS **C**ommon **C**ore **S**tate **S**tandards
W.7.2.d: Use precise language and domain-specific vocabulary to inform about or explain the topic. **W.7.5:** With some guidance and support from peers and adults, develop and strengthen writing as needed by planning, revising, editing, rewriting, or trying a new approach, focusing on how well purpose and audience have been addressed. **W.7.6:** Acquire and use accurately grade-appropriate general academic and domain-specific words and phrases; gather vocabulary knowledge when considering a word or phrase important to comprehension or expression.

Summary   **T207**

Write a Summary

Week 3 • Day 2

Student Objectives

- Revise for effective, communicative punctuation. (p. 208)

Revise

Focus on 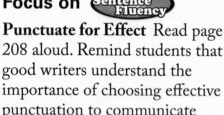 Sentence Fluency

Punctuate for Effect Read page 208 aloud. Remind students that good writers understand the importance of choosing effective punctuation to communicate with the audience. In a summary, well-written, declarative sentences effectively communicate meaning to the reader. Tell students to look back at Lidia Peretsky's summary on page 191 and notice that she did not confuse the reader by using questions or exclamations. It is clear that her purpose is to inform. Help students understand that a summary should not be littered with distracting questions and exclamations. Since the purpose of a summary is to state important information, declarative sentences are the best way to get the main ideas across in a summary. Encourage students to review their summaries and look for areas where they can use declarative sentences to present the facts found in the original source.

Online Writing Center

Provides **interactive proofreading activities** for each genre.

Revise

Focus on **Sentence Fluency**

The Rubric Says Well-written, declarative sentences effectively communicate meaning to the reader.

Writing Strategy Choose punctuation for effect.

The rubric says to use well-written, declarative sentences in my summary. I can see how questions and exclamations don't work well when the purpose is to give information to the reader. My essay should not be littered with distracting question marks and exclamations. Declarative sentences state facts, and that's exactly what I want to do. As I reread my draft, I found a sentence that needs some revision.

[DRAFT]

The Phoenicians and Arabs and even Christopher Columbus went in search of spices, but ~~did they~~ early people didn't know how spices worked?. Now we know that chemicles in it keep ~~all kinds of living~~ bacteria from growing in food, spoiling it, and making us humans sick.

[formed a declarative sentence]

Apply

Use declarative sentences to present the facts of your summary.

Optional Revising Lessons

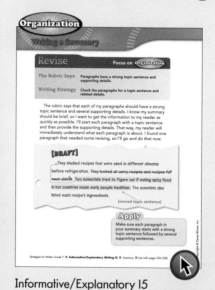

Organization

Writing a Summary

Revise Focus on **Organization**

The Rubric Says Paragraphs have a strong topic sentence and supporting details.

Writing Strategy Check the paragraphs for a topic sentence and related details.

The rubric says that each of my paragraphs should have a strong topic sentence and several supporting details. I know my summary should be brief, so I want to get the information to my reader as quickly as possible. I'll start each paragraph with a topic sentence and then provide the supporting details. That way, my reader will immediately understand what each paragraph is about. I found one paragraph that needed some revising, so I'll go and do that now.

[DRAFT]

They studied recipes that were used in different climates before refrigeration. They looked at curry recipes and recipes for meat dishes. Two scientists tried to figure out if eating spicy food in hot countries made early people healthier. The scientists also listed each recipe's ingredients.

[moved topic sentence]

Apply

Make sure each paragraph in your summary starts with a strong topic sentence followed by several supporting sentences.

Strategies for Writers Grade 7 ■ Informative/Explanatory Writing 15 ■ Summary ■ Use with pages 206–208

Informative/Explanatory 15

Voice

Writing a Summary

Revise Focus on **Voice**

The Rubric Says The writer establishes and maintains a formal style.

Writing Strategy Use a matter-of-fact, formal style.

The rubric says that my style should be formal throughout my summary. That doesn't mean I should try to impress my readers with long, fancy words. It does mean, however, that I should take a matter-of-fact tone to convey my information and avoid the kind of casual, chatty language I might use when talking with my friends. I think I did a good job of maintaining a formal style—right up until the last sentence! I'll go and revise that now.

[DRAFT]

Those people They also used the most bacteria-killing spices: onion, garlic, hot peppers, and cloves. For both early people and us, spices could add to better health. really make us a lot healthier.

[revised for formal style]

Apply

Make sure you use a formal style throughout your summary.

Strategies for Writers Grade 7 ■ Informative/Explanatory Writing 16 ■ Summary ■ Use with pages 206–208

Informative/Explanatory 16

Go to → *Strategies for Writers Grade 7 CD-ROM*

Edit Focus on Conventions

The Rubric Says	Pronouns are used correctly and have clear antecedents. The summary is easy to read and understand.
Writing Strategy	Recognize and correct inappropriate shifts in pronoun number and person.

✎ **Writer's Term**_____

Pronouns and Antecedents
A **pronoun** is a word that takes the place of a noun. Examples include *I, you, them, it, he, she, our, we,* and *they*. Pronouns must have clear antecedents. An **antecedent** is the word that a pronoun refers to or replaces.

It's time to check for mistakes and misspelled words, but according to the rubric, I should also check my use of pronouns.

[DRAFT]

[corrected pronoun]
scientists
at curry recipes and recipes for meat dishes. Two ~~scienctisf~~ ^

tried to figure out if eating spicy food in hot countries made

early people healthier. The scientists also listed each recipe's
                                        They
ingredients, ~~ingreedients. We~~ found that people in hot climates—where foods
                                Those people
spoil more quickly—used more spices. ~~They~~? also used the most

bacteria-killing spices: onion, garlic, hot peppers, and cloves. For
                                        [corrected an unclear antecedent]
both early people and us, spices could

Reflect
How did Emily's edits help make her summary easier to understand? Are all her pronouns correct and antecedents clear?

Apply Conventions
Check your draft for spelling, punctuation, and capitalization, making sure pronouns and antecedents are also used correctly.

For more practice with pronouns and antecedents, use the exercises on the next two pages.

Summary 209

Related Grammar Practice _____

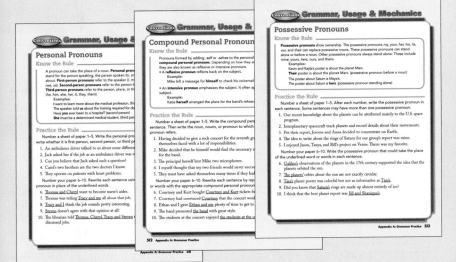

Student Edition pages 511–513

Go to ➡ **Appendix A: Grammar Practice**

Write
a Summary

Student Objectives

- Edit for correct use of pronoun number and person. *(p. 209)*

Edit

Focus on Conventions

Edit for Accurate Use of Pronouns and Antecedents Read aloud the Writer's Term box on page 209. Review the importance of and reasons for editing a piece of writing.

Use the mini-lessons on pages T210–211 for students having problems with pronoun-antecedent agreement. Then have students complete the exercises on pages 210–211. Go over the answers in class.

✎ **Writer's Term**_____

Pronouns and Antecedents A pronoun should also agree with its antecedent in number (singular or plural) and gender (male or female). There are three common groups of pronouns: subject pronouns (*I, you, he, she, it, we, they, who*), object pronouns (*me, you, him, her, it, us, them, whom*), and possessive pronouns (*my/mine, your/yours, his, her/hers, it/its, our/ours, their/theirs, whose*). An apostrophe is not used in a possessive pronoun.

CCSS **C**ommon **C**ore **S**tate **S**tandards
L.7.1: Demonstrate command of the conventions of standard English grammar and usage when writing or speaking.

Conventions
Mini-Lesson

Student Objectives

- Use pronouns and antecedents correctly. *(p. 210)*

Pronouns and Antecedents

Have students review the Know the Rule box on page 210. Then write the following sentence on the board:

- *Kellie shared the research report with me.*

Ask students how the pronoun *me* is used in this sentence. (object pronoun)

Now write the following on the board:

- *Her report is about community gardens.*

Ask students how the pronoun *Her* is used in this sentence. (possessive pronoun)

Then explain to students that pronouns often serve more than one function in writing. Finally, ask a volunteer to rewrite the first example sentence so that it contains both the pronoun *her* and an antecedent. (Possible response: Kellie shared her research report with me.)

Remind students that it is important to use pronouns and antecedents correctly in their summaries.

Online Writing Center

 Provides **interactive grammar games** and **practice activities** in student eBook.

Pronouns and Antecedents

Know the Rule

The pronouns *I, we, you, he, she, it,* and *they* are **subject pronouns**. Use them as subjects of sentences.

Subject of sentence: Irv and **I** like spicy food.

The pronouns *me, us, you, him, her, it,* and *them* are **object pronouns**. Use them as objects following verbs and as objects of prepositions.

Object of verb: A researcher informed Irv and **me**.

Object of preposition: He said, "Take some for **you** and **him**."

The pronouns *my, mine, our, ours, your, yours, his, hers, its, their,* and *theirs* are **possessive pronouns**. Use them to show possession. Do not use an apostrophe in a possessive pronoun.

Possession: Those samples are **mine**.

A pronoun should have a clear **antecedent**, or noun that it refers to. A pronoun must agree with its antecedent in number and gender.

Example: Irv took **his** samples because **he** liked **them**.

Practice the Rule

Read the sentences, looking for pronoun and antecedent errors. Then write each sentence correctly on a separate sheet of paper.

1. Frankie began to get very red after their first taste of Tepin peppers.   *his*
2. The peppers spread its heat through 300 gallons of salsa.   *their*
3. It should never be consumed in a concentrated form.   *They*
4. The next thing Denzel offered to we was a pepper soup.   *us*
5. Frankie and Jill were afraid to swallow any of our soup.   *their*
6. Them knew it would be too hot to handle.   *They*
7. The trick is to slice a pepper lengthwise and remove only a few of his seeds.   *its*
8. Frankie prefers a milder flavor, so him removes all of the seeds.   *he*
9. Me told Denzel that very spicy foods don't agree with me.   *I*
10. Because Denzel didn't want to make me uncomfortable, they made a mild dish.   *he*

Related Grammar Practice

Pages 73, 75, 77, 159, 161, 163, 165

Go to ⇨ **G.U.M. Student Practice Book**

Pronouns in Pairs

Know the Rule

Use a **subject pronoun** in a compound subject. Use an **object pronoun** in a compound direct object, a compound indirect object, or a compound object of a preposition.

> Examples: My **brother and I** both love to hike. (compound subject)
>
> Dad took **my brother and me** hiking. (compound direct object)

Practice the Rule

On a separate sheet of paper, write each sentence with the correct pronoun.

1. Every year, my parents and (I, me) camp for a week in New Hampshire's White Mountains.
2. This year, Dad invited his uncle to come along with my family and (I, me).
3. Before dawn, Dad woke Uncle Gerard and (I, me).
4. Uncle Gerard and (I, me) sat in the back with the family dog, Skipper.
5. Skipper took up so much space that (he, him) and Uncle Gerard had to squeeze over to one side of the car.
6. Soon we stopped for breakfast, which was good because Uncle Gerard and (I, me) were hungry!
7. Dad ordered eggs for (he, himself) and Mom, but Uncle Gerard and (I, me) had pancakes.
8. Mom said the campground looked the same as when (she, her) and her sister went there as children.
9. Dad set up two tents, one for Uncle Gerard and (I, me) and another for (he, him) and Mom.
10. At the end of the week, Dad, Mom, Uncle Gerard, Skipper, and (I, me) packed up our tents and went home.

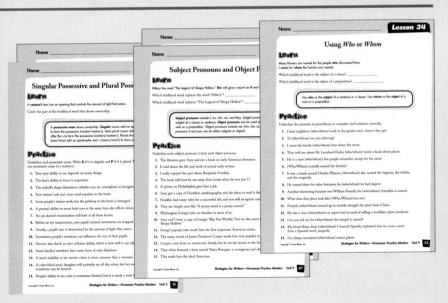

Pages 31, 33, 67, 71, 73

Go to ➡ **Grammar Practice Masters**

Conventions

Mini-Lesson

Student Objectives

- Use pronouns in pairs correctly. *(p. 211)*

Pronouns in Pairs

Have students review the Know the Rule box on page 211. Then write the following sentences on the board:

- *My dad and I are excited about our camping trip.*
- *My mom asked Dad and me to help pack the gear.*
- *While Dad packed the tent, Mom and I packed the food.*
- *Camping is a favorite activity for them and me.*

Ask students to identify the compound subject pronouns. (dad, I; Mom, I) Then ask students to identify the compound object pronouns. (Dad, me; them, me) Point out that the *I* in the first and third sentences is a subject pronoun. Also point out that *me* in the second and last sentences is an object pronoun. Assist students in using the correct pronouns in pairs by leaving out the other pronoun. For example, say: *My mom asked (I, me) to help pack the gear. Camping is a favorite activity for (I, me).*

CCSS **Common Core State Standards**

W.7.2: Demonstrate command of the conventions of standard English capitalization. **L.7.1:** Demonstrate command of the conventions of standard English grammar and usage when writing or speaking.

Write
a Summary

Week 3 • Day 4

Student Objectives

- Discuss preparation for publishing and presentation. *(p. 212)*
- Use a final editing checklist to publish their work. *(p. 212)*

Publish ⁺Presentation

Publishing Strategy Ask students if they like Emily's choice for sharing her summary in a class news magazine. Tell the class that her choice is not the only option for publishing her work. Invite students to name other ways they could publish their own summaries. Perhaps some students will want to include their summaries as part of a display in the nonfiction section of the library, while some may want to present theirs in a multimedia presentation to the class. Still others may want to publish their summaries on a class website.

Before publishing, have each student make a checklist and perform a final evaluation of the summary. Remind students that while typing their summaries on a computer allows them to choose their own fonts, they should remember to set clear margins and use a limited number of clear, readable fonts. When they have finished their final copies, encourage students to circulate them to friends and family members.

 Strategies for Writers Online
Go to **www.sfw.z-b.com** for additional online resources for students and teachers.

Publish ⁺Presentation

Publishing Strategy	Publish my summary in a class news magazine.
Presentation Strategy	Use visuals that enhance the text. Label the visuals.

Now I'm ready to publish my summary! But how, exactly, should I do this? I could read it to my friend Simone, or I could hang it on my science class's display board. It is about cooking ingredients, after all! But I'd really like to include it in the news magazine my class has been working on all year. I'll include some related, labeled visuals to enliven and enhance my summary. Then I'll read it through one last time to make sure I've done everything on my final checklist.

My Final Checklist

Did I—

✔ use all pronouns correctly?

✔ make sure each pronoun agreed with the number and gender of its antecedent?

✔ use appropriate visuals that enhance my summary?

✔ thoughtfully integrate my visuals with the text?

✔ label my visuals accurately?

Apply
Make a checklist to check your summary. Then make a final copy to publish.

212 Informative/Explanatory Writing

Differentiating Instruction

ENRICHMENT
Practice Makes Proficient Challenge students to read more articles or essays about their topics. Encourage them to use their summary as a good starting point. Encourage students to consult the Internet for information related to their topics.

REINFORCEMENT
Double Check Have students complete their checklists. Then have pairs of students exchange checklists and drafts to perform a final evaluation. Remind peer editors to check that pronouns are used correctly throughout the summary. Before students print their final copies, remind them that the grammar and spell checker may not catch every error, especially the pronoun *its*.

"What's So Hot About Spices?"

by Gail Jarrow and Paul Sherman

Summary by Emily

People have always known that spices are important in food preservation. Many early explorers actually were looking for routes to Asia, where they could find the spices they wanted. The Phoenicians and Arabs and even Christopher Columbus went in search of spices, but early people didn't know how spices worked. Now we know that chemicals in them keep bacteria from growing in food.

Two scientists tried to figure out if eating spicy food in hot countries made early people healthier. They studied recipes that were used in different climates before refrigeration. The scientists also listed each recipe's ingredients. They found that people in hot climates—where foods spoil more quickly—used more spices. Those people also used the most bacteria-killing spices: onion, garlic, hot peppers, and cloves. For both early people and us, spices could add to better health.

Hot red peppers

Garlic

Reflect

How did Emily do? Did she use all the traits of a good summary? Don't forget to use the rubric to check your own summary.

Summary **213**

Technology Tip — for 21st Century Literacies

Publishing content from students' summaries works as an information literacy exercise when students add their discoveries, ideas, and contributions to a wiki, or "knowledge community" site. In editing an article on a site like Wikipedia or Wikijunior, students need to not only have their facts correct, but they also need to add information in a way that contributes to the existing piece. Sometimes students' writing will be deleted or rejected in the process. Work with students to examine site elements, like the edit history, to see how the article has evolved and to "listen in" on discussions in the threads. Understanding the community will help students learn how to better contribute.

See **www.sfw.z-b.com** for further information about and links to these websites and tools.

Write a Summary

Week 3 • Day 5

Student Objectives

- Use a summary rubric. *(pp. 194–195)*
- Share a published summary. *(p. 213)*

Presentation Strategy Remind students of the importance of neatness when creating a final, polished copy of their work. Computers make it easy to use appropriate templates, set neat margins, indent paragraphs, and select clear fonts. Also remind students to use the header or footer function to label each page with the title, both the author's and the writer's name, and a page number. It is especially important to remember to label any visuals that have been added to enhance the text.

Reflecting on a Summary

Instruct students to refer to the rubric on pages 194–195 as they reread Emily's final copy on page 213. After students have finished reading, ask them what they think of Emily's changes. Did her revisions and edits strengthen or weaken her summary? What score would Emily have received for each writing trait?

CCSS Common Core State Standards

W.7.4: Produce clear and coherent writing in which the development, organization, and style are appropriate to task, purpose, and audience. **SL.7.5:** Include multimedia components and visual displays in presentations to clarify claims and findings and emphasize salient points.

Problem-Solution Essay Planner

WEEK 1

Day 1
Introduce
a Problem-Solution Essay

Student Objectives
- Review the elements of a problem-solution essay.
- Consider purpose and audience.
- Learn the traits of informative/explanatory writing.

Student Activities
- Read and discuss **What's in a Problem-Solution Essay?** and **Why Write a Problem-Solution Essay?** (pp. 214–215)
- Read **Linking Informative/Explanatory Writing Traits to a Problem-Solution Essay.** (p. 216)

Day 2
Analyze
Read a Problem-Solution Essay

Student Objectives
- Read a model problem-solution essay.

Student Activities
- Read **"The Best Way To Go."** (pp. 217–219)

Day 3
Analyze
Introduce the Rubric

Student Objectives
- Learn to read a rubric.

Student Activities
- Review **"The Best Way To Go."** (pp. 217–219)
- Read and discuss the **Problem-Solution Essay Rubric.** (pp. 220–221)

WEEK 2

Day 1
Write
Prewrite: Ideas

Student Objectives
- Read and understand a prewriting strategy.

Student Activities
- Read and discuss **Prewrite: Focus on Ideas.** (p. 226)
- Apply the prewriting strategy.

Day 2
Write
Prewrite: Organization

Student Objectives
- Make a Problem-Solution Frame to organize notes.

Student Activities
- Read and discuss **Prewrite: Focus on Organization.** (p. 227)
- Apply the prewriting strategy to create a Problem-Solution Frame.
- Participate in a peer conference.

Day 3
Write
Draft: Word Choice

Student Objectives
- Include domain-specific vocabulary.

Student Activities
- Read and discuss **Draft: Focus on Word Choice.** (p. 228)
- Apply the drafting strategy by using a Problem-Solution Frame to write a draft.

WEEK 3

Day 1
Write
Revise: Organization

Student Objectives
- Revise to include transitions to connect sentences and paragraphs.

Student Activities
- Read and discuss **Revise: Focus on Organization.** (p. 231)
- Reflect on a model draft.
- Apply the revising strategy.

Day 2
Write
Revise: Sentence Fluency

Student Objectives
- Revise for parallel sentence structures.

Student Activities
- Read and discuss **Revise: Focus on Sentence Fluency.** (p. 232)
- Reflect on a model draft.
- Apply the revising strategy.

Note: Optional Revising Lessons appear on the *Strategies for Writers* CD-ROM.

Day 3
Write
Edit: Conventions

Student Objectives
- Edit for correct use of verb tenses.

Student Activities
- Read and discuss **Edit: Focus on Conventions.** (p. 233)
- Reflect on a model draft.
- Apply the revising strategy.

Note: Teach the Conventions mini-lessons (pp. 234–235) if needed.

Day 4	Day 5

Analyze
Ideas, Organization, and Voice

Analyze
Word Choice, Sentence Fluency, and Conventions

Student Objectives
- Read a model problem-solution essay.
- Use the problem-solution essay rubric.
- Use the model problem-solution essay to study Ideas, Organization, and Voice.

Student Objectives
- Read a model problem-solution essay.
- Use the problem-solution essay rubric.
- Use the model problem-solution essay to study Word Choice, Sentence Fluency, and Conventions.

Student Activities
- Review **"The Best Way To Go."** *(pp. 217–219)*
- Read and discuss **Using the Rubric to Study the Model.** *(pp. 222–223)*

Student Activities
- Review **"The Best Way To Go."** *(pp. 217–219)*
- Read and discuss **Using the Rubric to Study the Model.** *(pp. 224–225)*

Day 4	Day 5

Write
Draft

Write
Revise: Ideas

Student Objectives
- Complete a draft.

Student Objectives
- Revise to include concrete and credible details.

Student Activities
- Finish the draft. *(p. 229)*
- Participate in a peer conference.

Student Activities
- Read and discuss **Revise: Focus on Ideas.** *(p. 230)*
- Reflect on a model draft.
- Apply the revising strategy.

Day 4	Day 5

Write
Publish: +Presentation

Write
Publish: +Presentation

Student Objectives
- Discuss preparation for publishing and presentation.
- Use a final editing checklist to publish their work.

Student Objectives
- Use a problem-solution essay rubric.
- Share a published problem-solution essay.

Student Activities
- Read and discuss **Publish: +Presentation.** *(p. 236)*
- Apply the publishing strategy.

Student Activities
- Share their work.
- Use the rubric to reflect upon and evaluate the model and their own writing. *(pp. 220–221, 237–239)*

To complete the chapter in fewer days, combine the learning objectives and activities in a way that supports students as they write.

Resources at-a-Glance

Grammar, Usage & Mechanics

Auxiliary Verbs T234
Irregular Verbs T235
Grammar Practice T233–T235

Differentiating Instruction

Using the Rubric T225
Draft T228
Publish T236

For additional Differentiating Instruction activities, see Strategies for Writers *Extensions Online at* **www.sfw.z-b.com.**

English Language Learners

Using the Rubric T222–T223
Prewrite T226
Revise T230

Conferencing

Peer to Peer T227, T229, T231
Peer Groups T227, T229, T231
Teacher-Led T227, T229, T231

Technology Tip

Using the Rubric T224
Publish T237

 Connection Letter
Reproducible letter (in English and Spanish) appears on the *Strategies for Writers* CD-ROM and at **www.sfw.z-b.com.**

Online Writing Center

Provides IWB resources, interactive games and practice activities, videos, eBooks, and a virtual file cabinet.

 Strategies for Writers Online

Go to **www.sfw.z-b.com** for free online resources for students and teachers.

Introduce
a Problem-Solution Essay

Week 1 • Day 1

Student Objectives

- Review the elements of a problem-solution essay. *(p. 214)*
- Consider purpose and audience. *(p. 215)*
- Learn the traits of informative/ explanatory writing. *(p. 216)*

What's a Problem-Solution Essay?

Discuss with students the definition of a problem-solution essay. Ask whether students enjoy solving problems. Ask if they ever encounter problems in the world for which they would like to find solutions. Point out that any time they explain a problem in writing and try to develop a possible solution, they are using the problem-solution genre.

What's in a Problem-Solution Essay?

Read and discuss with students each of the four elements of a problem-solution essay listed on page 214: Introduction, Body, Conclusion, and Style. Then discuss specific reasons that each element may be important to writing a problem-solution essay.

 Strategies for Writers Online
Go to **www.sfw.z-b.com** for additional online resources for students and teachers.

What's a **Problem-Solution Essay?**

A problem-solution essay sets out a problem and offers one or more solutions to the problem. Solving problems can be fun, and I would like to learn how to put problem-solving steps into writing.

What's in a **Problem-Solution Essay?**

Introduction
The introduction of a problem-solution essay states a problem and explains why the reader should care about it. The introduction should get the reader engaged and ready to follow along.

Body
The body of a problem-solution essay develops at least one solution thoroughly. The writer may describe more than one possible solution, explaining why one solution is better than the others.

Conclusion
The conclusion says something decisive about a solution or a combination of solutions. A good conclusion closes the essay in a way the reader will remember.

Style
The style of a problem-solution essay should not be too light or casual. The writer wants the reader to take the problem and proposed solutions seriously. The style should be fairly formal. At the same time, though, it should not be stiff or boring.

Informative/Explanatory Text Exemplars (Problem-Solution Essay)

Enzensberger, Hans Magnus. *The Number Devil: A Mathematical Adventure.* Translated by Michael Henry Heim. Henry Holt and Company, 1998. **CCSS** Robert, a 12 year-old boy, hates math. After his math teacher won't let him use a calculator to figure out word problems, Robert encounters a number devil that helps him with numbers.

Thimmesh, Catherine. *Girls Think of Everything: Stories of Ingenious Inventions by Women.* Houghton Mifflin, 2000. Learn about the many items we use every day that were invented by ingenious women. Thimmesh provides snippets of information about the creative female minds behind such products as windshield wipers and the chocolate chip cookie.

Why write a **Problem-Solution Essay?**

I'm thinking about why I might write a problem-solution essay. I am not ready to choose a topic yet, but here are some reasons I would want to write this kind of essay.

Understanding
If I want to solve a problem, I need to understand it first. Researching the problem and developing possible solutions would really help me expand my understanding.

Information
By the time I'm ready to write, I should have quite a bit of information I want to share. I will want to inform readers so that they'll understand the problem and solutions in my essay.

Explanation
In my essay, I need to explain not only the facts about my topic but how my topic connects to the wider world. I want readers to understand why the problem matters and why I have chosen a certain solution.

Why write a Problem-Solution Essay?

Read and discuss with students the reasons for writing a problem-solution essay listed on page 215. Point out that all writing has a purpose and is aimed at a specific audience. These authentic purposes help authors shape their writing. Someone writing to understand will research the problem and develop possible solutions. A writer who wants to inform will gather plenty of information to help readers grasp the problems and solutions. Someone who is writing to explain will offer not only facts but will also elaborate on how the topic connects to the world. Encourage students to share their own reasons for writing a problem-solution essay. Ask them to discuss how their reasons will affect the tone and focus of their writing.

Gore, Al. *An Inconvenient Truth: The Crisis of Global Warming.* **Viking Juvenile, 2007.** Adapted for a younger audience, Gore's book touches on the controversy of global warming and offers clear definitions of key terms related to the climate issue threatening our planet.

Bul Dau, John. *Lost Boy, Lost Girl: Escaping Civil War in Sudan.* **National Geographic Children's Books, 2010.** Read a firsthand account of John Bul Dau's and his wife, Martha's, experience enduring the remarkable hardships and famine of the war in Sudan. Learn about the struggles, pain, and sorrow they went through as children orphaned during the war, and experience their resilience and courage to survive.

CCSS **Common Core State Standards**
SL.7.1.c: Pose questions that elicit elaboration and respond to others' questions and comments with relevant observations and ideas that bring the discussion back on topic as needed.

Introduce
a Problem-Solution Essay

Linking Informative/ Explanatory Writing Traits to a Problem-Solution Essay

Read page 216 aloud to help students understand that they will follow Emily as she models using the writing process and the informative/explanatory writing traits together. A good problem-solution essay will be built around a clear, focused thesis supported by relevant facts and concrete details, appropriate transitions that connect ideas to show relationships, and domain-specific vocabulary. It will use a voice and tone that are appropriate for the purpose and audience.

Linking Informative/Explanatory Writing Traits to a **Problem-Solution Essay**

In this chapter, you will write an essay that explains a problem and proposes one or more solutions. This type of informative/explanatory writing is called a problem-solution essay. Emily will guide you through the stages of the writing process: Prewrite, Draft, Revise, Edit, and Publish. In each stage, Emily will show you important writing strategies that are linked to the Informative/Explanatory Writing Traits below.

Informative/Explanatory Writing Traits

Ideas	• a clear, focused thesis • relevant facts and concrete details that support and develop the thesis
 **Organization**	• a strong introduction, body, and conclusion • paragraphs that have a topic sentence and supporting details • appropriate and varied transitions that connect ideas and show relationships
Voice	• appropriate voice and tone for the purpose and audience
Word Choice	• precise language • domain-specific vocabulary that is used correctly and explained as necessary
Sentence Fluency	• clear sentences whose structure supports the purpose
Conventions	• no or few errors in grammar, usage, mechanics, and spelling

Before you write, read Alan Wong's problem-solution essay on the next three pages. Then use the problem-solution rubric on pages 220–221 to decide how well he did.

Informative/Explanatory Writing Traits in a Problem-Solution Essay

 **Ideas** The problem-solution essay contains a clear thesis that states the problem. Details are relevant and important.

 **Organization** A problem-solution essay is organized into an introduction, body, and conclusion. This makes it easier for the reader to understand the problem, its importance, and the recommended solution.

 **Voice** To ensure that the reader is engaged throughout the problem-solution essay, it's important to use an appropriate voice and tone. Using a formal style is the best way to achieve this in a problem-solution essay.

The Best Way To Go
by Alan Wong

Introduction

Formal Style

Our cities have been struggling with pollution and traffic for many years. Cars fill the highways and city streets, drivers complain about spending hours trapped in bottlenecks during rush hour, and everyone hates breathing the fumes from all those cars idling as they're stuck in traffic. What's the solution? How do we make the traffic flow more quickly and help clean up the air in the cities? More people should try these three ways to get around: carpooling, riding the bus, and biking.

Let's look at the pros and cons of each solution, starting with carpooling. When people carpool, they share a car to reach the same destination. For example, people who work in the same office building would drive to and from work together every day, instead of going in separate cars. The members of the carpool might take turns driving the others, or one person might be the driver and the others would contribute some money toward the cost of the gas used for the trip.

Carpooling has three obvious advantages: flexibility, companionship, and economy. Since carpools usually consist of just three or four people, members of the carpool have some control over what time they leave in the morning or return in the evening. If their work hours permit some flexibility, the group can decide to drive earlier or later to avoid the worst of rush hour. Carpool members can also enjoy each other's company as they travel in a quiet, comfortable car. And as members share the cost of gas, driving into town is cheaper for everyone.

Each advantage is mirrored by a disadvantage, however. The flexibility of a carpool only reaches so far. If one member needs to stay late at work, it's not fair to make everyone wait for that person. Each carpool member needs to have a back-up form of transportation for days when he or she can't ride with the rest of the group. When it comes to companionship, some people may find it hard to carpool with a person whose company they do not enjoy. And while it's true that carpoolers use less gas than if they traveled separately, the cars do still burn fuel—which means expense and pollution.

Body

Problem-Solution Essay 217

Word Choice A skilled writer uses domain-specific content vocabulary to make a problem-solution essay more credible. The terms are used effectively and defined clearly.

Sentence Fluency The writer uses clear sentences, including parallel structures that emphasize a relationship.

Conventions A good writer carefully edits his or her work prior to publishing. Correct use of grammar, particularly verbs, enhances the clarity of the writing in a problem-solution essay.

Analyze
the Model

Week 1 • Day 2

Student Objectives

• Read a model problem-solution essay. (pp. 217–219)

Read the Model

Read "The Best Way To Go" aloud to the class. Ask students to listen for the thesis statement and relevant details, and to notice how the details are organized. Also ask students to think about and discuss how a formal, serious tone affected how they connected to the problem-solution essay. How were their reactions different from their peers?

Elements of a Problem-Solution Essay

Have students refer to What's in a Problem-Solution Essay? on page 214 as you refer to the model. Discuss the notes "written" on the model to enhance students' understanding of the terms.

CCSS Common Core State Standards
R/Inf.7.1: Cite several pieces of textual evidence to support analysis of what the text says explicitly as well as inferences drawn from the text.

Riding the bus has similar advantages to those of a carpool. Bus riders can be flexible: you can catch a bus at different times of day, and usually buses run more frequently at rush hour. Riding the bus can be a more sociable experience than driving alone in a car, too. You may not chat with your fellow riders, but you can watch people of all sorts getting on and off the bus. Lastly, when it comes to fuel, the bus is even more economical than a carpool. One bus filled with thirty passengers burns a lot less gas than thirty separate cars driving the same distance.

What's the negative side to riding the bus? As with a carpool, the flexibility only extends so far. Buses stop only at certain points along their routes. You may have to transfer from one bus to another to get where you are going. Most likely, too, you'll have to walk a little distance from your bus stop to your home or workplace. On the social side, you have no control over who shares your space in a bus. In a carpool, you have some choice in your fellow riders; on a bus, if your fellow riders are loud and unpleasant, you're stuck with them until you reach your stop. In terms of fuel economy, the same comment applies to a bus as to a carpool: the bus does burn gas and create pollution, although riding a bus is a much more economical solution than driving a car.

Biking offers a non-motorized way to travel from point A to point B. Biking is probably the best solution in terms of flexibility, companionship, and economy. Bike riders have complete flexibility to decide what time they leave for work and what time they return. They are not limited by bus routes but can ride from their front door all the way to the office. Cyclists who live or work near each other can decide to ride together for companionship or ride alone when their schedules for the day do not match those of their friends. Best of all, it's the rider who provides the energy to make the bike go forward; no fuel is burned. In addition, biking is wonderful exercise and great for your health.

It's true, however, that even biking is not a perfect solution. In bad weather or icy conditions, a bike rider might decide to take a different means of transportation. In addition, it can be hard to carry a large load on a bicycle. Bike shops do sell saddlebags and offer other solutions for

Strategies for Writers Online
Go to **www.sfw.z-b.com** for additional online resources for students and teachers.

T218 Informative/Explanatory Writing

carrying all sorts of cargo, but a cyclist may still need to give some thought to what he or she will choose to bring to work each day. A bicycle is also a slower means of transportation than a car or bus. On the other hand, when you are biking, you are also getting your day's exercise, which might save you a trip to the gym. And on days when cars and buses are stalled in heavy traffic, a bike might just turn out to be the fastest way to move!

Knowing that there are three good alternatives to driving individual cars to work, how do we encourage people to try them? A solid program of education for riders, drivers, and all citizens of every community in the country would be a great start. Both the government and private organizations could work together to create signs and advertising campaigns to inform people about alternative choices in transportation. Since traffic and pollution are issues that concern everyone, it is appropriate to involve all areas of society.

Several cities have special carpool lanes on their highways to encourage people to share rides. More cities could adopt this helpful policy and make sure everyone knows that carpooling will allow them to get to their destinations faster. To encourage people to use buses, cities could make sure the buses are clean and pleasant to ride. Some cities are using technology to make bus riding easier, too. Riders can check online to see what time the next bus will arrive at their stop. City governments should also make sure information about routes and schedules is easy to get whether riders have access to the Internet or not.

To encourage biking, cities and private organizations could take several steps. Establishing special bike lanes along major streets would make biking much safer and easier in cities. City governments could also set up bike racks in convenient locations throughout the community so that cyclists could lock up their bikes. Private cycling organizations could launch education campaigns to teach drivers to look out for bikers and bikers to ride safely in city traffic. With just a little cooperation from governments, private organizations, and citizens, we can transform our cities into clean, low-traffic spaces!

Conclusion

CCSS **Common Core State Standards**
R/Inf.7.1: Cite several pieces of textual evidence to support analysis of what the text says explicitly as well as inferences drawn from the text.

Analyze
the Model

Student Objectives

- Learn to read a rubric. *(pp. 220–221)*

Use the Rubric

Explain the Rubric Explain that a rubric is a tool for planning, improving, and assessing a piece of writing. Tell students that a rubric helps a writer focus on key elements, or traits, in writing (**Ideas, Organization, Voice, Word Choice, Sentence Fluency, Conventions,** and **Presentation**).

Point out that column 6 describes a very good problem-solution essay, one that has received the highest score in all categories. This is what students should strive for in their own writing.

Discuss the Rubric Guide students in a discussion of the rubric. Read the descriptors that go with each trait. Discuss the difference between columns to be sure students fully understand the point system. Remind students to keep the rubric in mind when they write their own problem-solution essays and again when they revise them.

Online Writing Center

Provides a variety of **interactive rubrics,** including 4-, 5-, and 6-point models.

Problem-Solution Essay

Rubric

Use this 6-point rubric to plan and score a problem-solution essay.

	6	5	4
Ideas	A clear thesis statement states the problem, its importance, and a recommended solution. One or more solutions are fully developed with relevant facts and concrete details.	A thesis statement states the problem and a recommended solution. At least one solution is fully developed with some relevant facts and concrete details.	A thesis statement states the problem and a solution. One solution is partially developed with facts and details.
Organization	Ideas are organized logically in a strong introduction, body, and conclusion. Appropriate, effective transitions clarify relationships among ideas.	Ideas are organized logically in an introduction, body, and conclusion. Transitions link and clarify ideas.	Ideas are organized but the introduction, body, and/or conclusion could be stronger. Transitions are used.
Voice	The voice sounds knowledgeable and engages the reader. A formal tone is maintained consistently.	The voice informs and engages the reader most of the time. The tone may be overly formal (textbook-like).	The voice informs and engages the reader some of the time. The tone is informative in parts.
Word Choice	Domain-specific content vocabulary is used effectively and defined clearly.	Domain-specific content vocabulary is used correctly. One definition could be clearer.	Domain-specific content vocabulary is used correctly. Several definitions need clarification.
Sentence Fluency	Sentences are clear, including parallel structures that emphasize a relationship.	Sentences are clear most of the time, but one or two parallel structures are inconsistent.	Sentences are clear. Parallel structures are attempted.
Conventions	The writing has been carefully edited. All verbs are used correctly.	Minor errors are present but do not interfere with meaning. Verbs are used correctly.	A few errors cause confusion. Irregular verbs may be used incorrectly.
✚ Presentation	The format helps readers access the information.		

CCSS Common Core State Standards

Problem-Solution Essay

The lessons for problem-solution essay are based on the writing standards for Informative/Explanatory writing. The Organization and Ideas rubrics reflect standards **W.7.2, W.7.2.a,** and **W.7.2.f,** which address defining and introducing the topic as well as providing a concluding statement that follows from the topic. Additionally, standard **W.7.2.b** addresses developing the topic with relevant facts and concrete details, and standard **W.7.2.c** also aligns with the Organization rubric in stressing the use of transitions to clarify relationships among ideas. The Voice rubric, which stresses the use of a knowledgeable, formal tone relates to standard **W.7.2.e.** The Sentence Fluency and Word Choice rubrics are also drawn from the Informative/Explanatory standards. Standard **W.7.4** emphasizes producing clear and coherent writing in which the

3	2	1	
A thesis statement states the problem but not a solution. The solution is not well developed and details are lacking.	A thesis statement is present, but the problem and solution are not clear. No solution is fully developed.	No thesis statement is present. The ideas are incomplete.	Ideas
Ideas are presented but are not well organized. More or better transitions are needed to link ideas.	There is no clear introduction, body, or conclusion. Transitions are confusing or are used incorrectly.	The ideas are not organized. Transitions are not used.	Organization
The voice informs in the beginning then fades. An informative tone is not maintained.	The voice is weak or distant. The tone is too informal or casual to be informative.	The voice is absent. The tone is not established.	Voice
Domain-specific content vocabulary is used, but none are defined.	Some words are ordinary or overused. Domain-specific content vocabulary is not used.	Limited vocabulary and repetition dulls meaning. Some words are used incorrectly.	Word Choice
Sentences are clear some of the time. Parallel structures, if present, are not correct.	Many sentences are unclear. Parallel structures are not used.	Sentences are awkward to read or they are incomplete.	Sentence Fluency
Many errors are repeated and cause confusion. Irregular verbs may be used incorrectly.	Serious errors interfere with meaning. Verbs are used incorrectly.	The writing has not been edited.	Conventions

See Appendix B for 4-, 5-, and 6-point informative/explanatory rubrics.

Apply the Rubric

Assign Groups Divide the class into six small groups to examine the model. Assign a trait to each group. One person in each group should be responsible for recording one or two strong examples of the assigned trait. Each group should then decide on a score for the trait. Students should not assume that any trait should receive a 6. Instead, encourage the groups to discuss their traits thoroughly before scoring them.

Reassemble Class Bring the class back together and ask one person from each group to report the group's findings to the class. The point of this exercise is not to score the model, but rather to practice identifying and evaluating the traits within a piece of writing.

Additional Rubrics Appendix B includes 4-, 5-, and 6-point rubrics that can be used with any piece of informative/explanatory writing. The rubrics are also available as blackline masters in the back of this Teacher Edition, beginning on page T543.

development, organization, and style are appropriate to task, purpose, and audience. This standard aligns with the Sentence Fluency rubric, which stresses the use of parallel sentence structures to emphasize relationships. The Word Choice rubric aligns with standard **W.7.2.d,** which addresses the use of clearly defined domain-specific vocabulary.

The language standards (**L.7.1** and **L.7.2**) are addressed during editing and skills practice. In addition, there are multiple opportunities to address the speaking and listening standards during the writing process. Most important, this chapter will help your students produce coherent writing (**W.7.4**), improve their writing (**W.7.5**), and use technologies to publish and present their finished pieces (**W.7.6**).

CCSS **Common Core State Standards**
SL.7.1.b: Follow rules for collegial discussions, track progress toward specific goals and deadlines, and define individual roles as needed.

Analyze
the Model

Student Objectives

- Read a model problem-solution essay. *(pp. 217–219)*
- Use the problem-solution essay rubric. *(pp. 220–221)*
- Use the model problem-solution essay to study Ideas, Organization, and Voice. *(pp. 222–223)*

Study the Model

Assess the Model Have volunteers read aloud each section on pages 222–223. Discuss as a class whether students agree or disagree with each point in Emily's assessment of the problem-solution essay. Use questions such as the following to discuss the pages with students. Be sure students can back up their answers with concise examples from the essay:

- Does Alan Wong state the problem and a recommended solution at the beginning of the problem-solution essay? (Possible response: Yes, he states the problems, *traffic flow* and *clean air in cities,* in the first paragraph. He includes some solutions for different forms of transportation to help address the problems of *traffic flow* and *clean air in cities.*)

Strategies for Writers Online

Go to **www.sfw.z-b.com** for additional online resources for students and teachers.

Problem-Solution Essay
Using the Rubric to Study the Model

Did you notice that the model on pages 217–219 points out some key elements of a problem-solution essay? As he wrote "The Best Way to Go," Alan Wong used these elements to help him explain a problem and present solutions. He also used the 6-point rubric on pages 220–221 to plan, draft, revise, and edit the writing. A rubric is a great tool to evaluate writing during the writing process.

Now let's use the same rubric to score the model. To do this, we'll focus on each trait separately, starting with Ideas. We'll use the top descriptor for each trait (column 6), along with examples from the model, to help us understand how the traits work together. How would you score Alan on each trait?

- A clear thesis statement states the problem, its importance, and a recommended solution.
- One or more solutions are fully developed with relevant facts and concrete details.

Alan's introduction leads up to a crystal clear thesis statement. I know exactly what problem he plans to discuss and how he thinks it can be solved. Once he's set out his thesis, he goes on to explore each of his solutions using concrete details and relevant facts.

[from the writing model]

> How do we make the traffic flow more quickly and help clean up the air in the cities? More people should try these three ways to get around: carpooling, riding the bus, and biking.
>
> Let's look at the pros and cons of each solution, starting with carpooling.

222 Informative/Explanatory Writing

English Language Learners

BEGINNING

Negative Verbs Show a picture of ice cream. Ask, *Do you like ice cream?* If a student answers *yes,* model the complete sentence *Yes, I like ice cream,* and write it on the board. Have students say the sentence. Repeat for a *no* answer. Continue practicing with other verbs, such as *Is ice cream cold? Does ice cream taste sweet?* Repeat the activity with other photos.

INTERMEDIATE

Negative Verbs Ask students, *Do you come to school by _____?* After they answer, say, *I come/do not come to school by _____.* Write it on the board and have students read it. Underline *not* and explain that *not* is used with the verb in a negative sentence. Have partners ask questions and answer with *I do not* sentences.

Organization
- Ideas are organized logically in a strong introduction, body, and conclusion.
- Appropriate, effective transitions clarify relationships among ideas.

I like the way this essay is organized. The introduction states the problem and solution, the body develops each solution in detail, and the conclusion proposes ways the solutions could be implemented. In addition, Alan uses transitions at key points throughout the essay to show the reader how his ideas connect. In this paragraph, he uses *however* to show that he's about to offer a contrast and *in addition* to show that he's moving on to a new, connected thought.

[from the writing model]

It's true, however, that even biking is not a perfect solution. In bad weather or icy conditions, a bike rider might decide to take a different means of transportation. In addition, it can be hard to carry a large load on a bicycle.

Voice
- The voice sounds knowledgeable and engages the reader.
- A formal tone is maintained consistently.

Since Alan wants his reader to take his ideas seriously, he uses a formal tone and makes sure he sounds knowledgeable. That doesn't mean he sounds stiff or boring, though. Here, he keeps his tone formal, shows his knowledge of his topic, and uses *you* to add a personal note and engage the reader.

[from the writing model]

Riding the bus has similar advantages to those of a carpool. Bus riders can be flexible: you can catch a bus at different times of day, and usually buses run more frequently at rush hour. Riding the bus can be a more sociable experience than driving alone in a car, too. You may not chat with your fellow riders, but you can watch people of all sorts getting on and off the bus.

Problem-Solution Essay 223

- Does Alan include a strong introduction, body, and conclusion? (Possible response: Yes, the essay is well-organized with a strong introduction, a body that develops each solution, and a conclusion that proposes ways to implement the solutions.)

- Does Alan use a style and voice that are appropriate for the purpose and audience? (Possible response: Alan uses a knowledgeable, formal style to make sure he gets his message across.)

ADVANCED
Transition Words Write on the board: *Cell phone use while driving is dangerous. People are distracted. They are four times more likely to be in an accident. Annually 1.4 million crashes are caused by cell phone conversations.* Have students write a paragraph using the sentences on the board and transition words and phrases, such as *because, as a result, since, therefore, in addition, moreover, furthermore,* and *similarly.* Have partners read their paragraphs to each other.

ADVANCED HIGH
Transition Words Write on the board *Transition Words: as a result, because, since, therefore, in addition, moreover, furthermore,* and *similarly.* Have students write a brief problem-solution paragraph about cell phone use while driving. Remind them to include a few transition words.

CCSS **Common Core State Standards**
SL.7.1.b: Follow rules for collegial discussions, track progress toward specific goals and deadlines, and define individual roles as needed. **SL.7.1.c:** Pose questions that elicit elaboration and respond to others' questions and comments with relevant observations and ideas that bring the discussion back on topic as needed.

Analyze
the Model

Week 1 • Day 5

Student Objectives

- Read a model problem-solution essay. *(pp. 217–219)*
- Use the problem-solution essay rubric. *(pp. 220–221)*
- Use the model problem-solution essay to study Word Choice, Sentence Fluency, and Conventions. *(pp. 224–225)*

Continue the Discussion Use these questions to continue analyzing the model:

- Did Alan use clearly defined, domain-specific vocabulary? Which terms did he explain? (Possible response: Alan took care to define domain-specific vocabulary. It was helpful when he made a point to define *carpooling* for readers.)

- Which part of the model does an especially good job of including sentences that make the meaning of the essay clear? (Possible response: In the fourth paragraph, Alan uses parallel sentence structures to emphasize relationships. He writes about the pros and cons of bus riding and carpooling in a similar way. The relationship is easily understood.)

- Did Alan make correct use of verbs? (Possible responses: Yes, Alan used verbs correctly throughout his summary. His spelling, capitalization, and punctuation are also correct.)

 Strategies for Writers Online
Go to **www.sfw.z-b.com** for additional online resources for students and teachers.

 **Word Choice**
- Domain-specific content vocabulary is used effectively and defined clearly.

Carpooling is a key concept and a domain-specific term in Alan's essay, and he takes care to define the word for his readers. It's important to make sure your readers understand your terms. Otherwise, your solutions won't make sense to them!

[from the writing model]

When people carpool, they share a car to reach the same destination. For example, people who work in the same office building would drive to and from work together every day, instead of going in separate cars.

Sentence Fluency
- Sentences are clear, including parallel structures that emphasize a relationship.

Alan obviously took great care in composing his sentences. Each one conveys his meaning clearly. When he's discussing the pros and cons of bus riding and carpooling, for example, he introduces the cons in a similar way. That makes it easy for me to see the relationship between the ideas he is explaining.

[from the writing model]

Each advantage is mirrored by a disadvantage, however. The flexibility of a carpool only reaches so far. . . .

What's the negative side to riding the bus? As with a carpool, the flexibility only extends so far.

224 Informative/Explanatory Writing

Technology Tip for 21st Century Literacies

Real-world problems have stakeholders. Challenge student writers to interact with people whose lives are directly impacted by the problems addressed in their papers. Use tools like SurveyMonkey or Google Forms to design surveys that aid in the collection and analysis of information or points of view. If tools are available, use video cameras to collect and capture live interviews. Students will want to use the data tools that best fit their topics. Remind students that as they draft, these same contributors would be useful for readers as well.

See **www.sfw.z-b.com** for further information about and links to these websites and tools.

Conventions
- The writing has been carefully edited.
- All verbs are used correctly.

Alan must have checked punctuation, spelling, and capitalization very carefully: I don't see any errors. He uses verbs correctly throughout the essay. Notice the sentences in this example, where he uses the verbs *would* and *could* to help explain an idea he proposes as a solution.

> [from the writing model]
>
> A solid program of education for riders, drivers, and all citizens of every community in the country would be a great start. Both the government and private organizations could work together to create signs and advertising campaigns to inform people about alternative choices in transportation.

Presentation The format helps readers access the information.

Now it's my turn to write a problem-solution essay. I'll use the rubric and good writing strategies to help me. Read on to see how I do it.

Problem-Solution Essay **225**

Differentiating Instruction

ENRICHMENT

Create Problem-Solution Structures Encourage students to brainstorm several problems that they might like to solve. Then have them choose one and suggest solutions. After all students have contributed, ask them to prioritize the solutions. They should be able to defend their reasoning.

REINFORCEMENT

Evaluate Writing Traits Have students turn to the rubric on pages 220–221. Read column 6 for Ideas and then say: *Alan Wong states his thesis in the first paragraph. I can also see from the first paragraph that Alan has presented some solutions. Because I read the article, I know that he has included relevant and concrete details to develop the solutions.* Then call on volunteers to model the other traits. Coach students as needed.

Presentation Stress to students that neatness is always a priority. Text should be clearly handwritten in pen or typed, using a few readable fonts. Remind students that paragraphs should be indented (using the tab key if typed), or space should be left between block paragraphs. Talk about the use of white space to organize text. Good margins make the line lengths comfortable to read, and a centered title stands out on a page. Remind students that other text features, such as spacing and a bold font, can be used to highlight information.

Think About the Traits Once students have thoroughly discussed Alan Wong's model essay, ask them which traits they think are most important in a problem-solution essay. All the traits are important in every piece of writing, but some of the traits stand out more in some genres than in others. Students might say, for example, that in a problem-solution essay **Ideas** is very important because unless the writer includes a clear thesis and supporting details, the problem-solution essay makes no sense. Others may think that **Word Choice** is more important because domain-specific vocabulary helps the reader understand the problem and the solutions.

CCSS **Common Core State Standards**
SL.7.1.d: Acknowledge new information expressed by others and, when warranted, modify their own views.

Problem-Solution Essay **T225**

Write a Problem-Solution Essay

Week 2 • Day 1

Student Objectives

- Read and understand a prewriting strategy. *(p. 226)*

Prewrite

Focus on Ideas

Collect Information Direct students' attention to Emily's words on page 226. Remind them that in order to write their problem-solution essays, they will first have to choose and narrow a topic that can be explained in an essay. Point out that Emily chose to write about a topic that had been discussed in her social studies class. She didn't really understand the relationship between the problem and the solutions. That's why she decided to write about state involvement in nuclear power plants. Then point out Emily's notes on page 226. Explain that she will probably need more details about her topic as she starts to write. Tell students to use Emily's notes as a model and to keep track of their sources.

Online Writing Center

Provides **interactive graphic organizers** as well as a variety of graphic organizers in PDF format.

Prewrite Focus on Ideas

The Rubric Says	A clear thesis statement states the problem, its importance, and a recommended solution.
Writing Strategy	Choose and narrow a topic that can be explained in an essay. Take notes.

In social studies each week we discuss current events. That's how I learned that our state senate had voted not to renew the license of a nuclear power plant. I was concerned about the problems that came up in the discussion, but didn't have a clear understanding of how government and energy are related. I wanted to understand that idea better, and that's one reason I decided on the topic for my essay. It took me a while to state the problem clearly. Then I began to list solutions. I put stars beside the solutions I think are best, but I need to do more research to clarify my ideas.

Notes for Essay

Problem

What can people of Vermont do to replace energy that came from their only nuclear power plant?

Solutions

repair the nuclear plant and change management; vote to renew license

build a new power plant

buy more energy from Canada or other states

* explore alternatives to nuclear energy

* support safe, clean, green energy projects

Apply

Think about a problem and how to state it in your essay. List some solutions to research and consider.

English Language Learners

BEGINNING/INTERMEDIATE

Problem and Solution Read a language-level appropriate text with a clear problem and solution such as *Little Red Riding Hood*. Write on the board *problem* and *solution*. Read the words and have students repeat. Explain that the *problem* is what goes wrong in the story and the *solution* is how the problem is fixed. Have Intermediate ELL students share the problem and solution in the story. Ask, *What is the problem? What is the solution?* Write answers on the board and read as a group.

ADVANCED/ADVANCED HIGH

Problem and Solution Write a Problem-Solution Frame on the board and fill in the problem *Being Late to Class*. Ask students *Why is this a problem? Who has this problem?* As students share answers, fill in the Problem-Solution Frame.

The Rubric Says	Ideas are organized logically in a strong introduction, body, and conclusion.
Writing Strategy	Make a Problem-Solution Frame to organize the notes.

I can also use a Problem-Solution Frame to help me structure the paragraphs of my essay. The text in the Problem box will contain the information for my introduction and conclusion. The information in the Solution boxes will go into the body of my essay.

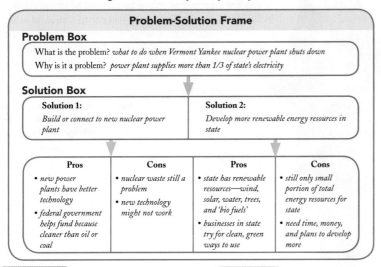

Problem-Solution Frame

Problem Box

What is the problem? *what to do when Vermont Yankee nuclear power plant shuts down*
Why is it a problem? *power plant supplies more than 1/3 of state's electricity*

Solution Box

Solution 1:	Solution 2:
Build or connect to new nuclear power plant	*Develop more renewable energy resources in state*

Pros	Cons	Pros	Cons
• *new power plants have better technology* • *federal government helps fund because cleaner than oil or coal*	• *nuclear waste still a problem* • *new technology might not work*	• *state has renewable resources—wind, solar, water, trees, and 'bio fuels'* • *businesses in state try for clean, green ways to use*	• *still only small portion of total energy resources for state* • *need time, money, and plans to develop more*

Reflect
What do you notice about the way Emily filled in the Problem-Solution Frame? How will this organizer help with her draft?

Apply
Use a Problem-Solution Frame or another organizer to prepare to write your essay.

Problem-Solution Essay **227**

Conferencing

PEER TO PEER When students have completed their Problem-Solution Frames, have pairs exchange organizers. Tell each student to check to see if the writer's problem is clear, if the solutions are reasonable, and if the details give enough information.

PEER GROUPS Separate students into small groups of three or four. Have them take turns reading their frames aloud. Listeners should raise their hands whenever they hear something that is confusing or misplaced. At this point, the writer should stop and reorganize the information to make sense. Remind students to refer to their notes to complete their organizers.

TEACHER-LED To demonstrate the importance of a focused organizer, create your own Problem-Solution Frame on the board, leaving several areas blank. Discuss how the missing information might affect the writing of an effective essay.

Write
a Problem-Solution Essay

Student Objectives

• Make a Problem-Solution Frame to organize notes. (p. 227)

Prewrite

Focus on **Organization**

Organize Ideas Explain that writers use a variety of organizers to get started writing. Encourage students to use note cards to keep track of information and sources as they conduct their research. Emily used a Problem-Solution Frame to help her organize her notes. Help students understand that the better organized their notes are, the easier it will be to write well-organized paragraphs. Ask students to study the organizer. Then ask how a Problem-Solution Frame can be an effective tool when writing a problem-solution essay. (Possible response: A Problem-Solution Frame helps you organize your thoughts and stay focused as you write.)

CCSS **Common Core State Standards**

W.7.2: Write informative/explanatory texts to examine a topic and convey ideas, concepts, and information through the selection, organization, and analysis of relevant content.

Problem-Solution Essay **T227**

Write a Problem-Solution Essay

Week 2 • Day 3

Student Objectives

• Include domain-specific vocabulary. (p. 228)

Draft

Focus on  Word Choice

Draft a Problem-Solution Essay
Remind students that drafting gives them a chance to get ideas on paper. Be sure that students understand that they will use their Problem-Solution Frames to guide them through the drafting process. Read page 228 aloud. Then ask students to read Emily's draft on page 229 on their own. Discuss whether the draft's length and structure reflect the purpose of the writing. (yes) Then have students compare Emily's draft to her Problem-Solution Frame. Ask students how her essay relates to the organizer. (Possible response: Her first paragraph states the problem and why it is a problem; her second paragraph gives possible solutions.) Point out that Emily also refers to the rubric as she writes. Encourage students to get into the habit of using the rubric as a guide for their own writing.

Online Writing Center

 Provides student eBooks with an **interactive writing pad** for drafting, revising, editing, and publishing.

Draft   Focus on Word Choice

The Rubric Says   Domain-specific content vocabulary is used effectively and defined clearly.

Writing Strategy   Define words that are unfamiliar to the audience.

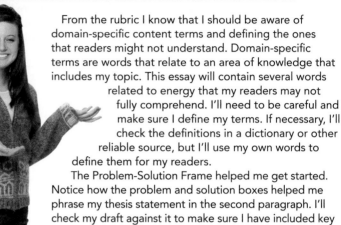

From the rubric I know that I should be aware of domain-specific content terms and defining the ones that readers might not understand. Domain-specific terms are words that relate to an area of knowledge that includes my topic. This essay will contain several words related to energy that my readers may not fully comprehend. I'll need to be careful and make sure I define my terms. If necessary, I'll check the definitions in a dictionary or other reliable source, but I'll use my own words to define them for my readers.

The Problem-Solution Frame helped me get started. Notice how the problem and solution boxes helped me phrase my thesis statement in the second paragraph. I'll check my draft against it to make sure I have included key points.

While writing the draft, I'll keep in mind that I will come back a few more times to revise and edit, so I won't try to fix everything at once.

228 Informative/Explanatory Writing

Differentiating Instruction

ENRICHMENT

Evaluate Sources Encourage students to evaluate different types of sources and then create a chart explaining the sources' strengths and weaknesses. For example, students might list an *editorial* as a source and then evaluate its strengths and/or weaknesses. Challenge students to include at least six types of sources in their charts. Place these charts in the classroom as a writer's resource.

REINFORCEMENT

Begin the Draft Before students begin to write, engage them in conversation about what they will write. The ability to phrase the problem and possible solutions verbally will help students when they begin to write.

Proofreading Marks

⌐ Indent   ℓ Take out something
≡ Make a capital   ⊙ Add a period
/ Make a small letter   ¶ New paragraph
∧ Add something   Ⓢⓟ Spelling error

[DRAFT]

State Power over Nuclear Power

Recently lawmakers in Vermont's State Senate voted not to renew the contract of Vermont Yankee, a nuclear power plant that has supplied a big portion of the state's electricity for almost forty years. Like other nuclear power plants, it generates and regulates high heat using nuclear fuel that comes from uranium, a radioactive element. *[defined domain-specific word]*

The decision of Vermont's Senate was based on difficulties at the plant, such as, broken equipment, fire hazards, security issues, communication failures, and possible leaks of radioactive materials. *[effective use of domain-specific words]* The lawmakers' vote against the nuclear power plant expressed the concerns of citizens throughout the state. However, the decision raised another problem: how to replace this major source of electricity for the state. Two possible solutions should be explored. The state could build a new, better nuclear power plant, or it could develop renewable energy sources. *[thesis statement]*

Reflect

How does Emily's use of domain-specific content words help you understand her essay?

Apply

When you draft your essay, make sure to define any domain-specific content words.

Problem-Solution Essay 229

Conferencing

PEER TO PEER Have pairs of students exchange drafts. Tell them to check that domain-specific vocabulary is well-defined and is used effectively. Ask students to think of two or three questions they might ask to help clarify information or supply missing details regarding domain-specific vocabulary.

PEER GROUPS Organize students into small groups. Have them take turns reading sections of their drafts aloud. Listeners should raise their hands when they hear an unfamiliar word. At this point, the writer should make notes on his or her draft about the vocabulary word and the missing definition.

TEACHER-LED Meet with individual students as they write their drafts. If a student is having trouble writing a strong introduction, revisit pages 226–227 together to make sure he or she has defined the problem and written a clear thesis statement.

Write
a Problem-Solution Essay

Week 2 • Day 4

Student Objectives

• Complete a draft. *(p. 229)*

Complete a Draft Encourage students to use the tools they have already created, their notes and their graphic organizers, when they write their drafts. Remind them to include and explain domain-specific (topic-related) vocabulary.

It is important that students are given ample time to draft their essays. As conferencing is important throughout the writing process, be sure to also plan time for peer-to-peer, peer group, or teacher-led conferences. Remind students that this is the time to get their ideas down on paper in a creative and engaging way. Assure them that they will have plenty of time to make changes and corrections later. Support them during the process by discussing their progress through conferencing.

CCSS **C**ommon **C**ore **S**tate **S**tandards

W.7.2.d: Use precise language and domain-specific vocabulary to inform about or explain the topic. **W.7.5:** With some guidance and support from peers and adults, develop and strengthen writing as needed by planning, revising, editing, rewriting, or trying a new approach, focusing on how well purpose and audience have been addressed. **W.7.6:** Acquire and use accurately grade-appropriate general academic and domain-specific words and phrases; gather vocabulary knowledge when considering a word or phrase important to comprehension or expression. **SL.7.1:** Engage effectively in a range of collaborative discussions (one-on-one, in groups, and teacher-led) with diverse partners on *grade 7 topics, texts, and issues,* building on others' ideas and expressing their own clearly.

Write
a Problem-Solution Essay

Week 2 • Day 5

Student Objectives

- Revise to include concrete and credible details. *(p. 230)*

Revise

Focus on Ideas

Add Credible Details Direct students to page 230, and read the text aloud. Discuss the importance of making sure details in a problem-solution essay are concrete and credible. Have one volunteer read the draft excerpt without the revisions, and then have another volunteer read the revised excerpt. Point out how much clearer the writing becomes with credible and factual details. Explain to students that if details are not relevant and plausible, readers will not take the problem-solution essay seriously. If students find that some of their details are not strong, they will want to do some additional research to develop their ideas. Encourage them to add facts and examples to strengthen their solutions.

Strategies for Writers Online
Go to **www.sfw.z-b.com** for additional online resources for students and teachers.

Revise
Focus on Ideas

The Rubric Says	One or more solutions are fully developed with relevant facts and concrete details.
Writing Strategy	Use details that are concrete and credible.

The rubric reminds me to develop one or more solutions. In my draft I tried to develop two solutions, but I want to add more concrete and relevant details to support my ideas. I did more research about nuclear and other kinds of energy. I mentioned the source for one very specific fact I found so that the reader will know my information is reliable. I think my revisions make my solution seem more complete and believable. Do you agree?

[DRAFT]

[added credible details]

These companies also are finding ways to use wood, crops, and animal waste products without polluting the air or harming the environment.

Vermont, like many other states, has a variety of renewable energy resources. It also has companies that have already developed clean and effective ways to use rivers, wind, and sunlight. Until now, Vermont's renewal resources have been only a small part of the state's 8% energy report (Page 2010, 2). , according to a recent official

[added factual detail]

[reliable source]

Apply
Make sure to include concrete and relevant facts from reliable sources to support your ideas.

230 Informative/Explanatory Writing

English Language Learners

BEGINNING/INTERMEDIATE
Past Tense Verbs Show students a picture of a child playing. Ask *What is the child doing?* After students respond, say and write on the board *Today the child plays.* Then say and write on the board *Yesterday the child played.* Read and have students repeat. Underline *-ed* in *played.* Explain that if something happens before now, or in the past, we add *-ed* to the verb. Repeat with several regular verbs.

ADVANCED/ADVANCED HIGH
Conclusion Read an article from the newspaper with a strong conclusion and an article with a weak conclusion. Talk about the characteristics of a strong and weak conclusion. Have students use the information they wrote in the Problem-Solution Frame to write a paragraph with a strong conclusion. Read a partner's paragraph and give feedback about the conclusion.

Revise

Focus on **Organization**

The Rubric Says	Appropriate, effective transitions clarify relationships among ideas.
Writing Strategy	Use transition words or phrases to connect sentences and paragraphs.

The rubric reminds me to guide my readers with appropriate transition words between sentences and paragraphs. I found a paragraph that needed transitions to lead the reader from one idea to the next. I was careful to choose transition words that would show clearly how my ideas are connected. What do you think? Do my ideas flow more smoothly with transitions?

Writer's Term___

Transitions

Transitions are words that guide the reader from one thought or paragraph to the next. Transitions that indicate results include *as a result*, *because*, *since*, and *therefore*. Transitions that indicate additional information include *in addition*, *moreover*, *furthermore*, and *similarly*.

[DRAFT]   [added transitions]

Laws and funds that support the promising efforts of clean energy companies in Vermont would generate new businesses, new jobs, and a greater supply of energy from within the state. In addition, A broader view of energy efficiency and available energy resources would save costs for customers. Furthermore, Improved technology with renewable energy resources in Vermont could lead the way for other states, the country, and the planet. As a result, A small state like Vermont could have a big impact.

Reflect

How do the added transition words make a difference in your reading of this part of the draft?

Apply

Read through your draft and find places to add appropriate, effective transition words.

Problem-Solution Essay 231

Conferencing

PEER TO PEER Have pairs of students exchange drafts. After reading the draft, each partner should offer helpful feedback, pointing out areas where transitions could be added to strengthen cohesion and clarify the relationships.

PEER GROUPS Separate students into small groups of three or four. Have students take turns reading sections of their drafts aloud. Encourage group members to suggest areas where transitions could be added to connect the writer's ideas and create smoother sentence flow.

TEACHER-LED Conference with pairs of students. Have them read each other's drafts and coach them in giving constructive criticism related to transition words and phrases.

Write
a Problem-Solution Essay

Week 3 • Day 1

Student Objectives

- Revise to include transitions to connect sentences and paragraphs. *(p. 231)*

Revise

Focus on

Add Transitions Transitions are important because they connect the writer's thoughts and help ensure smooth sentence flow. Remind students to check their drafts for transitions that connect ideas and make their writing flow smoothly. Refer students to page 542 for a list of transitions.

Also advise students to add short, precise headings to highlight and organize the sections of their essays. This will help connect the parts of the essay and make it easier for the reader to follow the organization.

Writer's Term___

Transitions When transitions are used effectively, the result is cohesion among ideas and smooth sentence flow. When ideas have cohesion, they connect well with one another. Transitions help connect ideas and indicate what is coming next in a piece of writing.

CCSS **Common Core State Standards**

W.7.2.b: Develop the topic with relevant facts, definitions, concrete details, quotations, or other information and examples. **W.7.2.c:** Use appropriate transitions to create cohesion and clarify the relationships among ideas and concepts.

Problem-Solution Essay T231

Write a Problem-Solution Essay

Week 3 • Day 2

Student Objectives

• Revise for parallel sentence structures. *(p. 232)*

Revise

Focus on  Sentence Fluency

Use Parallel Sentence Structure

Read page 232 aloud. Remind students that good writers understand the importance of using parallel sentence structures to show that certain ideas are related. Caution students not to repeat too many similar structures. They should use only enough to show the reader that a strong relationship exists between ideas. Tell students to notice how Emily revised her draft for parallel sentence structure. Her revisions connected her ideas and made her writing clearer. Encourage students to review their problem-solution essays and look for areas where they can use parallel sentence structures to strengthen the relationships between ideas.

Online Writing Center

Provides **interactive proofreading activities** for each genre.

Revise Focus on Sentence Fluency

The Rubric Says	Sentences are clear, including parallel structures that emphasize a relationship.
Writing Strategy	Use parallel sentence structures.

I know from the rubric that I should check for parallel structures in my sentences. Used thoughtfully, parallel structure can help show that certain ideas are related. I shouldn't repeat too many similar structures, but just enough to make a stronger connection for the reader. Here is one of my revisions, to strengthen the comparison of two types of energy.

[DRAFT] [revised for parallel structure]

The processes of burning Nuclear energy has been called a clean, green energy. When they are burned in power plants, coal, oil, or natural gas all release carbon dioxide, a gas that harmfully raises temperatures around on Earth. The processes of a nuclear power plant create heat and steam without releasing carbon dioxide.

Apply

Look for places where you can make a point by using sentences with parallel structure.

Optional Revising Lessons

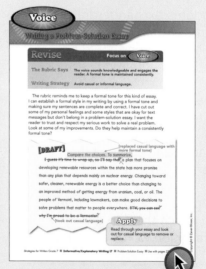

Voice

Informative/Explanatory 17

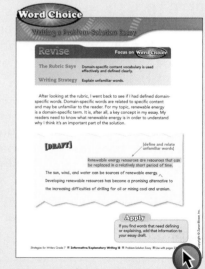

Word Choice

Informative/Explanatory 18

 Go to Strategies for Writers Grade 7 CD-ROM

Edit — Focus on **Conventions**

The Rubric Says	The writing has been carefully edited. All verbs are used correctly.
Writing Strategy	Recognize and correct inappropriate shifts in verb tense.

✏️ Writer's Term

Auxiliary Verbs

Auxiliary verbs, or helping verbs, are used with a main verb to show tense, for negatives and questions, and to convey possibilities. *Will, might,* and *could* are some auxiliary verbs that convey how likely an event is to happen.

I'm making corrections and paying special attention to verbs, as the rubric says. I want to use correct tenses and forms so my meaning is clear to the reader. I also made a proof mark to start a new paragraph.

[DRAFT]

[corrected auxiliary verbs]

To encourage this change, the federal government ~~begun~~ *has* begun to help fund construction of new nuclear power plants. Recent technology ~~made~~ *could make* them more safe and efficient than the early ones. However, the newest technologies ~~will not be~~ *have not been* tested over time. They might cost more or work less well than expected.

[corrected verb tense]

Reflect
Notice the edits. What changes did Emily make? How did they improve her draft?

Apply — Conventions
Edit your draft for spelling, grammar, punctuation, and capitalization. Look carefully at verb tenses.

For more practice in correctly using irregular verbs and auxiliary verbs, do the exercises on the next two pages.

Problem-Solution Essay 233

Related Grammar Practice

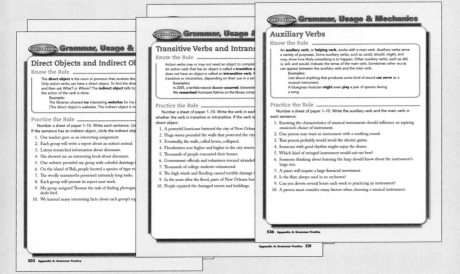

Student Edition pages 502, 503, 521, 524, 526

Go to ➡ Appendix A: Grammar Practice

Student Objectives
• Edit for correct use of verb tenses. *(p. 233)*

Edit

Focus on **Conventions**

Edit for Correct Verb Tense
Remind students to check their essays for proper spelling, capitalization, and punctuation, making sure that all verbs are used correctly.

Use the mini-lessons on pages T234–235 for students having problems with verb tenses and agreement. Then have students complete the exercises on pages 234–235. Go over the answers in class.

✏️ Writer's Term

Auxiliary Verbs Emphasize that an auxiliary verb assists a main verb by expressing shades of time and mood. To express time, auxiliary verbs determine the tense of a verb *(will drive, had driven)*. To express mood, auxiliary verbs can show, among other moods, obligation *(should study)* and willingness *(would study)*.

CCSS Common Core State Standards
L.7.1: Demonstrate command of the conventions of standard English grammar and usage when writing or speaking.

Problem-Solution Essay T233

Conventions

Mini-Lesson

Student Objectives

- Use auxiliary verbs correctly. (p. 234)

Auxiliary (Helping) Verbs

Have students review the Know the Rule box on page 234. Then write the following sentence on the board:

- *My class has read the book* Hatchet *by Gary Paulsen.*

Ask a volunteer to identify the main verb in the sentence. (read) Then ask a volunteer to identify the auxiliary verb. (has) Now write the following sentence on the board:

- *Can you recommend any other good books to read?*

Ask students to identify the main verb. (recommend) Now ask students to identify the auxiliary verb. (can) Then explain to students that auxiliary verbs are helping verbs that must be used with a main verb. They can be used to show tense, form negatives, form a question, or refer to a possible action.

Remind students that it is important to use auxiliary verbs correctly in their writing. Errors may distract or confuse the reader.

Online Writing Center

Provides **interactive grammar games** and **practice activities** in student eBook.

Auxiliary Verbs

Know the Rule

An **auxiliary verb**, or helping verb, works with a main verb. Auxiliary verbs have different purposes.

- to show tense
  Example: We **are** learning about Mayan societies.
- to form negatives
  Example: People today **do** not know about the Maya.
- to form a question
  Example: **Have** you ever studied the Maya?
- to refer to a possible action or tell how likely it is that something will happen
  Example: I **might** like to visit Belize or Guatemala some day.

Practice the Rule

Number a separate sheet of paper 1–10. For each sentence, write the auxiliary verb followed by the main verb. Then use the following letters to note the purpose of the auxiliary verb: **T** = show tense, **N** = form negatives, **Q** = form a question, **P** = refer to a possible action or how likely an action will be.

1. Throughout history, people have used renewable energy sources. *have used — T*
2. Until two hundred years ago, many societies had relied on wood, a renewable resource. *had relied — T*
3. Do you think of hydro-power as something new? *Do think — Q*
4. Do not forget that mills and other early industry depended on dammed rivers, a form of hydro-power. *Do forget — N*
5. Before the nineteenth century, industry had not relied on coal, a nonrenewable resource. *had relied — N*
6. The use of oil, another nonrenewable resource, has grown along with the major forms of transportation on the road today. *has grown — T*
7. Patterns of using renewable and nonrenewable energy might change in the near future. *might change — P*
8. Many people would prefer a greater development of renewable energy resources that don't harm the environment. *would prefer — P*
9. Some new research projects will focus on renewable energy sources called *biomass*. *will focus — T*
10. Did you know that biomass includes wood, animal waste, and fuels from vegetable crops? *Did know — Q*

Related Grammar Practice

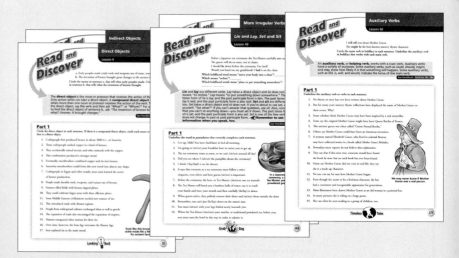

Pages 15, 17, 145, 147, 177

Go to **G.U.M. Student Practice Book**

Irregular Verbs

Know the Rule

Many verbs are **irregular**; they do not add -ed in the past tense. Here are some of the verbs, in three tenses:

Present	Past	Past Participle
break	broke	broken
bring	brought	brought
build	built	built
come	came	come
pay	paid	paid
speak	spoke	spoken
stand	stood	stood
take	took	taken
tell	told	told
write	wrote	written

Practice the Rule

Number a separate sheet of paper 1–10. Write each sentence with the underlined verb corrected for the tense given.

1. Do you know where you <u>stood</u> on every issue about our environment? (*present*) — *stand*
2. If you have not <u>took</u> a close look at some key issue, try writing an essay about it. (*past participle*) — *taken*
3. Studying an issue has <u>brung</u> out new ideas and perspectives for me. (*past participle*) — *brought*
4. I researched several news articles before I <u>write</u> my draft. (*past*) — *wrote*
5. I don't usually <u>spoke</u> with friends and family about an issue unless I have to write about it. (*present*) — *speak*
6. My parents <u>tell</u> me some points that they thought were important. (*past*) — *told*
7. The company that <u>build</u> the power plant is not the company that runs it now. (*past*) — *built*
8. For many years the management has <u>came</u> from outside our state. (*past participle*) — *come*
9. This company has not <u>pay</u> attention to the concerns of people in our state. (*past participle*) — *paid*
10. Now I know where I <u>have stood</u> on this particular issue, and I am ready to publish my essay. (*present*) — *stand*

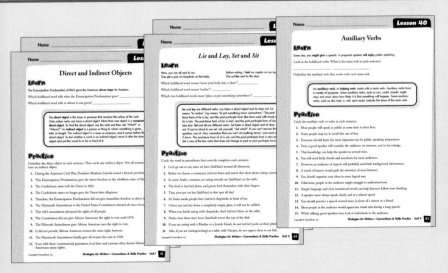

Pages 13, 37, 63, 65, 85

Go to ➡ *Grammar Practice Masters*

Student Objectives

- Use irregular verbs correctly. (*p. 235*)

Irregular Verbs

Have students review the Know the Rule box on page 235. Then write the following sentences on the board:

- *My little brother read me a funny poem last night.*
- *He has written some great stories and poems in his class.*
- *My family brought him to school for a special poetry presentation.*
- *He spoke clearly and audibly.*
- *He often finds really good poems and stories!*

Ask volunteers to identify the complete verbs in each sentence. (read, has written, brought, spoke, finds) Then ask students to identify the tense of each verb. (past, past participle, past, past, present) Remind students that many verbs are irregular. That means they do not add -ed in the past tense. The past tense of irregular verbs changes to become another word; the past participle needs help from an auxiliary verb. Remind students that it is important to use irregular verbs correctly in writing. Otherwise, readers can get confused. Encourage students to use online word resources to make sure they use irregular verbs correctly.

CCSS **Common Core State Standards**

L.7.2: Demonstrate command of the conventions of standard English capitalization, punctuation, and spelling when writing.

Write
a Problem-Solution Essay

Week 3 • Day 4

Student Objectives

- Discuss preparation for publishing and presentation. *(p. 236)*
- Use a final editing checklist to publish their work. *(p. 236)*

Publish **+Presentation**

Publishing Strategy Ask students if they like Emily's choice for sharing her problem-solution essay in a class news magazine. Tell the class that her choice is not the only option for publishing her work. Invite students to name other ways they could publish their own problem-solution essays individually or collectively. For example, if they have added visuals, they may want to compile their essays into a slideshow with other classes in the school.

Strategies for Writers Online

Go to **www.sfw.z-b.com** for additional online resources for students and teachers.

Publish **+Presentation**

Publishing Strategy	Publish my problem-solution essay in a class magazine.
Presentation Strategy	Use text features and illustrations.

Our essays will be published in a class magazine, so parents, classmates, and students in other grades will get to read them. My topic is pretty complicated, so I should pay special attention to organizing the presentation of my essay. I'll use text features such as spacing and bold font to help readers identify parts of my essay. I also plan to include a photo of a nuclear power plant and a photo of at least one kind of renewable energy. I might include a pie chart that shows the different kinds of energy used in Vermont. I'll ask my teacher if I need help inserting illustrations with my word processing program. I'll use my checklist as I prepare to publish.

My Final Checklist

Did I—

✔ correct all punctuation, capitalization, and spelling?

✔ correct grammar, including use of auxiliary and irregular verbs?

✔ use clear spacing, bold headings, and readable fonts to group topics?

✔ choose appealing visuals that bring out my ideas?

✔ place visuals to fit with the text?

Apply

Make a checklist to check your problem-solution essay. Then make a final copy to publish.

236 Informative/Explanatory Writing

Differentiating Instruction

ENRICHMENT

Copyedit Have pairs of students exchange papers to copyedit each other's work. When the partners have finished copyediting, have them return the drafts. Then have students discuss and defend their edits.

REINFORCEMENT

Use a Final Checklist Many students will be reluctant to revisit their essays to polish them for publication. Discuss the impact of a poorly presented product, whether it is a television commercial, a website, or a school paper.

State Power over Nuclear Power

by Emily

Recently lawmakers in Vermont's State Senate voted not to renew the contract of Vermont Yankee, a nuclear power plant that has supplied a big portion of the state's electricity for almost forty years. Like other nuclear power plants, it generates and regulates high heat using nuclear fuel that comes from uranium, a radioactive element.

The decision of Vermont's Senate was based on difficulties at the plant, such as broken equipment, fire hazards, security issues, communication failures, and possible leaks of radioactive materials. The lawmakers' vote against the nuclear power plant expressed the concerns of citizens throughout the state. However, the decision raised another problem: how to replace this major source of electricity for the state. Two possible solutions should be explored. The state could build a new, better nuclear power plant, or it could develop renewable energy sources.

Change to new improved nuclear power. Nuclear energy has been called a clean, green energy. The processes of burning coal, oil, or natural gas all release carbon dioxide, a gas that harmfully raises temperatures on Earth. The processes of a nuclear power plant create heat and steam without releasing carbon dioxide. Using more nuclear energy would help the United States meet world standards for a cleaner, greener environment. To encourage this change, the federal government has begun to help fund

Technology Tip for 21st Century Literacies

The problem-solution essay presents an opportunity for students to look outside of their own points of view to offer solutions that matter to others. Encourage students to put their findings into action. Use online, dynamic websites like DoSomething.org that bring together issues, resources, and suggestions for ways that adolescents can participate in enacting solutions or bringing awareness. Twenty-first century teaching invites a different sense of relevance and purpose to classroom work and requires information literacy skills that help students identify what is real and immediate.

Write
a Problem-Solution Essay

Week 3 • Day 5

Student Objectives

- Use a problem-solution essay rubric. *(pp. 220–221)*
- Share a published problem-solution essay. *(pp. 237–239)*

Presentation Strategy Remind students of the importance of neatness when creating a final, polished copy of their work. Their presentation (page design) has a great impact on readers. Messy or illegible work will turn readers away, while a neat and attractive format is inviting. Remind students of the numerous word-processing options available on computers. Computers make it easy to set neat margins, indent paragraphs, select clear fonts for creativity, and use various text features to enhance the writing. Also remind students to use the header or footer function to label each page with the essay's title, the writer's name, and a page number. It is especially important to remember to label any visuals that have been included in the essay.

CCSS Common Core State Standards

W.7.4: Produce clear and coherent writing in which the development, organization, and style are appropriate to task, purpose, and audience. **W.7.6:** Use technology, including the Internet, to produce and publish writing and link to and cite sources as well as to interact and collaborate with others, including linking to and citing sources.

Reflecting on a Problem-Solution Essay

Instruct students to refer to the rubric on pages 220–221 as they reread Emily's final essay on pages 237–239. As they read, remind them to pay close attention to all of Emily's changes. After students have finished reading, ask them to reflect on Emily's changes by asking: Did her revisions and edits strengthen her essay? What score would Emily have received for each writing trait? Ask volunteers to take a poll and tally the results. Be sure students can support the rubric scores with examples from Emily's writing.

Next have students reflect on their own essays. Depending on class size, you may want to write these questions on the board:

- *What was your favorite part of this assignment?*

- *Was there one part that was particularly challenging or easy?*

- *Name one thing you think you improved.*

- *Think about all the steps you took to complete your problem-solution essay. What will you do the same or differently next time?*

Allow time for students to share their thoughts in class, or organize students into smaller groups to facilitate a profitable discussion.

Strategies for Writers Online

Go to **www.sfw.z-b.com** for additional online resources for students and teachers.

construction of new nuclear power plants. Recent technology could make them more safe and efficient than the early ones.

However, the newest technologies have not been tested over time. They might cost more or work less well than expected. Also, any nuclear power plant creates nuclear waste. Unfortunately the nation has not yet worked out how to deal with hazards from transport and storage of nuclear waste. These are all good reasons to question any plans for a new nuclear power plant in Vermont.

Change to develop more renewable energy resources. The sun, wind, and water can be sources of renewable energy. Renewable energy resources are resources that can be replaced in a relatively short period of time. Developing renewable resources has become a promising alternative to the increasing difficulties of drilling for oil or mining coal and uranium.

Vermont, like many other states, has a variety of renewable energy resources. It also has companies that have already developed clean and effective ways to use rivers, wind, and sunlight. These companies also are finding ways to use wood, crops, and animal waste products without polluting the air or harming the environment. Until now, Vermont's renewable resources have been only 8% of the state's

energy, according to a recent official report (Page 2, 2010).

Laws and funds that support the promising efforts of clean energy companies in Vermont would generate new businesses, new jobs, and a greater supply of energy from within the state. In addition, a broader view of energy efficiency and available energy resources would save costs for customers. Furthermore, improved technology with renewable energy resources in Vermont could lead the way for other states, the country, and the planet. As a result, a small state like Vermont could have a big impact.

Compare the choices. To summarize, a plan that focuses on developing renewable resources within the state has more promise than any plan that depends mainly on nuclear energy. Changing toward safer, cleaner, renewable energy is a better choice than changing to an improved method of getting energy from uranium, coal, or oil. The people of Vermont, including lawmakers, can make good decisions to solve problems that matter to people everywhere.

Works Consulted

"Definition of a Nuclear Power Plant," eHow, accessed October 6, 2012, http://www.ehow.com/nuclear-power-plants.

"Energy Sources," Central Vermont Public Service, accessed October 8, 2012, http://www.cvps.com/ProgramsServices/EnergySources.aspx.

"Energy Sources," U.S. Energy Information Agency, Department of Energy, accessed October 6, 2012, http://www.eia.doe.gov/kids/energy.cfm?page=2.

Page, Guy. May 2010. "Renewable Energy Sources in Vermont, A Status Report, May 2010." Montpelier, VT: Vermont Energy Partnership.

Reflect

Read the essay and check it against the rubric. Which traits do you think are the strongest? When your own essay is complete, remember to check it against the rubric also.

CCSS **Common Core State Standards**

W.7.4: Produce clear and coherent writing in which the development, organization, and style are appropriate to task, purpose, and audience.

Informative/Explanatory Test Planner

WEEK 1

Day 1
Introduce
Informative/Explanatory Test Writing

Student Objectives
- Learn the components of the writing prompt. *(pp. 240–241)*

Student Activities
- Read and discuss **Read the Writing Prompt.** *(pp. 240–241)*

Day 2
Analyze
Introduce the Scoring Guide

Student Objectives
- Recognize the relationship of the scoring guide to the rubric and the six traits of writing.
- Read a model writing test response.

Student Activities
- Read **Writing Traits in the Scoring Guide.** *(p. 242)*
- Read the writing prompt response model. *(p. 243)*

Day 3
Analyze
Apply the Scoring Guide

Student Objectives
- Apply the scoring guide to the writing prompt response model.

Student Activities
- Read and discuss **Using the Scoring Guide to Study the Model.** *(pp. 244–245)*

WEEK 2

Day 1
Write
Prewrite: Ideas

Student Objectives
- Read and understand the writing prompt for informative/explanatory writing.
- Apply the six traits of writing to the writing prompt.

Student Activities
- Read and discuss **Prewrite: Focus on Ideas.** *(pp. 248–249)*

Day 2
Write
Prewrite: Ideas

Student Objectives
- Learn how to respond to the task in the writing prompt.

Student Activities
- Read and discuss **Prewrite: Focus on Ideas.** *(p. 250)*

Day 3
Write
Prewrite: Organization

Student Objectives
- Learn how to choose a graphic organizer for the writing prompt.

Student Activities
- Read and discuss **Prewrite: Focus on Organization.** *(p. 251)*

WEEK 3

Day 1
Write
Revise: Organization

Student Objectives
- Revise for logical presentation of details.

Student Activities
- Read and discuss **Revise: Focus on Organization.** *(p. 256)*

Day 2
Write
Revise: Voice

Student Objectives
- Revise to connect with readers.

Student Activities
- Read and discuss **Revise: Focus on Voice.** *(p. 257)*

Day 3
Write
Revise: Word Choice

Student Objectives
- Revise for precise language to eliminate wordiness and redundancy.

Student Activities
- Read and discuss **Revise: Focus on Word Choice.** *(p. 258)*

Note: Optional Revising Lessons appear on the *Strategies for Writers* CD-ROM.

Day 4	Day 5

Analyze
Apply the Scoring Guide

Day 4

Analyze
Time Management

Day 5

Student Objectives
- Continue to apply the scoring guide to a model test response.

Student Activities
- Read and discuss **Using the Scoring Guide to Study the Model.** (p. 246)

Student Objectives
- Learn how to plan time during a writing test.

Student Activities
- Read and discuss **Planning My Time.** (p. 247)

Day 4

Write
Prewrite: Organization

Day 5

Write
Draft: Ideas

Student Objectives
- Learn how to check the graphic organizer against the scoring guide.

Student Activities
- Read and discuss **Prewrite: Focus on Organization.** (pp. 252–253)

Student Objectives
- Draft an informative/explanatory writing test, using a clear and concise thesis statement.

Student Activities
- Read and discuss **Draft: Focus on Ideas.** (pp. 254–255)

Day 4

Write
Edit: Conventions

Day 5

Review
Test Tips

Student Objectives
- Edit the writing test for proper grammar, spelling, capitalization, and punctuation.

Student Activities
- Read and discuss **Edit: Focus on Conventions.** (pp. 259–260)

Student Objectives
- Review tips for writing for a test.

Student Activities
- Read and discuss the **Test Tips.** (p. 261)

To complete the chapter in fewer days, combine the learning objectives and activities in a way that supports students as they write.

Resources at-a-Glance

Differentiating Instruction

Using the Scoring
Guide.... T244–T245, T246–T247
Prewrite..............T250–T251
Edit.................T259–T260
For additional Differentiating Instruction activities, see Strategies for Writers Extensions Online at **www.sfw.z-b.com.**

English Language Learners

Using the Scoring Guide T242
Prewrite................... T248
Draft T254

 Connection Letter
Reproducible letter (in English and Spanish) appears on the *Strategies for Writers* CD-ROM and at **www.sfw.z-b.com.**

Online Essay Grader and Writing Tutor

Powered by Vantage Learning's MY Access!®, includes writing prompts and ongoing feedback for students as they write. Available for Grades 5–8.

Online Writing Center

Provides IWB resources, interactive games and practice activities, videos, eBooks, and a virtual file cabinet.

 Strategies for Writers Online

Go to **www.sfw.z-b.com** for free online resources for students and teachers.

Introduce
Informative/ Explanatory Test Writing

Week 1 • Day 1

Student Objectives

• Learn the components of the writing prompt. *(pp. 240–241)*

Read the Writing Prompt

Informative/Explanatory Test Writing In this chapter, students will apply what they have learned about informative/explanatory writing to write an informative/ explanatory test. Remind students that they will sometimes write on demand to complete assignments or tests. Tell students that when they write for tests, they will receive a writing prompt and a certain amount of time in which to write. Then their writing will be evaluated, just as with any test. Assure students that they do not need to be anxious about written tests. The skills they have already practiced will help them do a good job. Direct their attention to the three parts of the writing prompt.

Setup The setup does just what its name says: It sets writers up to do a good job. The setup gets writers to think about the writing topic in general before they narrow the topic.

 Strategies for Writers Online
Go to **www.sfw.z-b.com** for additional online resources for students and teachers.

Informative/ Explanatory test writing

Read the Writing Prompt

When you take a writing test, you will be given a writing prompt. Most writing prompts have three parts:

Setup This part of the writing prompt gives you the background information you need to get ready to write.

Task This part of the writing prompt tells you exactly what you are supposed to write: a cause-and-effect report.

Scoring Guide This section tells how your writing will be scored. To do well on the test, you should include everything on the list.

> **R**emember the rubrics you've been using? When you take a writing test, you don't always have all of the information that's on a rubric. But a scoring guide is a lot like a rubric. It lists everything you need to think about to write a good paper. Like the rubrics you've used, many scoring guides are based on the six traits of writing:

Ideas   Organization   Voice

Word Choice   Sentence Fluency   Conventions

Online Essay Grader and Writing Tutor

Powered by Vantage Learning's MY Access!®, this tool gives students

• immediate, ongoing, sentence-by-sentence feedback.

• helpful suggestions to improve their draft.

• a holistic score and a trait-specific score on their final draft.

• unlimited response submissions to the prompts.

Writing MODEL Prompt

Are you a spender or a saver? Think about how spending or saving your money affects your behavior.

Write a cause-and-effect report on the effects of your spending/saving habits.

Be sure your writing

- has a clear thesis statement and accurate, concrete supporting details.
- is well organized and uses appropriate transition words to clarify the relationship between causes and effects.
- uses a voice that matches the purpose and audience.
- is concise, not too wordy.
- has sentences that support the purpose.
- contains correct grammar, punctuation, capitalization, and spelling.

Task The task tells students not only what to write about but also what kind of writing to do: narrative, descriptive, informative/explanatory, or argument. Tell students that the best-written test will not receive a strong grade if it misses the topic or uses a form of writing other than the assigned form. Students must follow the instructions in the task.

Scoring Guide The scoring guide helps students plan and evaluate their writing. Help students understand how the scoring guide is similar to the rubric by asking these questions:

- Which bullets tell you how to organize your cause-and-effect report? (the first and second bullets)

- Which bullets help you extend and revise your writing? (the third and fourth bullets)

- Which bullet reminds you to look at sentences? (the fifth bullet)

- Which bullet reminds you about errors to look for during editing? (the sixth bullet)

Point out that in this chapter, students will use the informative/explanatory writing traits to review a model report before writing their own.

CCSS Common Core State Standards

W.7.2: Write informative/explanatory texts to examine a topic and convey ideas, concepts, and information through the selection, organization, and analysis of relevant content.

Analyze
the Scoring Guide

Week 1 • Day 2

Student Objectives

- Recognize the relationship of the scoring guide to the rubric and the six traits of writing. *(p. 242)*
- Read a model writing test response. *(p. 243)*

Writing Traits in the Scoring Guide

Scoring Guide as a Rubric

Remind students about how they used rubrics to guide, evaluate, and improve their writing of other informative/explanatory assignments. Point out that in a writing test the scoring guide acts as a rubric. Ask students for definitions and examples of each term in each category. For example, ask:

- What techniques have you used to organize other informative/ explanatory writing? (Possible response: Cause-and-Effect Chains, Outlines, Main-Idea Tables, Problem-Solution Frames)

- Which graphic organizer might help you write this test? (Possible response: Cause-and-Effect Chain)

- What voice would be appropriate when writing for an audience of business people? (Possible response: serious and formal)

Online Writing Center

Provides six **interactive anchor papers** for each mode of writing.

Writing Traits
in the Scoring Guide

The scoring guide in the prompt on page 241 has been made into this chart. Does it remind you of the rubrics you've used? Not all prompts include all of the writing traits, but this one does. Use them to do your best writing. Remember to work neatly and put your name on the test.

 **Ideas**
- Be sure your writing has a clear thesis statement and accurate, concrete supporting details.

 **Organization**
- Be sure your writing is well organized and uses appropriate transition words to clarify the relationship between causes and effects.

 **Voice**
- Be sure your writing uses a voice that matches the purpose and audience.

 **Word Choice**
- Be sure your writing is concise, not too wordy.

 Sentence Fluency
- Be sure your writing has sentences that support the purpose.

 **Conventions**
- Be sure your writing contains correct grammar, punctuation, capitalization, and spelling.

Look at Reginald James's cause-and-effect report on the next page. Did he follow the scoring guide?

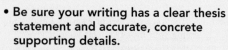
English Language Learners

BEGINNING/INTERMEDIATE

Graphic Organizer Help students practice using a Cause-and-Effect Chain by saying several cause-and-effect sentences. For example, *I slept too long* (cause), *so I was late* (effect). *I was late* (effect) *because I slept too long* (cause). Discuss with students how to use simple signal words and phrases, such as *so*, *because*, and *because of*. Then have partners work together to fill in a Cause-and-Effect graphic organizer.

ADVANCED/ADVANCED HIGH

Writing Prompt Have students read the informative/ explanatory writing prompt and write down no more than three words in each part of the prompt that they think are most important. Then have them compare with a partner and discuss the differences.

Saving for Bigger Things

by Reginald James

Have you ever heard the saying "A penny saved is a penny earned"? Well, I live by that statement! I put most of my allowance in my savings account and keep only what I really need. Although saving money means that I haven't been able to buy everything I want, it has taught me some important lessons.

Saving money has helped me understand the difference between what I want and what I need. For instance, I have a lot of friends who have big collections of DVDs and video games. While there are some cool DVDs and games that I would love to have, I don't really need them. Unless it's something that I feel is really necessary, I generally just don't buy it.

Another effect of saving money is that I have learned how to budget. I set aside $10 per week to use on the things I need, such as snacks and drinks after basketball practice. If I know I am going to need a little more one week for something like a new pair of shoes, then I try to save my spending money so that I won't have to dip into my savings.

Probably the best outcome of all my savings, though, is the fact that I am going to have enough money to buy something I've wanted for a long time. I love to go biking, and I know that if I want a new mountain bike, I'm going to have to pay for it myself. So I began saving money earlier this year, hoping to have enough saved up by next summer. Now, my savings account is quite large. I will have enough money to pay for a brand new bike as soon as spring arrives.

Sure, saving may not be as much fun as spending, but in the end, it teaches you important lessons while giving you the freedom to buy the things you really want.

Tell students that they will sometimes use writing prompts that do not include guidance for each of the six categories on the rubric by name. However, students can use their writing experience to remember the main requirements:

- a clear thesis statement and accurate, concrete supporting details
- well-organized paragraphs with appropriate transitions
- a voice that suits both purpose and audience
- precise, purposeful wording
- smooth sentences that support the writer's purpose
- good editing for spelling, punctuation, and capitalization.

If you have an old writing test that is no longer used, you might analyze its scoring guide with students to see which writing traits were included.

Read the Model

Writing Prompt Response Read "Saving for Bigger Things" aloud as students follow along in their books. Tell students to keep the requirements of the scoring guide in mind as they follow along. After reading the essay, invite students to summarize the text to be sure they understand it. Then have students move into small groups to discuss each element of the scoring guide and how it relates to the model.

CCSS Common Core State Standards
R/Inf.7.1: Cite several pieces of textual evidence to support analysis of what the text says explicitly as well as inferences drawn from the text.

Analyze
the Model

Student Objectives

- Apply the scoring guide to the writing prompt response model. (pp. 244–245)

Using the Scoring Guide to Study the Model

Review the Scoring Guide Remind students that the scoring guide is the tool that an evaluator—a teacher or other trained professional—will use to score the writing test. Students are given the scoring guide so they will know the criteria for judging their writing. They should use the scoring guide as they write to make sure they meet all the requirements.

Use the Scoring Guide Have students use the Writing Traits in the Scoring Guide chart on page 242 to evaluate the test written in response to the writing prompt on page 241. The chart is based on the scoring guide in the writing prompt.

Find More Examples Explain that pages 244–246 show how the writing model on page 243 meets all six writing traits. Have students look for other examples of each trait in the writing model. Remind them that they will use a scoring guide to evaluate their own writing tests later.

 Strategies for Writers Online
Go to **www.sfw.z-b.com** for additional online resources for students and teachers.

Using the Scoring Guide to Study the Model

Now let's use the scoring guide to check Reginald's writing test, "Saving for Bigger Things." Let's see how well his essay meets each of the six writing traits.

 Ideas
- The thesis statement is clear.
- The writing includes several accurate, concrete supporting details.

Reginald immediately introduced his thesis statement in a clear and easy-to-understand way. Then he provided several solid examples of what he actually learned from saving his money.

> Although saving money means that I haven't been able to buy everything I want, it has taught me some important lessons.
>
> Saving money has helped me understand the difference between what I want and what I need.

 **Organization**
- The writing is well organized and uses appropriate transition words to clarify the relationship between causes and effects.

Reginald guides the reader from one supporting example to the next with transition words such as *for instance* and *another effect*. These words signaled to me that although a new example was being given, all were related.

> Another effect of saving money is that I have learned how to budget. I set aside $10 per week to use on the things I need, such as snacks and drinks after basketball practice.

244 Informative/Explanatory Writing

Differentiating Instruction

ENRICHMENT

Explore Voice Have students explore voice by asking them to rewrite the first two paragraphs of the model essay from the third-person point of view. Get them started by writing the first two sentences on the board in third person: *Has anyone ever heard the saying "A penny saved is a penny earned?" Well, some people live by that statement.* Have students complete the two paragraphs and read their revisions aloud. Ask how the writer's voice in first-person point of view connects with the audience in a way that the third-person point of view would not. (Possible responses: Asking the reader (you) a question engages the reader immediately. Using the first-person point of view conveys credibility and connects with the reader.)

Voice

• The voice matches the purpose and audience.

It's clear that Reginald understands both his purpose and his audience. His voice is casual, which helps the reader connect with his writing, yet still informative.

Sure, saving may not be as much fun as spending, but in the end, it teaches you important lessons while giving you the freedom to buy the things you really want.

Word Choice

• The writing is concise and not too wordy.

I like how Reginald uses only the words necessary to get his point across. He never repeats himself. This made it so much easier to read, connect with, and understand his report.

Probably the best outcome of all my savings, though, is the fact that I am going to have enough money to buy something I've wanted for a long time.

Think About the Traits As students discuss Reginald James's cause-effect essay, ask them which traits they think are most important in a cause-effect essay. Of course, all the traits are important in every piece of writing, but some of the traits stand out more in some types of writing than in others. Students might say, for example, that the trait of **Organization** is very important because if a piece of writing is not well organized, the writer may lose track and the reader may lose interest. Or, they may say that **Word Choice** is very important because informative/explanatory test writing needs to be concise and to the point.

REINFORCEMENT

Review Transitions Remind students that one way to organize their writing and keep the audience's interest is to use transition words and phrases. Transitions keep the reader's interest by clarifying the relationship between causes and effects. Write these transitions on the board: *in addition, as a result,* and *furthermore*. Then read the second and third paragraphs of the model essay with students. Ask them to identify the transition words in those paragraphs. (*for instance, another effect*) Discuss the importance of connecting their thoughts with transition words and phrases when they are writing.

CCSS **Common Core State Standards**

SL.7.1: Engage effectively in a range of collaborative discussions (one-on-one, in groups, and teacher-led) with diverse partners on *grade 7 topics, texts, and issues,* building on others' ideas and expressing their own clearly.

Analyze
the Model

Student Objectives

- Continue to apply the scoring guide to the model writing test response. *(p. 246)*

Analyze the Model Help students focus on **Sentence Fluency** by telling them that the scoring guide reminds them that their writing should consist of sentences that support their purposes. Since the purpose in this assignment is to share information, they should use mostly declarative sentences.

Focus on **Conventions** by reminding students that they should use correct grammar, punctuation, and spelling in their writing test. It is important that they preserve time at the end to check their test for errors.

Strategies for Writers Online
Go to **www.sfw.z-b.com** for additional online resources for students and teachers.

Using the Scoring Guide to Study the Model

Sentence Fluency
- The writing consists of sentences that support the purpose.

Reginald uses mostly declarative sentences, which makes sense as his purpose is to inform. I'll keep this in mind as I write my own cause-and-effect report.

> I love to go biking, and I know that if I want a new mountain bike, I'm going to have to pay for it myself. So I began saving money earlier this year, hoping to have enough saved up by next summer.

Conventions
- The writing contains correct grammar, punctuation, capitalization, and spelling.

Using correct grammar and mechanics in a writing test is important, and I can tell that Reginald paid attention to this. I didn't see any errors in his grammar, punctuation, capitalization, or spelling. I'll be sure to check my test for errors, too!

Differentiating Instruction

ENRICHMENT

Set the Clock First ask students to explain the stopwatch visual on page 247. (Possible responses: Emily will have one hour to write the test. For this reason, the watch shows 60 minutes. The different-colored sections suggest what portion of the 60 minutes Emily should spend on each task.) Have students next describe the relationships between the lengths of time allotted to the tasks. (Possible response: Together, prewriting and drafting take most of the time. The least amount of time will be spent on editing.) Have students create two, colorized versions: one to represent a shorter period of time and one to represent a longer testing period. Have students assign approximate percentages of time to each segment on both clocks. Post this in the classroom and use the clocks for various timed projects.

Planning My Time

Before giving us a writing prompt, my teacher always tells us how much time we'll have to complete the test. Since I already know the steps of the writing process, I like to break up the total amount of time into each step. This way, I know I'll have enough time to do everything I need to do. If the test takes an hour, here's how I can organize my time. Planning your time will help you, too!

Step 4:
Edit
5 minutes

Step 1:
Prewrite
25 minutes

Step 3:
Revise
15 minutes

Step 2:
Draft
15 minutes

Informative/Explanatory Test Writing **247**

REINFORCEMENT

Start the Clock To prepare students for writing on demand, divide class periods for a variety of activities. Write a time schedule on the board to approximate the writing clock on page 247. Have students practice often enough so that they grow accustomed to dividing their time and completing the tasks. Talk about how setting time limits during test writing situations will help them succeed on writing tests. Recommend to students that they stay fairly close to the suggested time limits to ensure time for editing their drafts.

Analyze
Time Management

Student Objectives

• Learn how to plan time during a writing test. *(p. 247)*

Planning My Time

Time Management Explain to students that when they write for a test, they must complete all the steps of the writing process quickly. Students may be surprised that the student guide, Emily, has allotted so much of the writing time—25 minutes out of 60—to prewriting. Ask students why this time is necessary. (Possible responses: Without a plan for writing, students may write a draft that does not respond to the task. They will not have time to write another draft.)

Remind students also that revising is part of the writing task. Drafting and revising together take almost as much time—30 minutes—as prewriting; five minutes remain to edit. Tell students that when they have a shorter or longer time in which to write a test, they can use a similar time plan: about the same amount of time for prewriting as for drafting and revising combined, with a shorter amount of time for editing.

CCSS **Common Core State Standards**
W.7.10: Write routinely over extended time frames (time for research, reflection, and revision) and shorter time frames (a single sitting or a day or two) for a range of discipline-specific tasks, purposes, and audiences.

Informative/Explanatory Test Writing **T247**

Write
an Informative/ Explanatory Test

Week 2 • Day 1

Student Objectives

- Read and understand the writing prompt for informative/ explanatory writing. *(p. 248)*
- Apply the six traits of writing to the writing prompt. *(p. 249)*

Prewrite

Focus on Ideas

Study the Writing Prompt Make sure that students have copies of the writing prompt on page 248 so that they can practice marking them, following Emily's example. Tell students to mark any instructions that they find helpful. For example, a student whose writing often gets too wordy might mark the fourth bullet as a reminder.

Then walk students through page 249, encouraging them to add their own responses to Emily's. How will they gather concrete details and facts to help readers understand the relationship between causes and effects? What organizer will they use to plan their response? How will they make sure that their voice suits their purpose and audience?

▶ Strategies for Writers Online

Go to **www.sfw.z-b.com** for additional online resources for students and teachers.

Prewrite
Focus on (Ideas)

Writing Strategy Study the writing prompt to find out what to do.

When I take a writing test, I always study my writing prompt before I begin. A writing prompt usually has three parts (the setup, the task, and the scoring guide), but the parts aren't always labeled. Look for these sections on your writing prompt. Then label each one, like I did below. Also circle key words in the setup and the task that tell what kind of writing you will be doing and who your audience will be. I circled my topic in red. I also used blue to circle the kind of writing I'll be doing (a cause-and-effect report). My writing prompt doesn't say who my audience will be, so I'll write for my teacher.

My Writing Test Prompt

Setup — Have you ever overslept on a school day? This can cause a lot of problems for everyone involved.

Task — Write a cause-and-effect report on what happens when you get up late for school.

Scoring Guide — Be sure your writing

- has a clear thesis statement and accurate, concrete supporting details.
- is well organized and uses appropriate transition words to clarify the relationship between causes and effects.
- uses a voice that matches the purpose and audience.
- is concise, not too wordy.
- has sentences that support the purpose.
- contains correct grammar, punctuation, capitalization, and spelling.

248 Informative/Explanatory Writing

English Language Learners

BEGINNING

Writing Prompt Give students a copy of the standard informative/explanatory test writing prompt. Have them look at each word in the prompt and circle the words they do not know. Then teach the most important words, such as *over overslept, involved, report, cause, happens, late, problem.* You might have a higher-level ELL work with a lower-level ELL to review the meanings of these words.

INTERMEDIATE

Writing Prompt Have students read the informative/explanatory writing prompt and write down words they do not know. Review how to ask for help, such as, *What does* involved *mean? Does* involved *mean included?* Have them practice asking and answering with two other students. Finally, ask students to write their answers; for example, *If someone is involved, they are included.* Review as a class.

Think about how the scoring guide relates to the six traits of good writing you've studied in the rubrics. Not all of the traits are included in every scoring guide, but you'll still want to remember them to write a good report.

Ideas
- Be sure your writing has a clear thesis statement and accurate, concrete supporting details.

I'll clearly introduce my thesis statement and support it with concrete details and accurate facts.

Organization
- Be sure your writing is well organized and uses appropriate transition words to clarify the relationship between causes and effects.

I'll be sure to use carefully chosen transition words to guide my reader from point to point.

Voice
- Be sure your writing uses a voice that matches the purpose and audience.

As I write, I'll keep in mind both my purpose and my audience, and adjust my voice appropriately.

Word Choice
- Be sure your writing is concise, not too wordy.

I'll take the time to choose strong and accurate words.

Sentence Fluency
- Be sure your writing has sentences that support the purpose.

Before I start writing, I'll decide which sentence types are most appropriate for my purpose.

Conventions
- Be sure your writing contains correct grammar, punctuation, capitalization, and spelling.

This is important, so I'll make sure to check for mistakes in grammar and mechanics.

Summarize the Traits Once students have reviewed how the traits connect with the scoring guide, ask them to close their books and summarize how each trait plays an important role in a cause-and-effect report.

ADVANCED
Using Powerful Verbs After students have written their first drafts, have them circle all the verbs they used in the first paragraph. Then have them trade with a partner who will read the paragraph and change each of the circled verbs to a stronger one. Then have the partners discuss why they made each change. Monitor that students' changes were appropriate.

ADVANCED HIGH
Using Appropriate Voice Write the topic *Bald Eagles* on the board. Below it, write several introductory words, phrases, or sentences for a report about the desert; for example, *Raptors!*, *Bald eagles are large birds. Why is an eagle's nest so big? Fish and Rodents.* Ask students to rank the introductions according to how interesting they are. Remind students to use simple phrases, questions, or single words to capture the attention of the audience.

CCSS Common Core State Standards
SL.7.1.a: Come to discussions prepared, having read or researched material under study; explicitly draw on that preparation by referring to evidence on the topic, text, or issue to probe and reflect on ideas under discussion. R/Inf.7.5: Analyze the structure an author uses to organize a text, including how the major sections contribute to the whole and to the development of ideas.

Write
an Informative/ Explanatory Test

Week 2 • Day 2

Student Objectives

- Learn how to respond to the task in the writing prompt. *(p. 250)*

Prewrite

Focus on Ideas

Read page 250 aloud. Then work with students to brainstorm a list of problems they might encounter in their everyday lives. Ask them to think about some of the problems caused by decisions they may make on school days. Then ask them to think about some of the effects (results) that stem from their decisions. Point out Emily's notes on page 250. Explain that she will probably need more details about her topic as she starts to write.

Prewrite

Focus on **Ideas**

Writing Strategy   Respond to the task.

I've learned that good writers gather information before they begin writing, so that's what I'll do. I can gather a lot of information from the writing prompt. Let's take another look at the task, since that's the part of the writing prompt that explains what I'm supposed to write. When you write for a test, you don't have a lot of time, so you need to think about how you're going to respond before you start writing.

I'm supposed to write a cause-and-effect report on the problems caused by getting up late for school. I'll think about a time when I overslept. Then I'll jot down some notes.

Task — Write a cause-and-effect report on what happens when you get up late for school.

Notes

✔ I overslept.
✔ I missed the bus.
✔ My sister was late.
✔ I got my first tardy mark.

Apply

Since you won't have much time during a test, first think about how you'll respond to the task. Then jot down notes to help you gather information.

250   Informative/Explanatory Writing

Differentiating Instruction

ENRICHMENT

Determine Cause and Effect   Invite students to work in small groups and create several different sets of notes that could be developed into written responses that match the task on page 250. For example, suggest getting up late for school on one's birthday or the first day of school. Then have them create Cause-and-Effect Chains based on their sets of notes. Have students discuss what effects, if any, a topic change has on the chain reaction of events.

Online Writing Center

Provides **interactive graphic organizers** as well as a variety of graphic organizers in PDF format.

Prewrite

Focus on Organization

Writing Strategy   Choose a graphic organizer.

The next step is to arrange the details of my report. I'll choose a graphic organizer to help me do this quickly and efficiently. Since I'm writing a cause-and-effect report, I'll use a Cause-and-Effect Chain to show how one cause led to a chain reaction of events.

First I'll fill in the primary cause (oversleeping); then I'll list the effects. Next I'll fill in the three resulting causes of those effects, which in turn, led to three more final effects.

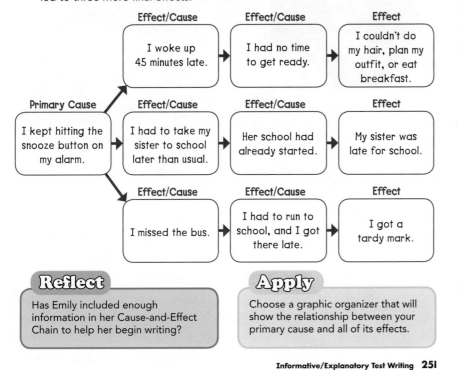

Reflect

Has Emily included enough information in her Cause-and-Effect Chain to help her begin writing?

Apply

Choose a graphic organizer that will show the relationship between your primary cause and all of its effects.

Write
an Informative/Explanatory Test

Week 2 • Day 3

Student Objectives

- Learn how to choose a graphic organizer for the writing prompt. (p. 251)

Prewrite

Focus on

Remind students that during a writing test, they will not be told what kind of graphic organizer to use. Instead they must think about how they have used graphic organizers in the past, and they must decide which one will be the most useful for a test. After students have chosen a problem to write about, have them create a Cause-and-Effect Chain to put their ideas in order.

REINFORCEMENT

Examine Cause-and-Effect Chains Work with students to review Emily's notes on page 250 and the Cause-and-Effect Chain on page 251. Discuss how the chain itself works by pointing out that all events are related to the primary cause. Trace the primary cause to the three primary effects and their causes. Then trace those to the secondary effects/causes, which result in the final effects. Finally, have students brainstorm similar "getting up late" experiences to make their notes. Assist as needed to connect their causes and effects logically in their organizers.

CCSS Common Core State Standards
W.7.2: Write informative/explanatory texts to examine a topic and convey ideas, concepts, and information through the selection, organization, and analysis of relevant content.

Write
an Informative/ Explanatory Test

Week 2 • Day 4

Student Objectives

- Learn how to check the graphic organizer against the scoring guide. *(pp. 252–253)*

Prewrite

Focus on

Check the Scoring Guide

Demonstrate how Emily has used each writing trait to make sure that her prewriting (gathering and organizing information) stays on track. Point out that each detail box on the Cause-and-Effect Chain is related to the primary cause. Then write this detail on the board:

When I got the alarm clock, I promised myself that I would never use the snooze button.

Ask students why this detail would not help Emily respond to the task and does not belong on Emily's organizer. (Possible response: It doesn't change the primary cause or affect the chain of events.) Ask students to check their Cause-and-Effect Chains to delete any details that are off-topic.

As they prepare their organizers, remind students to use the scoring guide. Doing so will help them write well-organized drafts that will require less revision.

Strategies for Writers Online

Go to **www.sfw.z-b.com** for additional online resources for students and teachers.

T252 Informative/Explanatory Writing

Prewrite · Focus on Organization

Writing Strategy Check my graphic organizer against the scoring guide.

Without much time to revise during a test, prewriting is really important. Before I begin drafting, I'll check my Cause-and-Effect Chain against the scoring guide in the writing prompt.

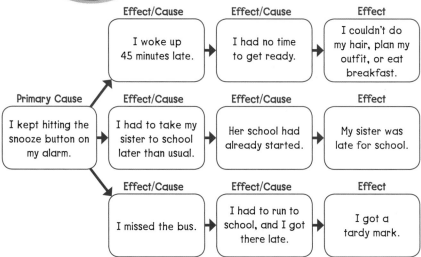

Effect/Cause	Effect/Cause	Effect
I woke up 45 minutes late.	I had no time to get ready.	I couldn't do my hair, plan my outfit, or eat breakfast.

Primary Cause
I kept hitting the snooze button on my alarm.

Effect/Cause	Effect/Cause	Effect
I had to take my sister to school later than usual.	Her school had already started.	My sister was late for school.

Effect/Cause	Effect/Cause	Effect
I missed the bus.	I had to run to school, and I got there late.	I got a tardy mark.

252 Informative/Explanatory Writing

Ideas
- Be sure your writing has a clear thesis statement and accurate, concrete supporting details.

Based on what I've written in my graphic organizer, I'm sure it'll be easy to write a good thesis statement and include concrete, factual supporting details.

Organization
- Be sure your writing is well organized and uses appropriate transition words to clarify the relationship between causes and effects.

To help readers follow the chain of causes and effects I'm explaining, I'll use clear and appropriate transitions.

Voice
- Be sure your writing uses a voice that matches the purpose and audience.

Since I'm telling an amusing story, my voice should be casual and entertaining. I'll also use first-person point of view.

Word Choice
- Be sure your writing is concise, not too wordy.

I'll be sure not to ramble or repeat myself. I'll use only accurate and descriptive words.

Sentence Fluency
- Be sure your writing has sentences that support the purpose.

I'll use mostly declarative sentences, as my purpose is to present facts.

Conventions
- Be sure your writing contains correct grammar, punctuation, capitalization, and spelling.

I'll check for proper grammar and mechanics when I edit my report.

Reflect

Emily's Cause-and-Effect Chain seems pretty complete. Can you think of anything that she might be missing?

Apply

Compare your graphic organizer with the scoring guide before you start to write. This way, you'll know what to do when you begin drafting.

Prepare to Draft Point out to students that Emily cannot check her work against all six writing traits yet. She will have to draft, for example, before she can check for smooth, flowing sentences. Ask students why, since this is the case, Emily stops to check her work against the scoring guide at this point. (Possible response: Emily does not want to start writing if she is off the topic and not responding to the task. She does not have much time to draft, so she must be sure she is on the right track before she starts drafting.) Explain to students that by reading each of the writing traits again, Emily is also reminding herself of what to keep in mind as she drafts.

CCSS Common Core State Standards

W.7.2.b: Develop the topic with relevant facts, definitions, concrete details, quotations, or other information and examples. **SL.7.1:** Engage effectively in a range of collaborative discussions (one-on-one, in groups, and teacher-led) with diverse partners on *grade 7 topics, texts, and issues,* building on others' ideas and expressing their own clearly.

Write
an Informative/ Explanatory Test

Week 2 • Day 5

Student Objectives

- Draft an informative/explanatory writing test, using a clear and concise thesis statement. (pp. 254–255)

Draft

Focus on Ideas

Tips for Test Writing As students prepare to draft, remind them to write on every other line of the paper. By leaving room in between lines, as Emily does, test writers make it easier to reread their drafts and leave spaces to make changes and insert new information such as supporting details. Encourage students to write as neatly as they can despite the time restraints. Not only will neat writing help the person grading the cause-and-effect report to read it easily, it will also help students during the revising and editing stages of their writing process.

Check the Thesis Statement Read Emily's words on page 254. Point out that she refers to her graphic organizer in order to write her draft. Emphasize to students the importance of using their graphic organizers as guidance during the

Online Writing Center

Provides student eBooks with an **interactive writing pad** for drafting, revising, editing, and publishing.

Draft Focus on Ideas

Writing Strategy Write a clear, concise thesis statement.

The scoring guide says that I should have a clear thesis statement. Making my Cause-and-Effect Chain reminded me of how many problems were caused by oversleeping on a school day. Using this information, it will be easy to come up with a clear and concise thesis statement.

[DRAFT]

Cause for Alarm

by Emily

Having to get up early for school can be a real bummer. But I learned the hard way that a few extra minutes of sleep, while pleasant at the time, can result in total chaos. So take it from me—don't use the snooze button in the morning. ◄——— [concise thesis statement]

I remember one Thursday morning when a few extra minutes of sleep disrupted my entire morning routine. Normally, my alarm goes off at 6:45 A.M., allowing me plenty of time to get ready for school. But on this perticular morning, I was so tired that I kept hitting the snooze button until 7:30—just ten minutes before I was supposed to catch the bus! I jumped out of bed and threw on an outfit that didn't even match. I didn't have time to take a shower, so I quickly brushed

---

English Language Learners

BEGINNING/INTERMEDIATE

Word Choice Remind students that when they draft, they should use powerful verbs. Write the following verbs on the board: *said, declared, exclaimed, cried, stated, answered,* and *uttered.* Have students work in pairs using the Continuum Scale to place words in order from boring and weak to strong and convincing.

ADVANCED/ADVANCED HIGH

Peer Review After students have drafted their cause-effect report, have them trade with another student. Partners should review the draft and look for specific details. Students should point out weak voice and suggest more descriptive words their partners could use. As you monitor, identify two or three examples of weak words or sentences, and discuss ways to strengthen them as a class.

my teeth and threw my hair up into a ponytale. Even though I was starved, there was no time to eat breakfast. I usually eat a bowl of cereal.

My parents leave early for work. I am responsable for walking my younger sister, Paige, to school before I catch the bus. She was already up and ready to go. I knew her teacher wasn't happy.

I feared the worst consaquence of all: getting my first tardy mark. With school starting right at 8:00 A.M., I ran as fast as I could. Even though I hurried, I arrived at 8:25 A.M. I was exhausted, hungry, and out of breath. When I walked into the classroom, my teacher gave me a stern look and said, Emily, you're late. Unless you have a good excuse, I have to give you a tardy mark."

There was no excuse for missing the morning lesson, but a lesson was learned that day Do not use the snooze button. It's only cause for alarm!

Reflect

What do you think? Is Emily's thesis statement clear and concise?

Apply

Include a clear and concise thesis statement in your cause-and-effect report.

Informative/Explanatory Test Writing   **255**

---

drafting process. Tell students to set their Cause-and-Effect Chains on their desks where they can look back frequently at the information they wrote. Remind them to make sure that they begin their reports with clear, concise thesis statements. Emily realized that making a Cause-and-Effect Chain showed her how many problems were caused by oversleeping on a school day. She used this information to come up with a clear and concise thesis statement. Students should read their thesis statements and ask themselves these questions:

- Is my thesis statement clear and concise so that the audience understands the point I will be making?

- Does my thesis statement focus on the cause-and-effect relationship to be discussed?

- If students answer *no* to either question, they should take another look at their thesis statements before they begin writing. Then they should use their Cause-and-Effect Chains to write more concise, focused thesis statements.

Finally, review the proofreading marks with students. Tell them that these marks will be helpful as they revise and edit their drafts.

CCSS **C**ommon **C**ore **S**tate **S**tandards

W.7.2.a: Introduce a topic clearly, previewing what is to follow; organize ideas, concepts, and information, using strategies, such as definition, classification, comparison/contrast, and cause/effect; include formatting (e.g. headings), graphics (e.g. charts, tables), and multimedia when useful to aiding comprehension.

Informative/Explanatory Test Writing   **T255**

Write
an Informative/ Explanatory Test

Week 3 • Day 1

Student Objectives

• Revise for logical presentation of details. *(p. 256)*

Revise

Focus on  Organization

Time Management Point out that students have about fifteen minutes to revise their drafts and that there are three revision tasks. Students might wish to subdivide their planned revising time into segments and tackle one writing strategy at a time.

Check for Appropriate Transition Words Remind students that a strong cause-and-effect report uses appropriate transition words to clarify the relationship between the causes and effects. This helps connect ideas and organize the information in the report. Students should follow Emily's example by checking to see that their transitions move the reader from one idea to the next in a logical order.

Refer students to page 542 for a list of transitions.

Online Writing Center

 Provides student eBooks with an **interactive writing pad** for drafting, revising, editing, and publishing.

T256 Informative/Explanatory Writing

Revise   Focus on Organization

Writing Strategy   Use appropriate transition words to show cause and effect.

Using transition words is a great way to keep my writing organized. Some transition words, such as *first*, *now*, and *after dinner*, help show the order of events. Other transition words, such as *so*, *because*, and *therefore*, show cause and effect. As I reread my draft, I found a place that could use some clarification, so I'll add some transition words now.

[DRAFT]   [used cause-effect transition word]

My parents leave early for work. , so I am responsible for walking my younger sister, Paige, to school before I catch the bus. She was already up and ready to go. I knew her teacher wasn't happy. Now I feared the worst consaquence of all: getting my first tardy mark.

[used time-order transition word]

 Apply

Use transition words to show the order of events and to connect causes and effects.

256   Informative/Explanatory Writing

Revise

Focus on **Voice**

Writing Strategy   Connect with the readers.

To truly connect with my reader, I have to use a voice that is appropriate for both my purpose and my audience. Since I'm telling a personal story, I'll keep my voice casual and engaging, and I'll use first-person point of view. I found a place where first person was needed. What do you think of my revisions?

[DRAFT]

I didn't have an ←———— [used first person] ————→ I did learn
There was no excuse for missing the morning lesson, but a lesson
———→ of my own
was learned that day Do not use the snooze button. It's only cause

for alarm!

Reflect

How do Emily's revisions help you better connect with the ending of her cause-and-effect paper?

Apply

To connect with your reader, use a voice that's appropriate for both your purpose and your audience.

Informative/Explanatory Test Writing **257**

Write
an Informative/ Explanatory Test

Week 3 • Day 2

Student Objectives

- Revise to connect with readers. (p. 257)

Revise

Focus on

Guide students to consider one paragraph of their drafts at a time, checking to make sure that they have used a voice that is appropriate for their purpose and audience. Emily's cause-and-effect report tells a personal story, so she used first-person pronouns like *I* and *me* to connect with the audience, yet still be informative. Although the style in her essay is personal, she definitely wants her audience to take her essay seriously. Ask students why Emily made the revisions in her draft. (Possible response: She wanted to use a first-person point of view to better connect with the reader.)

Remind students to draw a single neat line through unneeded sentences. This cuts the sentences without leaving a messy, hard-to-read draft behind.

CCSS **Common Core State Standards**

W.7.2.c: Use appropriate transitions to create cohesion and clarify the relationships among ideas and concepts.

Informative/Explanatory Test Writing **T257**

Write
an Informative/ Explanatory Test

Week 3 • Day 3

Student Objectives

• Revise for precise language to eliminate wordiness and redundancy. *(p. 258)*

Revise

Focus on

Use Precise Vocabulary Direct students to page 258, and read the text aloud. Discuss the importance of making sure that their writing is concise and not too wordy. Remind students that their writing is less credible when they repeat information or include unnecessary words. Guide students to Emily's deleted sentence. This sentence gave information that was unnecessary to the meaning of the draft. Leaving it in her report would have weakened Emily's writing.

Students may have time left in the revising period to check for other problems, such as run-on sentences and fragments. Encourage students to use every minute they have to improve their informative/ explanatory tests, even if they think they can finish early.

Online Writing Center

Provides **interactive proofreading activities** for each genre.

Revise — Focus on **Word Choice**

Writing Strategy — Choose language that expresses ideas precisely and concisely, recognizing and eliminating wordiness and redundancy.

The scoring guide says my writing should be concise and not too wordy. I know that when I repeat information or include unnecessary details, I weaken my writing and confuse my reader. I'll take a moment to reread my draft and delete any unnecessary words.

[DRAFT]

I didn't have time to take a shower, so I quickly brushed my teeth and threw my hair up into a ponytail. Even though I was starved, there was no time to eat breakfast. ~~I usually eat a bowl of cereal.~~

[deleted unnecessary words]

Reflect
What do you think? Does the deletion of repeated or unnecessary information strengthen Emily's writing?

Apply
To keep your writing clear and strong, use only necessary words and details.

258 Informative/Explanatory Writing

Optional Revising Lessons

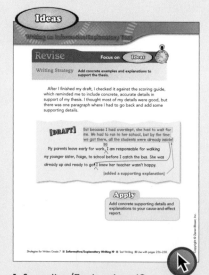

Informative/Explanatory 19

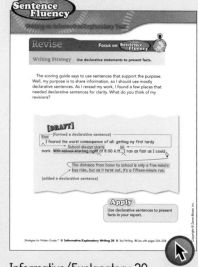

Informative/Explanatory 20

 Strategies for Writers Grade 7 CD-ROM

Writing Strategy   Check my grammar, punctuation, capitalization, and spelling.

I never turn in a paper without checking it for mistakes in grammar and mechanics. Editing my work after it is completed helps me find and correct mistakes that I made while drafting. I'll read through my report one last time, correcting mistakes as I read.

[FINAL DRAFT]   **Cause for Alarm**

by Emily

Having to get up early for school can be a real bummer. But I learned the hard way that a few extra minutes of sleep, while pleasant at the time, can result in total chaos. So take it from me—don't use the snooze button in the morning.

I remember one Thursday morning when a few extra minutes of sleep disrupted my entire morning routine. Normally, my alarm goes off at 6:45 A.M., allowing me plenty of time to get ready for school. But on this ~~perticular~~ *particular* morning, I was so tired that I kept hitting the snooze button until 7:30—just ten minutes before I was supposed to catch the bus! I jumped out of bed and threw on an outfit that didn't even match. I didn't have time to take a shower, so I quickly brushed my

Apply

Check your grammar, punctuation, capitalization, and spelling every time you write for a test.

Differentiating Instruction

ENRICHMENT

Clarify Ideas Provide students with a list of overused, worn-out words and expressions, such as *good, bad, really, very, as a matter of fact, in no time, for free, refer back,* etc. that weigh down and dull writing. Then have students consult online word resources for replacement words that express ideas precisely and concisely. Give students time to share their findings in class. Suggest that each student keep an active list of replacement words as a writer's resource.

Write
an Informative/ Explanatory Test

Week 3 • Day 4

Student Objectives

• Edit the writing test for proper grammar, spelling, capitalization, and punctuation. *(pp. 259–260)*

Edit

Focus on **Conventions**

Edit the Test Explain to students that while an informative/ explanatory report written for a test in a short period of time will rarely be perfect, they should find and correct as many errors as they can. Test graders know that students are writing quickly and watching the clock; graders know that a few errors may slip through. However, graders also look for evidence that students took time to edit. For example, when they see misspelled words crossed out and correctly spelled words inserted instead, graders know that students are paying attention to editing.

Review the proofreading marks on page 255 with students. Point out the insertions in Emily's draft. Remind students that they should not plan for time to recopy their drafts—every minute of writing time should be put to good use, making the report stronger, not to produce a perfectly neat final copy.

CCSS **C**ommon **C**ore **S**tate **S**tandards
L.7.2: Demonstrate command of the conventions of standard English capitalization, punctuation, and spelling when writing.

Review
Test Tips

Week 3 • Day 5

Student Objectives
- Review tips for writing for a test. (p. 261)

Test Tips

Reviewing Test Writing Explain to students that not all writing test prompts will be as clearly divided into parts as the writing prompt used in this chapter. However, students can still find and label the three important sections. Students can even generate a scoring guide if they must. Write this prompt on the board:

Write about how your life might be affected if a highway was built at the end of your street. Revise and edit your writing.

- **What is the setup?** (Possible response: One's life would be affected by the construction of a highway.)

Next ask the following:

- **What is the task?** (Write a cause-and-effect report about the effects of a nearby new highway.)

Strategies for Writers Online
Go to **www.sfw.z-b.com** for additional online resources for students and teachers.

[FINAL DRAFT] But because I had overslept, she had to wait for me. We had to run to her school, but by the time we got there, all the students were already inside!

teeth and threw my hair up into a ~~ponytale~~ ponytail. Even though I was starved, there was no time to eat breakfast. ~~I usually eat a bowl of cereal.~~ My parents leave early for work, so I am ~~responsable~~ responsible for walking my younger sister, Paige, to school before I catch the bus. She was already up and ready to go. I knew her teacher wasn't happy. Now I feared the worst ~~consaquence~~ consequence of all: getting my first tardy mark. ~~With school starting right~~ School always starts at 8:00 A.M., so I ran as fast as I could. Even though I hurried, I arrived at 8:25 A.M. I was exhausted, hungry, and out of breath. When I walked into the classroom, my teacher gave me a stern look and said, "Emily, you're late. Unless you have a good excuse, I have to give you a tardy mark."

I didn't have an ~~There was no~~ excuse for missing the morning lesson, but I did learn a lesson of my own ~~was learned~~ that day: Do not use the snooze button. It's only cause for alarm! The distance from home to school is only a five-minute bus ride, but as it turns out, it's a fifteen-minute run.

Reflect

Is Emily missing anything? Check her report against the scoring guide, and remember to check your work against your writing prompt's scoring guide, too.

260 Informative/Explanatory Writing

Differentiating Instruction

REINFORCEMENT

2-2-1 With only five minutes to edit, some students may become anxious during the editing stage of the writing process. Assist them in breaking down the time into easy-to-manage segments: two minutes to scan their drafts for spelling and capitalization errors, two minutes to look for punctuation errors, and one minute to check for common errors they often make. Looking for specific types of errors on consecutive readings will help students correct their writing and feel in control of the editing process.

Well now, that wasn't so bad! Just remember to use the writing process when you take a writing test. The process is just a little different for a test, but if you remember these important tips, I'm sure you'll do just fine!

Test Tips

1. **Study the writing prompt before you start to write.** Most writing prompts have three parts: the setup, the task, and the scoring guide. The parts probably won't be labeled. You'll have to figure them out for yourself!

2. **Make sure you understand the task before you start to write.**
   - Read all three parts of the writing prompt carefully.
   - Circle key words in the task part of the writing prompt that tell what kind of writing you need to do. The task might also identify your audience.
   - Make sure you know how you'll be graded.
   - Say the assignment in your own words to yourself.

3. **Keep an eye on the clock.** Decide how much time you will spend on each part of the writing process and try to stick to your schedule. Don't spend so much time on prewriting that you don't have enough time left to write.

4. **Reread your writing. Compare it to the scoring guide at least twice.** Remember the rubrics you've used? A scoring guide on a writing test is like a rubric. It can help you keep what's important in mind.

5. **Plan, plan, plan!** You don't get much time to revise during a test, so planning is more important than ever.

6. **Write neatly.** Remember: If the people who score your test can't read your writing, it doesn't matter how good your essay is!

Circle and label the task, and point out that it is missing some information. (Possible response: The task says to write a cause-and-effect report about a new highway, but it doesn't describe who the audience will be.)

Finally, ask students what they can do to make up a scoring guide since the writing prompt has only the general instructions to revise and edit. (Possible response: We know that we can make writing better by adding details and varying sentence lengths and types. We know that we always need to edit for correct grammar, spelling, punctuation, and capitalization.)

As students provide these responses, write them on the board in bulleted form. Show students that they have just figured out a useful scoring guide from their own experience. Students will see that even a brief writing prompt can give them the tools and guidance they need to write a successful test.

CCSS **C**ommon **C**ore **S**tate **S**tandards

W.7.5: With some guidance and support from peers and adults, develop and strengthen writing as needed by planning, revising, editing, rewriting, or trying a new approach, focusing on how well purpose and audience have been addressed. **SL.7.1.c:** Pose questions that elicit elaboration and respond to others' questions and comments with relevant observations and ideas that bring the discussion back on topic as needed.

Argument writing

Editorial

Pages T264A–T285

This genre opens the door to argument writing by encouraging students to develop an opinion on a real-world issue and build a reasonable argument that will convince others.

Prewrite   Brainstorm to choose a problem, or claim, for which there is a solution. Make a Problem-Solution Frame to organize the ideas.

Draft   Research the subject and gather accurate and relevant facts or statistics.

Revise   Strengthen the conclusion.
Use a blend of first-person and third-person point of view.
Replace vague words with specific ones.

Edit   Check the use of appositives and indefinite pronouns.

Publish   Submit editorial for publication in the school newspaper.

Business Letter

Pages T286A–T309

This genre gives students an opportunity to practice two important life skills—writing a business letter and concisely stating an argument.

Prewrite   Choose an issue. List explanations, facts, and examples to support the opinion. Make an Argument Map to show how reasons, facts, and examples support the call to action.

Draft   Write well-organized paragraphs that support the call to action.

Revise   Use a respectful and courteous tone.
Use homophones or other easily confused words correctly.
Use different sentence structures, such as conditional sentences.

Edit   Make sure that there are no double negatives and that infinitives are correct.

Publish   Mail the letter to the appropriate person.

Website Review

Pages T310A–T335

Students evaluate a website to determine whether it is reliable, up-to-date, and easy to use. This information is then presented in a way to convince others of the website's value.

Prewrite   Find a website about a topic of interest and list responses to it. Make a Pro-and-Con Chart to organize the responses.

Draft   Use credible sources of information and fair language.

Revise   State a clear claim and include at least one con.
Use words with the right connotation.
Vary sentences by using transition words.

Edit   Choose punctuation for effect.

Publish   Submit the review to the appropriate website.

Unit Overview

LITERATURE CONNECTION

Response to Literature

Pages T336A–T359

Students will respond to their reading by writing a literary analysis.

Prewrite	List the theme and reactions to the literature. Use a Paragraph Organizer to plan the literary analysis.
Draft	Use exact words.
Revise	Choose quotations that support the thesis. Strengthen the conclusion. Write different kinds of sentences.
Edit	Make sure to always use the right word.
Publish	Present the literary analysis as part of a class-published book.

Argument Test Writing

Pages T360A–T381

Students will learn and practice how to read an argument test prompt and how to plan their time. They will also learn and practice writing strategies for successful test writing in the mode of argument writing.

Prewrite	Study the writing prompt to find out what to do. Respond to the task. Choose a graphic organizer. Check the graphic organizer against the scoring guide.
Draft	Clearly state the claim for the reader.
Revise	Organize the ideas into an introduction, body, and conclusion. Sound convincing. Use words with the right connotation.
Edit	Check the grammar, punctuation, capitalization, and spelling.

Online Writing Center

Interactive Whiteboard Ready

Complete Digital Writing Instruction!

- My Writing Pad
- Interactive Rubrics
- Anchor Papers
- Graphic Organizers

- Content Area Writing Prompts
- Grammar Games
- Proofreading Activities
- Instructional Videos

- Virtual File Cabinet
- eBooks
- Assessments

For information, go to www.sfw.z-b.com

Also available: **Online Essay Grader and Writing Tutor,** powered by Vantage Learning's MY Access®.

21st Century Literacies
Technology, Digital Media & Writing

by Julie Coiro, Ph.D., University of Rhode Island & **Sara Kajder, Ph.D.,** Univeristy of Pittsburgh

 **INQUIRE First Locate, Then Evaluate**

Generating Keyword Searches

There are different keyword strategies you can use to quickly locate the Internet materials you need. If you are using a search engine such as **Google, Yahoo,** or **Bing,** you may wish to try the following:

- **Choose your keywords wisely.** Indicate in the search bar a subject area or specific topic. Use quotation marks to group two or more words together as a phrase. For example, if you are looking for a lesson on persuasive writing, you would enclose the phrase in quotation marks: "persuasive writing"

- **Narrow your search with a "topic+focus" keyword strategy.** If you preface both topic and focus words/phrases with a plus sign (+lesson+"persuasive writing"), the search engine will look only for hits that have both topic and focus words/phrases on the same webpage.

- **Specify the type of educational activity.** If you are searching for a specific type of educational activity, be sure to indicate this next to your topic. Common activities include Internet project, lesson plan, webquest (an online inquiry activity), cyberhunt, animation, simulation, quiz, game, or class project. Be sure to use quotation marks around phrases as needed.

- **Specify an appropriate grade level, if desired.** If you find your search results are not appropriate for students at your grade level, include the grade level or grade range in quotes (e.g., "seventh grade" or "middle school").

- **Think of a synonym or skim the search result annotations for more appropriate keywords.** Sometimes reading within the search results or on a few related websites creates more familiarity with the language around that topic. This will help you generate more appropriate search terms that better meet your needs.

Detecting Commercial Bias

Often, advertising is artfully woven into factual information or interactive games in ways that mask the author's underlying intentions. This is known as *commercial bias.* Commercially biased websites share information, but they also sell products. As your students learn more about argument writing, encourage them to consider the following questions to help them recognize the techniques that businesses use to persuade and influence those who use the Internet to gather information.

- Whose opinion does the information represent?
- What techniques does the business use to attract children to its website?
- What techniques does the business use to attract children to its products?
- Are there attempts to offer new ideas or teach something new?
- How does the advertising influence your opinions of products sold on the site?
- Who benefits most from the different types of information provided at this site?

For additional practice, discuss with students the 5 W's of evaluating websites:

- *Who* developed the content on the website and are they an expert?
- *What* is the author's purpose for the website?
- *When* was the site created and when was it last updated?
- *Where* does the information come from? Is there an "About Us" or "Contact" link?
- *Why* is (or isn't) this website useful for the purpose?

See also **Don't Buy It (http://pbskids.org/dontbuyit/),** where students can learn how to question, analyze, and become savvy consumers.

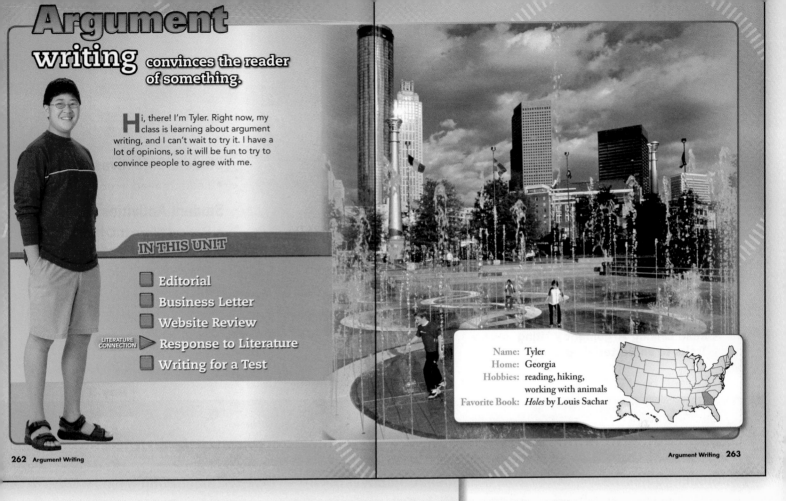

Argument

writing convinces the reader of something.

Hi, there! I'm Tyler. Right now, my class is learning about argument writing, and I can't wait to try it. I have a lot of opinions, so it will be fun to try to convince people to agree with me.

IN THIS UNIT

- [ ] Editorial
- [ ] Business Letter
- [ ] Website Review
- LITERATURE CONNECTION ▶ Response to Literature
- [ ] Writing for a Test

Name: Tyler
Home: Georgia
Hobbies: reading, hiking, working with animals
Favorite Book: *Holes* by Louis Sachar

Meet Your Writing Partner, Tyler

The writing partner for this chapter is Tyler, a boy from Georgia. You may wish to explore with students how Tyler's background, hobbies, interests, and personality connect with his choices of writing topics. Explain to students that Tyler will use what he knows to make decisions about his topics—a process that helps make his writing personal and real. Encourage students to use their own background knowledge, interests, and personalities as they write as well. Argument writing is based on personal opinion and your students will have many interesting and authentic points to make.

To differentiate instruction and maximize student achievement, use the Extensions Online activities available at **www.sfw.z-b.com.**

Created by Amy Humphreys, Ed.M., these engaging activities can be used to meet a wide range of learner needs. Each activity uses a combination of visual, written, oral, and kinesthetic elements, and deliberately leverages the power of collaboration and conversation so students learn to think like writers in fun and engaging ways. For more information on Differentiated Instruction, see page Z12.

Editorial Planner

WEEK 1

Day 1
Introduce
an Editorial

Student Objectives
- Review the elements of an editorial.
- Consider purpose and audience.
- Learn the traits of argument writing.

Student Activities
- Read and discuss **What's in an Editorial?** (p. 264)
- Read and discuss **Why Write an Editorial?** (p. 265)
- Read **Linking Argument Writing Traits to an Editorial.** (p. 266)

Day 2
Analyze
Read an Editorial

Student Objectives
- Read a model editorial.

Student Activities
- Read **"Turn It Off!"** (p. 267)

Day 3
Analyze
Introduce the Rubric

Student Objectives
- Learn to read a rubric.

Student Activities
- Review **"Turn It Off!"** (p. 267)
- Read and discuss **Editorial Rubric.** (pp. 268–269)

WEEK 2

Day 1
Write
Prewrite: Ideas

Student Objectives
- Read and understand a prewriting strategy.

Student Activities
- Read and discuss **Prewrite: Focus on Ideas.** (p. 274)
- Apply the prewriting strategy.

Day 2
Write
Prewrite: Organization

Student Objectives
- Make a Problem-Solution Frame to define a problem and organize the information that solves it.

Student Activities
- Read and discuss **Prewrite: Focus on Organization.** (p. 275)
- Reflect on the model Problem-Solution Frame.
- Apply the prewriting strategy to create a Problem-Solution Frame.

Day 3
Write
Draft: Ideas

Student Objectives
- Use a Problem-Solution Frame to begin writing.

Student Activities
- Read and discuss **Draft: Focus on Ideas.** (p. 276)
- Reflect on the model draft. (p. 277)
- Apply the drafting strategy by using a Problem-Solution Frame to begin a draft.

WEEK 3

Day 1
Write
Revise: Voice

Student Objectives
- Use a blend of first-person and third-person points of view.

Student Activities
- Read and discuss **Revise: Focus on Voice.** (p. 279)
- Reflect on the model draft.
- Apply the revising strategy.
- Participate in a peer conference.

Day 2
Write
Revise: Word Choice

Student Objectives
- Replace vague words with specific ones.

Student Activities
- Read and discuss **Revise: Focus on Word Choice.** (p. 280)
- Reflect on the model draft.
- Apply the revising strategy.

Note: Optional Revising Lessons appear on the *Strategies for Writers* CD-ROM.

Day 3
Write
Edit: Conventions

Student Objectives
- Check the use of appositives and indefinite pronouns.

Student Activities
- Read and discuss **Edit: Focus on Conventions.** (p. 281)
- Reflect on the model draft.
- Apply the editing strategy.

Note: Teach the Conventions mini-lessons (pp. 282–283) if needed.

Day 4

Analyze
Ideas, Organization, and Voice

Student Objectives
- Read a model editorial.
- Use the editorial rubric.
- Use the model editorial to study Ideas, Organization, and Voice.

Student Activities
- Review **"Turn It Off!"** (p. 267)
- Read and discuss **Using the Rubric to Study the Model.** (pp. 270–271)

Day 5

Analyze
Word Choice, Sentence Fluency, and Conventions

Student Objectives
- Read a model editorial.
- Use the editorial rubric.
- Use the model editorial to study Word Choice, Sentence Fluency, and Conventions.

Student Activities
- Review **"Turn It Off!"** (p. 267)
- Read and discuss **Using the Rubric to Study the Model.** (pp. 272–273)

Day 4

Write
Draft

Student Objectives
- Use a Problem-Solution Frame to complete a draft.

Student Activities
- Finish writing the draft. (p. 277)
- Participate in a peer conference.

Day 5

Write
Revise: Organization

Student Objectives
- Strengthen the conclusion.

Student Activities
- Read and discuss **Revise: Focus on Organization.** (p. 278)
- Reflect on the model draft.
- Apply the revising strategy.

Day 4

Write
Publish: +Presentation

Student Objectives
- Discuss preparation for publishing and presentation.
- Use a final editing checklist to publish their work.

Student Activities
- Read and discuss **Publish: +Presentation.** (p. 284)
- Apply the publishing strategy.

Day 5

Write
Publish: +Presentation

Student Objectives
- Use an editorial rubric.
- Share a published editorial.

Student Activities
- Share their work.
- Use the rubric to reflect upon and evaluate the model and their own writing. (pp. 268–269; 285)

Resources at-a-Glance

Grammar, Usage & Mechanics

Differentiating Instruction

For additional Differentiating Instruction activities, see Strategies for Writers *Extensions Online at* **www.sfw.z-b.com.**

English Language Learners

Conferencing

Technology Tip

 Connection Letter
Reproducible letter (in English and Spanish) appears on the *Strategies for Writers* CD-ROM and at **www.sfw.z-b.com.**

Online Writing Center

Provides IWB resources, interactive games and practice activities, videos, eBooks, and a virtual file cabinet.

 Strategies for Writers Online

Go to **www.sfw.z-b.com** for free online resources for students and teachers.

To complete the chapter in fewer days, combine the learning objectives and activities in a way that supports students as they write.

Introduce
an Editorial

Week 1 • Day 1

Student Objectives

- Review the elements of an editorial. *(p. 264)*
- Consider purpose and audience. *(p. 265)*
- Learn the traits of argument writing. *(p. 266)*

What's an Editorial?

Discuss with students the definition of an editorial. Ask students to bring in some magazines that they enjoy. Have them look through the tables of contents to see if the magazines have editorial or opinion sections. Point out that most newspapers, including those published online, have an editorial page. Tell students that any time they write to convince readers to agree with proposed solutions to problems, they are using the editorial genre.

What's in an Editorial?

Read and discuss with students the elements of an editorial listed on page 264. Explain that these elements—Three Parts, Supporting Evidence, and Clear Rationale—are also common to other forms of writing, such as cause-and-effect reports, summaries, and business letters. Then discuss why each element is important to keep in mind when writing a convincing editorial.

 Strategies for Writers Online
Go to **www.sfw.z-b.com** for additional online resources for students and teachers.

What's an **Editorial?**

It's writing that expresses the author's opinion. The writer of a problem-solution editorial states a problem and offers one or more solutions, hoping to convince readers to agree with the proposed solutions.

What's in an **Editorial?**

Three Parts
An editorial has an introduction that states a problem (or claim), a body that presents one or more solutions, and a conclusion that has a call to action.

Supporting Evidence
Facts and statistics can be used as supporting details in an editorial. You can cite statistics from a scientific study, or you can present facts from other sources. The goal is to support your argument with credible information.

Clear Rationale
A rationale is the thought process behind an opinion. All facts and details included in an editorial should support the writer's rationale. It's also important to acknowledge alternate or opposing claims to show that both sides of the story are understood.

Argument Text Exemplars (Editorial)

Clements, Andrew. *The Landry News.* Atheneum Books for Young Readers, 2000. Cara Landry is a new fifth-grade student who is excited and eager to learn. She is disappointed when she realizes that her teacher, Mr. Larson, prefers to read and sip coffee while his students work independently. To fight back, Cara writes an editorial about the state of teaching in the fifth-grade classroom that sparks a school-wide conversation about education, the First Amendment, and second chances.

Kelsey, Elin. *Not Your Typical Book About the Environment.* Owlkids Books, 2010. In a time when conversations about the future of the environment tend to be bleak, Kelsey's book presents a positive and encouraging view of things we already do, as well as new ideas of what we can do to lessen negative environmental impacts.

Why write an **Editorial?**

I can think of a bunch of reasons to write an editorial. I have as many reasons as I have opinions! I listed some purposes for writing here.

Solve a Problem
A good reason to write an editorial is to help solve a real-world problem. I can suggest a solution and try to convince other people to support it.

Logical Thinking
I can practice logical thinking while writing my editorial. If I am able to present a good, logical argument, my readers will be more likely to agree with my claims.

Information
Presenting information is another good reason to write. If I present a lot of relevant and accurate information in my editorial, people will be well informed about the issue I'm describing.

Organization
I can learn organizational skills while writing an editorial. I'll have to choose a problem, explain why it's a problem, and then offer at least one solution. I'll have to decide which points to make first and which to make last.

O'Neill, Terry. *The Homeless: Distinguishing Between Facts and Opinions*. Greenhaven Press, 1990. O'Neill's book provides students with an opportunity to think critically about a prevalent social issue. Students must distinguish between facts and opinions in several arguments focused on the best way to solve the issue of homelessness.

Wingate, Philippa. *Alien Abduction? The Evidence and the Arguments*. EDC Publishing, 1998. Through detailed accounts of eight cases of close encounters with extraterrestrial beings, Wingate explores the question of whether aliens really do exist.

Why write an Editorial?

Read and discuss with students the reasons for writing an editorial listed on page 265. Read the page aloud. Point out that all writing has a purpose and is aimed at a specific audience. Encourage students to discuss how authentic purposes help authors shape their writing. For example, someone writing to solve a problem will make sure the problem and solution(s) are clearly stated. A person practicing logical thinking and organization will make sure his or her editorial is presented as clearly as possible, excluding any extraneous information. A writer who is writing to inform will include many facts and examples to convince the reader. Encourage students to think about their own reasons for writing editorials and how these reasons for writing editorials will affect the tone and focus of their writing. Conclude the discussion by explaining to students that they are going to study and practice strategies for writing a good editorial.

CCSS **Common Core State Standards**

SL.7.1: Engage effectively in a range of collaborative discussions (one-on-one, in groups, and teacher-led) with diverse partners on *grade 7 topics, texts, and issues,* building on others' ideas and expressing their own clearly.

Introduce
an Editorial

Linking Argument Writing Traits to an Editorial

Read the introduction to page 266 aloud to help students understand that they will follow Tyler as he models using the writing process and the traits together. As they follow Tyler, students will see how the Argument Writing Traits have been adapted and applied to writing an editorial. They will see that an editorial can be used to express an opinion and, therefore, has many factors in common with other types of argument writing. However, the particular audience and purpose of an editorial determine how the traits are used.

Online Writing Center

 Provides six **interactive anchor papers** for each mode of writing.

T266 **Argument Writing**

Linking Argument Writing Traits to an

In this chapter, you will express your opinion about an important issue to a news source. This type of argument writing is called an editorial. Tyler will guide you through the stages of the writing process: Prewrite, Draft, Revise, Edit, and Publish. In each stage, Tyler will show you important writing strategies that are linked to the Argument Writing Traits below.

Argument Writing Traits

	• clearly stated claims, often balanced by alternate or opposing claims • supporting evidence from accurate and credible sources
	• a strong introduction that presents the writer's position • reasons and evidence that are organized logically • a conclusion that follows and supports the argument • transitions that clarify the relationships between the claim(s), the supporting evidence, and any counterclaims
	• a voice that supports the writer's purpose
	• language that is compelling
	• sentences that vary in length and begin in different ways
Conventions	• no or few errors in grammar, usage, mechanics, and spelling

Before you write, read the editorial on the next page. Then use the editorial rubric on pages 268–269 to evaluate the editorial. (You might want to look back at What's in an Editorial? on page 264, too!)

Argument Writing Traits in an Editorial

 **Ideas** The writer's claim (problem) is clearly stated, often balanced by other claims. The writer presents strong reasons and uses relevant evidence from credible sources.

 **Organization** The editorial includes a strong introduction. Reasons (main ideas) and evidence (supporting details) are organized logically in the body. Logical transitions connect ideas. The conclusion calls the reader to action.

 **Voice** The writer establishes and maintains a convincing, confident voice and a formal style that supports the writer's purpose.

TURN IT OFF!

by the editors of
The Springfield Middle School Gazette

**Part I:
Introduction**

Supporting Evidence

When was the last time you read a good book? How long ago was it that you went camping or took a weekend hike in the woods? There was a time when people were likely to get involved in pastimes like these. Now, though, the most common activity in many people's lives is watching television, but this isn't much of an "activity" at all. According to recent research compiled by RealVision, a program that states facts about television, the average teenager watches television more than twenty hours per week. He or she might even be bombarded with as many as 20,000 commercials per year. By the age of eighteen, that teenager will have seen more than 200,000 violent acts and more than 16,000 murders. At the same time, due to lack of any real activity, that teenager's likelihood of becoming seriously overweight rises steadily. Clearly, something is wrong here.

Clear Rationale

**Part II:
Body**

As a school, we can take steps to do something about excessive television watching and the problems it causes. Our suggestion is that we participate in the national TV-Turnoff Week next April. More than 3,000 groups, many of them schools, were part of this event last year. Most students who were involved thought it was great. They found that they had time to do many more things. Some listened to music. Others read or exercised. Still others cooked, made scrapbooks, and played board games. For a small fee, the TV-Turnoff Network, a not-for-profit organization that encourages less television watching, can provide our school with planning booklets to get us started. It can also supply posters and T-shirts to keep us motivated. Teachers can hold classroom discussions about activities to replace television. Once enough students become interested, it shouldn't be hard to get the whole school to participate.

But will one week away from staring at screens change our lives? It's hard to know. Many students who joined TV-Turnoff Week in the past said it really made a difference. It provided a springboard for breaking old viewing habits. With luck, the program can do the same for us.

— Part III: Conclusion

Editorial **267**

Word Choice The writer's language is compelling and convincing. Word choice creates meaning and cohesion among ideas.

Sentence Fluency Sentences vary in length and begin in different ways. The writer's ideas flow smoothly and hold the reader's attention.

Conventions The writer has proofread the writing carefully to make sure there are no or few errors in grammar, usage, mechanics, and spelling to distract the reader.

Analyze
the Model

Week 1 • Day 2

Student Objectives
• Read a model editorial. *(p. 267)*

Read the Model

Ask students to listen for the writing traits as you read "Turn It Off!" aloud. Ask students to note how the editorial is organized. Also ask students to think about how the writers reach out to the reader. They should agree that the writing voice supports the editors' purpose.

Elements of an Editorial

Have students refer to What's in an Editorial? on page 264 as you refer to the model on page 267. Discuss the notes written on the model to enhance students' understanding of the terms. Ask students to find additional evidence in the text to support their analysis of the model.

CCSS **C**ommon **C**ore **S**tate **S**tandards
R/Inf.7.1: Cite several pieces of textual evidence to support analysis of what the text says explicitly as well as inferences drawn from the text.

Analyze
the Model

Student Objectives

- Learn to read a rubric. (pp. 268–269)

Use the Rubric

Explain the Rubric Explain that a rubric is a tool for planning, improving, and assessing a piece of writing. Tell students that a rubric helps a writer focus on key elements, or traits, in writing (**Ideas, Organization, Voice, Word Choice, Sentence Fluency, Conventions,** and **Presentation**).

Point out that column 6 describes a very good editorial, one that has received the highest score in all categories. This is what students should strive for in their own writing.

Discuss the Rubric As students measure their own papers against the rubric, they should first decide whether the papers fall on the left of the rubric (use the trait well) or on the right (need improvement in using the trait). By examining their papers more closely, students can refine their scores for each trait to single numbers.

Editorial

Rubric

Use this 6-point rubric to plan and score an editorial.

	6	5	4	
Ideas	The claim (problem), solution, and relevant evidence are clear. Logical reasoning and quality evidence support the claim.	The claim (problem), solution, and relevant evidence are clear. The reasoning and evidence support the claim most of the time.	Either the claim (problem) or solution is not stated clearly. Some evidence is weak or not relevant.	
Organization	The introduction states the claim (problem), the body offers solutions, and the concluding section (conclusion) has a call to action.	The introduction states the claim (problem) and the body offers a solution. The call to action may be weak or missing.	The introduction states the claim (problem) and the writing is easy to follow. The solution is somewhat unclear and the call to action is weak or missing.	
Voice	The writer consistently maintains a confident voice and a formal style.	The writer uses a formal style throughout most of the writing.	The writer's voice often fades in and out. The voice starts out formal but lapses into casual language.	
Word Choice	Specific words are used effectively. Unfamiliar words are explained for the reader.	Specific words make the writing clear. Unfamiliar words are explained.	Most words are specific and communicate the meaning. Most unfamiliar words are explained.	
Sentence Fluency	Striking variety in sentence beginnings gives the text flow and rhythm and clarifies ideas.	Noticeable variety in sentence beginnings makes the text flow.	Most sentences have varied beginnings. The writing is choppy in a few places.	
Conventions	Appositives are punctuated correctly. Indefinite pronouns are clear. The writing is easy to understand.	Most appositives are punctuated correctly, and most indefinite pronouns are clear. The writing is not hard to read.	A few errors with appositives and indefinite pronouns don't interfere with the meaning.	

+Presentation The editorial is prepared neatly and legibly.

CCSS Common Core State Standards

Editorial

Strategies for Writers was designed and written to weave the Common Core State Standards (CCSS) throughout every unit. For **Argument** writing, the standards inform the unit's writing rubrics, objectives, and strategies. By presenting the standards in as many applications as possible, your students' exposure to them will be ensured. As a result, students are more likely to employ the Standards' language to write arguments, as well as in discussions about writing.

The editorial lessons are based principally on the writing standards for **Argument** writing. The rubrics and writing

---

Online Writing Center

Provides a variety of **interactive rubrics,** including 4-, 5-, and 6-point models.

3	2	1	
The problem and solution are identifiable but not clearly stated. Some evidence is weak or unrelated.	The problem or solution cannot be identified. Much of the evidence is weak or invented.	No problem or solution can be identified. Evidence is lacking.	**Ideas**
The introduction or conclusion needs work. The body is poorly organized, and the reader struggles to follow the writing.	Both the introduction and conclusion need work. Information is out of order and the reader feels lost.	There is no obvious introduction or conclusion. Details are listed but not organized.	**Organization**
The writer's voice is weak and does not connect with the audience. It wavers frequently between formal and informal.	The writer isn't interested in the topic. The voice isn't appropriate for the topic or audience.	The writing has no voice. The writer's lack of knowledge about the topic is obvious.	**Voice**
Words are often unclear and not explained, muddying the writer's meaning.	Many words are overused or used incorrectly. Unfamiliar words are not explained.	Words are vague and the text is often wordy. Reading takes work.	**Word Choice**
Some of the sentences are choppy, and beginnings are repetitious.	Many sentences begin the same way. Many parts of the writing are hard to read.	Sentences are incorrect or incomplete. The writing is hard to read out loud.	**Sentence Fluency**
Noticeable errors with appositives and indefinite pronouns slow down the reader.	Many errors with appositives and indefinite pronouns get in the way of reading.	Frequent serious errors with appositives and indefinite pronouns make the writing hard to understand.	**Conventions**

See Appendix B for 4-, 5-, and 6-point argument rubrics.

Editorial **269**

Apply the Rubric

Take a Poll Ask students to raise their hands to indicate what score they would give the editorial on one or more of the traits. Record the results. Ask students to offer examples from the editorial to support their scores. If there are students who seem to disagree with most of their classmates by a difference of more than two points, gently probe as to why they think so. If students score the editorial 5 or below, ask what the writer could do to bring up the score.

Additional Rubrics Appendix B includes 4-, 5-, and 6-point rubrics that can be used with any piece of argument writing. The rubrics are also available as blackline masters in this Teacher Edition, beginning on page T543.

strategies for the traits of Ideas and Organization in this chapter reflect writing standards **W.7.1.a**, **W.7.1.b**, and **W.7.3.e**, which focus on stating a claim (problem) and solution, and using logical reasoning and quality evidence to support a call to action. The rubrics and writing strategies for the traits of Voice, Word Choice, and Sentence Fluency in this chapter reflect writing standards **W.7.1.c** and **W.7.1.d**, which focus on using a formal style, strong, specific language, and sentence variety to support the writer's purpose and clarify ideas.

CCSS **Common Core State Standards**

SL.7.1.a: Come to discussions prepared, having read or researched material under study, explicitly draw on that preparation by referring to evidence on the topic, text, or issue to probe and reflect on ideas under discussion.

Analyze
the Model

Student Objectives

- Read a model editorial. *(p. 267)*
- Use the editorial rubric. *(pp. 268–269)*
- Use the model editorial to study Ideas, Organization, and Voice. *(pp. 270–271)*

Study the Model

Assess the Model Have volunteers read aloud each section on pages 270–271. Assign students to small writing groups or partners. Ask them to review Tyler's assessments of the model. Use questions such as the following to prompt discussion. Have students back up their answers for each trait with evidence from the model. Ask one student from each group or pair to record and report their findings to the class.

Do the authors

- state a claim (problem) clearly and use credible evidence to support the claim? (Possible response: Yes, the editors make and support their claim that excessive television viewing causes problems, such as lack of exercise and healthier activities. Because I watch a lot of television, I wanted to read on to see what solution(s) the writers suggest.)

 Strategies for Writers Online
Go to **www.sfw.z-b.com** for additional online resources for students and teachers.

Editorial
Using the Rubric to Study the Model

Did you notice that the model on page 267 points out some key elements of an editorial? As they wrote "Turn It Off!" the editors of the Springfield Middle School Gazette used these elements to help explain their claims. They also used the 6-point rubric on pages 268–269 to plan, draft, revise, and edit the writing. A rubric is a great tool to evaluate writing during the writing process.

Now let's use the same rubric to score the model. To do this, we'll focus on each trait separately, starting with Ideas. We'll use the top descriptor for each trait (column 6), along with examples from the model, to help us understand how the traits work together. How would you score the editors on each trait?

Ideas
- The claim (problem), solution, and relevant evidence are clear.
- Logical reasoning and quality evidence support the claim.

The authors clearly state the problem early on, as well as provide clearly outlined solutions to the issue at hand. They also provide so many relevant, accurate facts, it was easy to understand and agree with their point of view. It's clear they know what they're talking about!

[from the writing model]

Now, though, the most common activity in many people's lives is watching television, but this isn't much of an "activity" at all.

[from the writing model]

By the age of eighteen, that teenager will have seen more than 200,000 violent acts and more than 16,000 murders.

270 Argument Writing

English Language Learners

BEGINNING

Problem/Solution Show students a picture of trash on the sidewalk and ask, *Is this good or bad?* Explain it is a *problem.* Write *problem* on the board and have students repeat. Show students a picture of someone picking up the trash and ask, *Is this good or bad?* Explain it fixes the problem, it's the *solution.* Write *solution* and have students repeat. Repeat with one or two more pictures, emphasizing the words *problem* and *solution.*

INTERMEDIATE

Problem/Solution Show students a picture depicting a problem, such as trash on the sidewalk. Ask the students what they see in the picture. Explain to students this is a problem and it needs to be fixed. Show them several other pictures with one of the pictures showing a solution to the problem. Ask students what they see in each picture. Students choose the correct picture. Show other pictures that

Organization

- The introduction states the claim (problem), the body offers solutions, and the concluding section (conclusion) has a call to action.

The authors not only clearly define the problem and suggest a solution, but they also really inspire me to give their idea a try. The last paragraph's call to action is strong and clear—I know taking a break from television was the right thing to do.

> [from the writing model]
>
> But will one week away from staring at screens change our lives? It's hard to know. Many students who joined TV-Turnoff Week in the past said it really made a difference. It provided a springboard for breaking old viewing habits. With luck, the program can do the same for us.

Voice

- The writer consistently maintains a confident voice and a formal style.

It's clear that the authors have done their research and that they believe it themselves. Their voice is confident and informative, and the language, although formal, is still easy to connect with. The authors seem to truly want to help their readers get healthy and get moving.

> [from the writing model]
>
> At the same time, due to lack of any real activity, that teenager's likelihood of becoming seriously overweight rises steadily. Clearly, something is wrong here.

Editorial **271**

- organize the editorial in three parts (introduction, body, and conclusion)? (Possible response: The editorial leads with a strong introduction that states the problem, followed by a body that offers solutions, and a conclusion that urges readers to act. Readers can easily follow the writers' argument from beginning to end.)

- maintain a confident voice and formal style? (Possible response: The editorial opens with questions that immediately caught my attention. The writers sound knowledgeable about the topic and confident that the reader will agree with their opinion.)

depict problems and solutions. Have students work in pairs to match a problem to its appropriate solution.

ADVANCED

Relevant Facts Students must decide if a fact is relevant to the main idea. Give students the main idea, such as *There are many different kinds of pollution,* and list several facts and non-facts, such as *cars are one cause of air pollution; water pollution harms fish; smoke goes in the air;* and so on. Have students circle the facts that are relevant to the main idea.

ADVANCED HIGH

Relevant Facts Students use print and credible online resources to find several relevant facts that support a topic that you provide, such as *Water pollution is harmful to people and animals.* Have students write their findings on a Main Idea Table and use that information to write a paragraph.

CCSS Common Core State Standards

SL.7.1.b: Follow rules for collegial discussions, track progress toward specific goals and deadlines, and define individual roles as needed. **SL.7.1.c:** Pose questions that elicit elaboration and respond to others' questions and comments with relevant observations and ideas that bring the discussion back on topic as needed.

Analyze
the Model

Week 1 • Day 5

Student Objectives

- Read a model editorial. *(p. 267)*
- Use the editorial rubric. *(pp. 268–269)*
- Use the model editorial to study Word Choice, Sentence Fluency, and Conventions. *(pp. 272–273)*

Continue to Discuss the Model

Use questions such as these to continue to analyze the model:

Do the authors

- use specific words effectively?
(Possible response: Yes, the writers use formal-sounding words instead of casual-sounding ones. This helps the reader take the writers' point seriously. I also notice that the writers did not use words to intimidate the reader.)

- vary sentence beginnings to keep the text flowing smoothly?
(Possible response: The authors of "Turn It Off!" used a variety of sentences that hold the reader's interest throughout the editorial. It is easy and enjoyable to read.)

- use appositives and indefinite pronouns correctly? (Possible response: It's obvious that the editorial was carefully edited. There are no errors in spelling or grammar, so it's easy to understand. Also, appositives and pronouns are used correctly.)

 Strategies for Writers Online
Go to **www.sfw.z-b.com** for additional online resources for students and teachers.

T272 Argument Writing

 **Word Choice**
- Specific words are used effectively.
- Unfamiliar words are explained for the reader.

Strong and specific words help me get the most from this editorial. *Discussions* is more descriptive than *talks*. *Participate* is more accurate than *join in*. There were no difficult words left undefined. It's easier to respond to the authors' call to action when the writing is strong, specific, and fully understood.

[from the writing model]

Teachers can hold classroom discussions about activities to replace television. Once enough students become interested, it shouldn't be hard to get the whole school to participate.

Sentence Fluency
- Striking variety in sentence beginnings makes the text flow, gives it rhythm, and clarifies ideas.

I like how the authors use a variety of sentence structures throughout their editorial. Mixing up how sentences begin keeps me interested, helps me understand the information, and makes the text smooth and enjoyable to read.

[from the writing model]

As a school, we can take steps to do something about excessive television watching and the problems it causes. Our suggestion is that we participate in the national TV-Turnoff Week next April.

272 Argument Writing

Technology Tip for 21st Century Literacies

Recasting a piece of writing into another mode (e.g., audio or movement) changes what the writer is able to communicate. Have students recast a piece of editorial writing into a podcast while keeping a specific audience in mind. Challenge students to do more than just record a reading of their written work—the podcast has a specific audience and performance aspect. Keep reflection at the forefront of the work. How does using a document to create a podcast impact what writers can share? How does revisiting the written draft after recording the audio impact what writers include?

See **www.sfw.z-b.com** for further information about and links to these websites and tools.

Conventions
- Appositives are punctuated correctly.
- Indefinite pronouns are clear.
- The writing is easy to understand.

Wow! I can't find any spelling or grammatical errors at all in this editorial. Also, all appositives are correctly punctuated, and each indefinite pronoun is clear. I want my editorial to be perfect, too.

[from the writing model]

For a small fee, the TV-Turnoff Network, a not-for-profit organization that encourages less television watching, can provide our school with planning booklets to get us started.

+Presentation The editorial is prepared neatly and legibly.

My Turn!
Follow along to see how I use good writing strategies to write an editorial of my own. I'll use the rubric as a guide.

Presentation Explain to students that Presentation is just as important. Neatness is always a priority, and text should be neatly handwritten in pen or typed, using only a few readable fonts. White space should be used to create neat margins and to keep lines of text readable. Paragraphs should be indented (using the tab key if typed) or space should be left between block paragraphs. The title of the editorial should be centered at the top of the first page.

Think About the Traits After students have discussed the model, ask them which traits they think are the most important in an editorial. Some students may feel that **Organization** is very important because if the evidence is not presented in a logical order, the argument falls apart or simply cannot be followed. Others may feel that **Word Choice** is a more important trait because compelling language can help convince readers to agree with the claim and respond to the call to action.

Differentiating Instruction

ENRICHMENT
Understand a Writer's Rationale Have students look up *rationale* in the dictionary and then state the definition in their own words. Emphasize that they should look carefully at editorials to make sure the writers have based their solutions on good rationales.

REINFORCEMENT
Understand Elements of an Editorial Some students may benefit from seeing additional samples of editorials. Find some in your school or local newspaper or in the magazines that students brought in at the beginning of the chapter. Have students work in pairs to identify the problem and solution in each editorial. They should also note the supporting evidence that is presented in each piece.

CCSS Common Core State Standards

SL.7.1.c: Pose questions that elicit elaboration and respond to others' questions and comments with relevant observations and ideas that bring the discussion back on topic as needed. **SL.7.1.d:** Acknowledge new information expressed by others and, when warranted, modify their own views.

Write
an Editorial

Week 2 • Day 1

Student Objectives

- Read and understand a prewriting strategy. (p. 274)

Prewrite

Focus on Ideas

Brainstorm Topics Read page 274 aloud. Then work with students to brainstorm a list of problems for which they can propose solutions. Encourage students to choose one of the problems to research.

Point out Tyler's notes on page 274. Explain that because Tyler has taken notes, he will probably remember more details about the problem as he begins to write his draft.

Online Writing Center

 Provides **interactive graphic organizers** as well as a variety of graphic organizers in PDF format.

T274 Argument Writing

Prewrite — Focus on  Ideas

The Rubric Says The claim (problem), solution, and relevant evidence are clear.

Writing Strategy Brainstorm to choose a problem, or claim, for which there is a solution.

When our teacher told us we were going to be writing editorials, our class brainstormed some writing ideas. We came up with all kinds of potential topics: our cafeteria is dirty, our library needs to be open before school, there's too much bullying going on in the hallways, and activity period should be longer.

But I decided to write about bullying because I have some ideas on how to solve the problem. My claim will be that bullying is a problem that must be solved. I brainstormed by myself for more ideas. Then I wrote them down.

The Problem: Bullying

- happens in hallways, bathrooms
- could happen to anyone
- cause of violence in some schools (need examples)
- everyone afraid to rat on others
- some kids get hurt
- some kids are scared

We need:
- "no tolerance" policy
- help from teachers
- tables-turned activities
- more student involvement
- schoolwide campaign

Apply

Brainstorm to find a problem for which you can propose a solution. Then jot down some notes to get your thoughts together.

274 Argument Writing

English Language Learners

BEGINNING/INTERMEDIATE

Logical Order/Sequence Read a short narrative with a clear sequence of events, such as *The Three Billy Goats Gruff*. Using pictures from the book, have students sequence the story. Teach the words *first*, *next*, *then*, and *finally* for them to use as they retell the story.

ADVANCED/ADVANCED HIGH

Logical Order Ask students to write sentences about their morning routine using transition words such as *first*, *next*, *then*, and *finally*. Have them cut up the sentences, trade with another student, and put the sentences in order. Have students revise sentences to improve sentence fluency.

Prewrite

Focus on **Organization**

The Rubric Says	The introduction states the claim (problem), the body offers solutions, and the concluding section (conclusion) has a call to action.
Writing Strategy	Make a Problem-Solution Frame to organize the ideas.

Writer's Term___

Problem-Solution Frame
Use a **Problem-Solution Frame** to define a problem and organize the information that solves it.

I know from the rubric that it's important to organize my information. A Problem-Solution Frame will help me do this. I'll use the notes I gathered while brainstorming to help me think of possible results.

Problem-Solution Frame

Problem Box

What is the problem?
- bullying

Why is it a problem?
- some kids are scared
- some kids have been hurt
- cause of violence in some schools (need examples)
- everyone afraid to rat on others

Who has the problem?
- our school—in the hallways and in the bathrooms

End Result Box
- might not totally solve the problem, but will be a great start toward stopping it

Solution Box

Solutions
- schoolwide campaign
- "no tolerance" policy
- help from teachers
- tables-turned activities
- more student involvement

Results
- will make everyone more aware of the problem
- everyone will know rules and what will happen if they're broken
- will supervise bathrooms and little-used hallways to keep things from happening
- will show bullies what it feels like
- can show disapproval by recommending ways to change things

Reflect
How will Tyler's Problem-Solution Frame help him focus his writing?

Apply
Make a Problem-Solution Frame to organize your ideas.

Editorial **275**

Conferencing

PEER TO PEER When students' Problem-Solution Frames are complete, have pairs exchange frames. Instruct pairs to review each other's organizer and list the relevant details. Then have them exchange their findings to inform the writer.

PEER GROUPS Separate students into small groups. Have each group write a short rationale for using a Problem-Solution Frame to write their drafts. Then ask them to share their rationale and revise it based on feedback from other groups.

TEACHER-LED Conference with individuals, pairs of students, or small groups. To demonstrate how important the organizer is to writing a good editorial, create a Problem-Solution Frame, adding irrelevant details or leaving out key information. Discuss how extraneous or incomplete information would affect and weaken an editorial.

Student Objectives

- Make a Problem-Solution Frame to define a problem and organize the information that solves it. (*p. 275*)

Prewrite

Focus on **Organization**

Organize Ideas Explain that writers use different types of organizers to organize their ideas. Tyler used a Problem-Solution Frame to help him organize the details he had already written down in his notes. Have students study the organizer and then ask how a Problem-Solution Frame can be an effective tool when writing an editorial. (Possible response: A Problem-Solution Frame helps you keep track of the important information needed to write a good editorial.)

Writer's Term___

Problem-Solution Frame Point out how a Problem-Solution Frame is a useful tool when writing an editorial. The frame organizes the writer's ideas about solving a problem. Organizing ideas before writing helps writers put the important details in logical order. The frame will also alert a writer when information is not relevant or incomplete.

CCSS **Common Core State Standards**
W.7.1: Write arguments to support claims with clear reasons and relevant evidence.

Editorial **T275**

Write
an Editorial

Week 2 • Day 3

Student Objectives

• Use a Problem-Solution Frame to begin writing. *(p. 276)*

Draft

Focus on Ideas

Draft an Editorial Read page 276 aloud. Ask students to explain what it means to write a draft. Be sure that students understand that they will use their Problem-Solution Frames to guide them through the drafting process. Point out that, like Tyler, in the draft step writers should not be overly concerned with correctness. Tell students that the proofreader's marks are provided as a reference on page 277. To help them focus on writing, suggest that they circle any words or parts in their drafts that they might want to change later.

✏ Writer's Term _____

Credible Websites Demonstrate how to find trusted websites. Display the list of questions in the Writer's Term box in class as a reference and ask students to use the questions as they conduct research on their topic. If your school has an Internet policy, be sure to go over it with your students. Stress the importance of using reliable online sources.

Online Writing Center

Provides student eBooks with an **interactive writing pad** for drafting, revising, editing, and publishing.

Draft

Focus on **Ideas**

The Rubric Says	Logical reasoning and quality evidence support the claim.
Writing Strategy	Research the subject and gather accurate and relevant facts or statistics.

✏ Writer's Term

Credible Websites
How do you know a website can be trusted? Ask yourself these questions:
• Who wrote the website?
• What is the purpose of the website?
• Does the information match up with at least two other sources?
• Does the website look professionally designed?

Bullying is a big problem in my school and in schools all around the country. The rubric says I should include quality evidence and logical reasoning to support my claim. If I use reference sources in the library and search credible websites on the Internet, finding plenty of solid facts should not be difficult.

First, I'll focus on the bullying that's happening in my school and what could happen if we ignore the problem. Then, I'll follow my Problem-Solution Frame to develop the body, which will focus on the solution. This is where quality evidence and logical reasoning will really help convince my reader. Finally, my conclusion will summarize what could happen as a result of my proposed solutions.

Right now, I'll just focus on getting my ideas down. I'll worry about fixing any spelling or grammar mistakes later.

276 Argument Writing

Differentiating Instruction

ENRICHMENT

Propose Solutions Within small groups, have students brainstorm at least two reasonable solutions to a current problem or issue. Ask each group to list opposing viewpoints to the solutions. Have students discuss ways a writer might address opposing claims in an editorial.

REINFORCEMENT

Choose the Best Solution Some problems have two or more equally reasonable solutions. Offer these strategies:

• Present both solutions, arguing in favor of both. This way, the reader can decide which one is best.

• Present both solutions, arguing in favor of one of them.

• Present only the strongest of the solutions.

[DRAFT]

Stop the Bullying!

[introduction]

   Yesterday, a sixth grader was found hiding near the janitor's closet. Someone finally got him to admit, "XXX is after me." (XXX, an eighth grader has a reputation for bullying other students.) Last week, another sixth grader went to class with his shirt ripped and a scrach on his face. Though he wouldn't say what had happened, a lot of kids knew that he had had a run-in with YYY another bully. Allmost any student in our School could give more examples like these. Bullying the act of one kid terrorizing another, is happening all the time in our hallways and bathrooms. Some parents have even removed their children from school because the bullying has gotten so bad.

[claim/problem]

Reflect

What do you think of Tyler's introduction? In what ways does it grab your interest?

Apply

Write a draft that holds the reader's interest throughout. Remember to use quality evidence and logical reasoning. And don't forget a clear call to action!

Editorial **277**

Conferencing

PEER TO PEER Have partners exchange drafts to read. Tell students to think of two or three questions they would like to ask to clarify information or supply missing details. Have them write their questions on adhesive notes and affix them to the appropriate places on their partner's draft.

PEER GROUPS Have students work in groups of four. Each student passes his or her draft to the student on the right to read. That student writes one comment or suggestion on an adhesive note affixed to the draft and passes the draft along to the right. The review ends when everyone has received his or her own draft back with three comments.

TEACHER-LED Schedule conferences with pairs of students. Have them read each other's draft and coach them in giving constructive criticism.

Write
an Editorial

Week 2 • Day 4

Student Objectives

• Use a Problem-Solution Frame to complete a draft. (p. 277)

Draft an Editorial It is important that students are given ample time to draft their editorials. As conferencing is important throughout the writing process, be sure to plan time for peer to peer conferences, peer groups, or teacher-led conferences. Remind students that this is the time to get their ideas down on paper in a creative and engaging way. Assure them that they will have plenty of time to fix any mistakes later.

CCSS **C**ommon **C**ore **S**tate **S**tandards

W.7.5: With some guidance and support from peers and adults, develop and strengthen writing as needed by planning, revising, editing, rewriting, or trying a new approach, focusing on how well purpose and audience have been addressed.

Write
an Editorial

Week 2 • Day 5

Student Objectives

• Strengthen the conclusion. (p. 278)

Revise

Focus on Organization

Use a Question-Answer Pattern
After writing their drafts, help students prepare to revise by explaining how this step in the writing process gives them the chance to improve their editorials using the traits of writing. Because **Organization** is critical to a well-written editorial, help them use a question-answer pattern to engage the reader, support their claim(s), demonstrate their knowledge of the topic, and strengthen the conclusion. If students haven't begun their conclusions with a question, have them read their drafts and ask: *In the end, what do I want my reader to do?* Provide some sentence starters to stimulate asking a focused question, such as

How can we solve _____?

Can you help solve _____?

Have them answer the question as they revise their conclusions. Remind them that the conclusion should convince the reader to agree with the writer's solution and call the reader to action.

 Strategies for Writers Online
Go to **www.sfw.z-b.com** for additional online resources for students and teachers.

T278 Argument Writing

Revise   Focus on Organization

The Rubric Says	The introduction states the claim (problem), the body offers solutions, and the concluding section (conclusion) has a call to action.
Writing Strategy	Strengthen the conclusion.

I just read over my draft, and I'm really happy with the way I've presented both the problem, or claim, and the solution. But my conclusion is a bit weak. I want to do more than just inform my readers—I want to get them thinking and get them involved. Using a question-answer pattern will both engage the reader and make my conclusion stronger and more realistic. What do you think of my revision?

[DRAFT]   [strengthened the conclusion]

Can we get rid of bullying overnight? Probably not.
Bullying has been going on around here for a long time. But if we start some new policies and make sure everyone follows up on them, we can make a real start on solving the problem.

Apply
Strengthen your conclusion by engaging your reader.

278 Argument Writing

English Language Learners

BEGINNING/INTERMEDIATE
Action Verbs and Sentence Writing Demonstrate an action and say it while you do it; for example, *Mrs. Smith jumps.* Have students repeat. Write the sentence on the board. Point out the subject and the action verb. Show students pictures from magazines or newspapers. Then have them write a simple sentence about each picture.

ADVANCED/ADVANCED HIGH
Using Precise Words Write a generic word, such as *bad,* on the board. Use the Web or Continuum Scale graphic organizer to brainstorm other words that have the same meaning as *bad* or have stronger meanings. For example, on a Continuum Scale, you could write *bad, no good, awful, terrible, dreadful, shocking, unpleasant, ghastly,* and *horrific.* Tell students to use this idea when choosing words for their editorial.

Revise

Focus on **Voice**

The Rubric Says	The writer consistently maintains a confident voice and a formal style.
Writing Strategy	Use a blend of first-person and third-person points of view.

I know that an opinion needs to be expressed in an impartial way. If I get too personally involved in the writing, I'll drive my reader away. I also need to sound confident and use a formal style to be taken seriously. That means using third-person point of view will work best in my editorial. However, this *is* a subject I feel strongly about, and occasionally using first person will help me directly connect with the reader. If I establish a connection with my readers, they will feel more motivated to read and understand my argument.

[DRAFT]

[used first-person point of view]

we solve this problem

So how can ~~this problem be solved~~? The best solution is a schoolwide campaign against bullying. Everyone can play a part.

Reflect

How have Tyler's revisions helped? How has using the word *we* affected his writing?

Apply

Use a confident and formal voice as you write. Use a limited amount of first person to connect effectively with your reader.

Editorial **279**

Conferencing

PEER TO PEER Have pairs of students exchange drafts. After reading the draft, ask each student to offer helpful feedback regarding how to strengthen the piece, if needed.

PEER GROUPS Separate students into small groups. Have students take turns reading sections of their drafts aloud. Ask each group member to offer one suggestion on how to revise and strengthen one of the traits in the sections that have been read.

TEACHER-LED Schedule individual conferences. Read each student's draft. Point out its strengths and weaknesses. If needed, discourage students from "starting over." If a student seems stalled, revisit steps in the process to make improvements and keep going.

Student Objectives

• Use a blend of first-person and third-person points of view. (p. 279)

Revise

Focus on Voice

Connect With Audience Explain to students the importance of connecting with the audience, adding that establishing an appropriate writing **Voice** is one tool that writers use to accomplish this. The writer's tone, point of view, and writing style combine to communicate and connect with the audience.

Explain that when writing an editorial, third-person point of view establishes a formal tone and perspective. However, using first-person pronouns, such as *I* and *me*, at critical points in the editorial makes the writing more focused and urgent. By purposely using first-person pronouns, the writer will connect with readers on a personal level and move them to respond to the call to action.

Remind students that the writer's voice and tone should sound confident, knowledgeable, respectful, and convincing all the way through.

CCSS **C**ommon **C**ore **S**tate **S**tandards

W.7.1.b: Support claim(s) with logical reasoning and relevant evidence, using accurate, credible sources and demonstrating an understanding of the topic or text.
W.7.1.d: Establish and maintain a formal style.

Write
an Editorial

Week 3 • Day 2

Student Objectives

- Replace vague words with specific ones. *(p. 280)*

Revise

Focus on  Word Choice

Use Specific Words Read page 280 aloud. Explain to students that using vague words will not convince the audience. In fact, vague words can distract and confuse readers. On the other hand, using convincing language and specific words related to the topic increases readers' interest in the writer's topic.

Point out that Tyler's revisions are thoughtful and appropriate. By using stronger verbs, he is strengthening his message and, at the same time, making sure that the reader understands it. As students revise for **Word Choice,** remind them to consult print and online word resources such as dictionaries, thesauruses, and glossaries for replacement words that improve the message.

Revise

Focus on Word Choice

The Rubric Says	Specific words are used effectively. Unfamiliar words are explained for the reader.
Writing Strategy	Replace vague words with specific ones.

As I reread my draft, I looked for vague words I could replace with strong, specific words. I also made sure I explained any words that needed defining for my reader. For example, I explained both *bullying* and *no tolerance*. I found some vague words that need replacing. *Witness* is more accurate than *see,* and *disapprove* is stronger than *don't approve.* I'll make these changes now to strengthen my writing.

[DRAFT]

[used specific words]

witness

Students and teachers, the people most likely to ~~see~~ bullying, must

disapprove

play an active part. Students must learn to show that they ~~don't approve~~

of bullying, and they must understand that there is nothing wrong with

reporting it to an authority figure.

Apply

Fully explain all unfamiliar terms and use strong, specific words to strengthen your editorial.

Optional Revising Lessons

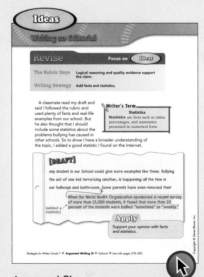

Argument 21

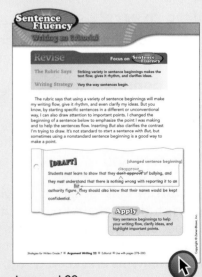

Argument 22

Edit

Focus on Conventions

The Rubric Says	Appositives are punctuated correctly. Indefinite pronouns are clear. The writing is easy to understand.
Writing Strategy	Check the use of appositives and indefinite pronouns.

Writer's Term

Appositives

An **appositive** is a word or a phrase that identifies a noun. An appositive usually follows the noun it identifies, and it is usually separated from the rest of the sentence by one or more commas.

The rubric says all appositives should be accurately punctuated and all indefinite pronouns should be clear. I'll find and fix any errors now.

[DRAFT]

[corrected appositive punctuation]

scratch
~~scrach~~ on his face. Though he wouldn't say what had happened, a lot

of kids knew that he had had a run-in with YYY, another bully. ~~Allmost~~ Almost

Reflect

What do you think? How have Tyler's choice of words and edits improved his writing?

Apply Conventions

Edit your draft for grammar and mechanics, making sure that appositives are set off with commas and indefinite pronouns are clear.

For more practice with appositives and indefinite pronouns, use the exercises on the next two pages.

Editorial **281**

Related Grammar Practice

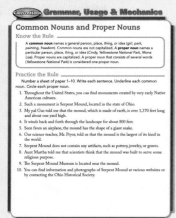

Student Edition page 509

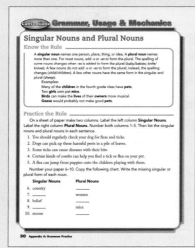

Student Edition page 510

Go to ▷ **Appendix A: Grammar Practice**

Write
an Editorial

Week 3 • Day 3

Student Objectives

• Check the use of appositives and indefinite pronouns. *(p. 281)*

Edit

Focus on

Remind students that editing is the step in the process where they can go back and correct any mistakes in spelling, grammar, punctuation, and capitalization. In this step, students should seek out editing partners to read and help them edit their writing. Explain that even very skilled writers can overlook errors in their own writing. Remind students that computers have a spell-check option that can be very helpful; however, this function may miss homophones that are used incorrectly. Use the mini-lessons on the following two pages of this Teacher Edition for students who need practice in using appositives and indefinite pronouns. Then have them complete pages 282 and 283.

Writer's Term

Appositives are useful when a writer needs to add more information to a sentence. The information is not essential to the sentence (restrictive), so it is separated by commas.

CCSS **C**ommon **C**ore **S**tate **S**tandards

L.7.1: Demonstrate command of the conventions of standard English grammar and usage when writing or speaking.

Editorial **T281**

Conventions

Mini-Lesson

Student Objectives

- Use appositives correctly. *(p. 282)*

Appositives

Explain to students that appositives are words or phrases that help explain or identify nouns and should be set off from the rest of the sentence by one or more commas. Then write the following example on the board: *The dog an Irish setter ran to catch the ball.*

Ask students to identify the appositive in this sentence. (an Irish setter) Explain that the appositive *an Irish setter* modifies the noun *dog.* Ask volunteers for suggestions on how to punctuate the sentence correctly. (The dog, an Irish setter, ran to catch the ball.)

Then write the following example on the board: *The dog obeyed its owner a girl named Kellie.* Ask students to identify the appositive in this sentence. (a girl named Kellie) Have a volunteer explain what the appositive modifies. (its owner) Ask volunteers for suggestions on how to punctuate the sentence correctly. (The dog obeyed its owner, a girl named Kellie.) Point out that writers use appositives to add information to their sentences.

Online Writing Center

Provides **interactive grammar games** and **practice activities** in student eBook.

Appositives

Know the Rule

An **appositive** is a word or a phrase that identifies a noun. An appositive usually follows the noun it identifies, and it's separated from the rest of the sentence by commas.

Examples: We volunteer one day each month at The Shelter, **a local nonprofit organization.**

Volunteers, **people who work for no money,** are important to nonprofit organizations.

Practice the Rule

Rewrite each sentence with correct punctuation on a separate sheet of paper.

1. Nonprofit organizations groups that work for a cause without expecting to make a profit can do a lot of good.
2. There are more than one million "recognized" organizations groups with official names and regular employees in the United States.
3. Some of these nonprofit organizations focus on social issues problems that affect many people across society.
4. Free legal representation a real issue for people unjustly accused of crimes is the focus of some groups.
5. A nonprofit organization that influences many people's lives is public television a source of excellent programming.
6. Donations gifts of money given freely by other groups or individuals are what help nonprofits survive.
7. After learning about nonprofit organizations, I was inspired to join Meals Door-to-Door a group that hand-delivers hot meals to the elderly during the winter months.
8. Nonprofit organizations are exempt from taxes money paid to the city based on the value of the property owned by the business.
9. Citizens people living in a community profit greatly when several nonprofits join together to help a cause.
10. Sometimes, the directors people who work full-time for the nonprofit groups get paid to compensate them for their time.

Related Grammar Practice

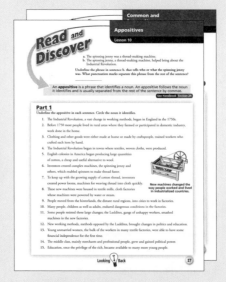

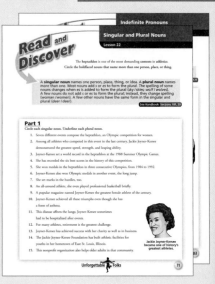

Pages 27, 69, 71, 83

Go to **G.U.M. Student Practice Book**

Indefinite Pronouns

Know the Rule

Indefinite pronouns refer to persons or things that are not identified as individuals. Indefinite pronouns include *all, anybody, anyone, both, either, anything, everyone, few, many, most, one, several, nobody,* and *someone.*

Example: Out of the twenty students in gym class, **most** signed up for the student-teacher basketball game.

Practice the Rule

Copy each sentence onto a separate sheet of paper. Circle the indefinite pronouns in each sentence.

1. (All) are invited to our Holiday Open-House celebration—the bigger the crowd, the better!
2. Ten of my friends are coming, and (some) are bringing their parents.
3. I think I've invited (everyone) I know—it should be a great party!
4. I invited two of my uncles from out of town, but (neither) could come.
5. Mom and I couldn't decide whether to serve pizza or tacos, so we're going to serve (both).
6. Four of my friends asked if they could bring (something) to the party.
7. Anna makes amazing brownies, so I asked her to bring (some).
8. I don't know what type of salad dressing all my friends like, so I bought (several).
9. We asked the neighbors if we could borrow their card tables for the party because we have (none).
10. We'll all be tired the next day, but (everybody) will be pleased they came to the party!

Editorial 283

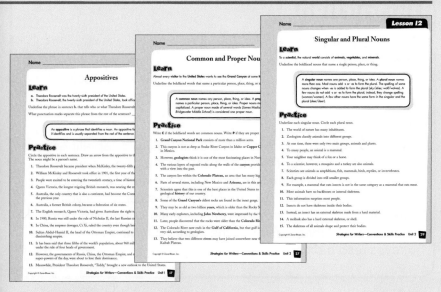

Pages 17, 27, 29

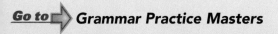

Go to **Grammar Practice Masters**

Mini-Lesson

Student Objectives

- Use indefinite pronouns correctly. *(p. 283)*

Indefinite Pronouns

Indefinite pronouns refer to persons or things that are not identified as individuals. Explain that in writing it's especially important to use indefinite pronouns correctly so the reader understands the meaning. Read aloud the list of pronouns and the example sentence in Know the Rule on page 283. Ask students to suggest additional examples that include indefinite pronouns. Tell them it's perfectly fine to use more than one pronoun in the same sentence, as long as the meaning is clear. Then ask them to identify only the indefinite pronouns in their examples.

You may want to provide one or two example sentences to get started:

- Jason kept his friends in the dark about the surprise until <u>all</u> had arrived.
- Although she had told <u>no one</u> about the concert tickets, <u>many</u> found them online.

CCSS Common Core State Standards

L.7.2: Demonstrate command of the conventions of standard English capitalization, punctuation, and spelling when writing.

Editorial T283

Write
an Editorial

Week 3 • Day 4

Student Objectives

- Discuss preparation for publishing and presentation. (p. 284)
- Use a final editing checklist to publish their work. (p. 284)

Publish +Presentation

Publish an Editorial Explain to students that Tyler's decision to publish his editorial in the school's newspaper is an excellent way to get the problem out in the open. He feels confident that a wider audience will help get more people involved in solving the problem. Tyler also mentions typing his submission so the editors of the newspaper can format it easily. Provide students with a template or guidelines for using a word processor that shows them where to place the title and their name and how to set the margins for a good layout. Remind them to indent paragraphs or leave a space between paragraphs. Encourage students to use a final checklist like the one on page 284 to prepare their final copies. Have each student print out a copy and check it one last time before submitting the editorial for publication.

Strategies for Writers Online

Go to **www.sfw.z-b.com** for additional online resources for students and teachers.

Publish +Presentation

Publishing Strategy	Submit the editorial for publication in the school newspaper.
Presentation Strategy	Prepare the editorial on a computer.

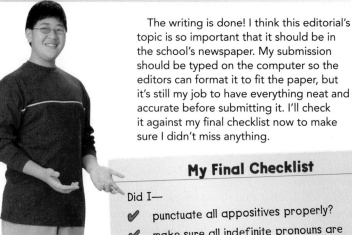

The writing is done! I think this editorial's topic is so important that it should be in the school's newspaper. My submission should be typed on the computer so the editors can format it to fit the paper, but it's still my job to have everything neat and accurate before submitting it. I'll check it against my final checklist now to make sure I didn't miss anything.

My Final Checklist

Did I—

- ✓ punctuate all appositives properly?
- ✓ make sure all indefinite pronouns are accurate and clear?
- ✓ type my editorial neatly on a word processor?
- ✓ indent each new paragraph and include my name on the page?

Apply

Make a checklist to check your editorial. Then make a final draft to publish.

284 Argument Writing

Differentiating Instruction

ENRICHMENT
Proofread Have pairs of students exchange papers to proofread each other's work. Then have students discuss their edits.

REINFORCEMENT
Check Spelling Discuss with students how misspellings interrupt the flow for the reader and give a poor impression of the writer, even if the sentence is still readable. Provide an example for students, such as *Many in the comunity voluntered to chaperoon our schol dance.* After correcting the sentence together, point out the value of having another pair of eyes read a draft.

STOP THE BULLYING!
by Tyler

Yesterday, a sixth grader was found hiding near the janitor's closet. Someone finally got him to admit, "XXX is after me." (XXX, an eighth grader, has a reputation for bullying other students.) Last week, another sixth grader went to class with his shirt ripped and a scratch on his face. What had happened? Although he wouldn't say, a lot of kids knew that he had had a run-in with YYY, another bully. Almost any student in our school could give more examples like these. Bullying, the act of one kid terrorizing another, is happening all the time in our hallways and bathrooms. When the World Health Organization sponsored a recent survey of more than 15,000 students, it found that more than 10 percent of the students were bullied "sometimes" or "weekly." Some parents have even removed their children from school because the bullying has gotten so bad.

Bullying is a problem that must be solved. So how can we solve this problem? The best solution is a schoolwide campaign against bullying. Everyone can play a part. First, the administration should make it clear that they don't approve of bullying. Then, they should announce a "No Tolerance" policy. This would mean that every time a bully is caught, he or she would be punished.

Students and teachers, the people most likely to witness bullying, must play an active part. Students must learn to show that they disapprove of bullying, and they must understand that there is nothing wrong with reporting it to an authority figure. But they should also know that their names would be kept confidential. Teachers should patrol hallways and bathrooms, the places where bullying goes on the most, and they should make it clear that bullies will be punished. They should also use homeroom periods to give individual guidance.

Can we get rid of bullying overnight? Probably not. Bullying has been going on around here for a long time. But if we start some new policies and make sure everyone follows up on them, we can make a real start on solving the problem.

Reflect

How did Tyler do? Did you notice how he used the rubric as he wrote? Don't forget to use the rubric to check your own editorial, too!

Technology Tip for 21st Century Literacies

An important part of writing an effective editorial requires anticipating readers' needs. Pair students and ask them to exchange written draft editorials. This could be done with Google Docs to facilitate sharing and additional digital literacy practices. Ask the reader to mark the text by highlighting supporting evidence and emotionally loaded words, and inserting questions where they arise. The comments field then becomes a collaborative discussion space where writers can interact with readers as they develop the editorial. Working online also makes it possible to share student work with readers outside your classroom.

See **www.sfw.z-b.com** for further information about and links to these websites and tools.

Write
an Editorial

Week 3 • Day 5

Student Objectives
- Use an editorial rubric. (pp. 268–269)
- Share a published editorial. (p. 285)

Share an Editorial Explain to students how important neatness is when creating a final copy of their work. Remind students of the many word processing features computers have to offer. The header and footer function is useful for labeling all pages of a piece of writing.

As an alternative to publishing their editorials in a school newspaper, explore other publishing options, such as a local newspaper, student magazines, or school website.

Reflecting on an Editorial

Ask students about their experiences writing editorials. What did they like about it? What was hard or easy? How would they score their editorials?

CCSS **C**ommon **C**ore **S**tate **S**tandards
W.7.4: Produce clear and coherent writing in which the development, organization, and style are appropriate to task, purpose, and audience. **W.7.6:** Use technology, including the Internet, to produce and publish writing and link to and cite sources as well as to interact and collaborate with others, including linking to and citing sources.

Business Letter Planner

WEEK 1

Introduce
a Business Letter
(Day 1)

Student Objectives
- Review the elements of a business letter.
- Consider purpose and audience.
- Learn the traits of argument writing.

Student Activities
- Read and discuss **What's in a Business Letter?** *(p. 286)*
- Read and discuss **Why Write a Business Letter?** *(p. 287)*
- Read **Linking Argument Writing Traits to a Business Letter.** *(p. 288)*

Analyze
Read a Business Letter
(Day 2)

Student Objectives
- Read a model business letter.

Student Activities
- Read the model business letter. *(p. 289)*

Analyze
Introduce the Rubric
(Day 3)

Student Objectives
- Learn to read a rubric.

Student Activities
- Review the model letter. *(p. 289)*
- Read and discuss the **Business Letter Rubric.** *(pp. 290–291)*

WEEK 2

Write
Prewrite: Ideas
(Day 1)

Student Objectives
- Read and understand a prewriting strategy.

Student Activities
- Read and discuss **Prewrite: Focus on Ideas.** *(p. 296)*
- Apply the prewriting strategy.

Write
Prewrite: Organization
(Day 2)

Student Objectives
- Make an Argument Map to organize the reasons, examples, and facts that support a call to action.

Student Activities
- Read and discuss **Prewrite: Focus on Organization.** *(p. 297)*
- Apply the prewriting strategy.
- Participate in a peer conference.

Write
Draft: Organization
(Day 3)

Student Objectives
- Use an Argument Map to write well-organized paragraphs that support the call to action.

Student Activities
- Read and discuss **Draft: Focus on Organization.** *(p. 298)*
- Apply the drafting strategy.

WEEK 3

Write
Revise: Word Choice
(Day 1)

Student Objectives
- Use homophones and other easily confused words correctly.

Student Activities
- Read and discuss **Revise: Focus on Word Choice.** *(p. 301)*
- Reflect on the model draft.
- Apply the revising strategy.
- Participate in a peer conference.

Write
Revise: Sentence Fluency
(Day 2)

Student Objectives
- Use different sentence structures, such as conditional sentences.

Student Activities
- Read and discuss **Revise: Focus on Sentence Fluency.** *(p. 302)*
- Reflect on the model draft.
- Apply the revising strategy.

Note: Optional Revising Lessons appear on the *Strategies for Writers* CD-ROM.

Write
Edit: Conventions
(Day 3)

Student Objectives
- Make sure negatives and infinitives are used correctly.

Student Activities
- Read and discuss **Edit: Focus on Conventions.** *(p. 303)*
- Reflect on the model draft.
- Apply the editing strategy.

Note: Teach the Conventions mini-lessons *(pp. 304–305)* if needed.

Analyze
Ideas, Organization, and Voice

Student Objectives
- Read a model business letter.
- Use the business letter rubric.
- Use the model business letter to study Ideas, Organization, and Voice.

Student Activities
- Review the model business letter.
- Read and discuss **Using the Rubric to Study the Model.** (pp. 292–293)

Analyze
Word Choice, Sentence Fluency, and Conventions

Student Objectives
- Read a model business letter.
- Use the business letter rubric.
- Use the model business letter to study Word Choice, Sentence Fluency, and Conventions.

Student Activities
- Review the model business letter.
- Read and discuss **Using the Rubric to Study the Model.** (pp. 294–295)

Write
Draft

Student Objectives
- Complete a draft.

Student Activities
- Finish writing the draft. (p. 299)
- Participate in a peer conference.

Write
Revise: Voice

Student Objectives
- Use a respectful and courteous tone.

Student Activities
- Read and discuss **Revise: Focus on Voice.** (p. 300)
- Reflect on the model draft.
- Apply the revising strategy.

Write
Publish: +Presentation

Student Objectives
- Discuss preparation for publishing and presentation.
- Use a final editing checklist to publish their work.

Student Activities
- Read and discuss **Publish: +Presentation.** (p. 306)
- Apply the publishing strategy.

Write
Publish: +Presentation

Student Objectives
- Use a business letter rubric.
- Share a published business letter.

Student Activities
- Share their work.
- Use the rubric to reflect upon and evaluate the model and their own writing. (pp. 290–291; 307–309)

Resources at-a-Glance

Grammar, Usage & Mechanics

Differentiating Instruction

For additional Differentiating Instruction activities, see Strategies for Writers *Extensions Online at* **www.sfw.z-b.com.**

English Language Learners

Conferencing

Technology Tip

 Connection Letter

Reproducible letter (in English and Spanish) appears on the *Strategies for Writers* CD-ROM and at **www.sfw.z-b.com.**

Online Writing Center

Provides IWB resources, interactive games and practice activities, videos, eBooks, and a virtual file cabinet.

 Strategies for Writers Online

Go to **www.sfw.z-b.com** for free online resources for students and teachers.

To complete the chapter in fewer days, combine the learning objectives and activities in a way that supports students as they write.

Introduce
a Business Letter

Week 1 • Day 1

Student Objectives

- Review the elements of a business letter. *(p. 286)*
- Consider purpose and audience. *(p. 287)*
- Learn the traits of argument writing. *(p. 288)*

What's a Business Letter?

Discuss with students the definition of *business letter* as stated on page 286. Ask students if they have ever written or received a business letter. Point out that business letters, including form letters that are mailed to many recipients at the same time, are often sent by regular mail. Tell students that any time they write a letter to an individual or an organization for the purpose of requesting action on the part of the recipient, they are writing a business letter.

What's in a Business Letter?

Read and discuss with students the elements of a business letter listed on page 286. Explain that some of these elements are also common to other forms of writing, such as essays, research reports, and editorials. Then discuss why each element may be important to writing a business letter.

 Strategies for Writers Online
Go to **www.sfw.z-b.com** for additional online resources for students and teachers.

T286 **Argument Writing**

What's a **Business Letter?**

It's a formal letter written to a person or a company. The writer of an argument-based business letter tries to convince the receiver to take action about a specific issue.

What's in a **Business Letter?**

Letter Form
A good business letter has six parts: heading, inside address, greeting, body, closing, and signature. The letter form makes it easy for the receiver to respond to the letter.

Important Issue
A business letter should always have a direct focus; otherwise, it's not worth writing. I'll use my business letter to explain an important issue to the recipient.

Call to Action
When a business letter is written to present an argument, it should have a clear call to action. The call to action explains what the writer wants the recipient to think, say, or do.

Evidence
The writer of a business letter will want to include enough details so that the recipient will understand the issue and possibly act upon a solution.

286 Argument Writing

Argument Text Exemplars (Business Letter)

Nobleman, Marc Tyler. *Extraordinary E-mails, Letters, and Resumés.* Children's Press, 2006. *Extraordinary E-mails, Letters, and Resumés* describes specific ways to write different forms of correspondence. The book also provides helpful information on how to start a writing assignment and prepare for an oral presentation.

Hackman, Peggy. *Dear Mr. President.* Avon Books, 1993. *Dear Mr. President* is a collection of letters written by children to President Clinton shortly after he took office. The letters range in topic from video games to health care, and prove that even young people are concerned about the matters of the nation. An afterword provides additional information on the importance of writing to our elected leaders.

Why write a **Business Letter?**

I can think of many reasons for writing a business letter. Here are some examples.

Make Something Happen
A business letter often contains the writer's request to the recipient to make something happen. Stating my case to the right person can result in the change that I am seeking.

Organize
Writing a business letter forces me to organize my ideas. I have to present everything in a logical, convincing form. This is a skill that will be helpful for years to come.

Get Help
Sometimes I can't solve problems on my own. But if I write a letter to the right person, I might be able to get the help that I need.

Inform
I can use a business letter to inform someone about an issue. I can educate the reader while explaining my solution to a problem.

Marcus, Leonard S. *Dear Genius: The Letters of Ursula Nordstrom.* HarperCollins, 2000. Ursula Nordstrom was the editorial director of Harper's Department of Books for Boys and Girls from 1940-1973. She played a key role in the publication of several children's classics, such as *Goodnight Moon* and *Charlotte's Web.* This book is a collection of letters written by Ms. Nordstrom during that exciting period that provide an insider's look at the challenges and triumphs she endured.

Waltz, Josephine M. *Write Out of the Oven! Letters and Recipes from Children's Authors.* Libraries Unlimited, 2005. *Write Out of the Oven!* is a collection of letters and recipes from more than 50 of the most beloved and award-winning children's authors of all time. In many cases, the letters address the most commonly asked questions and comments the authors have received from children over the years.

Why write a Business Letter?

Read page 287 aloud and discuss with students the reasons for writing a business letter. Point out that all writing has a purpose and is aimed at a specific audience. Encourage students to discuss how having authentic purposes helps authors shape their writing. For example, someone writing to make something happen may use a strong call to action. A person who is requesting help should use logical thinking and good organization to make sure his or her request is presented as clearly as possible. A writer who is writing to inform will include accurate facts and examples to convince the reader. Encourage students to think about their own reasons for writing letters and how these reasons affect the tone and focus of their writing. Conclude the discussion by explaining to students that they are going to study and practice strategies for writing a good business letter.

CCSS **C**ommon **C**ore **S**tate **S**tandards

SL.7.1: Engage effectively in a range of collaborative discussions (one-on-one, in groups, and teacher-led) with diverse partners on *grade 7 topics, texts, and issues,* building on each other's ideas and expressing their own clearly.

Introduce
a Business Letter

Linking Argument Writing Traits to a Business Letter

Read the introduction to page 288 aloud to help students understand that they will follow Tyler as he models using the writing process and the traits together. As they follow Tyler, students will see how the Argument Writing Traits have been adapted and applied to writing a business letter. They will see that a business letter can be used to express an opinion. When used to express an opinion, a business letter has many factors in common with other types of argument writing. However, the particular audience and purpose of an editorial determine how the traits are used.

Online Writing Center

Provides six **interactive anchor papers** for each mode of writing.

T288 Argument Writing

Linking Argument Writing Traits to a Business Letter

In this chapter, you will write to an organization to convince them to act in some way. This type of argument writing is called a business letter. Tyler will guide you through the stages of the writing process: Prewrite, Draft, Revise, Edit, and Publish. In each stage, Tyler will show you important writing strategies that are linked to the Argument Writing Traits below.

Argument Writing Traits

- clearly stated claims, often balanced by alternate or opposing claims
- supporting evidence from accurate and credible sources

- a strong introduction that presents the writer's position
- reasons and evidence that are organized logically
- a conclusion that follows and supports the argument
- transitions that clarify the relationships between the claim(s), the supporting evidence, and any counterclaims

- a voice that supports the writer's purpose

- language that is compelling

- sentences that vary in length and begin in different ways

- no or few errors in grammar, usage, mechanics, and spelling

Before you write, read Susan Bernini's letter on the next page. Then use the business letter rubric on pages 290–291 to decide how well she did. (You might want to look back at What's in a Business Letter? on page 286, too!)

Argument Writing Traits in a Business Letter

 **Ideas** The letter clearly states the writer's purpose and includes supporting evidence to convince the reader.

 **Organization** The letter includes a strong introduction that presents the writer's position. Reasons (main ideas) and evidence (supporting details) are organized logically. Logical transition words help the reader follow the writer's argument. The last paragraph calls the reader to action.

 **Voice** The writer uses a convincing voice and formal style that supports the writer's purpose and reaches out to the audience.

Business Letter Model

38 Oak Lane
Ridge Park, IL 60100 ⎤ **Letter Form: Heading**
November 12, 2012 ⎦

Director of Children's Services ⎤
Municipal Services of Ridge Park ⎟ **Letter Form: Inside Address**
455 Laurel Road ⎟
Ridge Park, IL 60100 ⎦

Dear Sir or Madam: ← **Letter Form: Greeting**

Important Issue

A group of families from Nigeria has recently moved into our area. About twenty students from these families are enrolled at my school, Trout Junior High. These students need special services to help them adapt to living here—help that your agency could provide. The following are some of the reasons I think you should assist them. ← **Call to Action**

Letter Form: Body

To begin with, these students are in dire need of translators or other language helpers. Our school has special classes for English-language learners. However, the teachers know little about these students' native languages. If translators could work with these students in their regular classes, it would really help them. Right now, these students just sit quietly and shake their heads when a teacher calls on them. Even after two months of school, they can barely communicate with us. *Evidence*

Another thing the students need help with is proper clothing for the winter. You might help them just by providing some warm hand-me-downs. However, it would be even better if you could get them some new, in-style clothing.

As you can see, there are many ways you could help our new students.

Yours truly, ← **Letter Form: Closing**

Susan Bernini ← **Letter Form: Signature**

Susan Bernini

Business Letter 289

Word Choice The writer's language is compelling and convincing. Word choice creates meaning and cohesion among the writer's claim, reasons, and evidence.

Sentence Fluency Sentences vary in length and begin in different ways. The writer's ideas flow smoothly and hold the reader's attention.

Conventions The writer has proofread carefully to make sure there are no or few errors in grammar, usage, mechanics, and spelling to distract the reader.

Analyze
the Model

Week 1 • Day 2

Student Objectives

• Read a model business letter. (p. 289)

Read the Model

Read the model business letter on page 289 aloud to the class. Ask students to listen for the writer's claim, reasons, and evidence. Then ask them to notice how the details are organized. Also ask students to think about and discuss how a formal, business-like style conveys the writer's purpose and suits the audience (the recipient of the letter).

Elements of a Business Letter

Have students refer to What's in a Business Letter? on page 286 as you refer to the model business letter. Discuss the notes written on the model to enhance students' understanding of the terms. Point out that they will also use the model to analyze the traits of a good business letter.

CCSS **Common Core State Standards**
R/Inf.7.1: Cite several pieces of textual evidence to support analysis of what the text says explicitly as well as inferences drawn from the text.

Business Letter T289

Analyze
the Model

Student Objectives

- Learn to read a rubric. (pp. 290–291)

Use the Rubric

Explain the Rubric Explain that a rubric is a tool for planning, improving, and assessing a piece of writing. Tell students that a rubric helps a writer focus on key elements, or traits, in writing (**Ideas, Organization, Voice, Word Choice, Sentence Fluency, Conventions,** and **Presentation**).

Point out that column 6 describes a very good business letter, one that has received the highest score in all categories. This is what students should strive for in their own writing.

Discuss the Rubric As students measure their own papers against the rubric, they should first decide whether the papers fall on the left of the rubric (use the trait well) or on the right (need improvement in using the trait). By examining their papers more closely, students can refine their scores for each trait to single numbers.

Online Writing Center

Provides a variety of **interactive rubrics,** including 4-, 5-, and 6-point models.

Rubric

Use this 6-point rubric to plan and score a business letter.

	6	5	4
Ideas	The claim is clear and balanced with an opposing claim. Accurate facts and examples are relevant and support the claim.	The claim is clear and an opposing claim is mentioned. Accurate facts, examples, and explanations support the claim.	The claim is clear, but there is no clear opposing claim. Some accurate and relevant information is included.
Organization	The letter is organized around a claim that inspires a call to action. Each body paragraph contains a strong and complete topic sentence.	The letter contains a call to action. Each body paragraph contains a topic sentence and supporting details.	Some parts of the letter are not related to the call to action. Some topic sentences may be hard to identify.
Voice	The writer's voice is convincing. The formal style is ideal for the topic and audience.	The writer's voice is convincing. The style is appropriate most of the time.	The writer's voice sounds convincing most of the time. The style, or tone, may be informal or inappropriate some of the time.
Word Choice	The language is striking. All words, including frequently confused words and homophones, are used correctly.	Words and phrases are clear. Frequently confused words and homophones are used correctly.	The language is clear, and most words are used correctly.
Sentence Fluency	Sentences are varied, interesting, and stand apart from other writing. The writing is smooth when read out loud.	Sentences are varied and interesting. The writing is easy to read.	There is some variety in sentence beginnings and lengths. Occasionally, the writing is choppy.
Conventions	Sentences are clear and correct: there are no double negatives, and infinitive phrases are effective.	A few double negatives or errors with infinitive phrases don't interfere with the meaning.	Some noticeable errors with infinitive phrases and double negatives do not interfere with reading.
+ Presentation	The letter and envelope are neat and in the correct format.		

290 Argument Writing

CCSS Common Core State Standards

Business Letter

Strategies for Writers was designed and written to weave the Common Core State Standards (CCSS) throughout every unit. For **Argument** writing, the standards inform the unit's writing rubrics, objectives, and strategies. By presenting the standards in as many applications as possible, your students' exposure to them will be ensured. As a result, students are more likely to employ the Standards' language to write arguments and in discussions about writing.

The business letter lessons are based principally on the writing standards for **Argument** writing. The rubrics and writing strategies for the traits of Ideas and Organization in this chapter reflect writing standards **W.7.1.a, W.7.1.b,** and **W.7.3.e,** which focus on stating a claim, addressing opposing claims, using

3	2	1	
The claim is somewhat clear. No opposing claim is mentioned. Some information is lacking or not relevant.	The claim is not clear. Little relevant information is included. Details are missing or inaccurate.	No claim is stated. No details are provided. The writer knows little about the topic.	**Ideas**
Several parts of the letter are not related to the call to action. Some paragraphs lack a topic sentence or supporting details.	The call to action is hard to identify. Several paragraphs lack a topic sentence and/or supporting details.	There is no call to action or organization to the writing. The writing is not organized into paragraphs.	**Organization**
The writer's voice sounds unconvincing. The tone may be uninterested, informal, or inappropriate.	The writer's voice is weak and not convincing. The tone may be rude, informal, or uninformed.	The voice is flat or absent. The writer does not connect with the audience.	**Voice**
Some vague words make the writing unclear. Several words are used incorrectly.	Much of the language is unclear, and many words are used incorrectly.	The language is vague. Words simply fill the page. Many words are used incorrectly.	**Word Choice**
Sentence beginnings are alike, and there is little variety in length.	Incomplete, choppy sentences are found throughout, making it hard to read.	Most sentences are incomplete or choppy. The writing is a challenge to read.	**Sentence Fluency**
Errors with infinitive phrases and double negatives are noticeable and interfere with reading out loud.	Many errors with infinitive phrases and double negatives interfere with meaning.	Frequent serious errors with infinitive phrases and double negatives make the writing hard to understand.	**Conventions**

See Appendix B for 4-, 5-, and 6-point argument rubrics.

Apply the Rubric

Assign Groups Assign students to small groups and ask them to check the model for each trait. One person in each group should be responsible for recording one or two strong examples of the trait as described by the rubric. Students should score the model for each trait accordingly. They should be able to support their scores. Note that although the models were written to score high in each trait, students should not assume each trait would receive a 6, the top score. Encourage students to discuss each trait thoroughly before assigning each score.

Reassemble Class Bring the class back together and ask one person from each group to report their findings to the class. The point of this exercise is to practice identifying and evaluating the traits within a piece of writing.

Additional Rubrics Appendix B includes 4-, 5-, and 6-point rubrics that can be used with any piece of argument writing. The rubrics are also available as blackline masters in this Teacher Edition, beginning on page T543.

accurate facts and examples to support the writer's claim, and providing a strong concluding statement or section. The rubrics and writing strategies for the traits of Voice, Word Choice, and Sentence Fluency in this chapter reflect writing standards **W.7.1.c** and **W.7.1.d,** which focus on using a convincing, appropriate voice and compelling language that are consistent with the writer's purpose and audience.

The language standards for grade 7 students are addressed during editing and skills practice. In addition, there are multiple opportunities to address the speaking and listening standards during the writing process. Most important, this chapter will help your students produce coherent writing (**W.7.4**) and improve their writing (**W.7.5**).

CCSS Common Core State Standards

SL.7.1.a: Come to discussions prepared, having read or researched material under study; explicitly draw on that preparation by referring to evidence on the topic, text, or issue to probe and reflect on ideas under discussion.

Analyze
the Model

Student Objectives

- Read a model business letter. (p. 289)
- Use the business letter rubric. (pp. 290–291)
- Use the model business letter to study Ideas, Organization, and Voice. (pp. 292–293)

Study the Model

Assess the Model Have volunteers read aloud each section on pages 292–293. Discuss as a class whether students agree or disagree with Tyler's assessments of the model. Use questions such as the following to discuss the pages with students. Be sure they can back up their answers with evidence from the model.

Does the writer

- state a claim (problem) clearly and use accurate evidence to support the claim? (Possible response: Yes, Susan Bernini makes and supports her claim that twenty new students from Nigeria need special services at her school.)

Strategies for Writers Online
Go to **www.sfw.z-b.com** for additional online resources for students and teachers.

Business Letter

Using the Rubric to Study the Model

Did you notice that the model on page 289 points out some key elements of a business letter? As she wrote her letter, Susan Bernini used these elements to help her explain why she wanted help for the new Nigerian students. She also used the 6-point rubric on pages 290–291 to plan, draft, revise, and edit the writing. A rubric is a great tool to evaluate writing during the writing process.

Now let's use the same rubric to score the model. To do this, we'll focus on each trait separately, starting with Ideas. We'll use the top descriptor for each trait (column 6), along with examples from the model, to help us understand how the traits work together. How would you score Susan on each trait?

> **Ideas**
> - The claim is clear and balanced with an opposing claim.
> - Accurate facts and examples are relevant and support the claim.
>
> I like how Susan clearly presents her concern right at the start of the letter. She explains the issue in a logical and direct way and provides solid, relevant examples and facts to support her requests.
>
> **[from the writing model]**
>
> A group of families from Nigeria has recently moved into our area. About twenty students from these families are enrolled at my school, Trout Junior High. These students need special services to help them adapt to living here—help that your agency could provide.

English Language Learners

BEGINNING
Facts Write this sentence on the board: *Birds are animals.* Ask students, *Is this always true?* and then say, *Facts are always true.* Write the word *fact* on the board, say it, and have students repeat it. Provide more examples of simple facts about birds to reinforce the meaning of *fact*.

INTERMEDIATE
Fact and Opinion Write a few simple facts about birds on the board. Explain that these are facts and facts are always true. Write *fact* on the board, say it, and have students repeat. Write a few opinions about birds on the board, such as *Birds are pretty. Birds are the best animal.* Explain that these are opinions, or what we think or feel. Write the word *opinion* on the board, say it, and have students repeat. Ask a student to make a statement about school and have other students determine whether the statement is a fact or an opinion.

Organization

- The letter is organized around a claim that inspires a call to action.
- Each body paragraph contains a strong and complete topic sentence.

What a strong letter! Every body paragraph relates back to Susan's call to action, which is clearly stated right at the beginning. Each point is made in a topic sentence, and then several supporting sentences provide all the information needed to fully understand her point of view.

[from the writing model]

> To begin with, these students are in dire need of translators or other language helpers. Our school has special classes for English-language learners. However, the teachers know little about these students' native languages.

Voice

- The writer's voice is convincing.
- The formal style is ideal for the topic and audience.

Susan understands her audience—an adult who is the Director of Children's Services. Her voice is strong and convincing, and her style remains appropriate and courteous throughout the letter.

[from the writing model]

> You might help them just by providing some warm hand-me-downs. However, it would be even better if you could get them some new, in-style clothing.

Business Letter 293

- organize the business letter into six parts (heading, inside address, greeting, body, closing, and signature)? (Possible response: The letter is organized as a business letter. It opens with a strong introduction that states the problem, followed by evidence that supports the writer's claim, and a conclusion that calls the recipient of the letter to action. Each body paragraph contains a strong and complete topic sentence. Readers can easily follow the letter from beginning to end.)

- maintain a convincing voice and a formal style? (Possible response: The writer uses a convincing voice throughout the letter because she wants to convince the reader that a solution is needed now. She maintains a formal business style because she wants the reader to take her reason for writing seriously.)

ADVANCED

Opinion and Reasons Read an editorial in the school newspaper. On the board write the author's opinion. Have partners highlight the reasons the author gives for that opinion. In small groups have students share the reasons they found. Have students write a short paragraph about *school lunch* giving their opinion and reasons for their opinion.

ADVANCED HIGH

Opinion and Reasons Introduce a Fact and Opinion Chart. Assign a topic to each pair of students, such as space travel or international travel. Have partners complete the Fact and Opinion Chart and then have the pair write a letter to their peers that makes a strong suggestion in support of a position. After their letters are complete, have students read their letters to the class. Then ask the class to vote on which arguments were presented most convincingly.

CCSS **C**ommon **C**ore **S**tate **S**tandards

SL.7.1.b: Follow rules for collegial discussions, track progress toward specific goals and deadlines, and define individual roles as needed. **SL.7.1.c:** Pose questions that elicit elaboration and respond to others' questions and comments with relevant observations and ideas that bring the discussion back on topic as needed.

Analyze
the Model

Week 1 • Day 5

Student Objectives

- Read a model business letter. (p. 289)
- Use the business letter rubric. (pp. 290–291)
- Use the model business letter to study Word Choice, Sentence Fluency, and Conventions. (pp. 294–295)

Continue Discussing the Traits

Use these questions to continue to analyze the model.

Does the writer

- use striking language? (Possible responses: Yes, the writer's words are purposeful and convincing. She uses simple, but direct words to make her reasons clear.)

- vary sentences to keep the text flowing smoothly? (Possible responses: The letter contains a variety of sentences that holds the reader's interest. It is easy to read aloud.)

- use correct grammar, mechanics, and spelling? (Possible responses: It's obvious that the letter was carefully edited. There are no errors, such as double negatives, so it's easy to understand the writer's ideas. I also noticed that infinitive phrases are used effectively.)

Word Choice

- The language is striking.
- All words, including frequently confused words and homophones, are used correctly.

Susan uses all words correctly—even tricky homophones and other easily confused words. In this example, she uses *here* (not *hear*) when discussing a place and *your* (not *you're*) when referring to the Director's agency. I'll work hard to use words accurately, too.

[from the writing model]

These students need special services to help them adapt to living here—help that your agency could provide.

Sentence Fluency

- Sentences are varied, interesting, and stand apart from other writing.
- The writing is smooth when read out loud.

I especially like how Susan varies her sentence structures. Using a variety of sentences is more effective and helps the writing sound natural. It's hard to pay attention to the same sentence type used over and over again. Susan's writing would sound smooth if it were read out loud.

[from the writing model]

If translators could work with these students in their regular classes, it would really help them. Right now, these students just sit quietly and shake their heads when a teacher calls on them.

294 Argument Writing

Technology Tip
for 21st Century Literacies

Real-world writing needs to be relevant and purposeful. Consider how to use this business-letter writing opportunity to engage students with their communities. Use the letter as an opportunity to make a contact resulting in a service project. Or use the letter to solicit assistance in planning a school event, contributions to the school library, and other needs. Remember, 21st century learning opportunities don't require technology, but they do require putting students' writing to work. Help students make these letters matter.

Strategies for Writers Online

Go to **www.sfw.z-b.com** for additional online resources for students and teachers.

Conventions
- Sentences are clear and correct: there are no double negatives, and infinitive phrases are effective.

I couldn't find a single mistake in Susan's letter! She even avoided using double negatives, a mistake that many people make. In the sentence below, she correctly uses *can barely* instead of *can't barely*.

[from the writing model]

Even after two months of school, they can barely communicate with us.

+ Presentation
The letter and envelope are neat and in the correct format.

My Turn!

I'm going to write a business letter about something that concerns me. I'll follow the rubric and use good writing strategies. Read on to see how I do it!

Business Letter **295**

Differentiating Instruction

ENRICHMENT
Experiment With Voice Discuss different types of voice with students. Have each student select a paragraph from the model and rewrite it using a voice that expresses a different feeling. Later, discuss how simply changing the voice of the writing can affect the meaning or tone of the paragraph.

REINFORCEMENT
Explore Sentence Fluency To help students appreciate how sentence fluency improves the flow of writing, rewrite one of the paragraphs from the model on the board using short declarative sentences. Explain that a series of short, abrupt sentences is described as "choppy." Discuss why choppy sentences are harder to read than ones that flow.

Presentation Explain to students that Presentation is just as important as any of the other traits. White space should be used to create neat margins, and the lines of text in each part of the letter should be spaced correctly. Paragraphs should be indented (using the tab key, if typed) or space should be left between block paragraphs. The text should follow business letter format.

Think About the Traits After students have thoroughly discussed the model business letter, ask them which traits they think are the most important in a letter. Remind them that all of the traits are important in every piece of writing; however, some traits play a more important role in specific types of writing. For example, some students may feel that **Organization** is very important in a letter because if the evidence is not presented in a logical order, the writer's facts and examples may be confusing or difficult to follow. Others may feel that **Word Choice** is a more important trait because strong, purposeful language helps strengthen the writer's message and convinces the reader to agree and respond.

CCSS **Common Core State Standards**

SL.7.1.c: Pose questions that elicit elaboration and respond to others' questions and comments with relevant observations and ideas that bring the discussion back on topic as needed. **SL.7.1.d:** Acknowledge new information expressed by others and, when warranted, modify their own views.

Business Letter **T295**

Write
a Business Letter

Week 2 • Day 1

Student Objectives

• Read and understand a prewriting strategy. (p. 296)

Prewrite

Focus on   Ideas

Choose a topic Read page 296 aloud. Work with students to brainstorm a list of issues about which they have strong opinions. Use the business letter model on page 289 and Tyler's topic on this page as jumping off points.

After creating a list of potential topics, have students circle their favorite topic. To help them determine their audience, have students ask and answer this question: *Which person or organization will help me address this issue?* Have them write down the name and address for the recipient(s). Go over their choices with them before they proceed. After confirming their selections, encourage students to research some facts and examples that they will use to support their opinions on the issue.

Online Writing Center

Provides **interactive graphic organizers** as well as a variety of graphic organizers in PDF format.

T296 Argument Writing

Prewrite   Focus on   Ideas

The Rubric Says The claim is clear and balanced with an opposing claim. Accurate facts and examples are relevant and support the claim.

Writing Strategy Choose an issue that you have a strong opinion about. List explanations, facts, and examples to support your opinion.

I had no trouble coming up with a topic for my business letter. The school board is planning to stop buying new books for our school library, and I am opposed to this. I decided to address my letter to the school board president, Ms. Williams. Then I listed explanations, facts, and examples that would support my opinion. I also thought about an opposing claim I want to mention, to show that I've really thought the issue through from all sides.

Opinion: Don't stop buying new books.

Explanations:
- need accurate, up-to-date information
- need recent books students can understand

Opposing Claim:
- students can find info they need on the Internet

Facts/Examples:
- a lot of research projects
- info about human genome project: library books really out of date
- Internet articles sometimes too difficult to help
- a lot of current nonfiction books written for students our age

Apply

Choose an important issue about which you have a strong opinion. Then list several reasons, facts, and examples to support your opinion.

296 Argument Writing

English Language Learners

BEGINNING/INTERMEDIATE

Write a List Write on the board *Things I Like To Do* and list a few activities such as *read books, talk to friends, play games*. Explain to students why we write lists of our ideas. Read the list one idea at a time and have students repeat. In groups of two or three, have students share activities they like to do. Compare lists as a group, add new activities to the list, and read one more time.

ADVANCED/ADVANCED HIGH

Homophones Explain that homophones are words that sound the same but have different meanings, such as *sea* and *see*. Give half of the group word cards with commonly confused homophones such as *their/there, threw/through, rode/road, write/right, close/clothes*. Give the other students cards with definitions. Students must match the word and definition and then write a sentence using the word correctly.

Prewrite
Focus on Organization

The Rubric Says	The letter is organized around a claim that inspires a call to action.
Writing Strategy	Make an Argument Map to show how the reasons, facts, and examples support the call to action.

My next step was to organize my ideas. Since I'd be using my letter to persuade Ms. Williams, I thought an Argument Map would be the best choice of a graphic organizer. I listed my call to action first, followed by my reasons. Then I filled in facts and examples wherever they fit best.

Writer's Term

Argument Map/Call to Action An **Argument Map** organizes reasons, examples, and facts that support your **call to action**. A call to action is a direct invitation to the audience to do something.

Argument Map

Call to Action Convince board members to change their minds.

Reason 1 Students need accurate, up-to-date information.

Example Our library has outdated information (human genome project).

Fact Internet information is often too hard to read.

Reason 2 Students need information they can understand.

Example There are many nonfiction books written for students our age.

Reflect
Do you think Tyler's Argument Map and notes are helpful? Has he included enough convincing information?

Apply
Use an Argument Map to organize your ideas.

Business Letter 297

Conferencing

PEER TO PEER Have pairs of students exchange Argument Maps. Tell them to ask themselves the following questions as they read the Map: *Is the writer's call to action clearly stated? Are the reasons and examples clear?* Then advise partners to write one or two comments on an adhesive note and return the Map with the note to the writer.

PEER GROUPS Have students work in groups of three or four. Ask each student to read his or her Argument Map aloud. Have the other students in the group take turns offering one comment or suggestion to the writer.

TEACHER-LED Schedule conferences with individual students about their Maps. Before they meet with you, tell students to think of questions to ask you about filling in the parts of the organizer or how they will use their Maps to organize their ideas and write their drafts.

Write
a Business Letter

Week 2 • Day 2

Student Objectives

- Make an Argument Map to organize the reasons, examples, and facts that support a call to action. (p. 297)

Prewrite

Focus on Organization

Organize Ideas Explain that writers use different types of organizers to organize their ideas. Tyler used an Argument Map to help him organize the details he had already written down in his notes. Ask how an Argument Map can be an effective tool when writing an editorial. (Possible response: An Argument Map helps writers organize their ideas. It lists a call to action that will go in the introduction, followed by the reasons, facts, and examples that will go in the body paragraphs.) Point out that Tyler's call to action indicates both his purpose and audience.

Writer's Term

Argument Map/Call to Action The purpose of the call to action is to prompt readers to do something, to react to the writing. It is a technique that writers use to motivate their readers.

CCSS **Common Core State Standards**
W.7.1: Write arguments to support claims with clear reasons and relevant evidence.

Business Letter **T297**

Write
a Business Letter

Week 2 • Day 3

Student Objectives

- Use an Argument Map to write well-organized paragraphs that support the call to action. *(p. 298)*

Draft

Focus on  Organization

Draft a Business Letter Read page 298 aloud. Then have students silently read Tyler's draft on page 299. Point out the correct business letter form, and ask students whether Tyler used it in his draft. (yes)

Remind students that they should not be overly concerned with correctness at this point. Also point out that the Proofreader's marks are provided as a reference on page 299. To help them focus on writing and avoid writing block, suggest that they circle any words or parts in their drafts they may want to change in revision.

The main goal is to get their ideas down on paper; they will have plenty of time to correct spelling, grammar, and punctuation later. Be sure that students understand that they will use their Argument Maps to guide them through the drafting process. If they are writing their drafts in class, plan time for writing, conferences, and reflection.

Online Writing Center

 Provides student eBooks with an **interactive writing pad** for drafting, revising, editing, and publishing.

Draft

Focus on **Organization**

The Rubric Says The letter is organized around a claim that inspires a call to action. Each body paragraph contains a strong and complete topic sentence.

Writing Strategy Write well-organized paragraphs that support the call to action.

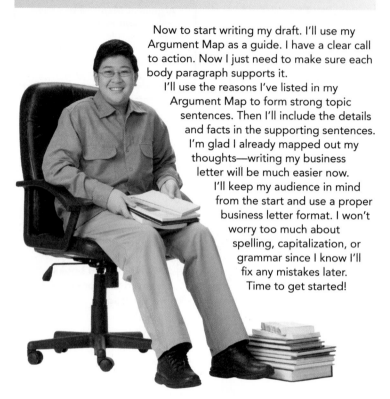

Now to start writing my draft. I'll use my Argument Map as a guide. I have a clear call to action. Now I just need to make sure each body paragraph supports it.

I'll use the reasons I've listed in my Argument Map to form strong topic sentences. Then I'll include the details and facts in the supporting sentences.

I'm glad I already mapped out my thoughts—writing my business letter will be much easier now.

I'll keep my audience in mind from the start and use a proper business letter format. I won't worry too much about spelling, capitalization, or grammar since I know I'll fix any mistakes later. Time to get started!

298 Argument Writing

Differentiating Instruction

ENRICHMENT

Include More Details Explain that for a business letter to be effective, it must present several legitimate reasons supported by specific facts and examples. Tell students that adding reasons and supporting details to their Argument Maps will help ensure that they have enough reasons and support for their opinions and help them to prioritize their evidence for the reader.

REINFORCEMENT

Supporting Details If students have trouble listing enough supporting details, ask them the following question for each reason they have given: What example or fact do you have that will convince me that your reason is true? If students cannot provide one, have them revisit their prewriting notes.

Proofreading Marks

⌐ Indent   ℓ Take out something
≡ Make a capital   ⊙ Add a period
/ Make a small letter   ⌗ New paragraph
∧ Add something   ⓢⓟ Spelling error

[DRAFT]

42 Georgia Pine Way
Atlanta, GA 30303
April 23, 2012   [heading]

Ms. Corrine Williams
School Board President
Consolidated District 2
456 South Peachtree Street   [inside address]
Atlanta, GA 30303

Dear Ms. Williams: ← [greeting]   [strong topic sentence]

I heard on the local news that the school board is having budget problems.
One perposed solution is to stop buying new books for our school libraries.
I am a student at Thompson Middle School, and I think that's really foolish
and I'm really upset! Here are the reasons for my opinion.

Students need accurite, up-to-date information on scientific and
political events. For example, I was recently asked to do a class report
on the human genome project. The book in our school library said that
all human genes would be identified "in the next ten years." My mother
told me, though, that the identification was already completed. None
of our library books weren't current enough to have this information.
Students can't hardly do accurite research in books like these.

Reflect

How do you think Ms. Williams
will respond to Tyler's opening
paragraphs?

Apply

Write a draft, making sure to use the
correct letter form and strong topic
sentences.

Business Letter 299

Write
a Business Letter

Week 2 • Day 4

Student Objectives

• Complete a draft. (p. 299)

Draft a Business Letter It is
important that students are given
ample time to draft their editorials.
As conferencing is important
throughout the writing process,
be sure to plan time for peer to
peer, peer group, or teacher-led
conferences. Remind students that
drafting is the time to get their
ideas down on paper in a creative
and engaging way. Assure them that
they will have plenty of time to fix
any mistakes later.

Conferencing

PEER TO PEER Have partners exchange their drafts. Tell
students to think of two or three questions they would like
to ask to clarify information or supply missing details. Have
them write their questions on adhesive notes and affix them
to the appropriate places on their partner's letter.

PEER GROUPS Have students work in groups of four.
Students pass their draft to the student on the right to read.
That student writes one comment or suggestion on an
adhesive note affixed to the draft and passes the draft along
to the right. The review ends when everyone has received
his or her own letter back with three comments.

TEACHER-LED Schedule conferences with pairs of students.
Have them read each other's draft and coach them in giving
constructive criticism on using the traits of Ideas and Organization as described in the rubric on page 290.

CCSS **C**ommon **C**ore **S**tate **S**tandards

W.7.5: With some guidance and support from peers
and adults, develop and strengthen writing as needed
by planning, revising, editing, rewriting, or trying a
new approach, focusing on how well purpose and
audience have been addressed.

Write
a Business Letter

Week 2 • Day 5

Student Objectives

• Use a respectful and courteous tone. *(p. 300)*

Revise

Focus on

Use a Formal Voice After writing their drafts, help students prepare to revise by explaining how this step in the writing process gives them the chance to improve their letter using the traits of writing. Read page 300 aloud. Explain that Tyler found a place where he needed to improve the voice. His changes will help maintain the formal voice he established in the beginning of his letter.

Stress to students the importance of maintaining a consistent voice. Have students read their drafts and ask themselves, *Do I address my reader in a respectful, courteous tone throughout the letter?* If they answer *maybe* or *not sure*, recommend that they work with a writing partner to make revisions. Like the recipient, the partner will be able to hear if the voice is appropriate and consistent.

 Strategies for Writers Online
Go to **www.sfw.z-b.com** for additional online resources for students and teachers.

T300 Argument Writing

Revise

Focus on **Voice**

The Rubric Says The writer's voice is convincing. The formal style is ideal for the topic and audience.

Writing Strategy Use a respectful and courteous tone.

The rubric says my voice should be convincing and my writing style should be appropriate for both my topic and audience. I am asking Ms. Williams to do something for me, and, if I want her to take my thoughts seriously, my letter should be formal, respectful, and polite. I want her to happily agree with me and not feel bullied in any way. As I reread my draft, I found a place that sounded too pushy. I'll fix it now.

[DRAFT]

problems. One perposed solution is to stop buying new books for our school libraries. I am a student at Thompson Middle School, and I think → that this is a big mistake. ~~that's really foolish and I'm really upset!~~ Here are the reasons for my opinion.
[used courteous tone]

Apply
Keep your voice convincing, yet respectful and courteous.

300 Argument Writing

English Language Learners

BEGINNING/INTERMEDIATE

Business Letter Format Pass out a blackline master of a simple business letter. Go over the different parts: inside address, heading, greeting, body, closing, and signature. Ask students: *To whom would you send a business letter? Your friend? The principal? Your mom? A store owner?* Elicit examples of who they would send it to. Then have students cut up the parts of the letter. Have students work with a partner to put the letter back together in correct letter form.

ADVANCED/ADVANCED HIGH

Conditional Sentences On the board, write *If I study, I will get good grades. I will get good grades if I study.* Explain these are conditional sentences, in which one thing depends on the other. Have students write one half of a conditional sentence. Then have them switch with a partner who must complete the sentence. Students should read the completed sentences to each other. Repeat several times.

Revise

Focus on Word Choice

The Rubric Says	All words, including frequently confused words and homophones, are used correctly.
Writing Strategy	Check the use of all homophones and other frequently confused words.

Writer's Term

Frequently Confused Words
Frequently confused words include **homophones** and words with similar sounds and/or meanings like **sit** and **set** or **lie** and **lay**. A homophone is a word that sounds the same as another word but has a different meaning and spelling like **they're, their,** and **there**.

The rubric tells me to check my use of words. I know that homophones and other words that sound similar can be tricky. I found a passage where I had made several errors by using the wrong words, so I went back and made some changes.

[DRAFT]

[corrected homophone errors]

we can get all the information we need on the Internet. The Internet, though, isn't hardly always ~~to~~ *too* helpful. I tried to find information on the human genome project ~~their~~ *there*. All I could find were papers written by scientists for other scientists. We need more ~~then~~ *than* that. We need

[corrected a frequently confused word]

Reflect

How have Tyler's revisions regarding voice and word accuracy strengthened his business letter?

Apply

Check your draft for errors in the use of homophones and other frequently confused words.

Business Letter **301**

Conferencing

PEER TO PEER Have partners exchange drafts. Tell them to read specifically for easily confused words, such as *accept/except, among/between, bad/badly, farther/further, its/it's, lay/lie, lead/led, learn/teach, past/passed, quiet/quit/quite, set/sit, their/there/they're, than/then, threw/through* and jot down all that they find. Then have writers use their partner's list to check the words and make changes, if needed. (Note: Comprehensive word lists are available online.)

PEER GROUPS Assign students to groups of three or four. Have them take turns reading their drafts aloud. Listeners should raise their hands whenever they hear an easily confused word. At this point, the writer should check to make sure the word is used (and spelled) correctly.

TEACHER-LED Schedule individual conferences. Review the revisions together. If they are incorrect or incomplete, make suggestions and recommend the lesson pages in their Student book that will assist them.

Write
a Business Letter

Week 3 • Day 1

Student Objectives

- Use homophones and other easily confused words correctly. (p. 301)

Revise

Focus on  Word Choice

Use the Right Word Have students identify the easily confused words and homophones that have tripped up Tyler. (*to, their, then*) Explain that homophones are words that sound alike but are spelled differently, such as *to, too, two*. Easily confused words have similar sounds and meanings, such as *sat, set, sit*. Then have students revise any misused homophones or easily confused words in their drafts.

Writer's Term

Frequently Confused Words Students will benefit from keeping their own personal list of words and consulting word resources in print and online. Explain that using the right word is the writer's responsibility and shows respect for the reader.

CCSS **C**ommon **C**ore **S**tate **S**tandards

W.7.1.c: Use words, phrases, and clauses to create cohesion and clarify the relationships among claim(s), reasons, and evidence. **W.7.1.d:** Establish and maintain a formal style.

Business Letter **T301**

Write
a Business Letter

Week 3 • Day 2

Student Objectives

• Use different sentence structures, such as conditional sentences. (p. 302)

Revise

Focus on  Sentence Fluency

Write Effective Conditional Sentences Explain to students that conditional sentences link probable outcomes (conditions) to the course of action in the main clause. Provide examples to show the structure of this type of sentence: *As long as I maintain good grades, my parents will let me see my friends on weekends. My parents will let me see my friends on weekends as long as I maintain good grades.* Underline the conditional clause in the examples and point out that it is followed by a comma when it begins the sentence. In argument writing, conditional sentences connect ideas ("If this is done/not done, then that will happen.") and help to convey a sense of immediacy.

 Writer's Term _____
Conditional Sentences are useful in argument writing to convince the reader to respond to the writer. Effective conditional sentences express, or lead to, a strong call to action.

Online Writing Center

Provides **interactive proofreading activities** for each genre.

T302 Argument Writing

Revise
Focus on **Sentence Fluency**

The Rubric Says	Sentences are varied, interesting, and stand apart from other writing. The writing is smooth when read out loud.
Writing Strategy	Use different sentence structures, such as conditional sentences.

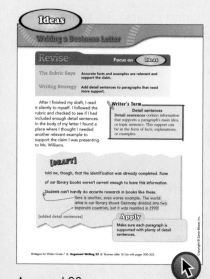

The rubric says to vary my sentences to keep my writing smooth. I'll add a few conditional sentences to mix things up. By explaining what might happen if we can't get new books, conditional sentences can also strengthen my overall message. Look below to see how I formed a conditional sentence.

✏️ **Writer's Term** _____
Conditional Sentences
A **conditional sentence** often contains **if, unless, provided, as long as,** or **would** to show that one thing depends on another. Conditional sentences also tell about situations that might happen.

[DRAFT]

The Internet, though, isn't hardly always ~~to~~ too helpful. I tried to find information on the human genome project ~~their~~ there. All I could find were papers written by scientists for other scientists. We need more ~~then~~ than that. We need nonfiction books by people who write just for students, if we're going to do a good job on our research.

[formed a conditional sentence]

Apply
Where can you add conditional sentences?

302 Argument Writing

Optional Revising Lessons

Ideas

Argument 23

Organization
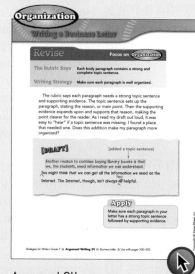

Argument 24

Go to ➡️ *Strategies for Writers Grade 7 CD-ROM*

Edit   Focus on **Conventions**

The Rubric Says	Sentences are clear and correct: there are no double negatives, and infinitive phrases are effective.
Writing Strategy	Make sure that there are no double negatives and that infinitives are correct.

✏ Writer's Term
Double Negatives
Negative words are words like **no, not, nothing, nobody, never, nowhere, neither, none, hardly, barely, scarcely, without,** and any contraction ending in **n't.** Using two negative words together creates the error called a **double negative**.

When rereading my draft, I found a few double negatives. I'll go and correct them now. While I'm at it, I'll also make sure all infinitive phrases are used effectively.

[DRAFT]

[corrected a double negative]
told me, though, that the indentification was already completed. None
                                                         were
[deleted a double negative]
of our library books ~~weren't~~ current enough to have this information.
                               accurate
Students can't ~~hardly~~ do ~~accurite~~ research in books like these.
Here is another, even worse example. The world atlas in our library shows Germany divided into two separate countries, but it was reunited in 1990!

Reflect

How do Tyler's revisions help his sentences to flow? In what ways have Tyler's edits helped his writing?

Apply   **Conventions**

Edit for spelling, punctuation, and capitalization. Be sure infinitives are correct and that there are no double negatives.

For more practice with infinitives and avoiding double negatives, complete the next two pages.

Business Letter 303

Write
a Business Letter

Week 3 • Day 3

Student Objectives

- Make sure negatives and infinitives are used correctly. *(p. 303)*

Edit

Focus on  Conventions

Edit for Accuracy Read page 303 aloud. Point out Tyler's edits and discuss how they improve the draft. Remind students that editing is the step in the process where they can go back and correct any mistakes in spelling, grammar, punctuation, and capitalization. Explain that even very skilled writers can overlook errors in their own writing. Writers tend to read what they intended to write and, therefore, they may miss things that jump out at the reader.

Use the mini-lessons on T304–305 for students who need practice to avoid double negatives and to use infinitives correctly. Then have students complete pages 304 and 305.

✏ Writer's Term _____
Double Negatives Mention to students several common misconstructions, such as *not hardly any* or *not barely enough.* Point out that the words *barely* and *hardly* are negative in meaning and should not be used with *no* or *not.*

CCSS Common Core State Standards
L.7.1: Demonstrate command of the conventions of standard English grammar and usage when writing or speaking.

Business Letter T303

Conventions

Mini-Lesson

Student Objectives

- Correct double negatives. (p. 304)

Double Negatives

Explain to the students that using more than one negative in a sentence is not only incorrect but also very confusing to the reader. Provide an example that includes a double negative, such as *Students do not have no right to decide this.* Underline the negative words, *not, no.* Ask students what they would do to fix this sentence. (Possible response: Change one of the negatives.) Then have students write or say the sentence correctly: (Possible response: Students do not have the right to decide this.) Make sure students understand the reason for the change before assigning the exercise on page 304.

Online Writing Center

Provides **interactive grammar games** and **practice activities** in student eBook.

Double Negatives

Know the Rule

Negative words are words like *no, not, nothing, nobody, never, nowhere, neither, none, hardly, barely, scarcely, without,* and any contraction ending in *n't.* A **double negative** occurs when more than one negative word is used to express a negative idea. Double negatives confuse the reader and confuse the writer's meaning. Avoid them whenever possible.

Double Negative: The school board doesn't have **no** money.
Corrected: The school board doesn't have any money.

Practice the Rule

Rewrite each sentence below on a separate sheet of paper, correcting the double negative used in each one.   **Possible responses given.**

1. It wasn't ~~hardly~~ *even* lunchtime, and Kellie was already hungry.
2. She couldn't ask her teacher ~~no~~ *any* questions about the menu.
3. So she distracted herself by sharpening a pencil that didn't have ~~no~~ *a* point.
4. She scarcely ~~never~~ *ever* had a pencil with a point.
5. While she was sharpening her pencil, she ~~couldn't~~ *could* barely wait to eat.
6. Kellie returned to her work, only to realize she didn't have ~~no~~ *enough* time to finish.
7. When the bell sounded, she ~~couldn't~~ *could* hardly run fast enough to the cafeteria.
8. Kellie waited and waited, but her friends weren't ~~nowhere~~ *anywhere* to be seen.
9. She got in line for a sandwich or salad, but the lunch lady said that neither ~~wasn't~~ *was* left.
10. Hungry and disappointed, Kellie decided to buy a yogurt, but her pocket didn't hold ~~no~~ *any* money!

Related Grammar Practice

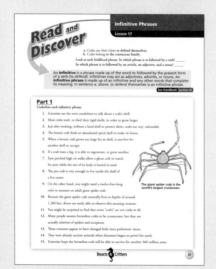

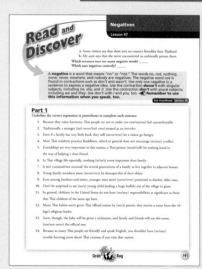

Pages 51, 141

 Go to G.U.M. Student Practice Book

Infinitive Phrases

Know the Rule

> An **infinitive** is a phrase made up of the word *to* followed by the present form of a verb (*to discover*). Infinitives may act as adjectives, adverbs, or nouns. An **infinitive phrase** is made up of an infinitive and any other words that complete its meaning.
>
> **Example:** My dream is **to learn how to walk on a tightrope.**

Practice the Rule

Copy the sentences onto a separate sheet of paper. Circle the infinitive phrases in each sentence.

1. Last night, Dad wanted us (to have dinner) early so that we could go out for ice cream afterward.
2. I was able (to get home) from school in time (to help him make dinner.)
3. Unfortunately, my brother had forgotten (to mention) that he had baseball practice after school.
4. Mom likes (to take) the bus home from work, and traffic was terrible.
5. She tried (to call) and let us know she was running late, but the battery in her cell phone died.
6. Of course, Dad and I didn't realize the rest of the family was going (to be late) for dinner.
7. We started (to chop) the vegetables and get everything ready.
8. As you can imagine, there was only one way for this story (to turn out.)
9. By the time Mom and my brother got home, dinner was far too burned (to eat.)
10. It's not very often that we go out (to eat) on a weeknight.

Mini-Lesson

Student Objectives

- Use infinitive phrases correctly. (p. 305)

Infinitive Phrases

Before assigning the practice page, discuss the example sentence on page 305 with students.

My dream is <u>to learn how to walk on a tightrope</u>. (phrase functions as a predicate noun)

Point out the infinitive phrase in the example sentence in Know the Rule on page 305. Circle the first two words in the phrase. Explain that the phrase begins with the word *to* followed by the present (infinitive) form of the verb *learn*. Go on to explain that unlike a prepositional phrase that begins with *to*, an infinitive phrase begins with *to* + a verb and any other words that complete its meaning (*how to walk on a tightrope*). Infinitive phrases can function as nouns, adjectives, or adverbs in a sentence.

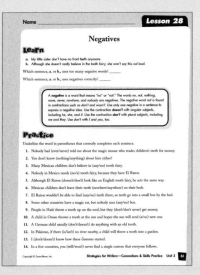

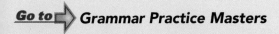 **Grammar Practice Masters**

CCSS Common Core State Standards

L.7.1.a: Explain the function of phrases and clauses in general and their function in specific sentences. **L.7.2:** Demonstrate command of the conventions of standard English capitalization, punctuation, and spelling when writing.

Write
a Business Letter

Week 3 • Day 4

Student Objectives

- Discuss preparation for publishing and presentation. (p. 306)
- Use a final editing checklist to publish their work. (p. 306)

Publish +Presentation

Publishing Strategy Explain to students that Tyler's decision to mail his letter shows commitment to expressing his opinion publicly. He feels confident that the recipient will help get more people involved in solving the problem. Tyler intends to type his letter using a word processor and to create address labels for his envelope.

Provide students with business letter templates or guidelines that show them how to set the margins for a good layout. Remind them to indent paragraphs or leave a space between paragraphs. Students should use a checklist like the one on page 306 to prepare their final copies. Encourage students to refer to the model on pages 307–308 to make sure their letters include all six parts. It's a good strategy to have students print out a copy of their own finished letters to check carefully before mailing.

Strategies for Writers Online
Go to **www.sfw.z-b.com** for additional online resources for students and teachers.

Publish +Presentation

Publishing Strategy	Mail the letter to the appropriate person.
Presentation Strategy	Make sure the letter has all six parts.

Now to mail my letter! I'll use the proper business letter format, so that the person who receives the letter will take it seriously. And I'll accurately address the envelope. The United States Postal Service won't be able to deliver my letter if I leave out vital information. In fact, I can check how to properly address my envelope by checking www.usps.com. But first I'll check it against my final checklist.

My Final Checklist

Did I—
- ✔ avoid using double negatives?
- ✔ include effective infinitive phrases?
- ✔ handwrite or type both my letter and envelope neatly?
- ✔ include all six parts in my letter?

Apply
Check your business letter against your checklist. Then make a final copy to publish.

306 Argument Writing

Differentiating Instruction

ENRICHMENT
Writing Letters 101 Students can look for examples of memorable letters that moved the recipient(s) to act in amazing or thoughtful ways. Provide time for students to use the Internet to collect information. Encourage them to share their findings in class.

REINFORCEMENT
Concentrated Copyediting Have pairs of students work together to edit their drafts for one specific thing. For example, have each pair begin by trading letters and proofreading only for punctuation or spelling. Then have pairs return the letters and discuss any edits on the page.

42 Georgia Pine Way
Atlanta, GA 30303
April 23, 2012

Ms. Corrine Williams
School Board President
Consolidated District 2
456 South Peachtree Street
Atlanta, GA 30303

Dear Ms. Williams:

I heard on the local news that the school board is having budget problems. One proposed solution is to stop buying new books for our school libraries. I am a student at Thompson Middle School, and I think that this is a big mistake. Here are the reasons for my opinion.

Students need accurate, up-to-date information on recent scientific and political events. For example, I was recently asked to do a class report on the Human Genome Project. The book in our school library said that all human genes would be identified "in the next ten years." My mother told me, though, that the identification was already completed. None of our library books were current enough to have this information. Here is another, even worse example. The world atlas in our library shows Germany divided into two separate countries, but it was reunited in 1990! Students can't do accurate research in books like these.

Technology Tip
for 21st Century Literacies

While students are developing purposeful business letters, they are also learning about themselves as writers. Consider using a podcasting site like iPadio or PodOmatic to house students' reflective comments and posts over time. Ask them to create posts that capture moments when they were confused or made an important discovery. This is meant to be a place that captures the "messiness" of their real learning where they reflect on the goals they want to set for future work. Revisit these posts so students can examine their growth and learning over time.

See **www.sfw.z-b.com** for further information about and links to these websites and tools.

Write
a Business Letter

Week 3 • Day 5

Student Objectives

- Use a business letter rubric. (pp. 290–291)
- Share a published business letter. (pp. 307–309)

Type a Business Letter Explain to students how important neatness is when creating a final copy of their work. Messy or illegible work will turn readers away, while a neat and interesting format draws readers in. Remind students of the many word processing features computers have to offer. Students should set neat margins, indent or use a space to separate paragraphs and lines of text, and select one, clear font so the recipient has no trouble reading the letter.

Encourage students to consult online resources such as dictionaries, thesauruses, and word glossaries to make sure they have correctly spelled all the words in their letters. Point out common mistakes, such as the spelling of the words *Sincerely* and *Yours truly*.

CCSS Common Core State Standards

W.7.4: Produce clear and coherent writing in which the development, organization, and style are appropriate to task, purpose, and audience. **W.7.6:** Use technology, including the Internet, to produce and publish writing and link to and cite sources as well as to interact and collaborate with others, including linking to and citing sources.

Reflecting on a Business Letter

Have a volunteer read aloud the questions in the Reflect box on page 309. Then ask the following:

- How did you use the rubric as you wrote your business letter?

- How effective do you think your letter will be? Why?

Ask students to jot down their responses in a personal writer's journal or in their notes on the chapter. Have them keep track of their responses for each genre in Argument Writing for future reference.

Another reason to continue buying library books is that we, the students, need information we can understand. You might think that we can get all the information we need on the Internet. The Internet, though, isn't always too helpful. I tried to find information on the Human Genome Project there. All I could find were papers written by scientists for other scientists. We need more than that. We need nonfiction books by people who write just for students if we're going to do a good job on our research.

I hope my letter has convinced you how important it is to keep buying new library books. Please try to convince the other school board members to change their minds on this issue.

Yours truly,

Tyler Lee

Tyler Lee

 Strategies for Writers Online

Go to **www.sfw.z-b.com** for additional online resources for students and teachers.

TYLER LEE
42 GEORGIA PINE WAY
ATLANTA GA 30303

MS CORRINE WILLIAMS
SCHOOL BOARD PRESIDENT
CONSOLIDATED DISTRICT 2
456 SOUTH PEACHTREE ST
ATLANTA GA 30303

Reflect

How did Tyler do? Did he use all the traits of a good business letter in his writing? Check it against the rubric. Then use the rubric to check your own business letter.

Website Review Planner

WEEK 1

Introduce
a Website Review

Student Objectives
- Review the elements of a website review.
- Consider purpose and audience.
- Learn the traits of argument writing.

Student Activities
- Read and discuss **What's in a Website Review?** (p. 310)
- Read and discuss **Why Write a Website Review?** (p. 311)
- Read **Linking Argument Writing Traits to a Website Review.** (p. 312)

Analyze
Read a Website Review

Student Objectives
- Read a model website review.

Student Activities
- Read **"Space Camp Anyone?"** (pp. 313–315)

Analyze
Introduce the Rubric

Student Objectives
- Learn to read a rubric.

Student Activities
- Review **"Space Camp Anyone?"** (pp. 313–315)
- Read and discuss the **Website Review Rubric.** (pp. 316–317)

WEEK 2

Write
Prewrite: Ideas

Student Objectives
- Read and understand a prewriting strategy.

Student Activities
- Read and discuss **Prewrite: Focus on Ideas.** (p. 322)
- Apply the prewriting strategy.

Write
Prewrite: Organization

Student Objectives
- Make a Pro-and-Con Chart to organize responses.

Student Activities
- Read and discuss **Prewrite: Focus on Organization.** (p. 323)
- Apply the strategy.
- Participate in a peer conference.

Write
Draft: Voice

Student Objectives
- Use credible sources of information and fair language.

Student Activities
- Read and discuss **Draft: Focus on Voice.** (p. 324)
- Apply the drafting strategy by using a Pro-and-Con Chart to begin a draft

WEEK 3

Write
Revise: Word Choice

Student Objectives
- Use words with the right connotation.

Student Activities
- Read and discuss **Revise: Focus on Word Choice.** (p. 327)
- Reflect on a model draft.
- Apply the revising strategy.
- Participate in a peer conference.

Write
Revise: Sentence Fluency

Student Objectives
- Vary sentences by using transition words.

Student Activities
- Read and discuss **Revise: Focus on Sentence Fluency.** (p. 328)
- Reflect on a model draft.
- Apply the revising strategy.

Note: Optional Revising Lessons appear on the *Strategies for Writers* CD-ROM.

Write
Edit: Conventions

Student Objectives
- Choose punctuation for effect.
- Use colons and semicolons correctly.

Student Activities
- Read and discuss **Edit: Focus on Conventions.** (p. 329)
- Reflect on a model draft.
- Apply the editing strategy.

Note: Teach the Conventions mini-lessons (pp. 330–331) if needed.

Analyze
Ideas, Organization, and Voice

Student Objectives
- Read a model website review.
- Use the website review rubric.
- Use the model website review to study Ideas, Organization, and Voice.

Student Activities
- Review **"Space Camp Anyone?"** (pp. 313–315)
- Read and discuss **Using the Rubric to Study the Model.** (pp. 318–319)

Analyze
Word Choice, Sentence Fluency, and Conventions

Student Objectives
- Read a model website review.
- Use the website review rubric.
- Use the model website review to study Word Choice, Sentence Fluency, and Conventions.

Student Activities
- Review **"Space Camp Anyone?"** (pp. 313–315)
- Read and discuss **Using the Rubric to Study the Model.** (pp. 320–321)

Write
Draft

Student Objectives
- Complete a draft.

Student Activities
- Finish writing the draft. (p. 325)
- Participate in a peer conference.

Write
Revise: Ideas

Student Objectives
- State a clear claim and include at least one con.

Student Activities
- Read and discuss **Revise: Focus on Ideas.** (p. 326)
- Reflect on a model draft.
- Apply the revising strategy.

Write
Publish: +Presentation

Student Objectives
- Discuss preparation for publishing and presentation.
- Use a final editing checklist to publish their work.

Student Activities
- Read and discuss **Publish: +Presentation.** (p. 332)
- Apply the publishing strategy.

Write
Publish: +Presentation

Student Objectives
- Use a website review rubric.
- Share a published website review.

Student Activities
- Share their work.
- Use the rubric to reflect upon and evaluate the model and their own writing. (pp. 316–317; 333–335)

Resources at-a-Glance

Grammar, Usage & Mechanics

Differentiating Instruction
For additional Differentiating Instruction activities, see Strategies for Writers Extensions Online *at* **www.sfw.z-b.com.**

English Language Learners

Conferencing

Technology Tip

 Connection Letter
Reproducible letter (in English and Spanish) appears on the *Strategies for Writers* CD-ROM and at **www.sfw.z-b.com.**

Online Writing Center

Provides IWB resources, interactive games and practice activities, videos, eBooks, and a virtual file cabinet.

 Strategies for Writers Online
Go to **www.sfw.z-b.com** for free online resources for students and teachers.

To complete the chapter in fewer days, combine the learning objectives and activities in a way that supports students as they write.

Introduce
a Website Review

Week 1 • Day 1

Student Objectives

- Review the elements of a website review. *(p. 310)*
- Consider purpose and audience. *(p. 311)*
- Learn the traits of argument writing. *(p. 312)*

What's a Website Review?

Discuss with students the definition of a website review. Explain that some websites are more credible than others and that Internet users often have to evaluate Web pages to decide which ones are the most reliable. Point out that any time students state the pros and cons of a website in writing, they are using the website review genre.

What's in a Website Review?

Read and discuss with students the elements of a website review listed on page 310. Explain that some of the elements are also common to other forms of writing, such as comparisons, essays, and argument writing. Then discuss why each element may be important when writing a website review.

Strategies for Writers Online

Go to **www.sfw.z-b.com** for additional online resources for students and teachers.

What's a **Website Review?**

It's a report about a particular website. It tells the reader how the website works, and it either recommends or discourages use of the site. Writing this will be fun because I can pretend I'm a Web master!

What's in a **Website Review?**

Selected Website
This is what I'm writing about. I'll be telling the reader about a selected website and whether or not I recommend it.

Pros and Cons
I'll have to inform my readers of the good features (pros) and bad features (cons) of the selected website.

Claim
The claim is the statement I will use to tell my readers whether or not I recommend the selected website. This will be the main idea of my review, and all the details should support it.

Organization
I will organize my report around the claim. Then I'll use my description of the website as support. I can use the introduction to clearly present my claim, the body to present supporting facts, and the conclusion to summarize my review and restate my claim.

Argument Text Exemplars (Website Review)

Burns, Tom. *Children's Literature Review: Excerpts from Reviews, Criticism, and Commentary on Books for Children and Young People, Volume 140.* Gale Cengage Learning, 2009. Burns presents an illustrated guide that features over 700 writers and illustrators for children and young adults. Entries focus on the major works and awards, as well as critical reviews and commentaries surrounding an author's or artist's works.

Horning, Kathleen T. *From Cover to Cover: Evaluating and Reviewing Children's Books.* Collins, 2010. *From Cover to Cover* provides an updated look at the world of children's literature. Horning outlines the publication process and highlights some of the best examples of children's literature. She exhibits how to write one's own book review in order to share new books with others.

Why write a **Website Review?**

What are some reasons for writing a website review? I listed some here, since I'm still thinking about why I want to write.

Entertain
A website review can be entertaining. I can write with a lively style and include information that interests my readers. It's always good for the reader to be pleased and entertained.

Convince
I can form my own opinion about a website and then, using details to support my opinion, write a review to try to convince others to agree with me.

Inform
Some websites are extremely useful. A website review can inform readers about a particular site. Then they can decide if the site would be useful to them.

Summarize
Sometimes websites are complicated and hard to navigate. Information is often hidden or lost because of flashy pictures, advertisements, or large titles. That's when it's important to summarize the details the reader really needs to know.

Why write a Website Review?

Read and discuss with students the reasons for writing a website review listed on page 311. Point out that all writing has a purpose and is aimed at a specific audience. These authentic purposes help writers shape their writing. Someone writing to entertain may use a lively tone and include fun information. A person writing to convince will provide lots of facts and examples to back up the writer's viewpoint. Someone writing to inform may include helpful information. A person writing to summarize will practice writing detail sentences to get the main point across. Encourage students to think about their own reasons for writing website reviews and how their reasons will affect the tone and focus of their writing.

SparkNotes Editors. *SparkNotes on The Giver.* SparkNotes LLC, 2003. *SparkNotes* is a literature guide that provides insight and analysis on Lois Lowry's *The Giver.*

SparkNotes Editors. *SparkNotes on The Outsiders.* SparkNotes LLC, 2002. *SparkNotes* is a literature guide that provides insight and analysis on S.E. Hinton's *The Outsiders.*

CCSS Common Core State Standards
SL.7.1: Engage effectively in a range of collaborative discussions (one-on-one, in groups, and teacher-led) with diverse partners on *grade 7 topics, texts, and issues,* building on each others' ideas and expressing their own clearly.

Introduce
a Website Review

Linking Argument Writing Traits to a Website Review

Read the introduction to page 312 aloud to help students understand that they will follow Tyler as he models using the writing process and the traits together. As they follow Tyler, students will see how the Argument Writing Traits have been adapted and applied to writing a website review. They will see that a website review expresses an opinion and, therefore, has many factors in common with other types of argument writing. However, the particular audience and purpose of a website review determine how the traits are used.

Online Writing Center

Provides six **interactive anchor papers** for each mode of writing.

T312   Argument Writing

Linking Argument Writing Traits to a **Website Review**

In this chapter, you will evaluate a website. This type of argument writing is called a website review. Tyler will guide you through the stages of the writing process: Prewrite, Draft, Revise, Edit, and Publish. In each stage, Tyler will show you important writing strategies that are linked to the Argument Writing Traits below.

Argument Writing Traits

Ideas
- clearly stated claims, often balanced by alternate or opposing claims
- supporting evidence from accurate and credible sources

Organization
- a strong introduction that presents the writer's position
- reasons and evidence that are organized logically
- a conclusion that follows and supports the argument
- transitions that clarify the relationships between the claim(s), the supporting evidence, and any counterclaims

Voice
- a voice that supports the writer's purpose

Word Choice
- language that is compelling

Sentence Fluency
- sentences that vary in length and begin in different ways

Conventions
- no or few errors in grammar, usage, mechanics, and spelling

Before you write, read Marie Tokonada's website review on the next three pages. Then use the website review rubric on pages 316–317 to decide how well she did. (You might want to look back at What's in a Website Review? on page 310, too!)

Argument Writing Traits in a Website Review

Ideas   The review clearly states and supports the writer's opinion. Evidence from accurate, credible sources is presented to convince the reader.

Organization   The review includes a strong introduction that presents the writer's opinion. Reasons (main ideas) and evidence (supporting details) are organized logically. Logical transitions guide the reader. The conclusion follows from and supports the writer's position.

Voice   The writer uses a convincing voice and formal style that support the writer's purpose and reaches out to the audience.

Space Camp Anyone?

by Marie Tokonada

Selected Website

Organization: Introduction

We all run across bad websites every now and then. Sometimes information is hard to retrieve because a site is too complex, or worse yet, the information is inaccurate or out of date. That's when we continue to search for a good site that loads quickly and contains just the information we're looking for. That's when we hope to run across a site like www.spacecamp.com. This site is easy to use, full of information, reliable, and up to date.

Claim

When I enter the Space Camp Web address in my computer's address bar, I am almost instantly taken to the site; I do not have to wait for images to load or for links to become functional. However, the opening screen is a bit cluttered. Menus run across the top, sides, and bottom of a box in the center of the page. The box shows alternating images of, and captions about, Space Camp, but the sequence sometimes moves so quickly that it is a little hard to follow.

Pros

Cons

Organization: Body

Website Review 313

Word Choice The writer's language is compelling and convincing. Word choice creates meaning and cohesion among the writer's claim, reasons, and evidence.

Sentence Fluency Sentences vary in length and begin in different ways. The writer's ideas flow smoothly and hold the reader's attention.

Conventions The writer has proofread carefully to make sure there are no or few errors in grammar, usage, mechanics, and spelling to distract the reader.

Analyze
the Model

Week 1 • Day 2

Student Objectives

• Read a model website review. *(pp. 313–315)*

Read the Model

Read the model website review on pages 313–315 aloud to the class. Ask students to listen for the writer's opinion, reasons, and evidence. Then ask them to notice how the details are organized. Also ask students to think about and discuss how a formal style conveys the writer's purpose to the audience.

Elements of a Website Review

Have students refer to What's in a Website Review? on page 310 as you refer to the model review. Discuss the notes written on the model to enhance students' understanding of the terms. Point out that they will also use the model to analyze the traits of a good website review.

CCSS **Common Core State Standards**
R/Inf.7.1: Cite several places of textual evidence to support analysis of what the text says explicitly as well as inferences drawn from the text.

Organization: Body

Pros The many menus offer multiple ways to find information; however,

Cons I found it difficult to decide which buttons would give me the best facts. For example, to find a schedule of Space Camp dates, you can click on "Space Camp" under Programs, "Dates & Rates" under Information, "Space Camp" on the bars running across the top of the page, or "Register Now" on one of the stamps running down the right side of the central screen. This kind of accessibility does have a positive side, however. I'd rather find the same information in several different places, than not find the information at all!

Cons Although the multiple buttons can be a bit confusing, they do work

Pros very well. Anything I clicked on loaded quickly. In this way, I could rapidly access any of the subpages on the site. It was easy to find the forms needed to make a reservation for a particular week or year. I could even name friends and siblings with whom I wanted to camp. Further, I could type in my name as I wanted it to appear on my Space Camp patch. I thought that was a fantastic feature!

Pros But what about the application form for Space Camp? Well, it was also easy to find. However, I was a bit let down at first because

Cons the form could not be completed online. But then I realized why: The application is long. I will have to write essays and get letters of recommendation. I will also have to list science projects with which I've been involved. It's good to know that this information is accessible and accurate, especially since the application process is so involved.

Pros The information on www.spacecamp.com is also very up to date; the home page shows a copyright date of this year. Not to mention, the simple click of a button allows you to check the availability of camps for the next year. Even the photographs were recent, showing people with up-to-date clothing and haircuts. All of this leads me to believe the site is credible and trustworthy.

314 Argument Writing

Books for Professional Development

Baines, Lawrence and Anthony Kunkel. *Going Bohemian: How to Teach Writing Like You Mean It.* 2nd ed. Newark, DE: International Reading Association, 2010. This award-winning collection of writing strategies sparks an artistic sensibility and enthusiasm for writing in adolescent students—including reluctant students and English language learners. Bohemian writing lessons rely on unconventional strategies such as competitive games, art and multimedia, and indirect approaches to encourage students to participate in the act of writing.

Calkins, Lucy McCormick. *The Art of Teaching Writing.* 2nd ed. Portsmouth, NH: Heinemann, 1994. This classic book contains chapters on assessment, thematic studies, writing throughout the day, reading-writing relationships, publication, curriculum development, nonfiction writing, and school-home connections.

Strategies for Writers Online
Go to **www.sfw.z-b.com** for additional online resources for students and teachers.

Organization: Body

Pros Finally, the site is very functional, which is excellent for a place that teaches about state-of-the-art technology. The site's interactive features also clearly state the security measures that were taken to protect my personal information, and contact information is clearly given on the home page as well as the "Contact Us" section.

In conclusion, I would strongly recommend www.spacecamp.com to anyone who is interested in learning about Space Camp. Even though it is a bit overdesigned, it is fast, reliable, and informative. So if you want to go to Space Camp, you should get online and download your application today!

Organization: Conclusion

Fletcher, Ralph, and JoAnn Portalupi. *Craft Lessons: Teaching Writing K-8.* **2nd ed. Portland, ME: Stenhouse, 2007.** Since its publication in 1998 *Craft Lessons* has become a mainstay of writing teachers. Purposeful, practical lessons—each printed on one page— are geared to three grade-level groupings: K–2, 3–4, and 5–8. The 95 lessons in this book, many based on veteran teachers' observations about typical student writing, provide a wealth of information for teaching leads, character, endings, stronger verbs, and much more.

Young, Art. *Teaching Writing Across the Curriculum.* **4th ed. Upper Saddle River: Prentice Hall, 2006.** This edition provides a comprehensive, accessible discussion of writing across the curriculum.

CCSS Common Core State Standards

W.7.6: Use technology, including the Internet, to produce and publish writing and link to and cite sources as well as to interact and collaborate with others, including linking to and citing sources.

Analyze
the Model

Week 1 • Day 3

Student Objectives

- Learn to read a rubric.
  (pp. 316–317)

Use the Rubric

Explain the Rubric Explain that a rubric is a tool for planning, improving and assessing a piece of writing. Tell students that a rubric helps a writer focus on key elements, or traits, in writing (**Ideas, Organization, Voice, Word Choice, Sentence Fluency, Conventions,** and **Presentation**).

Point out that column 6 describes a very good website review, one that has received the highest score in all categories. This is what students should strive for in their own writing.

Discuss the Rubric As students measure their own papers against the rubric, they should first decide whether the papers fall on the left of the rubric (use the trait well) or on the right (need improvement in using the trait). By examining their papers more closely, students can refine their scores for each trait to single numbers.

Online Writing Center

Provides a variety of **interactive rubrics,** including 4-, 5-, and 6-point models.

T316   **Argument Writing**

Rubric

Use this 6-point rubric to plan and evaluate a website review.

	6	5	4
Ideas	The claim is clearly stated. The review clearly presents both pros and cons about the website.	The claim is stated. The review presents pros and cons.	The claim is stated. Some pros and cons are presented.
Organization	The structure of the writing organizes the evidence logically and is perfect for the topic. The conclusion follows and supports the argument presented.	The structure of the writing is logically organized. The conclusion supports the argument.	The structure of the writing often works. The conclusion works.
Voice	The writer uses a confident, formal style. The voice is well suited for the audience and purpose.	The writer uses a strong voice. The style is suited for the audience and purpose.	The writer's voice is strong, and the style is appropriate most of the time.
Word Choice	The words support the author's purpose and help convince the reader. Site-specific terms are clearly defined.	The words are purposeful and convincing. Most site-specific terms are defined.	Most of the words are to the point and convincing. Most site-specific terms are defined.
Sentence Fluency	Transitions connect sentences, create variety, and clarify relationships among ideas.	Transitions connect sentences and create some variety.	Some sentences lack transitions, disrupting the flow of reading.
Conventions	Semicolons and colons are used correctly and effectively. The writing is easy to understand.	A few minor errors with semicolons and colons are present but do not interfere with meaning.	Some errors with semicolons and colons are noticeable but do not interfere with meaning.

+Presentation   All paragraphs are indented.

CCSS Common Core State Standards
Website Review

Strategies for Writers was designed and written to weave the Common Core State Standards (CCSS) throughout every unit. For **Argument** writing, the standards inform the unit's writing rubrics, objectives, and strategies. By presenting the standards in as many applications as possible, your students' exposure to them will be ensured. As a result, students are more likely to employ the Standards' language to write arguments and in discussions about writing.

The lessons for the website review are based principally on the writing standards for **Argument** writing. The rubrics and writing strategies for the traits of Ideas and Organization in this chapter reflect writing standards **W.7.1.a, W.7.1.b,** and **W.7.3.e,** which focus on stating a clear claim, presenting both pros and cons about a website, using evidence logically, and providing a strong concluding statement or section which

3	2	1	
The claim can be identified but is not clearly stated. Pros and cons are presented but not balanced.	The claim is hard to identify. Only pros or cons are stated, but not both.	The review lacks a claim. No pros or cons can be identified.	Ideas
The writing often isn't focused on the topic. The conclusion is present but may need work.	Information is out of order and creates confusion for the reader. The conclusion is vague or may be missing.	The writing is confusing and lacks any writing structure. No conclusion is present.	Organization
The writer's voice does not sound confident. The style may not be appropriate.	The writer's voice sounds weak and not convincing. The style doesn't work for the audience and purpose.	The voice is flat or absent from the writing. The writing lacks information about the topic.	Voice
Several words are weak or unrelated to the purpose. Some site-specific terms are not defined.	Many of the words are incorrect or are too general to be convincing. Site-specific terms, if used, are not defined.	The words don't make sense and are vague. Site-specific words are not used.	Word Choice
Sentences are too similar in sections. Transitions would help create variety and help clarify how ideas are related.	Sentences are choppy throughout the review. Transitions are missing. It's unclear how ideas are related.	Incomplete sentences run together. No transitions are used.	Sentence Fluency
Noticeable errors with semicolons and colons might slow down the reader.	Many obvious errors with semicolons and colons get in the way of reading the writing.	Errors with semicolons and colons are frequent and make reading difficult.	Conventions

See Appendix B for 4-, 5-, and 6-point argument rubrics.

Apply the Rubric

Assign Groups Assign students to small groups and ask them to check the model for each trait. One person in each group should be responsible for recording one or two strong examples of the trait as described by the rubric. Ask students to score each trait accordingly for the model. They should be able to support their scores. Note that although the models were written to score high in each trait, students should not assume each trait would receive a 6, the top score. Encourage students to discuss each trait thoroughly before assigning each score.

Reassemble Class Bring the class back together and ask one person from each group to report their findings to the class. The point of this exercise is to practice identifying and evaluating the traits within a piece of writing.

Additional Rubrics Appendix B includes 4-, 5-, and 6-point rubrics that can be used with any piece of argument writing. The rubrics are also available as blackline masters in this Teacher Edition, beginning on page T543.

follows from the writer's argument. The rubrics and writing strategies for the traits of Voice, Word Choice, and Sentence Fluency in this chapter reflect writing standards **W.7.1.c** and **W.7.1.d,** which focus on using a confident, formal style, convincing words, and site-specific terms that are defined and consistent with the writer's purpose and audience. In addition, this chapter addresses writing standard **W.7.6,** which focuses on using the Internet to link and cite sources.

The language standards for grade 7 students are addressed during editing and skills practice. In addition, there are multiple opportunities to address the speaking and listening standards during the writing process. Most important, this chapter will help your students produce coherent writing (**W.7.4**), improve their writing (**W.7.5**), and use technologies to publish and present their finished pieces (**W.7.6**).

CCSS **C**ommon **C**ore **S**tate **S**tandards

SL.7.1.a: Come to discussions prepared, having read or researched material under study, explicitly draw on that preparation by referring to evidence on the topic, text, or issue to probe and reflect on ideas under discussion.

Analyze
the Model

Student Objectives

- Read a model website review. *(pp. 313–315)*
- Use the website review rubric. *(pp. 316–317)*
- Use the model website review to study Ideas, Organization, and Voice. *(pp. 318–319)*

Study the Model

Assess the Model Have volunteers read aloud each section on pages 318–319. Discuss as a class whether students agree or disagree with Tyler's assessments of the model. Use questions such as the following to discuss the pages with students. Be sure they can back up their answers with evidence from the model.

Does the writer

- state an opinion clearly and use accurate evidence to support the claim? (Possible response: Yes, Marie Tokonada states her opinion clearly. She gives reasons for what she liked—the pros—and what she didn't like—the cons.)

Strategies for Writers Online
Go to **www.sfw.z-b.com** for additional online resources for students and teachers.

Website Review

Website Review
Using the Rubric to Study the Model

Did you notice that the model on pages 313–315 points out some key elements of a website review? As she wrote "Space Camp Anyone?" Marie Tokonada used these elements to help her review a website. She also used the 6-point rubric on pages 316–317 to plan, draft, revise, and edit the writing. A rubric is a great tool to evaluate writing during the writing process.

Now let's use the same rubric to score the model. To do this, we'll focus on each trait separately, starting with Ideas. We'll use the top descriptor for each trait (column 6), along with examples from the model, to help us understand how the traits work together. How would you score Marie on each trait?

Ideas
- The claim is clearly stated.
- The review clearly presents both pros and cons about the website.

Marie clearly states her claim early on. She then mentions several things she likes and doesn't like about the website. Her balanced comments gave credibility and weight to her opinion.

[from the writing model]

The many menus offer multiple ways to find information; however, I found it difficult to decide which buttons would give me the best facts.

English Language Learners

BEGINNING

Categorizing Good and Bad On the board draw two columns with the headings *good* and *bad* with visuals next to the word, such as smiley face/frown face. Say *good, bad*. Students repeat. Show a picture and corresponding word such as *friend, share, smile, hurt, crash, sick.* Say the word; have students repeat. Students then place the picture and word into the correct column.

INTERMEDIATE

Pros and Cons Explain that *pro* means "positive" or "good" and *con* means "negative" or "bad." Draw a Pros and Cons Chart on the board with the topic *Summer Vacation*. Write *no homework* and *too hot* on the board. Students determine whether these are pros or cons and write in the appropriate column on their own Pros and Cons Charts. Have volunteers put their written answers in this format: *Summer vacation is good/bad because _____.*

Organization

- The structure of the writing organizes the evidence logically and is perfect for the topic.
- The conclusion follows and supports the argument presented.

By organizing each observation into a separate paragraph, Marie makes it easy to follow her review, point by point. The concluding section reflects back to her opening claim, which helps me better understand her overall message.

[from the writing model]

> In conclusion, I would strongly recommend www.spacecamp.com to anyone who is interested in learning about Space Camp. Even though it is a bit overdesigned, it is fast, reliable, and informative.

Voice

- The writer uses a confident, formal style.
- The voice is well suited for the audience and purpose.

Marie uses a style and language that show me she understands what I may have experienced when surfing the Internet. Even though she's relating directly to the reader in this paragraph, she doesn't make the mistake of letting her language become too casual. This makes it easy to trust her opinion and connect with her purpose.

[from the writing model]

> We all run across bad websites every now and then. Sometimes information is hard to retrieve because a site is too complex, or worse yet, the information is inaccurate or out of date. That's when we continue to search for a good site that loads quickly and contains just the information we're looking for.

- organize the review in a way that guides the reader? (Possible responses: The review is well organized. The introduction tells what the review is about and the conclusion summarizes the writer's findings. The body paragraphs presented the main points. The review was easy to follow.)

- maintain a convincing voice and a formal style? (Possible responses: The writer established and maintained a confident voice and formal style. The serious tone is convincing and supports the writer's purpose.)

ADVANCED

Main Idea/Details Explain to students *Main Idea* is the big idea. Give students a short sentence paragraph about a nonfiction topic such as *Earth* or *World War II*. Have students highlight the main idea, and then have them exchange with another student who highlights a detail in a different color. Another student highlights another detail and so on. When finished highlighting, have students check their answers by filling in a Main Idea Table as a group.

ADVANCED HIGH

Main Idea/Details Remind students that the *Main Idea* is the big idea. Read a short nonfiction book. As a group, come up with the main idea. Write it on the board, and have students write it on their Main Idea Table. Have students independently write the details onto the table. Cut it apart and exchange with another student. Ask students to put their main idea and details in order and write a fluid paragraph.

CCSS **C**ommon **C**ore **S**tate **S**tandards

SL.7.1.b: Follow rules for collegial discussions, track progress toward specific goals and deadlines, and define individual roles as needed. **SL.7.1.c:** Pose questions that elicit elaboration and respond to others' questions and comments with relevant observations and ideas that bring the discussion back on topic as needed.

Analyze
the Model

Week 1 • Day 5

Student Objectives

- Read a model website review. *(pp. 313–315)*
- Use the website review rubric. *(pp. 316–317)*
- Use the model website review to study Word Choice, Sentence Fluency, and Conventions. *(pp. 320–321)*

Continue Discussing the Traits

Use the following questions to continue analyzing the model.

Does the writer

- use compelling language? (Possible response: Yes, the writer's words are purposeful and direct. She defines words the reader may not know and uses simple, but strong, words to convince her reader.)

- vary sentences to help the text flow smoothly? (Possible responses: The writer varied the structures of her sentences. She even uses exclamatory sentences to make strong points!)

- use correct grammar, mechanics, and spelling? (Possible response: It's obvious that the review was carefully edited. The punctuation is clear and accurate.)

 Strategies for Writers Online
Go to **www.sfw.z-b.com** for additional online resources for students and teachers.

 **Word Choice**
- The words support the author's purpose and help convince the reader.
- Site-specific terms are clearly defined.

Marie effectively uses strong, descriptive words like *credible* and *trustworthy* when describing the website. These words help shape my view of the site, too, even though I've never visited it. She's also careful to define any words used on the website that her reader might not understand.

[from the writing model]

Even the photographs were recent, showing people with up-to-date clothing and haircuts. All of this leads me to believe the site is credible and trustworthy.

Sentence Fluency
- Transitions connect sentences, create variety, and clarify relationships among ideas.

Marie is very good at using transition words, like *further*, to show how ideas are related. At the same time, she keeps her writing interesting and lively by using all kinds of sentence structures. Transitions provide variety in sentence patterns and length.

[from the writing model]

I could even name friends and siblings with whom I wanted to camp. Further, I could type in my name as I wanted it to appear on my Space Camp patch. I thought that was a fantastic feature!

320 Argument Writing

Technology Tip · for 21st Century Literacies

Blogs can offer multiple reviewers' points of view. Create a class blog for posting students' work. Doing so will help organize students' writing while allowing you to direct specific audiences to your students' work. You'll want to decide when setting up the blog whether to make it private (i.e., not listed in search engines) or public, and how you'd like students to make their identities known (e.g., using a pen name, just a first name and last initial, or other method).

See **www.sfw.z-b.com** for further information about and links to these websites and tools.

Conventions
- Semicolons and colons are used correctly and effectively. The writing is easy to understand.

Marie's review doesn't contain any spelling or capitalization errors. In addition, she uses colons and semicolons correctly.

[from the writing model]

When I enter the Space Camp Web address in my computer's address bar, I am almost instantly taken to the site; I do not have to wait for images to load or for links to become functional.

Here, Marie uses a colon to show that the second sentence further explains the first.

[from the writing model]

But then I realized why: The application is long.

Presentation All paragraphs are indented.

My Turn!

I can't wait to start my own website review. I'll use the rubric and good writing strategies. Read on to see how I do it!

Differentiating Instruction

ENRICHMENT
Collect Choice Words Encourage students to be on the lookout for words that are particularly appealing or well-suited for their jobs. Have students display their collection of choice words on a bulletin board or other place where all students can benefit from exposure to these words.

REINFORCEMENT
Use the Computer Some students may benefit from using a computer to compose their drafts and/or to format the final copy. Arrange for students to work with a mentor, perhaps in the computer lab, to learn the various formatting features of the computer.

Presentation Explain to students that Presentation is just as important as any of the other traits. Neatness is always a priority, and text should be clearly handwritten in pen or typed using only a few, readable fonts. White space should be used to create neat margins. The lines of text in each part of the review should be spaced correctly. Paragraphs should be indented (using the tab key) and space should be left between paragraphs for ease of reading.

Think About the Traits After students have thoroughly discussed the model website review, ask them which traits they think are the most important in a review. Remind them that all of the traits are important in every piece of writing; however some traits play a more important role in specific types of writing. For example, some students may feel that **Organization** is very important in a review because if the writer's reasons are not presented in a logical order, the reader may get lost or confused. Others may feel that **Voice** is important because the writer needs to sound confident and knowledgeable to convince the reader. Still others may feel that **Word Choice** is a more important trait because strong, purposeful language helps strengthen the writer's message and informs the reader.

CCSS **Common Core State Standards**

SL.7.1.c: Pose questions that elicit elaboration and respond to others' questions and comments with relevant observations and ideas that bring the discussion back on topic as needed. **SL.7.1.d:** Acknowledge new information expressed by others and, when warranted, modify their own views.

Write
a Website Review

Week 2 • Day 1

Student Objectives

- Read and understand a prewriting strategy. *(p. 322)*

Prewrite

Focus on Ideas

Find a Website Read page 322 aloud. Work with students to brainstorm a list of interesting topics about which they would like to learn more. Use the website model on pages 313–315 and the writing partner's topic on this page as jumping off points.

After creating a list of potential topics, have students circle their favorites. To help them determine their writing purpose and audience, have them ask and answer this question: *Who would value my opinion about a website on my topic?* Go over their choices with them before they proceed. Then encourage them to find reliable websites about their topics online. They should then take notes on the websites that offer the most current information about their topics.

Online Writing Center

Provides **interactive graphic organizers** as well as a variety of graphic organizers in PDF format.

Prewrite
Focus on **Ideas**

The Rubric Says	The claim is clearly stated. The review clearly presents both pros and cons about the website.
Writing Strategy	Find a website about a topic of interest and list responses to it.

When my teacher said to write a website review, I immediately thought of something: My family is going to Stone Mountain, a state park here in Georgia, for a weekend getaway. So I entered *Stone Mountain* in my search engine, and, out of several choices, I selected www.stonemountainpark.com, the official website for the park. Then I took notes on the site to see if it is reliable, valid, and easy to use. I also wanted to see if the site would help me plan our trip.

My Notes

- ✔ "Contact Us" and "FAQ" pages helpful for park information
- ✔ Too much information on "Contact Us" page
- ✔ Logical categories and links
- ✔ Cool trip planner
- ✔ Helpful "Maps & Directions" page
- ✔ No special-needs section
- ✔ Some pages a bit cluttered
- ✔ Attractive and easy to use

Apply

Do some online research, and select a website to review. Take good notes. You'll need them when you write.

English Language Learners

BEGINNING/INTERMEDIATE

Transition Words Read the book *The Three Little Pigs.* On the board, write the transition words *first, next, after that,* and *finally.* Read the words and have students repeat. Have Beginning ELLs put the story pictures in order next to the correct transition word. Then ask Intermediate ELLs to say what happened in each picture. Write each sentence on the board using the transition word. Read the sentences as a group.

ADVANCED/ADVANCED HIGH

Transition Words Divide students into groups of two or three. Write *Alexa had a great time at her birthday party, but she couldn't believe what happened.* Have students write a four-sentence story using the sentence on the board as a story starter. They will take turns adding a sentence. Each sentence must use a transition word. When stories are finished, have groups read them to the class.

Prewrite   Focus on (Organization)

The Rubric Says	The structure of the writing organizes the evidence logically and is perfect for the topic.
Writing Strategy	Make a Pro-and-Con Chart to organize the responses.

Writer's Term

Pro-and-Con Chart

A **Pro-and-Con Chart** can help you organize your opinions and evaluate opposing claims. By presenting a website's **pros** (positive points) and **cons** (negative points) in order of importance, you can summarize the site and explain why you liked and/or disliked it.

Since I am building an argument about whether a website should be recommended, I will use a Pro-and-Con Chart to organize my comments. Then I can decide whether to separate the pros and cons or mix them when I talk about a single feature.

Pro-and-Con Chart

Pros	Cons
"Contact Us" and "FAQ" pages helpful for park information	Too much information on "Contact Us" page
Logical categories and links	No special-needs section
Cool trip planner	Some pages a bit cluttered
Helpful "Maps & Directions" page	
Attractive and easy to use	

Reflect

How will Tyler's Pro-and-Con Chart help him organize his writing into paragraphs?

Apply

Use a Pro-and-Con Chart to organize your responses.

Website Review 323

Conferencing

PEER TO PEER After each student has chosen a website to review, have writing partners share their notes about their websites. Partners can then work together to create and complete their Pro-and-Con Charts.

PEER GROUPS Have students work in groups of three or four. Have each student read his or her Pro-and-Con Chart aloud. Ask the other students in the group to take turns offering one comment or suggestion to make it more helpful.

TEACHER-LED Conference with individual students about their Pro-and-Con Charts. Before they speak with you, tell students to think of questions to ask you about creating their charts or how they plan to use the chart to write their drafts.

Student Objectives

• Make a Pro-and-Con Chart to organize responses. (*p. 323*)

Prewrite

Focus on (Organization)

Pro-and-Con Chart Explain to students that creating a Pro-and-Con Chart is a good way to list what they like and don't like about their websites. Point out that the chart has two columns, one to list the *Pros* (the things Tyler liked) and one to list the *Cons* (the things Tyler did not like). Explain that making Pro-and-Con Charts will help students to build strong reviews about a website's usability, reliability, and accuracy. Then have students list evidence for both the pros and the cons on their charts. After completing their charts, students should be ready to write their drafts.

Writer's Term

Pro-and-Con Chart Have students refer to their charts to make sure they have listed at least one important con (a negative consideration) about their websites.

CCSS Common Core State Standards

W.7.8: Gather relevant information from multiple print and digital sources, using search terms effectively; assess the credibility and accuracy of each source; and quote or paraphrase the data and conclusions of others while avoiding plagiarism and following a standard format for citation.

Write
a Website Review

Week 2 • Day 3

Student Objectives

• Use credible sources of information and fair language. (p. 324)

Draft

Focus on ⬭Voice⬭

Draft a Website Review Read page 324 aloud. Ask students to explain what it means to write a draft. Be sure that students understand that they will use their Pro-and-Con Charts to guide them through the drafting process. Also point out that their writing voices should sound confident, knowledgeable, and convincing. It's important that they use a formal tone that is fair and balanced, and shows respect for the reader.

Point out that the proofreader's marks are provided as a reference on page 325. To help them focus on getting their thoughts down on paper, suggest that they circle any words or parts in their drafts that they might want to change later.

 Writer's Term _____
Credible Website Review your school's Internet use policy. Enlist help from the school computer lab instructor or librarian, if needed.

Online Writing Center

Provides student eBooks with an **interactive writing pad** for drafting, revising, editing, and publishing.

Draft

Focus on ⬭Voice⬭

The Rubric Says	The writer uses a confident, formal style. The voice is well suited for the audience and purpose.
Writing Strategy	Use credible sources of information and fair language.

✎ **Writer's Term** _____
Credible Website
A **credible website** is an online source that contains accurate, trustworthy, up-to-date information. An example of a credible website is www.britannica. com. Information on this site comes from the same people who write the **Encyclopaedia Britannica,** a current and respected source.

Now that my Pro-and-Con Chart is done, I need to decide whether I want to recommend www.stonemountainpark.com to others. I *did* list more pros than cons, and I *did* find the site both useful and fun, so I'll definitely recommend this site.

The rubric says to use a confident voice and formal style. Also, my teacher reminded me to use a credible source. Now that I think about it, the site I choose to review will affect my ability to use a confident voice. If I write about a website that lacks credibility and lists false information, my voice will reflect that. The site I've selected is sound, so I'm good there.

Of course, the words I use also create voice. I'll use fair and balanced language so my reader can trust my information. I'll keep my style fun but formal so I'll be taken seriously. Now to get writing!

324 Argument Writing

Differentiating Instruction

ENRICHMENT

Find Reliable Websites Before they begin writing their drafts, have students evaluate several trustworthy websites in small groups. First, write a selected topic on the board, such as *Early Space Exploration.* Then, ask each student to find two or three websites about the topic, such as **www.nasa.gov** or **www.thinkquest.org**.

REINFORCEMENT

Read a Review Bring to class some age-appropriate movie reviews. Have pairs of students work together to identify the pros and cons given in each review. Have them use one color of ink to mark the pros and a different color to mark the cons. Ask them to evaluate the information in the review.

[DRAFT]

When Are You Going to Stone Mountain?

A Website Review by Tyler

How do you find out about places you've never been? How would you find information about the grand canyon or Mexico city? You can find a reliable website. Credible websites have uptodate information, good contact information, and are easy to use. My family is going on

[interesting and formal voice]

a weekend getaway to Stone Mountain, a popular vacation spot for people in Georgia. It is a large park containing a huge, bare rock that you can see from far away. But when is the park open? What can you do there? I found a great website to help me plan my trip: www. stonemountainpark.com. It is a credible, attractive, and easy-to-use website that contains full information on the events and sights of Stone Mountain.

[formal, balanced language]

Reflect

How would you describe the language Tyler uses in the beginning of his review?

Apply

Be sure to use fair and balanced language when discussing your chosen website. Keep your voice interesting and formal.

Website Review 325

Conferencing

PEER TO PEER Have partners exchange drafts to read. Tell students to think of two or three questions they would like to ask to clarify information. Have each student write his or her questions on adhesive notes and affix them to the appropriate places on his or her partner's draft.

PEER GROUPS Have students work in groups of four. Ask each student to pass his or her draft to the student on the right to read. That student writes one comment or suggestion on an adhesive note affixed to the draft and passes the draft along to the right. The review ends when everyone has received his or her own draft back with three comments.

TEACHER-LED Schedule conferences with pairs of students. Have them read each other's draft and coach them in giving constructive criticism.

Write
a Website Review

Week 2 • Day 4

Student Objectives

• Complete a draft.

Continue Drafting It is important that students are given ample time to draft their reviews. As conferencing is important throughout the writing process, be sure to also plan time for peer-to-peer, peer group, or teacher-led conferences. Remind students that this is the time to get their ideas down on paper in a creative and engaging way. Assure them that they will have plenty of time to fix any mistakes later.

CCSS **C**ommon **C**ore **S**tate **S**tandards
W.7.5: With some guidance and support from peers and adults, develop and strengthen writing as needed by planning, revising, editing, rewriting, or trying a new approach, focusing on how well purpose and audience have been addressed.

Website Review T325

Write
a Website Review

Week 2 • Day 5

Student Objectives

• State a clear claim and include at least one con. *(p. 326)*

Revise

Focus on Ideas

State One Con Read page 326 aloud. Explain that a review is strengthened when it presents both pros and cons. In doing so, the reader is convinced that the writer has researched the topic (website) objectively. Have students compare the changes Tyler made to his draft and ask whether he stated a con in a balanced, fair way. Have students defend their responses.

Read aloud the Apply text at the bottom of the page. Then refer students to their Pro-and-Con Charts and remind them to include important cons about their websites and support their claims with relevant evidence.

Strategies for Writers Online
Go to **www.sfw.z-b.com** for additional online resources for students and teachers.

Revise
Focus on (Ideas)

The Rubric Says	The claim is clearly stated. The review clearly presents both pros and cons about the website.
Writing Strategy	State a clear claim and include at least one con.

My claim is clear and supported by plenty of relevant information. But I need to include both pros *and* cons about the site. When I include a comment that's the opposite of my overall opinion, my reader is more likely to believe my claim, because I'm being fair to both sides.

[DRAFT]

There were even links embedded in the answer to almost every

Although, I must say, there was so much information listed here that it did seem a bit overwhelming.

question.

∧

[added a con]

Apply

Include both pros and cons in your website review for credibility.

326 Argument Writing

English Language Learners

BEGINNING/INTERMEDIATE
Descriptive Writing Show students a picture of a landscape. Ask students what they see in the picture. Write responses on the board. Read the words and point to the object in the picture. Have students repeat. Ask students questions about how things might look, feel, smell, sound, or taste. For example, *How does the grass feel?* Write students' responses on the board, read them, and have students repeat.

ADVANCED/ADVANCED HIGH
Descriptive Writing Show students a picture of a landscape or city. Tell students they are going to write a descriptive paragraph about the picture. Encourage them to visualize themselves in the picture. Ask, *What do you smell, hear, feel, taste, and see?* Have students fill in an Observation Chart. Finally, have students use information from the chart to write a descriptive paragraph.

Revise

Focus on Word Choice

The Rubric Says	The words support the author's purpose and help convince the reader. Site-specific terms are clearly defined.
Writing Strategy	Use words with the right connotation.

The rubric says I should use words that support my purpose. I think www.stonemountainpark.com is an excellent site, and I want my reader to agree. One way I can convince the reader is to use words with positive connotations, that is, words that have positive ideas or images associated with them. As I reread my draft, I came across some descriptive words that could be stronger. By using words with a positive connotation, like *top-notch*, I'll strengthen my writing and message.

[DRAFT]

You can edit your trip planner at any time so that it shows only the things you want to do. I printed out my trip planner so that I could go over it with Mom and Dad. This tool is ~~great~~ top-notch; it really helped me.

[used strong positive word]

Reflect

How have Tyler's revisions affected your opinion of his review?

Apply

Use words with appropriate associations to describe your website.

Website Review **327**

Conferencing

PEER TO PEER Have partners exchange drafts. Ask them to list any words that may be slang expressions or sound too casual for a review. Also have them list any domain-specific words they find that are not clearly defined for the reader.

PEER GROUPS Working in groups of three or four, have each student pass his or her draft to the student on his or her right to read. Ask readers to list any confusing or general words on an adhesive note and attach it to the draft.

TEACHER-LED Schedule conferences with individual students to read their drafts. Discuss any words that may not convey the writer's intended meaning. Be sure students use a word resource to find replacement words and supply definitions for domain-specific vocabulary.

Write
a Website Review

Student Objectives

- Use words with the right connotation. *(p. 327)*

Revise

Focus on Word Choice

Avoid Overused Words Ask a volunteer to read page 327 aloud. Have students talk about **Word Choice,** beginning with Tyler's revision in his draft. Explain that the connotation of a word is the feeling one gets from a word, as opposed to the denotation, which is the dictionary meaning. Tyler chose a word that has a very strong positive connotation. Discuss how the meaning of the sentence would change if Tyler used another word, for example, *helpful, nice,* or *excellent.*

Encourage students to use a thesaurus to choose the words that convey the desired meaning.

CCSS **C**ommon **C**ore **S**tate **S**tandards

L.7.4.c: Consult general and specialized reference materials (e.g., dictionaries, glossaries, thesauruses), both print and digital, to find the pronunciation of a word or determine or clarify its precise meaning or its part of speech. **W.7.1.b:** Support claim(s) with logical reasoning and relevant evidence, using accurate, credible sources and demonstrating an understanding of the topic or text. **W.7.1.c:** Use words, phrases, and clauses to create cohesion and clarify the relationships among claim(s), reasons, and evidence.

Write a Website Review

Week 3 • Day 2

Student Objectives

• Vary sentences by using transition words. *(p. 328)*

Revise

Focus on  Sentence Fluency

Transition Words Discuss how to use transition words to make connections, clarify relationships between ideas, and improve the flow of sentences. Provide a set of short, related sentences, such as: *The homepage is colorful and interactive. It takes a long time to load.* Then ask students to connect the ideas by using compare-and-contrast transition words. (Possible responses: 1. Even though the homepage is colorful and interactive, it takes a long time to load. 2. The homepage is colorful and interactive, but it takes a long time to load.) Point out that a comma is needed to separate the clauses.

Writer's Term _____

Transition Words Explain that the example transition words are used to connect details for comparison/contrast and to show time. Other transition words add information, clarify, emphasize, and summarize.

Writing a Website Review

Revise — Focus on Sentence Fluency

The Rubric Says	Transitions connect sentences, create variety, and clarify relationships among ideas.
Writing Strategy	Vary sentences by using transition words.

The rubric says to use transitions to connect sentences and ideas and add variety. Transitions make the flow of the sentences and the ideas smooth. A paper with smooth sentences is enjoyable to read and holds the reader's attention. Here's a paragraph that could use some transitions. I'll add them now.

Writer's Term _____

Transition Words

Transition words tie ideas together and move writing from one idea to the next. **Compare-and-contrast transition words** include **similarly, likewise, although, however, yet,** and **but.** **Time-order transition words** include **before, after, during, first, second, third, next, soon, later, finally,** and **then.**

[DRAFT] — [added transition words]

Although
~~The~~ website is excellent in most areas, one area is weak, what about accesability for special-needs patrons? My father will go with us to Stone Mountain and he uses a wheelchair. I couldn't find a section on the site that discusses acomodations for people with special needs. Other websites I've looked at have sections that explain special parking ramps, and general accesability of attractions; however,
I had to search through the information on each sub page of this site just to find one or two sentences on accesability.

Apply

Use transition words to write smooth and interesting sentences.

328 Argument Writing

Optional Revising Lessons

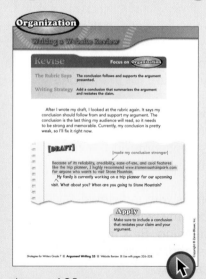

Argument 25

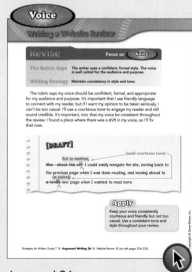

Argument 26

Go to ▶ *Strategies for Writers Grade 7 CD-ROM*

| The Rubric Says | Semicolons and colons are used correctly and effectively. The writing is easy to understand. |
| Writing Strategy | Choose punctuation for effect. |

✏ Writer's Term

Colons and Semicolons

A **colon** is used after the greeting in a business letter, between the city of publication and the publisher in a bibliographic entry, to introduce a list or series, and to separate two clauses when the second clause further explains the first. A **semicolon** is used in place of a comma and a conjunction when combining two related independent clauses.

Before I'm done, I need to check my spelling, punctuation, and capitalization. The rubric also says to make sure I used colons and semicolons correctly, so I'll check that now.

[DRAFT]

[correct use of a semicolon]

The Stone Mountain website also has a great tool called a trip planner; it helps people plan their trips. It works a bit like an online shopping cart. There is an "Add to My Trip Plan" link at the top of most of the park's events and activities pages. If you click on the link, the activity will immediately be added to your planner; a description of the event will then show up in your trip planner.

[corrected a colon error]

Reflect

Did Tyler catch all his errors? How have his edits improved his writing? What effect does punctuation have on the writer's message?

Apply — **Conventions**

Edit your draft for spelling and grammar, making sure to use colons and semicolons correctly.

For more practice with colons and semicolons, use the exercises on the next two pages.

Website Review **329**

elated Grammar Practice _____

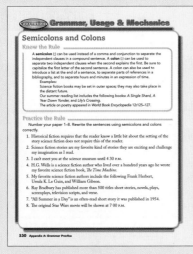

Student Edition page 530

Go to ▷ Appendix A: Grammar Practice

Write
a Website Review

Student Objectives

- Choose punctuation for effect.
- Use colons and semicolons correctly. *(p. 329)*

Edit

Focus on  Conventions

Edit for Accuracy Read page 329 aloud. Point out Tyler's edits and discuss how they improve the draft.

Use the mini-lessons on pages T330–T331 for students who need practice to use colons and semicolons correctly. Then have students complete pages 330 and 331.

✏ Writer's Term _____

Colons and Semicolons Point out that a colon has a very specific job to do. A colon alerts the reader to information, similar to "sounding a drum roll." Go on to explain that a semicolon is a "sophisticated" comma. Its job is to combine longer sentences of closely related ideas.

CCSS **C**ommon **C**ore **S**tate **S**tandards

W.7.1.c: Use words, phrases, and clauses to create cohesion and clarify the relationships among claim(s), reasons, and evidence. **L.7.1:** Demonstrate command of the conventions of standard English grammar and usage when writing or speaking.

Conventions

Mini-Lesson

Student Objectives

• Use semicolons correctly. *(p. 330)*

Semicolons

Have students read the Know the Rule box on page 330. Then write the following on the board: *Julie filled her suitcase with the following items; suntan lotion, a bathing suit, a robe, a beach towel, sandals, and lip gloss.*

Ask students if the sentence is punctuated correctly. (no) Now call on a volunteer to explain how to edit the sentence. (Change the semicolon to a colon.) Remind students that a colon, not a semicolon, should be used to introduce a list.

Now write the following on the board: *Many are called few are chosen.*

Ask students if this sentence is punctuated correctly. (no) Call on a volunteer to explain how to edit the sentence. (Add a semicolon after *called.*) Ask why a semicolon should be used instead of a colon. (because two related independent clauses are being combined)

Remind students that colons and semicolons have very specific uses and that they should be careful not to confuse these punctuation marks with commas or periods.

Online Writing Center

 Provides **interactive grammar games** and **practice activities** in student eBook.

Semicolons

Know the Rule

> A **semicolon** is used in place of a comma and a conjunction when combining two related independent clauses to make a compound sentence. Note that a semicolon goes outside quotation marks.
>   **Example:** Bicycles used to be much harder to ride; they didn't come with multiple speeds.
> Semicolons are often misused in writing. Understanding the function of semicolons will help you use them properly when you write.

Practice the Rule

Write each sentence with correct punctuation on a separate sheet of paper.

1. Last year's dance was horrible. it rained so heavily, the school roof leaked.
2. Buckets were placed all over the gym floor to catch the water dripping from the roof. people kept tripping over them.
3. Students were soaked by the heavy downpour when they arrived. many joked that they should have worn bathing suits!
4. The funny thing is that bathing suits would have been appropriate. the theme of the dance was "Let's Have a Beach Party."
5. Happily, the students were good sports about it all. everyone had fun in spite of the water.
6. The rain cleared up during the dance. by the time we left the sky was clear and dry.
7. This year things should be better. the roof has been repaired.
8. The theme for the dance is "Desert Moon". maybe the weather will be hot and dry to match!
9. I'm the chair of the dance committee. I'm really hoping everything goes right this year.
10. I'll do my best to make sure the refreshments, music, and decorations are great. there's nothing I can do about the weather, though.

Related Grammar Practice

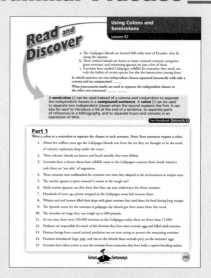

Page 201

Go to ➡ **G.U.M. Student Practice Book**

Colons

Know the Rule

Use a **colon**
- to introduce a list or a series at the end of a complete sentence.
  Example: The art kit included the following: paint, brushes, and crayons.
- after the greeting in a business letter.
  Example: Dear Madam:
- between the city of publication and the publisher in a bibliographic entry.
  Example: Columbus: Zaner-Bloser
- to separate two clauses when the second clause is a direct result of the first.
  Example: The cupboards were bare: We went shopping.

Colons, like semicolons, are often misused. Understanding the function of colons will help you use them correctly in your own writing.

Practice the Rule

Write each sentence or word group with correct punctuation on a separate sheet of paper.

1. A good first-aid kit contains the following items: antibiotic cream, cotton gauze, and bandages.
2. Dad forgot to set his alarm last night: he missed the train this morning.
3. Chicago: Fun Books, Inc.
4. Uncle Joel's package contained several things: two books, six packs of gum, and a feather.
5. Watch for these birds on our hike: chickadees, cardinals, and doves.
6. Dear Mr. Puglia:
7. Boston: Beacon Press
8. Adam didn't know the answer: he grabbed a dictionary and looked it up.
9. Dear Principal O'Toole:
10. Here's what I like on my tacos: lettuce, tomato, avocado, and cheese.

Conventions

Mini-Lesson

Student Objectives
- Use colons correctly. *(p. 331)*

Colons

Have students practice using colons in the examples in this exercise. Review their answers and go over possible rewrites with them. Before asking students to exchange drafts to have their editing partners proofread them, make sure students can use colons and semicolons in their own writing. Suggest places in their reviews where they can utilize a semicolon or a colon. Then have writing partners trade papers and proofread one another's work. When they finish, have pairs exchange reviews and discuss the edits.

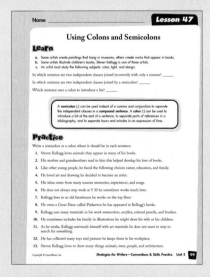

Page 99

Go to ➡ *Grammar Practice Masters*

CCSS Common Core State Standards
L.7.2: Demonstrate command of the conventions of standard English capitalization, punctuation, and spelling when writing.

Write
a Website Review

Week 3 • Day 4

Student Objectives

- Discuss preparation for publishing and presentation. (p. 332)
- Use a final editing checklist to publish their work. (p. 332)

Publish ⁺Presentation

Publishing Strategy Use the final website review to discuss publishing and presentation. Ask students to point out the presentation elements that make it stand out as a polished piece. (Possible responses: interesting title; strong introduction, indented paragraphs; sentence variety, visuals) Then ask students if they like Tyler's choice for sharing his website review. Tell the class that his choice is not the only option for publishing his work. Invite students to name other ways they could publish their own website reviews.

Have each student make a checklist to prepare a final copy. Encourage students to make a final evaluation of their reviews before publishing them. Then have students publish copies of their work in a class book or on the school's website.

Strategies for Writers Online
Go to **www.sfw.z-b.com** for additional online resources for students and teachers.

Publish ⁺Presentation

Publishing Strategy   Submit the review to the appropriate website.

Presentation Strategy   Indent or add space between the paragraphs.

I'm done! Since the concern I had about the information on accessibility was pretty serious, I've decided to submit my website review to the park's director. Hopefully, my report can help bring about actual change! Before I send it though, I need to make sure I indent each paragraph, or, if I use block-style paragraphs, I'll leave space between them to help the reader visually. Then I'll read my review one last time to make sure I've done everything on my final checklist.

My Final Checklist

Did I—

- ✔ fix any spelling, grammar, and punctuation errors?
- ✔ use semicolons correctly in my writing?
- ✔ use colons properly and effectively?
- ✔ indent or leave space between paragraphs?

Apply

Make a checklist to check your work. Then make a final copy to publish.

332   Argument Writing

Differentiating Instruction

ENRICHMENT

Publishing Options After polishing their own website reviews, have students brainstorm ways to publish them, such as a collection in a class e-book, a handy reference on a school website, or a series of reviews in the school newspaper. Have them make a list of three or four ideas. Encourage them to discuss the pros and cons of each idea before presenting them to the class. Have all students vote on their favorite option.

ENRICHMENT

Adding Pictures and Illustrations Allow students time to add pictures and illustrations to their reviews. If possible, demonstrate how to access and position visuals on the page. After enhancing their reviews, have students write a set of tips to use anytime they need to incorporate visuals into their writing.

When Are You Going to Stone Mountain?

A Website Review by Tyler

How do you find out about places you've never been? How would you find information about the Grand Canyon or Mexico City? You can find a reliable website. Credible websites have up-to-date information, good contact information, and are easy to use. My family is going on a weekend getaway to Stone Mountain, a popular vacation spot for people in Georgia. It is a large park containing a huge, bare rock that you can see from far away. But when is the park open? What can you do there? I found a great website to help me plan my trip: www.stonemountainpark.com. It is a credible, attractive, and easy-to-use website that contains full information on the events and sights of Stone Mountain.

Several features of www.stonemountainpark.com show that it is credible. A main feature is the many ways to contact the park for information. First, the "Contact Us" button leads to a well-organized subpage that contains several links such as "Directions to the Park," "Operating Schedule," and "Tickets/Prices." Here, you can also find 24-hour local and nationwide park phone numbers, along with the option to fill in some personal information so that park employees can electronically answer your questions and send you an e-newsletter. Second, the "FAQ" button leads to yet another subpage that contains categorized answers to frequently asked questions. This page was very helpful since many of my own questions were the same as some of the FAQs. There were even links embedded in the answer to almost every question. Although, I must say, there was so much information listed here that it did seem a bit overwhelming.

Technology Tip for 21st Century Literacies

Posting to a blog is as much about offering a review as it is about opening your thoughts to the comments and feedback of others. Invite students to post comments in response to class blog entries or others you identify as appropriate. Evaluate different kinds of feedback and discuss what writers find helpful and genuinely responsive. Remind students that along with posts, images, and other digital content they post online, the comments they share with others are also part of their ongoing, searchable digital footprints.

See **www.sfw.z-b.com** for further information about and links to these websites and tools.

Write a Website Review

Week 3 • Day 5

Student Objectives

- Use a website review rubric. (pp. 316–317)
- Share a published website review. (pp. 333–335)

Indent Paragraphs Refer students to the final website review on pages 333–335. Ask them to notice how the writer indented the paragraphs as he typed. Demonstrate how to use the tab feature on a word processor to indent paragraphs. Also point out that students should set neat margins, indent or use a space to separate paragraphs, and select one or two clear fonts.

Reflecting on a Website Review

Have a volunteer read aloud the question in the Reflect box on page 335. Then ask students the following:

- How did you do using all the traits of a website review?

Have students jot down their response to the question in a personal writer's journal or in their notes on the chapter.

CCSS Common Core State Standards

W.7.4: Produce clear and coherent writing in which the development, organization, and style are appropriate to task, purpose, and audience. **W.7.6:** Use technology, including the Internet, to produce and publish writing and link to and cite sources as well as to interact and collaborate with others, including linking to and citing sources.

The Stone Mountain website also has a great tool called a trip planner; it helps people plan their trips. It works a bit like an online shopping cart. There is an "Add to My Trip Plan" link at the top of most of the park's events and activities pages. If you click on the link, the activity will immediately be added to your planner: A description of the event will then show up in your trip planner. You can edit your trip planner at any time so that it shows only the things you want to do. I printed out my trip planner so that I could go over it with Mom and Dad. This tool is top-notch; it really helped me.

In addition, the maps on www.stonemountainpark.com are a great feature; they can be accessed from the homepage by clicking on the "Maps & Directions" button. Grid patterns overlay the park map. When you click on one square in the grid, that segment pops up larger and more detailed. When you click on the "Written Driving Directions" link, you are given a written description of driving directions to the park, from any one of nine different regions. This is great because some people aren't very good at reading maps!

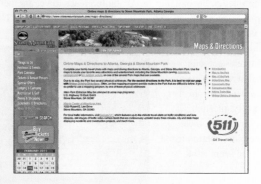

Although the website is excellent in most areas, one area is weak: What about accessibility for special-needs patrons? My father will go with us to Stone Mountain, and he uses a wheelchair. I couldn't find a section on the site that discusses accommodations for people with special needs. Other websites I've looked at have sections that explain special parking, ramps, and general accessibility of attractions; however, I had to search through the information on each subpage of this site just to find one or two sentences on accessibility.

Other than that one complaint, though, I found this website to be very attractive and easy to use. It loads almost instantly, as do all of the features. Although some of the pages are a bit cluttered, most of the pages are spacious and easy to read. Not to mention, I could easily navigate the site, moving back to the previous page when I was done reading, and moving ahead to an entirely new page when I wanted to read more.

Because of its reliability, credibility, ease-of-use, and cool features like the trip planner, I highly recommend www.stonemountainpark.com for anyone who wants to visit Stone Mountain. My family is currently working on a trip planner for our upcoming visit. What about you? When are you going to Stone Mountain?

Reflect

How did Tyler do using all the traits of a website review? Check his writing against the rubric, and don't forget to use the rubric to check your own work, too.

Response to Literature Planner

WEEK 1

Day 1
Introduce
a Response to Literature

Student Objectives
- Review the elements of a response to literature.
- Consider purpose and audience.
- Learn the traits of argument writing.

Student Activities
- Read and discuss **What's in a Response to Literature?** *(p. 336)*
- Read and discuss **Why Write a Response to Literature?** *(p. 337)*
- Read **Linking Argument Writing Traits to a Response to Literature.** *(p. 338)*

Day 2
Analyze
Read a Response to Literature

Student Objectives
- Read a model response to literature.

Student Activities
- Read **"Tables Turned."** *(p. 339)*

Day 3
Analyze
Introduce the Rubric

Student Objectives
- Learn to read a rubric.

Student Activities
- Review **"Tables Turned."** *(p. 339)*
- Read and discuss **Response to Literature Rubric.** *(pp. 340–341)*
- Participate in a peer conference.

WEEK 2

Day 1
Write
Prewrite: Ideas

Student Objectives
- List the theme and reactions to the literature.

Student Activities
- Read and discuss **Prewrite: Focus on Ideas.** *(p. 346)*
- Apply the prewriting strategy.

Day 2
Write
Prewrite: Organization

Student Objectives
- Use a Paragraph Organizer to plan the writing.

Student Activities
- Read and discuss **Prewrite: Focus on Organization.** *(p. 347)*
- Apply the strategy.
- Participate in a peer conference.

Day 3
Write
Draft: Organization

Student Objectives
- Use exact words.

Student Activities
- Read and discuss **Draft: Focus on Word Choice.** *(p. 348)*
- Apply the drafting strategy by usin a Paragraph Organizer to begin a draft.

WEEK 3

Day 1
Write
Revise: Organization

Student Objectives
- Strengthen the conclusion.

Student Activities
- Read and discuss: **Revise: Focus on Organization.** *(p. 351)*
- Reflect on a model draft.
- Apply the revising strategy.
- Participate in a peer conference.

Day 2
Write
Revise: Sentence Fluency

Student Objectives
- Write different kinds of sentences.

Student Activities
- Read and discuss: **Revise: Focus on Sentence Fluency.** *(p. 352)*
- Reflect on the model draft.
- Apply the revising strategy.

Note: Optional Revising Lessons appear on the *Strategies for Writers* CD-ROM.

Day 3
Write
Edit: Conventions

Student Objectives
- Make sure to use the right word.

Student Activities
- Read and discuss **Edit: Focus on Conventions.** *(p. 353)*
- Reflect on a model draft.
- Apply the editing strategy.

Note: Teach the Conventions mini-lessons *(pp. 354–355)* if needed.

Analyze
Ideas, Organization, and Voice

Student Objectives
- Read a model response to literature.
- Use the response to literature rubric.
- Use the model response to literature to study Ideas, Organization, and Voice.

Student Activities
- Review **"Tables Turned."** *(p. 339)*
- Read and discuss **Using the Rubric to Study the Model.** *(pp. 342–343)*

Analyze
Word Choice, Sentence Fluency, and Conventions

Student Objectives
- Read a model response to literature.
- Use the response to literature rubric.
- Use the model response to literature to study Word Choice, Sentence Fluency, and Conventions.

Student Activities
- Review **"Tables Turned."** *(p. 339)*
- Read and discuss **Using the Rubric to Study the Model.** *(pp. 344–345)*

Write
Draft

Student Objectives
- Complete a draft.

Student Activities
- Finish writing the draft. *(p. 349)*
- Participate in a peer conference.

Write
Revise: Ideas

Student Objectives
- Choose quotations that support the thesis.

Student Activities
- Read and discuss **Revise: Focus on Ideas.** *(p. 350)*
- Reflect on the model draft.
- Apply the revising strategy.

Write
Publish: +Presentation

Student Objectives
- Discuss preparation for publishing and presentation.
- Use a final editing checklist to publish their work.

Student Activities
- Read and discuss **Publish: +Presentation.** *(p. 356)*
- Apply the publishing strategy.

Write
Publish: +Presentation

Student Objectives
- Use a response to literature rubric.
- Share a published response to literature.

Student Activities
- Share their work.
- Use the rubric to reflect upon and evaluate the model and their own writing. *(pp. 340–341; 357–359)*

complete the chapter in fewer days, combine the learning objectives and activities in a way that supports students as they write.

Resources at-a-Glance

Grammar, Usage & Mechanics

Differentiating Instruction

For additional Differentiating Instruction activities, see Strategies for Writers *Extensions Online at* **www.sfw.z-b.com.**

English Language Learners

Conferencing

Technology Tip

 Connection Letter
Reproducible letter (in English and Spanish) appears on the *Strategies for Writers* CD-ROM and at **www.sfw.z-b.com.**

Online Writing Center

Provides IWB resources, interactive games and practice activities, videos, eBooks, and a virtual file cabinet.

 Strategies for Writers Online

Go to **www.sfw.z-b.com** for free online resources for students and teachers.

Introduce
a Response to Literature

Week 1 • Day 1

Student Objectives

- Review the elements of a response to literature. *(p. 336)*
- Consider purpose and audience. *(p. 337)*
- Learn the traits of argument writing. *(p. 338)*

What's a Response to Literature?

Discuss with students the definition of a response to literature. Explain to students that the purpose of this type of argument writing is to convince others to read a book, poem, or play that the writer has read and recommends. Point out to students that this chapter will help them collect ideas and organize a response, specifically, a literary analysis. Also tell students that they will be asked to respond to a variety of literature over the course of their studies.

What's in a Response to Literature?

Read and discuss with students the elements of a response to literature listed on page 336. Explain that some of the elements are also common to other forms of argument writing, such as editorials and website reviews.

 Strategies for Writers Online
Go to **www.sfw.z-b.com** for additional online resources for students and teachers.

What's a **Response to Literature?**

It's an essay I write to share my ideas about something I've read. I just read a great story, and I will be writing a literary analysis that I hope will convince people to accept my interpretation of the story.

What's in a **Response to Literature?**

Summary
A response to literature starts out with a summary of what the writer read. The summary of a story should give a brief description of the main ideas of the plot and important characters.

Claim
The claim is the heart of the response to literature. It states the writer's opinion of the story.

Supporting Evidence
These are details that support the claim and build the argument. Supporting evidence can include quotations from the story, paraphrases (restating text or passages in the writer's own words), details from the story, and the writer's own knowledge.

Analysis
In a literary analysis, the writer offers an interpretation of the literature. For example, a writer could examine the theme and then discuss what it means or how the characters get the theme across to the readers.

Argument Text Exemplars (Response to Literature)

Johnston, Norma. *Harriet: The Life and World of Harriet Beecher Stowe.* **Beech Tree Books, 1994.** Complete with 20 black-and-white photos, this biography explores the compelling life and works of Harriet Beecher Stowe, author of *Uncle Tom's Cabin.*

Nel, Philip. *The Annotated Cat: Under the Hats of Seuss and His Cats.* **Random House Books for Young Readers, 2007.** Nel provides insight into the evolution of Dr. Suess' books, *The Cat in the Hat* and *The Cat in the Hat Comes Back,* two books that changed the landscape of children's literature and learning to read.

Why write a **Response to Literature?**

Here are some reasons I can think of to respond to literature.

Argument

When I get excited about a story, or have ideas about what I've read, I like to share them and try to convince others to agree with my opinion. That way they might decide to read the story themselves!

Information

Responding to literature is a way to let other readers know about a story they might enjoy. Or it might be a way to let readers know that this is a story that would not interest them.

Understanding

As I write, I can learn a lot about how I think or feel about something I've read. Sometimes I surprise myself!

Why write a Response to Literature?

Read and discuss with students the reasons for writing a response to literature listed on page 337. Point out that all writing has a purpose and is aimed at a specific audience. These authentic purposes help writers shape their writing. Someone writing to convince others of their opinion will include compelling examples from the piece of literature that support the writer's main points. A person writing to inform may include memorable examples and factual information. A person writing to understand will share personal feelings and reflections. Encourage students to think about their own reasons for writing a response to literature and how their reasons, or rationale, will affect the tone and style of their responses.

Petit, Jayne. *Maya Angelou: Journey of the Heart.* Puffin, 1998. Drawn from Maya Angelou's autobiographies, *Journey of the Heart* presents the life and challenges of this devoted writer, activist, and poet. Readers catch a glimpse into the events that inspired her work in a book that is true to the voice of Maya Angelou.

Wheeler, Jill C. *R.L. Stine.* ABDO & Daughters, 1996. Learn more about this humorous author whose mission is to have children turn to reading for entertainment and who is not afraid to tackle frightening story lines in his novels.

CCSS **C**ommon **C**ore **S**tate **S**tandards

SL.7.1: Engage effectively in a range of collaborative discussions (one-on-one, in groups, and teacher-led) with diverse partners on *grade 7 topics, texts, and issues,* building on each others' ideas and expressing their own clearly.

Introduce
a Response to Literature

Linking Argument Writing Traits to a Response to Literature

Read the introduction to page 338 aloud to help students understand that they will follow Tyler as he models using the writing process and the argument writing traits together. As they follow Tyler, students will see how the Argument Writing Traits have been adapted and applied to writing a response to literature. They will see that a response to literature can be used to express an opinion and, therefore, has many factors in common with other types of argument writing. However, the particular audience and purpose of a response to literature determine how the traits are used.

Online Writing Center

Provides six **interactive anchor papers** for each mode of writing.

T338 Argument Writing

Linking Argument Writing Traits to a Response to Literature

In this chapter, you will try to convince your reader to believe your claim about a piece of literature. This type of argument writing is called a response to literature. Tyler will guide you through the stages of the writing process: Prewrite, Draft, Revise, Edit, and Publish. In each stage, Tyler will show you important writing strategies that are linked to the Argument Writing Traits below.

Argument Writing Traits

 Ideas
- clearly stated claims, often balanced by alternate or opposing claims
- supporting evidence from accurate and credible sources

 Organization
- a strong introduction that presents the writer's position
- reasons and evidence that are organized logically
- a conclusion that follows and supports the argument
- transitions that clarify the relationships between the claim(s), the supporting evidence, and any counterclaims

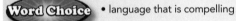 **Voice**
- a voice that supports the writer's purpose

Word Choice
- language that is compelling

 Sentence Fluency
- sentences that vary in length and begin in different ways

 Conventions
- no or few errors in grammar, usage, mechanics, and spelling

Before you write, read Lucinda Juarez's response to literature on the next page. Then use the response to literature rubric on pages 340–341 to decide how well she did. (You might want to look back at What's in a Response to Literature? on page 336, too!)

338 Argument Writing

Argument Writing Traits in a Response to Literature

 Ideas The review clearly states and supports the writer's opinion. Evidence from the source is presented to convince the reader.

 **Organization** The review includes a strong introduction that presents the writer's opinion. Reasons (main ideas) and evidence (supporting details) are organized logically. Logical transitions guide the reader. The conclusion follows from and supports the writer's position.

 **Voice** The writer uses a convincing voice and formal style that support the writer's purpose and connect to the audience.

Tables Turned
by Lucinda Juarez

I just read a story that really made me laugh, "The Ransom of Red Chief," by O. Henry. The characters were funny, the story just did not let up, and the plot has a surprise twist that I guarantee you have never come across before in any of your reading. It was over the top, strange, and hilarious. ←Claim

The three main characters are two kidnappers, Sam and Bill, and their victim, if you can call him that. Actually, it is the kidnappers who become the victims. But let me backtrack a bit. The two kidnappers are con men who need some extra money to pull off a fraudulent land scheme. They decide that the most brilliant way to get their needed funds is to kidnap the son of the richest man in town and make the father pay a steep ransom. They accomplish this and take him to a cave. What the kidnappers didn't count on was that, instead of feeling kidnapped, the boy is thrilled to be out. "I've never had so much fun in all my life," he tells them. The kid imagines himself to be an Indian chief (the "Red Chief" in the story's title). His boundless imagination comes up with various, relentless activities.

Summary

As Sam tries to work out the setup and details of collecting the kidnap money, Bill's job is to try to keep the kid amused. "Red Chief" finds endless ways to torture Bill, including trying to scalp him, putting a red-hot boiled potato down his back, and riding him like a horse. As the kidnappers' unexpected ordeal continues, Sam and Bill actually lower the ransom they had in mind. In the end, they go one step further—they actually pay the father money in order to get rid of him! That's a very original plot and turn of events. ⌐Supporting Evidence⌐

The author, O. Henry, is a fantastic storyteller. He really knows how to give life to his characters. I thoroughly enjoyed myself, and at times had to laugh out loud, too. The tale is outrageously ironic, to be sure, and it makes you think about how the tables can turn regardless of how well and cleverly you think you have planned! The kidnappers certainly did not plan on having to pay a ransom to be able to return "Red Chief" to his father.

Work Cited
Analysis

Henry, O. "The Ransom of Red Chief." *The Literature Network.* Jalic, n.d.
    Web. 21 April 2011.

Word Choice The writer's language is convincing. Word choice creates meaning and cohesion among the writer's claim and supporting evidence.

Sentence Fluency Sentences vary in length and begin in different ways. The writer's ideas flow smoothly and hold the reader's attention from beginning to end.

Conventions The writer has proofread carefully to make sure there are no or few errors in grammar, usage, mechanics, and spelling to distract the reader.

Analyze
the Model

Student Objectives

• Read a model response to literature. *(p. 339)*

Read the Model

Read "Tables Turned" on page 339 aloud to the class. Ask students to listen for the writer's claim and supporting evidence as you read the model. Then ask them to notice how the response is organized. Also ask students to think about how the formal writing style conveys the writer's purpose and assures the audience that the writer knows the topic well.

Elements of a Response to Literature

Have students refer to What's in a Response to Literature? on page 336 as you refer to the model response. Discuss the notes written on the model to enhance students' understanding of the terms. Be sure to talk about how the writer avoids plagiarism by citing the source in the Work Cited section at the end of the response. Point out that they will now use the model to analyze the traits of a good response to literature.

CCSS **Common Core State Standards**
R/Inf.7.1: Cite several pieces of textual evidence to support analysis of what the text says explicitly as well as inferences drawn from the text.

Analyze
the Model

Student Objectives

- Learn to read a rubric. (pp. 340–341)

Use the Rubric

Explain the Rubric Explain that a rubric is a tool for planning, improving, and assessing a piece of writing. Tell students that a rubric helps a writer focus on key elements, or traits, in writing (**Ideas, Organization, Voice, Word Choice, Sentence Fluency, Conventions,** and **Presentation**).

Point out that column 6 describes a very good response to literature, one that has received the highest score in all categories. This is what students should strive for in their own writing.

Discuss the Rubric As students measure their own papers against the rubric, they should first decide whether the papers fall on the left of the rubric (use the trait well) or on the right (need improvement in using the trait). By examining their papers more closely, students can refine their scores for each trait to single numbers.

Online Writing Center

Provides a variety of **interactive rubrics,** including 4-, 5-, and 6-point models.

Rubric

Use this 6-point rubric to plan and score a response to literature.

	6	5	4
Ideas	The writing shows an in-depth understanding of the literature. Quotations support the writer's claim and are accurately referenced.	The writing shows an understanding of the literature. Quotations support the writer's claim.	The writing shows a partial understanding of the literature. Quotations do not fully support the writer's claim.
Organization	The introduction is engaging and states the claim, the body organizes the reasons in a compelling way, and the concluding section is strong.	The introduction states the claim, the body organizes the reasons, and the concluding section refers back to the claim.	The introduction introduces the literature and the body provides reasons, but the concluding section is weak.
Voice	A consistent formal style and personal voice engage the reader and support the writer's claim.	A formal style and personal voice engage the reader and support the writer's claim most of the time.	The reader catches glimpses of the writer's style and voice, but they are inconsistent.
Word Choice	Precise language conveys the message to the reader.	Precise language is used most of the time.	Precise language is used occasionally but not consistently.
Sentence Fluency	A variety of sentence structures contributes to the rhythm and flow. The writer's ideas are easy to follow.	Most of the sentence structures are varied. Most of the writer's ideas are easy to follow.	Several sentences in a row share the same structure. They slow the flow of ideas.
Conventions	The writing has been carefully edited. Homophones, if used, are correct.	Minor errors are present but do not interfere with meaning. Homophones are correct.	A few errors may cause confusion. One or two homophones may be used incorrectly.

✛ Presentation The literary analysis is neat and legible.

CCSS Common Core State Standards

Response to Literature

Strategies for Writers was designed and written to weave the Common Core State Standards throughout every unit. For **Argument** writing, the standards inform the unit's writing rubrics, objectives, and strategies.

The lessons for response to literature are based principally on the writing standards for **Argument** writing. The rubrics and writing strategies for the traits of Ideas and Organization in this chapter reflect writing standards **W.7.1.a, W.7.1.b,** and **W.7.3.e,** which focus on showing a clear understanding of the literature, using accurate quotations that support the writer's ideas, and organizing the review in three parts: an introduction, a body, and a conclusion. The rubrics and writing

3	2	1	
The writing shows only a basic understanding of the literature. Quotations do not support the writer's claim.	The writer's ideas need development and support. Quotations are not used.	The writing reflects a lack of understanding of the literature.	Ideas
There is an introduction, a body, and a conclusion.	There is no introduction or conclusion. The writing has little organization or direction.	The writing is not organized as a response.	Organization
Some style and voice come through in the beginning then fade.	The voice sounds distant or tentative. A personal style is not established.	The voice is absent. The reader does not have a sense of who the writer is.	Voice
The language is mostly clear. Some vague words could cause misunderstanding.	Some of the writing is unclear or too general. It lacks precision.	Vague or wrong word choice takes away from the writing. The writing doesn't make sense.	Word Choice
Many sentences in a row share the same structure. They dull the flow of ideas.	Most sentences are very short. The writing sounds choppy, especially when read aloud.	The writing contains fragments and run-on sentences. The ideas are incomplete or hard to follow.	Sentence Fluency
Many errors are repeated and cause confusion. Homophones may be used incorrectly.	Serious errors interfere with meaning. Homophones are not used correctly.	The writing has not been edited.	Conventions

See Appendix B for 4-, 5-, and 6-point argument rubrics.

Apply the Rubric

Identify Traits Read aloud or display a short excerpt from any text. Go through the traits one by one, asking students to identify examples of the traits. Ask questions such as the following to guide students:

- What is the excerpt about? How can you tell?

- How is the excerpt organized?

- What can you tell about the intended purpose or audience from the way the author sounds?

- What do you think of the author's choice of words?

- Are there sentences that flow particularly well? Are there places where the author could use more variety?

Additional Rubrics Appendix B includes 4-, 5-, and 6-point rubrics that can be used with any piece of argument writing. The rubrics are also available as blackline masters in this Teacher Edition, beginning on page T543.

strategies for the traits of Voice, Word Choice, and Sentence Fluency in this chapter reflect writing standards **W.7.1.c** and **W.7.1.d**, which focus on using a consistent formal style, a personal voice, precise language, and a variety of sentences that engage the reader and support the writer's purpose.

The language standards for grade 7 students are addressed during editing and skills practice. In addition, there are multiple opportunities to address the speaking and listening standards during the writing process. Most important, this chapter will help your students produce coherent writing (**W.7.4**), improve their writing (**W.7.5**), and use technologies to publish and present their finished pieces (**W.7.6**).

CCSS Common Core State Standards

SL.7.1.a: Come to discussions prepared, having read or researched material under study; explicitly draw on that preparation by referring to evidence on the topic, text, or issue to probe and reflect on ideas under discussion.

Analyze
the Model

Week 1 • Day 4

Student Objectives

- Read a model response to literature. *(p. 339)*
- Use the response to literature rubric. *(pp. 340–341)*
- Use the model response to literature to study Ideas, Organization, and Voice. *(pp. 342–343)*

Study the Model

Assess the Model Have volunteers read aloud each section on pages 342–343. Discuss as a class whether students agree or disagree with Tyler's assessments of the model. Use questions such as the following to discuss the pages with students. Be sure they can back up their answers with evidence from the model.

Does the writer

- state an opinion clearly and use accurate evidence to support the claim? (Possible response: Yes, Lucinda Juarez presents her opinion about the book clearly. She also summarizes it for readers who may not have read "The Ransom of Red Chief," and she references the source in her response. She also includes a Work Cited section at the end of the response.)

Strategies for Writers Online
Go to **www.sfw.z-b.com** for additional online resources for students and teachers.

Using the Rubric to Study the Model
Response to Literature

Did you notice that the model on page 339 points out some key elements of a response to literature? As she wrote "Tables Turned," Lucinda Juarez used these elements to help her respond to the short story "The Ransom of Red Chief." She also used the 6-point rubric on pages 340–341 to plan, draft, revise, and edit the writing. A rubric is a great tool to evaluate writing during the writing process.

Now let's use the same rubric to score the model. To do this, we'll focus on each trait separately, starting with Ideas. We'll use the top descriptor for each trait (column 6), along with examples from the model, to help us understand how the traits work together. How would you score Lucinda on each trait?

Ideas

- The writing shows an in-depth understanding of the literature.
- Quotations support the writer's claim and are accurately referenced.

Lucinda seems to really understand and appreciate the story and what the author's intentions were. To show how tables are turned in the story, she uses a striking quote. Note that Lucinda found the story online and provided information about it at the bottom of her essay.

[from the writing model]

What the kidnappers didn't count on was that, instead of feeling kidnapped, the boy is thrilled to be out. "I've never had so much fun in all my life," he tells them.

English Language Learners

BEGINNING/INTERMEDIATE

Respond to Text Read a language-level appropriate story. After reading, ask *Who likes the story?* Use nonverbal motions to support your question, such as nod head, thumbs-up, smile. Students give a thumbs-up for indication. Say, *I like the story.* Students repeat. Do the same process for *Who doesn't like the story?* Beginning ELL students draw a picture about the story. Intermediate ELL students draw a picture of their favorite part and write simple sentences to tell about it.

- The introduction is engaging and states the claim, the body organizes the reasons in a compelling way, and the concluding section is strong.

Right off the bat, Lucinda tells the reader her response to the story and gives us a glimpse into her reasoning. After reading the introduction, I was eager to know more. Lucinda follows up with a body that gives solid reasons for her reactions and a conclusion that makes me want to read "The Ransom of Red Chief" myself.

[from the writing model]

I just read a story that really made me laugh, "The Ransom of Red Chief," by O. Henry. The characters were funny, the story just did not let up, and the plot has a surprise twist that I guarantee you have never come across before in any of your reading. It was over the top, strange, and hilarious.

- A consistent formal style and personal voice engage the reader and support the writer's claim.

Lucinda's writing is very lively and not stiff. She is comfortable with her readers and connects with them using a style that is warm but not too casual. Her writing has a sense of humor that seems to reflect the amusement she felt while reading "The Ransom of Red Chief." Look how she gives a hint about who is really the victim in this story, and then how she brings the reader back to the beginning of the plot.

[from the writing model]

The three main characters are two kidnappers, Sam and Bill, and their victim, if you can call him that. Actually, it is the kidnappers who become the victims. But let me backtrack a bit. The two kidnappers are con men who need some extra money to pull off a fraudulent land scheme.

Response to Literature 343

- organize the review in a way that guides the reader? (Possible responses: The response is well organized and easy to follow. The introduction states the writer's opinion about the book, the body paragraphs include examples from the book that support the writer's opinion, and the conclusion is strong and convincing.)

- maintain a convincing voice and a formal style? (Possible responses: The writer establishes and maintains a confident, friendly style that seems to match the tone of the book. The writer sounds knowledgeable and engaging throughout the response.)

ADVANCED/ADVANCED HIGH

Parts of a Story: Climax Explain the climax is the most exciting part of the book where all the events come together. Prepare to read a simple story that has an obvious climax, such as *Little Red Riding Hood*. Prior to reading the story, tell the students to listen/think/be prepared to tell the climax of the story. After reading, give students a paper with different parts of the story. They must choose the climax of the story.

CCSS Common Core State Standards

SL.7.1.b: Follow rules for collegial discussions, track progress toward specific goals and deadlines, and define individual roles as needed. **SL.7.1.c:** Pose questions that elicit elaboration and respond to others' questions and comments with relevant observations and ideas that bring the discussion back on topic as needed.

Analyze
the Model

Week 1 • Day 5

Student Objectives

- Read a model response to literature. *(p. 339)*
- Use the response to literature rubric. *(pp. 340–341)*
- Use the model response to literature to study Word Choice, Sentence Fluency, and Conventions. *(pp. 344–345)*

Continue Discussing the Traits

Use questions such as the following to continue to analyze the model.

Does the writer

- use compelling language? (Possible response: The writer's words are purposeful and precise. She uses the literary term *ironic* to explain the book's ending.)

- vary sentences to keep the text flowing smoothly? (Possible response: The writer varied the structures of her sentences.)

- use correct grammar, mechanics, and spelling? (Possible response: It's obvious that the response was carefully edited. Frequently confused words are used correctly.)

- Precise language conveys the message to the reader.

Lucinda's writing is very descriptive and precise. She is precise when referring to parts of the story, using words such as *characters, plot, twist, story's title,* and *author*. She is also not afraid to use a literary term. Look at how she used the word *ironic* when describing the twist at the end.

[from the writing model]

> It's outrageously ironic, to be sure, and makes you think about how the tables can turn regardless of how well and cleverly you think you have planned! The kidnappers certainly did not plan on having to pay a ransom to be able to return "Red Chief" to his father.

- A variety of sentence structures contributes to the rhythm and flow.
- The writer's ideas are easy to follow.

It was easy to follow Lucinda's ideas. Her response never gets boring, because her writing has a fluid rhythm. A variety of sentence structures keeps things interesting throughout the essay. Look at how she describes the way Red Chief makes life miserable for the kidnappers.

[from the writing model]

> The kid imagines himself to be an Indian chief (the "Red Chief" in the story's title). His boundless imagination comes up with various relentless activities.
>
> As Sam tries to work out the setup and details of collecting the kidnap money, Bill's job is to try to keep the kid amused. "Red Chief" finds endless ways to torture Bill, including trying to scalp him, putting a red-hot boiled potato down his back, and riding him like a horse.

344 Argument Writing

Technology Tip — for 21st Century Literacies

Ask students to create a digital, multimedia book review poster using Glogster. Posters should include a minimum of three media types and offer a consistent and appropriate visual design. Require students to create their own media (e.g., a video book trailer, an audio review, or a visual movie poster) and also to submit reflective writing in which they consider how each individual component and the poster as a whole is intentionally created to engage a specific audience. Students could also exchange posters and rewrite for a completely different audience.

See **www.sfw.z-b.com** for further information about and links to these websites and tools.

Strategies for Writers Online

Go to **www.sfw.z-b.com** for additional online resources for students and teachers.

Conventions
- The writing has been carefully edited.
- Homophones, if used, are correct.

Lucinda's analysis has been carefully edited. I do not see any errors in spelling, grammar, or punctuation. I also see that she uses homophones correctly. For example, the words *to*, *two*, and *too* are homophones—they sound the same, but they are spelled differently and have different meanings. Look at how Lucinda uses these homophones correctly.

[from the writing model]

> The three main characters are two kidnappers, Sam and Bill, and their victim, if you can call him that.

[from the writing model]

> As Sam tries to work on the set-up and details of collecting the kidnap money, Bill's job is to try to keep the kid amused.

[from the writing model]

> I thoroughly enjoyed myself, and at times had to laugh out loud, too.

+Presentation The literary analysis is neat and legible.

My Turn!

Now it's my turn to respond to literature. I'll use the rubric and good writing strategies to help me. Read on to see how I do it.

Response to Literature **345**

Differentiating Instruction

ENRICHMENT

Use the Rubric to Score a Model Have students work in pairs to score the model response to literature on page 339, using the top descriptors (column 6) for each trait in the rubric on pages 340–341. Make sure they include **Presentation**. When the groups have reached a consensus, ask the groups to share and defend their scores for each trait.

REINFORCEMENT

Focus on a Single Trait To help students who have trouble grasping the concept of the traits, focus on one trait at a time. Collect multiple examples of text that exemplify a trait. Talk through each one with students until they are able to identify **Ideas**, for example, on their own.

Presentation Explain to students that Presentation is just as important as any of the other traits. Neatness is always a priority, and text should be clearly handwritten in pen or typed, using only a few, readable fonts. White space should be used to create neat margins, and the lines of text in each part of the review should be spaced correctly. Paragraphs should be indented (using the tab key) or space should be left between paragraphs for ease of reading.

Think About the Traits After students have thoroughly discussed the model response to literature, ask them which traits they think are the most important in a response. Remind them that all of the traits are important in every piece of writing; however some traits play a more important role in specific types of writing. For example, some students may feel that **Organization** is very important in a response because if the writer's evidence is not presented in a logical order, the reader may get lost or confused. Others may feel that **Voice** is important because the writer needs to sound confident and knowledgeable to convince the reader. Still others may feel that **Word Choice** is a more important trait because strong, purposeful language helps strengthen the writer's message.

Common Core State Standards

SL.7.1.c: Pose questions that elicit elaboration and respond to others' questions and comments with relevant observations and ideas that bring the discussion back on topic as needed. **SL.7.1.d:** Acknowledge new information expressed by others and, when warranted, modify their own views.

Write
a Response to Literature

Week 2 • Day 1

Student Objectives

- List the theme and reactions to the literature. *(p. 346)*

Prewrite

Focus on Ideas

Make Notes About a Story Read page 346 aloud. Have students make a short list of memorable stories, including ones they have read in class. If students mentioned specific stories during their discussions of the model and writing traits, encourage them to include them as potential writing topics by jotting the titles on the board.

Be sure students have access to the stories, either as hand-held books or online. Have them page through the stories to refresh their memories of the plot lines, characters, and themes. After students complete their brainstorming, tell each student to choose his or her favorite story on the short list. Then have them use Tyler's notes on page 346 to list the details from that story. To help them state a claim, ask this question:

- What message or lesson does the story teach?

Have them write their responses under "My Claim" in their notes.

Online Writing Center

 Provides **interactive graphic organizers** as well as a variety of graphic organizers in PDF format.

Prewrite — Focus on Ideas

The Rubric Says The writing shows an in-depth understanding of the literature.

Writing Strategy List the theme and reactions to the literature.

We've read several short stories in class this year. Our teacher has asked us to write a literary analysis of our favorite one. I know which story was my favorite: "The Tell-Tale Heart" by Edgar Allan Poe. I'm looking forward to explaining why that story speaks to me. I made a list of some details from the story and thoughts I have about it.

My List

Story
"The Tell-Tale Heart" by Edgar Allan Poe

Summary
The narrator of the story tells about murdering another man. He goes crazy, even though he keeps saying he's not. He keeps hearing a heartbeat—the heartbeat of the man he murdered, he thinks. The murderer confesses at the end.

My Claim
You can't commit a crime and get away with it. Your conscience will get you in the end.

Supporting Evidence
The narrator murdered a man and was able to hide all the evidence. Even though he could have gotten away with the murder, his heartbeat drives him to confess to the murder.

Apply

Choose your favorite story. Then make a list of some details from the story and thoughts you have about it.

346 Argument Writing

English Language Learners

BEGINNING/INTERMEDIATE

Writing Sentences Write on the board *My mom cooks dinner.* Read it all together. Explain that sentences have subjects (who) and verbs (action). Underline the subject and verb in different colors when you talk about them. On strips of paper, write subjects and predicates. Give each student one strip. They must find the match to create a sentence.

ADVANCED/ADVANCED HIGH

Quotation Marks Explain that we use quotation marks to separate dialogue in text. On the board, write *The teacher asked What is your next class?* Show students the correct placement of the comma and quotation marks. Then write the student's answer in this way: *The student replied Math is my next class.* Have a student insert quotes and a comma. Have partners create their own correctly punctuated dialogues and read them to the class.

Prewrite

The Rubric Says	The introduction is engaging and states the claim, the body organizes the reasons in a compelling way, and the concluding section is strong.
Writing Strategy	Use a Paragraph Organizer to plan the writing.

My next step is to plan my literary analysis. I'll use a Paragraph Organizer to plan each of the sections. In the **introduction**, I'll draft my claim. In the **body**, I'll include a summary, support for the claim, and personal observations. In the **conclusion**, I'll wrap it all up.

Writer's Term

Paragraph Organizer
A **Paragraph Organizer** organizes information that will go in the **introduction, body,** and **conclusion** of your writing.

Paragraph Organizer

Introduction
- You can't get away with murder. You can get rid of evidence, but you can't get rid of your conscience.

Body
- The narrator of the story is a murderer. He is trying to convince the reader that he is not crazy. Then he tells how he killed an old man. The heartbeat enters the story as he is about to kill the man. The narrator thinks the heartbeat belongs to the old man, but the heartbeat remains even after the man is dead. The police don't suspect the murderer because he's done such a good job of covering up the crime. But the heartbeat the murderer keeps hearing finally drives him to confess to the police.

Conclusion
- The heartbeat is the murderer's conscience. The murderer confesses to the police, but this may not bring him relief. He'll have to live with his conscience for as long as his tell-tale heart keeps beating.

Reflect
How will the Paragraph Organizer help Tyler plan out his writing?

Apply
Use a Paragraph Organizer to plan the introduction, body, and conclusion of your response.

Conferencing

PEER TO PEER After each student has chosen a story to analyze, have writing partners share their notes about their stories. Partners can then work together to create and complete their Paragraph Organizers.

PEER GROUPS Have students work in groups of three or four. Have each student read his or her Paragraph Organizer aloud. Ask the other students in the group to take turns offering one comment or suggestion to make it more helpful.

TEACHER-LED Conference with individual students about their Paragraph Organizers. Before they speak with you, tell students to think of questions to ask you about creating their organizers or how they plan to use them to write their drafts.

Write
a Response to Literature

Week 2 • Day 2

Student Objectives
- Use a Paragraph Organizer to plan the writing. (*p. 347*)

Prewrite

Focus on **Organization**

Paragraph Organizer Explain to students that creating a Paragraph Organizer is a good way to plan the three parts of their responses to literature: the introduction, body, and conclusion. Point out that the introduction states Tyler's claim. Have them refer to Tyler's notes on page 346 and their own notes to fill in the remainder of the organizer. Tell them it's a good idea to include more information from the story than they may use in their analysis.

Writer's Term

Paragraph Organizer Have students refer to their notes to make sure they have written enough details about their stories in the corresponding parts of the organizer. Also have them mark the page numbers of direct quotes and examples they can use to support their claims when they write their drafts.

CCSS **C**ommon **C**ore **S**tate **S**tandards
W.7.4: Produce clear and coherent writing in which the development, organization, and style are appropriate to task, purpose, and audience.

Write
a Response to Literature

Week 2 • Day 3

Student Objectives

• Use exact words. *(p. 348)*

Draft

Focus on Word Choice

Draft a Response to Literature
Read page 348 aloud. Be sure that students understand that they will use their Paragraph Organizers to guide them through the drafting process. Also point out that their writing voice should sound confident, knowledgeable, and convincing. It's important that they use a formal tone that is fair and balanced, and shows respect for the reader.

Point out the list of literary terms mentioned on this page that students can utilize. (*irony, simile, personification,* and *foreshadowing*) If needed, provide a quick refresher and refer students to a glossary of literary terms (see Enrichment below) to help them understand the terms.

Then remind them that they should not be overly concerned with correctness of grammar and mechanics at this point. Point out that the proofreader's marks are provided as a reference on the next page.

Online Writing Center

 Provides student eBooks with an **interactive writing pad** for drafting, revising, editing, and publishing.

T348 Argument Writing

Draft

Focus on Word Choice

The Rubric Says	Precise language conveys the message to the reader.
Writing Strategy	Use exact words.

All the planning I did should make writing my draft go pretty smoothly. The paragraph organizer really helped me to get my ideas on paper, especially my claim.

As I write, I'll try to remember to use exact words. Using exact words will help capture the reader's interest in the writing and will help the reader understand and appreciate the story and my claim. Examples of exact words to use when describing parts of the story include *plot, character, conflict, resolution,* and *theme.* Literary terms include *irony, simile, personification,* and *foreshadowing.*

As I draft my literary analysis, I'll try to avoid mistakes in grammar and spelling, but I know I can fix my mistakes later.

You can read the beginning of my draft on the next page. What do you think?

348 Argument Writing

Differentiating Instruction

ENRICHMENT

Use Literary Terms Ask for volunteers to prepare a poster of literary terms for use in class. Include those listed on page 348 and ask students to suggest others. Using a glossary of terms in the literature anthology or in an online source, have students add to the list from time to time.

REINFORCEMENT

Read a Literary Analysis Bring to class samples of literary analyses or reviews. Have pairs of students identify the writer's claim. Have students circle the claim and underline direct quotations and examples from the source. Ask them whether the analysis contained enough information to convince them to read the story.

[DRAFT]

You Can't Get Away with Murder

by Tyler

[claim]

Even if you commit a perfect crime and have gotten rid of all the evidence, there is one piece of evidence you can never get rid of—your conscience. That's the message I got from reading Edgar Allan Poe's "The Tell-Tale Heart." This short, intense story is the scariest and most disturbing I've ever read. It's a horror story of a murder told by a psychologically disturbed narrator who also happens too be the murderer. In the end, even after he has successfully covered up his crime, he does not get away with what he has done because his own guilty conscience gives him away What sets off his guilty conscience is the steady heartbeat that he keeps hearing.

[precise words]

Reflect

What do you think about the writing process so far? How have the prewriting activities helped?

Apply

Use your Paragraph Organizer to respond to a favorite story that you've read.

Response to Literature **349**

Conferencing

PEER TO PEER Have partners exchange drafts to read. Tell students to think of two or three questions they would like to ask to clarify information. Have them write their questions on adhesive notes and affix them to the appropriate places on their partner's draft.

PEER GROUPS Have students work in groups of four. Ask students to pass their drafts to the student on the right to read. That student writes one comment or suggestion on an adhesive note affixed to the draft and passes the draft along to the right. The review ends when everyone has received his or her own draft back with three comments.

TEACHER-LED Schedule conferences with pairs of students. Have them read each other's draft and coach them in giving constructive criticism.

Write
a Response to Literature

Week 2 • Day 4

Student Objectives

• Complete a draft. *(p. 349)*

Continue Writing a Draft It is important that students are given ample time to write their drafts. As conferencing is important throughout the writing process, be sure to also plan time for peer to peer, peer groups, or teacher-led conferences. Remind students that this is the time to get their ideas down on paper in a creative and engaging way. Assure them that they will have plenty of time to fix any mistakes later.

CCSS **C**ommon **C**ore **S**tate **S**tandards

W.7.9: Draw evidence from literary or informational texts to support analysis, reflection, and research. **L.7.4.c:** Consult general and specialized reference materials (dictionaries, glossaries, thesauruses), both print and digital, to find the pronunciation of a word or determine or clarify its precise meaning or its part of speech. **L.7.6:** Acquire and use accurately grade-appropriate general academic and domain-specific words and phrases; gather vocabulary knowledge when considering a word or phrase important to comprehension or expression.

Response to Literature **T349**

Write
a Response to Literature

Week 2 • Day 5

Student Objectives

- Choose quotations that support the thesis. *(p. 350)*

Revise

Focus on Ideas

Illustrate the Point Read page 350.

Using Quotations Review that it is important to back up one's claims in a literary analysis with evidence from the story. One good way to do this is to use quotations. Quotations both give a flavor of the writing style and also provide specific evidence. Explain to students that quotations must be blended smoothly into the writing; they can't be unrelated to the sentences around them. Also explain that the exact words from the text must be enclosed in quotation marks and properly credited.

✏ Writer's Term _____

Plagiarism Review any policies that your school has in place for teaching and handling plagiarism. Emphasize to students that plagiarism is, essentially, stealing.

 Strategies for Writers Online
Go to **www.sfw.z-b.com** for additional online resources for students and teachers.

T350 Argument Writing

Revise Focus on Ideas

The Rubric Says	Quotations support the writer's claim and are accurately referenced.
Writing Strategy	Choose quotations that support the claim.

I know that an opinion, or claim, has to be backed up with details and other kinds of information. When writing about literature, it is common to use quotations to support the claim. After I finished my draft, I read it silently to myself and checked to see whether I backed up my claim with details. I found a place to add a quote that perfectly illustrates my point that the narrator is not sane.

✏ Writer's Term _____

Plagiarism

Plagiarism is using someone else's words and ideas without giving credit. Avoid plagiarizing by using quotation marks around exact words from the story and by including full references.

[DRAFT]

You get a sense that something is terribly wrong, but you don't know what it is. Also, you don't have any idea if you can really trust the point of view and judgment of the narrator. He then reveals that he has taken the life of the man he lives with. This was not a crime of passion or one done for money. Actually, he says he loved the man. He did it because of the man's eye! "He had the eye of a vulture—a pale blue eye, with a film over it." (p. 228)

[added quotation]

Apply

Make sure that you use quotations that support your claim.

350 Argument Writing

English Language Learners

BEGINNING/INTERMEDIATE

Using Capitals and Periods Write on the board *My dog is big.* Point to the *M* and say, *capital M.* Students repeat. Explain capital is a big letter and point at the capitals on an alphabet chart. Point to the period in the sentence on the board and say *period.* Have students repeat. Write *the cat is black* on the board. Have a student add a capital and period and repeat the terms with the class.

ADVANCED/ADVANCED HIGH

Fact/Opinion Write on the board *The Earth rotates around the sun. It is fun to swim in the ocean.* Explain to the students a fact is something that can be proven. An opinion is what they think or feel about something. Read the sentences. Have students decide which one is fact and which one is opinion. Have partners work together to find examples of fact and opinion in a magazine or newspaper article.

Revise Focus on **Organization**

The Rubric Says	The introduction is engaging and states the claim, the body organizes the reasons in a compelling way, and the concluding section is strong.
Writing Strategy	Strengthen the conclusion.

I've reread my draft, and I'm really happy with most of it. The introduction engages the reader and clearly states my claim, and the body presents well-organized supporting reasons. But the essay just ends. I need to strengthen my conclusion and make it meaningful. The conclusion should refer to the claim, summarize some of the reasons, and include a personal insight. Look at how I revised my conclusion. Do you think it works better now?

[DRAFT]

[referred to claim]

The beating heart the killer heard was not the heartbeat of his victim. It was his own heartbeat.

No crime can ever be perfect, because the criminal must live with his own conscience. Throughout the story, he deceived himself into

A heartbeat is very powerful. Hearts beat faster when we are anxious—the more anxious, the faster.

thinking that all was fine with him, that he wasn't crazy. But he was.

The heartbeat of the murderer was a relentless, steady reminder of

the heartbeat he took away. In the end, he sought relief from it by

But we do not know if even the confession will bring him relief, as he will
confessing. have to live with the knowledge of what he has done for the rest of his
life, for as long as his tell-tale heart keeps beating.

[added personal insights]

Reflect

How did Tyler's revisions help to make his essay stronger?

Apply

Check your draft and make sure your conclusion is strong.

Response to Literature 351

Conferencing

PEER TO PEER Have partners exchange and read drafts. Tell students to think of two or three questions they would like to ask to clarify information or supply missing details. Have them write their questions on adhesive notes and affix them to the appropriate place on their partners' drafts.

PEER GROUPS In groups of three or four, have each student pass his or her draft to the student on their right to read. That student writes one comment or suggestion about its organization on an adhesive note affixed to the draft and passes the draft along to the right. The review of drafts ends when everyone has received his or her draft back with three constructive comments.

TEACHER-LED Conference with writing partners. Coach them on giving constructive criticism to improve the organization of the drafts.

Write
a Response to Literature

Week 3 • Day 1

Student Objectives

• Strengthen the conclusion. (p. 351)

Revise

Focus on

Evaluate the Conclusion Discuss what it means to organize writing logically. List responses on the board. (Possible responses: The response has an introduction, body, and conclusion. The introduction grabs the reader's attention. It's easy for the reader to read and follow. The conclusion is memorable.)

Discuss how the changes Tyler made strengthens his conclusion. Then help students strengthen their concluding statements, ask questions such as these:

• If you could boil the story down to one sentence, what would it be?

• In which important way(s) will the story stay with you for a long time?

Also refer them to the well-written conclusion in the first model on page 339, the traits rubric on page 340, and the analysis of **Organization** on page 343.

CCSS Common Core State Standards
W.7.1.e: Provide a concluding statement or section that follows from and supports the argument presented.
W.7.5: With some guidance and support from peers and adults, develop and strengthen writing as needed by planning, revising, editing, rewriting, or trying a new approach, focusing on how well purpose and audience have been addressed.

Write a Response to Literature

Week 3 • Day 2

Student Objectives

- Write different kinds of sentences. *(p. 352)*

Revise

Focus on 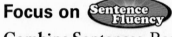 Sentence Fluency

Combine Sentences Read the introduction to page 352 and direct students' attention to Tyler's draft. Discuss the changes Tyler made. Help students understand that Tyler's changes eliminated choppiness and improved the flow of the writing.

Point out that the suggestion to vary sentences is akin to using a variety of colors. Using the same colors everywhere would result in a boring color scheme after awhile. It's true for writing, too. Using the same kinds of sentences makes for a boring writing pattern. Encourage students to read their drafts aloud to partners. Tell partners to listen for too many sentences in a row that share the same structure (predictable) or length (choppy or overly long). Also remind writers to use transition words and phrases to connect ideas smoothly.

Online Writing Center

 Provides **interactive proofreading activities** for each genre.

Revise   Focus on **Sentence Fluency**

The Rubric Says   A variety of sentence structures contributes to the rhythm and flow. The writer's ideas are easy to follow.

Writing Strategy   Write different kinds of sentences.

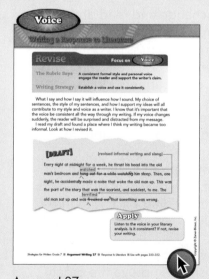

The rubric says that a variety of sentences will help the flow of my writing. When the sentences all sound the same, the writing can sound choppy, causing the reader to get bored and lose interest. Smooth, flowing writing is much more enjoyable for the reader.

To get an idea about how my writing sounded, I read my draft out loud to myself. I listened for places where I needed some variety. I can add phrases or clauses to lengthen some sentences. I can also break apart rambling sentences. Here's what I did to combine some short, choppy sentences. Now I've got two longer, flowing sentences followed by a short, punchy quote.

[DRAFT]

The police came shortly thereafter. They were checking up. A
                                               because

neighbor had reported hearing a cry. It was the only sound the

victim had made when he was about to be killed. The killer was

            that

confident. He had erased all signs of the crime. He let them in.

"I smiled—for what had I to fear?" (p. 232)

[combined short, choppy sentences]

Apply

Read your draft aloud to yourself and listen for places where you may want to vary your sentences.

352 Argument Writing

Optional Revising Lessons

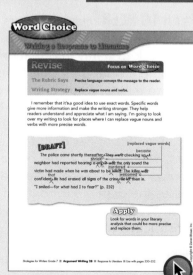

Voice

Word Choice

Argument 27   Argument 28

Go to ➡ *Strategies for Writers Grade 7 CD-ROM*

Edit

Focus on **Conventions**

The Rubric Says — The writing has been carefully edited. Homophones, if used, are correct.

Writing Strategy — Make sure to always use the right word.

Writer's Term
Homophones
Homophones are words that sound alike but that have different meanings. A few examples of homophones are **to/two/too**, **ate/eight**, **be/bee**, and **right/write**.

Now it's time to check my draft for spelling, punctuation, grammar, and capitalization. While checking my draft, I found an incorrectly used homophone. It's easy to confuse homophones, and the computer spell checker will not find those errors. I'm going to correct it now. I'll also correct any other errors I see.

[DRAFT]

[changed to correct homophone]

It's a horror story of a murder told by a psychologically disturbed

narrator who also happens ~~too~~ to be the murderer. In the end, even after

he has successfully covered up his crime, he does not get away with

what he has done because his own guilty conscience gives him away.

[corrected punctuation]

Reflect
What do you think of Tyler's edits? How do they make the literary analysis easier to read and understand?

Apply **Conventions**
Edit for spelling, punctuation, and capitalization. Also make sure that you haven't used any incorrect homophones.

For practice with homophones and frequently confused words, see the exercises on the next two pages.

Response to Literature 353

Write
a Response to Literature

Week 3 • Day 3

Student Objectives
• Make sure to use the right word. (p. 353)

Edit

Focus on **Conventions**

Edit for Accuracy Read page 353 aloud. Point out Tyler's corrections and discuss how Tyler edited the draft. Remind students that editing is the time to correct any mistakes in spelling, grammar, punctuation, and capitalization.

Remind students that computers have a spell-check function, but it will not catch homophones or frequently confused words. Use the mini-lessons on the following two pages for students who need practice to use easily confused words correctly. Then have students complete pages 354 and 355.

Writer's Term
Homophones Other sound-alike words that are easily confused in literary writing include *allusion/illusion; cite/sight/site; coarse/course; hear/here; past/passed; scene/seen; their/there/they're; vary/very; wear/where.*

CCSS Common Core State Standards
L.7.1: Demonstrate command of the conventions of standard English grammar and usage when writing or speaking.

Conventions

Mini-Lesson

Student Objectives

- Use homophones correctly. (p. 354)

Homophones

Have students read the Know the Rule box on page 354. Have students suggest other examples of homophones that have given them problems. (Possible responses: *its/it's; to/too/two; their/there/ they're*) Suggest others that you have noticed in your students' writing. Ask students to share tips for associating the variations in spellings with the correct meanings. Invite them to look up the most problematic of words in print and online resources. Encourage students to keep a personal list of the homophones that trip them up from time to time. They should consult the list whenever they are writing to make sure they've used the words correctly.

Online Writing Center

Provides **interactive grammar games** and **practice activities** in student eBook.

Conventions Grammar, Usage & Mechanics

Homophones

Know the Rule

Homophones are words that sound the same but that are spelled differently and have different meanings.
Examples: **pair, pear,** and **pare**
toe and **tow**

Practice the Rule

Accept sentences that use homophones correctly.
Complete each sentence with the correct homophone on a separate sheet of paper. Write your own sentence for the unused homophone.

1. The climbers wanted to reach the _____ of the mountain and see the spectacular view of the valley below. (peek/**peak**)
2. A giant cone dropped down from the ancient _____ tree. (**fir**/fur)
3. The cyclists felt hot and tired and decided to _____ in the shade for a drink of water. (paws/**pause**)
4. The divers were ecstatic to catch a glimpse of the huge, rarely _____ oarfish. (**seen**/scene)
5. The _____ had to make an emergency landing when the pilot detected problems with one of the engines. (plain/**plane**)
6. Let's take a _____ in the class to see how many students can speak a second language. (pole/**poll**)
7. The last thing you would want to come across while hiking in the jungle is a wild _____ charging at you. (bore/**boar**)
8. It was a difficult _____ to finish first in the marathon. (**feat**/feet)
9. The speaker was _____ from talking so long to the group. (horse/**hoarse**)
10. Make sure you don't drop that vase and _____ it! (brake/**break**)

Related Grammar Practice

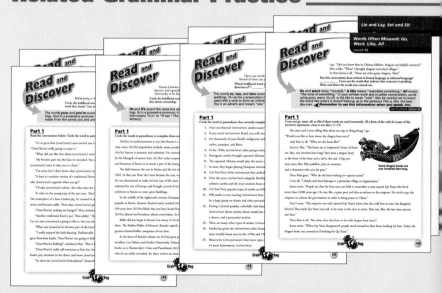

Pages 129, 131, 133, 135, 137, 139, 143, 145

Go to G.U.M. Student Practice Book

Frequently Confused Words

Know the Rule

People often confuse **words that look or sound similar**. If a writer uses the wrong word, the reader may not understand the intended message. Be sure to check the words carefully when you compose on the computer because the spell checker will not catch this kind of error!

> **Example:** A **desert** is a very dry place that gets little rainfall.
> A **dessert** is a sweet treat eaten after a meal.

Practice the Rule

Write each sentence with the correct word or words on a separate sheet of paper.

1. Please _____ my apology for being so late. (except/accept)
2. Everyone _____ Millie was at the soccer game this afternoon. (except/accept)
3. Martine donated dresses, coats, and other _____ to the clothing drive. (clothes/cloths)
4. For the car wash, we'll need a box full of _____ to use for drying cars. (clothes/cloths)
5. On the _____ of July, this country celebrates its independence. (Fourth/Forth)
6. The explorers went _____ around the globe and brought back many riches from faraway lands. (fourth/forth)
7. Be careful not to _____ your keys. (loose/lose)
8. You are not allowed to let your dog run _____ in the park. (loose/lose)
9. Hank bought a _____ cake at the bakery and brought _____ it to the birthday party. (brought/bought)
10. Sometimes when you breathe _____, it's good to take a deep breath _____. (breathe/breath)

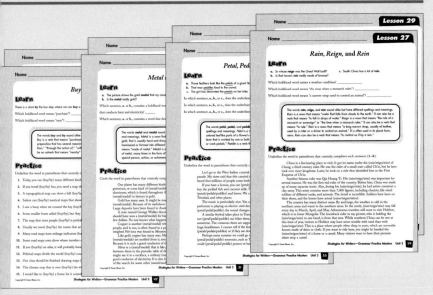

Pages 47, 49, 51, 53, 55, 57, 59, 63

Go to → Grammar Practice Masters

Mini-Lesson

Student Objectives

- Use frequently confused words correctly. (p. 355)

Frequently Confused Words

Have students read the Know the Rule on page 355. Point out that once a piece of writing is published, it's too late to catch errors. Unintended meanings or humor can be avoided by careful editing. Encourage students to find a reliable editing partner who will hone in on easily confused words that spell checkers will miss.

Also encourage students to consult word resources as they write and revise. A good strategy is to circle words and phrases in their drafts for editing later. This way, they are less likely to overlook something they intended to double check.

CCSS Common Core State Standards
L.7.2: Demonstrate command of the conventions of standard English capitalization, punctuation, and spelling when writing.

Write
a Response to Literature

Week 3 • Day 4

Student Objectives

- Discuss preparation for publishing and presentation. (p. 356)
- Use a final editing checklist to publish their work. (p. 356)

Publish +Presentation

Publishing Strategy Use Tyler's finished response to discuss publishing and presentation. Ask students to point out the presentation elements that make it stand out as a polished piece. (Possible responses: interesting title; good handwriting or word processing; indented paragraphs; illustrations, etc.) Then ask students if they like Tyler's choice for publishing (a class book). Tell the class that his choice is not the only publishing option. Invite students to name other ways they could publish their work.

Have each student make a checklist to prepare a final copy. Encourage each student to make a final evaluation of his or her writing before publishing it. Then have students publish copies of their work in a class book or on the library's website.

 Strategies for Writers Online
Go to **www.sfw.z-b.com** for additional online resources for students and teachers.

Publish +Presentation

Publishing Strategy	Present the literary analysis as part of a class-published book.
Presentation Strategy	Use neat handwriting or word processing.

My writing will be in a class-published book that will be on display in the library. I'll use my best handwriting, or, even better, I'll use the computer to make sure my analysis is neat and readable. I can use the word-processing features to make good margins, put a heading at the top of my essay, and choose clear, readable fonts. I might be able to find a picture of the author on the Internet to use in my response. I may even consider making a short video of my favorite scene from the story to share with the class. First, though, I'll make a final checklist.

My Checklist

Did I—

✔ check for correct capitalization, punctuation, grammar, and spelling?

✔ make sure all homophones and frequently confused words are used correctly?

✔ use a computer or good handwriting to make sure my essay is neat and readable?

✔ look for a picture of the author to include with my response?

Apply

Check your literary analysis against your final checklist. Then make a final copy to publish.

356 Argument Writing

Differentiating Instruction

ENRICHMENT

Publishing Options After polishing their own writing, have students brainstorm ways to publish, such as a collection in a class e-book or a handy reference on the library's website. Have them make a list of three or four ideas and agree on the best option.

REINFORCEMENT

Adding Pictures and Illustrations If students are using a word processor to prepare their final copies, invite those with computer experience to share their finished work and demonstrate the various formatting options for designing pages and incorporating visuals.

YOU CAN'T GET AWAY WITH MURDER

by Tyler

Even if you commit a perfect crime and have gotten rid of all the evidence, there is one piece of evidence you can never get rid of—your conscience. That's the message I got from reading Edgar Allan Poe's "The Tell-Tale Heart." This short, intense story is the scariest and most disturbing I've ever read. It's a horror story of a murder told by a psychologically disturbed narrator who also happens to be the murderer. And, in the end, even after he has successfully covered up his crime, he does not get away with what he has done because his own guilty conscience gives him away. What sets off his guilty conscience is the steady heartbeat that he keeps hearing.

Right at the start, the reader knows that there is something wrong with the narrator. He begins the story trying to convince the reader, and probably himself, that though he's "very, very, dreadfully nervous," (p. 228) he's not crazy. You get a sense that something is terribly wrong, but you don't know what it is. Also, you don't have any idea if you can really trust the point of view and judgment of the narrator. He then reveals that he has taken the life of the man he lives with. This was not a crime of passion or one done for money. Actually, he says he loved the man. He did it because of the man's eye! "He had the eye of a vulture—a pale blue eye, with a film over it." (p. 228)

As the story unfolds, the narrator describes the creepy way he went about preparing to murder the man, all the while saying that he is not a madman. Every night at midnight for a week, he thrust his head into the old man's bedroom and watched

Write
a Response to Literature

Week 3 • Day 5

Student Objectives

- Use a response to literature rubric. *(pp. 340–341)*
- Share a published response to literature. *(pp. 357–359)*

Cite the Work Refer students to the finished work on pages 357–359. Point out that Tyler added a "Work Cited" reference at the end of his paper. Explain that it is formatted according to Modern Language Association (MLA) style guidelines for documenting citations. Go over the entry carefully, making sure students have followed the example precisely. Explain that this is an example of using conventions in writing. For more information, see **www.mla.org**.

Technology Tip for 21st Century Literacies

Readers often share their opinions and reviews of the books they read within peer groups or groups with shared interests. To capture the need to talk with others about our reading, use a computer with a webcam to create video e-mail with a tool like EyeJot, or a video blog post in which students share their thinking with others. Identify the recipient or audience ahead of time, and work with students to find a balance between reading a pre-written script to the camera and speaking impromptu as they think about their reading.

See **www.sfw.z-b.com** for further information about and links to these websites and tools.

CCSS Common Core State Standards

W.7.4: Produce clear and coherent writing in which the development, organization, and style are appropriate to task, purpose, and audience. **W.7.6:** Use technology, including the Internet, to produce and publish writing and link to and cite sources as well as to interact and collaborate with others, including linking to and citing sources.

Reflecting on a Response to Literature

Have a volunteer read aloud the question in the Reflect box on page 359. Then ask students the following questions:

- How did you do using all the traits of a response to literature?

- How did writing a response to literature deepen or change your understanding of the literature?

Have students jot down their answers to the question in a personal writer's journal or in their notes on the chapter and save it for future reference.

him sleep. Then, one night, he accidentally made a noise that woke the old man up. This was the part of the story that was the scariest, and saddest, to me. The old man sat up and was terrified that something was wrong. The killer waited for the old man to lie back down again, which he finally did. The killer then opened his lantern a tiny bit, to get some light, and saw the man's open eye, the eye that he hated so much. At that moment, he also started hearing "a low, dull quick sound." (p. 230) He recognized the sound as the beating of the old man's terrified heart.

The sound became louder and louder, until the killer was afraid that the neighbors would hear it. In an instant, he jumped into the room and killed the old man. To cover his crime, he dismembered the old man's body, cutting "off the head and the arms and the legs." (p. 231) He then hid the body parts under the flooring of the room, so that no evidence of his crime could be seen. All this he did very quickly, and, he thought, cleverly to conceal his gruesome crime.

The police came shortly thereafter, checking up because a neighbor had reported hearing a shriek, the only sound the victim had made when he was about to be murdered. The killer, confident that he had erased all signs of the crime, welcomed them in. "I smiled—for what had I to fear?" (p. 232)

The killer could have gotten away with his crime. The police were satisfied that everything was fine. But he started to hear the steady noise again, the beating heart. "—much such a sound as a watch makes when enveloped in cotton. I gasped for breath—and yet the officers heard it not." (p. 232)

The sound grew louder and louder to the killer. The policemen continued as if all was fine. But the murderer became convinced that the policemen knew, that they heard the sound,

Strategies for Writers Online

Go to **www.sfw.z-b.com** for additional online resources for students and teachers.

too. How could they not? It was becoming louder and louder and louder. Finally he could not take it any longer, and he confessed. "I admit the deed!—tear up the planks! here, here!—it is the beating of his hideous heart." (p. 233)

No crime can ever be perfect, because the criminal must live with his own conscience. The beating heart the killer heard was not the heartbeat of his victim; it was his own heartbeat. Throughout the story, he deceived himself into thinking that all was fine with him, that he wasn't crazy. But he was. A heartbeat is very powerful. Hearts beat faster when we are anxious—the more anxious, the faster. The heartbeat of the murderer was a relentless, steady reminder of the heartbeat he took away. In the end, he sought relief from it by confessing. But we do not know if even the confession will bring him relief, as he will have to live with the knowledge of what he has done for the rest of his life, for as long as his tell-tale heart keeps beating.

Work Cited

Poe, Edgar Allan. "The Tell-Tale Heart." *The Fall of the House of Usher and Other Writings.* Ed. David Galloway. London: Penguin, 2003. 228–233. Print.

Reflect

How did Tyler do? Did he include all the traits of a response to literature? Check it against the rubric. Then use the rubric to check your own literary analysis.

Argument Test Planner

WEEK 1

Day 1
Introduce
Argument Test Writing

Student Objectives
- Learn the components of the writing prompt.

Student Activities
- Discuss the components of the writing prompt. *(pp. 360–361)*

Day 2
Analyze
Introduce the Scoring Guide

Student Objectives
- Recognize the relationship of the scoring guide to the rubric and the six traits of writing.
- Read a model writing test response.

Student Activities
- Read and discuss **Writing Traits in the Scoring Guide.** *(p. 362)*
- Read the writing prompt response model. *(p. 363)*

Day 3
Analyze
Apply the Scoring Guide

Student Objectives
- Apply the scoring guide to the writing prompt response model.

Student Activities
- Read and discuss **Using the Scoring Guide to Study the Model.** *(pp. 364–365)*

WEEK 2

Day 1
Write
Prewrite: Ideas

Student Objectives
- Read and understand the writing prompt for argument writing.
- Apply the six traits of writing to the writing prompt.

Student Activities
- Read and discuss **Prewrite: Focus on Ideas.** *(pp. 368–369)*

Day 2
Write
Prewrite: Ideas

Student Objectives
- Learn how to respond to the task in the writing prompt.

Student Activities
- Read and discuss **Prewrite: Focus on Ideas.** *(p. 370)*

Day 3
Write
Prewrite: Organization

Student Objectives
- Learn how to choose a graphic organizer for the writing prompt.

Student Activities
- Read and discuss **Prewrite: Focus on Organization.** *(p. 371)*

WEEK 3

Day 1
Write
Revise: Organization

Student Objectives
- Organize the ideas into an introduction, body, and conclusion.

Student Activities
- Read and discuss **Revise: Focus on Organization.** *(p. 376)*

Day 2
Write
Revise: Voice

Student Objectives
- Sound convincing.

Student Activities
- Read and discuss **Revise: Focus on Voice.** *(p. 377)*

Day 3
Write
Revise: Word Choice

Student Objectives
- Use words with the right connotation.

Student Activities
- Read and discuss **Revise: Focus on Word Choice.** *(p. 378)*

Note: Optional Revising Lessons appear on the *Strategies for Writers* CD-ROM.

Day 4	Day 5

Analyze
Apply the Scoring Guide

Student Objectives

Continue to apply the scoring guide to the writing prompt response model.

Student Activities

• Read and discuss **Using the Scoring Guide to Study the Model.** *(p. 366)*

Analyze
Time Management

Student Objectives

• Learn how to plan time during a writing test.

Student Activities

• Read and discuss **Planning My Time.** *(p. 367)*

Day 4	Day 5

Write
Prewrite: Organization

Student Objectives

• Learn how to check the graphic organizer against the scoring guide.

Student Activities

• Read and discuss **Prewrite: Focus on Organization.** *(pp. 372–373)*

Write
Draft: Ideas

Student Objectives

• Draft an argument writing test, stating the claim clearly.

Student Activities

• Read and discuss **Draft: Focus on Ideas.** *(pp. 374–375)*
• Draft an argument writing test.

Day 4	Day 5

Write
Edit: Conventions

Student Objectives

• Check the grammar, punctuation, capitalization, and spelling.

Student Activities

Read and discuss **Edit: Focus on Conventions.** *(pp. 379–380)*

Review
Test Tips

Student Objectives

• Review tips for writing for a test.

Student Activities

• Read and discuss the **Test Tips.** *(p. 381)*

...mplete the chapter in fewer days, combine the learning objectives and activities in a way that supports students as they write.

Resources at-a-Glance

Differentiating Instruction

For additional Differentiating Instruction activities, see Strategies for Writers *Extensions Online at* **www.sfw.z-b.com.**

English Language Learners

 Connection Letter

Reproducible letter (in English and Spanish) appears on the *Strategies for Writers* CD-ROM and at **www.sfw.z-b.com.**

Online Essay Grader and Writing Tutor

Powered by Vantage Learning's MY Access!®, includes writing prompts and ongoing feedback for students as they write. Available for Grades 5–8.

Online Writing Center

Provides IWB resources, interactive games and practice activities, videos, eBooks, and a virtual file cabinet.

 Strategies for Writers Online

Go to **www.sfw.z-b.com** for free online resources for students and teachers.

Introduce
an Argument Test

Week 1 • Day 1

Student Objectives

- Learn the components of the writing prompt. *(pp. 360–361)*

Read the Writing Prompt

Argument Test Writing In this chapter, students will apply what they have learned about argument writing to the challenge of taking an argument writing test. Remind students that they will sometimes write on demand to complete an assignment or test. Tell students that when they write for a test, they will receive a writing prompt and a certain amount of time in which to write. Then their writing will be evaluated, just as with any test. Assure students that they do not need to be anxious about a writing test. The skills they have already practiced will help them do a good job. Direct their attention to the three parts of the writing prompt.

Setup The setup does just what its name says: it sets the writer up to do a good job. The setup gets writers to think about the writing topic in general before they choose a narrow topic.

Strategies for Writers Online
Go to **www.sfw.z-b.com** for additional online resources for students and teachers.

Argument
test writing

Read the Writing Prompt

When you take a writing test, you will be given a writing prompt. Most writing prompts have three parts:

Setup This part of the writing prompt gives you the background information you need to get ready to write.

Task This part of the writing prompt tells you exactly what you are supposed to write: an argument essay.

Scoring Guide This section tells how your writing will be scored. To do well on the test, you should include everything on the list.

> **R**emember the rubrics you've used in writing class? When you take a writing test, you don't always have all of the information that's on a rubric. But a scoring guide is a lot like a rubric. It lists everything you need to think about to write a good paper. Like the rubrics you've used, many scoring guides are based on the six traits of writing:

| Ideas | Organization | Voice |
| Word Choice | Sentence Fluency | Conventions |

Online Essay Grader and Writing Tutor

Powered by Vantage Learning's MY Access!®, this tool gives students

- immediate, ongoing, sentence-by-sentence feedback.
- helpful suggestions to improve their draft.
- a holistic score and a trait-specific score on their final draft.
- unlimited response submissions to the prompts.

Writing MODEL Prompt

The parent-teacher group at your school has proposed a Turn-Off-the-TV Week for students in your school.

Write an argument essay for your teacher telling why you support or oppose this plan.

Be sure your writing

- clearly states your claim and provides relevant evidence.

- is well organized. State your claim, give a new reason in each paragraph, and restate your claim at the end.

- uses a voice that sounds convincing.

- uses words that support your purpose.

- has varied sentences.

- has correct grammar, punctuation, capitalization, and spelling.

Task The task tells students not only what to write about but also what kind of writing to do: narrative, informative/explanatory, argument, or descriptive. Tell students that the best-written test will not receive a strong grade if it misses the topic or uses a form of writing other than the assigned form. Students must follow the instructions in the task.

Scoring Guide The scoring guide helps students plan and evaluate their writing. Help students understand how the scoring guide is similar to the rubrics they have seen by asking these questions:

- Which bullet focuses on **Ideas**? (the first bullet)

- Which bullet focuses on **Organization**? (the second bullet)

- Which bullets help you improve **Voice** and **Word Choice**? (the third and fourth bullet)

- Which bullet encourages you to improve **Sentence Fluency**? (the fifth bullet)

- Which bullet reminds you to edit your writing? (the sixth bullet)

Point out that in this chapter, students will use the argument writing traits to review a model essay before writing their own.

CCSS Common Core State Standards

W.7.1: Write arguments to support claims with clear reasons and relevant evidence.

Analyze
the Scoring Guide

Week 1 • Day 2

Student Objectives

- Recognize the relationship of the scoring guide to the rubric and the six traits of writing. *(p. 362)*
- Read a writing prompt response model. *(p. 363)*

Writing Traits in the Scoring Guide

Scoring Guide as a Rubric

Remind students about how they used rubrics to guide, evaluate, and improve their writing of other argument pieces. Point out that in a writing test, the scoring guide acts as a rubric. Ask students for definitions and examples of each item in each category. For example, ask the following:

- What type of voice would be appropriate when writing for an audience of parents and school administrators? (serious and formal)
- What organizers have you used to organize details in the types of argument writing you have done? (problem-and-solution frames, argument maps, pro-and-con charts, paragraph organizers)
- Which graphic organizer might help you write this test? (Argument Map)

Online Writing Center

 Provides six **interactive anchor papers** for each mode of writing.

Writing Traits
in the Scoring Guide

The scoring guide in the prompt on page 361 has been made into this chart. Does it remind you of the rubrics you've used? Not all prompts include all of the writing traits, but this one does. Use them to do your best writing. Remember to work neatly and put your name on each page.

- Be sure your writing clearly states your claim and provides relevant evidence.

- Be sure your writing is well organized. State your claim, give a new reason in each paragraph, and restate your claim at the end.

- Be sure your writing uses a voice that sounds convincing.

- Be sure your writing uses words that support your purpose.

- Be sure your writing has varied sentences.

- Be sure your writing has correct grammar, punctuation, capitalization, and spelling.

Look at Leah Alexander's argument essay on the next page. Did she follow the scoring guide?

362 Argument Writing

English Language Learners

BEGINNING

The Writing Process Review the steps in the writing process using simple words. Use the following words to substitute for *prewrite, draft, revise, edit,* and *publish: about/plan, write, change, fix,* and *show.* Remind students to follow all of these steps during a writing test.

INTERMEDIATE

Word Choice Remind students that when they draft, they should use powerful verbs. Write the following verbs on the board or on index cards: *have to, perhaps, possibly, be required to, might, need to.* Then have students work in pairs to sort the words that mean *maybe* and *must.* Ask which words are more powerful and convincing.

Turn It Off? No Way!

by Leah Alexander

If my school planned to have a Turn-Off-the-TV Week, I would be the first to protest. There are several reasons why I feel this way.

First of all, television is an excellent way of discovering what is going on in the world. Others might disagree and say that you can always read a news magazine or the newspaper instead, but sometimes there is important news that changes from minute to minute. For example, in the 2000 presidential election, people did not know which candidate had gotten more votes. For several weeks, TV was the best source of up-to-date information. Besides, a picture is worth a thousand words. You just can't get the same kind of visual experience from other media.

Another reason for watching TV is that sometimes we kids need a break. After spending an hour on the school bus, six hours in school, and a couple of hours doing homework (not to mention an hour or two of sports and afterschool clubs), we need some time off! I can't think of anything more relaxing than a good sitcom. That doesn't mean I want to watch TV all night. I'm the first one to pick up a good book in my free time. I just think that it's important not to work so hard all the time.

There is a third reason I don't support a week without television. I want to be an actress when I grow up. I think it's really helpful to watch both good and bad actors to see how—or how not—to act. Some people might say I should just go to the movies, but they are too expensive. Since television is usually free, you don't waste your money if the show isn't good.

I can see skipping a night of TV now and then. I do it myself, especially if I have to study for a big test. But a whole week without television seems like overkill.

I have no doubt that there are many reasons why people support the idea of a week of no television for kids. But for responsible students like me, the reasons *not* to turn off the TV outweigh them.

Argument Test Writing 363

Tell students that they will sometimes use writing prompts that do not include guidance for each of the six categories in the rubric by name.

However, students can use their writing experience to remember the main requirements:

- a clear claim, supported by strong reasons and evidence from credible sources
- logical organization that includes helpful transition words that guide the reader
- a voice that sounds convincing and appropriate for both purpose and audience
- language that is compelling and supports the writer's purpose
- sentences that flow well with a variety in length and structure
- conscientious editing for spelling, punctuation, and capitalization

Read the Model

Writing Prompt Response

Read "Turn It Off? No Way!" aloud as students follow along in their books. Tell students to keep the requirements of the scoring guide in mind as they follow along. After reading the essay aloud, ask students how the writing is organized. (according to well-supported reasons) Ask which evidence they found most effective and why.

ADVANCED
Writing Prompt Make a few copies of the argument writing prompt. Cut apart the sentences in the scoring guide. Have partners work together to assign the sentences to one of the rubric writing traits—Ideas, Organization, Voice, Word Choice, Sentence Fluency, and Conventions.

ADVANCED HIGH
Using Different Kinds of Sentences Tell students they can make their writing more interesting by varying the types of sentences they write. Write the following sentences on the board: *Do you know a foreign language? Let me tell you why you should learn a foreign language. You should learn a foreign language because….* Ask students which sentence sounds more dramatic. Write other plain sentences on the board, and have students suggest ways to make them more dramatic by using questions, exclamations, or commands.

CCSS Common Core State Standards
R/Inf.7.1: Cite several pieces of textual evidence to support analysis of what the text says explicitly as well as inferences drawn from the text.

Argument Test Writing T363

Analyze
the Model

Student Objectives

- Apply the scoring guide to the writing prompt response model. *(pp. 364–365)*

Using the Scoring Guide to Study the Model

Review the Scoring Guide Remind students that the scoring guide is the tool that an evaluator—a teacher or other trained professional—will use to score the writing test. Students are given the scoring guide so they will know the criteria on which the writing will be judged.

Use the Scoring Guide Have students use the writing traits in the Scoring Guide chart on page 362 to evaluate the test written in response to the writing prompt on page 361. The chart is based on the scoring guide.

Find More Examples Explain that pages 364–366 show how the writing model on page 363 meets all six writing traits. Have students read pages 364–365 and look for additional examples of **Ideas, Organization, Voice,** and **Word Choice** in the model.

Strategies for Writers Online
Go to **www.sfw.z-b.com** for additional online resources for students and teachers.

Using the Scoring Guide to Study the Model

Now let's use the scoring guide to check Leah's writing test, "Turn It Off? No Way!" Let's see how well her essay meets each of the six writing traits.

Ideas

- The claim is clearly stated.
- Relevant evidence is included.

I like how Leah gets right to the point and gives the reader her opinion, or claim, in the very first sentence. There's no questioning the way she feels about the topic.

> If my school planned to have a Turn-Off-the-TV Week, I would be the first to protest.

Throughout her essay, Leah provides plenty of relevant supporting evidence to back up her point of view.

> First of all, television is an excellent way of discovering what is going on in the world. Others might disagree and say that you can always read a news magazine or the newspaper instead, but sometimes there is important news that changes from minute to minute.

Organization

- The writing is well organized.
- The claim is stated, a new reason is given in each body paragraph, and the claim is restated at the end.

Leah's writing is so well organized, I had no trouble understanding, and even agreeing with, her argument. She even restates her opinion in the conclusion, just to be sure her point is completely clear.

> I have no doubt that there are many reasons why people support the idea of a week of no television for kids. But for responsible students like me, the reasons *not* to turn off the TV outweigh them.

364 Argument Writing

ENRICHMENT

Explore Word Choice Have students explore and practice word choice more deeply by choosing one paragraph from the model and rewriting it, replacing as many words as they can with different precise words. The goal is not necessarily to write a better or more precise paragraph but to compare the effects produced by choosing different precise words. Have students exchange their rewritten paragraphs with partners or with other members of a small group and discuss how the changes affected the experience of reading the paragraphs.

- The writer's voice sounds convincing.

Leah's voice is so confident, and her arguments are so solid, that I found it easy to agree with her point of view. She's clearly thought her opinion through.

That doesn't mean I want to watch TV all night. I'm the first one to pick up a good book in my free time. I just think that it's important not to work so hard all the time.

- The writer uses words that support the purpose.

Leah was clever to use words like *best source of up-to-date information, visual experience,* and *media.* These words are appropriate for the topic, and give her writing strength and credibility.

For several weeks, TV was the best source of up-to-date information. Besides, a picture is worth a thousand words. You just can't get the same kind of visual experience from other media.

Think About the Traits Once students have thoroughly discussed the model argument essay on page 363, ask them which traits they think are most important in this type of essay. Of course, all the traits are important in every piece of writing, but some of the traits stand out more in some types of writing than in others. Students might say, for example, that the trait **Organization** is very important because the writer must present his or her ideas in a way that helps the reader follow the argument. Or, they may say that **Word Choice** is important because precise, carefully chosen words help convince the reader.

REINFORCEMENT

Support Voice Remind students that voice is the way the writer "speaks" to the reader through his or her writing. A voice can be informal and convincing, like Leah's voice in the model. Or it can be formal and serious, as in a business letter or a report presented to the school board. Help students "hear" Leah's voice by reading the model aloud with expression and phrasing. Ask volunteers to read short portions of the model aloud to help them better hear the voice.

CCSS **Common Core State Standards**

SL.7.1: Engage effectively in a range of collaborative discussions (one-on-one, in groups, and teacher-led) with diverse partners on *grade 7 topics, texts, and issues,* building on others' ideas and expressing their own clearly.

Analyze
the Model

Week 1 • Day 4

Student Objectives

- Continue to apply the scoring guide to the writing prompt response model. *(p. 366)*

Analyze the Model Ask students to find other example passages in the model that flow well because of sentence variety. Have them explain why the mix of sentence lengths and types makes the passages they chose enjoyable to read. Also have them look for how the writer uses punctuation for effect.

Remind students that using conventions correctly is crucial to making their writing accessible to readers. The most interesting ideas will be lost on readers if poor grammar and spelling make the writing hard to understand. Ask students to think about areas of grammar, spelling, or punctuation where they often make mistakes. Have them look for examples of those conventions being used correctly in the model.

Strategies for Writers Online
Go to **www.sfw.z-b.com** for additional online resources for students and teachers.

Using the Scoring Guide to Study the Model

- **The writing contains a variety of sentences.**

Reading Leah's writing is enjoyable and it really got me thinking. She uses a variety of sentence structures to keep the writing smooth and lively. I especially like her use of parentheses in the example below.

> After spending an hour on the school bus, six hours in school, and a couple of hours doing homework (not to mention an hour or two of sports and afterschool clubs), we need some time off! I can't think of anything more relaxing than a good sitcom.

- **The writing contains correct grammar, punctuation, capitalization, and spelling.**

As far as I can see, Leah did not make any serious mistakes in capitalization, punctuation, sentence structure, or spelling. But don't forget to check for mistakes in your own work. For example, if you know you often misspell words, you should make sure to pay close attention to spelling. Editing for grammar and mechanics at every step of the writing process will help you avoid errors on your writing test.

366 Argument Writing

Differentiating Instruction

ENRICHMENT

Set the Clock First ask students to explain the stopwatch visual on page 367. (Possible response: Tyler will have one hour to write the test. For this reason, the watch shows 60 minutes. The different-colored sections suggest what portion of the 60 minutes Tyler should spend on each task.) Have students next describe the relationships between the lengths of time allotted to the tasks. (Possible response: Prewriting takes about as much time as drafting and editing combined.) Have students create two, colorized versions: one to represent a shorter period of time and one to represent a longer testing period. Have students assign approximate percentages of time to each segment on both clocks. Post in the classroom and use the clocks for various writing projects.

Planning My Time

Before giving us a writing prompt, my teacher always tells us how much time we'll have to complete the test. Since I'm familiar with the steps of the writing process, I can think about how much time I need for each one. If I break up the total amount of time into small sections to complete each step, I'll be sure to have enough time to do everything I need. If the test takes an hour, here's how I can organize my time. Planning your time will help you, too!

Step 4:
Edit
5 minutes

Step 1:
Prewrite
25 minutes

Step 3:
Revise
15 minutes

Step 2:
Draft
15 minutes

Argument Test Writing 367

REINFORCEMENT

Start the Clock To prepare students for writing on demand, divide class periods for a variety of activities. Write a time schedule on the board to approximate the writing clock on page 367. Have students practice often enough so that they grow accustomed to dividing their time and completing the tasks. Talk about how setting time limits during test writing situations will help them succeed on writing tests. Recommend to students that they stay fairly close to the suggested time limits to ensure time for editing their drafts.

Analyze
Time Management

Student Objectives

• Learn how to plan time during a writing test. *(p. 367)*

Planning My Time

Time Management Explain to students that when they write for a test, they must complete all the steps of the writing process quickly. Students may be surprised that Tyler has allotted so much of the writing time—25 minutes out of 60—to prewriting. Ask students why this time is necessary. (Possible response: Without a plan for writing, students may write a draft that does not respond to the task. Then they will not have time to write another draft.)

Remind students also that revising is part of the writing task. Drafting and revising together take more time—30 minutes—than prewriting; five minutes remain to edit. Tell students that when they have a shorter or longer time in which to write a test, they can use a similar time plan: about the same amount of time for prewriting and for drafting/revising, with a shorter time left for editing.

CCSS Common Core State Standards

W.7.10: Write routinely over extended time frames (time for research, reflection, and revision) and shorter time frames (a single sitting or a day or two) for a range of discipline-specific tasks, purposes, and audiences.

Argument Test Writing T367

Write
an Argument Test

Week 2 • Day 1

Student Objectives

- Read a writing prompt for argument writing. *(p. 368)*
- Apply the six traits of writing to the writing prompt. *(p. 369)*

Prewrite

Focus on Ideas

Study the Writing Prompt Make sure students have copies of the writing prompt on page 368 so that they can follow Tyler's example and practice marking them. Tell students to mark any instructions that they find helpful. For example, a student who often has trouble organizing his or her writing might mark the second bullet as a reminder.

Then walk students through the think-aloud on page 369, encouraging them to add their own responses to Tyler's. For example, how will they introduce their claims? How will they organize their essays?

Strategies for Writers Online

Go to **www.sfw.z-b.com** for additional online resources for students and teachers.

Prewrite   Focus on   Ideas

Writing Strategy   Study the writing prompt to find out what to do.

I always study my writing prompt before I take a test. A writing prompt usually has three parts (the setup, task, and scoring guide), but they're not always labeled. When you study your writing prompt, look for these sections and label each one, just like I did below. Then circle key words in the setup and the task that tell what kind of writing you will be doing and who your audience will be. I circled my topic in purple. I also used red to circle what kind of writing I'll be doing (an argument essay) and who my audience is (others). I'll assume that my classmates are the "others."

My Writing Test Prompt

Setup — You believe that a special holiday should be created to honor a particular person or event. Think about a person or event that is important enough to you to be honored in this way.

Task — Write an essay to convince others that this person or event should be honored.

Scoring Guide — Be sure your writing
- clearly states your claim and provides relevant evidence.
- is well organized. State your claim, give a new reason in each paragraph, and restate your claim at the end.
- uses a voice that sounds convincing.
- uses words that support your purpose.
- has varied sentences.
- has correct grammar, punctuation, capitalization, and spelling.

368 Argument Writing

English Language Learners

BEGINNING

Writing Prompt Give students a copy of the standard argument test writing prompt. Have them look at each word in the prompt and circle the words they do not know. Then teach the most important words, such as *remember, holiday, honor, convince, why.* You might have a higher-level ELL work with a lower-level ELL to review the meanings of these words.

INTERMEDIATE

Writing Prompt Have students read the argument writing prompt and write down words they do not know. Review how to ask for help by asking questions, such as, *What does* honor *mean? Does* honor *mean "remember"?* Have them practice asking and answering with two other students. Finally, ask students to write their answers; for example, *To honor someone is to remember why they are special.* Review as a class.

Think about how the scoring guide relates to the six traits of good writing you've studied in the rubrics. Not every trait will be included in every scoring guide, but you'll still want to remember them all in order to write a good essay.

Ideas
- Be sure your writing clearly states your claim and provides relevant evidence.

I'll begin my essay with my claim, or opinion, so it's clear early on. Then, I'll include lots of relevant evidence in the body paragraphs.

Organization
- Be sure your writing is well organized. State your claim, give a new reason in each paragraph, and restate your claim at the end.

I'll be sure to give a new supporting reason in each paragraph and then clearly repeat my claim in the conclusion.

Voice
- Be sure your writing uses a voice that sounds convincing.

Strong yet friendly language will help me connect with the reader and persuade my audience to agree with my opinion.

Word Choice
- Be sure your writing uses words that support your purpose.

Word choice is so important. I'll work hard to use words appropriate for both my subject and audience.

Sentence Fluency
- Be sure your writing has varied sentences.

To keep my writing smooth and energetic, I'll use a variety of sentence structures.

Conventions
- Be sure your writing has correct grammar, punctuation, capitalization, and spelling.

I don't want to have any mistakes in my essay, so I'll be sure to leave enough time for editing.

Argument Test Writing 369

Discuss the Traits Explain that the purpose of this chapter is to help students prepare for a writing test. Help them build confidence in using the traits to guide and inform their writing. Divide students into small groups and assign each group a trait on page 369. Have the group discuss why that trait is important and how Tyler's ideas will help him write a good observation report. Then ask each group to share their ideas with the other groups.

ADVANCED

Supporting Arguments To help with organization during an argument writing test, suggest students use an Opinion Chart graphic organizer. Give partners a topic, and have them complete a graphic organizer to record their opinions.

ADVANCED HIGH

Writing Prompt Have students read the argument writing prompt and write down no more than three words in each part of the prompt that they think are most important. Then have them compare with a partner and discuss the differences.

CCSS Common Core State Standards

SL.7.1.a: Come to discussions prepared, having read or researched material under study; explicitly draw on that preparation by referring to evidence on the topic, text, or issue to probe and reflect on ideas under discussion.

Write
an Argument Test

Week 2 • Day 2

Student Objectives

• Learn how to respond to the task in the writing prompt. *(p. 370)*

Prewrite

Focus on (Ideas)

Encourage students to spend some time brainstorming a list of special events or a list of people who have helped them in memorable ways. To get them thinking about their purpose and audience, prompt them with questions such as the following:

• Who would you like to thank and honor for helping you or someone close to you?

• Whom should you notify about creating a day to honor your special person?

• What event had an effect on you? Why?

After choosing one from their lists, have students share their choice with a writing partner. Encourage them to also share their reasons for their choice.

Online Writing Center

Provides **interactive graphic organizers** as well as a variety of graphic organizers in PDF format.

T370 Argument Writing

Prewrite

Focus on (Ideas)

Writing Strategy   Respond to the task.

Before you start writing for a test, you should collect information. The first place to look for information is the writing prompt. Although I don't have a whole lot of time to complete my test, I know that prewriting is important because it will help me get my ideas together before I begin drafting.

My writing prompt instructs me to write an argument essay to convince others that a holiday should be created to honor a person or an event. First I have to think of someone or something that should be honored. My dog, Cato, was sick not too long ago, and our vet, Dr. Lamb, saved his life. I remember how happy I was when I found out that Cato would be OK, so I think I'll honor Dr. Lamb with this essay. I'll begin by quickly writing down some notes.

Task — [Write an essay to convince others that this person or event should be honored.

Notes

✔ Dr. Lamb saved my dog's life.

✔ She cares for pets whose owners can't pay her.

✔ Everyone likes her because she really cares about pets and people.

Apply

Think about how you'll respond to the task before you begin writing. Then jot down notes to help you gather information.

370   Argument Writing

Differentiating Instruction

ENRICHMENT

Prioritize Ideas   Challenge students to choose the strongest topic. If students are having difficulty choosing between two people or events, have them think of more than three reasons for each one. The topic with the strongest reasons and evidence should be their choice.

REINFORCEMENT

Decide on a Topic   Read aloud the Writing Prompt on page 368. Ask students to explain what it means in their own words and, if needed, guide them in restating the direction. Then draw a simple chart on the board with three columns. Label the columns: *School, Home,* and *Community.* Then ask each student to offer suggestions of helpful people or events they associate with each category. When all students have contributed, ask them to choose their favorite from the list.

Writing Strategy   Choose a graphic organizer.

Now that I've decided on a topic, it's time to start organizing my ideas. Since I'm writing an argument essay, I'll use an Argument Map. I'll use the information from the setup and task sections of the writing prompt as my call to action, and I'll fill in the rest of my Argument Map with the notes I took earlier, as well as other ideas.

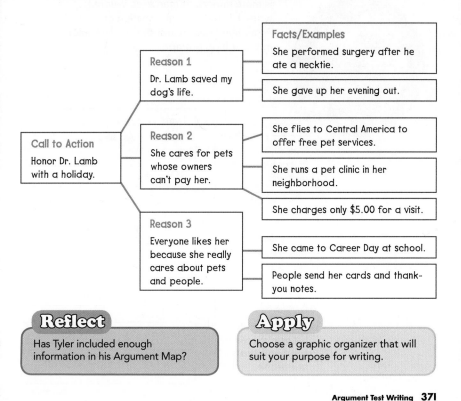

		Facts/Examples
	Reason 1 Dr. Lamb saved my dog's life.	She performed surgery after he ate a necktie.
		She gave up her evening out.
Call to Action Honor Dr. Lamb with a holiday.	**Reason 2** She cares for pets whose owners can't pay her.	She flies to Central America to offer free pet services.
		She runs a pet clinic in her neighborhood.
		She charges only $5.00 for a visit.
	Reason 3 Everyone likes her because she really cares about pets and people.	She came to Career Day at school.
		People send her cards and thank-you notes.

Reflect

Has Tyler included enough information in his Argument Map?

Apply

Choose a graphic organizer that will suit your purpose for writing.

Argument Test Writing   371

Write
an Argument Test

Week 2 • Day 3

Student Objectives

- Learn how to choose a graphic organizer for the writing prompt. (p. 371)

Prewrite

Focus on **Organization**

Once students have chosen their topics, have them create graphic organizers and list the reasons and evidence for their argument essays. Tell students that while an Argument Map is an effective tool for prewriting an argument essay, other organizers might work just as well. Explain that their first response to a writing prompt usually will be to make quick notes about a potential topic. Assure them that whether they use a list, chart, or map, the organizer they use should help them get ready to write their drafts. Ask students to discuss other organizers they have used. Have them demonstrate how other organizers would work to organize their ideas.

CCSS **Common Core State Standards**

W.7.1.b: Support claim(s) with logical reasoning and relevant evidence, using accurate, credible sources, and demonstrating an understanding of the topic or text.

Write
an Argument Test

Week 2 • Day 4

Student Objectives

- Learn how to check the graphic organizer against the scoring guide. *(pp. 372–373)*

Prewrite

Focus on

Check the Graphic Organizer

Have students evaluate Tyler's Argument Map on page 372. Initiate discussion by asking these questions:

- Are the reasons in logical order?

- Are they well supported?

- Is anything missing?

Read the **Ideas** and **Organization** descriptors and commentaries on page 373 aloud to demonstrate how Tyler has used each writing trait to help him prewrite his draft. Have students follow the traits to complete their organizers.

After students complete their organizers, have them complete the activity in the Apply box on page 373.

Strategies for Writers Online

Go to **www.sfw.z-b.com** for additional online resources for students and teachers.

T372 **Argument Writing**

Prewrite

Focus on **Organization**

Writing Strategy Check the graphic organizer against the scoring guide.

You don't always get much time to revise during a writing test. So prewriting is more important than ever. Before I write, I'll check the information on my Argument Map against the scoring guide in the writing prompt.

Call to Action
Honor Dr. Lamb with a holiday.

Reason 1
Dr. Lamb saved my dog's life.

Facts/Examples
She performed surgery after he ate a necktie.

She gave up her evening out.

Reason 2
She cares for pets whose owners can't pay her.

She flies to Central America to offer free pet services.

She runs a pet clinic in her neighborhood.

She charges only $5.00 for a visit.

Reason 3
Everyone likes her because she really cares about pets and people.

She came to Career Day at school.

People send her cards and thank-you notes.

372 **Argument Writing**

- Be sure your writing clearly states your claim and provides relevant evidence.

I'll begin with the call to action from my Argument Map. Relevant facts and examples strengthen my point of view.

- Be sure your writing is well organized. State your claim, give a new reason in each paragraph, and restate your claim at the end.

I'll use the reasons in the Argument Map to write the body paragraphs. Then I'll restate the opinion in the conclusion.

- Be sure your writing uses a voice that sounds convincing.

I'll be sure to use language that reflects how strongly I feel about my topic—and how it would only make sense for others to agree with me.

- Be sure your writing uses words that support your purpose.

My choice of words is really important. I'll use clear and concise words that are appropriate for my purpose.

- Be sure your writing has varied sentences.

To keep my reader interested, I'll use a variety of sentences. This will also help my writing flow.

Conventions

- Be sure your writing has correct grammar, punctuation, capitalization, and spelling.

I know to watch my spelling, grammar, capitalization, and punctuation.

Reflect

Can you think of anything that's missing from Tyler's Argument Map?

Apply

Compare your graphic organizer with the scoring guide before you start to write. This way you'll be sure you know what to do when you begin drafting.

Argument Test Writing 373

Prewrite

Prepare to Draft Compare the scoring guide to the instructions that come with assemble-it-yourself furniture. The building instructions usually advise you through several preparatory steps, including laying out all the pieces included in the kit and gathering the correct tools. If you just dive right into the task, you'll end up with a mess.

Discuss where Tyler is in the process right now. (He has done the preparation work and is ready to draft.) Ask students why it's necessary for Tyler to re-read and think about the traits that come after **Ideas** and **Organization,** even though he has not begun to write. (Possible response: He needs to keep the other traits in mind as he writes.) Have students discuss strategies for using the traits to shape their drafts before beginning to write.

CCSS **C**ommon **C**ore **S**tate **S**tandards
W.7.1: Write arguments to support claims with clear reasons and relevant evidence.

Argument Test Writing T373

Write
an Argument Test

Week 2 • Day 5

Student Objectives

- Draft an argument writing test, stating the claim clearly. (pp. 374–375)

Draft

Focus on

Tips for Test Writing As students prepare to draft, remind them to write on every other line of paper. This leaves space for students to make their corrections when they revise and edit their drafts. Mention that in a testing situation, students will not have time to create a fresh final copy of their writing.

Tell students to refer to their Argument Maps frequently as they draft. If a new detail occurs to students while they draft, they should add it only if it will add something important to the reader's understanding of the argument.

Have students read pages 374–375 and discuss how the highlighted text helps the reader understand Tyler's claim. **(Possible response: Tyler's claim is clear and stated in the first sentence. This tells his purpose for writing and helps the reader prepare to read his essay.)**

Encourage students to follow this model to write their drafts.

Online Writing Center

 Provides student eBooks with an **interactive writing pad** for drafting, revising, editing, and publishing.

Draft   Focus on (Ideas)

Writing Strategy   Clearly state the claim for the reader.

It's time to start writing. The scoring guide says that I should clearly state my claim for the reader. I'll begin my draft with my call to action so that my essay is convincing and easy to follow, right from the start.

[DRAFT]   Dr. Kitty Lamb Day
by Tyler   [clear claim statement]

The person I nominate to be honored with a special holiday is Dr. Kitty Lamb, our veterinarian. Believe it or not, that's her real name. Dr. Lamb has been my dogs' doctor since he was a pup. There are several reasons why I think she is a hero.

Since it looks like she kind of saved my dog's life, the first reason is personal. Cato likes to chew on things. Once he even chewed up the tire on my bicycle! The time he really got into trouble, however, was when he swallowed one of my dad's neckties. We didn't know he had done anything wrong until he stopped eating and started whining a lot. Thats when we called Dr. Lamb. She said to bring Cato right over. When we got there, she was all dressed up because her and her husband were on there way to a party. She had to perform surgery for five ours to save that silly dog's life. After a few weeks Cato completely recovered.

374 Argument Writing

English Language Learners

BEGINNING

Word Order On the board, write *recycle, should, and, paper, cans, You.* Ask, is this a sentence? Tell students that the words need to be rearranged. Ask partners to fix the order of words in the sentence: *You should recycle paper and cans.* Underline, *You* and circle *should recycle.* Point out that this sentence has a subject and a verb, so it is complete.

INTERMEDIATE

Using Strong Words After students have written their first drafts, have them circle all the verbs they used in the first paragraph. Then have them trade with a partner who will read the paragraph and change each of the circled verbs to a stronger one. Then have the partners discuss why they made each change. Monitor that students' changes were appropriate.

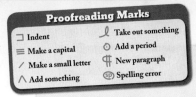
[DRAFT]

The second reason I think Dr. Lamb should be recognized is because of the volunteer work that she do. Every year, she flies to Central America with a group of other vets. There they care for the pets of people who don't have enough money for proper pet care. Even at home, Dr. Lamb helps people and their pets. Once a month, she runs a pet clinic here in town where you can have your pet examined for just five dollars.

Dr. Lamb came to our school on Career Day to tell about the work she does. If you ever visit her office. You will be amazed at all the cards and letters on her bulletin board. These are all thank-you notes from pet owners that she has helped.

I am so happy with Dr. Lamb that I would like to become a veterinarian when I grow up. I think a great way to recognize her would be to hold a pet parade on the street in front of her office. Maybe she could even wear a crown that says Top Dog! Although there are many other heroes who might deserve a holiday of their won, Dr. Lamb definitely gets my vote!

Reflect

Do you think Tyler's claim is clear?

Apply

You may not get a chance to recopy your paper in a writing test, so try to be neat when you write.

ADVANCED

Writing Arguments Have students use the Opinion Chart they created to write a paragraph or two. Monitor as they write to make sure they are beginning with the main idea, or what they want to persuade their reader to think or do. The rest of the essay should include strong sentences that support the writer's opinions.

ADVANCED HIGH

Peer Review After students have drafted their argument essays, have them trade with another student. Partners should review the drafts and look for specific details. Students should point out weak voice and suggest more persuasive words their partners could use. As you monitor, identify two or three examples of weak words or sentences, and discuss ways to strengthen them as a class.

Introduce and Support Claim As students write their drafts, tell them to pay attention to presenting and supporting their reasons logically. Have them ask themselves these questions:

- Have I stated my claim (purpose for writing) clearly in the introduction?
- Do I present each reason in its own paragraph?
- Do I support each reason with relevant facts and examples?

Remind students to present their reasons logically, stating the most important reason first.

CCSS **Common Core State Standards**

W.7.1.a: Introduce claim(s), acknowledge alternate or opposing claims, and organize the reasons and evidence logically. **W.7.1.b:** Support claim(s) with logical reasoning and relevant evidence, using accurate, credible sources and demonstrating an understanding of the topic or text.

Write
an Argument Test

Week 3 • Day 1

Student Objectives

• Organize the ideas into an introduction, body, and conclusion. (p. 376)

Revise

Focus on  Organization

Time Management Remind students that they have about fifteen minutes to revise their drafts and that there are three revision tasks. Students might wish to subdivide their planned revising time into three, five-minute segments and tackle one strategy at a time.

Check for Logical Order Read the Writing Strategy aloud, and have students read the rest of page 376. The draft shows changes that Tyler made to the end of his essay to help the reader follow all of his reasons. Point out that Tyler revised the beginning of this paragraph to connect ideas for the reader. Also mention that the revision announces the last reason in the essay.

Tell students to review their writing to make sure their essays are well organized. If they followed their organizers, their paragraphs should make sense and be easy to follow.

 Strategies for Writers Online
Go to **www.sfw.z-b.com** for additional online resources for students and teachers.

T376 Argument Writing

Revise

Focus on **Organization**

Writing Strategy   Organize the ideas into an introduction, body, and conclusion.

My Argument Map was so helpful when writing my draft. I put my call to action in the first paragraph and supporting details in the body. Then I restated my claim in the conclusion. But there's one paragraph where it's not clear that I'm mentioning a new reason, and it's confusing. I'll strengthen my organization by adding a line to let my reader know a new point is being made.

[DRAFT]

The last reason I think Dr. Lamb is a hero is because of the way she treats both animals and people.

She
~~Dr. Lamb~~ came to our school on Career Day to tell about the work she does. If you ever visit her office. You will be amazed at all the cards and letters on her bulletin board.

[organized writing]

Apply

Make sure your ideas are organized logically and clearly.

376 Argument Writing

Revise

Focus on Voice

Writing Strategy   Sound convincing.

As with any writing assignment, my voice should match my purpose and audience. My purpose in this paper is to convince others that Dr. Lamb deserves her own holiday. I need to sound confident, include strong and relevant reasons to back up my opinion, and use balanced, positive language. Mostly I did a great job, but there's one line where I don't sound too sure of myself. I'll rewrite that line now to sound more confident.

[DRAFT]

[used convincing tone]

Since ~~it looks like~~ she ~~kind of~~ saved my dog's life, the first reason is personal. Cato likes to chew on things. Once he even chewed up the tire on my bicycle! The time he really got into trouble, however, was when he swallowed one of my dad's neckties.

Reflect

How have Tyler's organization and voice revisions affected his writing?

Apply

Use strong, relevant reasons and positive language to sound convincing.

Argument Test Writing   377

Write
an Argument Test

Week 3 • Day 2

Student Objectives

• Sound convincing. (p. 377)

Revise

Focus on Voice

Review Voice Have students read page 377. Ask students how Tyler's revisions make his voice sound more convincing. (Possible response: The deleted text did not sound certain or confident. Tyler's changes improved the tone and made the writing stronger in this part.) Explain that a writer's voice should connect with the reader from the first sentence to the last sentence in an essay. In other words, writers need to establish and maintain a convincing voice and tone.

Have students review their essays for consistent voice. Point out that during a writing test, students will not be able to read their drafts aloud to share them with partners.

Remind students also to utilize clear proofreading marks and make their changes as neatly as possible in the lines above or below their original writing.

CCSS **Common Core State Standards**

W.7.1.d: Establish and maintain a formal style.

Write
an Argument Test

Week 3 • Day 3

Student Objectives

- Use words with the right connotation. *(p. 378)*

Revise

Focus on Word Choice

Use the Right Words Have students read page 378 and discuss Tyler's revisions. Ask students how his changes improve this part of the essay. (Possible responses: He chose replacement words that convey a positive meaning. Tyler's changes are consistent with his purpose to convince others to honor his hero.) Tell students that as they revise for word choice they should look for and replace any words that sound too casual or unconvincing. Allow students to use word resources during this revising practice and have them record new words and definitions on a personal writing vocabulary list.

Revise
Word Choice

Writing Strategy Use words with the right connotation.

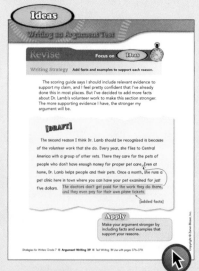

I know from the scoring guide that I should choose words that support my purpose. My goal is to convince my reader to agree with my point of view. The words I choose will directly affect how my reader responds to my claim. I need to use words that are associated with positive emotions or reactions—words with positive connotations. As I reread my draft, I found some words I could replace with others that have stronger positive connotations. I'll change them now.

[DRAFT]

[used strong positive words]

impressed by

I am so happy with Dr. Lamb that I would like to become a

honor

veterinarian when I grow up. I think a great way to recognize her

would be to hold a pet parade on the street in front of her office.

Apply

Make your point with words that have the right connotations.

378 Argument Writing

Optional Revising Lessons

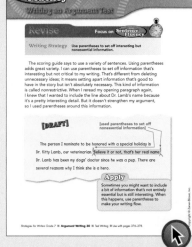

Argument 29

Argument 30

Online Writing Center

Provides **interactive proofreading activities** for each genre.

Writing Strategy   Check the grammar, punctuation, capitalization, and spelling.

It's always a good idea to check your writing test one last time before turning it in. The scoring guide says to use correct grammar, punctuation, capitalization, and spelling. I always leave plenty of time to correct errors in these important areas.

[FINAL DRAFT]

Dr. Kitty Lamb Day
by Tyler

The person I nominate to be honored with a special holiday is Dr. Kitty Lamb, our veterinarian. (Believe it or not, that's her real name.) Dr. Lamb has been my ~~dogs~~ dog's doctor since he was a pup. There are several reasons why I think she is a hero.

Since she saved my dog's life, the first reason is personal. Cato likes to chew on things. Once he even chewed up the tire on my bicycle! The time he really got into trouble, however, was when he swallowed one of my dad's neckties. We didn't know he had done anything wrong until he stopped eating and started whining a lot. That's when we called Dr. Lamb. She said to bring Cato right over. When we got there, she was all dressed up because ~~her~~ she and her husband were on ~~there~~ their way to a party. She had to perform surgery for five ~~ours~~ hours to save that silly dog's life. After a few weeks, Cato completely recovered.

Argument Test Writing   379

Student Objectives

- Check the grammar, punctuation, capitalization, and spelling. *(pp. 379–380)*

Edit

Focus on **Conventions**

Edit the Test Explain to students that while an argument essay written for a test in a short period of time will rarely be perfect, they should find and correct as many errors as they can. Test graders know that students are writing quickly and watching the clock; graders know that a few errors may slip through. However, graders also look for evidence that students took time to edit. When they see misspelled words crossed out and correctly spelled words inserted instead, for example, graders know that students are paying attention to editing.

Review the proofreading marks on page 375 with students. Then point out the changes in Tyler's draft and the proofreader's marks he used for the insertions. Remind students that they should not plan on having enough time to recopy a test writing draft. Their goal is to make their changes legible, not to produce a perfectly neat final copy.

CCSS **Common Core State Standards**
L.1: Demonstrate the command of the conventions of standard English grammar and usage when writing or speaking. **L.2:** Demonstrate command of the conventions of standard English capitalization, punctuation, and spelling when writing.

Differentiating Instruction

ENRICHMENT
Reaching the Finish Line Advanced students who often finish writing tests early may fall into the habit of simply waiting for the testing period to be over. Remind them that utilizing available time to re-check their writing is an excellent strategy. If students have finished revising their essays for **Organization, Voice,** and **Word Choice,** refer them to the list of traits on page 373 to make sure they covered all the traits. Then have them read their essays one more time while keeping the writing traits and the writing task in mind.

Argument Test Writing   T379

Review
Test Tips

Student Objectives

- Review tips for writing a test. (p. 381)

Test Tips

Reviewing Test Writing Explain to students that not all writing test prompts will be as clearly divided into parts as the writing prompt they used in this chapter. However, students can still find and label the three important parts of a writing prompt. Students can even generate a scoring guide if they must. Write this prompt on the board:

Think about an issue that affects you and express your opinion on the issue. Revise and edit your response.

Now ask:

- What is the setup? (Think about an issue that affects you.)

Circle and label the setup, and point out that it is rather brief. Ask students how they might expand on it to get a better sense of the background for this writing prompt. (Possible response: What kind of an issue? Where would the issue be of concern? For example, does the issue exist in school, at home, or in the community?)

Strategies for Writers Online
Go to **www.sfw.z-b.com** for additional online resources for students and teachers.

[FINAL DRAFT]

The second reason I think Dr. Lamb should be recognized is because of the volunteer work that she ~~do~~ does. Every year, she flies to Central America with a group of other vets. There, they care for the pets of people who don't have enough money for proper pet care. Even at home, Dr. Lamb helps people and their pets. Once a month, she runs a pet clinic here in town where you can have your pet examined for just five dollars. The doctors don't get paid for the work they do there, and they even pay for their own plane tickets.

She ~~Dr. Lamb~~ came to our school on Career Day to tell about the work she does. If you ever visit her office, ~~Y~~you will be amazed at all the cards and letters on her bulletin board. These are all thank-you notes from pet owners that she has helped.

I am so ~~happy with~~ impressed by Dr. Lamb that I would like to become a veterinarian when I grow up. I think a great way to ~~recognize~~ honor her would be to hold a pet parade on the street in front of her office. Maybe she could even wear a crown that says Top Dog! Although there are many other heroes who might deserve a holiday of their ~~won~~ own, Dr. Lamb definitely gets my vote! The last reason I think Dr. Lamb is a hero is because of the way she treats both animals and people.

Reflect

Before Tyler turns in his test, he should check it against the scoring guide one last time. Remember to use your writing prompt's scoring guide to check your writing whenever you take a test.

Apply

Don't turn in a test paper until you've done a final edit to check for grammar and spelling mistakes.

380 Argument Writing

Differentiating Instruction

REINFORCEMENT

Focus the Edit All writers tend to repeat mistakes until the rules are mastered. Tell students that when they edit their work, they should spend the most time on the conventions that give them trouble. For example, a student may need to spend less time checking grammar, capitalization, and punctuation, and spend more time on spelling. To make the most of their editing time during a test situation, have students focus on their most frequent errors and fix them first.

I'm done! That was easy! When you take a writing test, remember to use the writing process. The process is just a little different for a test, but if you keep in mind these important tips, you'll do just fine.

TEST TIPS

1. **Study the writing prompt before you start to write.** Most writing prompts have three parts: the setup, the task, and the scoring guide. The parts probably won't be labeled. You'll have to figure them out for yourself!

2. **Make sure you understand the task before you start to write.**
   - Read all three parts of the writing prompt carefully.
   - Circle key words in the task part of the writing prompt that tell what kind of writing you need to do. The task might also identify your audience.
   - Make sure you know how you'll be graded.
   - Say the assignment in your own words to yourself.

3. **Keep an eye on the clock.** Decide how much time you will spend on each part of the writing process and try to stick to your schedule. Don't spend so much time on prewriting that you don't have enough time left to write.

4. **Reread your writing. Compare it to the scoring guide at least twice.** Remember the rubrics you've used? A scoring guide on a writing test is like a rubric. It can help you keep what's important in mind.

5. **Plan, plan, plan!** You don't get much time to revise during a test, so planning is more important than ever.

6. **Write neatly.** Remember: If the people who score your test can't read your writing, it doesn't matter how good your story or essay is!

Next ask:

- **What is the task?** (Express an opinion on an issue.)

Circle and label the task, and point out that it is missing some information. It does not tell specifically what kind of writing is called for. Ask students how they can tell what kind of writing the task requires. (Possible response: The task is about an issue that concerns me. It states *express your opinion.* An argument essay states the writer's opinion about an issue, backed up by credible evidence. So the prompt is calling for an argument essay.)

Finally, ask students what they can do to make up a scoring guide, since the writing prompt provides only general instructions to *revise and edit.* (Possible response: We know that we can use the writing drafts to prewrite, draft, revise, and edit. We can write a quick list of the traits for an argument essay to guide our planning and writing time.)

Have students volunteer the names of the traits and how they apply to this prompt. Write students' responses on the board in bulleted form. Show students that they have just figured out a useful scoring guide from their own writing experiences. Students will see that even a brief writing prompt can give them the information they need to write a successful test.

CCSS Common Core State Standards
W.7.1: Write arguments to support claims with clear reasons and relevant evidence.

Descriptive writing

Biographic Sketch

Pages T384A–T405

This genre opens the door to descriptive writing by encouraging students to draw on their own experiences to describe someone they know.

Prewrite Describe someone you know very well.
Make a Character Chart.

Draft Use plenty of sensory details to provide a clear mental picture for the reader.

Revise Introduce the character right away. Add sayings or quotes that the subject frequently uses.
Use a thesaurus to replace vague words with vivid, descriptive ones.

Edit Check prepositional phrases and avoid misplaced participial phrases (dangling modifiers).

Publish Display the biographic sketch on a "Who Am I?" bulletin board in the school hallway.

Observation Report

Pages T406A–T427

This genre gives students an opportunity to explore the natural world. It is also a beginning stage of writing for science.

Prewrite Choose an aspect of nature to observe. Make notes (with sketches) of what you observe.
Make an Observation Chart to organize all notes around the five senses.

Draft Write transitions that connect ideas.

Revise Show thoughtfulness about and caring for the subject.
Replace ordinary, vague words with specific words.
Vary sentence patterns for meaning, reader interest, and style.

Edit Check to see that the subject and verb in each sentence agree.

Publish Add the account to the class's science journal.

Geographic Description

Pages T428A–T455

This genre gives students a chance to do research—an important skill—while they learn about and describe a place they've never been to.

Prewrite Use an atlas to find a place to describe. Then research the place in three other appropriate sources.
Make a Web to organize descriptive details.

Draft Use third-person point of view and an objective tone.

Revise Use a comparison to make the description more complete.
Add some figurative language, including similes and metaphors.
Combine short, choppy sentences.

Edit Check to see that adjectives and adverbs are used correctly.

Publish Choose visuals that will work with the text.

MATH CONNECTION

Poem

Pages T456A–T477

Students will express their understanding of a mathematical concept or event in the creative form of a poem.

Prewrite   Choose a topic. Make a list of descriptive details.
Use a Web to plan the poem.

Draft   Choose words and phrases for effect.

Revise   Choose details that bring the topic to life.
Check the order of the lines and stanzas.
Place line breaks where they make sense.

Edit   Check the use and punctuation of adjective and adverb clauses.

Publish   Present the poem in a multimedia presentation.

Descriptive Test Writing

Pages T478A–T499

Students will learn and practice how to read a descriptive test prompt and how to plan their time. They will also learn and practice writing strategies for successful test writing in the descriptive mode.

Prewrite   Study the writing prompt to find out what to do.
Respond to the task.
Choose a graphic organizer.
Check the graphic organizer against the scoring guide.

Draft   Draw the reader in with sensory details that paint a visual image.

Revise   Make sure details are presented in a logical, natural order.
Connect with the readers.
Replace vague words and phrases with precise ones.

Edit   Check grammar, punctuation, capitalization, and spelling.

Online Writing Center

Interactive Whiteboard Ready

Complete Digital Writing Instruction!

- My Writing Pad
- Interactive Rubrics
- Anchor Papers
- Graphic Organizers

- Content Area Writing Prompts
- Grammar Games
- Proofreading Activities
- Instructional Videos

- Virtual File Cabinet
- eBooks
- Assessments

For information, go to www.sfw.z-b.com

Also available: **Online Essay Grader and Writing Tutor,** powered by Vantage Learning's MY Access®.

21ˢᵗ Century Literacies
Technology, Digital Media & Writing

by **Julie Coiro, Ph.D.,** University of Rhode Island & **Sara Kajder, Ph.D.,** University of Pittsburgh

INSPIRE **Websites to Spark Ideas**

Publishing Biographic Sketches

Many websites can spark ideas for students who are not quite sure who to write about for a biographic sketch or for those simply looking for more information about a particular person. These websites offer opportunities for students to link their writing to topics such as science, math, social studies, and art. Here are a few online biography collections your students may wish to visit:

• **The Academy of Achievement (www.achievement. org)** In the Achiever Gallery, the focus is on extraordinary individuals who have shaped the twentieth century with their courage, commitment, and ingenuity. The website also includes Achievement TV—an electronic forum that allows students to meet and learn from individuals who have shaped the history of our times—via live and interactive teleconferences that are simulcast nationwide.

• **I WAS Wondering (www.iwaswondering.org),** a project of the National Academy of Sciences, highlights the lives and accomplishments of contemporary women in science. Students will be inspired by biographies, interactive games, fun facts, and opportunities to ask questions about science.

• **The HistoryMakers (www.thehistorymakers. com)** includes biographical information and audio and video clips about African Americans who have influenced history. The website aims to capture the stories of accomplished African Americans across all walks of life, and to use new technologies to create an accessible digital collection for students, teachers, and scholars.

Writing Science Observation Reports

As part of this descriptive writing unit, students may wish to check out some of the following online collections. These websites may spark ideas for science experiments they can do at home. Students can then formally write up their procedures and results in an observation report.

• **PBS Science Activities (http://pbskids.org/zoom/ activities/sci)** includes experiments especially designed for children to explore concepts such as chemistry, engineering, the five senses, forces, life science, patterns sound, structures, and water.

• **Energy Quest Science Projects (http://www. energyquest.ca.gov/projects/index.html)** offers fun experiments to guide an exploration of simplified concepts related to chemical energy, geothermal energy, and nuclear energy.

• **Exploratorium Science Snacks (www.exploratorium. edu/snacks)** are miniature versions of some of the most popular exhibits at the Exploratorium Museum of Science, Art, and Human Perception located in San Francisco, California. Each features ideas about what to do and notice after setting up an experiment.

• **Science Experiments at Home (http://members. ozemail.com.au/~macinnis/scifun/miniexp.htm)** is an interesting collection of short experiments and explanations of what's happening that is sure to prompt writing ideas.

Descriptive writing brings clear word pictures to the reader.

Hi, there! My name is Andre. Welcome to the world of descriptive writing. Descriptive writing sounds like fun. I'll get to paint pictures with words as I describe objects, people, places, and events. Living in Alaska gives me a lot of stuff to describe, and I can't wait to get started!

IN THIS UNIT

- ☐ Biographic Sketch
- ☐ Observation Report
- ☐ Geographic Description
- MATH CONNECTION ▶ ☐ Poem
- ☐ Writing for a Test

Name:	Andre
Home:	Alaska
Hobbies:	snowboarding, camping, hiking, astronomy
Favorite Book:	*Water Sky* by Jean Craighead George
Favorite Food:	hamburgers

To differentiate instruction and maximize student achievement, use the Extensions Online activities available at **www.sfw.z-b.com.**

Created by Amy Humphreys, Ed.M., these engaging activities can be used to meet a wide range of learner needs. Each activity uses a combination of visual, written, oral, and kinesthetic elements, and deliberately leverages the power of collaboration and conversation so students learn to think like writers in fun and engaging ways. For more information on Differentiated Instruction, see page Z12.

Meet Your Writing Partner, Andre

The writing partner for this chapter is Andre, a boy from Alaska. Read the information about Andre to find out more about him. Explain that Alaska is known for its vast wilderness areas, cold climate, and fascinating wildlife. Review the personal information given about Andre. Discuss what kinds of things Andre might describe. Also, point out that Andre will go through the steps in the writing process: prewrite, draft, revise, edit, and publish. At each stage, Andre will blend good writing strategies with the traits of writing: ideas, organization, voice, word choice, sentence fluency, and conventions.

Biographic Sketch Planner

WEEK 1

Day 1
Introduce
a Biographic Sketch

Student Objectives
- Review the elements of a biographic sketch.
- Consider purpose and audience.
- Learn the traits of descriptive writing.

Student Activities
- Read and discuss **What's in a Biographic Sketch?** (p. 384)
- Read and discuss **Why Write a Biographic Sketch?** (p. 385)
- Read **Linking Descriptive Writing Traits to a Biographic Sketch.** (p. 386)

Day 2
Analyze
Read a Biographic Sketch

Student Objectives
- Read a model biographic sketch.

Student Activities
- Read **"Jane Ellis: Teacher, Alaskan."** (p. 387)

Day 3
Analyze
Introduce the Rubric

Student Objectives
- Learn to read a rubric.

Student Activities
- Review **"Jane Ellis: Teacher, Alaskan."** (p. 387)
- Read and discuss the **Biographic Sketch Rubric.** (pp. 388–389)

WEEK 2

Day 1
Write
Prewrite: Ideas

Student Objectives
- Read and understand a prewriting strategy.

Student Activities
- Read and discuss **Prewrite: Focus on Ideas.** (p. 394)
- Apply the prewriting strategy.

Day 2
Write
Prewrite: Organization

Student Objectives
- Make a Character Chart to organize details about the biography's subject.

Student Activities
- Read and discuss **Prewrite: Focus on Organization.** (p. 395)
- Reflect on the model Character Chart.
- Apply the prewriting strategy.
- Participate in a peer conference.

Day 3
Write
Draft: Ideas

Student Objectives
- Begin writing, using sensory details.

Student Activities
- Read and discuss **Draft: Focus on Ideas.** (pp. 396–397)
- Reflect on a model draft.
- Apply the drafting strategy.

WEEK 3

Day 1
Write
Revise: Voice

Student Objectives
- Revise for effective use of quotations.

Student Activities
- Read and discuss **Revise: Focus on Voice.** (p. 399)
- Apply the revising strategy.
- Participate in a peer conference.

Day 2
Write
Revise: Word Choice

Student Objectives
- Use a thesaurus to revise for vivid, descriptive words.

Student Activities
- Read and discuss **Revise: Focus on Word Choice.** (p. 400)
- Apply the revising strategy.

Note: Optional Revising Lessons appear on the *Strategies for Writers* CD-ROM.

Day 3
Write
Edit: Conventions

Student Objectives
- Edit for dangling modifiers and prepositional phrases.

Student Activities
- Read and discuss **Edit: Focus on Conventions.** (p. 401)
- Apply the editing strategy.

Note: Teach the Conventions mini-lessons (pp. 402–403) if needed.

Day 4	Day 5
Analyze Ideas, Organization, and Voice	**Analyze** Word Choice, Sentence Fluency, and Conventions

Student Objectives
- Read a model biographic sketch.
- Use the biographic sketch rubric.
- Use the model biographic sketch to study Ideas, Organization, and Voice.

Student Activities
- Review **"Jane Ellis: Teacher, Alaskan."** (p. 387)
- Read and discuss **Using the Rubric to Study the Model.** (pp. 390–391)

Student Objectives
- Read a model biographic sketch.
- Use the biographic sketch rubric.
- Use the model biographic sketch to study Word Choice, Sentence Fluency, and Conventions.

Student Activities
- Review **"Jane Ellis: Teacher, Alaskan."** (p. 387)
- Read and discuss **Using the Rubric to Study the Model.** (pp. 392–393)

Day 4	Day 5
Write Draft	**Write** Revise: Organization

Student Objectives
- Complete a draft.

Student Activities
- Finish the draft.
- Participate in a peer conference.

Student Objectives
- Revise for strong character introduction.

Student Activities
- Read and discuss **Revise: Focus on Organization.** (p. 398)
- Reflect on a model draft.
- Apply the revising strategy.

Day 4	Day 5
Write Publish: +Presentation	**Write** Publish: +Presentation

Student Objectives
- Discuss preparation for publishing and presentation.
- Use a final editing checklist to publish their work.

Student Activities
- Read and discuss **Publish: +Presentation.** (p. 404)
- Apply the publishing strategy.

Student Objectives
- Use a biographic sketch rubric.
- Share a published biographic sketch.

Student Activities
- Share their work.
- Use the rubric to reflect upon and evaluate the model and their own writing. (pp. 388–389, 405)

complete the chapter in fewer days, combine the learning objectives and activities in a way that supports students as they write.

Resources at-a-Glance

Grammar, Usage & Mechanics
Dangling Modifiers T402
Prepositional Phrases T403
Grammar Practice T401–T403

Differentiating Instruction
Using the Rubric T393
Draft T396
Publish T404
For additional Differentiating Instruction activities, see Strategies for Writers *Extensions Online at* **www.sfw.z-b.com.**

English Language Learners
Using the Rubric T390–T391
Prewrite T394
Revise T398

Conferencing
Peer to Peer T395, T397, T399
Peer Groups T395, T397, T399
Teacher-Led T395, T397, T399

Technology Tip
Using the Rubric T392
Publish T405

 Connection Letter
Reproducible letter (in English and Spanish) appears on the *Strategies for Writers* CD-ROM and at **www.sfw.z-b.com.**

Online Writing Center
Provides IWB resources, interactive games and practice activities, videos, eBooks, and a virtual file cabinet.

 Strategies for Writers Online
Go to **www.sfw.z-b.com** for free online resources for students and teachers.

Introduce
a Biographic Sketch

Week 1 • Day 1

Student Objectives

- Review the elements of a biographic sketch. *(p. 384)*
- Consider purpose and audience. *(p. 385)*
- Learn the traits of descriptive writing. *(p. 386)*

What's a Biographic Sketch?

Ask students whether any of them have read a biography. Then ask them to imagine that they want to write a biography. What questions would they ask? What details do they think are important? Point out that a biographic sketch is a short form of a biography—a sketch rather than a whole painting.

What's in a Biographic Sketch?

Have students give examples that illustrate each element of a biographic sketch. Start the conversation by providing examples:

- Subject—Hank Aaron, J. K. Rowling, a grandparent
- The senses—"the pin-pricks of icy snowflakes on his skin," "the deep, rich flavor of chocolate"
- Quotations—"Grandpa always said, 'Never let a day go to waste!'"

Strategies for Writers Online

Go to **www.sfw.z-b.com** for additional online resources for students and teachers.

What's a Biographic Sketch?

It's a true account of a period of a real person's life. I think I'll like writing one because I like finding out about people.

What's in a Biographic Sketch?

Subject
That's the person I'm going to write about. I'll need to do some research and maybe interview the subject of my biographic sketch. It's my job to tell his or her story.

The Senses
I'll need to use my senses to write good details. I'll include details that appeal to whichever senses are appropriate for my subject. I'll use these to paint a picture for my audience.

Quotations
I'll use quotations to bring my subject to life. I'll listen carefully for sayings or quotes my subject uses. The quotations will say a lot about my subject.

384 Descriptive Writing

Descriptive Text Exemplars (Biographic Sketch)

Freedman, Russell. *The Voice That Challenged a Nation: Marian Anderson and the Struggle for Equal Rights.* Houghton Mifflin Harcourt, 2011. Marian Anderson was one of the great vocal artists of the 20th century. However, because of her race, she could not sing at Constitution Hall, Washington's largest concert hall. With the help of Eleanor Roosevelt, Anderson broke racial barriers when she gave a landmark performance on the steps of the Lincoln Memorial.

Myers, Walter Dean. *I've Seen the Promised Land: The Life of Dr. Martin Luther King, Jr.* HarperCollins, 2004. Dr. Martin Luther King, Jr., was a crusader of the civil rights movement, preaching nonviolent social justice and equality for African Americans. Dr. King was a powerful, spiritual leader and believed nonviolence could be used to end racial discrimination.

Why write a Biographic Sketch?

I'm going to think about reasons to write a biographic sketch. Maybe that will help me figure out whose life I want to write about.

Entertainment
I have met people who are funny, exciting, or influential. I want to share these people with an audience. Entertaining the reader is one good reason to write a biographic sketch.

Personal Reflection
Writing helps me reflect, or make sense out of the things I see. A biographic sketch can help me understand how I've been affected by someone I've met.

Honoring
There are some people who make a big difference in the world. A biographic sketch is a way to honor them. I could even use my sketch to nominate someone for an award.

Biographic Sketch **385**

Partridge, Elizabeth. *This Land Was Made for You and Me: The Life and Songs of Woody Guthrie.* Viking, 2002. `CCSS` This biography chronicles the life of Woody Guthrie, a talented songwriter and folksinger who traveled across the country and experienced political and social conflicts. Many of these conflicts helped inspire some of his most memorable songs.

Sills, Leslie. *In Real Life: Six Women Photographers.* Holiday House, 2002. *In Real Life* celebrates the lives and works of photographers Imogene Cunningham, Dorothea Lange, Lola Alvarez Bravo, Carrie Mae Weems, Elsa Dorfman, and Cindy Sherman. These six women, whose careers span nearly a century, broke ethnic and gender barriers in the field of photography.

Why write a Biographic Sketch?

Remind students that all writing has a purpose. Writers write for many reasons and for a variety of audiences, and these authentic purposes help shape the writing. In the case of a biographic sketch, the purpose will help dictate what types of details the writer chooses to include. Read and discuss page 385 with students. Mention that because a biographic sketch is short, they will want to focus on details that support their purpose. For example, a writer who wants to entertain will likely focus on humorous, exciting, or suspenseful incidents in the life of the subject. When engaging in personal reflection, a writer might look for turning points in the subject's life—events that formed that person's character. A biographic sketch written to honor someone will include details that illustrate why the subject is special and worthy of admiration.

Encourage students to think about their reasons for writing a biographic sketch and how these reasons will affect the tone and focus of their writing.

`CCSS` **C**ommon **C**ore **S**tate **S**tandards
SL.7.1: Engage effectively in a range of collaborative discussions (one-on-one, in groups, and teacher-led) with diverse partners on *grade 7 topics, texts, and issues,* building on each others' ideas and expressing their own clearly.

Biographic Sketch **T385**

Introduce
a Biographic Sketch

Linking Descriptive Writing Traits to a Biographic Sketch

Have students read page 386. Emphasize that they will follow Andre as he models using the writing process and the traits together. As they follow Andre, students will see how the Descriptive Writing Traits have been adapted and applied to writing a biographic sketch. They will see that a biographic sketch has many factors in common with other types of descriptive writing. However, the particular audience and purpose of a biographic sketch determine how the traits are used.

Discuss with students how each trait applies to a biographic sketch. Ask students to explain why poor use of any one of the traits would weaken the quality of a sketch and possibly confuse the reader.

Online Writing Center

Provides six **interactive anchor papers** for each mode of writing.

Linking Descriptive Writing Traits to a Biographic Sketch

In this chapter, you will write about a real person. This type of descriptive writing is called a biographic sketch. Andre will guide you through the stages of the writing process: Prewrite, Draft, Revise, Edit, and Publish. In each stage, Andre will show you important writing strategies that are linked to the Descriptive Writing Traits below.

Descriptive Writing Traits

 Ideas
- a clear topic that is developed by relevant supporting details
- descriptive details that are well chosen for the topic

 Organization
- well-organized paragraphs that logically follow the order of the description, whether by time, location, or another order
- varied and appropriate transitions that show the relationship between ideas and concepts

 Voice
- a voice that is appropriate for the purpose and audience

 Word Choice
- precise words and phrases, possibly including figurative language, that create an accurate picture for the reader

 Sentence Fluency
- sentences that vary in length and type to add flow to the writing

 Conventions
- no or few errors in grammar, usage, mechanics, and spelling

Before you write, read Elaine Dixon's biographic sketch on the next page. Then use the biographic sketch rubric on pages 388–389 to decide how well she did. (You might want to look back at What's in a Biographic Sketch? on page 384, too!)

Descriptive Writing Traits in a Biographic Sketch

 **Ideas**   For a biographic sketch, the focus should be limited to specific events or a key theme in the subject's life. Relevant supporting details explain why the topic is worthy of attention.

 **Organization**   In a biographic sketch, the paragraphs will most likely be in chronological order. Transitions show the order of events and how they relate to each other.

 **Voice**   A sketch that is written for entertainment should have a different tone than a sketch written to honor the subject.

Jane Ellis: Teacher, Alaskan

by Elaine Dixon

Who is the oldest person you know? For the students at Nell Scott Middle School, it is a math teacher, Mrs. Jane Ellis. Mrs. Ellis was born **Subject** in 1923 in San Francisco, California. This was 30 years before the school principal was even born and 70 years before the building she now teaches in was built!

In 1944, Mrs. Ellis started teaching in Modesto, California. Then the U.S. Army sent her and her husband to Alaska in 1948. The cold, crisp landscape was beautiful to Mrs. Ellis. She got a teaching job right away at a government school and taught all grades and all subjects. "Those children taught me to be a teacher," Mrs. Ellis explains. "When I got it right, they learned like kittens lapping up milk. If they weren't learning, I had only one place to look—in the mirror!" **Quotation**

Mrs. Ellis is a special teacher! But she's special not just because she's been teaching for a long time. She's special because she loves a good joke, remembers the name of each student she ever taught, and makes students think math is fun and important. She does this with her creative teaching methods. For instance, after ringing a shiny brass bell on her desk, she likes to call out in a strong voice, "Time for a lightning drill." Soon the room is filled with shouting as students call out the times tables for their assigned number. When she's satisfied, Mrs. Ellis rings the bell again and says, "Class, what have you achieved?" And the class shouts back: "The times tables!" **Sensory details**

Besides being a good teacher, Mrs. Ellis is simply hard to forget. Tall and thin, she wears a flowery perfume that trails behind her. She often wears purple slacks with a purple sweater and fur-lined boots. "I always want to be ready for anything!" she says. Her hair is silver and tightly curled. And her eyes sparkle on a face that is covered with wrinkles. "These aren't wrinkles," Mrs. Ellis says. "They're wisdom lines!" She has a quip or a quote for everything!

When is Mrs. Ellis going to retire? Not any time soon! As she likes to say, "My students still have a lot to teach me!"

Biographic Sketch 387

Word Choice Precise words and phrases will help the reader gain an understanding of the subject in the short length of a biographic sketch.

Sentence Fluency Variety in sentence lengths and types gives writing a pleasing rhythm and flow.

Conventions Too many errors in grammar, usage, mechanics, and spelling will make the writing confusing and hard to read. The writer's message is easily lost or misunderstood when conventions are not correctly applied.

Analyze
the Model

Week 1 • Day 2

Student Objectives

- Read a model biographic sketch. (p. 387)

Read the Model

Have students read "Jane Ellis: Teacher, Alaskan" silently. Then ask students to tell you what is the focus of each paragraph. Discuss how the paragraphs are organized. Ask students whether they feel the organization is logical and if they might have chosen a different order.

Elements of a Biographic Sketch

Use the notes on the model to discuss the various elements of a biographic sketch. Refer students to What's in a Biographic Sketch? on page 384 if they need to review the elements. Ask students what the quotations and sensory details tell the reader about Mrs. Ellis. Have students discuss whether they feel the sketch uses the elements effectively to convey a clear picture of Mrs. Ellis.

CCSS **Common Core State Standards**

R/Lit.7.1: Cite several pieces of textual evidence to support analysis of what the text says explicitly as well as inferences drawn from the text.

Analyze the Model

Student Objectives

- Learn to read a rubric. (pp. 388–389)

Use the Rubric

Explain the Rubric Explain that a rubric is a tool for planning, improving, and assessing a piece of writing. Tell students that a rubric helps a writer focus on key elements, or traits, in writing (**Ideas, Organization, Voice, Word Choice, Sentence Fluency, Conventions,** and **Presentation**). Point out that column 6 describes a very good biographic sketch, one that has received the highest score in all categories. This is what students should strive for in their own writing.

Discuss the Rubric Guide students in a discussion of the rubric. Read the descriptors that go with each trait and take a moment to note the progression from the top descriptor to the lowest one. Remind students to keep the rubric in mind when they write their own biographic sketch and again when they revise it.

Online Writing Center

Provides a variety of **interactive rubrics,** including 4-, 5-, and 6-point models.

Biographic Sketch

Rubric

Use this 6-point rubric to plan and evaluate a biographic sketch.

	6	5	4
Ideas	Relevant descriptive details, including sensory details, capture the subject.	Relevant details, including sensory details, describe the subject.	Several sensory details describe the subject, but some details are not relevant.
Organization	The beginning introduces the character and draws the reader in. Details are organized logically.	The beginning is interesting and introduces the character. Most details are organized logically.	The beginning introduces the character. Most details are organized logically.
Voice	Quotations are effective and give voice to the character.	Quotations are used to help the reader understand the character.	Some quotations are used, but not all of them help the reader understand the character.
Word Choice	Vivid, descriptive language gives the reader a clear picture of the subject.	Clear language helps the reader understand the subject.	Some vague or dull language sometimes muddies the picture of the subject.
Sentence Fluency	Well-placed prepositional phrases add flow and information to sentences.	Prepositional phrases are used and enhance sentence flow in several places.	Prepositional phrases are used but not consistently.
Conventions	Phrases are clear and enhance the meaning of sentences.	Phrases are clear and add meaning to sentences.	Some phrases are used and don't interfere with the meaning.

+Presentation The biographic sketch is neat and legible.

CCSS Common Core State Standards

Biographic Sketch

Writing in the Descriptive mode can engage the Common Core State Standards for both Narrative and Informative/Explanatory writing. The rubrics and strategies for the biographic sketch are based principally on Narrative standards. The Organization and Voice rubrics reflect standards **W.7.3.a** and **W.7.3.b,** which address character introduction and development. In the biographic sketch, the concept of character translates easily to the subject of the sketch. Additionally, standard **W.7.3.b** lists several narrative techniques, including dialogue. In the Voice rubric, the effective use of dialogue is addressed as quotations that give voice to the subject.

3	2	1	
Few sensory details are included, and the subject is hard to picture.	Very few sensory details are used. Most details are irrelevant. The subject is not described.	Few or no details describe the subject. No sensory details are used.	**Ideas**
The character is not clearly introduced. The organization can be followed, but several details are out of place.	It is hard to tell who is the subject of the writing. The details are poorly organized and hard to follow.	The writing has no clear subject. The details are not organized at all.	**Organization**
Quotations are poorly used; they do not give voice to the character.	Few quotations are included, and their meaning is confusing.	No quotations are used; the character does not have a voice.	**Voice**
Vague or dull language is used in several places. The reader does not have a clear picture of the subject.	Most of the language is vague or dull. It is easy to lose interest in the subject.	The language is hard to follow. The writer has not tried to describe the subject.	**Word Choice**
Some prepositional phrases are used, but not all of them are correct.	Prepositional phrases are placed incorrectly and interfere with meaning.	Prepositional phrases are missing from the writing.	**Sentence Fluency**
Some phrases are placed incorrectly in sentences. They may interfere with meaning.	Phrases are placed incorrectly and interfere with meaning.	Phrases are missing from the writing.	**Conventions**

See Appendix B for 4-, 5-, and 6-point descriptive rubrics.

Apply the Rubric

Assign Individuals Assign each student a trait and give students five to ten minutes to find as many examples as they can of their assigned traits in the model.

Group Discussion Have the students who were assigned the same trait discuss their findings and agree among themselves on the best one or two examples of the trait. One student in the group should write the example and take notes on the group's reasons for choosing that example.

Reassemble Class Bring the class back together and ask one person from each group to share the group's example and reasoning.

Additional Rubrics Appendix B includes 4-, 5-, and 6-point rubrics that can be used with any piece of descriptive writing. The rubrics are also available as blackline masters beginning on page T543.

The Ideas, Organization, and Word Choice rubrics are also drawn from the Narrative standards. Standard **W.7.3.d** addresses precise wording, relevant details, and sensory language. These concepts are emphasized in the Ideas rubric, which focuses on relevant descriptive and sensory details, and the Word Choice rubric, which specifies the use of vivid, descriptive language.

CCSS **Common Core State Standards**

SL.7.1: Engage effectively in a range of collaborative discussions (one-on-one, in groups, and teacher-led) with diverse partners on *grade 7 topics, texts, and issues*, building on others' ideas and expressing their own clearly. **SL.7.1.a:** Come to discussions prepared, having read or researched material under study; explicitly draw on that preparation by referring to evidence on the topic, text, or issue to probe and reflect on ideas under discussion. **SL.7.1.b:** Follow rules for collegial discussions, track progress toward specific goals and deadlines, and define individual roles as needed. **SL.7.1.d:** Acknowledge new information expressed by others and, when warranted, modify their own views.

Analyze
the Model

Week 1 • Day 4

Student Objectives

- Read a model biographic sketch. (p. 387)
- Use the biographic sketch rubric. (pp. 388–389)
- Use the model biographic sketch to study Ideas, Organization, and Voice. (pp. 390–391)

Study the Model

Assess the Model Read each section on pages 390–393 with students. In one large group or several small ones, discuss whether students agree or disagree with each point in Andre's assessment of the biographic sketch. Use questions such as the following to discuss the model and the traits with students. Encourage students to back up each other's answers with additional examples from the model.

- Which details tell you Mrs. Ellis is a good teacher? (Possible responses: her creative teaching methods, such as the lightning drill; the fact that she makes students think math is fun and important)

![Strategies for Writers Online logo] **Strategies for Writers Online**
Go to **www.sfw.z-b.com** for additional online resources for students and teachers.

Using the Rubric to Study the Model

Biographic Sketch

Did you notice that the model on page 387 points out some key elements of a biographic sketch? As she wrote "Jane Ellis: Teacher, Alaskan," Elaine Dixon used these elements to help describe her subject. She also used the 6-point rubric on pages 388–389 to plan, draft, revise, and edit the writing. A rubric is a great tool to evaluate writing during the writing process.

Now let's use the same rubric to score the model. To do this, we'll focus on each trait separately, starting with Ideas. We'll use the top descriptor for each trait (column 6), along with examples from the model, to help us understand how the traits work together. How would you score Elaine on each trait?

Ideas

- Relevant descriptive details, including sensory details, capture the subject.

I like the way Elaine describes not only how Mrs. Ellis looks, but also how she smells. The picture of Mrs. Ellis in my mind is vivid and alive, and this makes the writing stronger and more interesting.

[from the writing model]

Besides being a good teacher, Mrs. Ellis is simply hard to forget. Tall and thin, she wears a flowery perfume that trails behind her. She often wears purple slacks with a purple sweater and fur-lined boots.

390 Descriptive Writing

English Language Learners

BEGINNING
Identifying Characteristics Show a photo of a person who students know. Say, *Describe the person.* If students supply one-word answers, model a few descriptive sentences using their answers. For example, *He is Mr. Warrick. He is a principal. He is 50 years old.* Write the sentences on the board and have students repeat them. Then ask students to write the sentences on paper. Have students repeat the activity with a photo of a family member.

INTERMEDIATE
Describing an Important Person Have students identify an important person in their lives. Ask each student to write answers to the following questions. *Who is the important person? Why is the person important to you? What is your relationship to the person? What did you learn from the person?* Have students discuss their answers with a partner.

Organization

- The beginning introduces the character and draws the reader in.
- Details are organized logically.

I like how Elaine opens her sketch with a question. I automatically felt connected to the topic and couldn't wait to read more. Elaine's details are well-organized and give me a complete picture of Mrs. Ellis.

[from the writing model]

Who is the oldest person you know? For the students at Nell Scott Middle School, it is a math teacher, Mrs. Jane Ellis. Mrs. Ellis was born in 1923 in San Francisco, California.

Voice

- Quotations are effective and give voice to the character.

Elaine does a great job of choosing quotations that make an impression and really show me Mrs. Ellis's personality—funny, smart, and witty. Now I can envision the whole person, not just what she looks like on the outside.

[from the writing model]

"These aren't wrinkles," Mrs. Ellis says. "They're wisdom lines!" She has a quip or a quote for everything!

Biographic Sketch 391

- In what order is the essay organized? (chronological) What time frame does the last paragraph address? (the future)

- Read just the quotations in the biographic sketch. What additional adjectives would you use to describe Mrs. Ellis's attitude, based only on the quotations? (Possible responses: upbeat, enthusiastic, energetic, self-reliant)

ADVANCED

Personality Descriptions As a class, brainstorm different personality traits, such as *funny, thoughtful, brave, charitable,* and so on. Have partners think of a person who exemplifies each personality trait.

ADVANCED HIGH

Role-Play Assign partners a personality trait, and have them write a role-play in which they can demonstrate the meaning of the word. For example, if the trait is *thoughtfulness,* the students might act out a situation in which one student has the flu and the other student delivers hot soup for his or her friend. You might ask the class to use the clues in each role-play to guess the trait that was assigned to each pair.

CCSS Common Core State Standards

SL.7.1.b: Follow rules for collegial discussions, track progress toward specific goals and deadlines, and define individual roles as needed. **SL.7.1.c:** Pose questions that elicit elaboration and respond to others' questions and comments with relevant observations and ideas that bring the discussion back on topic as needed.

Analyze
the Model

Week 1 • Day 5

Student Objectives

- Read a model biographic sketch. *(p. 387)*
- Use the biographic sketch rubric. *(pp. 388–389)*
- Use the model biographic sketch to study Word Choice, Sentence Fluency, and Conventions. *(pp. 392–393)*

Continue the Discussion Continue to discuss how well the writing traits were used in the model biographic sketch. Use the following questions to begin the discussion:

- Choose the sentence or sentences that you think give the most striking description of Mrs. Ellis. Why do you find that sentence so vivid or appealing? (Possible response: *Besides being a good teacher, Mrs. Ellis is simply hard to forget. Tall and thin, she wears a flowery perfume that trails behind her. I can imagine what it's like to be near Mrs. Ellis.*)

- Choose an example of a sentence with at least one prepositional phrase. How does the phrase improve the sentence? (Possible response: *For instance, after ringing a shiny brass bell on her desk, she likes to call out in a strong voice, "Time for a lightning drill." The phrases add information about the sequence of events and describe Mrs. Ellis's voice.*)

 Strategies for Writers Online
Go to **www.sfw.z-b.com** for additional online resources for students and teachers.

 **Word Choice**
- Vivid, descriptive language gives the reader a clear picture of the subject.

Elaine has really inspired me to work hard at describing the subject of my own sketch. Her descriptions are so strong and creative—I want my reader to have the same reaction to my writing.

[from the writing model]

Her hair is silver and tightly curled. And her eyes sparkle on a face that is covered with wrinkles.

 **Sentence Fluency**
- Well-placed prepositional phrases add flow and information to sentences.

Elaine uses lots of prepositional phrases to add variety to her sentences. These phrases mix things up and made reading her work easier and more enjoyable. They also contain interesting facts!

[from the writing model]

In 1944, Mrs. Ellis started teaching in Modesto, California. Then the U.S. Army sent her and her husband to Alaska in 1948.

392 Descriptive Writing

Technology Tip for 21st Century Literacies

Engaging others in the stories of our lives is often about telling those stories to raise empathy or to examine something from a different perspective. Challenge students to collect multiple resources and media (e.g., digital images, audio recordings captured on a cell phone) that capture as many emotions, feelings, facts, and points of view as possible. When the biographic sketch focuses on sharing a slice of an individual's story, what we learn from that as readers and writers often comes from how we relate new perspectives and ideas to what is known. Use that discussion to inform students' writing.

Conventions
- Phrases are clear and enhance the meaning of sentences.

Elaine has very good spelling and punctuation. I couldn't find any errors in her work. I read her sketch another time to see if she has any dangling modifiers. She does not!

[from the writing model]

For instance, after ringing a shiny brass bell on her desk, she likes to call out in a strong voice, "Time for a lightning drill."

✛Presentation The biographic sketch is neat and legible.

My Turn!

I'm going to write a biographic sketch about someone in my school. I'm glad to have the rubric and good writing strategies to use as a guide. Keep reading to see how I do!

Biographic Sketch **393**

Differentiating Instruction

ENRICHMENT
Practice Descriptive Language Find a piece of descriptive text. Display it without the adjectives or other descriptive language. Ask students how they would rewrite it. Compare the results with the original.

REINFORCEMENT
Understand Sensory Details Read part of the model without sensory details. For example, *Besides being a teacher, Mrs. Ellis is hard to forget. She wears perfume. She wears slacks, a sweater, and boots. Her hair is silver. Her face has wrinkles.* Then read the passage as written. Help students compare the two versions.

Presentation Remind students that they must consider how their papers will look when they prepare their final copies.

Using a computer is an excellent way to create clean, legible text. Encourage students to use a word processing program and choose one legible font for the text of their sketches. They may use another, more decorative font for the title of the sketch, as long as it is also clear and readable.

Think About the Traits Once students have thoroughly discussed the model biographic sketch, ask them which traits they think are most important in a biographic sketch. Of course, all the traits are important in every piece of writing, but some of the traits stand out more in some genres than in others. Students might say, for example, that in a biographic sketch **Ideas** are very important because the facts and details about the subject are central to the sketch. Or, they may say that **Organization** is key to understanding the sequence of events in the subject's life. Encourage students to ask each other clarifying questions if their fellow students are not clear in their answers.

CCSS **Common Core State Standards**

SL.7.1.c: Pose questions that elicit elaboration and respond to others' questions and comments with relevant observations and ideas that bring the discussion back on topic as needed. **SL.7.1.d:** Acknowledge new information expressed by others and, when warranted, modify their own views.

Biographic Sketch **T393**

Write
a Biographic Sketch

Week 2 • Day 1

Student Objectives

• Read and understand a prewriting strategy. *(p. 394)*

Prewrite

Focus on Ideas

Gather Information Read page 394 aloud. Point out that Andre started by brainstorming a list of people and then deciding which one he wanted to write about. Tell students to jot down a list of possible subjects and ask themselves the following questions:

• What person is the most interesting to me?

• Do I know enough about this person to write a biographic sketch about him or her?

• Will the reader find this person interesting?

• What is my purpose in writing this sketch: to entertain the reader, reflect on my subject, or honor my subject?

Once students have chosen a subject, have them jot down notes about the person.

Online Writing Center

Provides **interactive graphic organizers** as well as a variety of graphic organizers in PDF format.

Prewrite
Focus on Ideas

The Rubric Says	Relevant descriptive details, including sensory details, capture the subject.
Writing Strategy	Describe someone at school (a teacher, a classmate, or other close friend) in a biographic sketch.

My big question is: who should be the subject of my sketch? There are plenty of interesting people here in Alaska. I've thought about some of my Aleut friends and about an old man I know who still digs for gold. But I think I'll write about my best friend, Seth. He and his family raise dogs that pull sleds in races like the Iditarod. He's quite a character! I'll start by listing details about Seth, and then choose the most interesting details to include in my sketch.

Description of Seth

- tall, skinny, won't play basketball
- loves dogs more than anything
- feeding dogs is daily chore
- knows how to hook up the dog sled and drive the dogs
- almost always wears jeans, parka, boots, Seawolves cap
- lets the dogs lick him on the face (gross!)
- sled dogs are part of his family
- funny sense of humor

Apply

Choose a person you think is interesting. Jot down some descriptions of that person.

394 Descriptive Writing

English Language Learners

BEGINNING/INTERMEDIATE
Character Chart Have students use the information they wrote about their special person to fill in a character chart. Review the meanings of the words *Looks, Personality,* and *Actions.* In the *Actions* column, students should answer the question, *Why is he or she important?*

ADVANCED/ADVANCED HIGH
Sensory Details After students have selected the subject of their biographic sketches, have them close their eyes and imagine exactly how the person looks, smells, feels, and sounds. For example, a favorite grandmother may look kind or have white hair. She may smell like roses. Her skin might feel soft. Her voice might sound gentle and soothing. There may even be a taste that comes to mind, such as her special recipe. Have students write sensory details about their subjects.

Prewrite

Focus on **Organization**

The Rubric Says   Details are organized logically.

Writing Strategy   Make a Character Chart.

OK, the rubric tells me to organize my details logically. That makes sense. I will describe Seth in a way that won't confuse my reader. I think a Character Chart will help me organize my details and keep track of them.

CHARACTER CHART

Character: My friend Seth

Looks	Personality	Actions
• red hair • tall and skinny • grew 3 inches in one summer • changes clothes after school • jeans, parka, rubber boots, Seawolves cap	• steady and easy-going • knows his mind • loves dogs more than anything else • knows what he wants in life (to raise dogs)	• feeds the sled dogs every night • dogs lick him (yuck!) • can hitch up the sled • can drive the sled

Reflect
How does Andre's chart look? Does he have enough information to write his sketch?

Apply
Use your notes to make a Character Chart about your subject.

Biographic Sketch   **395**

Conferencing

PEER TO PEER Have partners exchange Character Charts. Tell them to ask themselves the following questions as they read their partners' drafts: Is there any information the writer could add to help me understand the subject? Are the categories clear? Tell partners to write one or two comments on an adhesive note and return the chart to its writer.

PEER GROUPS Have students work in groups of three or four. Each student reads his or her Character Chart aloud. The other students in the group take turns offering one comment or suggestion.

TEACHER-LED Hold conferences with individual students about their Character Charts. Before they speak with you, tell students to think of questions to ask you about points they found difficult when creating the chart or that they want to improve.

Write
a Biographic Sketch

Week 2 • Day 2

Student Objectives

• Make a Character Chart to organize details about the biography's subject. (p. 395)

Prewrite

Focus on

Organize Ideas Discuss how a Character Chart can help students write a biographic sketch. (Possible response: Each category can be the basis of a paragraph.)

Explain that as they work on their charts, they may decide not to include items from their notes that don't fit the categories—or they may think of items they want to add.

Writer's Term

Character Chart Encourage students to use more than three categories if they feel it's necessary. More than five categories would probably not be useful for a short biographic sketch.

CCSS **Common Core State Standards**
W.7.3.a: Engage and orient the reader by establishing a context and point of view and introducing a narrator and/or characters; organize an event sequence that unfolds naturally and logically. **W.7.3.d:** Use precise words and phrases, relevant descriptive details, and sensory language to capture the action and convey experiences and events. **SL.7.1.a:** Come to discussions prepared, having read or researched material under study; explicitly draw on that preparation by referring to evidence on the topic, text, or issue to probe and reflect on ideas under discussion. **SL.7.6:** Adapt speech to a variety of contexts and tasks, demonstrating command of formal English when indicated or appropriate.

Biographic Sketch   **T395**

Write
a Biographic Sketch

Week 2 • Day 3

Student Objectives

• Begin writing, using sensory details. *(pp. 396–397)*

Draft

Focus on Ideas

Draft a Biographic Sketch
Explain that writing a draft is a chance for writers to get ideas on paper without having to worry about making too many mistakes. However, remind students that their first draft still has to be readable!

Read the information about sensory details in the Writer's Term box and Andre's words on page 396 with the students. Then read Andre's draft on page 397 together. Ask if Andre used sensory details in his draft and have students find sensory details other than the highlighted ones. Also discuss whether Andre's draft includes the details from his Character Chart.

Point out that Andre repeatedly refers to the rubric as he writes. Encourage students to get into the habit of using the rubric to guide their own writing as well.

Have students use the details in their Character Charts to write drafts of their biographic sketches. Remind them to use sensory details.

Online Writing Center

 Provides student eBooks with an **interactive writing pad** for drafting, revising, editing, and publishing.

Draft

Focus on Ideas

The Rubric Says   Relevant descriptive details, including sensory details, capture the subject.

Writing Strategy   Draft a biographic sketch. Use plenty of sensory details to provide a clear mental picture for the reader.

> **Writer's Term** _____
> **Sensory Details**
> **Sensory details** appeal directly to one of the five senses (seeing, feeling, smelling, tasting, and hearing).

It's time to start writing my draft. I've picked out the person I want to write about—my friend Seth. Then I organized what I want to say about him. I want to show my readers a side of Seth that they don't see at school. I want them to feel as if they are right beside him as he feeds his dogs and takes them out for a ride.

The rubric tells me to use sensory details. Sensory details will help me help my readers to see, feel, smell, and hear a part of Seth's life. I don't think any tasting is involved—except for the dog kibbles!

I think I'll start my biographic sketch by telling the audience some facts about Seth. Then I'll give them a word picture of Seth at home. When he's working with the dogs, he's really in his zone. I'm just going to get started. I won't worry about grammar and spelling mistakes yet. I know I'll be fixing them later.

396 Descriptive Writing

Differentiating Instruction

ENRICHMENT

Add Figurative Language Encourage students to use similes and metaphors to convey sensory details. Remind them that similes and metaphors compare two concepts and that similes specifically include the words *like* or *as*. Give examples such as, *light as a feather* and *The hot sunlight was an added burden on our shoulders.*

REINFORCEMENT

Brainstorm With a Partner Before they begin writing, have students work with a partner to think of sensory details for their drafts. The first student shares his or her Character Chart or describes the subject of the sketch, and both partners brainstorm ideas for sensory details, which the first student writes down. Then the partners brainstorm ideas for the second student's sketch.

Proofreading Marks

⊐ Indent ℓ Take out something
≡ Make a capital ⊙ Add a period
/ Make a small letter ¶ New paragraph
∧ Add something SP Spelling error

[DRAFT]

My Friend, Sled Dog Seth

Seth is a seventh grader at Nell Scott Middle School. At school, Seth is just like anybody else. But after school, most often, you see Seth dressed in blue jeans, an unzipped parka, and shiny green rubber boots, carrying a bucket of smelly brown kibbles. A steel scoop sticks out the top. He is heading out to feed the sled dogs.

[sensory details]

His boots make a squishing sound in the spongey ground. Nearing the dog pens, the squishing sound is drowned out by barking. The dogs' metal food pans go skitering as the dogs run up to the fence. Seth rubs their soft fur and lets each dog like his face. He is kind and affectionut as he feeds the dogs.

Reflect

How does Andre's draft sound to you? How do his sensory details bring the subject of his biographic sketch alive?

Apply

Use your Character Chart to write a draft of your biographic sketch. Make sure to put in some sensory details to help your readers get a clear mental picture.

Biographic Sketch **397**

Conferencing

PEER TO PEER Have partners exchange drafts to read. Tell students to think of two or three questions they would like to ask to clarify information or supply missing details. Have them write their questions on sticky notes and affix them to the appropriate place on their partners' drafts.

PEER GROUPS Have students work in groups of four. Students pass their drafts to the student on the right to read. That student writes one comment or suggestion on a sticky note affixed to the draft and passes the draft along to the right once again. The review ends when everyone has received their drafts back with three comments.

TEACHER-LED Hold conferences with pairs of students. Have them read each other's drafts and coach them in giving constructive criticism.

Write
a Biographic Sketch

Week 2 • Day 4

Student Objectives

• Complete a draft.

Writer's Term

Sensory Details Sensory details explain exactly what the writer perceives through his or her senses. They are especially important in a biographic sketch because the writer's goal is to make the subject come alive for readers through a fairly short piece of writing. Tell students to take moment to close their eyes and visualize their subject or the scenes they want to describe. Some students may benefit from drawing pictures to evoke sensory details.

CCSS Common Core State Standards

W.7.5: With some guidance and support from peers and adults, develop and strengthen writing as needed by planning, revising, editing, rewriting, or trying a new approach, focusing on how well purpose and audience have been addressed. **W.7.3.d:** Use precise words and phrases, relevant descriptive details, and sensory language to capture the action and convey experiences and events. **SL.7.6:** Adapt speech to a variety of contexts and tasks, demonstrating command of formal English when indicated or appropriate.

Biographic Sketch **T397**

Write
a Biographic Sketch

Week 2 • Day 5

Student Objectives

- Revise for strong character introduction. *(p. 398)*

Revise

Focus on  Organization

Introduce the Subject Remind students that a strong beginning is a way to make a good first impression. An exciting, intriguing, or appealing opening makes readers want to continue reading and predisposes them to like what they read next. In a biographic sketch, a strong beginning means introducing the character in a way that will make the reader want to know more about him or her.

Read Andre's words on page 398 with students. Then read the draft excerpt and Andre's revision. Discuss why the new sentence revision makes a stronger introduction. (Possible responses: It addresses the reader directly; it gives Seth's nickname and makes you wonder how he got it; it's short and punchy.)

 Strategies for Writers Online
Go to **www.sfw.z-b.com** for additional online resources for students and teachers.

T398 Descriptive Writing

Revise
Focus on **Organization**

The Rubric Says	The beginning introduces the character and draws the reader in.
Writing Strategy	Introduce the character right away.

So now it's time to revise my draft. The rubric says I should introduce my character right away and in a way that grabs my reader's attention. I did introduce Seth in the beginning, but not in a very exciting way. I want my reader to be interested in finding out more about him. I will revise the first paragraph now to really draw the reader in.

[DRAFT]   [used exciting introduction]

Meet Sled Dog Seth!
Seth is a seventh grader at Nell Scott Middle School. At school, Seth is just like anybody else. But after school, most often, you see Seth dressed in blue jeans, an unzipped parka, and shiny green rubber boots, carrying a bucket of smelly brown kibbles.

Apply
Introduce your character in the beginning in an attention-grabbing way.

398 Descriptive Writing

English Language Learners

BEGINNING/INTERMEDIATE
Using Quotations Tell students to think about the subject of their biographic sketch and ask, *What does your person often say?* Write students' answers on the board. The quotes are most likely in the students' native language. Ask students to describe the meaning of the quote in English. Model how students might include the quote in their writing. For example, *My grandmother always says, "Que será, será," which means "What will be, will be."*

ADVANCED/ADVANCED HIGH
Using Vivid Words Identify a few vague words that students wrote in their Character Charts; for example, *nice* or *soft*. Challenge partners to come up with more precise words; for example, *kindhearted* or *silky smooth*. Then have each student revise their sensory details to include more vivid descriptive words.

Revise

Focus on Voice

The Rubric Says	Quotations are effective and give voice to the character.
Writing Strategy	Add several sayings or quotes that the subject frequently uses.

The rubric says that I should use quotations in my biographic sketch. Using my subject's own words will help bring him to life for the reader. I want my readers to really hear Seth's unique voice! I will mix some of Seth's quotes throughout my writing. This will liven up the sketch and help the writing flow. I already found a place where a quote would fit in perfectly.

[DRAFT]

[added quotes]

"I love my dogs," Seth always says. "They are a part of my family, just like my mom and dad and my sister, Katie."

Reflect

What do you think? Does Andre's introduction grab your attention? How do his details and quotes bring his subject to life?

Apply

Add some quotes or sayings to bring your character to life for your audience.

Biographic Sketch 399

Conferencing

PEER TO PEER Have partners read their introductory paragraphs aloud to each other. Have the pairs discuss ways they could introduce their subjects in a more engaging way.

PEER GROUPS Have students work in groups of three or four. Tell students to read the introductory paragraphs of the other's drafts, and then write one or two words that describe the subject on an adhesive note affixed to the draft. When students get their own drafts back, have them revise as necessary.

TEACHER-LED Hold conferences with individual students about their drafts. Point out places where a quotation might be effectively placed and ask students if there is a quote or saying they can add.

Write
a Biographic Sketch

Week 3 • Day 1

Student Objectives

• Revise for effective use of quotations. *(p. 399)*

Revise

Focus on Voice

Incorporate Quotations On the board write the title *We Hear It Here.* Ask students to tell you phrases they hear frequently in the classroom. Start them off by listing a few of the phrases you use frequently. Tell students the list is special for each class and indicates the unique personality of each class. In the same way, including quotations in a biographic sketch brings the unique personality of the subject to life. Go through Andre's draft on page 397. Make sure students can identify how quotes and sayings are used in Andre's sketch.

Have students look for places in their biographic sketches where they can add quotations that bring out their subjects' personalities.

CCSS **Common Core State Standards**
W.7.3.a: Engage and orient the reader by establishing a context and point of view and introducing a narrator and/or characters; organize an event sequence that unfolds naturally and logically. **W.7.3.b:** Use narrative techniques, such as dialogue, pacing, and description, to develop experiences, events, and/or characters. **SL.7.6:** Adapt speech to a variety of contexts and tasks, demonstrating command of formal English when indicated or appropriate.

Write
a Biographic Sketch

Week 3 • Day 2

Student Objectives

• Use a thesaurus to revise for vivid, descriptive words. (p. 400)

Revise

Focus on  Word Choice

Revise Language Have students examine the vivid words and details Andre added. Note that Andre's vivid details are also sensory details. Review the use of proofreading marks with students. (See page 397.)

✏️ Writer's Term _____

Thesaurus Remind students that synonyms are not identical in meaning and that a lively synonym found in a thesaurus might not be an appropriate replacement for a duller word in their writing.

Revise   Focus on **Word Choice**

The Rubric Says	Vivid, descriptive language gives the reader a clear picture of the subject.
Writing Strategy	Use a thesaurus to replace vague words with vivid, descriptive ones.

✏️ Writer's Term _____

Thesaurus
A **thesaurus** is a book of words and their synonyms (words with a similar meaning) and antonyms (words with an opposite meaning). You can use either a print or an online thesaurus.

The rubric says to use vivid and descriptive language to describe Seth. Thinking of creative and different words is sometimes difficult, so I will use a thesaurus to help me out. It's fun using unique words to describe things. What do you think of my choices?

[DRAFT]

[replaced vague word]

silky

up to the fence. Seth rubs their ~~soft~~ fur and lets each dog like his

face. He is kind and affectionut as he feeds the dogs.

[vivid details]

right up to the roots of his carrot-colored hair

With a crunch, the scoop hits the kibbles. With a clatter, the kibbles hit the pans.

Apply

Use a thesaurus to find and use vivid and descriptive words to describe your subject.

400   Descriptive Writing

Optional Revising Lessons _____

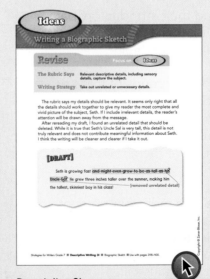

Ideas

Writing a Biographic Sketch

Revise   Focus on Ideas

The Rubric Says	Relevant descriptive details, including sensory details, capture the subject.
Writing Strategy	Take out unrelated or unnecessary details.

The rubric says my details should be relevant. It seems only right that all the details should work together to give my reader the most complete and vivid picture of the subject, Seth. If I include irrelevant details, the reader's attention will be drawn away from the message.

After rereading my draft, I found an unrelated detail that should be deleted. While it is true that Seth's Uncle Sal is very tall, this detail is not truly relevant and does not contribute meaningful information about Seth. I think the writing will be cleaner and clearer if I take it out.

[DRAFT]

Seth is growing fast ~~and might even grow to be as tall as his Uncle Sal~~. He grew three inches taller over the summer, making him the tallest, skinniest boy in his class!   [removed unrelated detail]

Strategies for Writers Grade 7 ■ Descriptive Writing 31 ■ Biographic Sketch ■ Use with pages 398–400.

Descriptive 31

Sentence Fluency

Writing a Biographic Sketch

Revise   Focus on Sentence Fluency

The Rubric Says	Well-placed prepositional phrases add flow and information to sentences.
Writing Strategy	Add prepositional phrases.

I reread my draft to check for sentence fluency, and I found a few sentences were too short and choppy. The rubric says that well-placed prepositional phrases can help with flow and add information to sentences. I'll go back and add prepositional phrases to the sentences that didn't read well. My writing will flow better, and I'll be adding important information at the same time.

✏️ Writer's Term _____

Preposition
A **preposition** shows a relationship between the noun or pronoun that follows the preposition (the object of the preposition) and another word or group of words in the sentence. *The book is on the table.*

[DRAFT]

[added prepositional phrase]

to a sled

After the dogs' dinner, Seth hitches them up. He checks each dog's paws and adjusts reins and harnesses.

Strategies for Writers Grade 7 ■ Descriptive Writing 32 ■ Biographic Sketch ■ Use with pages 398–400.

Descriptive 32

Go to ➡ Strategies for Writers Grade 7 CD-ROM

Edit

Focus on Conventions

The Rubric Says	Phrases are clear and enhance the meaning of sentences.
Writing Strategy	Check prepositional phrases and avoid misplaced participial phrases (dangling modifiers).

Writer's Term

Dangling Modifier
A modifier describes, clarifies, or gives more detail about a concept. A **dangling modifier** is a word or phrase that modifies a word not clearly stated in the sentence.

Different kinds of phrases add meaning to my writing. However, I have to be careful how I place them in my sentences. For example, a participial phrase that doesn't clearly relate to the subject will mislead my readers.

[DRAFT]

[corrected dangling modifier]

His boots make a squishing sound in the ~~spongey~~ spongy ground.

~~As he nears~~
~~Nearing~~ the dog pens, the squishing sound is drowned out by barking. The dogs' metal food pans go ~~skitering~~ skittering as the dogs run up to the fence.

Reflect

Andre used lots of vivid, descriptive words. He also worked hard to fix any dangling modifiers and ensure correct use of phrases. Can you find any mistakes he might have missed?

Apply Conventions

Edit your draft for spelling, punctuation, and capitalization. Be sure to use all phrases correctly.

For more practice fixing dangling modifiers and using prepositional phrases, use the exercises on the next two pages.

Biographic Sketch 401

Related Grammar Practice

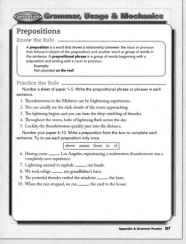

Student Edition page 517

Go to ➡ **Appendix A: Grammar Practice**

Write
a Biographic Sketch

Week 3 • Day 3

Student Objectives

- Edit for dangling modifiers and prepositional phrases. (p. 401)

Edit

Focus on Conventions

Review with students the difference between revising (improving text) and editing (correcting text). Explain that it is sometimes easier to catch someone else's mistakes than your own. Suggest that students exchange drafts with a partner and have the partner proofread the draft for spelling and grammar errors.

Use the mini-lessons on T402–403 for students who need help writing clear sentences. After students complete the exercises on pages 402–403, review the answers in class.

Writer's Term

Dangling Modifier Dangling modifiers must be corrected because they force the reader to pause and figure out what the writer is trying to say. Even if the meaning of the sentence becomes clear with a little thought, the flow of the writing has been interrupted and the reader may become frustrated.

CCSS **C**ommon **C**ore **S**tate **S**tandards

L.7.1: Demonstrate command of the conventions of standard English grammar and usage when writing or speaking.

Conventions

Mini-Lesson

Student Objectives

• Identify and correct dangling modifiers. *(p. 402)*

Dangling Modifiers

Explain to students that dangling modifiers contain words that accidentally modify the wrong thing. When writing, students need to express clearly who is doing what in every sentence. Dangling modifiers can confuse and frustrate readers.

Write the following on the board: *Using a pencil, the drawing went quickly.*

Ask students what is unclear in this sentence: *Using a pencil* is unclear because we don't know who used a pencil. Ask volunteers for suggestions on how to fix this dangling modifier. (Possible response: When I used a pencil, the drawing went quickly.)

Dangling Modifiers

Know the Rule

> **Dangling modifiers** most frequently occur at the beginning of sentences as introductory participial phrases.
>
> **Incorrect:** After reading the original study, the article remains unconvincing.
>
> The article—the subject of the main clause—did not read the original study. Who did? When you figure that out, you can fix the sentence.
>
> **Correct:** After reading the original study, I found the article unconvincing.

Practice the Rule

Read each sentence below. Find the dangling modifiers. Write each sentence correctly on a separate sheet of paper. Possible answers are given.

1. Looking for a certain breed, sled dogs are often not purebreds.
   Sled dogs are often not purebreds, so I won't look for a certain breed.
2. After examining them, the dogs are ready to be identified.
   After being examined, the dogs are ready to be identified.
3. Using a syringe, a microchip gives each dog a code.
   Each dog is given a code on a microchip that is inserted with a syringe.
4. After doing a blood test, the dogs can be hitched to the sled.
   After a vet does a blood test, the dogs can be hitched to the sled.
5. While waiting to start, the crowd is restless.
   While waiting for the race to start, the crowd is restless.
6. Wearing dog booties, the jagged ice won't hurt their paws.
   The jagged ice won't hurt the paws of dogs wearing dog booties.
7. Panting and barking eagerly, the drivers ready the dog sleds.
   Panting and barking eagerly, the dogs are hitched to the dog sleds.
8. When fired, the dogs leap forward at the sound of the starting gun.
   When the starting gun is fired, the dogs leap forward.
9. Riding on the back of the sled, the dogs respond to the commands of the drivers.
   The dogs respond to the commands of the drivers, who ride on the back of the sled.
10. After winning the race, a prize is awarded to the lead dog team.
    After winning the race, the lead dog team receives a prize.

Related Grammar Practice

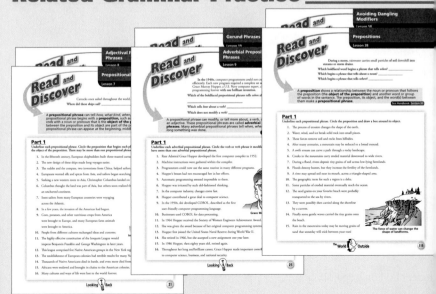

Pages 21, 23, 25, 55, 113, 173

Go to ➡ **G.U.M. Student Practice Book**

Online Writing Center

Provides **interactive grammar games** and **practice activities** in student eBook.

Prepositional Phrases

Know the Rule

A **prepositional phrase** can tell how, what kind, when, how much, or where. A prepositional phrase begins with a **preposition**, such as *in, over, of, to,* or *by*. It ends with a noun or pronoun that is the **object of the preposition**. The words between the preposition and its object are part of the prepositional phrase. A prepositional phrase can be anywhere in a sentence.

> **Example:** Please place this book **on the second shelf of the bookcase** that is **in the corner of my office.**

Practice the Rule

Find the prepositional phrases in each sentence. Write them on a separate sheet of paper.

1. In the morning, we are driving out of town and across the state toward our favorite amusement park.
2. It's a long ride to the park, but we entertain ourselves by reading books and listening to music in the car.
3. When we arrive, we will pass through the gates and head to the roller coaster.
4. We're told by our parents that we should meet near the park entrance before lunchtime.
5. After a picnic lunch, I hope to sit beside my brother and sail above the treetops on the relaxing gondola ride.
6. There are hundreds of games in the arcade located in the southeast corner of the park.
7. After sundown, all the lights turn on and transform the park into a magical world of light and sound and fun.
8. During the ride home, I fall asleep with my head on my big sister's shoulder and dream about my wonderful day.
9. When we arrived home, I stumbled up the steps and into the house.
10. Minutes later, my head was on my pillow and I was dreaming again.

Conventions

Mini-Lesson

Student Objectives

- Identify and correctly use prepositional phrases. *(p. 403)*

Prepositional Phrases

Prepositional phrases link the parts of sentences and provide information that tells where, what kind, when, or how much. A prepositional phrase always begins with a preposition and includes an object of the preposition.

Before students do the activity, practice using prepositional phrases as a class. Begin by asking questions and giving simple commands, such as the following: *Who is sitting near the door? Diego, please put a pencil on your desk.* Point out the prepositional phrases in each sentence, and then explain what kind of information the phrase provides. Then call on students to ask each other questions or give simple commands using prepositional phrases. Be sure they can identify the prepositional phrases they use, as well as explain what information each phrase is providing.

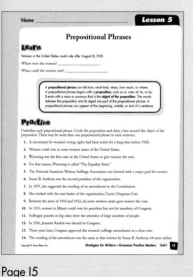

Page 15

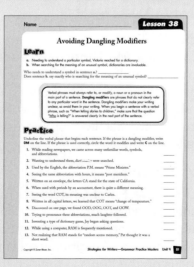

Page 81

Go to ➡️ *Grammar Practice Masters*

CCSS **Common Core State Standards**

L.7.1.c: Place phrases and clauses within a sentence, recognizing and correcting misplaced and dangling modifiers. **L.7.2:** Demonstrate command of the conventions of standard English capitalization, punctuation, and spelling when writing.

Write
a Biographic Sketch

Week 3 • Day 4

Student Objectives

- Discuss preparation for publishing and presentation. (p. 404)
- Use a final editing checklist to publish their work. (p. 404)

Publish +Presentation

Publishing Strategy Ask students what they think of Andre's decision to post his sketch on a bulletin board. Remind the class that he might also include this sketch in his journal, send it to a friend or relative, or send it to the person he wrote about. Invite students to name other ways they could publish their own biographic sketches.

Have students make final checklists to check their own sketches. Along with their chosen methods of publishing, encourage them to give or send copies to friends and relatives who would enjoy reading about the people they described.

Strategies for Writers Online
Go to **www.sfw.z-b.com** for additional online resources for students and teachers.

Publish   +Presentation

Publishing Strategy	Display the biographic sketch on a "Who Am I?" bulletin board in the school hallway.
Presentation Strategy	Use clear, readable fonts or neat handwriting.

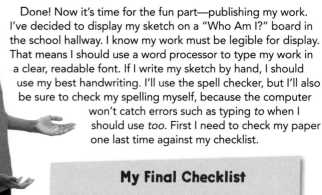

Done! Now it's time for the fun part—publishing my work. I've decided to display my sketch on a "Who Am I?" board in the school hallway. I know my work must be legible for display. That means I should use a word processor to type my work in a clear, readable font. If I write my sketch by hand, I should use my best handwriting. I'll use the spell checker, but I'll also be sure to check my spelling myself, because the computer won't catch errors such as typing *to* when I should use *too*. First I need to check my paper one last time against my checklist.

My Final Checklist

Did I—

✔ fix any dangling modifiers?

✔ correctly and effectively use all prepositional phrases?

✔ correct any spelling, grammar, or punctuation errors?

✔ neatly handwrite or type out my biographic sketch?

Apply

Make a final checklist to check your own biographic sketch. Then make a final copy to publish.

404   Descriptive Writing

Differentiating Instruction

ENRICHMENT
Create a Multimedia Presentation Have students create a multimedia presentation to accompany their biographic sketches. Students could include photos of the subjects, if available; photos or video clips relating to events in the subjects' lives or interests; or sound or music clips that relate to the topics.

REINFORCEMENT
Limit the Final Checklist Help students create short final checklists focusing on a limited number of skills, such as fixing dangling modifiers, correcting spelling errors, and using neat and legible handwriting or fonts. Have students focus on the items in their limited checklists.

SLED DOG SETH

by Andre

Meet Sled Dog Seth! Seth is a seventh grader at Nell Scott Middle School. At school, Seth is just like anybody else. But after school, most often, you see Seth dressed in blue jeans, an unzipped parka, and shiny green rubber boots, carrying a bucket of smelly brown kibbles. A steel scoop sticks out the top. He is heading out to feed the sled dogs.

"I love my dogs!" Seth always says. "They are a part of my family, just like my mom and dad and my sister, Katie." His boots make a squishing sound in the spongy ground. As he nears the dog pens, the squishing sound is drowned out by barking. The dogs' metal food pans go skittering as the dogs run up to the fence. Seth rubs their silky fur and lets each dog lick his face right up to the roots of his carrot-colored hair. He is kind and affectionate as he feeds the dogs. With a crunch, the scoop hits the kibbles. With a clatter, the kibbles hit the pans.

After the dogs' dinner, Seth hitches them up to a sled. He checks each dog's paws and adjusts reins and harnesses. He pulls up his hood and zips up the parka. Then he yells, "Mush!" and off he goes! Snowflakes hit his face like a thousand needles. The cold wind turns his nose bright red.

Seth is growing fast. He grew three inches taller over the summer, making him the tallest, skinniest boy in his class! He always gets invited to play on the school's basketball team, but he always shakes his head no. "I don't have time. After school, I work with the dogs," he says. That's his life. His parents have cared for sled dogs all their lives, and so will Seth!

Reflect

Check Andre's biographic sketch against the rubric. Did he do a good job? Use the rubric and your checklist to check your own biographic sketch.

Technology Tip   for 21st Century Literacies

Gathering responses to students' writing can be challenging, especially when they are posted online. We need to prepare student writers to share feedback that will help improve a piece while also protecting them from receiving comments that aren't helpful. Consider using an online survey tool such as Google Forms or SurveyMonkey as a tool for collecting responses to student work. This provides both specific prompts for a reader to consider when responding, but it also presents the comments in a searchable, sortable way that will help you and the class consider what worked (or didn't) in individual pieces.

See **www.sfw.z-b.com** for further information about and links to these websites and tools.

Write
a Biographic Sketch

Week 3 • Day 5

Student Objectives

- Use a biographic sketch rubric. *(pp. 388–389)*
- Share a published biographic sketch. *(p. 405)*

Presentation Strategy When using a computer, it can be tempting to use decorative fonts or to change fonts often, but these practices can also make the reader's job difficult. Fancy fonts are sometimes hard to read, and changing fonts is distracting. Students may wish to use a more decorative font for the title, but it should still be easy to read.

Reflecting on a Biographic Sketch

Ask students to reflect on the experience of writing a biographic sketch. Ask:

- What did you enjoy the most about writing your biographic sketch?

- Which part was the most difficult for you?

- What did you learn about improving your writing from this experience?

CCSS **C**ommon **C**ore **S**tate **S**tandards

W.7.4: Produce clear and coherent writing in which the development, organization, and style are appropriate to task, purpose, and audience. **W.7.6:** Use technology, including the Internet, to produce and publish writing and link to and cite sources as well as to interact and collaborate with others, including linking to and citing sources.

Observation Report Planner

WEEK 1

Day 1
Introduce an Observation Report

Student Objectives
- Review the elements of an observation report.
- Consider purpose and audience.
- Learn the traits of descriptive writing.

Student Activities
- Read and discuss **What's in an Observation Report?** (p. 406)
- Read and discuss **Why Write an Observation Report?** (p. 407)
- Read **Linking Descriptive Writing Traits to an Observation Report.**

Day 2
(p. 408)
Analyze
Read an Observation Report

Student Objectives
- Read a model observation report.

Student Activities
- Read **"Observations of a Bird Watcher."** (p. 409)

Day 3
Analyze
Introduce the Rubric

Student Objectives
- Learn to read a rubric.

Student Activities
- Review **"Observations of a Bird Watcher."** (p. 409)
- Read and discuss the **Observation Report Rubric.** (pp. 410–411)

WEEK 2

Day 1
Write
Prewrite: Ideas

Student Objectives
- Read and understand a prewriting strategy.

Student Activities
- Read and discuss **Prewrite: Focus on Ideas.** (p. 416)
- Apply the prewriting strategy.

Day 2
Write
Prewrite: Organization

Student Objectives
- Make an Observation Chart to organize notes.

Student Activities
- Read and discuss **Prewrite: Focus on Organization.** (p. 417)
- Reflect on the model Observation Chart.
- Apply the prewriting strategy to create an Observation Chart.
- Participate in a peer conference.

Day 3
Write
Draft: Organization

Student Objectives
- Begin writing, using transitions to connect ideas.

Student Activities
- Read and discuss **Draft: Focus on Organization.** (pp. 418–419)
- Reflect on a model draft.
- Apply the drafting strategy by using the Observations Chart and by using transitions.

WEEK 3

Day 1
Write
Revise: Word Choice

Student Objectives
- Revise for use of precise words.

Student Activities
- Read and discuss **Revise: Focus on Word Choice.** (p. 421)
- Reflect on a model draft.
- Apply the revising strategy.
- Participate in a peer conference.

Day 2
Write
Revise: Sentence Fluency

Student Objectives
- Revise to vary sentence lengths and patterns.

Student Activities
- Read and discuss **Revise: Focus on Sentence Fluency.** (p. 422)
- Reflect on a model draft.
- Apply the revising strategy.

Note: Optional Revising Lessons appear on the *Strategies for Writers* CD-ROM.

Day 3
Write
Edit: Conventions

Student Objectives
- Edit for subject-verb agreement.

Student Activities
- Read and discuss **Edit: Focus on Conventions.** (p. 423)
- Reflect on a model draft.
- Apply the editing strategy.

Note: Teach the Conventions mini-lessons (pp. 424–425) if needed.

Day 4	Day 5
Analyze Ideas, Organization, and Voice	**Analyze** Word Choice, Sentence Fluency, and Conventions

Student Objectives
- Read a model observation report.
- Use the observation report rubric.
- Use the model observation report to study Ideas, Organization, and Voice.

Student Activities
- Review **"Observations of a Bird Watcher."** (p. 409)
- Read and discuss **Using the Rubric to Study the Model.** (pp. 412–413)

Student Objectives
- Read a model observation report.
- Use the observation report rubric.
- Use the model observation report to study Word Choice, Sentence Fluency, and Conventions.

Student Activities
- Review **"Observations of a Bird Watcher."** (p. 409)
- Read and discuss **Using the Rubric to Study the Model.** (pp. 414–415)

Day 4	Day 5
Write Draft	**Write** Revise: Voice

Student Objectives
- Complete a draft.

Student Activities
- Continue to draft.
- Participate in a peer conference.

Student Objectives
- Revise for informative, enthusiastic voice.

Student Activities
- Read and discuss **Revise: Focus on Voice.** (p. 420)
- Reflect on a model draft.
- Apply the revising strategy.

Day 4	Day 5
Write Publish: +Presentation	**Write** Publish: +Presentation

Student Objectives
- Discuss preparation for publishing and presentation.
- Use a final editing checklist to publish their work.

Student Activities
- Read and discuss **Publish: +Presentation** (p. 426)
- Apply the publishing strategy.

Student Objectives
- Use an observation report rubric.
- Share a published observation report.

Student Activities
- Share their work.
- Use the observation report rubric to reflect on the model and their own writing. (pp. 410–411, 427)

complete the chapter in fewer days, combine the learning objectives and activities in a way that supports students as they write.

Grammar, Usage & Mechanics

Subject-Verb Agreement....... T424
More Subject-Verb Agreement. . T425
Grammar Practice.......T423–T425

Differentiating Instruction

Using the Rubric............ T415
Draft T418
Publish.................... T426
For additional Differentiating Instruction activities, see Strategies for Writers *Extensions Online at* **www.sfw.z-b.com.**

English Language Learners

Using the Rubric........T412–T413
Prewrite T416
Revise...................... T420

Conferencing

Peer to Peer T417, T419, T421
Peer Groups...... T417, T419, T421
Teacher-Led T417, T419, T421

Technology Tip

Using the Rubric............ T414
Publish.................... T427

 Connection Letter
Reproducible letter (in English and Spanish) appears on the *Strategies for Writers* CD-ROM and at **www.sfw.z-b.com.**

Online Writing Center
Provides IWB resources, interactive games and practice activities, videos, eBooks, and a virtual file cabinet.

 Strategies for Writers Online
Go to **www.sfw.z-b.com** for free online resources for students and teachers.

Introduce
an Observation Report

Week 1 • Day 1

Student Objectives

- Review the elements of an observation report. *(p. 406)*
- Consider purpose and audience. *(p. 407)*
- Learn the traits of descriptive writing. *(p. 408)*

What's an Observation Report?

Discuss the definition of an observation report with students. Ask students if any of them describe things in their journals or blogs. Point out that any time they describe something they have seen, they are using the observation report genre.

What's in an Observation Report?

Read and discuss the elements of an observation report with students. Explain that many of these elements are also common to other forms of writing, such as a biography, personal account, and historical narrative. Discuss how each element may be used by a writer to communicate what he or she observed.

 Strategies for Writers Online
Go to **www.sfw.z-b.com** for additional online resources for students and teachers.

What's an Observation Report?

It's a report that describes an object, person, event, or process that the writer has seen. It's my chance to describe something amazing.

What's in an Observation Report?

Information
An observation report is about facts. It presents a lot of information by using descriptive language to help the reader "see" the subject.

Concrete Details
Sometimes I read things that make no sense to me because there are no concrete details to support the ideas. I'll include plenty of concrete details to help my readers grasp exactly what I'm describing. I'll include some pictures, too.

Personal Experiences
Writing lets me tell about things that have happened to me or things that I have experienced. In Alaska, there are so many things that other people don't often see. I can bring those things to life for people who have never been to the North.

Organization
Ideas can't be all jumbled up or just presented in an unconnected list! I'll need to group my observations into paragraphs and lead the reader through them with logical transitions.

Descriptive Text Exemplars (Observation Report)

Isaacson, Philip. *A Short Walk Around the Pyramids and Through the World of Art.* **Knopf, 1993.** CCSS Isaacson provides the reader with an exciting tour from the pyramids of Egypt to the skyscrapers of New York City and discusses the many different forms art can take. Using sculpture, pottery, painting, photographs, furniture, and cities, Isaacson shows how art is all around us.

Lasky, Kathryn. *Interrupted Journey: Saving Endangered Sea Turtles.* **Candlewick, 2006.** This book describes the true story of a community's attempt to protect and save an endangered Kemp's ridley turtle. The author also discusses the turtle's life cycle, the hazards they face, as well as efforts to help the turtle reproduce.

Why write an Observation Report?

There are plenty of reasons for writing an observation report. I listed some here.

Entertainment
Some things that I see are so strange, beautiful, or mysterious that I just want to share them with someone else. Entertaining the reader is one good reason to write an observation report.

Personal Reflection
Writing about something I've seen will help me to understand it better because I have to think it through in order to put my thoughts in words.

Information
Some observations can inform the reader. My story can bring experiences from Alaska down to the mainland.

Contribution to Science
Most science involves observation. Astronomers observe the stars. Biologists watch and observe animals and plants. Their observations build understanding and knowledge. I can contribute, too! Sharpening my observation skills will be important to my success in science.

Leroe, Ellen. *Disaster! Three Real-Life Stories of Survival.* **Hyperion Books, 2000.** Read three harrowing tales of survival surrounding the 1914 sinking of the Empress of Ireland, the 1928 Arctic crash of airship Italia, and the 1930 crash of the R-101 dirigible.

Paulsen, Gary. *Woodsong.* **Simon and Schuster, 2007.** Gary Paulsen, a Newbery Award winning author known for his man-in-nature adventure stories, writes about his own experience and adventures competing in the Iditarod race in Alaska. Paulsen uses descriptive language and vivid imagery as he recounts many of the lessons learned during the events surrounding the iconic race that shaped his life and his writing.

Why write an Observation Report?

Read and discuss with students the reasons for writing an observation report on page 407. Point out that all writing has a purpose. Writers write for many reasons and for a variety of audiences, and these authentic purposes help to shape the writing. Someone writing to entertain may use a tone that conveys excitement, humor, or suspense. When writing for personal reflection, a writer may focus on building understanding. A person whose goal is to inform may include many facts and explanations to help his or her audience understand the report's topic. A writer who is writing to contribute to science will make sure all observations are accurate and clearly stated. Encourage students to think about their reasons for writing observation reports, as well as who will be reading them, and how these elements will affect the tone and focus of their writing. For example, if the purpose is to contribute to science, yet the audience consists of younger children, a good writer would adjust the type of language used throughout the report.

CCSS Common Core State Standards
SL.7.1: Engage effectively in a range of collaborative discussions (one-on-one, in groups, and teacher-led) with diverse partners on *grade 7 topics, texts, and issues,* building on others' ideas and expressing their own clearly.

Introduce
an Observation Report

Linking Descriptive Writing Traits to an Observation Report

Have students read page 408. Emphasize that they will follow Andre as he models using the writing process and the traits together. As they follow Andre, students will see how the Descriptive Writing Traits have been adapted and applied to writing an observation report. They will see that an observation report has many factors in common with other types of descriptive writing. However, the particular audience and purpose of an observation report determine how the traits are used.

Discuss with students how each trait applies to an observation report. For example, using precise words and phrases to create an accurate picture for the reader is crucial to the purpose of an observation report.

Online Writing Center

Provides six **interactive anchor papers** for each mode of writing.

Linking Descriptive Writing Traits to an Observation Report

In this chapter, you will describe an object, person, event, or process. This type of descriptive writing is called an observation report. Andre will guide you through the stages of the writing process: Prewrite, Draft, Revise, Edit, and Publish. In each stage, Andre will show you important writing strategies that are linked to the Descriptive Writing Traits below.

Descriptive Writing Traits

Trait	Description
Ideas	• a clear topic that is developed by relevant supporting details • descriptive details that are well chosen for the topic
 Organization	• well-organized paragraphs that logically follow the order of the description, whether by time, location, or another order • varied and appropriate transitions that show the relationship between ideas and concepts
Voice	• a voice that is appropriate for the purpose and audience
Word Choice	• precise words and phrases, possibly including figurative language, that create an accurate picture for the reader
Sentence Fluency	• sentences that vary in length and type to add flow to the writing
Conventions	• no or few errors in grammar, usage, mechanics, and spelling

Before you write, read Naomi Greenberg's observation report on the next page. Then use the observation report rubric on pages 410–411 to decide how well she did. (You might want to look back at What's in an Observation Report? on page 406, too!)

Descriptive Writing Traits in an Observation Report

 **Ideas** An observation report must have a clear, specific topic, since the goal is to describe one thing, place, or event in detail for the reader. Supporting details should all be relevant, and descriptive details should help the reader more clearly "see" the observations.

 **Organization** Writing that is organized into clear paragraphs is easy to follow. Transitions move the readers from one paragraph to the next.

 **Voice** Depending on the report's topic, the writer may want to share amusement, excitement, awe, or interest.

Observations of a Bird Watcher

by Naomi Greenberg

An outdoor bird feeder can be fun to observe any time of the year. Watching the one in my backyard for just a few months gave me a real education in bird behavior.

Factual information — *Personal experience*

Cardinals, for example, are not only beautiful, they are also very clever. The all-red, crested male approaches the feeder on his own and checks out the territory. When he has made sure no enemies (that is, cats) are nearby, he leaves, and then the female, more brown than red, arrives to feed at her leisure. Mr. Cardinal still keeps watch, though, from a nearby branch. Later, he and his mate may perch together in an out-of-the-way spot, with the male transferring tasty tidbits from his beak to hers. At such moments the two may "cheep" softly to each other. At other times, though, their call may be loud, almost strident.

Concrete details

Other loud birds around the feeder are the blue jays. These crested fellows are good-looking, but they have very poor manners, pushing smaller birds away in their eagerness to eat. Only recently did I realize that some of the jay's noisiness has a purpose. Listening to the bird's loud, repeated "jay, jay" call one day, it occurred to me that it sounded like a warning siren. I looked out at the feeder, and sure enough, a cat was stalking nearby.

Organized with logical transitions

Besides the beautiful cardinals and jays, several more ordinary-looking birds often crowd around the feeder. Flocks of gray-brown sparrows usually arrive in groups but politely wait their turn, perching on the telephone wire just above the feeder. House finches, sparrow-like birds with a reddish forehead and breast, show the same good manners, chattering to each other as they sit and wait. Mourning doves often pick at seeds that have fallen from the feeder.

During spring migration, new species arrive. Tiny, bright yellow goldfinches dropped by one day late last April. But the biggest thrill was the visit of the gorgeous grosbeaks. One or two of the black, white, and gold-colored males came first, in early May, followed the next day by at least ten companions. After a day or two of feeding, the birds lost their bedraggled look and moved on, perhaps to other bird feeders.

Observation Report 409

Word Choice The writer's goal is to convey an accurate image of what he or she has observed. Precise language will help paint a clear picture for the reader.

Sentence Fluency Variety in sentence lengths and types gives writing a pleasing rhythm and flow.

Conventions Too many errors in grammar, usage, mechanics, and spelling will make the writing hard to read. The writer's observations will be lost on the reader if poor use of conventions leads to confusion or misunderstanding. At the worst, readers will give up in frustration if they cannot make out the meaning.

Analyze
the Model

Week 1 • Day 2

Student Objectives
• Read a model observation report. (*p. 409*)

Read the Model

Read "Observations of a Bird Watcher" as students follow along in their books. Ask students which details helped them most clearly visualize the action around the bird feeder.

Elements of an Observation Report

Use the notes on the model to discuss the various elements of an observation report. Refer students to What's in an Observation Report? on page 406 if they need to review the elements. Discuss why concrete details are important in this type of writing. Point to the sentence underlined in blue and then write on the board: *Blue jays are very aggressive.* Ask students to compare the two sentences and discuss why the one with more concrete details is better. (Possible responses: It explains exactly how the blue jays are aggressive; it gives the reader a more precise picture of what happens at the feeder.)

CCSS Common Core State Standards
R/Lit.7.1: Cite several pieces of textual evidence to support analysis of what the text says explicitly as well as inferences drawn from the text.

Analyze
the Model

Week 1 • Day 3

Student Objectives

- Learn to read a rubric.
  (pp. 410–411)

Use the Rubric

Explain the Rubric Explain that a rubric is a tool for planning, improving, and assessing a piece of writing. Tell students that a rubric helps a writer focus on key elements, or traits, in writing (**Ideas, Organization, Voice, Word Choice, Sentence Fluency, Conventions,** and **Presentation**). Point out that column 6 describes a very good observation report, one that has received the highest scores in all categories. This is what students should strive for in their own writing.

Discuss the Rubric Guide students in a discussion of the rubric. Read the descriptors that go with each trait, and take a moment to point out the ways the traits support each other (e.g., using precise, descriptive words helps the writer best understand what you are describing). Remind students to keep the rubric in mind when they write their own observation report and again when they revise it.

Online Writing Center

Provides a variety of **interactive rubrics,** including 4-, 5-, and 6-point models.

Rubric

Use this 6-point rubric to plan and evaluate an observation report.

	6	5	4	
Ideas	Concrete details support each topic sentence. Visuals support the text.	Concrete details support most topic sentences. Visuals support the text.	Some details are vague and do not support the topic sentences. Visuals are included.	
Organization	Varied, appropriate transitions create cohesion and make the paragraphs easy to follow.	Appropriate transitions create cohesion and help the paragraphs flow.	Transitions are appropriate and helpful most of the time but lack variety.	
Voice	The writer's voice is informative and enthusiastic. It draws the reader into the text.	The writer's voice is informative and enthusiastic.	The writer's voice loses energy as the report progresses. More knowledge of the topic would help.	
Word Choice	Precise words and phrases capture the experience and bring it to life for the reader.	Precise words and phrases describe the experience clearly.	In some places, imprecise words and phrases create a fuzzy picture for the reader.	
Sentence Fluency	Varied sentence lengths and patterns make the report enjoyable to read.	Varied sentence lengths and patterns are noticeable.	There is some variety in sentence lengths and beginnings.	
Conventions	Subjects and verbs agree. The meaning is clear.	A few minor errors in subject-verb agreement are present, but they do not interfere with the meaning.	A few problems with subject-verb agreement may confuse the reader.	

✛ Presentation Paragraphs are indented.

CCSS Common Core State Standards

Observation Report

Writing in the Descriptive mode can engage the Common Core State Standards for both Narrative and Informative/Explanatory writing. The rubrics and strategies for the observation report are based principally on Informative/Explanatory standards. The descriptors for the Ideas rubric are drawn from standards **W.7.2.a** and **W.7.2.b**. Standard **W.7.2.a** includes the use of graphics to aid comprehension; the Ideas descriptor reflects this in its requirement for visuals. Standard **W.7.2.b** calls for writers to use concrete details, which is also echoed in the rubric.

3	2	1	
Several topic sentences lack supporting details. Visuals are included but do not relate to the text.	Few or no concrete details are included. Topic sentences are missing or unsupported. Visuals are missing or unrelated.	The writer has included neither topic sentences nor concrete details. No visuals are used.	**Ideas**
Transitions are lacking in some places. Transitions that are included may be inappropriate or lack variety.	Transitions are lacking, dull, and/or incorrectly used.	The writer has included no transitions.	**Organization**
The writer's voice is flat and poorly informed in places.	The writer's voice is sometimes difficult to identify.	The writer's voice is missing.	**Voice**
Words and phrases are vague in several places; the reader has to work to understand the experience.	The descriptions are very hard to follow because the words and phrases are too broad or vague.	The description is impossible to understand because the language is too vague.	**Word Choice**
Sentence beginnings and lengths tend to be the same.	Many sentences are too short or too similar. The report is choppy to read.	Some sentences are incomplete or incorrect.	**Sentence Fluency**
Many problems with subject-verb agreement interfere with meaning.	Many problems with subject-verb agreement are present, and they constantly interfere with meaning.	Frequent, serious errors with subject-verb agreement make the writing very hard to understand.	**Conventions**

See Appendix B for 4-, 5-, and 6-point descriptive rubrics.

Observation Report **411**

The Organization rubric restates standard **W.7.2.c** with its emphasis on the use of appropriate transitions to create cohesion and link ideas. The Word Choice rubric, specifying the use of precise language to inform the reader, is drawn from standard **W.7.2.d**.

Apply the Rubric

Small Groups Have students work in groups of four or five to find one good example of each trait in the model. One student in each group can write down the examples, or each student can write the examples for one or two traits.

Class Discussion Bring the class back together. Discussing one trait at a time, ask each group to give the examples they chose. Note whether groups tended to choose the same examples or whether they came up with a variety. Ask groups who chose different examples to explain their choices. You may wish to have the class decide which example best represents each trait. The point of this exercise is not to score the model, but to practice identifying the traits in an observation report.

Additional Rubrics Appendix B includes 4-, 5-, and 6-point rubrics that can be used with any piece of descriptive writing. The rubrics are also available as blackline masters in the back of the Teacher Edition, beginning on T543.

CCSS **Common Core State Standards**
SL.7.1: Engage effectively in a range of collaborative discussions (one-on-one, in groups, and teacher-led) with diverse partners on *grade 7 topics, texts, and issues*, building on others' ideas and expressing their own clearly. **SL.7.1.a:** Come to discussions prepared, having read or researched material under study; explicitly draw on that preparation by referring to evidence on the topic, text, or issue to probe and reflect on ideas under discussion. **SL.7.1.b:** Follow rules for collegial discussions, track progress toward specific goals and deadlines, and define individual roles as needed. **SL.7.1.d:** Acknowledge new information expressed by others and, when warranted, modify their own views.

Analyze
the Model

Student Objectives

- Read a model observation report. *(p. 409)*
- Use the observation report rubric. *(pp. 410–411)*
- Use the model observation report to study Ideas, Organization, and Voice. *(pp. 412–413)*

Study the Model

Assess the Model Use questions such as the following to discuss the model and the traits with students. Encourage students to back up their answers with examples from the model.

- Which concrete details give you a clear picture of the spring migration? (Possible responses: the tiny, bright yellow goldfinches; the specific number of colorful grosbeaks that show up at the feeder)

 Strategies for Writers Online
Go to **www.sfw.z-b.com** for additional online resources for students and teachers.

Observation Report
Using the Rubric to Study the Model

Did you notice that the model on page 409 points out some key elements of an observation report? As she wrote "Observations of a Bird Watcher," Naomi Greenberg used these elements to help her describe her experience. She also used the 6-point rubric on pages 410–411 to plan, draft, revise, and edit the writing. A rubric is a great tool to evaluate writing during the writing process.

Now let's use the same rubric to score the model. To do this, we'll focus on each trait separately, starting with Ideas. We'll use the top descriptor for each trait (column 6), along with examples from the model, to help us understand how the traits work together. How would you score Naomi on each trait?

Ideas
- Concrete details support each topic sentence.
- Visuals support the text.

Naomi uses many concrete details to support her ideas. Look how she follows her topic sentence about cardinals with solid information that explains just why she thinks cardinals are clever. The picture she uses adds to my understanding by providing a great visual of these interesting birds.

[from the writing model]

Cardinals, for example, are not only beautiful, they are also very clever. The all-red, crested male approaches the feeder on his own and checks out the territory. When he has made sure no enemies (that is, cats) are nearby, he leaves, and then the female, more brown than red, arrives to feed at her leisure.

English Language Learners

BEGINNING
The Five Senses Demonstrate the meanings of *sight, sound, touch, taste,* and *smell,* and make sure students understand that each sense corresponds to a certain part of the body. For example, our sense of sight is fulfilled by the eyes. Say a word, such as *salty, loud,* or *green,* and have students point to the body part that we use to perceive the idea of the word. Then model a sentence for students to repeat, such as *I can taste something salty.*

INTERMEDIATE
Observation Chart Briefly review the five senses. Present students with a familiar object, such as a carrot or an apple. Have partners complete an Observation Chart for the object, making sure to include at least one idea for each of the five senses.

Organization
- Varied, appropriate transitions create cohesion and make the paragraphs easy to follow.

Writing that has cohesion is writing that fits together well. All parts are logically connected and flow together smoothly. Naomi uses transitions to connect ideas and paragraphs, so it is easy to follow along. Here, she uses the phrase *Other loud birds* to make a graceful transition to discussing blue jays.

[from the writing model]

> Other loud birds around the feeder are the blue jays. These crested fellows are good-looking, but they have very poor manners, pushing smaller birds away in their eagerness to eat.

Voice
- The writer's voice is informative and enthusiastic.
- It draws the reader into the text.

Naomi definitely knows what she's talking about. Her voice is energetic and respectful of these tiny creatures. Bird watching sounds like fun!

[from the writing model]

> Listening to the bird's loud, repeated "jay, jay" call one day, it occurred to me that it sounded like a warning siren. I looked out at the feeder, and sure enough, a cat was stalking nearby.

- What transition does the writer use in the second paragraph? (for example) How does this transition help connect the first two paragraphs? (Possible response: It tells that the information about cardinals is one of the things the writer learned by watching the feeder.)

- What are some other ways Naomi expresses her enthusiasm for the subject? (Possible responses: She uses the phrase *But the biggest thrill was*; she talks about the birds as if they were people—*but they have very poor manners.*)

ADVANCED

Main Idea/Details Explain to students that the main idea is the big idea. Give students a short paragraph about a scientific topic such as *metamorphosis*. Have students highlight the main idea, and then have them exchange with another student who highlights a detail in a different color. Another student highlights another detail and so on. When finished highlighting, have students check their answers by filling in a Main Idea Table as a group.

ADVANCED HIGH

Relevant Facts Students must decide if a fact is relevant to the main idea. Give students the main idea, such as *Butterflies go through a process called metamorphosis*, and list several related and unrelated facts, such as *most snakes hatch from eggs, one stage of metamorphosis is the larva stage, the caterpillar forms a chrysalis*, and so on. Have students circle the facts that are relevant to the main idea.

CCSS **Common Core State Standards**

SL.7.1.b: Follow rules for collegial discussions, track progress toward specific goals and deadlines, and define individual roles as needed. **SL.7.1.c:** Pose questions that elicit elaboration and respond to others' questions and comments with relevant observations and ideas that bring the discussion back on topic as needed.

Analyze
the Model

Week 1 • Day 5

Student Objectives

- Read a model observation report. *(p. 409)*
- Use the observation report rubric. *(pp. 410–411)*
- Use the model observation report to study Word Choice, Sentence Fluency, and Conventions. *(pp. 414–415)*

Continue the Discussion Use the following questions to continue to analyze the model:

- Which words did you find most precise and descriptive? What duller words might these words replace? (Possible responses: *stalking* might replace *walking*; *chattering* might replace *making noises*; *companions* might replace *others*.)

- Do all the verbs agree with their subjects in the model? (yes)

- Precise words and phrases capture the experience and bring it to life for the reader.

Naomi uses words that accurately and clearly describe what she sees. Precise words such as *perch* and *tasty tidbits* create a stronger image than general words such as *sit* and *food*.

[from the writing model]

Later, he and his mate may perch together in an out-of-the-way spot, with the male transferring tasty tidbits from his beak to hers.

- Varied sentence lengths and patterns make the report enjoyable to read.

Naomi has a nice mix of short and long sentences, and there is variety in their structure. Here are some examples. The first example starts with a dependent clause; the second example starts with a prepositional phrase.

[from the writing model]

When he has made sure no enemies (that is, cats) are nearby, he leaves. . .

[from the writing model]

During spring migration, new species arrive.

414 Descriptive Writing

Technology Tip — for 21st Century Literacies

Sometimes when writing a summary or report, we lose the details that readers need, often because an individual sees one event through a specific lens or point of view. We counter this by capturing evidence from the event, often from multiple points of view. Use VoiceThread, Glogster, or a different multimodal authoring space/tool to collect images and video that reflect different stances, positions, and/or interpretations. Challenge students to return to this resource as they draft their report.

See **www.sfw.z-b.com** for further information about and links to these websites and tools.

 Strategies for Writers Online
Go to **www.sfw.z-b.com** for additional online resources for students and teachers.

Conventions

- Subjects and verbs agree.
- The meaning is clear.

I didn't notice any problems with Naomi's subject-verb agreement in the report. The following sentences show you how carefully she avoids this error.

[from the writing model]

Other loud birds around the feeder are the blue jays.

[from the writing model]

House finches, sparrow-like birds with a reddish forehead and breast, show the same good manners . . .

+Presentation Paragraphs are indented.

Now it's my turn to write! I'm going to write an observation report of my own. Watch to see how I use the rubric to practice good writing strategies.

Observation Report 415

Differentiating Instruction

ENRICHMENT

Experiment With Voice Brainstorm attitudes a writer might want to convey through voice, such as anger, amazement, sorrow, or excitement. Have students rewrite a paragraph from the model using a voice that expresses a different feeling. Discuss how changing the voice affects the meaning or tone of the paragraph.

REINFORCEMENT

Explore Sentence Fluency Rewrite one of the model paragraphs using only short declarative sentences. Read aloud the two versions and discuss what makes one version easier or harder to read and understand.

Presentation Remind students that they must consider how their papers will look when they prepare their final copies. Paragraph indents provide the reader with a visual guide to paragraph breaks. When you look away from the report, you can quickly reorient yourself when you return to it by using the indents to help you find the paragraph you want. By creating a little space on the page, paragraph indents also break up the text so that it does not appear as a single, intimidating block. Readers find it easier and more enjoyable to read text that is presented in a way that is easy on the eyes.

Think About the Traits Once students have thoroughly discussed the model observation report, ask them which traits they think are most important in this type of writing. Of course, all the traits are important in every piece of writing, but some of them stand out more in some genres than in others. Students might say, for example, that in an observation report **Organization** is of special importance because placing details into clear, easy-to-understand categories or sequences makes it easier for the reader to follow the observations. Students might also mention **Word Choice** because precise, descriptive wording is needed to convey the writer's observations clearly and accurately.

CCSS **C**ommon **C**ore **S**tate **S**tandards

SL.7.1.c: Pose questions that elicit elaboration and respond to others' questions and comments with relevant observations and ideas that bring the discussion back on topic as needed. **SL.7.1.d:** Acknowledge new information expressed by others and, when warranted, modify their own views.

Observation Report T415

Write an Observation Report

Week 2 • Day 1

Student Objectives

- Read and understand a prewriting strategy. *(p. 416)*

Prewrite

Focus on Ideas

Gather Information As students think about possible topics for their own observation reports, have them ask themselves the following questions: Do I think this topic will be interesting to readers? Does my topic have the right scope—not too broad or too narrow—for this observation report? That is, will I be able to supply enough concrete details to fill several paragraphs? Will I be able to explain my observations completely without having to write a paper that's simply too long?

Once subjects are chosen, have students make their observations and take notes. Tell students to sketch out visuals they may want to include with their reports. Mention that they will not necessarily have to draw their final visuals—the sketches may serve as a starting point for a search for appropriate photos or clip art.

Online Writing Center

 Provides **interactive graphic organizers** as well as a variety of graphic organizers in PDF format.

Prewrite

Focus on **Ideas**

The Rubric Says   Concrete details support each topic sentence.

Writing Strategy   Choose an aspect of nature to observe. Make notes (with sketches) about the observations.

Last week Mom and I saw the aurora borealis, or northern lights, in the sky above our woods. I decided the lights would be a perfect topic for my observation report. Last night the northern lights were back, and the show was amazing! To plan my report, I made notes and drew sketches of what I saw. I'll use both to add lots of concrete details to my report. I want my reader to understand exactly what I experienced.

My Notes on the Aurora Borealis

- ✔ cold night, crisp breezes, smell of fresh pine
- ✔ one arc of light spreads across the sky, followed by several more (white, with red and purple at edges)
- ✔ rays of light form "drapes" across the sky, seem to blow softly in the wind (light up whole sky)
- ✔ hissing noises as sky lights up
- ✔ drapes disappear and reappear as new rays shoot down from space (white with purple in between)
- ✔ after 10–15 minutes drapes start to spread wider, color starts to fade
- ✔ lights blink on and off, then disappear

Apply
Think about things you have seen. Choose one to write about and gather information by making notes on what you saw.

416   Descriptive Writing

English Language Learners

BEGINNING/INTERMEDIATE

Order Words Show photographs of the metamorphosis of a butterfly. On the board, write the transition words *first, next, after that,* and *finally.* Read the words and have students repeat. Have Beginning ELLs put the photos in order next to the correct transition word. Then ask Intermediate ELLs to say what happened in each picture. Write each sentence on the board using the transition word. Read the sentences as a group.

ADVANCED/ADVANCED HIGH

Cause-and-Effect Transition Words On the board, write *The temperature dropped. A cold front moved into the area.* Ask students, *Which is the cause and which is the effect?* Then demonstrate the different ways to express the cause-and-effect relationship using various transition words, such as *because, so,* or *as a result.* For example, *The temperature dropped because a cold front moved into the area.*

Prewrite

Focus on Organization

The Rubric Says	Varied, appropriate transitions create cohesion and make the paragraphs easy to follow.
Writing Strategy	Make an Observation Chart to organize the notes around the five senses.

Writer's Term

Observation Chart

An **Observation Chart** organizes information that has been gathered by using sight, sound, touch, taste, and smell. Appealing to as many senses as possible is a good way to get the reader involved in the experience.

So I thought it would be helpful to organize my notes into an Observation Chart. Organizing my notes will also help me write strong, well-focused paragraphs. Once I have my observations organized by senses, it will be easy to think about a variety of transitions between paragraphs.

OBSERVATION CHART

TOPIC: aurora borealis

SIGHT	SOUND	TOUCH	TASTE	SMELL
• arcs of white light spread across the sky (red and purple at edges) • rays of light form "drapes" that seem to sway in the wind • drapes disappear, then reappear (mostly white; purple in between) • lights spread thinner, blink on and off, fade out	• hissing noises at height of light show	• crisp evening breezes		• sweet smell of pine trees in the air

Reflect

How will organizing details according to the senses help Andre write a logical report?

Apply

Use an Observation Chart to organize your ideas around the five senses.

Observation Report **417**

Conferencing

PEER TO PEER Have partners review each other's Observation Charts. Tell students to ask their partners questions to clarify any items in the charts that they don't fully understand.

PEER GROUPS Have students work in groups of three or four. Each student passes his or her Observation Chart to the student on the left. Students use adhesive notes to indicate the detail they think is the most interesting and one detail they think needs clarification. Students continue passing the charts around the group until each student has reviewed all the charts.

TEACHER-LED Hold conferences with individual students about their Observation Charts. Give students suggestions for the types of details they might include in categories that are giving them trouble.

Write
an Observation Report

Week 2 • Day 2

Student Objectives

• Make an Observation Chart to organize notes. *(p. 417)*

Prewrite

Focus on  Organization

Organize Ideas Read and discuss Andre's Observation Chart. Ask which sense has no details (taste) and which has the most details. (sight) Ask students why this might be the case. (Possible responses: There was nothing to taste in Andre's experience; sight is how people can perceive the aurora borealis.)

Writer's Term

Observation Chart If students have difficulty thinking of details to include outside of the Sight category, have them go back to their notes and use them as a springboard for remembering the observations they made in more detail.

CCSS **Common Core State Standards**

W.7.2.a: Introduce a topic clearly, previewing what is to follow; organize ideas, concepts, and information, using strategies such as definition, classification, comparison/contrast, and cause/effect; include formatting (e.g., headings), graphics (e.g., charts, tables), and multimedia when useful to aiding comprehension. **W.7.2.b:** Develop the topic with relevant facts, definitions, concrete details, quotations, or other information and examples. **W.7.4:** Produce clear and coherent writing in which the development, organization, and style are appropriate to task, purpose, and audience. **W.7.10:** Write routinely over extended time frames (time for research, reflection, and revision) and shorter time frames (a single sitting or a day or two) for a range of discipline-specific tasks, purposes, and audiences.

Write
an Observation Report

Week 2 • Day 3

Student Objectives

- Begin writing, using transitions to connect ideas. *(pp. 418–419)*

Draft

Focus on  Organization

Draft an Observation Report
Read the information about transitions in the Writer's Term box and Andre's words on page 418 with students. Then read Andre's draft on page 419 together. Have students find details from the Observation Chart in the model and discuss Andre's organization. Point out the highlighted transitions and ask students how these transitions help create cohesion. Make sure students understand that *cohesion* means the quality of holding together well.

Point out that Andre repeatedly refers to the rubric as he writes. Encourage students to get into the habit of using the rubric to guide their own writing.

Have students use the details in their Observation Charts to write drafts of their observation reports. Remind them to include transitions within and between paragraphs.

Online Writing Center

 Provides student eBooks with an **interactive writing pad** for drafting, revising, editing, and publishing.

T418 Descriptive Writing

Draft

Focus on **Organization**

The Rubric Says	Varied, appropriate transitions create cohesion and make the paragraphs easy to follow.
Writing Strategy	Use transitions to connect ideas.

Once I collected all my information, I was ready to draft my report. I decided to describe the light show in the order in which things happened. This wasn't too difficult because I had listed the sights on my observation chart in chronological, or time, order.

The rubric reminds me that transitions are important. Well-chosen transitions will guide my reader through my paragraphs. They'll also connect my ideas in a logical way. That's what *cohesion* means—it's what happens when the ideas in an essay are clearly and strongly linked. Since I'm writing my essay in chronological order, I'll think about including time-order transitions in logical places.

When I drafted my report, I worried mainly about getting my ideas down. I figured I could check for errors later.

> **Writer's Term**
>
> **Transitions**
> **Transitions** are words or phrases that link ideas between or within paragraphs. Some time-order transition words are *first, while,* and *then.*

418 Descriptive Writing

Differentiating Instruction

ENRICHMENT
Add Research Have students use the Internet or other sources to research the phenomenon they observed. Tell them to incorporate the new details from their research into their drafts.

REINFORCEMENT
Write With a Partner Allow students to work in pairs to write a single observation, create Observation Charts, and/or write drafts. One student can be in charge of writing notes and drafting, or each student can take turns writing details in the Observation Chart and paragraphs in the draft.

[DRAFT]

Observing the Aurora Borealis, or Northern Lights

Sometimes I'm really happy that we live so far north. This is the reason. If you are lucky, on certin nights you may see the aurora borealis, or northern lights.   [transition within paragraph]

It is a perfect night for a light show. The air feels crisp and cold as a gentle breeze touches my skin. I can smell the fresh pine trees growing in the nearby woods. Stars are twinkeling.

[time-order transition]

→ While I watch the sky, a great white arc of light begin to appear. It stretches larger and larger. Several more follow it. They expand. They become red and purple, especially at the edges.

→ Then the formation changes. Green and white rays of light seems to drop straight down from above. The rays flow and form themselves into drapes that spred across the entire sky. The drapes are mostly white, but with some purple in between. A hissing noise begins as the drapes slowly disappear and then reppear in new forms.

Reflect

How did Andre do? How did his transitions help link his ideas together?

Apply

Write a draft using observations from your Observation Chart and including a variety of appropriate transitions.

Observation Report 419

Write
an Observation Report

Week 2 • Day 4

Student Objectives

• Complete a draft.

✎ Writer's Term

Transitions Transitions are one important way to create meaning for the reader. By showing the relationship between ideas, they enable the reader to follow the writer's reasoning and understand the writing. A lack of transitions can lead to misunderstandings, as the reader is left to figure out why the writer has jumped from one idea to another. In addition to time order, transitions can show cause and effect (*so, because, therefore*), comparison and contrast (*nevertheless, in contrast, similarly*), and conditions (*if, in that case*). See the list of transitions on page 542.

Conferencing

PEER TO PEER Instruct partners to exchange and read each other's drafts. Have students pick out a transition they think works especially well and point out a place where they think a transition (or a stronger transition) would be useful.

PEER GROUPS Have students work in groups of three or four. Each student reads aloud a section of his or her draft that he or she had trouble writing. Then, for three to five minutes, the students discuss ways the section could be improved. The group discusses a draft section for each member.

TEACHER-LED Hold conferences with individual students. Discuss the transitions in students' reports and how they can be improved. Allow students to ask any questions they may have about drafting their reports.

CCSS Common Core State Standards

W.7.2.b: Develop the topic with relevant facts, definitions, concrete details, quotations, or other information and examples. **W.7.2.c:** Use appropriate transitions to create cohesion and clarify the relationships among ideas and concepts. **W.7.5:** With some guidance and support from peers and adults, develop and strengthen writing as needed by planning, revising, editing, rewriting, or trying a new approach, focusing on how well purpose and audience have been addressed.

Write an Observation Report

Week 2 • Day 5

Student Objectives

• Revise for informative, enthusiastic voice. (p. 420)

Revise

Focus on Voice

Engage the Reader Read the rubric descriptor and writing strategy on page 420 aloud. Explain to students that enthusiasm is contagious; if readers sense a writer's excitement about a topic, they will be intrigued and want to know more. Once readers have been drawn in, maintaining the enthusiastic voice and providing good information will keep them interested.

Read Andre's words on page 420 with students. Then read the draft excerpt and Andre's revision. Ask how the added sentence affects the voice in the paragraph. (Possible response: It gives energy and excitement by describing exactly how the writer feels.)

✏ Writer's Term _____

Personal Reaction Writers share personal reactions to set the voice and help the reader relate to their experiences. In Andre's observation report, the personal reaction helps Andre convey his enthusiasm.

▶ Strategies for Writers Online

Go to **www.sfw.z-b.com** for additional online resources for students and teachers.

T420 **Descriptive Writing**

Revise   Focus on **Voice**

The Rubric Says	The writer's voice is informative and enthusiastic. It draws the reader into the text.
Writing Strategy	Show that I know and care a lot about the subject.

✏ Writer's Term _____
Personal Reaction
A **personal reaction** tells how an observation made you feel and what it made you think about.

I like what I've written so far. I think my reader will picture the aurora borealis vividly. But my voice seems a little flat and boring. I think I need to add my personal reactions to my observations to liven things up. Watching the lights was thrilling, and I want my audience to feel my excitement as they read.

[DRAFT]

[added personal reaction] → Inside, my heart is beating faster. Seeing the northern lights is exciting!

It is a perfect night for a light show. The air feels crisp and cold as a gentle breeze touches my skin. I can smell the fresh pine trees growing in the nearby woods. Stars are twinkling.

While I watch the sky, a great white arc of light begin to appear. It stretches larger and larger. Several more follow it.

Apply
How did your observation make you feel? Add some personal reactions to your writing.

420 **Descriptive Writing**

English Language Learners

BEGINNING/INTERMEDIATE

Subject-Verb Agreement Write *A dog, A cat, A bird, A cow,* and *A mouse* on five index cards. Write the plural partner for each word on five more index cards. Shuffle the cards and have students sort the words into plural and singular categories. Add ten more cards: *bark, barks, meow, meows, chirp, chirps, moo, moos, squeak,* and *squeaks.* Then have students match each verb to an appropriate singular or plural noun. Point out that the subject must agree with the verb in number.

ADVANCED/ADVANCED HIGH

Voice: Personal Reaction Write *roller coaster ride* on the board. Give partners one minute to brainstorm words that would describe the feeling of riding a roller coaster, such as *terrifying, exhilarating, exciting, scary.* Repeat for other experiences, such as winning a race or seeing a shooting star. Remind students to include their personal feelings in their observations reports.

Revise

Focus on Word Choice

The Rubric Says	Precise words and phrases capture the experience and bring it to life for the reader.
Writing Strategy	Replace ordinary, vague words with specific words.

The rubric says I should use specific words to bring my experience to life for my reader. As I reread my draft, I notice some of my words are vague and overused. It only makes sense that the more creative and specific my words are, the easier it will be for the reader to share my experience with the aurora borealis. I'll replace the vague words with stronger, more specific words now. What do you think of my revisions?

[DRAFT]

fade

After ten or fifteen minutes, the aurora borealis starts to go away. The formation of drapes get wider and wider but becomes

distinct

less and less there.

[replaced vague words]

Reflect

Now that Andre has replaced vague words with specific words, can you better envision the lights?

Apply

Replace overused, vague words with colorful, specific words in your report.

Observation Report 421

PEER TO PEER Have partners read their drafts aloud to each other. Have the pairs discuss the voice in their drafts and what they could revise to add energy and enthusiasm.

PEER GROUPS Have students work in groups of three or four. Have each student choose a sentence from his or her draft that contains language that could be made more precise. Tell the groups to discuss the sentences and suggest more precise words for each one.

TEACHER-LED Hold conferences with small groups of students about revising for voice. Choose an example of voice from each student's draft. Suggest ways students can make their voices more enthusiastic and engaging.

Write
an Observation Report

Week 3 • Day 1

Student Objectives

- Revise for use of precise words. (p. 421)

Revise

Focus on Word Choice

Choose Precise Words On the board write the words *good, said,* and *bad.* Ask students to call out precise words that could be used to replace each of these words and write their suggestions beneath the appropriate word. (Possible responses: wonderful, marvelous, delicious; whispered, responded, exclaimed; terrible, tragic, dreadful) Discuss why writing that features precise language is more successful than vague writing.

Read the rubric and writing strategy aloud and then have students read Andre's words and the draft excerpt silently. Point out the revisions and ask if students can think of other precise words Andre might have used to replace the vague ones.

Have students review their observation reports for vague language and replace it with more precise wording.

CCSS **Common Core State Standards**

W.7.2.d: Use precise language and domain-specific vocabulary to inform about or explain the topic. **W.7.4:** Produce clear and coherent writing in which the development, organization, and style are appropriate to task, purpose, and audience. **L.7.3.a:** Choose language that expresses ideas precisely and concisely, recognizing and eliminating wordiness and redundancy.

Write
an Observation Report

Week 3 • Day 2

Student Objectives

• Revise to vary sentence lengths and patterns. (p. 422)

Revise

Focus on

Vary Sentence Patterns Read the Writer's Term box on page 422 aloud. Then invite students to tell a short story about a person running away from a lion (or choose a different topic, as long as it is exciting). Call on students to take turns contributing sentences to the story. The only rule is that all sentences must follow the subject-verb or subject-verb-object pattern. Discuss the way dull, repetitive sentence patterns can make even a thrilling topic dull.

✎ Writer's Term _____

Sentence Pattern The variety of possible sentence patterns is endless. The basic subject-verb-object structure can be varied with prepositional phrases, clauses, and compound subjects and objects. Students can also join two simple subject-verb-object sentences with a conjunction to create variety.

Revise
Focus on **Sentence Fluency**

The Rubric Says Varied sentence lengths and patterns make the report enjoyable to read.

Writing Strategy Vary sentence patterns for meaning, reader interest, and style.

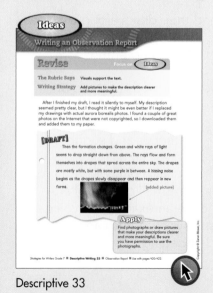

✎ Writer's Term _____

Sentence Pattern

A **sentence pattern** is the order in which the parts of a sentence are arranged. Sentence patterns include subject-verb (*The dog ate*) and subject-verb-object (*The dog ate her dinner*). Using the same sentence pattern over and over makes your writing boring.

Now to check for sentence fluency. The rubric tells me I should vary my sentence lengths and patterns to keep things interesting. I found one paragraph that needed work, so I revised it to add variety. I think the meaning comes through more clearly in my revised sentences, too.

[DRAFT]

[combined sentences]

, and soon

It stretches larger and larger. Several more follow it. ~~They expand.~~

as they expand.

They become red and purple, especially at the edges.

Apply

Do your sentence beginnings all sound the same? If so, replace some of them with a descriptive clause or phrase.

422 Descriptive Writing

Optional Revising Lessons _____

Ideas

Writing an Observation Report

Revise
Focus on **Ideas**

The Rubric Says Visuals support the text.

Writing Strategy Add pictures to make the description clearer and more meaningful.

After I finished my draft, I read it silently to myself. My description seemed pretty clear, but I thought it might be even better if I replaced my drawings with actual aurora borealis photos. I found a couple of great photos on the Internet that were not copyrighted, so I downloaded them and added them to my paper.

[DRAFT]

Then the formation changes. Green and white rays of light seems to drop straight down from above. The rays flow and form themselves into drapes that spred across the entire sky. The drapes are mostly white, but with some purple in between. A hissing noise begins as the drapes slowly disappear and then reappear in new forms. [added picture]

Apply

Find photographs or draw pictures that make your descriptions clearer and more meaningful. Be sure you have permission to use the photographs.

Strategies for Writers Grade 7 ■ **Descriptive Writing 33** ■ Observation Report ■ Use with pages 420–422.

Descriptive 33

Organization

Writing an Observation Report

Revise
Focus on **Organization**

The Rubric Says Varied, appropriate transitions create cohesion and make the paragraphs easy to follow.

Writing Strategy Connect one paragraph to another.

The rubric says I should use appropriate transitions to make the paragraphs easy to follow. I was careful to write a clear topic sentence for each paragraph and then include several supporting sentences to keep my information organized. But as I reread my draft, I noticed that some paragraphs could flow together better. Using a transition sentence at the end of one paragraph to help set up the next is a great way to connect separate paragraphs. Transition sentences help the reader move from one topic to the next without feeling like they've missed something. I'll add a transition sentence now.

[DRAFT]

[added transition sentence]

Sometimes I'm really happy that we live so far north. This is the reason. If you are lucky, on certin nights you may see the aurora Here is my observation from a night last week when the lights appeared, borealis, or northern lights.

It is a perfect night for a light show. The air feels crisp and cold as a gentle breeze touches my skin.

Apply

Use transition sentences to connect separate paragraphs in your report.

Strategies for Writers Grade 7 ■ **Descriptive Writing 34** ■ Observation Report ■ Use with pages 420–422.

Descriptive 34

Go to **Strategies for Writers Grade 7 CD-ROM**

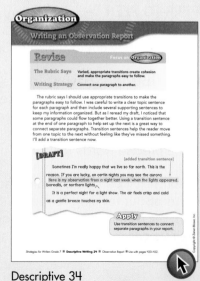

Edit

Focus on Conventions

The Rubric Says	Subjects and verbs agree. The meaning is clear.
Writing Strategy	Check to see that the subject and verb in each sentence agree.

Writer's Term

Subject-Verb Agreement
Singular subjects name only one thing and must be used with singular verbs. Singular verbs usually end in -s or -es. Plural subjects name more than one thing and must be used with plural verbs. The pronoun *you* also uses a plural verb. Compound subjects joined with *and* are generally plural.

Now I have to look for errors. I always check for grammar mistakes and misspelled words. According to the rubric, I should also make sure subjects agree with verbs.

[DRAFT]

[corrected subject-verb agreement error]

Then the formation changes. Green and white rays of light seems to drop straight down from above.

Reflect

Check over Andre's writing. Has he fixed all subject-verb agreement errors? Can you find any other mistakes?

Apply Conventions

Edit your draft for spelling, punctuation, and capitalization. Check for and fix subject-verb agreement errors.

For more practice fixing errors with subject-verb agreement, use the exercises on the next two pages.

Observation Report **423**

Related Grammar Practice

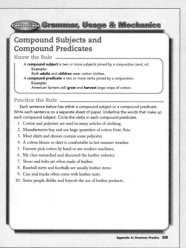

Student Edition Page 50I

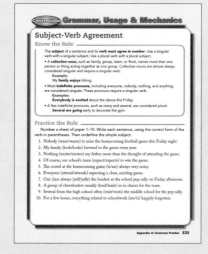

Student Edition Page 525

 Appendix A: Grammar Practice

Write an Observation Report

Week 3 • Day 3

Student Objectives

• Edit for subject-verb agreement. (p. 423)

Edit

Focus on Conventions

Discuss the difference between revising and editing. Be sure students understand that in the revising steps they looked for ways to improve the story. The editing step is the place where errors are corrected. Explain that while the strategy in the editing lesson is to check subject-verb agreement, Andre will be marking other errors in his paper as well, and these corrections will appear in the final copy.

Writer's Term

Subject-Verb Agreement
Mistakes in subject-verb agreement are fairly common and easy to make. In word-processed text, mistakes are sometimes typographical errors, where the final *s* is accidentally left off a verb. More commonly, writers make errors in subject-verb agreement when there is a compound subject or when the verb is separated from the subject by a prepositional phrase.

CCSS Common Core State Standards
L.7.1: Demonstrate command of the conventions of standard English grammar and usage when writing or speaking.

Observation Report **T423**

Student Objectives

- Correct subject-verb agreement. (p. 424)

Subject-Verb Agreement

Write the following on the board: *The dog chase the cat.* Ask students to identify the subject and verb in the sentence. (dog, chase) Ask:

- Do the subject and verb agree? (no)

- Is the subject singular or plural? (singular)

- Is the verb singular or plural? (plural)

- How could you correct the sentence? (The dog chases the cat.)

Write the following on the board: *Tom and Becky was lost in the cave.*

Ask students to identify the subject and verb in the sentence. (Tom and Becky, was) Ask:

- Do the subject and verb agree? (no)

- Is the subject singular or plural? (plural)

- Is the verb singular or plural? (singular)

- How could you correct the sentence? (Tom and Becky were lost in the cave.)

Online Writing Center

GAMES Provides **interactive grammar games** and **practice activities** in student eBook.

Conventions ## Grammar, Usage & Mechanics

Subject-Verb Agreement

Know the Rule

Use **singular subjects** with **singular verbs**. Use **plural subjects** and the pronoun *you* with **plural verbs**.

Example: Singular: The **dog runs** fast. Plural: The **dogs run** fast.

Compound subjects joined with *and* are nearly always plural. In compound subjects joined with *or* or *nor*, the verb agrees with the last item in the subject.

Example: The **dog and the cat like** to play in the snow. The **dog or the cat likes** to play in the snow.

Be sure that the verb agrees with the subject and not with the object of a preposition that comes before the verb.

Example: One of the dogs **is** hungry.

To make sure the subject and verb agree in a question, reword the sentence as an answer to the question in subject-verb order.

Example: Question: Where **are** the **collars** for the dogs? Reworded: The **collars** for the dogs **are** in the basement.

Practice the Rule

Write each sentence correctly on a separate sheet of paper.

1. An aurora borealis (is/are) not the only unusual sight in the night sky.
2. The region above storm clouds also (contain/contains) remarkable lights.
3. Sprites, elves, and blue jets (is/are) the names given to these light forms.
4. (Has/Have) you ever heard of these formations before?
5. The flashes of light given off by a sprite (creates/create) a curtain-like effect above thunderstorm clouds.
6. The core of a storm's clouds (is/are) the source of a blue jet.
7. Elves (is/are) disk-shaped and (last/lasts) only thousandths of a second.
8. Pictures of blue jets (has/have) been taken from airplanes.
9. Scientists (is/are) still learning about these light forms.
10. I (am/are) lucky to have seen these light forms.

Related Grammar Practice

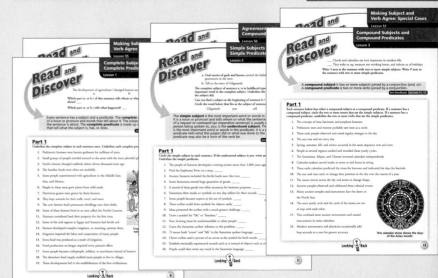

Pages 9, 11, 13, 167, 169, 171

Go to ⟹ **G.U.M. Student Practice Book**

More Subject-Verb Agreement

Know the Rule

A **collective noun**—such as *collection, group, team, country,* or *family*—names more than one person or object acting together as one group. These nouns are almost always considered singular.

   Example: My whole **family is** moving to Iowa.

Most **indefinite pronouns**, including *everyone, nobody, nothing, something,* and *anything,* are considered singular.

   Example: I know **someone** who **likes** broccoli on pizza.

A few indefinite pronouns, such as *many* and *several,* are considered plural.

   Example: I know **many** who **like** plain cheese pizza.

Practice the Rule

Choose the correct verb in each sentence below. Then write the complete sentences on a separate sheet of paper.

1. Everyone (has/have) a favorite seasonal tradition.
2. Several (is/are) specific to just one family.
3. For example, every summer around the Fourth of July, my whole family (gathers/gather) at my grandparents' lake house.
4. Everyone (knows/know) to take a nap in the afternoon because we'll be up late.
5. In the afternoon, a group of us (goes/go) for a swim in the cold lake.
6. Later, nothing (beats/beat) a bonfire by the lake with all my relatives gathered together to watch it.
7. Someone always (brings/bring) marshmallows we can roast.
8. We play charades by the light of the fire, and my team always (wins/win).
9. Some of us, especially the younger ones, (goes/go) to bed after charades.
10. Many (stays/stay) up until midnight talking quietly and enjoying the night.

Conventions

Mini-Lesson

Student Objectives

• Correct subject-verb agreement with collective nouns and indefinite pronouns. (*p. 425*)

More Subject-Verb Agreement

Read Know the Rule on page 425 aloud as students follow along in their books. Practice the concepts of collective nouns and indefinite pronouns by saying words from both categories, while having students call out "collective" or "indefinite," depending on which type of word you say.

Write these sentence starters on the board: *My family, Nobody, Many; Our school _____ team,* and *Several.* Ask volunteers to create sentences that begin with these starters.

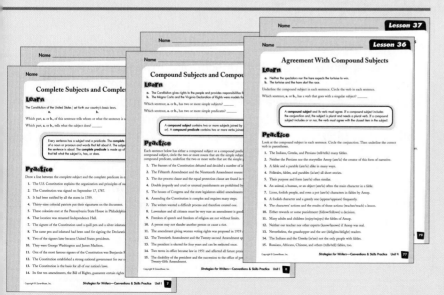

Pages 7, 9, 11, 75, 77, 79

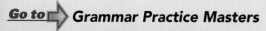

Go to ➡ *Grammar Practice Masters*

CCSS **Common Core State Standards**

L.7.2: Demonstrate command of the conventions of standard English capitalization, punctuation, and spelling when writing.

Write
an Observation Report

Week 3 • Day 4

Student Objectives

- Discuss preparation for publishing and presentation. *(p. 426)*
- Use a final editing checklist to publish their work. *(p. 426)*

Publish ⁺Presentation

Publishing Strategy Ask students if they can think of another way Andre might share his observation report. Remind the class that he might also include this report in his journal or send it to a website that collects observations regarding the natural world. Invite students to name other ways they could publish their own observation reports.

Take a moment to review and discuss Andre's final checklist. Are there any important items he has forgotten? Have students use Andre's final checklist or make their own to check their reports. Along with including the reports in a class journal, encourage them to give or send copies to friends and relatives who would enjoy reading about the experience they described.

Strategies for Writers Online
Go to **www.sfw.z-b.com** for additional online resources for students and teachers.

Publish ⁺Presentation

Publishing Strategy	Add the report to the class's science journal.
Presentation Strategy	Indent every paragraph.

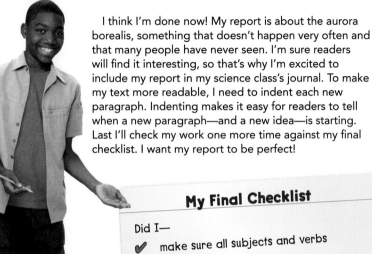

I think I'm done now! My report is about the aurora borealis, something that doesn't happen very often and that many people have never seen. I'm sure readers will find it interesting, so that's why I'm excited to include my report in my science class's journal. To make my text more readable, I need to indent each new paragraph. Indenting makes it easy for readers to tell when a new paragraph—and a new idea—is starting. Last I'll check my work one more time against my final checklist. I want my report to be perfect!

My Final Checklist

Did I—
- ✓ make sure all subjects and verbs agree?
- ✓ indent each new paragraph?
- ✓ use proper grammar, spelling, and punctuation?

Apply
Make your own final checklist to check your observation report. Then make a final copy to publish.

426 Descriptive Writing

Differentiating Instruction

ENRICHMENT
Create a Web Page If your school permits, encourage students to create a page on the school website on which to publish their observation reports. Have students expand their reports for the web page and add more photos and other graphics.

REINFORCEMENT
Reinforce Paragraphs Work with students who are having trouble separating paragraphs. Help students type their final copies on a computer, then review the paragraph breaks with them. Help students make sure they have broken up text correctly and indented each paragraph.

Observing the Aurora Borealis, or Northern Lights

by Andre J.

Sometimes I'm really happy that we live so far north. This is the reason. If you are lucky, on certain nights you may see the aurora borealis, or northern lights. Here is my observation from a night last week when the lights appeared.

It is a perfect night for a light show. The air feels crisp and cold as a gentle breeze touches my skin. I can smell the fresh pine trees growing in the nearby woods. Stars are twinkling. Inside, my heart is beating faster. Seeing the northern lights is exciting!

While I watch the sky, a great white arc of light begins to appear. It stretches, larger and larger, and soon several more follow it. They become red and purple, especially at the edges, as they expand.

Then the formation changes. Green and white rays of light seem to drop straight down from above. The rays flow and form themselves into drapes that spread across the entire sky. The drapes are mostly white, but I see some purple in between. A hissing noise begins as the drapes slowly disappear and then reappear in new forms.

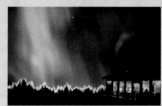

After ten or fifteen minutes, the aurora borealis starts to fade away. The formation of drapes gets wider and wider but becomes less and less distinct. The lights seem to blink on and off. Finally, they disappear altogether.

Reflect

What do you think? Did Andre use all the traits of a good observation report? Check it against the rubric. Then use the rubric to check your own report.

Technology Tip for 21st Century Literacies

Student writers need real readers. Consider making this a community-specific report, asking students to report on events occurring within their homes and then to share their writing in online spaces that invite feedback and commentary. For example, students could capture observational reports (or oral histories) using Historypin (for photos), iPadio (live broadcasting), or PodOmatic (for audio podcasts). Post students' work on a website or blog, or share students' writing with a local historical society for its display and use. Asking students to report for authentic readers lifts a "school" piece of writing and creates purpose.

See **www.sfw.z-b.com** for further information about and links to these websites and tools.

Write
an Observation Report

Week 3 • Day 5

Student Objectives

- Use an observation report rubric. *(pp. 410–411)*
- Share a published observation report. *(p. 427)*

Presentation Strategy Indenting gives readers a simple visual cue to indicate the start of each new paragraph. If they are writing their reports by hand, students should indent their paragraphs with a consistent space, about one inch. If students are using a computer, they may find that their word processing program automatically indents new paragraphs. If it does not, they should use the tab key to indent paragraphs. If your class uses block-style paragraphs, remind students to put space between the paragraphs.

Reflecting on an Observation Report

Ask students to reflect on the experience of writing an observation report. Prompt them to think about what worked well and what they would do differently next time.

CCSS Common Core State Standards

W.7.4: Produce clear and coherent writing in which the development, organization, and style are appropriate to task, purpose, and audience. W.7.6: Use technology, including the Internet, to produce and publish writing and link to and cite sources as well as to interact and collaborate with others, including linking to and citing sources.

Geographic Description Planner

WEEK 1

Day 1
Introduce
a Geographic Description

Student Objectives
- Review the elements of a geographic description.
- Consider purpose and audience.
- Learn the traits of descriptive writing.

Student Activities
- Read and discuss **What's in a Geographic Description?** (p. 428)
- Read and discuss **Why Write a Geographic Description?** (p. 429)
- Read **Linking Descriptive Writing Traits to a Geographic Description.** (p. 430)

Day 2
Analyze
Read a Geographic Description

Student Objectives
- Read a model geographic description.

Student Activities
- Read **"A Visit to the Past."** (p. 431)

Day 3
Analyze
Introduce the Rubric

Student Objectives
- Learn to read a rubric.

Student Activities
- Review **"A Visit to the Past."** (p. 431)
- Read and discuss the **Geographic Description Rubric.** (pp. 432–43)

WEEK 2

Day 1
Write
Prewrite: Ideas

Student Objectives
- Read and understand a prewriting strategy.

Student Activities
- Read and discuss **Prewrite: Focus on Ideas.** (pp. 438–440)
- Apply the prewriting strategy.

Day 2
Write
Prewrite: Organization

Student Objectives
- Make a Web to organize notes.

Student Activities
- Read and discuss **Prewrite: Focus on Organization.** (p. 441)
- Reflect on the model Web.
- Apply the prewriting strategy to create a Web.
- Participate in a peer conference.

Day 3
Write
Draft: Voice

Student Objectives
- Begin writing, using third-person point of view and an objective to

Student Activities
- Read and discuss **Draft: Focus on Voice.** (pp. 442–445)
- Reflect on a model draft.
- Apply the drafting strategy.

WEEK 3

Day 1
Write
Revise: Word Choice

Student Objectives
- Revise for use of figurative language.

Student Activities
- Read and discuss **Revise: Focus on Word Choice.** (p. 447)
- Reflect on a model draft.
- Apply the revising strategy.

Day 2
Write
Revise: Sentence Fluency

Student Objectives
- Revise to combine short, choppy sentences.

Student Activities
- Read and discuss **Revise: Focus on Sentence Fluency.** (p. 448)
- Reflect on a model draft.
- Apply the revising strategy.

Note: Optional Revising Lessons appear on the *Strategies for Writers* CD-ROM.

Day 3
Write
Edit: Conventions

Student Objectives
- Edit for correct use of adjectives and adverbs.

Student Activities
- Read and discuss **Edit: Focus on Conventions.** (p. 449)
- Reflect on a model draft.
- Apply the editing strategy.

Note: Teach the Conventions mini-lessons (pp. 450–451) if needed.

Day 4

Analyze
Ideas, Organization, and Voice

Student Objectives
- Read a model geographic description.
- Use the geographic description rubric.
- Use the model geographic description to study Ideas, Organization, and Voice.

Student Activities
- Review **"A Visit to the Past."** (p. 431)
- Read and discuss **Using the Rubric to Study the Model.** (pp. 434–435)

Day 5

Analyze
Word Choice, Sentence Fluency, and Conventions

Student Objectives
- Read a model geographic description.
- Use the geographic description rubric.
- Use the model geographic description to study Word Choice, Sentence Fluency, and Conventions.

Student Activities
- Review **"A Visit to the Past."** (p. 431)
- Read and discuss **Using the Rubric to Study the Model.** (pp. 436–437)

Day 4

Write
Draft

Student Objectives
- Complete a draft.

Student Activities
- Finish the draft.
- Participate in a peer conference.

Day 5

Write
Revise: Ideas

Student Objectives
- Revise for the use of comparisons to make the description more complete.

Student Activities
- Read and discuss **Revise: Focus on Ideas.** (p. 446)
- Reflect on a model draft.
- Apply the revising strategy.

Day 4

Write
Publish: +Presentation

Student Objectives
- Discuss preparation for publishing and presentation.
- Use a final editing checklist to publish their work.

Student Activities
- Read and discuss **Publish: +Presentation.** (p. 452)
- Apply the publishing strategy.

Day 5

Write
Publish: +Presentation

Student Objectives
- Use a geographic description rubric.
- Share a published geographic description.

Student Activities
- Share their work.
- Use the rubric to reflect upon and evaluate the model and their own writing. (pp. 432–433, 453–455)

...mplete the chapter in fewer days, combine the learning objectives and activities in a way that supports students as they write.

Resources at-a-Glance

Grammar, Usage & Mechanics

Differentiating Instruction

For additional Differentiating Instruction activities, see Strategies for Writers *Extensions Online at* **www.sfw.z-b.com.**

English Language Learners

Conferencing

Technology Tip

 Connection Letter
Reproducible letter (in English and Spanish) appears on the *Strategies for Writers* CD-ROM and at **www.sfw.z-b.com.**

Online Writing Center

Provides IWB resources, interactive games and practice activities, videos, eBooks, and a virtual file cabinet.

 Strategies for Writers Online

Go to **www.sfw.z-b.com** for free online resources for students and teachers.

Introduce
a Geographic Description

Student Objectives

- Review the elements of a geographic description. *(p. 428)*
- Consider purpose and audience. *(p. 429)*
- Learn the traits of descriptive writing. *(p. 430)*

What's a Geographic Description?

Discuss the definition of a geographic description with students. Ask students whether any of them have ever sent a postcard while on a trip or described a place they have seen. Point out that any time they describe a place they've seen, they are using the geographic description genre.

What's in a Geographic Description?

Read and discuss the elements of a geographic description with students. Ask students to point out ways in which the elements are related. For example, the real-place focus dictates that the descriptive details must be accurate. Also, because the place is not imaginary, it does not make sense to use first-person point of view to describe it if the writer has not been there.

 Strategies for Writers Online
Go to **www.sfw.z-b.com** for additional online resources for students and teachers.

What's a Geographic Description?

It's a detailed report about a particular place. I think this kind of writing will be interesting because I get to do some research.

What's in a Geographic Description?

Point of View
My description can be from either first-person or third-person point of view. If I write about a place I've actually been to, then I'll use first-person point of view. Otherwise, it makes more sense to write from the third-person point of view.

Real-Place Focus
The report is focused on one real place. This means that my report must be true. And the facts must come from a good source. I'll need to use reference books such as an atlas and reliable websites.

Descriptive Details
I want my readers to really know what it's like to be at this place, so I'll bring it to life with lots of accurate details and make sure I include only facts that are relevant to my description.

Organization
I'll organize my description with an introduction, body, and conclusion. The body is where I'll give most of the details about the place. Further, I'll organize the information into categories that make sense to the reader.

428 Descriptive Writing

Descriptive Text Exemplars (Geographic Description)

Gorrell, Gena K. *In the Land of the Jaguar.* Tundra Books, 2007. *In the Land of the Jaguar* examines the fascinating history of South America. Using beautiful illustrations and maps, this book takes the reader on an exciting journey that explores South America's history from the past to the present.

Myers, Walter Dean. *Antarctica: Journeys to the South Pole.* Scholastic Press, 2004. Myers reveals the adventure, danger, failures, and triumphs that dotted the discovery and exploration of Antarctica. Readers get a glimpse into some of the best known explorers, such as Amundsen, Scott, and Cook.

Why write a Geographic Description?

There are all kinds of reasons to write a geographic description. Here are some of them. I'll have to think about them to help me decide what to write about.

Entertainment
I've read about many interesting places. I can entertain readers with my own description of a place. Entertainment is a good reason to write a geographic description.

Virtual Travel
I can travel all over the world and even to worlds that have never existed by reading about them. Now I'll help other people to travel virtually with my own geographic description.

Share Information
Writing a geographic description is a great way to share information about a place. I can write a description to educate, instruct, or inform my reader.

Understanding
Sometimes reading about places can feel like fact overload. Deciding which details to use in a piece of writing, however, helps me think through how they are important.

Why write a Geographic Description?

Read and discuss with students the reasons for writing a geographic description listed on page 429. Point out that all writing has a purpose. Writers write for many reasons and for a variety of audiences. Good writers know that both purpose and audience will help shape their writing. Someone writing to entertain may use figurative language and comparisons. A writer who is writing for virtual travel may focus on feelings and thoughts. A person who is writing to inform may include many facts and explanations to help his or her audience understand the topic. Encourage students to think about their reasons for writing a geographic description and how these reasons will affect the tone and focus of their writing.

Arnold, Caroline. *Easter Island: Giant Stone Statues Tell of a Rich Past*. Clarion Books, 2000. Arnold explores the history of the Rapanui people, beginning with the arrival of the first settlers back in A.D. 400 and taking us through the time of the giant stone statues to the Easter Island of today. Beautiful pictures contribute to a text that sheds light on the mysterious theories surrounding this island population and these great stone statues.

Woronov, Naomi. *China Through My Window*. M.E. Sharpe, 1988. *China Through My Window* is Woronov's personal reflection of the culture and landscape of China as she experienced it during her two years spent there as a teacher. She draws from the journals and letters she wrote during that time, transporting the reader to another world.

CCSS **Common Core State Standards**
SL.7.1: Engage effectively in a range of collaborative discussions (one-on-one, in groups, and teacher-led) with diverse partners on *grade 7 topics, texts, and issues*, building on others' ideas and expressing their own clearly.

Introduce
a Geographic Description

Linking Descriptive Writing Traits to a Geographic Description

Have students read page 430. Emphasize that they will follow Andre as he models using the writing process and the traits together. As they follow Andre, students will see how the Descriptive Writing Traits have been adapted and applied to writing a geographic description. They will see that a geographic description has many factors in common with other types of descriptive writing. However, the particular audience and purpose of a geographic description determine how the traits are used.

Discuss with students how each trait applies to a geographic description. For example, well-chosen descriptive details will be very important for conveying a clear picture of the geographic location to the reader. In addition, choosing an appropriate voice will help the reader believe the writer knows the topic well.

Linking Descriptive Traits to a Geographic Description

In this chapter, you will describe a place. This type of descriptive writing is called a geographic description. Andre will guide you through the stages of the writing process: Prewrite, Draft, Revise, Edit, and Publish. In each stage, Andre will show you important writing strategies that are linked to the Descriptive Writing Traits below.

Descriptive Writing Traits

 Ideas
- a clear topic that is developed by relevant supporting details
- descriptive details that are well chosen for the topic

 Organization
- well-organized paragraphs that logically follow the order of the description, whether by time, location, or another order
- varied and appropriate transitions that show the relationship between ideas and concepts

 Voice
- a voice that is appropriate for the purpose and audience

 Word Choice
- precise words and phrases, possibly including figurative language, that create an accurate picture for the reader

 Sentence Fluency
- sentences that vary in length and type to add flow to the writing

 Conventions
- no or few errors in grammar, usage, mechanics, and spelling

Before you write, read Timothy O'Malley's geographic description on the next page. Then use the geographic description rubric on pages 432–433 to decide how well he did. (You might want to look back at What's in a Geographic Description? on page 428, too!)

Descriptive Writing Traits in a Geographic Description

 **Ideas** All details should be relevant to the place, and they should be descriptive enough to give the reader a good picture of it.

 **Organization** The paragraphs may be ordered in a variety of ways, perhaps moving from one part of the place to another. Transitions show how the aspects described in the paragraphs are related.

 **Voice** The writer's purpose will determine the voice. In a geographic description, the ideal voice will likely be a more formal one.

A Visit to the Past
by Timothy O'Malley

Third-person point of view

Introduction

In August of A.D. 79, life ended for the Italian city of Pompeii. Mount Vesuvius, a volcano just to the north, exploded with violent force. Most of the city's citizens escaped, but some refused to leave their homes. Everyone who stayed behind was either asphyxiated by poisonous gases or buried alive under pumice, ash, and other materials. Buried in more than 15 feet of volcanic debris, Pompeii remained untouched for centuries. Excavations have now uncovered the remains of a city that was literally stopped dead in its tracks.

In Pompeii today, it is possible to see evidence of the citizens' everyday life and of the sudden, terrible death of many. The remains help to paint a picture of the city as it was when time stood still on that August day.

Relevant facts

The Forum is where major religious and government events took place. Much of it is still standing. Several two-story marble columns that marked off the open meeting area remain. They hover like sentinels standing guard. Nearby are half-destroyed temples and other buildings. East of the city lies the amphitheater. Grass covers much of it now with a soft green blanket. But it is easy to imagine audiences shouting and applauding as they watched gladiators perform here.

Stores and businesses are on many of the streets. These provide a close look at where citizens bought and sold their wares. Baked goods, fine woven cloth, and drinking vessels were just a few of the items that citizens could buy. Some of the stores stood separate from other buildings. Others were tucked into corners of larger homes. Still others were storefronts, with families living behind them.

Accurate details

One fascinating aspect of Pompeii is the large number of private houses. Nowhere else is it possible to see such a wide range of structures from so many time periods. One structure is called the House of the Faun. It fills a full city block. Its walls feature beautiful mosaics and murals. Other large homes feature elaborate, pillared entrances. Most are decorated with floor mosaics worked into detailed patterns. Such houses generally enclose lovely courtyards and gardens.

The excavations of the buildings and streets of Pompeii show a well-off, bustling city. Other remains show just how quickly the volcano did its work. Many human remains were found. Covered with layers of smoothed-down molten ash, the bodies look like sculptures made of soft clay. Many were found in completely natural positions. They probably never knew what hit them.

A site like Pompeii can show us many things. It can show how citizens of ancient Roman cities lived and worked. It can show us their art and culture. It also points out very clearly how overwhelming natural forces can be. There are indeed many lessons to learn from Pompeii.

Body

Conclusion

Geographic Description 431

Word Choice Precise words and phrases are especially important in a geographic description because the writer's goal is to describe a location as clearly and accurately as possible.

Sentence Fluency Variety in sentence lengths and types gives writing a pleasing rhythm and flow.

Conventions Many mistakes in conventions will hinder the reader's ability to understand the geographic description. They will also frustrate the reader and leave him or her with a poor impression of the writer.

Analyze
the Model

Week 1 • Day 2

Student Objectives

• Read a model geographic description. *(p. 431)*

Read the Model

Have students read "A Visit to the Past." Tell students to look for the descriptive writing traits in the model as they read.

Elements of a Geographic Description

Use the notes on the model to discuss the various elements of a geographic description. Ask:

• How does the introduction draw the reader in? (Possible response: It gets the reader interested with a dramatic scene, and it explains why Pompeii is important.)

• How does the conclusion wrap up the description? (Possible response: It reiterates why Pompeii is important and explains its relevance.)

CCSS **C**ommon **C**ore **S**tate **S**tandards

SL.7.1: Engage effectively in a range of collaborative discussions (one-on-one, in groups, and teacher-led) with diverse partners on *grade 7 topics, texts, and issues,* building on others' ideas and expressing their own clearly. **SL.7.1.c:** Pose questions that elicit elaboration and respond to others' questions and comments with relevant observations and ideas that bring the discussion back on topic as needed. **R/Lit.7.1:** Cite several pieces of textual evidence to support analysis of what the text says explicitly as well as inferences drawn from the text.

Analyze
the Model

Student Objectives

- Learn to read a rubric. *(pp. 432–433)*

Use the Rubric

Explain the Rubric Explain that a rubric is a tool for planning, improving, and assessing a piece of writing. Tell students that a rubric helps a writer focus on key elements, or traits, in writing (**Ideas, Organization, Voice, Word Choice, Sentence Fluency, Conventions,** and **Presentation**). Point out that column 6 describes a very good geographic description, one that has received the highest score in all categories. This is what students should strive for in their own writing.

Discuss the Rubric Guide students in a discussion of the rubric. Read the descriptors for each trait aloud, pausing after each trait to help students note the differences between the descriptors for each score. Focus on words such as *thoughtful* and *attention-getting* that distinguish a score of 6. Remind students to keep the rubric in mind when they write their own geographic descriptions and again when they revise them.

Online Writing Center

 Provides a variety of **interactive rubrics,** including 4-, 5-, and 6-point models.

Rubric

Use this 6-point rubric to plan and evaluate a geographic description.

	6	**5**	**4**
Ideas	Relevant facts and accurate details develop the topic. Thoughtful comparisons clarify the writer's ideas.	Many accurate details are used, and most facts are relevant. Comparisons are used effectively.	Some imprecise details and irrelevant facts are used, but the topic is developed. At least one comparison is used effectively.
Organization	Information is logically organized into categories. The introduction, body, and conclusion work well together.	Most information is organized into logical categories. There is a clear introduction, body, and conclusion.	Some information is not in a logical category. Introduction, body, and conclusion are present but may not work well together.
Voice	The writer's voice suits the purpose and draws the reader in.	The writer's voice is strong. It connects consistently with the audience.	The voice comes and goes. It is acceptable for the writer's purpose and audience.
Word Choice	Figurative language is used in ways that are attention-getting and unusual. It enhances the description.	Figurative language is used in clear and original ways and is effective.	Figurative language is often clear and somewhat effective.
Sentence Fluency	Great variety in sentence lengths and beginnings make the writing a pleasure to read.	The writing contains a significant variety in sentence length. It flows well.	Some of the sentences vary in length and are easy to read.
Conventions	Adjectives and adverbs are used correctly and enhance the writing.	A few minor errors in the use of adjectives and adverbs do not distract the reader.	Some noticeable errors in the use of adjectives and adverbs may distract the reader.
➕ Presentation	Visuals are thoughtfully integrated with the text.		

CCSS Common Core State Standards

Geographic Description

Writing in the Descriptive mode can engage the Common Core State Standards for both Narrative and Informative/Explanatory writing. The rubrics and strategies for the geographic description are based principally on Informative/Explanatory standards. The descriptor for the Ideas rubric is drawn from standard **W.7.2.b**. Both standard and rubric emphasize developing the topic with relevant facts and details.

3	2	1	
Several imprecise details or irrelevant facts distract the reader. The writer uses comparisons, but they are not clear.	The writing is hard to follow because many details and facts are wrong or irrelevant. No comparisons are used.	Facts and details are vague and not connected to the topic. No comparisons are used.	Ideas
The logic of the categories is hard to follow. The introduction or conclusion is missing.	Information is not organized into categories. The introduction and conclusion are missing.	Information is random and unconnected. There is no sign of introduction, body, or conclusion.	Organization
The writer's voice is sincere. The voice may not be acceptable for the topic.	The voice isn't always identifiable and isn't a good match for the purpose and audience.	This is the wrong voice for this piece of writing. It is not appropriate for the purpose and audience.	Voice
Figurative language is vague and unclear.	Figurative language is misused.	The writing contains no figurative language.	Word Choice
The writing sounds choppy. Many sentences are about the same length.	The writing may contain run-on and choppy or incomplete sentences. There is little variety in length.	Fragments and choppy sentences make the writing difficult to read.	Sentence Fluency
Several errors in the use of adjectives and adverbs make the reader pause.	Many errors in the use of adjectives and adverbs make the writing hard to understand in places.	Many serious errors in the use of adjectives and adverbs make the writing very hard to understand.	Conventions

See Appendix B for 4-, 5-, and 6-point descriptive rubrics.

Apply the Rubric

Individual Work Have students decide how they would score the model on each of the traits.

Class Discussion Bring the class together. Take a survey of students and note the score that was most frequently given for each trait. Ask a few students who assigned that score to explain their reasons and give examples. Ask students who gave a different score to explain their reasons and find out whether any other students are convinced to change their minds.

Additional Rubrics Appendix B includes 4-, 5-, and 6-point rubrics that can be used with any piece of descriptive writing. The rubrics are also available as blackline masters beginning on page T543.

The Organization rubric reflects standard **W.7.2.a**, which deals with organization. The rubric calls for information to be organized into categories, echoing the standard's mention of using classification as an organizational strategy. The Organization rubric also picks up the emphasis in standard **W.7.2.f** on a conclusion that flows from the rest of the writing. Standard **W.7.2.e** is echoed in the Voice rubric, with its mention of using a suitable voice for the topic.

CCSS **C**ommon **C**ore **S**tate **S**tandards

SL.7.1: Engage effectively in a range of collaborative discussions (one-on-one, in groups, and teacher-led) with diverse partners on *grade 7 topics, texts, and issues*, building on others' ideas and expressing their own clearly. **SL.7.1.a:** Come to discussions prepared, having read or researched material under study; explicitly draw on that preparation by referring to evidence on the topic, text, or issue to probe and reflect on ideas under discussion. **SL.7.1.b:** Follow rules for collegial discussions, track progress toward specific goals and deadlines, and define individual roles as needed. **SL.7.1.d:** Acknowledge new information expressed by others and, when warranted, modify their own views.

Analyze
the Model

Student Objectives

- Read a model geographic description. *(p. 431)*
- Use the geographic description rubric. *(pp. 432–433)*
- Use the model geographic description to study Ideas, Organization, and Voice. *(pp. 434–435)*

Study the Model

Assess the Model Read each section on pages 434–435 with students. Discuss whether students agree or disagree with each point in Andre's assessment of the geographic description. Use questions such as the following to discuss the model and the traits with students. Encourage students to back up their answers with examples from the model.

- How do the various facts mentioned in the model help develop the topic? (Possible response: They give a very clear picture of everyday life in Pompeii.)

Strategies for Writers Online

Go to **www.sfw.z-b.com** for additional online resources for students and teachers.

Using the Rubric to Study the Model
Geographic Description

Did you notice that the model on page 431 points out some key elements of a geographic description? As he wrote "A Visit to the Past," Timothy O'Malley used these elements to help him write a geographic description. He also used the 6-point rubric on pages 432–433 to plan, draft, revise, and edit the writing. A rubric is a great tool to evaluate writing during the writing process.

Now let's use the same rubric to score the model. To do this, we'll focus on each trait separately, starting with Ideas. We'll use the top descriptor for each trait (column 6), along with examples from the model, to help us understand how the traits work together. How would you score Timothy on each trait?

 **Ideas**

- Relevant facts and accurate details develop the topic.
- Thoughtful comparisons clarify the writer's ideas.

Timothy definitely did some research before writing his geographic description. The way he easily blends accurate facts and creative comparisons keeps me interested and informs me about Pompeii.

[from the writing model]

In August of A.D. 79, life ended for the Italian city of Pompeii. Mount Vesuvius, a volcano just to the north, exploded with violent force.

[from the writing model]

Covered with layers of smoothed-down molten ash, the bodies look like sculptures made of soft clay.

434 Descriptive Writing

English Language Learners

BEGINNING

Maps, Atlases, and Globes Have at least one map, atlas, and globe available to introduce to students. On a map or globe, identify geographic directions *north, south, east,* and *west.* Check students' concept of directions by having them point to a direction as you say it. Then go a step further by naming a place on the map and having students locate it and give the location using the words *north, south, east,* or *west.*

INTERMEDIATE

Describing Position Introduce maps, atlases, and globes as above. Using a map of the world, then ask, *Where is the United States?* After students give an answer, model the answer in a complete sentence, *The United States is in the north.* Repeat for each student's native country.

Organization
- Information is logically organized into categories.
- The introduction, body, and conclusion work well together.

Timothy introduces his topic in the introduction. He then logically organizes his information into categories, with each body paragraph describing a different type of building. Finally he neatly wraps up his discussion in a brief conclusion.

[from the writing model]

A site like Pompeii can show us many things. It can show how citizens of ancient Roman cities lived and worked. It can show us their art and culture. It also points out very clearly how overwhelming natural forces can be. There are indeed many lessons to learn from Pompeii.

Voice
- The writer's voice suits the purpose and draws the reader in.

As I read Timothy's paper, I could feel his respect and awe for Pompeii. His voice reflects that, although something tragic occurred there, Pompeii is beautiful and rich with history. It was easy to share his excitement and want to learn more about it all.

[from the writing model]

One fascinating aspect of Pompeii is the large number of private houses. Nowhere else is it possible to see such a wide range of structures from so many time periods.

Geographic Description 435

- What categories did the writer use to organize the model? (types of buildings) Did you find this to be a logical system? Why or why not? (Possible response: Yes. The categories allowed the writer to describe life in different parts of the city.)

- What words would you use to describe the writer's voice in the model? (Possible responses: serious, informative, enthusiastic about the topic)

ADVANCED
Reliable Sources Ask students where they can find useful information about a topic. Students might answer *the Internet, encyclopedias, books, magazines, atlases,* and *textbooks.* Discuss the pros and cons of each type of source. Assign a geographic location, and have partners use at least three types of sources to discover information about it. Have students report their information to the class.

ADVANCED HIGH
Organizing Details Have students use a Web to organize details about their selected geographic locations. They should write the name of the location in the center circle. Each of the next layer of circles can be the main idea of each paragraph in the essay. Supporting details would be added to the next layer of circles. Once students have researched a few main ideas and supporting details, have them use their notes to give a brief oral presentation to the class.

CCSS **C**ommon **C**ore **S**tate **S**tandards

SL.7.1.b: Follow rules for collegial discussions, track progress toward specific goals and deadlines, and define individual roles as needed. **SL.7.1.c:** Pose questions that elicit elaboration and respond to others' questions and comments with relevant observations and ideas that bring the discussion back on topic as needed.

Analyze
the Model

Week 1 • Day 5

Student Objectives

- Read a model geographic description. *(p. 431)*
- Use the geographic description rubric. *(pp. 432–433)*
- Use the model geographic description to study Word Choice, Sentence Fluency, and Conventions. *(pp. 436–437)*

Continue the Discussion Use the following questions to continue discussing the model:

- Pick another use of figurative language you find striking. Why did this image catch your eye? (Possible response: *They hover like sentinels standing guard.* The image is a little spooky, and it also gives the impression that Pompeii has something valuable that needs guarding.)

- Look at the first paragraph. Why do these sentences flow well? (The paragraph starts with a short, startling sentence, then follows with longer sentences that give more information. One sentence begins with a clause, giving added variety.)

- Choose two adjectives and two adverbs that you think do a good job of making the writing more interesting. (Possible responses: *violent, lovely, literally, quickly*)

 **Strategies for Writers Online**
Go to **www.sfw.z-b.com** for additional online resources for students and teachers.

 **Word Choice**
- Figurative language is used in ways that are attention-getting and unusual. It enhances the description.

Timothy's use of figurative language, such as similes and metaphors, created powerful and vivid images in my mind as I read. Picturing grass as a soft green blanket, spread out across the amphitheater, enlivened the scene and really held my attention.

[from the writing model]

East of the city lies the amphitheater. Grass covers much of it now with a soft green blanket. But it is easy to imagine audiences shouting and applauding as they watched gladiators perform here.

Sentence Fluency
- Great variety in sentence lengths and beginnings make the writing a pleasure to read.

Timothy uses both long and short sentences throughout his geographic description. This made reading it easier and more enjoyable. I will follow his lead and mix up my sentence lengths, too.

[from the writing model]

The Forum is where major religious and government events took place. Much of it is still standing. Several two-story marble columns that marked off the open meeting area remain. They hover like sentinels standing guard.

436 Descriptive Writing

Technology Tip for 21st Century Literacies

As much as writing a geographic description requires exercising some specialized vocabulary, it is still written with a purpose, for an audience, and for our use. To ratchet up the options for this work, consider using Google Earth and an audio tool like Vocaroo to have students post their descriptions to the actual location in Google Earth that they are describing. Embed examples for students to consider as models and ask which locations they would find most compelling to mark/describe. Which audiences would find this writing useful?

See **www.sfw.z-b.com** for further information about and links to these websites and tools.

Conventions
- Adjectives and adverbs are used correctly and enhance the writing.

The writer uses adjectives and adverbs correctly. Here are a few examples.

> [from the writing model]
>
> The excavations of the buildings and streets of Pompeii show a well-off, bustling city. Other remains show just how quickly the volcano did its work. Many human remains were found. Covered with layers of smoothed-down molten ash, the bodies look like sculptures made of soft clay.

✛ Presentation Visuals are thoughtfully integrated with the text.

My Turn!

I can't wait to get started on my own geographic description. I can follow the rubric and make sure I use good writing strategies. Read on to see how it turns out!

Geographic Description 437

ENRICHMENT

Creative Comparisons Have each student write a one-paragraph geographic description of your classroom, using as many comparisons as he or she can to illustrate ideas. Tell students that it's acceptable to be humorous but that their comparisons should still make sense and help the reader understand more clearly how something looks or feels.

REINFORCEMENT

Understand Voice Illustrate the concept of voice by asking questions such as the following: "If I use words like *fascinating* or *amazing*, is my voice enthusiastic or bored? If I use lots of contractions and expressions like *LOL*, is my voice formal or casual? If I use words like *awful* and *unpleasant* is my voice expressing criticism or approval?"

Presentation Remind students that they must consider how their papers will look when they prepare their final copies. In the case of a geographic description, visuals are a key part of presentation because they give the readers a chance to see for themselves what the writer is describing. The writer can use photographs or drawings to highlight specific parts or aspects of the location, or they can select visuals that give an overview of the entire area. By choosing visuals thoughtfully and placing them appropriately within the text, the writer can greatly enhance the reader's understanding and enjoyment of the description.

Think About the Traits Once students have thoroughly discussed the model geographic description, ask them which traits they think are most important in this type or writing. Students might say, for example, that in a geographic description **Organization** is of special importance because it allows the reader to consider the location one aspect at a time. Students might also mention **Voice** because an informed, appealing voice draws the reader in and makes the reading more enjoyable.

CCSS **Common Core State Standards**

SL.7.1.c: Pose questions that elicit elaboration and respond to others' questions and comments with relevant observations and ideas that bring the discussion back on topic as needed. **SL.7.1.d:** Acknowledge new information expressed by others and, when warranted, modify their own views.

Geographic Description T437

Write
a Geographic Description

Week 2 • Day 1

Student Objectives

• Read and understand a prewriting strategy. *(pp. 438–440)*

Prewrite

Focus on Ideas

Choose a Location Have students read page 438 silently. Once students have read the page, discuss Andre's choice of location for his geographical description. Point out that Andre used an atlas to make his decision. Ask students what other resources they might use to think of places they might want to write about. (Possible responses: the Internet, books, magazines, television shows) Mention that students may also want to use their own experiences and choose to write about a place they have visted.

✎ **Writer's Term**_____
Atlas Many atlases contain not just information about a place's location on the planet but also data about the place's climate, topography, political divisions, and a variety of other categories.

▶ **Strategies for Writers Online**
Go to **www.sfw.z-b.com** for additional online resources for students and teachers.

Prewrite
Focus on (Ideas)

The Rubric Says Relevant facts and accurate details develop the topic.

Writing Strategy Use an atlas to find a place to describe. Then research the place in three other appropriate sources.

✎ **Writer's Term**_____
Atlas
An **atlas** is a book that contains maps and geographic information.

I went to the atlas to choose a place for my topic, but I didn't have to look long. I picked a place where it gets even colder than Alaska. I chose Antarctica!

The atlas showed the location of Antarctica and gave information about its terrain. When we talk about places in social studies class, though, we always include topics like climate, animals that live there, the people who live there, and other things. I know my audience will want to read information that will surprise as well as inform. So I'll do my research carefully to ensure my facts are accurate *and* interesting.

438 Descriptive Writing

English Language Learners

BEGINNING

Point of View Write the following sentence frame on the board: _____ *visited Machu Picchu last year.* As you insert different subjects into the sentence, have students tell whether the sentence is told from the first- or the third-person point of view. Use the following subjects: *I, José and Ramón, The youth group, We, Our family, Mr. Potts, My brothers and I.*

INTERMEDIATE

Point of View Briefly review the Beginning activity above. Write a new sentence frame on the board: _____ *visit/visits the beach every summer.* Write the following subjects on the board: *I, José and Ramón, The youth group, We, Our family, Mr. Potts, My brothers and I.* Have students say the sentence with one of the subjects and the appropriate verb.

I came up with a list of questions I thought my audience would want answers for, so I jotted them down on an index card.

> What does Antarctica look like?
> What is the weather like in Antarctica?
> What plants and animals live in Antarctica?
> Do people live in Antarctica?

I followed the strategy and chose three sources, besides the atlas, to use for more information. It was fun to do research online, but I chose my Internet source carefully. Most Internet sites are good, but some are put together sloppily or offer opinions not supported by facts. And, as I said before, accuracy is key!

Writer's Term

Appropriate Source

An **appropriate source** is a place to get information that is suitable, right, or proper for your purpose. Here are some good sources of information about specific places:
- An **encyclopedia** to get a good overview of the place
- An **almanac** to get current facts and figures about things such as government, population, and dimensions of mountains and rivers
- A **travel guidebook** to learn about specific areas and what to see in them
- A **website** to get answers to common questions about the place and to see pictures of it

Geographic Description 439

Plan for Research Have students read pages 439–440 silently. Discuss Andre's questions. Ask students if they can think of any other questions they might ask about Antarctica if they were preparing to write Andre's geographical description.

Have students jot down their own questions to guide their research. Tell them to use the information they found in the atlas to help them think of questions. For example, they might ask whether a place that's near the Equator gets very hot.

Writer's Term _____

Appropriate Source Once students have found a source that contains information that suits their purpose, they should check to make sure the source is up-to-date. Travel guidebooks and almanacs often display the year of their publication on the cover. If the date is not prominently displayed, students should check the copyright page. Websites do not always display the date on which they were last modified. Students should be sure to use reputable sites such as www.nationalgeographic.com or sites created by the United States government.

ADVANCED
Relevant Facts Students must decide if a fact is relevant to the main idea. Give students the main idea, such as *New York is the American capital for business,* and list several related and unrelated facts, such as *thousands of businesses are located in New York City, the stock market is located there, many international restaurants are found in New York,* and so on. Have students circle the facts that are relevant to the main idea.

ADVANCED HIGH
Adding Description to Details Using the details they researched, have students add descriptive words to their facts in order to paint a clear picture in the reader's mind about what the place is truly like. Have students trade papers with another student who should then refer to reliable resources to check that all facts in the description are accurate.

CCSS **C**ommon **C**ore **S**tate **S**tandards

W.7.8: Gather relevant information from multiple print and digital sources, using search terms effectively; assess the credibility and accuracy of each source; and quote or paraphrase the data and conclusions of others while avoiding plagiarism and following a standard format for citation.

Gather Information Discuss how the questions students wrote down will help guide their research. Ask volunteers to reveal the place they chose and read one of their questions. Have the class brainstorm suggestions for sources the student could use to answer the question.

Remind students that they should scrutinize websites carefully to make sure they are reliable. Ask students to name ways they can tell if a site is good to use. Make sure the following points are mentioned:

- The site is run by a reputable source, such as a university, the National Geographic Society, or the government (.gov).

- The site is up-to-date.

- The site has more facts than opinions.

- Facts students already know are presented accurately on the site.

Have students research their place and use note cards to take notes.

The three sources I chose were an encyclopedia, a website, and a recent book about Antarctica that I found in the school library. I jotted down notes from each source that would help me answer my questions.

Website:
mostly scientists live in Antarctica
they live in science "stations"
Amundsen-Scott Station—huge geodesic dome
McMurdo Station—more than 100 buildings
temperatures as low as −128°F

Encyclopedia:
fierce, biting winds
covered with huge sheet of ice
Emperor and Adélie penguins live there
huge birds called skuas live there

Library Book:
East Antarctica—a high, flat plateau
West Antarctica—mountainous islands
too dry to snow much
lichen and mosses grow

Apply

Choose an interesting place. Gather information by making notes on what you read.

440 Descriptive Writing

Online Writing Center

Provides **interactive graphic organizers** as well as a variety of graphic organizers in PDF format.

The Rubric Says	Information is logically organized into categories.
Writing Strategy	Make a Web to organize the descriptive details.

I got a lot of information from my sources, but I needed to make it all work together. My strategy was to use a Web to organize the most important descriptive details into categories. My main categories came from my list of questions. They are in the green shapes.

Writer's Term
Web
A **Web** organizes details around a central topic.

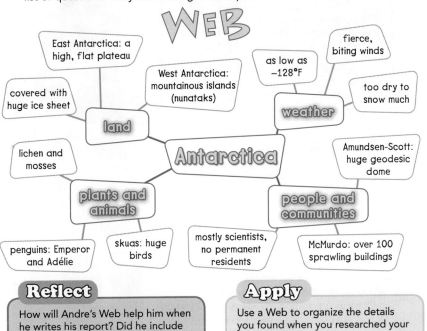

WEB

- East Antarctica: a high, flat plateau
- West Antarctica: mountainous islands (nunataks)
- covered with huge ice sheet
- **land**
- as low as −128°F
- fierce, biting winds
- too dry to snow much
- **weather**
- **Antarctica**
- lichen and mosses
- Amundsen-Scott: huge geodesic dome
- **plants and animals**
- **people and communities**
- penguins: Emperor and Adélie
- skuas: huge birds
- mostly scientists, no permanent residents
- McMurdo: over 100 sprawling buildings

Reflect

How will Andre's Web help him when he writes his report? Did he include all the details he'll need?

Apply

Use a Web to organize the details you found when you researched your geographic description.

Geographic Description **441**

Conferencing

PEER TO PEER Have partners review each other's Webs. Have students indicate one or two categories they would like to know more about if they were reading a geographic description of the place.

PEER GROUPS Have students work in groups of four. Have students take turns sharing their places and the categories they chose with the group. The group suggests possible categories each student could add to his or her Web. Students decide individually whether or not to accept the suggestions.

TEACHER-LED Hold conferences with pairs of students about their Webs. Have the pairs look at each other's Webs and offer comments as you coach them in giving constructive criticism.

Write
a Geographic Description

Week 2 • Day 2

Student Objectives

- Make a Web to organize notes. *(p. 441)*

Prewrite

Focus on **Organization**

Organize Ideas Make sure students understand the purpose and organization of the Web. Ask volunteers to name the central topic, the categories, and the details for each category. Discuss why a Web is a useful way to organize information visually (it shows how the different categories and details are connected). Point out that the categories in the Web are drawn from Andre's questions on page 439.

Writer's Term

Web One advantage of a Web is that it can be as complex as the writer wants. For a shorter essay, a simpler Web such as the one shown is generally adequate. You may wish to explain to students, however, that they can add subcategories to their Webs if needed.

CCSS **C**ommon **C**ore **S**tate **S**tandards

W.7.2.a: Introduce a topic clearly, previewing what is to follow; organize ideas, concepts, and information, using strategies such as definition, classification, comparison/contrast, and cause/effect; include formatting (e.g., headings), graphics (e.g., charts, tables) and multimedia when useful to aiding comprehension. **W.7.2.b:** Develop the topic with relevant facts, definitions, concrete details, quotations, or other information and examples.

Geographic Description　T441

Write
a Geographic Description

Week 2 • Day 3

Student Objectives

- Begin writing, using third-person point of view and an objective tone. *(pp. 442–445)*

Draft

Focus on Voice

Draft a Geographic Description

Explain that writing a draft is a chance for writers to get ideas on paper without having to worry about making mistakes. Students should focus on developing their ideas and establishing a consistent point of view and tone.

Read the information about objective tone in the Writer's Term box and Andre's words on page 442 with the students. Then read Andre's draft on pages 443–445 together. Have students refer back to Andre's questions on page 439 and discuss whether he answered them to their satisfaction. Discuss how Andre used his Web to organize his writing.

Point out that Andre repeatedly refers to the rubric as he writes. Encourage students to get into the habit of using the rubric to guide their own writing.

Online Writing Center

 Provides student eBooks with an **interactive writing pad** for drafting, revising, editing, and publishing.

Draft   Focus on (Voice)

The Rubric Says   The writer's voice suits the purpose and draws the reader in.

Writing Strategy   Use third-person point of view and an objective tone.

> ✏️ **Writer's Term____**
>
> **Objective Tone**
> *Objective* means sticking to the facts and avoiding emotions or opinions. When writing about a topic you have not experienced yourself, it's best to use an **objective tone**. This allows you to provide information creatively without sharing personal opinions or biases. Use third-person point of view (*he, she, it*) to support an objective tone.

The rubric says my voice should match my purpose and connect with my audience. Well, my purpose is to inform and my audience is my class. Using third-person point of view is perfect. Third person allows me to give the facts without providing my opinion or bias, while also making clear that I've never been to Antarctica myself. Although using third person takes me out of the writing, I can still give my writing a personality by crafting the words and sentences carefully. That will help keep my audience interested.

First I'll focus on getting my ideas down; I'll find and fix mistakes later. Now to start writing!

442 Descriptive Writing

Differentiating Instruction

ENRICHMENT

Compare and Contrast Two Places You may wish to have students write a geographic description that compares and contrasts two places. Before students write, have them decide on categories to compare and contrast. Have students create two Webs (one for each location) that use the same categories, and then use the Webs to organize and write their descriptions.

[DRAFT]

[third-person point of view]   **A White World**

    "Everywhere you look, all you see is white." This is how many travelers to Antarctica explain their reaction to this isolated continent. Antarctica is not a place where most people would want to live. However, to many visitors it appears quite remarkably.

Antarctica is covered almost complete with a huge ice sheet. It extends almost five and a half million square miles, and the thickly part averages about 6,500 feet. The land is divided into sections. East Antarctica is a high, flat plateau. West Antarctica is smallest. It is a series of mountainus islands held together by the ice sheet. Nunataks are mountains buried so deep that only their tips peek through the ice. Between East and West Antarctica are the Transantarctic mountains. They cut the land into two neat chunks. On either side of West Antarctica are big floating ice sheets. One, the Ross Ice Shelf, is as large as France.

[facts about the land]

Geographic Description 443

Write
a Geographic Description

Week 2 • Day 4

Student Objectives
• Complete a draft.

✎ Writer's Term

Objective Tone An objective tone is ideal for a geographic description because the writer's purpose is to give the audience a clear picture of a location, using text that is unclouded with the writer's personal opinions or feelings. Students should be careful to avoid presenting opinions as if they are facts. Tell them to make sure all their statements can be supported by the facts they found in their research.

REINFORCEMENT
Review Point of View Review the concept of point of view with students. Tell students that one simple definition of point of view is "who is telling the story." Say: *When I use first-person point of view, I [your name] am telling a story about things I have experienced, and I use the words I and we to talk about what I did. When I use third-person point of view, I'm not speaking about my personal experiences. I use the words he, she, it, and them to talk about the people and things in my writing.* Help students practice by saying several sentences in first- and third-person points of view and having them identify the point of view of each sentence.

CCSS Common Core State Standards

W.7.2.b: Develop the topic with relevant facts, definitions, concrete details, quotations, or other information and examples. **W.7.4:** Produce clear and coherent writing in which the development, organization, and style are appropriate to task, purpose, and audience. **L.7.5:** With some guidance and support from peers and adults, develop and strengthen writing as needed by planning, revising, editing, rewriting, or trying a new approach, focusing on how well purpose and audience have been addressed.

Focus on Point of View Discuss the use of third-person point of view in the model. Point out the note in the first paragraph of the model and ask students to find additional examples of third-person point of view. Discuss with students how third-person point of view affects them as readers. Guide the discussion by asking:

- Does the use of third person make you more likely to believe the writer?

- Does third-person point of view give the writing a more formal or a more casual tone?

[DRAFT]

[facts about weather]

The weather in Antarctica is real cold. Winter temperatures drop as low as –128 degrees Fahrenheit. The average winter temperature range is from –40 to –94 degrees inland. These temperatures can freeze spit in midair! You have to take them serious. Winds are fierce and biting. Gusts over 100 miles per hour are not uncommon. Even in summer, in warmer coastal areas, +32 degrees is the average temperature. But no snow falls in many parts of Antarctica. Strong winds kick up existing snow, but the air is usually so dry that new snow cannot form. This is why Antarctica is sometimes called *The White Desert*.

Plants and animals are more commonlier in Antarctica than you might expect. There are several hundred species of lichens. They grow good along the rocks. They create colorful colonies of yellow, green, and black. Mosses can also be found. The main animals living in Antarctica are penguins, of which the emperor penguin, about three or four feet tall, scoots around the ice like an industrious headwaiter. The Adélie are slightly smaller and also live in large colonies. The South Polar skua is a huge and powerful flying bird. It has been seen as far inland as the Pole. It has also been seen as far north as the Equator.

[facts about plants and animals]

444 Descriptive Writing

Conferencing

PEER TO PEER Have partners exchange drafts. Tell students to read each other's drafts, paying special attention to organization and voice. Have each student write two or three suggestions for his or her partner's draft on a separate sheet of paper. Allow students a few minutes to discuss and clarify the suggestions.

PEER GROUPS Have students work in groups of four. Have each student read one or two paragraphs aloud from his or her draft. After each student reads, have the group discuss the paragraphs. Each student in the group should tell what he or she likes best about the paragraphs and give one suggestion.

TEACHER-LED Hold conferences with individual students about their drafts. Point out any places where they have used a tone that is not objective or stated an opinion as a fact.

 Strategies for Writers Online
Go to **www.sfw.z-b.com** for additional online resources for students and teachers.

[DRAFT]

Surprisingly, people also live in Antarctica. Nearly all of them are scientists. (No one, though, makes this cold continent a permanent home.) Including the United States, 29 countries have research stations. The largest is the American facility called McMurdo Station. It is on Ross Island in the Ross Ice Shelf. This community contains about 100 low, sprawling buildings. There are dormitories, a gymnasium, a science lab, and other structures. About 250 people spend the winter there. In summer, the population rises to 1,000. A smaller facility is the Amundsen-Scott South Pole Station. It is very close to the Pole. The main building is a huge aluminum geodesic dome. It is more than 55 feet high at its highest point. Housing space for 27 people, equipment depots, and various research areas are either within it or connected to it by covered passageways. Glinting in the sun in the empty Antarctic plain, the station looks like the hom of visitors from another planet.

Tourists do visit Antarctica. However, it can cost as much as $40,000 to get all the way to the South Pole. If they have the money and are adventuraous enough to make the trip, they can visit this unique isolated continent.

[conclusion]

Reflect
How did Andre do? Did he organize his details? Does his voice match his purpose and audience?

Apply
It's your turn to write a draft using details from your Web. Don't forget to start generally, then get specific, and go back to general for your conclusion.

Geographic Description 445

Focus on an Objective Tone
Discuss the use of an objective tone in the model. Ask students to find examples of an objective tone in the model. Discuss why an objective tone is suitable for a geographic description. Tell students that the opposite of *objective* is *subjective*. Ask students what type of writing might present similar information but in a subjective tone. (Possible responses: reviews of tourist destinations, editorials)

English Language Learners

BEGINNING/INTERMEDIATE
Modifiers: Adjectives and Adverbs On the board, write the sentences *She looks _____.* and *He sings _____.* Write the following words on index cards: *tired, hungry, poorly, angry, happy, loudly, well.* As you show students a card, have them say the word and tell which sentence the word goes with. Then say the sentence. Use this as a starting point for illustrating the differences between adjectives and adverbs.

ADVANCED/ADVANCED HIGH
Figurative Language Describe personification, simile, and metaphor to students. On the board, write *Bangkok is the grandest jewel in the crown of Asia, Bangkok is like a jewel in the crown of Asia,* and *Bangkok sings to her visitors.* Have students tell what type of figurative language is used in each sentence. Then have students revise one sentence in their geographic descriptions to include figurative language.

CCSS **Common Core State Standards**
W.7.2.b: Develop the topic with relevant facts, definitions, concrete details, quotations, or other information and examples. **W.7.5:** With some guidance and support from peers and adults, develop and strengthen writing as needed by planning, revising, editing, rewriting, or trying a new approach, focusing on how well purpose and audience have been addressed. **SL.7.1:** Engage effectively in a range of collaborative discussions (one-on-one, in groups, and teacher-led) with diverse partners on *grade 7 topics, texts, and issues,* building on others' ideas and expressing their own clearly.

Write
a Geographic Description

Week 2 • Day 5

Student Objectives

- Revise for use of comparisons to make the description more complete. *(p. 446)*

Revise

Focus on Ideas

Use Comparisons Read the rubric descriptor and writing strategy on page 446 aloud. Explain to students that a comparison can help put information in perspective for a reader, or help them to visualize an aspect of the description more clearly.

Have students read Andre's words and the draft excerpt. Ask students whether Andre's revision gives perspective or helps visualize. (gives perspective) How does comparing the information about Antarctica with more familiar information help the reader better understand the topic? (Possible response: It helps the reader understand just how cold it gets in Antarctica in the winter.)

Strategies for Writers Online
Go to **www.sfw.z-b.com** for additional online resources for students and teachers.

Revise
Focus on ⬤ **Ideas**

The Rubric Says Thoughtful comparisons clarify the writer's ideas.

Writing Strategy Use a comparison to make the description more complete.

The rubric tells me to use thoughtful comparisons to clarify my ideas. I know *I* learn new information best when it is paired up with something I already know. Comparing the new information with familiar knowledge really helps me grasp the idea. So I'll do this for my reader, too.

[DRAFT]

In Alaska, the average winter temperature ranges from 12 to –20 degrees. ← [used a comparison]

The weather in Antarctica is real cold. Winter tempertures drop as low as –128 degrees Fahrenheit. The average winter temperature in Antarctica range is from –40 to –94 degrees inland. These tempertures can freeze spit in midair!

Apply

Include some thoughtful comparisons in your geographic description to make your writing more complete.

446 Descriptive Writing

Revise

Focus on **Word Choice**

The Rubric Says	Figurative language is used in ways that are attention-getting and unusual.
Writing Strategy	Add some figurative language, including similes and metaphors.

Writer's Term

Figurative Language

Figurative language is language that goes beyond the normal meaning of the words in it. Figurative language, which includes similes and metaphors, creates a mental picture for the reader. A simile compares two different things by using the words *like* or *as*. A metaphor compares two different things by calling one thing another.

I read my draft to my writing partner, Jill. She liked most of my descriptive details, but she said that my description of the land itself was kind of dull. So I went back and added some figurative language, including some similes and metaphors.

[DRAFT]

thickly part averages about 6,500 feet. The land is divided into [added a metaphor] —an icy table of land

sections. East Antarctica is a high, flat plateau. West Antarctica is

smallest. It is a series of mountainus islands held together by the ice

sheet. Nunataks are mountains buried so deep that only their tips

peek through the ice. Between East and West Antarctica are the

In some areas, nunataks dot the [added a simile]
surface like punctuation marks.

Reflect

How did using comparisons and figurative language affect Andre's writing?

Apply

Add some figurative language to your geographic description. Try to include at least one simile and at least one metaphor.

Geographic Description 447

Write

a Geographic Description

Student Objectives

- Revise for use of figurative language. *(p. 447)*

Revise

Focus on

Incorporate Figurative Language
Read the Writer's Term box aloud. Then give examples of similes and metaphors, such as the following: *The tree's bare branches were like hooked claws.* (simile) *His reaction to the insult was a hurricane of fury.* (metaphor) Encourage students to think of their own similes and metaphors.

Have students read the rest of the text on the page, including the draft excerpt. Point out the revisions and discuss with students how the figures of speech help deepen their understanding of the topic.

Writer's Term

Figurative Language You may also wish to introduce *personification*, which is giving human qualities to animals or things. *The sun smiled warmly upon us* is a somewhat clichéd example you can give students.

CCSS Common Core State Standards

W.7.4: Produce clear and coherent writing in which the development, organization, and style are appropriate to task, purpose, and audience. **W.7.5:** With some guidance and support from peers and adults, develop and strengthen writing as needed by planning, revising, editing, rewriting, or trying a new approach, focusing on how well purpose and audience have been addressed.

Write
a Geographic Description

Week 3 • Day 2

Student Objectives

• Revise to combine short, choppy sentences. *(p. 448)*

Revise

Focus on  Sentence Fluency

Combine Sentences Have students read page 448 and look at Andre's revisions. Discuss how combining short sentences can improve the flow of the writing.

Explain that one good way to make sure writing does not contain too many short sentences in a row is to read it aloud. Sometimes a writer hears problems with sentence fluency that are not as obvious when reading silently. Help students find relatively private spaces where they can read their drafts aloud. Tell them to read their drafts aloud two or three times and then revise any passages that contain too many short, choppy sentences.

Online Writing Center

Provides **interactive proofreading activities** for each genre.

Revise
Focus on Sentence Fluency

The Rubric Says Great variety in sentence lengths and beginnings make the writing a pleasure to read.

Writing Strategy Combine short, choppy sentences.

Jill commented on some of my sentences. She mentioned that some were really short and started in similar ways. My description sounded choppy. The way I fixed one of my paragraphs was to combine two or three short sentences that were about the same subject. As a result, I not only created sentences of different lengths, but I also varied the beginnings of the sentences.

[DRAFT] [combined short sentences]

Plants and animals are more commonlier in Antarctica than you might expect. ~~There are~~ several hundred species of lichens. ~~They~~ grow good along the rocks. They create colorful colonies of yellow, green, and black. Mosses can also be found.

Apply

Check the length of your sentences. Do short, choppy ones need to be combined? Put a couple of them together.

448 Descriptive Writing

Optional Revising Lessons

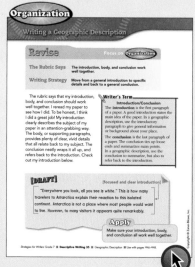

Descriptive 35

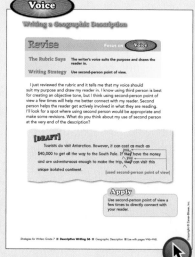

Descriptive 36

Go to **Strategies for Writers Grade 7 CD-ROM**

Edit
Focus on **Conventions**

The Rubric Says	Adjectives and adverbs are used correctly and enhance the writing.
Writing Strategy	Check to see that adjectives and adverbs are used correctly.

Writer's Term

Adjective and Adverb
An **adjective** is a word that describes a noun or pronoun. An **adverb** is a word that describes a verb, an adjective, or another adverb.

Now I need to proofread my geographic description for errors. I always check for spelling, punctuation, and capitalization errors. The rubric also tells me to check my adjectives and adverbs. I know that sometimes it's easy to get the two mixed up.

[DRAFT]

[corrected adjective] [corrected adverb] → completely [changed adverb to adjective]

Antarctica is covered almost ~~complete~~ with a huge ice sheet.

It extends almost five and a half million square miles, and the thickest
~~thickly~~ part averages about 6,500 feet. The land is divided into
—an icy table of land.
sections. East Antarctica is a high, flat plateau. West Antarctica is
→ smaller   mountainous
~~smallest~~ It is a series of ~~mountainus~~ islands held together by the ice sheet.

Reflect
What do you think? Can you find any mistakes that Andre has missed? How have his revisions helped his writing?

Apply **Conventions**
Edit your draft for spelling, punctuation, and capitalization. Be sure to fix any mistakes in adjectives and adverbs.

For more practice using adjectives and adverbs correctly, use the exercises on the next two pages.

Geographic Description **449**

Related Grammar Practice

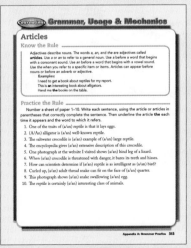

Student Edition page 515

Conventions Grammar, Usage & Mechanics
Demonstrative Pronouns and Demonstrative Adjectives

Student Edition page 516

Go to ➡ **Appendix A: Grammar Practice**

Write
a Geographic Description

Week 3 • Day 3

Student Objectives
• Edit for correct use of adjectives and adverbs. *(p. 449)*

Edit

Focus on

Check for Errors Remind students that adjectives and adverbs are describing words that describe different things. Review the material in the Writer's Term box.

Use the mini-lesson on page T450 for students having problems with adjectives and adverbs and the mini-lesson on page T451 for students having problems with the comparative and superlative forms. Then have students complete the exercises on pages 450 and 451. Go over their answers in class.

Writer's Term
Adjective and Adverb Adverbs often end in *-ly*, although some common adverbs, such as *soon*, *fast*, and *late*, do not. It should be noted that some words, such as *late*, can function either as an adjective or an adverb. (*Oh no, I'm late!* or *The teacher does not accept late homework.*)

CCSS **Common Core State Standards**

L.7.1: Demonstrate command of the conventions of standard English grammar and usage when writing or speaking.

Geographic Description **T449**

Conventions

Mini-Lesson

Student Objectives

- Correctly identify and use adjectives and adverbs. (p. 450)

Adjectives and Adverbs

Explain to students that an adjective describes a noun or pronoun while an adverb describes a verb, an adjective, or another adverb. Review the basic parts of speech. Write *noun, verb, adjective, adverb,* and *pronoun* on the board. To the side, write *adjective* and *adverb.* Have students help you draw arrows from *adjective* to the parts of speech it describes. Then do the same with *adverb.* Ask:

- What questions are answered by an adjective? (which one, what kind, or how many)

- What questions are answered by an adverb? (how, when, where, or to what extent)

Write a mixed list of adverbs and adjectives on the board. Have students identify which ones are which. For example:

Adjectives	Adverbs
colorful	coldly
wooden	soon
fuzzy	swiftly
awkward	awkwardly
blue	colorfully

Online Writing Center

Provides **interactive grammar games** and **practice activities** in student eBook.

Conventions Grammar, Usage & Mechanics

Adjectives and Adverbs

Know the Rule

An **adjective** describes a noun or pronoun. An adjective
- tells which one, what kind, or how many.
  Examples: **blue** car, **shiny** star, **eight** caterpillars
- may follow a linking verb.
  Examples: The rug feels **soft**.

The articles *a, an,* and *the* are adjectives that indicate the presence of a noun.
  Examples: **The** cat chases **a** mouse.

An **adverb** describes a verb, an adjective, or another adverb. An adverb
- tells how, when, where, or to what extent.
  Examples: The train whistled **loudly**.
- may end in *-ly,* although many common ones do not.
  Examples: **deep, deeply; fair, fairly**

Practice the Rule

Write each sentence on a separate sheet of paper. Underline the words that are adjectives. Circle the words that are adverbs.

1. The preparations for a long and adventurous trip can be exhausting.
2. Detailed lists must be written carefully to make sure supplies are appropriate.
3. Properly packing your supplies into suitcases and backpacks takes great patience and much practice.
4. Thorough planning will certainly help to make the trip enjoyable.
5. For an efficient departure, you must learn how to quickly eat a nutritious breakfast and dress appropriately for the weather.
6. If you accidentally forget something, you will just have to be very calm.
7. While on your adventure, don't forget to politely ask for directions and leave generous tips to the hard-working hotel staff.
8. When you finally return, you will be amazed at your wonderful accomplishments.
9. Offer your friends and family a complete description of your trip.
10. They will be thoroughly impressed.

Related Grammar Practice

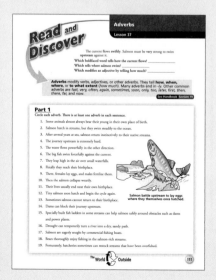

Page III

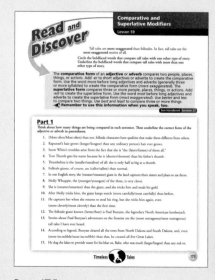

Page 175

Go to G.U.M. Student Practice Book

Comparative and Superlative Forms

Know the Rule

Use the **comparative form** of an adjective or adverb when comparing two things. Use the **superlative form** when comparing three or more things. Make the comparative form of an adjective or adverb by adding *-er* or using the word *more*. To make the superlative form of an adjective or adverb, add *-est* or use *most*.

> **Examples:** The oak tree is **taller** than the maple tree. The redwood, though, is the **tallest** of the three. (adjectives)
>
> English class starts **earlier** than social studies. Math starts **earliest**. (adverbs)

Practice the Rule

On a separate sheet of paper, write the correct form of the underlined adjective or adverb.

1. Being the first person to reach the Pole was the <u>great</u> goal of many explorers. *(greatest)*
2. Of the two poles, the North Pole was reached <u>soonest</u>. *(sooner)*
3. Robert Peary, an American explorer, made his <u>earlier</u> of six tries in 1893. *(earliest)*
4. On the first trip, Peary's sled dogs <u>quicker</u> became sick or froze to death. *(quickly)*
5. Matthew Henson was the <u>better</u> of all of Peary's assistants. *(best)*
6. On May 8, 1900, Peary and Henson passed a point <u>farthest</u> north than anyone had ever gone. *(farther)*
7. In 1906, President Roosevelt awarded Peary National Geographic's <u>high</u> honor, the Hubbard Medal. *(highest)*
8. Henson was awarded the same medal much <u>latest</u>, in 2000. *(later)*
9. Some have questioned whether the conquest of the Pole, Peary's <u>greater</u> accomplishment, actually happened. *(greatest)*
10. They believe he reached the <u>farther</u> point north for his time but did not reach the North Pole. *(farthest)*

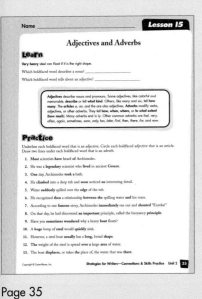

Page 35

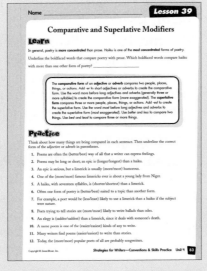

Page 83

Go to Grammar Practice Masters

Conventions

Mini-Lesson

Student Objectives

- Identify and use comparative and superlative forms correctly. *(p. 451)*

Comparative and Superlative Forms

Read Know the Rule on page 451 with students. Note that both adjectives and adverbs take the same endings to form the comparative and superlative forms.

Place a chart on the board. The second and third columns should be labeled *Comparative Form* and *Superlative Form*. In the first column, write common adjectives. Have students fill in the comparative and superlative forms. For example:

Adjective	Comparative Form	Superlative Form
sick	sicker	sickest
tall	taller	tallest
red	redder	reddest

Make a similar chart for adverbs, such as *quickly, soon, honestly,* and *constantly.*

CCSS Common Core State Standards
L.7.2: Demonstrate command of the conventions of standard English capitalization, punctuation, and spelling when writing.

Write
a Geographic Description

Week 3 • Day 4

Student Objectives

• Discuss preparation for publishing and presentation. *(p. 452)*

• Use a final editing checklist to publish their work. *(p. 452)*

Publish ⁺Presentation

Publishing Strategy Ask students if they like Andre's choice for sharing his geographic description. Remind the class that he might also include this description in his journal or send it to a friend or relative. Invite students to list real-life applications for the geographic description genre. (Possible responses: geography textbook, informational book or travelogue, travel brochure or website, website sponsored by a location such as a state or national park)

Have students make a final checklist to check their descriptions. Ask students if they feel Andre left out any important items on the checklist. Along with posting their work on a bulletin board, encourage them to give or send copies to friends and relatives who would enjoy reading about the place they described.

 Strategies for Writers Online
Go to **www.sfw.z-b.com** for additional online resources for students and teachers.

T452 Descriptive Writing

Publish ⁺Presentation

Publishing Strategy	Submit the description to the school's magazine.
Presentation Strategy	Choose visuals that will work with the text.

Guess what? I'm almost done! I can't wait to show my parents and submit my piece to my school's magazine. But I think I need to add one more thing: some great visuals. I'll search the Internet for related photographs, maps, or illustrations that are OK to use. I'll insert them near the text they describe and include captions for my readers to understand what each visual shows. It's easy to do with my word-processing program! Finally, I'll check my writing against this checklist to make sure I did everything right.

My Final Checklist

Did I—

✓ use all adjectives and adverbs correctly?

✓ use comparative and superlative forms accurately?

✓ fix all spelling, grammar, and punctuation mistakes?

✓ use effective and appropriate visuals?

Apply

Make a final checklist to check your geographic description. Then publish your final copy.

452 Descriptive Writing

Differentiating Instruction

ENRICHMENT

Submit for Publication Encourage students to submit their geographic descriptions for publication to magazines or websites that publish the work of young people. Tell students they must research the publication's submission guidelines and follow them precisely.

REINFORCEMENT

Research Visuals With a Partner Allow students to include just one visual that illustrates some aspect of the location they described. Pair struggling students with more advanced students to search for appropriate visuals. Have the advanced student assist in placing the visual appropriately within the geographic description.

A WHITE WORLD

by Andre

"Everywhere you look, all you see is white." This is how many travelers to Antarctica explain their reaction to this isolated continent. Antarctica is not a place where most people would want to live. However, to many visitors it appears quite remarkable.

Antarctica is covered almost completely with a huge ice sheet. It extends almost five and a half million square miles, and the thickest part averages about 6,500 feet. The land is divided into sections. East Antarctica is a high, flat plateau—an icy table of land. West Antarctica is smaller. It is a series of mountainous islands held together by the ice sheet. In some areas, nunataks dot the surface like punctuation marks. Nunataks are mountains buried so deep that only their tips peek through the ice. Between East and West Antarctica are the Transantarctic Mountains. They cut the land into two neat chunks. On either side of West Antarctica are huge floating ice sheets that hug the land like armrests on a chair. One, the Ross Ice Shelf, is as large as France.

SOUTH PACIFIC OCEAN

Elephant Island

Antarctic Peninsula

Paulet Island

Antarctic Circle

Ocean Camp

Weddell Sea

ANTARCTICA

Geographic Description 453

Revising our writing in response to feedback is very different from making editing corrections. Making feedback multimodal often helps students see and hear themselves as readers-writers and genuinely see ways to rethink or revise their work. Using screencasting tools like Jing, recording audio responses, or embedding comments in Google Docs encourages peer review. Students become responsible for both using the feedback they receive and thinking connectively about how their writing presents and captures them working in that reader-writer role.

See **www.sfw.z-b.com** for further information about and links to these websites and tools.

Write
a Geographic Description

Week 3 • Day 5

Student Objectives

- Use a geographic description rubric. *(pp. 432–433)*
- Share a published geographic description. *(pp. 453–455)*

Presentation Strategy It's important that students choose visuals that show important aspects of the places and do not contradict the content of the text. Students should also take time to think about the appropriate placement of the visuals within the text so that they don't confuse the reader.

Remind students that they should look for visuals that are not copyrighted. Explain that using another person's work, including visual images, without permission is plagiarism, which is a serious offense.

CCSS **Common Core State Standards**

W.7.2.a: Introduce a topic clearly, previewing what is to follow; organize ideas, concepts, and information, using strategies such as definition, classification, comparison/contrast, and cause effect; include formatting (e.g., headings), graphics (e.g., charts, tables), and multimedia when useful to aiding comprehension. W.7.4: Produce clear and coherent writing in which the development, organization, and style are appropriate to task, purpose, and audience. SL.7.1: Engage effectively in a range of collaborative discussions (one-on-one, in groups, and teacher-led) with diverse partners on *grade 7 topics, texts, and issues,* building on others' ideas and expressing their own clearly. SL.7.5: Include multimedia components and visual displays in presentations to clarify claims and findings and emphasize salient points.

Reflecting on a Geographic Description

Ask students to return to the rubric to evaluate Andre's geographic description. Divide the class into groups and have them discuss how they would score Andre on each of the six traits. Have the groups compare their scores to the ones assigned by the other groups. Ask students to give examples to support their scores.

Have students write in journals or discuss as a class thoughts about their progress in writing. Use questions such as these to stimulate students' thoughts:

- What did you like about this assignment? What did you dislike?

- What aspect of the assignment was the most difficult for you? Why?

- What surprised you about writing a geographic description?

- What is one thing you will do differently the next time you write a geographic description?

The weather in Antarctica is really cold. Winter temperatures drop as low as –128 degrees Fahrenheit. In Alaska, the average winter temperature ranges from 12 to –20 degrees. The average winter temperature range in Antarctica is from –40 to –94 degrees inland. These temperatures can freeze spit in midair! You have to take them seriously. Winds are fierce and biting. Gusts over 100 miles per hour are not uncommon. Even in summer, in warmer coastal areas, +32 degrees is the average temperature. But no snow falls in many parts of Antarctica. Strong winds kick up existing snow, but the air is usually so dry that new snow cannot form. This is why Antarctica is sometimes called *The White Desert*.

Plants and animals are more common in Antarctica than you might expect. Several hundred species of lichens grow well along the rocks. They create colorful colonies of yellow, green, and black. Mosses can also be found. The main animals living in Antarctica are penguins. The emperor penguin, about three or four feet tall, scoots around the ice like an industrious headwaiter. The Adélie, slightly smaller, also live in large colonies there. The South Polar skua is a huge and powerful flying bird. It has been seen as far inland as the Pole and as far north as the Equator.

454 Descriptive Writing

 Strategies for Writers Online
Go to **www.sfw.z-b.com** for additional online resources for students and teachers.

Surprisingly, people also live in Antarctica. Nearly all of them are scientists. (No one, though, makes this cold, forbidding region a permanent home.) Including the United States, 29 countries have research stations. The largest is the American facility called McMurdo Station. It is on Ross Island in the Ross Ice Shelf. This community contains about 100 low, sprawling buildings. There are dormitories, a gymnasium, a science lab, and other structures. About 250 people spend the winter there. In summer the population rises to 1,000. A smaller facility is the Amundsen-Scott South Pole Station. It is very close to the Pole. The main building is a huge aluminum geodesic dome. It is more than 55 feet high at its highest point. Housing space for 27 people, equipment depots, and various research areas are either within it or connected to it by covered passageways. Glinting in the sun in the empty Antarctic plain, the station looks like the home of visitors from another planet.

Tourists do visit Antarctica. However, it can cost as much as $40,000 to get all the way to the South Pole. If you have the money and are adventurous enough to make the trip, you can visit this unique isolated continent.

Reflect

How did Andre do? Did he use all the traits of a good geographic description? Would you give him a top score for each item of the rubric? Don't forget to use the rubric to check your geographic description, too.

CCSS **Common Core State Standards**

W.7.5: With some guidance and support from peers and adults, develop and strengthen writing as needed by planning, revising, editing, rewriting, or trying a new approach, focusing on how well purpose and audience have been addressed. **W.7.6:** Use technology, including the Internet, to produce and publish writing and link to and cite sources as well as to interact and collaborate with others, including linking to and citing sources.

Poem Planner

WEEK 1

Introduce
a Poem

Student Objectives
- Review the elements of a poem.
- Consider purpose and audience.
- Learn the traits of descriptive writing.

Student Activities
- Read and discuss **What's in a Poem?** (p. 456)
- Read and discuss **Why Write a Poem?** (p. 457)
- Read **Linking Descriptive Writing Traits to a Poem.** (p. 458)

Analyze
Read a Poem

Student Objectives
- Read a model poem.

Student Activities
- Read **"Pythagoras."** (p. 459)

Analyze
Introduce the Rubric

Student Objectives
- Learn to read a rubric.

Student Activities
- Review **"Pythagoras."** (p. 459)
- Read and discuss the **Poem Rubric.** (pp. 460–461)

WEEK 2

Write
Prewrite: Ideas

Student Objectives
- Read and understand a prewriting strategy.

Student Activities
- Read and discuss **Prewrite: Focus on Ideas.** (p. 466)
- Apply the prewriting strategy.

Write
Prewrite: Organization

Student Objectives
- Make a Web to plan the poem.

Student Activities
- Read and discuss **Prewrite: Focus on Organization.** (p. 467)
- Reflect on the model Web.
- Apply the prewriting strategy to create a Web.
- Participate in a peer conference.

Write
Draft: Word Choice

Student Objectives
- Begin writing, using figurative language.

Student Activities
- Read and discuss **Draft: Focus on Word Choice.** (pp. 468–469)
- Reflect on a model draft.
- Apply the drafting strategy by using the Web to help write a poem with figurative language.

WEEK 3

Write
Revise: Organization

Student Objectives
- Revise for order of lines and stanzas.

Student Activities
- Read and discuss **Revise: Focus on Organization.** (p. 471)
- Reflect on a model draft.
- Apply the revising strategy.
- Participate in a peer conference.

Write
Revise: Sentence Fluency

Student Objectives
- Revise for line breaks.

Student Activities
- Read and discuss **Revise: Focus on Sentence Fluency.** (p. 472)
- Reflect on a model draft.
- Apply the revising strategy.

Note: Optional Revising Lessons appear on the *Strategies for Writers* CD-ROM.

Write
Edit: Conventions

Student Objectives
- Edit for correct use of adverb and adjective clauses.

Student Activities
- Read and discuss **Edit: Focus on Conventions.** (p. 473)
- Reflect on a model draft.
- Apply the editing strategy.

Note: Teach the Conventions mini-lessons (pp. 474–475) if needed.

<table>
<tr><td>

Day 4
Analyze
Ideas, Organization, and Voice

Student Objectives
- Read a model poem.
- Use the poem rubric.
- Use the model poem to study Ideas, Organization, and Voice.

Student Activities
- Review **"Pythagoras."** (p. 459)
- Read and discuss **Using the Rubric to Study the Model.** (pp. 462–463)

</td><td>

Day 5
Analyze
Word Choice, Sentence Fluency, and Conventions

Student Objectives
- Read a model poem.
- Use the poem rubric.
- Use the model poem to study Word Choice, Sentence Fluency, and Conventions.

Student Activities
- Review **"Pythagoras."** (p. 459)
- Read and discuss **Using the Rubric to Study the Model.** (pp. 464–465)

</td></tr>
</table>

<table>
<tr><td>

Day 4
Write
Draft

Student Objectives
- Complete a draft.

Student Activities
- Finish the draft.
- Participate in a peer conference.

</td><td>

Day 5
Write
Revise: Ideas

Student Objectives
- Revise for well-chosen details.

Student Activities
- Read and discuss **Revise: Focus on Ideas.** (p. 470)
- Reflect on a model draft.
- Apply the revising strategy.

</td></tr>
</table>

<table>
<tr><td>

Day 4
Write
Publish: +Presentation

Student Objectives
- Discuss preparation for publishing and presentation.
- Use a final editing checklist to publish their work.

Student Activities
- Read and discuss **Publish: +Presentation.** (p. 476)
- Apply the publishing strategy.

</td><td>

Day 5
Write
Publish: +Presentation

Student Objectives
- Use a poem rubric.
- Share a published poem.

Student Activities
- Share their work.
- Use the rubric to reflect upon and evaluate the model and their own writing. (pp. 460–461, 477)

</td></tr>
</table>

...omplete the chapter in fewer days, combine the learning objectives and activities in a way that supports students as they write.

Resources at-a-Glance

Grammar, Usage & Mechanics

Adjective Clauses T474
Adverb Clauses T475
Grammar Practice T473–T475

Differentiating Instruction

Using the Rubric T465
Draft T468
Publish T476
For additional Differentiating Instruction activities, see Strategies for Writers *Extensions Online at* **www.sfw.z-b.com.**

English Language Learners

Using the Rubric T462–T463
Prewrite T466
Revise T470

Conferencing

Peer to Peer T467, T469, T471
Peer Groups T467, T469, T471
Teacher-Led T467, T469, T471

Technology Tip

Using the Rubric T464
Publish T477

 Connection Letter
Reproducible letter (in English and Spanish) appears on the *Strategies for Writers* CD-ROM and at **www.sfw.z-b.com.**

Online Writing Center

Provides IWB resources, interactive games and practice activities, videos, eBooks, and a virtual file cabinet.

 Strategies for Writers Online

Go to **www.sfw.z-b.com** for free online resources for students and teachers.

Introduce
a Poem

Student Objectives

- Review the elements of a poem. *(p. 456)*
- Consider purpose and audience. *(p. 457)*
- Learn the traits of descriptive writing. *(p. 458)*

What's a Poem?

Ask students to tell the names of poems they have read. Note the different forms of the poems students mention and emphasize that not all poems rhyme.

What's in a Poem?

Read and discuss the elements of a poem with students. Give examples—or have students give examples—of each element. Write a section of a poem students have read in class on the board to show lines. Remind students of the definitions of *simile*, *metaphor*, and *personification*, and give examples of these examples of figurative language. For rhythm, say a line from a poem with a strong rhythm (e.g., *Listen my children and you shall hear/Of the midnight ride of Paul Revere*) and clap to emphasize the beats. To illustrate rhyme, quote something familiar, though cliché, such as *Roses are red, violets are blue....*

Strategies for Writers Online
Go to **www.sfw.z-b.com** for additional online resources for students and teachers.

What's a Poem?

It's a piece of writing that expresses the thoughts or feelings of the writer. A poem can also describe or explain an event, object, or subject. Poems can take many different forms.

What's in a Poem?

Line
A poem is made up of a number of lines, each ending where the writer feels there should be a break, not necessarily at a comma or period. Punctuation rules are not always followed in poems.

Figurative Language
Figurative language such as simile, personification, and metaphor are often found in poetry. Creative use of language can help the reader "see" an everyday event or object in an entirely new way.

Rhythm
Poems are meant to be both read and heard. The writer uses line breaks to control the poem's rhythm or speed. This controlled rhythm adds a whole new dimension to the poem when spoken out loud.

Rhyme
Not every poem rhymes, but many do. Rhyming words can be found on the same line, at the ends of alternating lines, or anywhere else in a poem. Rhyming words help connect ideas within the poem—and they're fun to read and hear.

456 Descriptive Writing

Descriptive Text Exemplars (Poem)

Carlson, Lori Marie. *Red Hot Salsa: Bilingual Poems on Being Young and Latino in the United States.* Henry Holt and Co., 2005. Carlson has put together a collection of poems that addresses the complexities that come with being bicultural. Poems appear in both Spanish and English and focus on topics from language and amor to family moments and neighborhoods.

Frost, Helen. *The Braid.* Frances Foster Books, 2006. The Braid is the tale of two sisters, separated during the Highland Clearances of the 1850s. While apart geographically, the sisters stay connected through a piece of each other's hair that is woven into their own braid. Alternating narrative poems told by each sister add to the beauty of this story.

Why write a Poem?

There are plenty of reasons to write a poem. Here are just a few.

Description
A poem is a great way to describe something—an object, an event, even a feeling—in a completely different way. You can be as creative and experimental as you like when you write a poem. That way, you can offer the reader a totally new way of looking at something.

Personal Reflection
Writing poems is a wonderful way to safely explore our inner thoughts and feelings. Words are powerful. Even if you never share your poem with a reader, the act of writing a poem itself can be a great way to gain personal insights.

Enjoyment
Writing poetry is fun! Experimenting with the sounds of words, figurative language, and poem structure is an exciting form of self-expression. Also, the feeling of satisfaction when the poem is finished can't be beat.

Understanding
Poetry can be used as a different approach when trying to help the reader understand a specific idea or topic. No subject is off limits when it comes to poetry, so why not explain an event in history, current events, science, or even math through a poem?

Poem **457**

Why write a Poem?

Read and discuss with students the reasons for writing a poem on page 457. Point out that all writing has a purpose. Writers write for many reasons and for a variety of audiences, and these authentic purposes help to shape the writing. A poet writing to describe something will focus on how that thing looks, sounds, and feels. When writing a poem for personal reflection, a poet focuses inward to explore his or her feelings. When the purpose is enjoyment, the poet might cut loose and experiment with unusual forms, sounds, and ideas. A poem written with the goal of understanding might explore a familiar topic in a new way. Encourage students to think about their reasons for writing a poem and how these reasons will affect the tone and focus of their writing.

Rylant, Cynthia. *Boris*. Graphia, 2006. Rylant tells the story of Boris the cat and the owner who adopted him. Told in a series of free verse poems, this book explores far more than life with a cat. Rylant touches on love and loss, kindness, and the give and take of companionship.

Myers, Walter Dean. Street Love. Amistad, 2007. Street Love is a collection of short poems that tell the story of Damien, a 17-year-old academic and athletic star, and Junice, a 16 year old trying to keep her family together after her mother is taken to prison for dealing drugs. The poems chronicle the ups and downs of Damien and Junice's taboo relationship, and show the true power of love.

CCSS Common Core State Standards

SL.7.1: Engage effectively in a range of collaborative discussions (one-on-one, in groups, and teacher-led) with diverse partners on *grade 7 topics, texts, and issues,* building on others' ideas and expressing their own clearly.

Introduce
a Poem

Linking Descriptive Writing Traits to a Poem

Have students read page 458. Emphasize that they will follow Andre as he models using the writing process and the Descriptive Writing Traits together.

Discuss with students how each trait applies to a poem. For example, precise words and figurative language are important forms of expression for a poet as he or she tries to create crystal-clear images in the reader's mind.

When students read the model on page 459, tell them to think about how well the model applies each of the traits. Have students score the poem from 1 to 6 on each trait, then ask volunteers to share their scores. Ask other students whether they agree or disagree with the scores. Be sure students give examples to support their opinions.

Online Writing Center

 Provides six **interactive anchor papers** for each mode of writing.

Linking Descriptive Writing Traits to a **Poem**

In this chapter, you will describe or explain a math concept in a poem. Andre will guide you through the stages of the writing process: Prewrite, Draft, Revise, Edit, and Publish. In each stage, Andre will show you important writing strategies that are linked to the Descriptive Writing Traits below.

Descriptive Writing Traits

 Ideas
- a clear topic that is developed by relevant supporting details
- descriptive details that are well chosen for the topic

 Organization
- well-organized paragraphs that logically follow the order of the description, whether by time, location, or another order
- varied and appropriate transitions that show the relationship between ideas and concepts

 Voice
- a voice that is appropriate for the purpose and audience

 Word Choice
- precise words and phrases, possibly including figurative language, that create an accurate picture for the reader

 Sentence Fluency
- sentences that vary in length and type to add flow to the writing

 Conventions
- no or few errors in grammar, usage, mechanics, and spelling

Before you write, read Sage Quintley's poem on the next page. Then use the poem rubric on pages 460–461 to decide how well she did. (You might want to look back at What's in a Poem? on page 456, too!)

458 Descriptive Writing

Descriptive Writing Traits in a Poem _____

 **Ideas** Whether or not it is expressed in grammatically correct sentences, a poem must have a topic that is clear to the reader. Well-chosen descriptive details will support the images created in the poem.

 **Organization** A poem is organized by lines and stanzas, not paragraphs. Still, the organization of lines and stanzas should have logic within the poem. Transitions may be used where necessary to help the reader follow the poem.

 **Voice** The voice should be appropriate for the feeling the poet wants to convey.

Pythagoras
by Sage Quintley

Just a man, you say?
  No way!
Born on the Isle of Samos
  In the year 570 B.C.E.   ← Rhyme

His mind, it shone like
  The crystal waters flowing   ← Figurative language (simile)
Through the Aegean Sea.

He discovered a secret
  About right triangles,
    A truth about the lengths of their sides.   ← Varied line lengths to control rhythm
So listen up now,
  And let me explain.
    His genius cannot be denied!

Three sides to a right triangle—
  Side a, side b, side c.
Side c is the hypotenuse,
  Let that be as clear as can be.

Now square the lengths of sides a and b,
  Then add them,
      And what you'll discover—
Is that *that* number equals
  The square of side c.

(Just a man, you say?
  No way!)

The Pythagorean Theorem—it's more than just a theory!

Poem **459**

Word Choice Poems aim to convey clear, striking images to the reader with just a few, carefully chosen words. Precise words and figurative language are two of a poet's principal tools for accomplishing this.

Sentence Fluency In a poem, sentence fluency translates to rhythm: the lengths and patterns of the lines should be carefully planned to create flow and rhythm.

Conventions If the poet chooses to alter or ignore a conventional practice, such as capitalization or punctuation, he or she should do it in a way that is consistent and comprehensible.

Analyze
the Model

Week 1 • Day 2

Student Objectives

• Read a model poem. *(p. 459)*

Read the Model

Read "Pythagoras" aloud as students follow along in their books. Then have students close their books as you read the poem again. Tell them to listen for the rhythm and rhyme of the poem, as well as the voice of the poet.

Elements of a Poem

Use the notes on the model to discuss the various elements of a poem. Refer students to What's in a Poem? on page 456 if they need to review the elements. Have students find the rhyming words in the poem. (say, way; BCE, Sea; sides, denied; c, be; b, c; say, way) Point out that the rhyme scheme in a poem does not have to be perfectly regular. Have students clap the beats as you read the poem slowly to help them understand the rhythm. Ask students to consider both the voice of the poet and the structure of the poem, and then decide what the poet's purpose was in writing this poem. (Possible response: The poet wanted to inform the reader, but in an entertaining way.)

CCSS **C**ommon **C**ore **S**tate **S**tandards

SL.7.1: Engage effectively in a range of collaborative discussions (one-on-one, in groups, and teacher-led) with diverse partners on *grade 7 topics, texts, and issues,* building on others' ideas and expressing their own clearly. **R/Lit.7.5:** Analyze how a drama's or poem's form or structure (e.g. soliloquy, sonnet) contributes to its meaning.

Analyze the Model

Student Objectives

- Learn to read a rubric. (pp. 460–461)

Use the Rubric

Explain the Rubric Explain that a rubric is a tool for planning, improving, and assessing a piece of writing. Tell students that a rubric helps a writer focus on key elements, or traits, in writing (**Ideas, Organization, Voice, Word Choice, Sentence Fluency, Conventions,** and **Presentation**). Point out that column 6 describes a very good poem, one that has received the highest score in all categories. This is what students should strive for in their own writing.

Discuss the Rubric Guide students in a discussion of the rubric. Read the descriptors that go with each trait and take a moment to point out the ways the traits support each other. For example, **Ideas** and **Organization** are closely related: When a poem focuses on a single subject, it's easy to organize descriptive details around that subject. Remind students to keep the rubric in mind when they write their own poem and again when they revise it.

Online Writing Center

Provides a variety of **interactive rubrics,** including 4-, 5-, and 6-point models.

T460 **Descriptive Writing**

Poem

Rubric

Use this 6-point rubric to plan and evaluate a poem.

	6	5	4
Ideas	The poem focuses on a single subject. Well-chosen descriptive details create clear images.	The poem focuses on a single subject. Most of the details create clear images.	The poem focuses on a single subject. A few details create clear images.
Organization	The poem is organized for description. Ideas are easy to follow.	The poem is organized for description. Most of the ideas are easy to follow.	The poem is organized. One or two ideas may not be in the best order.
Voice	The poet's voice connects with the audience from beginning to end.	The poet's voice connects with the audience most of the time.	The poet's voice is clear at first but then fades.
Word Choice	Precise vocabulary and figurative language are used purposefully and effectively.	Most words are used purposefully. One comparison could be more effective.	Most of the words are used purposefully. Several comparisons could be more effective.
Sentence Fluency	The lines and line breaks establish an appropriate cadence and rhythm.	Rhythm and flow are maintained most of the time. One or two lines may need improvement.	Rhythm and flow are maintained some of the time. Several lines need improvement.
Conventions	The writing has been carefully edited. Adjective and adverb clauses are used correctly.	Minor errors are present but do not interfere with meaning. Clauses are used correctly.	A few errors cause confusion. Several clauses may be used incorrectly.
✛ Presentation	The poem is placed attractively and neatly on the page.		

460 **Descriptive Writing**

CCSS Common Core State Standards

Poem

Writing in the Descriptive mode can engage the Common Core State Standards for a variety of modes. For example, the Ideas and Organization descriptors relate best to informative/explanatory standard **W.7.2.a,** which deals with establishing a clear topic and choosing an organizational scheme.

3	2	1	
The focus is somewhat clear. Details are few; some are not clear.	The focus is not clear. Some details may be unrelated.	The writing is not a poem. Details are not clear or are unrelated.	Ideas
Some of the ideas seem to be out of order.	The poem is not organized. The ideas are incomplete or hard to follow.	The writing is not organized. Ideas are difficult or impossible to follow.	Organization
The voice is weak and does not get or hold the audience's attention.	The voice is not clear. The audience does not know who is speaking.	The poet's voice is absent. The audience does not know who is speaking.	Voice
Most of the words are used purposefully. Comparisons may be unclear.	Many words are ordinary or overused. Comparisons are unclear or absent.	Words are very basic and limited. Some words may be used incorrectly.	Word Choice
The rhythm is inconsistent. Some line breaks interrupt the flow.	Rhythm is not established. The lines do not flow.	The lines do not make a poem.	Sentence Fluency
Many errors are repeated and cause confusion. Several clauses are used incorrectly.	Serious errors interfere with meaning. Clauses are used incorrectly.	The writing has not been edited.	Conventions

See Appendix B for 4-, 5-, and 6-point descriptive rubrics.

Apply the Rubric

Take a Poll Ask students to raise their hands to indicate what score they would give the poem on one or more of the traits. Record the results. Ask students to offer examples from the poem to support their scores. If there are students who seem to disagree with most of their classmates by a difference of two or more points, gently probe as to why they think so. If students score the poem 5 or below, ask students to suggest what the writer should do to bring up the score.

Additional Rubrics Appendix B includes 4-, 5-, and 6-point rubrics that can be used with any piece of descriptive writing. The rubrics are also available as blackline masters beginning on page T543.

The Word Choice rubric reflects narrative standard **W.7.3.d** with its emphasis on precise language and description. The voice rubric picks up the emphasis found in standard **W.7.4** on producing writing with a style that is appropriate to the purpose and audience.

CCSS **Common Core State Standards**
SL.7.1: Engage effectively in a range of collaborative discussions (one-on-one, in groups, and teacher-led) with diverse partners on *grade 7 topics, texts, and issues,* building on others' ideas and expressing their own clearly. **SL.7.1.a:** Come to discussions prepared, having read or researched material under study; explicitly draw on that preparation by referring to evidence on the topic, text, or issue to probe and reflect on ideas under discussion. **SL.7.1.b:** Follow rules for collegial discussions, track progress toward specific goals and deadlines, and define individual roles as needed. **SL.7.1.d:** Acknowledge new information expressed by others and, when warranted, modify their own views.

Analyze
the Model

Week 1 • Day 4

Student Objectives

- Read a model poem. *(p. 459)*
- Use the poem rubric. *(pp. 460–461)*
- Use the model poem to study Ideas, Organization, and Voice. *(pp. 462–463)*

Study the Model

Assess the Model Read each section on pages 462–463 with students. Discuss whether students agree or disagree with each point in Andre's assessment of the poem. Use questions such as the following to discuss the model and the traits with students. Encourage students to back up their answers with examples from the model.

- What other details tell you something about Pythagoras? (Possible responses: *He discovered a secret/About right triangles; His genius cannot be denied!*)

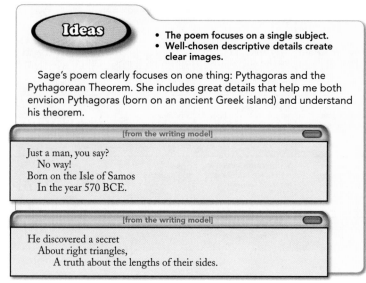

Using the Rubric to Study the Model

Did you notice that the model on page 459 points out some key elements of a poem? As she wrote "Pythagoras," Sage Quintley used these elements to help her describe a mathematical concept. She also used the 6-point rubric on pages 460–461 to plan, draft, revise, and edit the writing. A rubric is a great tool to evaluate writing during the writing process.

Now let's use the same rubric to score the model. To do this, we'll focus on each trait separately, starting with Ideas. We'll use the top descriptor for each trait (column 6), along with examples from the model, to help us understand how the traits work together. How would you score Sage on each trait?

Ideas
- The poem focuses on a single subject.
- Well-chosen descriptive details create clear images.

Sage's poem clearly focuses on one thing: Pythagoras and the Pythagorean Theorem. She includes great details that help me both envision Pythagoras (born on an ancient Greek island) and understand his theorem.

> [from the writing model]
>
> Just a man, you say?
>   No way!
> Born on the Isle of Samos
>   In the year 570 BCE.

> [from the writing model]
>
> He discovered a secret
>   About right triangles,
>   A truth about the lengths of their sides.

462 Descriptive Writing

English Language Learners

BEGINNING
Rhyme Time Use masking tape to make a dividing line on the floor. Use blue and red as the labels for each side. When you say a word, students should decide whether the word rhymes with *blue* or *red* and stand on that side of the line. Use words that students should know, such as *you, head, said, do, grew, two, led, bed.* After each word, say, *That's right. The words* red *and* bed *rhyme.*

INTERMEDIATE
Elements of a Poem Write this simple four-line poem on the board: *Roses are red/Violets are blue/Your smile is like sunshine/And your laughter is too!* Clarify any vocabulary students may not know, such as *roses, violets,* and *laughter.* Then identify the following elements of the poem: lines, figurative language (simile), rhythm, and rhyme.

Strategies for Writers Online
Go to **www.sfw.z-b.com** for additional online resources for students and teachers.

Organization
- The poem is organized for description.
- Ideas are easy to follow.

Sage's ideas are organized in a clear and logical way. She introduces her subject and then provides supportive, explanatory details. I had no problem understanding her description of Pythagoras's great discovery.

[from the writing model]

> Now square the lengths of sides a and b,
>   Then add them,
>   And what you'll discover—
> Is that *that* number equals
>   The square of side c.

Voice
- The poet's voice connects with the audience from beginning to end.

I really enjoyed reading Sage's poem. Her voice is casual and friendly, with a slight hint of humor. I felt like she was speaking directly to me, and this connection helped me stay engaged and better understand the topic.

[from the writing model]

> So listen up now,
>   And let me explain.
>   His genius cannot be denied!

Poem **463**

- How would you describe the sequence of ideas in the poem? (Possible response: introduction of Pythagoras, explanation of his theorem, explanation of why the theorem is important)

- Find another example of the direct, casual voice Sage uses in the poem. (Possible response: *Just a man, you say?/No way!*)

ADVANCED/ADVANCED HIGH

Rhyme and Rhythm To introduce the idea of poetic rhyme and rhythm, write a simple limerick on the board: *There once was a princess from Glog/Who met a nice prince with a dog/She soon married the prince/But hasn't seen him since/A spell turned him into a frog!* Ask students what they notice about the poem. If necessary, point out that lines 1, 2, and 5 all rhyme and have the same number of "beats." The same is true of lines 3 and 4. Have partners write a limerick about a geometric shape.

CCSS **C**ommon **C**ore **S**tate **S**tandards

SL.7.1: Engage effectively in a range of collaborative discussions (one-on-one, in groups, and teacher-led) with diverse partners on *grade 7 topics, texts, and issues,* building on others' ideas and expressing their own clearly. **SL.7.1.a:** Come to discussions prepared, having read or researched material under study; explicitly draw on that preparation by referring to evidence on the topic, text, or issue to probe and reflect on ideas under discussion. **SL.7.1.b:** Follow rules for collegial discussions, track progress toward specific goals and deadlines, and define individual roles as needed. **SL.7.1.c:** Pose questions that elicit elaboration and respond to others' questions and comments with relevant observations and ideas that bring the discussion back on topic as needed.

Analyze
the Model

Week 1 • Day 5

Student Objectives

- Read a model poem. *(p. 459)*
- Use the poem rubric. *(pp. 460–461)*
- Use the model poem to study Word Choice, Sentence Fluency, and Conventions. *(pp. 464–465)*

Continue the Discussion Use these questions to continue the discussion of the traits in the model poem:

- Find some examples of precise mathematical words in the poem. (*right triangles, hypotenuse*) Why is it important for Sage to use these words? (Possible response: Readers won't understand the Pythagorean Theorem if Sage is not clear and precise about her terms.)

- Identify a section of the poem that has a faster rhythm than other sections of the poem? (Possible response: *Just a man you say? No way!*) How did Sage accomplish this faster rhythm? (Possible response: The words and sentences are shorter.)

- How does Sage's use of punctuation help you follow the rhythm of the poem? (Possible response: The punctuation tells you when to pause at the end of a line and when to keep reading.)

 Strategies for Writers Online
Go to **www.sfw.z-b.com** for additional online resources for students and teachers.

 • Precise vocabulary and figurative language are used purposefully and effectively.

Sage uses an effective and clever simile at the beginning of her poem. She describes Pythagoras's mind as being so brilliant, it shines like the "crystal waters" in the Aegean Sea—the sea that just happens to surround Samos. This simile energizes the poem and adds to my vision of Pythagoras.

> [from the writing model]
>
> His mind, it shone like
>   The crystal waters flowing
> Through the Aegean Sea.

 • The lines and line breaks establish an appropriate cadence and rhythm.

While reading Sage's poem out loud, I noticed a beat or rhythm. She uses line breaks and word repetition in such a way that I can't help but read some sections faster and some slower. This rhythm was fun to read aloud and listen to.

> [from the writing model]
>
> Three sides to a right triangle—
>   Side a, side b, side c.
> Side c is the hypotenuse,
>   Let that be as clear as can be.

Technology Tip — for 21st Century Literacies

Writing doesn't have to be solitary. Use this opportunity to nudge students toward writing collaboratively and, if possible, to do so with someone outside of the classroom. Use the connective resources discussed in earlier tips to find partner classes with whom students can work. Then use an online writing tool with real-time updates (such as Google Docs or EtherPad) to have students compose their poems together. You'll want to establish some means of keeping track of versions of their work for unpacking later, another benefit of most online tools. Again, the goal is to create a cohesive poem—together.

See **www.sfw.z-b.com** for further information about and links to these websites and tools.

Conventions
- The writing has been carefully edited.
- Adjective and adverb clauses are used correctly.

Even though poems have more flexibility as far as structure and form, conventions are still important. Sage did a nice job of using grammar, capitalization, and punctuation in a way that is not only clear but also effective for her poem. She even used parentheses correctly.

[from the writing model]

(Just a man, you say?
  No way!)
The Pythagorean Theorem—it's more than just a theory!

✚ Presentation The poem is placed attractively and neatly on the page.

My Turn!

Now it's my turn to write a poem. I'll use the rubric and good writing strategies to help me. Follow along to see how I do it.

Differentiating Instruction

ENRICHMENT
Research Poems Have students work individually or in groups to find a poem they like that represents the traits described in the rubric. Have students find examples that illustrate each trait in the poem.

REINFORCEMENT
Practice Reading Aloud To help students understand the function of line breaks and punctuation in a poem, choose a poem such as "Sick" by Shel Silverstein and read it aloud. Discuss how you knew where to pause and where to read on.

Presentation Remind students that they must consider presentation when they prepare their final copy. Visual presentation is especially important with a poem. Students' poems should be centered vertically on the page, set flush left (unless the poem's structure requires something specific), and include space between stanzas, if stanzas are used. Readers will be more attracted to a poem that is visually appealing, and the neat presentation will make the poem easier to read and appreciate. This is a great time to emphasize how a poem's structure can help affect its tone and/or meaning.

Think About the Traits Once students have thoroughly discussed the model poem, ask them which traits they think are most important in this type or writing. Of course, all the traits are important in every piece of writing, but some of them stand out more in some genres than in others. Students might say, for example, that in a poem **Word Choice** is of special importance because clear and precise images are so important. Students might also mention **Sentence Fluency** because line lengths and breaks are important in establishing and maintaining the poem's rhythm.

CCSS **Common Core State Standards**

SL.7.1: Engage effectively in a range of collaborative discussions (one-on-one, in groups, and teacher-led) with diverse partners on *grade 7 topics, texts, and issues,* building on others' ideas and expressing their own clearly. **SL.7.1.c:** Pose questions that elicit elaboration and respond to others' questions and comments with relevant observations and ideas that bring the discussion back on topic as needed. **SL.7.1.d:** Acknowledge new information expressed by others and, when warranted, modify their own views.

Write
a Poem

Week 2 • Day 1

Student Objectives

• Read and understand a prewriting strategy. *(p. 466)*

Prewrite

Focus on Ideas

Brainstorm Ideas Have students read page 466 silently. Once students have read the page, discuss Andre's notes and his choice of topic. Point out that he chose a topic that has a variety of aspects he could describe. Tell students to start by making a list of mathematical concepts they know well—it will be difficult to write a poem about a concept they are not sure they understand clearly. Then have students review their notes and jot down descriptive details for two or three of the concepts. Students may then choose a concept they are comfortable with and that allows them to easily think of several descriptive details.

Once students have chosen their topic, have them take a few moments to think about it and add any more descriptive details that come to mind.

Online Writing Center

Provides **interactive graphic organizers** as well as a variety of graphic organizers in PDF format.

T466 Descriptive Writing

Prewrite

Focus on **Ideas**

The Rubric Says	The poem focuses on a single subject.
Writing Strategy	Choose a topic. Make a list of descriptive details.

Well, this is different! My math teacher has asked everyone in class to explain a mathematical concept—*in a poem.* I've never thought to do that, but this assignment sounds like fun. Each student gets to choose a subject, but we have to make it clear through the use of descriptive details that we fully understand the topic. What will I write about? I'm excited to use my creativity and unique point of view. I'll start by taking some notes on the possible topics I could cover. Then I'll decide which to use and take it from there.

Possible Math Poem Topics

— pi and circles—finding the circumference and diameter
— understanding mean, median, mode, and range
— identifying angles—right, acute, obtuse *This is the one!*
   —right angle is ninety degrees
     —corner of a room, corner of a street
   —acute angle is less than ninety degrees
     —clothespin, alligator jaws
   —obtuse angle is greater than ninety degrees
     —open magazine, mostly extended arm

Apply

Brainstorm possible topics for your poem. Jot down a few notes about each. Then choose one for your poem's subject.

466 Descriptive Writing

English Language Learners

BEGINNING/INTERMEDIATE

Math Words As a class, brainstorm a list of math words. Define any words students do not know. Have students categorize their words into operations, symbols, names of mathematicians, and types of math. Have students tell what math topic they would like to write a poem about.

ADVANCED/ADVANCED HIGH

Descriptive Details Have students use a Web graphic organizer to write down ideas about their selected math concepts. Each "branch" of the web should contain an aspect of the math concept that they want to explore. For each aspect, have students list words they can use to accurately and creatively describe it.

Prewrite

Focus on **Organization**

The Rubric Says	The poem is organized for description.
Writing Strategy	Use a Web to plan the poem.

I've decided to focus on different types of angles. I've worked hard this year learning how to differentiate between right, acute, and obtuse angles, and I'd like to share my knowledge with my reader. I'll organize the facts and details in a Web. This graphic organizer will be a huge help when I draft my poem. All the details will be right there in front of me, guiding me as I write.

Web

- **angles**
  - **right**
    - street intersections, my road
    - no curves at all
    - 90 degrees
    - corners of my room
  - **acute**
    - less than 90 degrees
    - alligator's mouth
    - looks like greater-than and less-than symbols
    - wooden clothespins
  - **obtuse**
    - an open book or magazine
    - internal angles of certain shapes
    - most rooftops
    - greater than 90 degrees
    - an arm or leg bent only a little

Reflect
Review Andre's Web. In what ways will it help him draft his poem?

Apply
Create a Web using facts and details about your topic.

Poem 467

Conferencing

PEER TO PEER Have partners exchange Webs. Tell students to suggest one detail or category that could be added to their partner's web.

PEER GROUPS Have students work in groups of three or four. Each student passes his or her Web to the student on the left. Students use sticky notes to indicate the details they think are the most interesting and one detail they think needs clarification. Students continue passing the Webs until each student has reviewed each group member's Web.

TEACHER-LED Hold conferences with individual students about their Webs. Review the Webs to make sure all details are accurate and offer suggestions to students who are having trouble thinking of details or categories.

Write
a Poem

Week 2 • Day 2

Student Objectives

- Make a Web to plan the poem. (p. 467)

Prewrite

Focus on

Organize Ideas Make sure students understand the organization of the Web. Ask volunteers to name the central topic, the categories, and the details for each category. Discuss why a Web is a useful way to organize information visually. (It shows how the different categories and details are connected.) Have students compare Andre's Web to his notes on page 466. Has Andre added or left out any details from the notes? (added)

Have students create Webs based on their notes. Then instruct them to take some time to review their Webs to see whether they want to add more details.

CCSS **Common Core State Standards**

W.7.2.a: Introduce a topic clearly, previewing what is to follow; organize ideas, concepts, and information, using strategies such as definition, classification, comparison/contrast, and cause/effect; include formatting (e.g., headings), graphics (e.g., charts, tables), and multimedia when useful to aiding comprehension. **W.7.2.b:** Develop the topic with relevant facts, definitions, concrete details, quotations, or other information and examples.

Poem T467

Write
a Poem

Week 2 • Day 3

Student Objectives

- Begin writing, using figurative language. (pp. 468–469)

Draft

Focus on **Word Choice**

Draft a Poem In drafting, students should focus on developing the basic structure of their poems, as well as the use of precise and figurative language, to help them clearly and effectively get their ideas across.

Have students read Andre's poem on page 469. Ask for students' personal reactions to the use of personification in Andre's poem. Does it make the poem more personal? Is the image humorous or dull? Ask students which images they liked best and found most effective in the second half of the poem.

Point out that Andre repeatedly refers to the rubric as he writes. Encourage students to get into the habit of using the rubric to guide their own writing.

Tell students they may use a poetry form they are familiar with or they may write their poems in free verse. Remind them to use precise language and figures of speech.

Online Writing Center

Provides student eBooks with an **interactive writing pad** for drafting, revising, editing, and publishing.

Draft

Focus on  **Word Choice**

The Rubric Says	Precise vocabulary and figurative language are used purposefully and effectively.
Writing Strategy	Choose words and phrases for effect.

With all of my details organized in a Web, I'm ready to draft my poem. The rubric reminds me to use vocabulary and figurative language purposefully and effectively. There are typically fewer words in poems, so I have to be sure to use only words and phrases that will help me clearly describe my topic—angles.

The more descriptive language I use—such as adjectives, adjective clauses, adverbs, and adverb clauses—the more clearly my reader will "see" each angle I describe. I also used personification—a type of figurative language—to help engage the reader and present my topic in a new and creative way.

As I draft, I won't worry about making mistakes. I just want to get my ideas down on paper first. I'll fix any errors later on.

> **Writer's Term**_____
> **Personification**
> **Personification** is giving an inanimate object (such as a mountain) or abstract quality (such as honor) human or lifelike qualities (such as thoughts, feelings, or personalities). *The mountain hungered for the morning sun* is one example.

468 Descriptive Writing

Differentiating Instruction

ENRICHMENT

Choose a Complex Form Have students research poetry forms and choose a more complex form, such as a sonnet or ballad, in which to write their poems. Students may want to write their poems as a series of shorter poems in challenging forms such as a haiku or a limerick.

REINFORCEMENT

Choose a Simple Form Help students choose a simple mathematical concept, or assign a concept if students are having trouble thinking of one. Offer students a selection of poetic forms that are more straightforward, such as quatrain, cinquain, or acrostic, from which to choose.

[DRAFT]

Angles
by Andre

So I decided, to invite some over
And settle it once and for all.
Soon a crowd of angles
Were standing in my front hall.

Angels can be hard
When you don't know them by name.
If you've never met
They all might look the same

Each one introduced itself and a
Pattern was quickly shown.
I wrote it down and now I know
What my math teachers have always known.

[used personification]

Right angles: 90 degrees—
　　The corners of my room
　　Lines that go up and across,
　　At the corner of my street.

Acute angles: less than 90—
　　A "less than" or "greater than" sign
　　A clothespin, an open alligators mouth
　　But no more than 90 degrees by design.

Obtuce angles: greater than 90—
　　My father's mostly extended arm
　　An open magazine, the library roof
　　Each internal angle of a regular octagon.

Now I know each angle's name
Which all depends on the degrees.
but can someone help me figure out
How to serve angles biscits and tea.

Reflect

How did Andre do? In what ways did his Web help him organize his poem?

Apply

Use your Web to draft your poem. Remember to focus on one topic, use precise words, and have fun with figurative language.

Poem **469**

Conferencing

PEER TO PEER Have partners read their drafts aloud to each other. If students are uncomfortable with reading aloud, allow them to exchange drafts to read silently. Have each student tell which image he or she liked best in his or her partner's poem and ask one question about an image that may need clarification.

PEER GROUPS Have students work in groups of three or four. Have each student describe one figure of speech from his or her draft and have the group discuss ways the figure of speech might be changed or improved. Students may or may not choose to adopt the suggestions.

TEACHER-LED Hold conferences with individual students. Read students' drafts aloud if they are comfortable with you doing so. Comment on rhythm as well as on the use of language.

Write
a Poem

Week 2 • Day 4

Student Objectives
• Complete a draft.

✏ Writer's Term
Personification can be used to convey any tone the poet chooses, but images and words must be chosen carefully to ensure that the intended tone is portrayed. For example, when poorly used, personification can be unintentionally humorous (e.g., *They gazed in terror at the mad scientist and knew they were in the hands of a brain with very evil intentions.*) Have students think about what emotional overtones they want to convey before they choose how they will personify their chosen mathematical concept. Tell students to read over any instances where they use personification to ensure they have not accidentally created a mental image or tone that contradicts their purpose.

CCSS **C**ommon **C**ore **S**tate **S**tandards
W.7.3.d: Use precise words and phrases, relevant descriptive details, and sensory language to capture the action and convey experiences and events. **W.7.4:** Produce clear and coherent writing in which the development, organization, and style are appropriate to task, purpose, and audience. **W.7.5:** With some guidance and support from peers and adults, develop and strengthen writing as needed by planning, revising, editing, rewriting, or trying a new approach, focusing on how well purpose and audience have been addressed. **SL.7.1.b:** Follow rules for collegial discussions, track progress toward specific goals and deadlines, and define individual roles as needed.

Write
a Poem

Week 2 • Day 5

Student Objectives

- Revise for well-chosen details. (p. 470)

Revise

Focus on Ideas

Choose Details Carefully Have students read page 470. Have them discuss why *Lines that go up and across* and *At the corner of my street* are ineffective. (Possible response: The images are too vague and don't necessarily describe right angles. "Up and across" could indicate any direction, and streets don't always cross at right angles.) Have students discuss why Andre's revisions are an improvement. (Possible responses: They give clearer, more concrete examples of things that have right angles; the image of a balloon with no right angles is surprising and different.)

Have students review their poems and look for vague details that can be replaced with more specific or lively ones.

Strategies for Writers Online
Go to **www.sfw.z-b.com** for additional online resources for students and teachers.

Writing a Poem

Revise

Focus on Ideas

The Rubric Says   Well-chosen descriptive details create clear images.

Writing Strategy   Choose details that bring the topic to life.

After rereading my poem, I realized that some of my details were confusing and ineffective. The details *Lines that go up and across* and *At the corners of my street* don't effectively or vividly "show" a right angle at all. So I revised these details for more accurate and creative images, and I'm happy with my changes. What do you think?

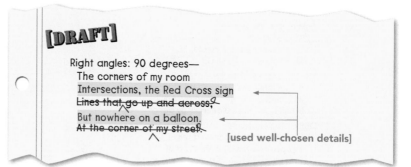

[DRAFT]

Right angles: 90 degrees—
The corners of my room
Intersections, the Red Cross sign
~~Lines that go up and across;~~
But nowhere on a balloon.
~~At the corner of my street.~~

[used well-chosen details]

Apply

Use details that creatively and vividly describe or explain the subject of your poem.

English Language Learners

BEGINNING/INTERMEDIATE

Lines and Stanzas Select a simple two-stanza poem and read it to students. Explain any unknown vocabulary. Have students point out an example of a line and a stanza. Tell students that each stanza tells a different idea about the subject. Cut apart the lines of the poem and have partners work together to put the lines in order. Remind them that all poetry should have a logical order.

ADVANCED/ADVANCED HIGH

Organizing a Poem Distribute a short, nonfiction essay to students. Have them identify the main idea and details in the essay. Then have partners work together to create a poem using the information from the essay. Their poem may have rhyme or rhythm, but it must be separated into lines and stanzas. Each stanza should tell about one aspect of the subject of the original essay.

Revise

The Rubric Says	The poem is organized for description. Ideas are easy to follow.
Writing Strategy	Check the order of the lines and stanzas.

When I reread the first two stanzas of my poem, even I felt some confusion. As I read the first line, I felt like I had missed something. Then I realized that if I switched the order of the stanzas, everything made more sense. I needed to explain *why* I invited angles to my house *first* for the reader to easily follow along. Then the crowd of angles in my front hall made sense.

[DRAFT]

So I decided, to invite some over

And settle it once and for all.

Soon a crowd of angles

Were standing in my front hall.

Angles
~~Angels~~ can be hard

When you don't know them by name.

If you've never met

They all might look the same

[revised stanza order for clarity]

Reflect

What do you think? How has Andre's revision helped clarify the ideas and images in his poem?

Apply

Organize your poem's lines and stanzas effectively, so that the reader can easily follow along.

Poem **471**

Conferencing

PEER TO PEER Have partners exchange drafts and read them silently. Then have each partner point out a detail that he or she feels needs improvement. Tell the pairs to discuss how the details can be revised to be clearer and/or more interesting.

PEER GROUPS Have small groups pass their drafts around for each member to read silently. Then have students discuss how they chose the details they included in their poems. Encourage group members to offer helpful suggestions if necessary.

TEACHER-LED Hold conferences with pairs or groups of students about revising for order. Have students read the drafts silently, and then coach them on how to offer helpful suggestions.

Write
a Poem

Week 3 • Day 1

Student Objectives

- Revise for order of lines and stanzas. *(p. 471)*

Revise

Focus on  Organization

Order Lines and Stanzas Make sure students know the definition of a stanza. Point to a stanza in the model and explain that a stanza has a function similar to that of a paragraph in prose. Like a paragraph, a stanza focuses on one idea or image. Mention, however, that stanzas are generally much less structured than paragraphs and are not required to have topic sentences or transitions.

Read the rubric and writing strategy on page 471 aloud. Then have students read Andre's words and the draft excerpt silently. Discuss Andre's revision and why the order of ideas in a poem has to make sense, just as it does in prose.

Remind students to revise their poems so that the meaning is clear to the audience.

CCSS Common Core State Standards

W.7.2.a: Introduce a topic clearly, previewing what is to follow; organize ideas, concepts, and information, using strategies such as definition, classification, comparison/contrast, and cause/effect; include formatting (e.g., headings), graphics (e.g., charts, tables), and multimedia when useful to aiding comprehension. **W.7.3.d:** Use precise words and phrases, relevant descriptive details, and sensory language to capture the action and convey experiences and events. **W.7.5:** With some guidance and support from peers and adults, develop and strengthen writing as needed by planning, revising, editing, rewriting, or trying a new approach, focusing on how well purpose and audience have been addressed.

Write
a Poem

Week 3 • Day 2

Student Objectives

• Revise for line breaks. *(p. 472)*

Revise

Focus on

Vary Sentence Patterns Have students read page 472 silently. Discuss Andre's words and talk about why it's important to read a poem aloud in order to get a feel for the line breaks. Read the entire model on page 469 aloud once and then read the draft excerpt on page 472 aloud twice. The first time, have students follow along as you read; the second time have them listen with their eyes closed. Ask students whether listening to the poem helped them understand Andre's revision.

Tell students to read their poems aloud a few times and make any necessary changes to the line breaks.

Online Writing Center

 Provides **interactive proofreading activities** for each genre.

Revise
Focus on **Sentence Fluency**

The Rubric Says	The lines and line breaks establish an appropriate cadence and rhythm.
Writing Strategy	Place line breaks where they make sense.

When you work with prose (any writing that is not poetry), using a variety of complete sentences helps the writing flow easily. In poetry, you create rhythm and flow by grouping words together and carefully placing the breaks between lines. A poet needs to read the poem out loud several times to know exactly where to break a line and which words should be spoken together. As I read my poem out loud, I found a spot where the rhythm was off. So I revised the line break for the cadence, or beat, I wanted.

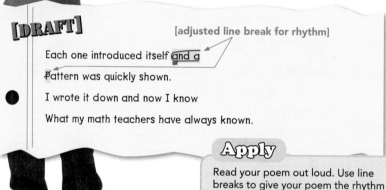

[DRAFT]

[adjusted line break for rhythm]

Each one introduced itself and a

Pattern was quickly shown.

I wrote it down and now I know

What my math teachers have always known.

Apply

Read your poem out loud. Use line breaks to give your poem the rhythm you want to achieve.

472 Descriptive Writing

Optional Revising Lessons

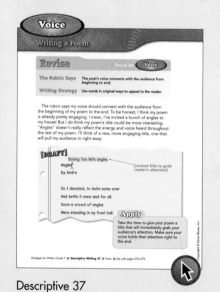

Descriptive 37

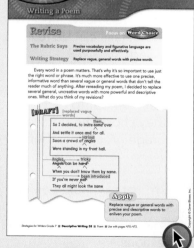

Descriptive 38

Go to **Strategies for Writers Grade 7 CD-ROM**

The Rubric Says   The writing has been carefully edited. Adjective and adverb clauses are used correctly.

Writing Strategy   Check the use and punctuation of adjective and adverb clauses.

Writer's Term_____

Adjective and Adverb Clauses
An **adjective clause** always begins with a relative pronoun and describes a noun. An **adverb clause** always begins with a subordinating conjunction and tells why, where, when, under what circumstances, or to what degree.

Time to fix all spelling, grammar, and punctuation mistakes. I'll also make sure adjective and adverb clauses are used correctly. If a dependent clause begins a sentence, a comma should immediately follow the clause.

[DRAFT]

Now I know each angle's name,

Which all depends on the degrees.   [fixed spelling and punctuation errors]

but can someone help me figure out

How to serve angles biscits and tea

Reflect

How did Andre do with his editing? Can you find any mistakes he might have missed?

Apply   **Conventions**

Edit your draft for spelling, punctuation, and capitalization. Check all adjective and adverb clauses.

For more practice identifying adjective and adverb clauses, use the exercises on the next two pages.

Poem **473**

Related Grammar Practice _____

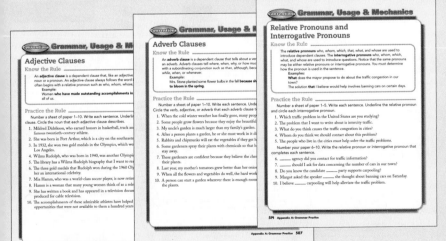

Student Edition pages 506, 507, 514

Go to ➡ **Appendix A: Grammar Practice**

Write
a Poem

Week 3 • Day 3

Student Objectives

• Edit for correct use of adverb and adjective clauses. (p. 473)

Edit

Focus on **Conventions**

Explain that while the strategy in the editing lesson is to check adjective and adverb clauses, students should also look for and fix any other errors. Suggest that they read their poems over several times, checking a different type of convention each time.

Use the mini-lessons on pages T474–475 for students having problems with adjective and adverb clauses. Then have students complete the exercises on pages 474–475. Go over their answers in class.

✏ **Writer's Term_____**

Adjective and Adverb Clauses
To recognize adjective clauses, students should look for relative pronouns such as *which, who, whom, whose,* or *that.* To recognize adverb clauses, students should look for subordinating conjunctions such as *although, because, if, as, as if, than, while, when,* or *whenever.*

CCSS Common Core State Standards
L.7.1: Demonstrate command of the conventions of standard English grammar and usage when writing or speaking. **L.7.1.c:** Place phrases and clauses within a sentence, recognizing and correcting misplaced and dangling modifiers.

Poem **T473**

Student Objectives

- Identify adjective clauses and use them correctly. *(p. 474)*

Adjective Clauses

Explain to students that an adjective clause has the same function as an adjective—it modifies a noun or a pronoun. Write the following on the board: *Look at that cute baby! That's my sister, who is really cute when she giggles.* Circle *cute* in the first sentence and draw a line to *baby* to show the noun it modifies. Circle *who is really cute when she giggles* in the second sentence and draw a line to *sister* to show the noun it modifies.

Read Know the Rule on page 474 aloud to students, and then discuss restrictive and nonrestrictive clauses. Write the following on the board and have students call out *restrictive* or *nonrestrictive* as you point to each one. Be sure that students can explain their answers.

You have the book that I need to finish the assignment. (restrictive)

My math book, which I need for my assignment tonight, is awfully heavy. (nonrestrictive)

The math teacher, who looks a little like my Uncle Lou, is really very nice. (nonrestrictive)

Online Writing Center

Provides **interactive grammar games** and **practice activities** in student eBook.

Conventions Grammar, Usage & Mechanics

Adjective Clauses

Know the Rule

A clause has a subject and a verb. An **adjective clause** is a dependent clause that describes a noun or a pronoun. An adjective clause always follows the word it describes and begins with a relative pronoun such as *who, whom, whose, which,* or *that.*

Example: Ming has math in the room that overlooks the parking lot.

When a clause is essential to the meaning of a sentence, it is restrictive. If the clause can be removed without affecting the meaning of the sentence, it is nonrestrictive. Separate nonrestrictive clauses from the rest of the sentence with commas.

Example: I need my math book, which is on the kitchen table.

Practice the Rule

Read the following sentences. On a separate sheet of paper, write each adjective clause and then indicate whether it is restrictive or nonrestrictive.

1. I'm off for a week's vacation with my aunt, who just happens to be this year's state poet laureate. nonrestrictive
2. A poet laureate is a poet whom the state might call upon when a poem needs to be written for an official event. restrictive
3. Aunt Grace has written many poems that have been published in literary magazines all over the country. restrictive
4. She lives in a small, antique house with my Uncle Gabe, whose real name happens to be Gabriel. nonrestrictive
5. Aunt Grace says that the wildflowers in her fields whisper to her, which sounds so magical I wish it were true. nonrestrictive
6. My cousin River, who has grown up already and moved to the city, is also an accomplished poet. nonrestrictive
7. But River writes musical poems, or songs, that are designed to help injured children heal faster. restrictive
8. His music is used as a form of therapy in hospitals whose patients are mostly children. restrictive
9. Listening to or singing the songs strengthens the children's immune systems, which is essential for healing to take place. nonrestrictive
10. I'm so lucky to have family members who inspire me in so many ways. restrictive

Related Grammar Practice

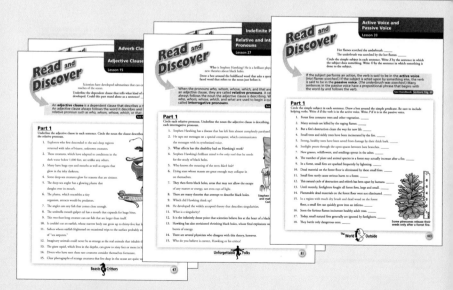

Pages 47, 49, 81, 83, 103

Go to ➡ G.U.M. Student Practice Book

Adverb Clauses

Know the Rule

An **adverb clause** is a dependent clause that tells about a verb, an adjective, or an adverb. Adverb clauses tell where, when, why, to what degree, or under what circumstances. They begin with a subordinating conjunction such as *than*, *although*, *because*, *if*, *as*, *as if*, *while*, *when*, or *whenever*. When an adverb clause begins a sentence, follow it with a comma.

Example: Before I go to the library, I'll call to be sure they are open.

Practice the Rule

Read the following sentences. On a separate sheet of paper, copy each adverb clause that you find. Then circle each subordinating conjunction.

1. I'm nearly jumping out of my skin with excitement (because) tomorrow I leave for Camp Wahoo!
2. (While) staying at Camp Wahoo last summer, I made some of the greatest friends, and I can't wait to see them again.
3. Well, I've finally arrived at Camp Wahoo's gates, and it feels (as if) I never left.
4. (Before) my parents went back home, they gave me a special gift: a beautiful, handmade journal.
5. (Although) we hike and swim here, Camp Wahoo is basically a camp for budding poets, like me!
6. (If) learning to write better poetry is your goal, this camp was designed just for you.
7. (After) we wake up, we start our day with morning exercise and breakfast, just like other summer camps.
8. (When) breakfast is over, we break into groups and study the style and writings of several famous poets from around the world.
9. I've been writing poetry in my new journal (whenever) I have time to myself.
10. I can't wait to show my journal to my teacher (after) I get home.

Mini-Lesson

Student Objectives

- Identify adverb clauses and use them correctly. *(p. 475)*

Adverb Clauses

Explain to students that an adverb clause has the same function as an adverb—it modifies an adjective, a verb, or another adverb. Write the following on the board: *I like to go to the library whenever I get the chance.* Underline *whenever I get the chance* and tell students it is an adverb clause. Draw an arrow from the clause to *go* and tell students that the adverb clause adds information about the verb *go*.

Write the following items on the board and have students tell you which are adverb clauses.

Sometimes I go walking in the woods

Because he always gets lost (adverb clause)

While you were out (adverb clause)

That's why she fell down

If I were you (adverb clause)

Never eat a berry off that bush

Tomorrow we leave for our trip

Although we knew it was a bad idea (adverb clause)

CCSS **C**ommon **C**ore **S**tate **S**tandards

L.7.1.c: Place phrases and clauses within a sentence, recognizing and correcting misplaced and dangling modifiers. **L.7.2:** Demonstrate command of the conventions of standard English capitalization, punctuation, and spelling when writing.

Write
a Poem

Week 3 • Day 4

Student Objectives

- Discuss preparation for publishing and presentation. (p. 476)
- Use a final editing checklist to publish their work. (p. 476)

Publish ⁺Presentation

Publishing Strategy Use the following questions to ask students what they think of Andre's publishing strategy:

- How do you think the multimedia presentation will enhance Andre's poem?
- What types of music and images do you think Andre should choose?

Discuss Andre's final checklist. Do students feel Andre left out any important items on his checklist? Have students make final checklists to check their own poems. Then have students think of other ways they could publish their poems, such as binding them into a class book, e-mailing them to relatives or friends, or keeping them in a poem journal.

Strategies for Writers Online
Go to **www.sfw.z-b.com** for additional online resources for students and teachers.

Publish ⁺Presentation

Publishing Strategy	Present the poem in a multimedia presentation.
Presentation Strategy	Display information clearly.

I did it! I'm so proud of my finished poem. Now to publish it in an exciting way. I think it would be fun to present my poem as a multimedia experience. I can play music and project fun images on a screen behind me as I read "Having Tea With Angles." I'll also neatly print out my poem to make it easy to read. But first I want to use my final checklist to make sure I haven't forgotten anything.

My Final Checklist

Did I—

- ✓ use and punctuate all adjective and adverb clauses correctly?
- ✓ edit for spelling, grammar, and punctuation mistakes?
- ✓ present my poem in a clear and interesting way?
- ✓ remember to put my name beneath the title?

Apply

Make your own final checklist to check your poem. Then write a final copy and publish it.

476 Descriptive Writing

Differentiating Instruction

ENRICHMENT

Create a Poem Collage Have students research images and words associated with the mathematical concepts they have chosen to illustrate in their poems and create collages on poster board. Allow students to use design software to create their posters, if they prefer.

REINFORCEMENT

Extra Practice Give students extra time to practice presenting their poems aloud and coach them in techniques for speaking to a group. If a student is unable to speak before the class, allow him or her to present his or her poem to you individually.

Having Tea With Angles

by Andre

Angles can be tricky
When you don't know them by name.
If you've never been introduced
They all might look the same.

So I decided to invite them over
And settle it once and for all.
Soon a crowd of various angles
Were standing in my front hall.

Each one introduced itself
And a pattern was quickly shown.
I wrote it down and now I know
What my math teachers have always known.

Right angles: 90 degrees—
   The corners of my room
   Intersections, the Red Cross sign
   But nowhere on a balloon.

Acute angles: less than 90—
   A "less than" or "greater than" sign
   A clothespin, an open alligator's mouth
   But no more than 90 degrees by design.

Obtuse angles: greater than 90—
   My father's mostly extended arm
   An open magazine, the library's roof
   Each internal angle of a regular octagon.

Now I know each angle's name,
Which all depends on the degrees.
But can someone help me figure out
How to serve angles biscuits and tea?

Reflect

What do you think? Did Andre use all the traits of a good poem? Check it against the rubric. Then use the rubric to check your own poem.

Technology Tip for 21st Century Literacies

Publishing work for a global audience requires that writers carefully consider how their ideas fit the modes of expression they are using. Ask students to move their written poem into a collaborative and multimodal writing space like Glogster or Popplet. Working in pairs (either with a face-to-face or electronic writing partner), create a presentation of the poem that uses at least three different modes (e.g., audio, image, motion). Then ask students to provide a rationale for their choices. How does each mode communicate? How did the partners come together to make those decisions?

See **www.sfw.z-b.com** for further information about and links to these websites and tools.

Write
a Poem

Week 3 • Day 5

Student Objectives

- Use a poem rubric. *(pp. 460–461)*
- Share a published poem. *(p. 477)*

Presentation Strategy Encourage students to search online for images to use with their presentations. Remind them to avoid copyrighted images because plagiarism is a serious offense. Remind students to use appropriate eye contact, adequate volume, and clear pronunciation when they speak in front of their classmates. Encourage students to practice their presentations at least once for a friend or family member before they present to the class.

Reflecting on a Poem

Ask students to share their thoughts about writing a poem. What surprised them? What worked well for them?

CCSS **C**ommon **C**ore **S**tate **S**tandards

W.7.4: Produce clear and coherent writing in which the development, organization, and style are appropriate to task, purpose, and audience. **W.7.5:** With some guidance and support from peers and adults, develop and strengthen writing as needed by planning, revising, editing, rewriting, or trying a new approach, focusing on how well purpose and audience have been addressed. **SL.7.1:** Engage effectively in a range of collaborative discussions (one-on-one, in groups, and teacher-led) with diverse partners on *grade 7 topics, texts, and issues,* building on others' ideas and expressing their own clearly. **SL.7.4:** Present claims and findings, emphasizing salient points in a focused, coherent manner with pertinent descriptions, facts, details, and examples; use appropriate eye contact, adequate volume, and clear pronunciation. **SL.7.5:** Include multimedia components and visual displays in presentations to clarify claims and findings and emphasize salient points.

Descriptive Test Planner

WEEK 1

Day 1
Introduce
Descriptive Test Writing

Student Objectives
- Learn the components of the writing prompt.

Student Activities
- Read and discuss **Read the Writing Prompt.** (*pp. 478–479*)

Day 2
Analyze
Introduce the Scoring Guide

Student Objectives
- Recognize the relationship of the scoring guide to the rubric and the six traits of writing.
- Read a model writing test response.

Student Activities
- Read and discuss **Writing Traits in the Scoring Guide.** (*p. 480*)
- Read **"The Ice Storm."** (*p. 481*)

Day 3
Analyze
Apply the Scoring Guide

Student Objectives
- Apply the scoring guide to a model test response.

Student Activities
- Read and discuss **Using the Scoring Guide to Study the Model.** (*pp. 482–483*)

WEEK 2

Day 1
Write
Prewrite: Ideas

Student Objectives
- Read and understand a writing test prompt for descriptive writing.
- Apply the six traits of writing to the writing prompt.

Student Activities
- Read and discuss **Prewrite: Focus on Ideas.** (*pp. 486–487*)

Day 2
Write
Prewrite: Ideas

Student Objectives
- Learn how to respond to the task in the writing prompt.

Student Activities
- Read and discuss **Prewrite: Focus on Ideas.** (*p. 488*)

Day 3
Write
Prewrite: Organization

Student Objectives
- Learn how to choose a graphic organizer for the writing prompt.

Student Activities
- Read and discuss **Prewrite: Focus on Organization.** (*p. 489*)

WEEK 3

Day 1
Write
Revise: Organization

Student Objectives
- Revise for logical presentation of details.

Student Activities
- Read and discuss **Revise: Focus on Organization.** (*p. 494*)

Day 2
Write
Revise: Voice

Student Objectives
- Revise to connect with readers.

Student Activities
- Read and discuss **Revise: Focus on Voice.** (*p. 495*)

Note: Optional Revising Lessons appear on the *Strategies for Writers* CD-ROM.

Day 3
Write
Revise: Word Choice

Student Objectives
- Revise to replace vague words and phrases with precise ones.

Student Activities
- Read and discuss **Revise: Focus on Word Choice.** (*p. 496*)

Day 4	**Day 5**

Analyze
Apply the Scoring Guide

Student Objectives
- Continue to apply the scoring guide to a model test response.

Student Activities
- Read and discuss **Using the Scoring Guide to Study the Model.** (p. 484)

Analyze
Time Management

Student Objectives
- Learn how to plan time during a writing test.

Student Activities
- Read and discuss **Planning My Time.** (p. 485)

Day 4	**Day 5**

Write
Prewrite: Organization

Student Objectives
- Learn how to check the graphic organizer against the scoring guide.

Student Activities
- Read and discuss **Prewrite: Focus on Organization.** (pp. 490–491)

Write
Draft: Ideas

Student Objectives
- Use the graphic organizer to begin a writing test response that uses sensory details to paint a visual image.

Student Activities
- Read and discuss **Draft: Focus on Ideas.** (pp. 492–493)
- Draft a descriptive writing test.

Day 4	**Day 5**

Write
Edit: Conventions

Student Objectives
- Edit the writing test response for proper grammar, spelling, capitalization, and punctuation.

Student Activities
- Read and discuss **Edit: Focus on Conventions.** (pp. 497–498)

Review
Test Tips

Student Objectives
- Review tips for writing for a test.

Student Activities
- Read and discuss the **Test Tips.** (p. 499)

complete the chapter in fewer days, combine the learning objectives and activities in a way that supports students as they write.

Resources at-a-Glance

Differentiating Instruction

Using the Scoring
For additional Differentiating Instruction activities, see Strategies for Writers *Extensions Online at* **www.sfw.z-b.com.**

English Language Learners

Using the Scoring

 Connection Letter
Reproducible letter (in English and Spanish) appears on the *Strategies for Writers* CD-ROM and at **www.sfw.z-b.com.**

Online Essay Grader and Writing Tutor

Powered by Vantage Learning's MY Access!®, includes writing prompts and ongoing feedback for students as they write. Available for Grades 5–8.

Online Writing Center

Provides IWB resources, interactive games and practice activities, videos, eBooks, and a virtual file cabinet.

 Strategies for Writers Online

Go to **www.sfw.z-b.com** for free online resources for students and teachers.

Introduce
Descriptive Test Writing

Student Objectives

• Learn the components of the writing prompt. (pp. 478–479)

Introduce the Writing Prompt

Descriptive Test Writing In this chapter, students will apply what they have learned about descriptive writing to the challenge of taking a descriptive writing test. Remind students that they will sometimes write on demand to complete an assignment or test. Tell students that when they write for a test, they will receive a writing prompt and a certain amount of time in which to write. Then their writing will be evaluated, just as with any test. Assure students that they do not need to be anxious about writing a test. The skills they have already practiced will help them do a good job. Direct their attention to the three parts of the writing prompt on pages 478–479.

Setup The setup does just what its name says: it sets the writer up to do a good job. The setup gets writers to think about the writing topic in general before they choose a topic that is appropriate for a writing assignment this size.

Strategies for Writers Online
Go to **www.sfw.z-b.com** for additional online resources for students and teachers.

Descriptive
test writing

Read the Writing Prompt

When you take a writing test, you will be given a writing prompt. Most writing prompts have three parts:

Setup This part of the writing prompt gives you the background information you need to get ready to write.

Task This part of the writing prompt tells you exactly what you are supposed to write: an observation report.

Scoring Guide This section tells how your writing will be scored. To do well on the test, you should include everything on the list.

Remember the rubrics you used earlier in the unit? When you take a writing test, you don't always have all of the information that's on a rubric. However, the scoring guide is a lot like a rubric. It lists everything you need to think about to write a good paper. Like the rubrics you've used in this unit, many scoring guides are based upon these important traits of writing:

Ideas · Organization · Voice · Word Choice · Sentence Fluency · Conventions

Online Essay Grader and Writing Tutor

Powered by Vantage Learning's MY Access!®, this tool gives students

• immediate, ongoing, sentence-by-sentence feedback.

• helpful suggestions to improve their draft.

• a holistic score and a trait-specific score on their final draft.

• unlimited response submissions to the prompts.

Think about a time of extreme or out-of-the-ordinary weather, such as a thunderstorm, hail, or even snow. It can be something you saw in person or that you learned about on the news.

Write an observation report that describes in detail what you saw or experienced.

Be sure your writing

- has sensory details that paint a visual image.
- has details arranged in a natural and logical order.
- uses a voice that suits the audience and purpose.
- uses precise words and phrases to develop the topic.
- uses a variety of sentence lengths and types.
- contains correct grammar, punctuation, capitalization, and spelling.

Task The task tells students not only what to write about but also what kind of writing to do: narrative, descriptive, informative/explanatory, or argument. Tell students that even the best-written test will not receive a strong grade if it misses the topic or uses a form of writing other than the assigned form. Students must follow the instructions in the task.

Scoring Guide The scoring guide helps students plan and evaluate their writing. Help students understand how the scoring guide is similar to the rubrics they have seen by asking these questions:

- Which bullet focuses on the ideas in the writing? (the first bullet)

- Which bullet encourages you to improve your sentence fluency? (the fifth bullet)

- Which bullet focuses on the organization of the writing? (the second bullet)

CCSS **C**ommon **C**ore **S**tate **S**tandards

SL.7.1: Engage effectively in a range of collaborative discussions (one-on-one, in groups, and teacher-led) with diverse partners on *grade 7 topics, texts, and issues,* building on others' ideas and expressing their own clearly. **SL.7.1.b:** Follow rules for collegial discussions, track progress toward specific goals and deadlines, and define individual roles as needed.

Analyze
the Scoring Guide

Week 1 • Day 2

Student Objectives

• Recognize the relationship of the scoring guide to the rubric and the six traits of writing.

• Read a writing prompt response model. (pp. 480–481)

Writing Traits in the Scoring Guide

Scoring Guide as a Rubric

Remind students how they used rubrics to guide, evaluate, and improve their writing of other descriptive pieces. Point out that in a writing test, the scoring guide acts as a rubric. Ask students for definitions and examples of each item in each category. For example, ask:

• What type of voice would be appropriate when writing for an audience of parents and school administrators? (Possible response: serious and formal)

• What order have you used to organize details in the types of descriptive writing you have done? (Possible responses: chronological, 5 W's, the five senses)

• What are some precise words you could use to replace the vague word *good*? (Possible responses: wonderful, suitable, tasty, talented)

Writing Traits
in the Scoring Guide

The scoring guide in the prompt on page 479 has been made into this chart. Does it remind you of the rubrics you've used? Not all prompts include all the writing traits, but this one does. Use them to do your best writing. Remember to write neatly and put your name on each page.

• Be sure your writing has sensory details that paint a visual image.

• Be sure your writing has details arranged in a natural and logical order.

• Be sure your writing uses a voice that suits the audience and purpose.

• Be sure your writing uses precise words and phrases to develop the topic.

• Be sure your writing uses a variety of sentence lengths and types.

• Be sure your writing contains correct grammar, punctuation, capitalization, and spelling.

Look at Merritt Graves's story on the next page. Did she follow the scoring guide?

480 Descriptive Writing

English Language Learners

BEGINNING

The Writing Process Review the steps in the writing process using simple words. Use the following words to substitute for *prewrite, draft, revise, edit,* and *publish: about/plan, write, change, fix,* and *show.* Remind students to follow all of these steps during a writing test.

INTERMEDIATE

Logical Order To help with organization during a descriptive writing test, suggest students use a Sequence Chain graphic organizer. Give partners a brief story to read. Have them complete a graphic organizer to track the events of the story. Then have them trade stories and Sequence Chains with another pair who will read the story and verify the correct order of events.

The Ice Storm

by Merritt Graves

Snow! Awakening early, I peek outside to glimpse what looks like snow on the ground. I go out to get a closer look and thump! I slip and fall to the ground. This isn't snow; it's something much meaner and more deceiving. It's a North Texas ice storm, and I've fallen right into its frigid, slippery trap.

I push myself up with my bare hands. The ice on the ground is numbing, and my fingers get a chill. I blow on them and see the puffs of white come out of my mouth. The air is cold and damp and feels as though it's going right through my body. Carefully, I navigate my way back inside. I'd rather view the ice storm from the warmth of our house.

Now I take a closer look at what nature has dealt us. The trees are frosted. Their branches look burdened with the weight of the ice pulling them down. The grass has a layer of frost on it, its blades each coated with rain and dampness that's been frozen overnight. The metal on our patio furniture has a glaze to it, and the cushions are coated with a frosty layer.

I let our dog, Muzzles, a small, white Maltese, go outside. Crunch, crunch, crunch, go his little paws on the grass, leaving behind indentations in the ice with each step he takes. I notice Muzzles's footsteps are the only sounds; today, no cars rush by on their morning commute. Muzzles quickly turns around and heads for the door, sliding along the ice-covered patio before making it inside.

The skies still look angry—cloudy and gray and still. It's as though they want to make sure the ice doesn't melt any time soon. I know that until it does melt, much of the town will stay tucked indoors.

Descriptive Test **481**

Tell students that they will sometimes use writing prompts that do not include guidance for each of the six categories in the rubric by name. However, students can use their writing experience to remember the main requirements:

- clear details that put readers in the picture
- logical organization
- a voice that is appropriate to both topic and audience
- language that is clear and precise
- sentences that flow well with a variety in lengths and patterns
- accurate and thorough editing for spelling, punctuation, and capitalization

Read the Model

Writing Prompt Response Read "The Ice Storm" aloud as students follow along in their books. Tell students to keep the requirements of the scoring guide in mind as they follow along. After reading the story aloud, ask students how the story is organized. (according to the senses) Call on volunteers to explain which sensory details they found most effective and why.

ADVANCED
Using Precise Words Write a generic word, such as *fine*, on the board. Use the Web or Continuum Scale graphic organizer to brainstorm other words that have the same meaning as *fine* or have stronger meanings. For example, on a Continuum Scale, you could write *good, all right, fine, fantastic, incredible,* and *amazing.* Tell students to use this idea when choosing words for their descriptive writing.

ADVANCED HIGH
Using Appropriate Voice Write the topic *The Desert* on the board. Below it, write several introductory words, phrases, or sentences for a report about the desert; for example, *Heat!, The desert is very hot. Why is the desert so hot? Cacti and lizards.* Ask students to rank the introductions according to how interesting they are. Remind students to use a tone of voice in their writing that draws the reader in and keeps them interested.

CCSS **C**ommon **C**ore **S**tate **S**tandards

SL.7.1.b: Follow rules for collegial discussions, track progress toward specific goals and deadlines, and define individual roles as needed. **SL.7.1.d:** Acknowledge new information expressed by others and, when warranted, modify their own views.

Analyze
the Model

Student Objectives

- Apply the scoring guide to a model test response. (pp. 482–483)

Using the Scoring Guide to Study the Model

Review the Scoring Guide
Remind students that the scoring guide is the tool that an evaluator—a teacher or other trained professional—will use to score the writing test. Students are given the scoring guide so they will know the criteria on which the writing will be judged. They should use the scoring guide as they write to make sure they meet all requirements.

Use the Scoring Guide
Have student use the Writing Traits in the Scoring Guide chart on page 480 to evaluate the test written in response to the writing prompt on page 479.

Find More Examples
Explain that pages 482–484 show how the writing model on page 481 meets all six writing traits. Have students read pages 482–483 and look for additional examples of Ideas, Organization, Voice, and Word Choice in the model.

 Strategies for Writers Online
Go to **www.sfw.z-b.com** for additional online resources for students and teachers.

Using the Scoring Guide to Study the Model

Now let's use the scoring guide to check Merritt's writing test, "The Ice Storm." Let's see how well her essay meets each of the writing traits.

 **Ideas**
- The writing has sensory details that paint a visual image.

Merritt's description of the North Texas ice storm is so vivid, so complete, that I can almost feel the brutal cold and hear Muzzles walk across the crunchy, frozen grass.

The trees are frosted. Their branches look burdened with the weight of the ice pulling them down. The grass has a layer of frost on it, its blades each coated with rain and dampness that's been frozen overnight.

Crunch, crunch, crunch, go his little paws on the grass, leaving behind indentations in the ice with each step he takes.

 **Organization**
- The details are in a natural and logical order.

Merritt organizes her details in a natural and logical order. Her goal is to share a sensory experience, so she focuses on one sense at a time. As I read, I could easily and vividly imagine what the cold felt like, as well as how the day looked and sounded.

I let our dog, Muzzles, a small, white Maltese, go outside. Crunch, crunch, crunch, go his little paws on the grass, leaving behind indentations in the ice with each step he takes.

482 Descriptive Writing

Differentiating Instruction

ENRICHMENT
Explore Word Choice Have students explore and practice word choice more deeply by choosing one paragraph from the model and rewriting it, replacing as many words as they can with different precise words. The goal is not necessarily to write a better or more precise paragraph but to compare the effects produced by choosing different precise words. Have students then exchange their rewritten paragraphs with partners or with other members of a small group and discuss how the changes affected the experience of reading the paragraphs.

Voice

- The voice suits the audience and purpose.

Merritt grabbed my attention with the very first word! She definitely knew who she was writing for—other kids her own age. Her voice throughout the story reflects the excitement she felt on the day of the ice storm. As I read, I couldn't help but feel that excitement, too.

> Snow! Awakening early, I peek outside to glimpse what looks like snow on the ground. I go out to get a closer look and thump! I slip and fall to the ground.

Word Choice

- The writing uses precise words and phrases to develop the topic.

Merritt clearly worked hard at using strong, specific words and phrases to describe her experience. *Numbing* is more powerful and accurate than *cold*. *Puffs of white* is a more colorful and creative phrase than *my breath*. Precise words and phrases add clarity and energy to her story.

> I push myself up with my bare hands. The ice on the ground is numbing, and my fingers get a chill. I blow on them and see the puffs of white come out of my mouth.

Descriptive Test 483

REINFORCEMENT

Support Voice Remind students that *voice* is the way the writer speaks to the reader through his or her writing. A voice can be friendly and engaging, like Merrit's voice in the model, or it can be serious and formal, as in a business letter or a report presented to the school board. Help students hear Merritt's voice by reading the model aloud with expression. Ask volunteers to read short portions of the model with expression to help them better hear the voice.

CCSS Common Core State Standards

SL.7.1.b: Follow rules for collegial discussions, track progress toward specific goals and deadlines, and define individual roles as needed. **SL.7.1.d:** Acknowledge new information expressed by others and, when warranted, modify their own views. **R/Inf.7.1:** Cite several pieces of textual evidence to support analysis of what the text says explicitly as well as inferences drawn from the text.

Analyze
the Model

Week 1 • Day 4

Student Objectives

- Continue to apply the scoring guide to a writing test response. *(p. 484)*

Analyze the Model Ask students to find other examples in the model of passages that flow well because of sentence variety. Have them explain why the mix of sentence lengths and types makes the passages they chose enjoyable to read.

Ask students to think about areas of grammar, spelling, or punctuation where they often make mistakes. Have them look for examples of those conventions being used correctly in the model.

Think About the Traits Once students have thoroughly discussed the model test response, ask them which traits they think are most important in an observation report. Students might say, for example, that the trait of **Ideas** is very important because the reader wants to know all the details of what the writer observed. They may also say that **Word Choice** is important because precise, carefully chosen words help the reader get a clear picture of the writer's observations.

Strategies for Writers Online
Go to **www.sfw.z-b.com** for additional online resources for students and teachers.

Using the Scoring Guide to Study the Model

Sentence Fluency
- The writing uses a variety of sentence lengths and types.

I like how Merritt uses both short and long sentences throughout her writing. It's more enjoyable and easier to read a variety of sentence structures.

The air is cold and damp and feels as though it's going right through my body. Carefully, I navigate my way back inside. I'd rather view the ice storm from the warmth of our house.

Conventions
- The writing has correct grammar, punctuation, capitalization, and spelling.

I can tell that Merritt has edited her story and made sure that there were no mistakes. I know how important it is to check for mistakes in my own work, and I will be sure to keep that in mind as I write. Don't forget to check for mistakes in your work, too! Be sure to check for proper grammar and mechanics at every step of the writing process so you can avoid having errors on your final test.

Planning My Time

Before giving us a writing test prompt, my teacher tells us how much time we'll have to complete the test. Since I'm already familiar with the writing process, I can think about how much total time I need and then divide it up into the different parts of the writing process. If the test takes an hour, here's how I can organize my time. Planning your time will help you, too!

Step 4:
Edit
5 minutes

Step 1:
Prewrite
25 minutes

Step 3:
Revise
15 minutes

Step 2:
Draft
15 minutes

Descriptive Test **485**

Student Objectives

• Learn how to plan time during a writing test. (p. 485)

Planning My Time

Time Management Explain to students that when they write for a test, they must complete all the steps of the writing process quickly. Students may be surprised that the student guide, Andre, has allotted so much of the writing time—25 minutes out of 60—to prewriting. Ask students why this time is necessary. (Possible response: Without a plan for writing, students may write a draft that does not respond to the task. Then they will not have time to write another draft.)

Remind students also that revising is part of the writing task. Drafting and revising together take about as much time—30 minutes—as prewriting; five minutes remain to edit. Tell students that when they have a shorter or longer time in which to write a test, they can use a similar time plan: allocate an equal amount of time for prewriting and for drafting/revising, with less time for editing.

Differentiating Instruction

REINFORCEMENT

Support the Visual Help students read the stopwatch visual. Explain that in the example, Andre will have one hour to write the test. For this reason, the watch shows 60 minutes. Explain that the different-colored sections show what portion of the 60 minutes Andre should spend on each task. Help students observe the relationships between the lengths of time allotted to the tasks (Drafting takes a little more than half the time of prewriting, revising and editing take the same amount of time, etc.) Help students observe that if they take a test in which they have more or less than 60 minutes to write, they should divide their time into proportions similar to those shown on the page.

CCSS **C**ommon **C**ore **S**tate **S**tandards

W.7.4: Produce clear and coherent writing in which the development, organization, and style are appropriate to task, purpose, and audience. **W.7.10:** Write routinely over extended time frames (time for research, reflection, and revision) and shorter time frames (a single sitting or a day or two) for a range of discipline-specific tasks, purposes, and audiences.

Write
a Descriptive Test

Week 2 • Day 1

Student Objectives

- Read and understand a writing test prompt for descriptive writing.
- Apply the six traits of writing to the writing prompt. *(pp. 486–487)*

Prewrite

Focus on Ideas

Study the Writing Prompt Review the parts of the prompt that Andre marked. Ask students if they would annotate any other key words. (Possible response: Some students might want to identify important words in the scoring guide, such as *sensory details* or *logical order*.)

Then walk students through the "think-aloud" on page 487, encouraging them to add their own responses to Andre's. How will they make sure that their language is precise and develops the topic? How will they determine what order is natural and logical for their writing?

Discuss the Traits Divide students into small groups and assign each group a trait. Have the group discuss why that trait is important when writing an observation report and how Andre's ideas will help him write a good test response.

 Strategies for Writers Online
Go to **www.sfw.z-b.com** for additional online resources for students and teachers.

T486 Descriptive Writing

Prewrite Focus on Ideas

Writing Strategy Study the writing prompt to be sure I know what to do.

Once I receive my writing prompt, I study it to make sure I know exactly what I'm supposed to do. A writing prompt usually has three parts, even though they aren't always labeled. Take a closer look at the prompt, though, and you should be able to find the setup, task, and scoring guide. I labeled all three of those in my writing prompt. You'll want to circle key words in the setup and the task that tell what kind of writing you need to do. I circled my topic in blue. You'll also want to circle what kind of writing you'll be doing, as I did, and study what the scoring guide says.

My Writing Test Prompt

Setup — Think about your favorite meal. Where do you go to get it, what does it look like, what does it smell like, and how does it taste?

Task — Write an observation report about experiencing your favorite meal that will make your reader practically be able to taste it.

Scoring Guide — Be sure your writing
- has sensory details that paint a visual image.
- has details arranged in a natural and logical order.
- uses a voice that suits the audience and purpose.
- uses precise words and phrases to develop the topic.
- uses a variety of sentence lengths and types.
- contains correct grammar, punctuation, capitalization, and spelling.

486 Descriptive Writing

English Language Learners

BEGINNING

Writing Prompt Give students a copy of the descriptive test writing prompt. Have them look at each word in the prompt and circle the words they do not know. Then teach the most important words, such as *think about, favorite, look, smell, taste, observation report, sensory details, arranged, voice, audience*. You might have a higher-level ELL work with a lower-level ELL to review the meanings of these words.

INTERMEDIATE

Writing Prompt Have students read the descriptive writing prompt and write down words they do not know. Review how to ask for help, such as, *What does* sensory details *mean? Does* sensory details *mean "things about the five senses"?* Have them practice asking and answering with two other students. Finally, ask students to write their answers; for example, *Sensory details tell about how something feels, sounds, smells, tastes, or looks*. Review as a class.

Before you get started, think about how the scoring guide relates to the writing traits you've studied in the rubrics. Even though not all of the traits may be included in every scoring guide, you'll want to remember them all in order to write a good essay.

- Be sure your writing has sensory details that paint a visual image.

I want my reader to be able to almost smell and taste my favorite meal. Using lots of sensory details will help.

- Be sure your writing has details arranged in a natural and logical order.

I'll introduce my subject, and then provide details in an order that makes the most sense.

- Be sure your writing uses a voice that suits the audience and purpose.

I'll keep my voice casual and entertaining. Reading about food should be fun, not boring and dry.

- Be sure your writing uses precise words and phrases to develop the topic.

I want to give my reader a "taste" of my favorite meal, so I'll be sure to use precise words and phrases.

- Be sure your writing uses a variety of sentence lengths and types.

Using a mixture of short and long sentences will help my writing flow smoothly.

- Be sure your writing contains correct grammar, punctuation, capitalization, and spelling.

I'm going to need to leave time to check my grammar, punctuation, and capitalization. I'll be sure to check and double check my spelling, too!

Descriptive Test 487

ADVANCED

Writing Prompt Make a few copies of the descriptive writing prompt. Cut apart the sentences in the scoring guide. Have partners work together to assign the sentences to one of the rubric writing traits—Ideas, Organization, Voice, Word Choice, Sentence Fluency, and Conventions.

ADVANCED HIGH

Writing Prompt Have students read the descriptive writing prompt and write down no more than three words in each part of the prompt that they think are most important. Then have them compare with a partner and discuss the differences.

CCSS **Common Core State Standards**

SL.7.1: Engage effectively in a range of collaborative discussions (one-on-one, in groups, and teacher-led) with diverse partners on *grade 7 topics, texts, and issues,* building on others' ideas and expressing their own clearly.

Write
a Descriptive Test

Week 2 • Day 2

Student Objectives

- Learn how to respond to the task in the writing prompt. *(p. 488)*

Prewrite

Focus on Ideas

Gather Information Encourage students to spend some time brainstorming foods they like and meals they have enjoyed. To help get them thinking, prompt them with questions such as the following:

- Does someone in your family cook a dish you really like?

- What's your favorite restaurant? What's your favorite thing to order when you're there?

- Can you think of a special occasion when you had a meal you especially enjoyed?

- What's your favorite meal among the things you eat on a regular basis?

Prewrite   Focus on (Ideas)

Writing Strategy   Respond to the task.

One thing I've learned about writing is that writers gather information before they begin writing. So to get started, I'll take a look at the information that's provided in the writing prompt. You can get a lot of information from the writing prompt! You won't have forever to finish a test, so it's important to think about how you're going to respond before you start writing.

My task is to write an observation report describing my favorite meal. Choosing my favorite meal is easy: I'll talk about the hamburgers at the Tick Tock Diner. Speaking of tick-tock, the clock is ticking on my test time so I'd better get going!

Task — [Write an (observation report) about experiencing your favorite meal that will make your reader practically be able to taste it.]

Notes

✔ Tick Tock has the best burgers in town!

✔ They're big and juicy and loaded with toppings.

✔ The place is great, too.

Apply

Before you start writing, think about how you'll respond to the task part of the prompt. Next write down notes to help you gather information.

488 **Descriptive Writing**

Differentiating Instruction

ENRICHMENT

More About the Meal Challenge students to provide some background information about the meal, in addition to the sensory descriptions. For example, they can tell what they know about some of the ingredients, or the cultural or historical background of an ethnic dish. Encourage students to add a Background Details column to their charts.

Online Writing Center

Provides **interactive graphic organizers** as well as a variety of graphic organizers in PDF format.

Prewrite

Focus on **Organization**

Writing Strategy Choose a graphic organizer.

Time is limited, so I need to get my ideas on paper fast! Since I know what I'm going to be writing about, my next step is to organize all the details. Because sensory details are so important, it feels natural to organize my observations according to the five senses. I'll use an Observation Chart to keep them all straight.

I'll start out by writing down the topic of my essay, which came out of the setup and task in the writing prompt. Then I'll write down five columns and label them Sight, Sound, Touch, Taste, and Smell.

TOPIC: Tick Tock Diner's Tasty Burgers

SIGHT	SOUND	TOUCH	TASTE	SMELL
-counter with the grill behind it -a few booths along the window -mostly red and white inside -vinyl-covered stools -burgers served on white plastic plate with fries on side -old-fashioned	-kind of noisy -people talking -wait staff and cooks yell orders back and forth -burgers sizzling on the grill -jukebox plays old music	-buns are always soft when you pick up your burger -slightly warm since they put them on the griddle	-juicy, slightly salty, and delicious! -tangy ketchup and creamy mayo -comes with crisp lettuce, sweet tomato, and sour pickles	-whole place smells like a burger -smell the grease from the fries and the grill

Reflect

What do you think? Did Andre record enough details in his Observation Chart?

Apply

Choose a graphic organizer that helps you organize the information you need to appeal to your reader's senses.

Descriptive Test **489**

REINFORCEMENT

Support Sensory Details If students are having trouble thinking of details for the senses other than taste and smell, prompt them with questions such as these: Hearing—Who else was at the meal? Was there laughter or conversation? Sight—What made the food appetizing to look at? What was the room like? Touch—Where did you sit? Were you comfortable? Was the room hot or cold?

Write
a Descriptive Test

Week 2 • Day 3

Student Objectives

- Learn how to choose a graphic organizer for the writing prompt. (p. 489)

Prewrite

Focus on **Organization**

Organize Information Once students have chosen their topic, have them create a graphic organizer and write the details for their observation reports. Tell students that while the five senses are a useful way to organize their details for a description of a meal, they could choose other organizers. Discuss with students what other types of organizers they could use for an observation report. (Possible responses: A sequence chain would allow details to be organized in the order in which they occurred; a Web would allow details to be organized in various types of categories.) If students decide to use an Observation Chart, encourage them to consider adding a column for additional details they might want to include.

CCSS **C**ommon **C**ore **S**tate **S**tandards

W.7.2.a: Introduce a topic clearly, previewing what is to follow; organize ideas, concepts, and information, using strategies such as definition, classification, comparison/contrast, and cause/effect; include formatting (e.g., headings), graphics (e.g., charts, tables), and multimedia when useful to aiding comprehension. **SL.7.1.d:** Acknowledge new information expressed by others and, when warranted, modify their own views.

Write
a Descriptive Test

Week 2 • Day 4

Student Objectives

• Learn how to check the graphic organizer against the scoring guide. *(pp. 490–491)*

Prewrite

Focus on

Check the Graphic Organizer
Have students evaluate Andre's Observation Chart on page 490.

Ask:

• Are all the details correctly classified? (yes)

• Which details are most important, and which could be omitted without harming the report? (Accept answers that students can justify.)

Read out loud the **Ideas** and **Organization** descriptors and commentary on page 491 to demonstrate how Andre has used each writing trait to make sure his prewriting (gathering and organizing information) has stayed on track. Have students look at their own graphic organizers, evaluate them in light of the traits, and make any necessary changes.

Have students read the rest of page 491 silently.

Strategies for Writers Online
Go to **www.sfw.z-b.com** for additional online resources for students and teachers.

Prewrite

Focus on **Organization**

Writing Strategy Check my graphic organizer against the scoring guide.

During a test, you won't have a lot of time for revising. That makes prewriting an essential part of your test writing process. Before I even begin writing my draft, I'm going to check my Observation Chart against the scoring guide in the writing prompt.

TOPIC: Tick Tock Diner's Tasty Burgers				
SIGHT	**SOUND**	**TOUCH**	**TASTE**	**SMELL**
-counter with the grill behind it -a few booths along the window -mostly red and white inside -vinyl-covered stools -burgers served on white plastic plate with fries on side -old-fashioned	-kind of noisy -people talking -wait staff and cooks yell orders back and forth -burgers sizzling on the grill -jukebox plays old music	-buns are always soft when you pick up your burger -slightly warm since they put them on the griddle	-juicy, slightly salty, and delicious! -tangy ketchup and creamy mayo -comes with crisp lettuce, sweet tomato, and sour pickles	-whole place smells like a burger -smell the grease from the fries and the grill

490 Descriptive Writing

Ideas
- Be sure your writing has sensory details that paint a visual image.

My Observation Chart has all the senses covered!

 Organization
- Be sure your writing has details arranged in a natural and logical order.

I'll state my topic early on and then give the details in a logical order according to the five senses.

 Voice
- Be sure your writing uses a voice that suits the audience and purpose.

I'll keep my voice friendly and energetic.

 Word Choice
- Be sure your writing uses precise words and phrases to develop the topic.

As I look at my Observation Chart, I see some precise and descriptive words and phrases I'll use in my writing.

 Sentence Fluency
- Be sure your writing uses a variety of sentence lengths and types.

I want to hold my reader's attention, so I'll use a variety of sentences to keep my writing interesting.

 Conventions
- Be sure your writing contains correct grammar, punctuation, capitalization, and spelling.

I'll pay attention to this as I write, but I'll be sure to double check things when I edit my draft.

Reflect

What do you think? How will Andre's Observation Chart help him write a good report?

Apply

The steps you take before you start writing your draft will ensure that you have a well-organized and well-written observation report!

Prepare to Draft Discuss where Andre is in the writing process right now. (Possible response: He has done the preparation work and is ready to draft.) Ask students why it's necessary for Andre to reread and think about the traits, even though he has not begun to draft. (Possible response: to remind himself of what he'll have to keep in mind as he writes)

CCSS Common Core State Standards

W.7.2.b: Develop the topic with relevant facts, definitions, concrete details, quotations, or other information and examples. **SL.7.1.a:** Come to discussions prepared, having read or researched material under study; explicitly draw on that preparation by referring to evidence on the topic, text, or issue to probe and reflect on ideas under discussion.

Write
a Descriptive Test

Week 2 • Day 5

Student Objectives

- Use the graphic organizer to begin a writing test response that uses sensory details to paint a visual image. *(pp. 492–493)*

Draft

Focus on Ideas

Tips for Test Writing As students prepare to draft, remind them to write on every other line of paper, as Andre does. This leaves space for students to make their corrections when they revise and edit their drafts. Mention that in a testing situation, students will not have time to create a fresh final copy of their writing.

Tell students they should keep their graphic organizers out as they draft and refer to them frequently. If a new detail occurs to students while they draft, they might consider including it if it will enhance the reader's understanding. Overall, though, students should stick with the information in their organizers. Throwing in too many new details as they draft could muddy the organization of the writing.

Have students read pages 492–493 and discuss how the highlighted details help readers share Andre's experience.

Online Writing Center

Provides student eBooks with an **interactive writing pad** for drafting, revising, editing, and publishing.

Draft

Focus on (Ideas)

Writing Strategy Draw the reader in with sensory details that paint a visual image.

According to the scoring guide, I need to include sensory details that paint a visual image. My Observation Chart has a lot of information about what the diner looks like, and I think that'll help to draw the reader into my story.

[DRAFT]

The Tastiest Burger

by Andre

Four oclock is always burger time. That's the time the old broke clock above the Tick Tock Diner has displayed for as long as anyone can remember. But even though the clock no longer functions, the burgers inside are much appreciated by all the customers.

The aroma of burgers cooking on the grill and fries cooking in the deep fryer grabs me from the moment I walk into the old-fashioned diner on saturday night. Its packed. I can hear the buzz of people talking. I hear the wait staff and cooks yelling orders to each other

The diner is decked out in red white, and chrome. Red vinyl covers the seats of the booths and stools, while white-topped tables have chrome legs. An old jukebox rests in one corner of the diner, with tunes from a previous decade. Even the employees there look as though they came from another time, seeing name tags that display names like "Betty" and "Midge" and "Johnny" and "Suzy." [sensory details]

492 Descriptive Writing

English Language Learners

BEGINNING

Proofreading After students have written and revised their writing tests, have them trade papers and proofread another student's paper. Ask them to circle any words whose spelling looks incorrect and then look up the word in a dictionary. Remind students to use knowledge of spelling patterns (for example, **/n/** can be spelled **n, kn,** or **gn**); search in alphabetical order; compare the dictionary spelling; and correct any misspellings.

INTERMEDIATE

Using Strong Descriptors After students have written their first drafts, have them circle all the adjectives and adverbs they used in the first paragraph. Then have them trade with a partner who will read the paragraph and change each of the circled words to a more descriptive one. Have the partners discuss why they made each change.

[DRAFT]

Norma, my server, doesn't need to ask what I want. My order is always the same burger, fries, and a soda. I take an empty seat at the counter, which puts me closer to the kitchen action. Here, I can hear the burgers sizzling on the grill, inviting me to order. Soon, she places the white plastic plate in front of me. On it sits perfection: a juicy burger and fries still glisening with grease and salt.

[sensory details]

The bun is soft and slightly warm as I lift it to take my first bite. The burger is juicy, salty, and delicious. Crisp lettuce, a thick slab of tomato, and sour pickles surround the patty. While tangy Ketchup and creamy mayyonaise make perfect-tasting accompaniments.

I take a sip of the cold soda, which leaves me ready for a salty fry. I bite into one. Its crisp and salty on the outside, concealing the soft potato inside. Then I go to back the burger, which seems to get messier and harder to eat with every delicious bite I take. I suddenly remember—I have a math quiz in three days!

Before I know it, all that's left on my plate are a few splatters of Ketchup, mayyonaise, and burger grease, along with one lonely fry. On second thought, I devour that as well and leave full and satisfied.

Reflect

What do you think? Can you practically smell and taste the burgers Andre has described?

Apply

Use vivid words and details to make the experience real for your reader. Make sure to include these in your observation report.

Descriptive Test 493

Check Sensory Details Have students begin drafting their observation reports. As they write, tell them to pay attention to the sensory details they include. Students should keep the following in mind:

- Does each detail relate clearly to the topic?
- Does each detail help the reader experience some aspect of the topic through the senses?
- Does each detail relate well to the other details in the paragraph?

Remind students that they are not obligated to include every detail that appears in their graphic organizers. Students may find as they write that one or two details seem less important or relevant than they seemed at first.

ADVANCED

Observation Chart Briefly review the five senses. Present students with a familiar object, such as a flower or tree. Have partners complete an Observation Chart for the object, making sure to include one idea for each of the five senses, if applicable. Then have them create an Observation Chart for their selected weather phenomenon that they can use as a basis for their descriptive writing test.

ADVANCED HIGH

Peer Review After students have drafted their descriptive essays, have them trade with another student. Partners should review the draft and look for specific details. Students should point out weak voice and suggest more descriptive words their partners could use. As you monitor, identify two or three examples of weak words or sentences, and discuss ways to strengthen them as a class.

CCSS **Common Core State Standards**

W.7.3.d: Use precise words and phrases, relevant descriptive details, and sensory language to capture the action and convey experiences and events.

Descriptive Test Writing T493

Write
a Descriptive Test

Week 3 • Day 1

Student Objectives

• Revise for logical presentation of details. (p. 494)

Revise

Focus on Organization

Time Management Point out that students have about fifteen minutes to revise their drafts and that there are three revision tasks. Students might wish to subdivide their planned revising time into three five-minute segments and tackle one strategy at a time. (If you are using the Optional Revising pages, you will need to plan accordingly. See page T496.)

Check for Logical Order Read the Writing Strategy aloud, and have students read the rest of page 494. Point out that Andre chose an order that felt natural to him and organized his paragraphs accordingly. The draft excerpt shows that details must be placed logically within paragraphs as well.

Tell students to review their writing to make sure details are grouped into paragraphs in a way that makes sense and that details within the paragraphs follow a logical order.

 Strategies for Writers Online
Go to www.sfw.z-b.com for additional online resources for students and teachers.

Revise
Focus on Organization

Writing Strategy Make sure details are presented in a logical, natural order.

The scoring guide says details should be presented in a logical and natural order. I accomplished that by focusing on one sense at a time as I lead readers through a meal at the Tick Tock Diner. It makes sense to let readers experience the meal through a different sense in each paragraph. Checking my writing, though, I see that I've put one detail out of place. In my draft, Norma takes my order before I even sit down! I'll fix that now.

[DRAFT]

[placed sentence in logical order]

Norma, my server, doesn't need to ask what I want. My order is always the same burger, fries, and a soda. I take an empty seat at the counter, which puts me closer to the kitchen action. Here, I can hear the burgers sizzling on the grill, inviting me to order. Soon, she places the white plastic plate in front of me. On it sits perfection: a juicy burger and fries still glisening with grease and salt.

Apply

When you reread your writing, make sure details are organized logically and naturally.

Revise

Focus on **Voice**

Writing Strategy   Connect with the readers.

For this paper, I used first person to help pull the readers into my experience. It's the best way to connect with them when sharing a personal experience. I also want to keep my voice friendly and casual for my audience—my classmates and teachers. But as I read my paper aloud to myself, I heard some words that just don't sound like me. I'll revise them so that my writing sounds more like my speaking voice.

[DRAFT]

————— [used casual voice] —————
An old jukebox rests in one corner of the diner, with tunes from a

~~previous decade~~. Even the ~~employees~~ there look as though they came
                 servers

from another time, seeing name tags that display names like "Betty" and

"Midge" and "Johnny" and "Suzy."

Reflect

How do Andre's revisions help strengthen his voice?

Apply

You want to connect with your readers. Be sure to use a voice that's appropriate for both your audience and your purpose.

Descriptive Test 495

Write a Descriptive Test

Week 3 • Day 2

Student Objectives

- Revise to connect with readers. (p. 495)

Revise

Focus on

Review Voice Have students read page 495. Ask students why first-person point of view makes sense for an observation report. (Possible response: The goal of an observation report is to share something that the writer experienced, so it makes sense for the writer to speak from his or her own point of view.) Explain that whatever voice they choose to use to connect with the reader, they need to maintain that voice consistently throughout their writing.

Have students review their reports for voice. Tell them to focus especially on the later portions of their reports, where writers often lose track of the voice they established at the beginning and become inconsistent.

Point out that students should make their changes as neatly as possible. They should keep in mind that their writing will be scored by another person who has to be able to read it to understand it. Neatness counts!

CCSS **Common Core State Standards**

W.7.3.a: Engage and orient the reader by establishing a context and point of view and introducing a narrator and/or characters; organize an event sequence that unfolds naturally and logically.

Write
a Descriptive Test

Week 3 • Day 3

Student Objectives

- Revise to replace vague words and phrases with precise ones. (p. 496)

Revise

Focus on Word Choice

Check for Vague Words Have students read page 496 and discuss Andre's revisions. Ask students what precise words they might use to replace *old* in the second sentence. (**Possible responses:** *ancient, antiquated, old-fashioned, retro*) Tell students that as they revise for word choice they should look for commonly used, vague words such as *is/are/am, have, good, bad, there,* and *said.* Explain that while these words are sometimes perfectly appropriate, oftentimes they can and should be replaced by more precise, vivid words.

Online Writing Center

Provides **interactive proofreading activities** for each genre.

Revise

Focus on **Word Choice**

Writing Strategy Replace vague words and phrases with precise ones.

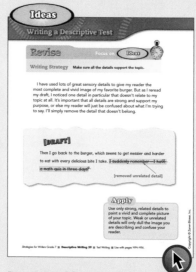

Now I'll reread my paper to be sure I've used specific words, as the scoring guide says to do. I think some of my descriptions about the restaurant are a little too vague. I'll add more precise and specific words.

[DRAFT]

[added specific words]

Red vinyl covers the seats of the booths and stools, while white-topped tables ~~have~~ stand supported by chrome legs. An old jukebox rests in one corner of the diner, ~~with~~ belting out tunes from ~~a previous decade~~ another era. Even the ~~employees~~ servers there look as though they came from another time, ~~seeing~~ their white shirts emblazoned with name tags that display names like "Betty" and "Midge" and "Johnny" and "Suzy."

Apply

Word choice is important. Vague words and phrases don't help your reader get a clear picture of what you're describing, so replace them with precise ones.

Optional Revising Lessons

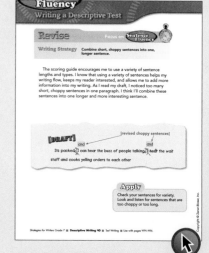

Ideas
Writing a Descriptive Test

Revise
Focus on **Ideas**

Writing Strategy Make sure all the details support the topic.

I have used lots of great sensory details to give my reader the most complete and vivid image of my favorite burger. But as I reread my draft, I noticed one detail in particular that doesn't relate to my topic at all. It's important that all details are strong and support my purpose, or else my reader will just be confused about what I'm trying to say. I'll simply remove the detail that doesn't belong.

[DRAFT]

Then I go back to the burger, which seems to get messier and harder to eat with every delicious bite I take. ~~I suddenly remember—I have a math quiz in three days!~~

[removed unrelated detail]

Apply
Use only strong, related details to paint a vivid and complete picture of your topic. Weak or unrelated details will only dull the image you are describing and confuse your reader.

Descriptive 39

Sentence Fluency
Writing a Descriptive Test

Revise
Focus on **Sentence Fluency**

Writing Strategy Combine short, choppy sentences into one, longer sentence.

The scoring guide encourages me to use a variety of sentence lengths and types. I know that using a variety of sentences helps my writing flow, keeps my reader interested, and allows me to add more information into my writing. As I read my draft, I noticed too many short, choppy sentences in one paragraph. I think I'll combine these sentences into one longer and more interesting sentence.

[DRAFT]

[revised choppy sentences]

Its packed. I can hear the buzz of people talking. I hear the wait staff and cooks yelling orders to each other

Apply
Check your sentences for variety. Look and listen for sentences that are too choppy or too long.

Descriptive 40

Go to **Strategies for Writers Grade 7 CD-ROM**

Edit

Writing Strategy Check my grammar, punctuation, capitalization, and spelling.

Before I turn in my paper, I'll need to do a final check for grammar, punctuation, capitalization, and spelling.

[FINAL DRAFT]

The Tastiest Burger
by Andre [revised choppy sentences]

Four o'clock is always burger time. That's the time the old broken clock above the Tick Tock Diner has displayed for as long as anyone can remember. But even though the clock no longer functions, the burgers inside are much appreciated by all the customers.

The aroma of burgers cooking on the grill and fries cooking in the deep fryer grabs me from the moment I walk into the old-fashioned diner on saturday night. It's packed, and I can hear the buzz of people talking. I hear the wait staff and cooks yelling orders to each other.

The diner is decked out in red, white, and chrome. Red vinyl covers the seats of the booths and stools, while white-topped tables ~~have~~ stand supported by chrome legs. An old jukebox rests in one corner of the diner, ~~with~~ belting out tunes from ~~a previous decade~~ another era. Even the ~~employees~~ servers there look as

Apply

Check your grammar, punctuation, capitalization, and spelling every time you write for a test.

Descriptive Test 497

Differentiating Instruction

ENRICHMENT

Early Finishers Advanced students often finish tests early and fall into the habit of simply waiting for the testing period to be over. If students have revised for writing traits and checked for conventions once, instruct them to reread the writing prompt on page 486, and then carefully read their reports one more time while keeping the writing traits and the writing task in mind.

Write
a Descriptive Test

Week 3 • Day 4

Student Objectives

- Edit the writing test for proper grammar, spelling, capitalization, and punctuation. *(pp. 497–498)*

Edit

Focus on **Conventions**

Edit the Test Explain to students that while an observation report written for a test in a short period of time will rarely be perfect, they should find and correct as many errors as possible. Test evaluators know that students are writing quickly and watching the clock and that a few errors may slip through. However, evaluators also look for evidence that students took time to edit. For example, when they see misspelled words crossed out and correctly spelled words inserted instead, they know that students are paying attention to editing.

Review the proofreading marks on page 493 with students. Point out the insertions in Andre's draft. Remind students that they should not plan for time to recopy their drafts—every minute of writing time should be put to making the report stronger, not to produce a perfectly neat final copy.

CCSS **C**ommon **C**ore **S**tate **S**tandards

W.7.2.d: Use precise language and domain-specific vocabulary to inform about or explain the topic. **W.7.3.d:** Use precise words and phrases, relevant descriptive details, and sensory language to capture the action and convey experiences and events. **L.7.3.a:** Choose language that expresses ideas precisely and concisely, recognizing and eliminating wordiness and redundancy.

Descriptive Test Writing T497

Review
Test Tips

Week 3 • Day 5

Student Objectives

- Review tips for writing for a test. (*pp. 498–499*)

Test Tips

Reviewing Test Writing Explain to students that not all writing test prompts will be as clearly divided into parts as the writing prompt used in this chapter. However, students can still find and label the three important sections. Students can even generate a scoring guide if they must. Write this prompt on the board: *Think about your favorite place to relax. Write a description about this place. Revise and edit your report.*

Now ask these questions:

- What is the setup? (Think about your favorite place to relax.)

Circle and label the setup, and point out that it is rather brief. Ask students how they might expand on it to get a better sense of the background for this writing prompt. (Possible response: Ask questions such as *Why is this place special? What do I see, hear, feel, and think while I'm there?*)

- What is the task? (Write a description about this place.)

Strategies for Writers Online
Go to **www.sfw.z-b.com** for additional online resources for students and teachers.

[FINAL DRAFT]

though they came from another time, ~~seeing~~ name tags that display
their white shirts emblazoned with
names like "Betty" and "Midge" and "Johnny" and "Suzy."

Norma, my server, doesn't need to ask what I want. My order is always the same, burger, fries, and a soda. I take an empty seat at the counter, which puts me closer to the kitchen action. Here, I can hear the burgers sizzling on the grill, inviting me to order. Soon, she places the white plastic plate in front of me. On it sits perfection: a juicy burger and fries still ~~glisening~~ glistening with grease and salt.

The bun is soft and slightly warm as I lift it to take my first bite. The burger is juicy, salty, and delicious. Crisp lettuce, a thick slab of tomato, and sour pickles surround the patty. While tangy Ketchup and creamy ~~mayyonaise~~ mayonnaise make perfect-tasting accompaniments.

I take a sip of the cold soda, which leaves me ready for a salty fry. I bite into one. Its crisp and salty on the outside, concealing the soft potato inside. Then I go back to the burger, which seems to get messier and harder to eat with every delicious bite I take. ~~I suddenly remember I have a math quiz in three days!~~

Before I know it, all that's left on my plate are a few splatters of Ketchup, ~~mayyonaise~~ mayonnaise, and burger grease, along with one lonely fry. On second thought, I devour that as well and leave full and satisfied.

Reflect

When writing for a test, remember to use your time wisely. Be sure to use your writing prompt's scoring guide to check over your writing and make any necessary revisions. Good luck!

498 Descriptive Writing

Differentiating Instruction

REINFORCEMENT

Customize Editing Everyone has a mistake they tend to make consistently. Tell students that when they edit their work, they should break the process down to make it more manageable and to focus on their own particular weaknesses. For example, a student might take two minutes to check grammar, spelling, and capitalization and leave three minutes for punctuation, if punctuation is that student's most frequent area of concern. Set aside time to conference with individual students to help them determine what their areas of relative weaknesses are in conventions and to determine how they should allocate their editing time.

Time's up, and it wasn't bad at all. Keep in mind these important steps when you write for a test.

TEST TIPS

1. **Study the writing prompt before you start to write.** Most writing prompts have three parts: the setup, the task, and the scoring guide. The parts probably won't be labeled. You'll have to figure them out for yourself!

2. **Make sure you understand the task before you start to write. Remember to:**
   - Read all three parts of the writing prompt carefully.
   - Circle key words in the task part of the writing prompt that tell what kind of writing you need to do and who your audience is.
   - Make sure you know how you'll be graded.
   - Say what you need to do in your own words.

3. **Keep an eye on the clock.** Decide how much time you will spend on each part of the writing process and try to stick to it. Don't spend so much time on prewriting that you don't have enough time to write!

4. **Reread your writing. Compare it to the scoring guide at least twice.** Remember the rubrics you have used in the chapter? A scoring guide on a writing test is like a rubric. It can help you keep in mind what's important.

5. **Plan, plan, plan!** You don't get much time to revise during a test, so planning is more important than ever.

6. **Write neatly.** Remember: If the people who score your test can't read your writing, it doesn't matter how good your story or essay is!

Descriptive Test 499

Circle and label the task and point out that it is missing some information. For example, it does not tell specifically what kind of writing is called for. Ask students how they can decide what kind of writing the task requires. (Possible response: The task says to write about a place the writer knows well, and it mentions the word *description*. An observation report gives a description of a place the writer has been or an experience the writer has had.)

Finally ask students what they can do to make up a scoring guide, since the writing prompt has only the general instructions to *revise and edit*. (Possible response: We know that we can make writing better by using the six traits. We can write a quick list of the traits for an observation report.)

Have students volunteer the names of the traits and how they apply to an observation report. Write students' responses on the board in bulleted form. Show students that they have just figured out a useful scoring guide from their own experiences. Students will see that even a brief writing prompt can give them the tools and guidance they need to write a successful test.

CCSS **Common Core State Standards**

L.7.1: Demonstrate command of the conventions of standard English grammar and usage when writing or speaking. **SL.7.1.c:** Pose questions that elicit elaboration and respond to others' questions and comments with relevant observations and ideas that bring the discussion back on topic as needed.

Grammar Practice The mini-lessons in this section are designed to reinforce targeted grammar, usage, and mechanics skills that students can transfer to their writing. These pages are referenced throughout the Teacher Edition in the Related Grammar section. Or you may wish to use the Table of Contents on this page to choose specific lessons that will benefit your students. To provide valuable additional practice, follow up each mini-lesson with an exercise from **More Practice,** which begins on page 532.

Appendix A
Grammar Practice

Compound Subjects and Compound Predicates

Know the Rule

A **compound subject** is two or more subjects joined by a conjunction (*and, or*).
   Example:
   Both **adults** and **children** wear cotton clothes.
A **compound predicate** is two or more verbs joined by a conjunction.
   Example:
   American farmers still **grow** and **harvest** large crops of cotton.

Practice the Rule

Each sentence below has either a compound subject or a compound predicate. Write each sentence on a separate sheet of paper. Underline the words that make up each compound subject. Circle the verbs in each compound predicate.

1. Cotton and polyester are used in many articles of clothing.
2. Manufacturers (buy) and (use) huge quantities of cotton from Asia.
3. Most shirts and dresses contain some polyester.
4. A cotton blouse or shirt is comfortable in hot summer weather.
5. Farmers (pick) cotton by hand or (use) modern machines.
6. My class (researched) and (discussed) the leather industry.
7. Shoes and belts are often made of leather.
8. Baseball mitts and footballs are usually leather items.
9. Cars and trucks often come with leather seats.
10. Some people (dislike) and (boycott) the use of leather products.

Conventions

Mini-Lessons

Student Objectives

- Identify and correctly use compound subjects and compound predicates. *(p. 501)*

Compound Subjects and Compound Predicates

A compound subject is two or more subjects joined by a conjunction *(and, or)*. A compound predicate is two or more verbs joined by a conjunction.

Display these sentences on the board. Ask students to combine the pairs of sentences by writing a sentence with a compound subject or a compound predicate. Remind them to use a plural verb with a compound subject.

- *Baseball requires upper body strength. Swimming also requires upper body strength.* (Baseball and swimming require upper body strength.)

- *The store owner sells baseball mitts. The store owner repairs baseball mitts.* (The store owner sells and repairs baseball mitts.)

Tell students that using compound subjects and predicates in their writing can help them vary their sentence structure and avoid repetitive sounding sentences. For more practice with this skill, see page 532.

CCSS **C**ommon **C**ore **S**tate **S**tandards
L.7.1: Demonstrate command of the conventions of standard English grammar and usage when writing or speaking.

Conventions Mini-Lesson

Student Objectives

• Identify direct objects and indirect objects. *(p. 502)*

Direct Objects and Indirect Objects

A direct object is a noun or pronoun that receives the action of a verb. An indirect object tells to whom or for whom the action of the verb is done. Both direct and indirect objects can be compound. Display these sentences on the board. Have students find and identify the direct objects and indirect objects.

• *My aunt gave me a new jacket and boots.* (*me*: indirect object; *jacket, boots*: direct objects)

• *I showed Erin and Jim my presents.* (*Erin, Jim*: indirect objects; *presents*: direct object)

Tell students that using direct objects and indirect objects in their writing will help them clarify whom or what receives the action of the verb and who or what is affected by the action of the verb. For more practice with this skill, see page 532.

CCSS Common Core State Standards

L.7.1: Demonstrate command of the conventions of standard English grammar and usage when writing or speaking.

Direct Objects and Indirect Objects

Know the Rule

> The **direct object** is the noun or pronoun that receives the action of the verb. Only action verbs can have a direct object. To find the direct object, say the verb and then ask *What?* or *Whom?* The **indirect object** tells to whom or for whom the action of the verb is done.
>
> **Example:**
> The librarian showed **me** interesting **websites** for my report.
> (The direct object is *websites*. The indirect object is *me*.)

Practice the Rule

Number a sheet of paper 1–10. Write each sentence. Underline the direct object. If the sentence has an indirect object, circle the indirect object.

1. Our teacher gave us an interesting assignment.
2. Each group will write a report about an extinct animal.
3. Latoya researched information about dinosaurs.
4. She showed me an interesting book about dinosaurs.
5. One website provided my group with colorful drawings of extinct animals.
6. On the island of Bali, people hunted a species of tiger to extinction.
7. The woolly mammoths possessed extremely long tusks.
8. Each group will present its report next week.
9. My group assigned Thomas the task of finding photographs or drawings of the dodo bird.
10. We learned many interesting facts about each group's topic.

Predicate Nouns and Predicate Adjectives

Know the Rule

A **predicate noun** follows a linking verb and renames the subject of the sentence. A **predicate adjective** follows a linking verb and describes the subject. A linking verb does not show action. Rather, it "links" a subject with either another noun or an adjective. The forms of the verb *be* are commonly used as linking verbs. Other verbs that may be linking verbs include *become, seem, feel, taste, look,* and *appear*.

> **Example:**
> *The Music Man* is a famous **musical** from the 1950s. (predicate noun)
> Our class seems **excited** about seeing *The Music Man*. (predicate adjective)

Practice the Rule

Number a sheet of paper 1–10. Write each sentence. Underline the subject of the sentence. Then circle the predicate noun or predicate adjective in the sentence. At the end of each sentence, write whether the word is a predicate noun or a predicate adjective.

1. The songs in the play are very entertaining. predicate adjective
2. A small town in the state of Iowa is the setting of the play. predicate noun
3. In 1957, the show was a great success on Broadway. predicate noun
4. Broadway is a famous avenue in New York City. predicate noun
5. It is the site of many large theaters. predicate noun
6. In 1962, a movie of *The Music Man* was very popular. predicate adjective
7. The film actually became one of the biggest hits of the year. predicate noun
8. In the beginning of the play, the main character appears honest. predicate adjective
9. He is, however, really a scoundrel after everyone's money. predicate noun
10. In the end, though, the scoundrel becomes an honest man. predicate noun

Mini-Lesson

Student Objectives

- Identify predicate nouns and predicate adjectives. *(p. 503)*

Predicate Nouns and Predicate Adjectives

Predicate nouns and predicate adjectives follow linking verbs. A predicate noun renames the subject. A predicate adjective describes the subject. Like direct objects and indirect objects, predicate nouns and predicate adjectives can be compound. Display these sentences on the board. Have students find the predicate nouns and predicate adjectives in the sentences.

- *Helen Keller was an inspirational person.* (**person:** predicate noun)

- *She was courageous and intelligent.* (**courageous, intelligent:** predicate adjectives)

- *Annie Sullivan was a gifted teacher.* (**teacher:** predicate noun)

Tell students that using predicate nouns and predicate adjectives in their writing will help them tell more about the subject of a sentence. For more practice with this skill, see page 532.

CCSS **Common Core State Standards**
L.7.1: Demonstrate command of the conventions of standard English grammar and usage when writing or speaking.

Conventions

Mini-Lesson

Student Objectives

• Identify the four kinds of sentences. *(p. 504)*

Kinds of Sentences

Display these sentences on the board. Discuss how the meaning changes depending on the punctuation.

• *Get the fire extinguisher.* (gives a command; imperative sentence)

• *Get the fire extinguisher!* (shows excitement; exclamatory sentence)

Display these sentences on the board. Have students tell the kind of sentence and add the correct punctuation.

• *Oh no, I am totally lost* (exclamatory; !)

• *Will you give me directions* (interrogative; ?)

• *Tell me which way to go* (imperative; .)

• *I thanked the person for helping me.* (declarative; .]

Tell students that writing different kinds of sentences is one way to vary sentence structure and make their writing more interesting. Using the right kind of sentence is especially important when writing dialogue. For more practice with this skill, see page 533.

CCSS **Common Core State Standards**

L.7.1: Demonstrate command of the conventions of standard English grammar and usage when writing or speaking.

Kinds of Sentences

Know the Rule

A sentence always begins with a capital letter and ends with a type of punctuation. A **declarative sentence** makes a statement and ends with a period. An **interrogative sentence** asks a question and ends with a question mark. An **imperative sentence** gives a command and ends with a period or an exclamation point. An **exclamatory sentence** shows excitement and ends with an exclamation point. When you write, use the punctuation mark based on the effect you want to convey to your readers.

Examples:

Please tell me the year in which the Second World War ended. (imperative sentence)

The Second World War, often written as World War II, ended in 1945. (declarative sentence)

Practice the Rule

Number a sheet of paper 1–10. Write each sentence, adding the correct end punctuation. Then write the kind of sentence it is.

1. World War II lasted from 1939 to 1945. declarative
2. Which countries were involved in this war? interrogative
3. Many powerful countries as well as less powerful countries from around the world were involved. declarative
4. Name the countries that were allies of the United States during the war. imperative
5. A principle ally of the United States was the United Kingdom. declarative
6. Did the United States really fight against Japan and Germany? interrogative
7. How unbelievable that Germany was once our enemy! exclamatory
8. Have you ever seen the famous photograph taken in New York City on the day that Japan surrendered? interrogative
9. That photograph shows a sailor kissing a nurse. declarative
10. Wow! Everyone must have been happy that the war had finally ended! exclamatory

Dependent Clauses and Independent Clauses

Know the Rule

An **independent clause** is a group of words with a subject and a predicate that expresses a complete thought. An independent clause can stand alone as a sentence. A **dependent clause** has a subject and a predicate, but it does not express a complete thought and cannot stand alone as a sentence. Independent clauses and dependent clauses can be used together to form sentences. A dependent clause often begins with a subordinating conjunction such as *although, as, because, if,* or *when.* When a dependent clause begins a sentence, it is separated from the independent clause by a comma.

> **Examples:**
> after we eat lunch (dependent clause)
> We will go to the museum. (independent clause)
> After we eat lunch, we will go to the museum. (complex sentence with a dependent and an independent clause)
> We will go to the museum after we eat lunch. (complex sentence with an independent and a dependent clause)

Practice the Rule

Number a sheet of paper 1–10. Identify the underlined clause in each sentence by writing **independent** or **dependent** after the appropriate number.

1. James wanted to go to a science museum <u>because he is interested in dinosaurs</u>. *dependent*
2. Because Felipe is studying the history of ships, <u>he suggested a maritime museum</u>. *independent*
3. <u>As Lauren had hoped</u>, the class decided to visit an art museum. *dependent*
4. We looked at some modern sculptures, <u>which not all of my classmates liked</u>. *dependent*
5. Although the photography exhibit was free, <u>we didn't have time to go</u>. *independent*
6. <u>While we walked past the old paintings</u>, a guard watched us closely. *dependent*
7. <u>We ate lunch in the museum cafe</u> because it was raining outside. *independent*
8. This is the same museum <u>that I visited last year with my parents</u>. *dependent*
9. <u>When my father goes to a museum</u>, he quickly becomes bored. *dependent*
10. Although I am often bored in museums, <u>I always find something of interest</u>. *independent*

Mini-Lesson

Student Objectives

- Identify dependent and independent clauses. *(p. 505)*

Dependent Clauses and Independent Clauses

A clause is a group of words with a subject and a predicate. An independent clause expresses a complete thought. A dependent clause does not express a complete thought. Tell students not to confuse phrases that begin with *after, before, since,* or *until* with dependent clauses. Remember: a clause has a subject and a predicate. Display these sentences. Ask students to find and label the dependent and independent clauses.

- *After she had finished cooking, my mother finally relaxed.* (After she had finished cooking: dependent clause; my mother finally relaxed: independent clause)

- *After dinner, we usually go for a walk.* (we usually go for a walk: independent clause)

Tell students that using dependent clauses in sentences is a way to vary their sentence structure and add clarifying details to their writing. For more practice with this skill, see page 533.

CCSS **C**ommon **C**ore **S**tate **S**tandards

L.7.1.a: Explain the function of phrases and clauses in general and their function in specific sentences.
L.7.1.c: Place phrases and clauses within a sentence, recognizing and correcting misplaced and dangling modifiers.

Conventions

Mini-Lesson

Student Objectives

- Identify adjective clauses. *(p. 506)*

Adjective Clauses

An adjective clause is a dependent clause that describes a noun or pronoun. If the adjective clause gives essential information about a noun, no comma is needed. If the adjective clause gives extra, but nonessential information, use a comma to separate it from the main clause. Display these sentences on the board. Have students identify the adjective clause and the noun it modifies. Then have students explain why the sentences are punctuated as they are.

- *Young-Hee is living in the house that her father built.* (that her father built; modifies: *house*; essential clause: no comma needed)

- *Her brother, who is a world-class musician, lives with her.* (who is a world class musician; modifies: *brother*; nonessential clause: comma needed)

Tell students that using adjective clauses will add clarifying and descriptive details to their writing. For more practice with this skill, see page 533.

CCSS Common Core State Standards

L.7.1.a: Explain the function of phrases and clauses in general and their function in specific sentences. **L.7.1.c:** Place phrases and clauses within a sentence, recognizing and correcting misplaced and dangling modifiers. **L.7.2:** Demonstrate command of the conventions of standard English capitalization, punctuation, and spelling when writing.

Adjective Clauses

Know the Rule

An **adjective clause** is a dependent clause that, like an adjective, describes a noun or a pronoun. An adjective clause always follows the word it describes and often begins with a relative pronoun such as *who, whom, whose, which,* or *that.*
Example:
Women **who have made outstanding accomplishments in sports** inspire all of us.

Practice the Rule

Number a sheet of paper 1–10. Write each sentence. Underline the adjective clause. Circle the noun that each adjective clause describes.

1. Mildred Didrikson, who earned honors in basketball, track and field, and golf, was a famous twentieth-century athlete.
2. She was born in Port Arthur, which is a city on the southeastern coast of Texas.
3. In 1932, she won two gold medals in the Olympics, which were held in Los Angeles.
4. Wilma Rudolph, who was born in 1940, was another Olympic gold medalist.
5. The library has a Wilma Rudolph biography that I want to read.
6. The three gold medals that Rudolph won during the 1960 Olympics in Rome made her an international celebrity.
7. Mia Hamm, who was a world-class soccer player, is now retired.
8. Hamm is a woman that many young women think of as a role model.
9. She has written a book and has appeared in a television documentary, which was produced for cable television.
10. The accomplishments of these admirable athletes have helped women gain opportunities that were not available to them a hundred years ago.

Adverb Clauses

Know the Rule

An **adverb clause** is a dependent clause that tells about a verb, an adjective, or an adverb. Adverb clauses tell *where, when, why,* or *how much.* They often begin with a subordinating conjunction such as *than, although, because, if, as, as if, while, when,* or *whenever.*

> **Example:**
> Mrs. Stone planted some flower bulbs in the fall **because she wanted flowers to bloom in the spring**.

Practice the Rule

Number a sheet of paper 1–10. Write each sentence. Underline the adverb clause. Circle the verb, adjective, or adverb that each adverb clause tells about.

1. When the cold winter weather has finally gone, many people (plant) their gardens.
2. Some people (grow) flowers because they enjoy the beautiful blossoms.
3. My uncle's garden is much (larger) than my family's garden.
4. After a person plants a garden, he or she (must work) in it diligently.
5. Rabbits and chipmunks will (eat) the vegetables if they get half a chance.
6. Some gardeners (spray) their plants with chemicals so that harmful insects will stay away.
7. These gardeners are (confident) because they believe the chemicals will protect their plants.
8. Last year, my mother's tomatoes grew (better) than her onions.
9. When all the flowers and vegetables do well, the hard work (seems) worthwhile.
10. A person (can start) a garden wherever there is enough room and sunlight for the plants.

Conventions

Mini-Lesson

Student Objectives

- Identify adverb clauses. *(p. 507)*

Adverb Clauses

An adverb clause tells about a verb, an adjective, or another adverb. An adverb clause that begins a sentence is followed by a comma. An adverb clause at the end of a sentence needs no comma. Display these sentences on the board. Have students identify each adverb clause and the word it modifies. Then have students explain why the sentences are punctuated as they are.

- *When I got home from practice, I took a nap.* (When I got home from practice; took; clause begins the sentence)

- *I woke up feeling tired because I took such a short nap.* (because I took such a short nap; tired; clause ends the sentence)

Tell students that using adverb clauses will add clarifying and descriptive details to their writing and help vary their sentence structure. For more practice with this skill, see page 534.

CCSS **Common Core State Standards**

L.7.1.a: Explain the function of phrases and clauses in general and their function in specific sentences.
L.7.1.c: Place phrases and clauses within a sentence, recognizing and correcting misplaced and dangling modifiers.

Conventions

Mini-Lesson

Student Objectives

- Identify and correct run-on sentences and comma splices. (p. 508)

Run-on Sentences and Comma Splices

A run-on sentence results when no punctuation is used between two complete sentences. A comma splice results when two complete sentences are separated only by a comma. Display this sentence on the board. Discuss with students possible ways to correct it.

- *We began rehearsing the play last Thursday everyone involved was present.* (Possible response: We began rehearsing the play last Thursday. Everyone involved was present. Possible response: We began rehearsing the play last Thursday, and everyone involved was present. Possible response: We began rehearsing the play last Thursday; everybody involved was present.)

Advise students to read their writing aloud so that they can hear where the pauses are in natural speech. This will give them a clue about where the punctuation should go. For more practice with this skill, see page 534.

CCSS **Common Core State Standards**

L.7.2: Demonstrate command of the conventions of standard English capitalization, punctuation, and spelling when writing.

Conventions Grammar, Usage & Mechanics

Run-on Sentences and Comma Splices

Know the Rule

A **run-on sentence** results when no punctuation is used between two complete sentences. A **comma splice** results when two complete sentences are separated by only a comma. You can correct a run-on sentence or a comma splice in several ways. You may decide to add a conjunction, such as *and* or *but,* after the comma. You may decide to separate the two sentences by a period. You may join the sentences with a semicolon.

Examples:
Incorrect:
Vaccinations help to immunize people against diseases, they have not always been popular with the general population.
Correct:
Vaccinations help to immunize people against disease, **but** they have not always been popular with the general population.
Vaccinations help to immunize people against disease. **T**hey have not always been popular with the general population.
Vaccinations help to immunize people against disease; **they** have not always been popular with the general population.

Practice the Rule

Correct sentences 1 and 2 with a semicolon. Correct sentences 3 and 4 by adding a comma and a conjunction. Correct sentence 5 by making two sentences. Possible responses.

1. We heard at the beginning of the school year that we needed flu vaccinations; medical agencies warned parents and students that a flu epidemic was on the way.

2. Many people objected to having vaccinations; their objections were often based on ethical, religious, or medical reasons.

3. Some people were afraid that the flu shot was dangerous, and they thought that they could avoid the flu by washing their hands and not coughing in other people's faces.

4. The flu and the vaccination were constantly in the news, but they disappeared from the news when the actual number of cases was much lower than expected.

5. Nevertheless, over the years vaccinations have been extremely beneficial to people. vaccinations have helped control dreaded diseases such as polio and smallpox.

Common Nouns and Proper Nouns

Know the Rule

A **common noun** names a general person, place, thing, or idea (*girl, park, painting, freedom*). Common nouns are not capitalized. A **proper noun** names a particular person, place, thing, or idea (*Cindy, Yellowstone National Park, Mona Lisa*). Proper nouns are capitalized. A proper noun that consists of several words (*Yellowstone National Park*) is considered one proper noun.

Practice the Rule

Number a sheet of paper 1–10. Write each sentence. Underline each common noun. Circle each proper noun.

1. Throughout the United States, you can find monuments created by very early Native American cultures.
2. Such a monument is Serpent Mound, located in the state of Ohio.
3. My pal Gus told me that the mound, which is made of earth, is over 1,370 feet long and about one yard high.
4. It winds back and forth through the landscape for about 800 feet.
5. Seen from an airplane, the mound has the shape of a giant snake.
6. Our science teacher, Mr. Pryor, told us that the mound is the largest of its kind in the world.
7. Serpent Mound does not contain any artifacts, such as pottery, jewelry, or graves.
8. Aunt Martha told me that scientists think that the mound was built to serve some religious purpose.
9. The Serpent Mound Museum is located near the mound.
10. You can find information and photographs of Serpent Mound at various websites or by contacting the Ohio Historical Society.

Mini-Lesson

Student Objectives

- Identify common nouns and proper nouns. *(p. 509)*

Common Nouns and Proper Nouns

Display these sentences on the board. Have students identify and label the common nouns and proper nouns.

- *My relatives live in Austin, Texas.* (*relatives*; common; *Austin, Texas*: proper)

- *Jason believes that honesty is important.* (*Jason*: proper; *honesty*: common)

- *My best friend lives on Commercial Street.* (*friend*: common; *Commercial Street*: proper)

- *Mr. Chin wants to hire people with creative abilities.* (*Mr. Chin*: proper; *people*: common; *abilities*: common)

Explain, too, that nouns can be either concrete or abstract. Concrete nouns—such as *bridge, spaghetti, car*—are ones that can be experienced through the senses. Abstract nouns—such as *bravery, jealousy, love*—cannot be sensed. For more practice with this skill, see page 534.

CCSS **C**ommon **C**ore **S**tate **S**tandards

L.7.2: Demonstrate command of the conventions of standard English capitalization, punctuation, and spelling when writing.

Conventions

Mini-Lesson

Student Objectives

- Identify and correctly use singular nouns and plural nouns. *(p. 510)*

Singular Nouns and Plural Nouns

A singular noun names one person, place, thing, or idea. A plural noun names more than one. For most nouns, add *–s* or *–es* to the singular. Sometimes the spelling changes *(wife, wives; child, children).* Display the following nouns on the board. Have students write the plural form of each noun. Then have students explain how they formed the plural.

- *crutch* (*crutches*; add *–es* because the noun ends in *–ch*)

- *knife* (*knives*; spelling of certain nouns changes when *–es* is added to form the plural)

- *cuff* (*cuffs*; for most singular nouns, add *–s* to form the plural)

- *valley* (*valleys*; for most singular nouns, add *–s* to form the plural)

Write a collection of words from around the room on the board. Ask students to spell the plural forms.

Tell students that using singular and plural nouns correctly will help them avoid distracting errors in their writing. For more practice with this skill, see page 535.

CCSS **Common Core State Standards**

L.7.2: Demonstrate command of the conventions of standard English capitalization, punctuation, and spelling when writing.

Singular Nouns and Plural Nouns

Know the Rule

A **singular noun** names one person, place, thing, or idea. A **plural noun** names more than one. For most nouns, add *-s* or *-es* to form the plural. The spelling of some nouns changes when *-es* is added to form the plural (*baby/babies; knife/knives*). A few nouns do not add *-s* or *-es* to form the plural; instead, the spelling changes (*child/children*). A few other nouns have the same form in the singular and plural (*sheep*).

Examples:

Many of the **children** in the fourth grade class have **pets**.

Two **girls** own pet **mice**.

Birds can make the **lives** of their **owners** more musical.

Geese would probably not make good **pets**.

Practice the Rule

On a sheet of paper make two columns. Label the left column **Singular Nouns**. Label the right column **Plural Nouns**. Number both columns 1–5. Then list the singular nouns and plural nouns in each sentence.

1. You should regularly check your dog for fleas and ticks. dog; fleas, ticks
2. Dogs can pick up these harmful pests in a pile of leaves. pile; dogs, pests, leaves
3. Some ticks can cause diseases with their bite. bite; ticks, diseases
4. Certain kinds of combs can help you find a tick or flea on your pet. tick, flea, pet; kinds, combs
5. A flea can jump from puppies onto the children playing with them. flea; puppies, children

Number your paper 6–10. Copy the following chart. Write the missing singular or plural form of each noun.

Singular Nouns	Plural Nouns
6. country	_____ countries
7. _____ woman	women
8. belief	_____ beliefs
9. _____ mouse	mice
10. moose	_____ moose

Personal Pronouns

Know the Rule

A pronoun can take the place of a noun. **Personal pronouns** can be used to stand for the person speaking, the person spoken to, or the person spoken about. **First-person pronouns** refer to the speaker (*I, me*) or include the speaker (*we, us*). **Second-person pronouns** refer to the person being spoken to (*you*). **Third-person pronouns** refer to the person, place, or thing being spoken about (*he, him, she, her, it, they, them*).

Examples:

I want to learn more about the medical profession. (first person)

The speaker told **us** about the training required for doctors. (first person)

Have **you** ever been to a hospital? (second person)

She must be a determined medical student. (third person)

Practice the Rule

Number a sheet of paper 1–5. Write the personal pronoun in each sentence. Then write whether it is first person, second person, or third person.

1. An ambulance driver talked to us about some different jobs in medicine. us–first person
2. Jack asked her if the job as an ambulance driver was very demanding. her–third person
3. Can you believe that Jack asked such a question? you–second person
4. Carol's two brothers are the two doctors I know. I–first person
5. They operate on patients with heart problems. They–third person

Number your paper 6–10. Rewrite each sentence using the appropriate personal pronoun in place of the underlined words.

6. <u>Thomas and Cheryl</u> want to become nurse's aides. They
7. Thomas was telling <u>Tracy and me</u> all about that job. us
8. <u>Tracy and I</u> think the job sounds pretty interesting. We
9. <u>Steven</u> doesn't agree with that opinion at all! He
10. The librarian told <u>Thomas, Cheryl, Tracy, and Steven</u> to quiet down as they discussed jobs. them

Conventions

Mini-Lesson

Student Objectives

- Identify and correctly use personal pronouns. *(p. 511)*

Personal Pronouns

A pronoun can take the place of a noun. Display these sentences. Have students rewrite the sentences using the correct personal pronoun in place of the underlined words. Then have students label the personal pronoun as first person *(I, me, we, us)*, second person *(you)*, and third person *(he, him, she, her, it, they, them)*.

- <u>Eileen and I</u> *work for Mr. Gonzalez.* (We: first person)
- <u>Alan</u> *chose three books.* (He: third person)
- *I invited* <u>Tracy, Jose, and Kim</u> *to my party.* (them: third person)

Tell students that using personal pronouns in their writing will help them avoid the repetition of using the same noun over and over again. However, they must be sure that the antecedent of the pronoun is clear. For more practice with this skill, see page 535.

CCSS **C**ommon **C**ore **S**tate **S**tandards

L.7.1: Demonstrate command of the conventions of standard English grammar and usage when writing or speaking.

Appendix A: Grammar Practice T5II

Conventions

Mini-Lesson

Student Objectives

• Identify compound personal pronouns. *(p. 512)*

Compound Personal Pronouns

Compound personal pronouns are formed by adding *-self* or *-selves* to personal pronouns. Reflexive and intensive pronouns are kinds of compound personal pronouns. A reflexive pronoun refers back to the subject. An intensive pronoun emphasizes the subject and often appears right after the subject. Display these sentences on the board. Have students find the compound personal pronouns and tell whether they are reflexive or intensive pronouns.

• *Katie cooked the entire meal by herself.* (herself; reflexive)

• *Katie herself did all the preparation for the meal.* (herself; intensive)

• *We enjoyed ourselves at Katie's dinner.* (ourselves; reflexive)

• *Katie presented herself and her meal with a real sense of style.* (herself; reflexive)

Tell students that using compound personal pronouns correctly will help them add clarity and emphasis to their writing. For more practice with this skill, see page 535.

CCSS **C**ommon **C**ore **S**tate **S**tandards
L.7.1: Demonstrate command of the conventions of standard English grammar and usage when writing or speaking.

T512   Appendix A: Grammar Practice

Compound Personal Pronouns

Know the Rule

Pronouns formed by adding *-self* or *-selves* to the personal pronouns are called **compound personal pronouns**. Depending on how they are used in a sentence, they are also known as reflexive or intensive pronouns.

• A **reflexive pronoun** reflects back on the subject.
   Example:
   Mike left a message for **himself** to check his voicemail.

• An **intensive pronoun** emphasizes the subject. It often appears right after the subject.
   Example:
   Katie **herself** arranged the plans for the band's rehearsal.

Practice the Rule

Number a sheet of paper 1–5. Write the compound personal pronoun in each sentence. Then write the noun, nouns, or pronoun to which the compound personal pronoun refers.

1. Having decided to give a rock concert for the seventh grade, Mike and Katie found themselves faced with a lot of responsibilities. themselves–Mike, Katie

2. Mike decided that he himself would find the necessary amplifiers and microphones for the band. himself–he

3. The principal herself lent Mike two microphones. herself–principal

4. I myself thought that my two friends would never succeed at their task. myself–I

5. They must have asked themselves many times if they had made a smart decision. themselves–They

Number your paper 6–10. Rewrite each sentence by replacing the underlined word or words with the appropriate compound personal pronoun.

6. Courtney and Kurt bought <u>Courtney and Kurt</u> tickets for the concert. themselves

7. Courtney had convinced <u>Courtney</u> that the concert would be fun. herself

8. Ethan and I gave <u>Ethan and me</u> plenty of time to get to the concert. ourselves

9. The band presented <u>the band</u> with great style. itself

10. The students at the concert enjoyed <u>the students at the concert</u>. themselves

Possessive Pronouns

Know the Rule

Possessive pronouns show ownership. The possessive pronouns *my, your, her, his, its, our,* and *their* can replace possessive nouns. These possessive pronouns can stand alone or before a noun. Other possessive pronouns always stand alone. These include *mine, yours, hers, ours,* and *theirs.*

Examples:

Kevin and Kayla's poster is about the planet Mars.

Their poster is about the planet Mars. (possessive pronoun before a noun)

The poster about Saturn is Maya's.

The poster about Saturn is **hers.** (possessive pronoun standing alone)

Practice the Rule

Number a sheet of paper 1–5. After each number, write the possessive pronoun in each sentence. Some sentences may have more than one possessive pronoun.

1. Our recent knowledge about the planets can be attributed mainly to the U.S. space program. **Our**

2. Interplanetary spacecraft track planets and record details about their movements. **their**

3. For their report, Jerome and Anna decided to concentrate on Earth. **their**

4. The idea to write about the rings of Saturn for our group's report was mine. **our, mine**

5. I enjoyed Jason, Tanya, and Bill's project on Venus. Theirs was my favorite. **Theirs, my**

Number your paper 6–10. Write the possessive pronoun that could take the place of the underlined word or words in each sentence.

6. <u>Galileo's</u> observations of the planets in the 17th century supported the idea that the planets orbited the sun. **His**

7. <u>The planets'</u> orbits about the sun are not exactly circular. **Their**

8. <u>Tara's</u> planet poster was colorful but not as informative as <u>Tim's.</u> **Her, his**

9. Did you know that <u>Saturn's</u> rings are made up almost entirely of ice? **its**

10. I think that the best planet report was <u>Jill and Shaniqua's.</u> **theirs**

Conventions

Mini-Lesson

Student Objectives

- Identify and correctly use possessive pronouns. *(p. 513)*

Possessive Pronouns

Possessive pronouns show ownership and replace possessive nouns. Display these sentences on the board. Have students tell the possessive pronoun that could take the place of the underlined word or words in each sentence.

- *The book is not <u>Mia's</u> book.* (her)

- *If students knew that, they would be more careful about recycling <u>students'</u> trash.* (their)

- *<u>Ben's</u> report is on active volcanoes.* (His)

- *<u>The school's</u> location made it very easy to find.* (Its)

Some possessive pronouns stand alone in a sentence. Display the following sentences. Have students identify the possessive pronouns.

- *Is that cell phone yours?* (yours)

- *No, it is hers.* (hers)

Tell students that identifying and correctly using possessive pronouns will help them to vary sentence structure and avoid repetition in their writing. For more practice with this skill, see page 536.

CCSS **C**ommon **C**ore **S**tate **S**tandards

L.7.1: Demonstrate command of the conventions of standard English grammar and usage when writing or speaking.

Conventions

Mini-Lesson

Student Objectives

- Identify and correctly use relative pronouns and interrogative pronouns. *(p. 514)*

Relative Pronouns and Interrogative Pronouns

Relative pronouns are used to introduce dependent clauses. Interrogative pronouns are used to introduce questions. Display these sentences on the board. Remind students to use *who* as the subject or predicate nominative of a clause and to use *whom* as an object. Have students tell the relative pronoun or interrogative pronoun that best completes each sentence. Then, have them discuss their answers.

- *(Who, Whom) is the best photographer?* (Who; predicate nominative of the clause)

- *(Who, Whom) should I talk to about my project?* (Whom; object of a preposition)

- *We want to talk with someone (who, that) knows about photography.* (who; subject of the dependent clause)

Tell students that using relative and interrogative pronouns in their writing can help them vary their sentence structure and make their writing more interesting. For more practice with this skill, see page 536.

CCSS Common Core State Standards

L.7.1: Demonstrate command of the conventions of standard English grammar and usage when writing or speaking.

Relative Pronouns and Interrogative Pronouns

Know the Rule

> The **relative pronouns** *who, whom, which, that, what,* and *whose* are used to introduce dependent clauses. The **interrogative pronouns** *who, whom, which, what,* and *whose* are used to introduce questions. Notice that the same pronouns may be either relative pronouns or interrogative pronouns. You must determine how the pronoun is used in the sentence.
>
> **Examples:**
> **What** does the mayor propose to do about the traffic congestion in our town?
> The solution **that** I believe would help involves banning cars on certain days.

Practice the Rule

Number a sheet of paper 1–5. Write each sentence. Underline the relative pronoun and circle each interrogative pronoun.

1. (Which) traffic problem in the United States are you studying?
2. The problem <u>that</u> I want to write about is intercity traffic.
3. (What) do you think causes the traffic congestion in cities?
4. (Whom) do you think we should contact about this problem?
5. The people <u>who</u> live in the cities must help solve the traffic problems.

Number your paper 6–10. Write the relative pronoun or interrogative pronoun that completes each sentence.

6. _____ agency did you contact for traffic information? Which (or *What*)
7. _____ should I ask for data concerning the number of cars in our town? Whom
8. Do you know the candidate _____ party supports carpooling? whose
9. Margot asked the speaker _____ she thought about banning cars on Saturday. what
10. I believe _____ carpooling will help alleviate the traffic problem. that

Articles

Know the Rule

Adjectives describe nouns. The words *a*, *an*, and *the* are adjectives called **articles**. Use *a* or *an* to refer to a general noun. Use *a* before a word that begins with a consonant sound. Use *an* before a word that begins with a vowel sound. Use *the* when you refer to a specific item or items. Articles can appear before nouns or before an adverb or adjective.

Examples:
I need to get **a** book about reptiles for my report.
This is **an** interesting book about alligators.
Hand me **the** books on the table.

Practice the Rule

Number a sheet of paper 1–10. Write each sentence, using the article or articles in parentheses that correctly complete the sentence. Then underline the article **the** each time it appears and the word to which it refers.

1. One of the traits of (a/an) reptile is that it lays eggs.
2. (A/An) alligator is (a/an) well-known reptile.
3. The saltwater crocodile is (a/an) example of (a/an) large reptile.
4. The encyclopedia gives (a/an) extensive description of this crocodile.
5. One photograph at the website I visited shows (a/an) hind leg of a lizard.
6. When (a/an) crocodile is threatened with danger, it bares its teeth and hisses.
7. How can scientists determine if (a/an) reptile is as intelligent as (a/an) bird?
8. Curled up, (a/an) adult thread snake can fit on the face of (a/an) quarter.
9. This photograph shows (a/an) snake swallowing (a/an) egg.
10. The reptile is certainly (a/an) interesting class of animals.

Conventions

Mini-Lesson

Student Objectives

• Identify and correctly use articles. *(p. 515)*

Articles

The words *a*, *an*, and *the* are adjectives called articles. Articles can appear before nouns or before an adjective or adverb. Display these sentences. Have students choose the correct articles and explain their answers.

• *One of (a, the) dogs in the race was (a, an) border collie.* (**the:** refers to a specific dog; **a:** refers to a general class of dogs, comes before a consonant sound)

• *He was (a, an) outstanding dog.* (**an:** refers to a general class of dogs, comes before a vowel sound)

• *(The, A) dog's name was Barney.* (**The:** refers to a specific dog)

Tell students that using articles correctly can help them avoid distracting grammatical errors in their writing. For more practice with this skill, see page 536.

CCSS **C**ommon **C**ore **S**tate **S**tandards
L.7.1: Demonstrate command of the conventions of standard English grammar and usage when writing or speaking.

Conventions

Mini-Lesson

Student Objectives

• Identify and correctly use demonstrative pronouns and demonstrative adjectives. (p. 516)

Demonstrative Pronouns and Demonstrative Adjectives

Display these sentences on the board. Have students find and label the demonstrative pronoun or demonstrative adjective.

• *(This, These) are my favorite books.* (*These:* demonstrative pronoun)

• *(That, Those) books are mysteries.* (*Those:* demonstrative adjective)

• *(That, Those) looks like a good book.* (*That:* demonstrative noun)

• *(This, These) is my absolute favorite book.* (*This:* demonstrative pronoun)

• *(This, Those) students belong to a book club.* (*Those:* demonstrative adjective)

Tell students that identifying and correctly using demonstrative pronouns and demonstrative adjectives will help them add clarifying details and avoid unnecessary repetition in their writing. For more practice with this skill, see page 537.

CCSS **Common Core State Standards**

L.7.1: Demonstrate command of the conventions of standard English grammar and usage when writing or speaking.

Demonstrative Pronouns and Demonstrative Adjectives

Know the Rule

This, these, that, and *those* can be either **demonstrative adjectives** or **demonstrative pronouns**. *This* and *these* refer to a thing or things nearby. *That* and *those* refer to a thing or things farther away.
Demonstrative adjectives are used with nouns. They tell "which one."
Examples:
I like **these** cartoons in my book.
That book isn't very funny.

Demonstrative pronouns take the place of nouns or pronouns.
Example:
This is a much funnier collection of early comics.

Practice the Rule

Number a sheet of paper 1–10. Write the demonstrative adjective or demonstrative pronoun in each sentence. After each demonstrative adjective, write the noun that it describes. After each demonstrative pronoun, write the noun or pronoun it takes the place of.

1. I love this cartoon by Dr. Seuss. this–cartoon

2. That artist must have been really talented. That–artist

3. This is the book on cartoons I requested last week from the library. This–book

4. Do these websites describe the history of cartoons and comic strips? these–websites

5. This series of panels makes up a comic strip. This–series

6. These are reproductions of drawings from *Hogan's Alley,* one of the first newspaper comic strips in the United States. These–reproductions

7. That is the funniest cartoon I have ever seen. That–cartoon

8. Among the cartoons you've shown me, this one is the most colorful. this–one

9. It's difficult to understand the point of these old political cartoons. these–cartoons

10. If it hadn't been for those early cartoonists, we might not have today's animated cartoons. those–cartoonists

Prepositions

Know the Rule

A **preposition** is a word that shows a relationship between the noun or pronoun that follows it (object of the preposition) and another word or group of words in the sentence. A **prepositional phrase** is a group of words beginning with a preposition and ending with a noun or pronoun.

Example:
Rain pounded **on the roof**.

Practice the Rule

Number a sheet of paper 1–5. Write the prepositional phrase or phrases in each sentence.

1. Thunderstorms in the Midwest can be frightening experiences. in the Midwest
2. You can usually see the dark clouds of the storm approaching. of the storm
3. The lightning begins, and you can hear the deep rumbling of thunder. of thunder
4. Throughout the storm, bolts of lightning flash across the sky. Throughout the storm, of lightning, across the sky
5. Luckily, the thunderstorms quickly pass into the distance. into the distance

Number your paper 6–10. Write a preposition from the box to complete each sentence. Try to use each preposition only once.

> above   across   from   in   of

6. Having come _____ Los Angeles, experiencing a midwestern thunderstorm was a completely new experience. from
7. Lightning seemed to explode _____ our heads. above
8. We took refuge _____ my grandfather's barn. in
9. The powerful thunder rattled the windows _____ the barn. of (or in)
10. When the rain stopped, we ran _____ the yard to the house. across (or in)

Conventions

Mini-Lesson

Student Objectives

- Identify and correctly use prepositions and prepositional phrases. *(p. 517)*

Prepositions

A prepositional phrase is a group of words beginning with a preposition and ending with a noun or pronoun. Display these prepositions on the board. Have students use the prepositions to write sentences with prepositional phrases. Remind students that prepositional phrases do not have verbs; only clauses have a subject and a verb.

- *about* (Possible response: I asked a question about plant life.)
- *after* (Possible response: After the game, we went out to eat.)
- *behind* (Possible response: Adrianna left her notebook behind the bookcase.)
- *during* (Possible response: During the storm, we played games.)
- *with* (Possible response: I went to the movies with my friend.)

Tell students that using prepositional phrases will help them vary their sentence structure and add clarifying details to their writing. For more practice with this skill, see page 537.

CCSS **C**ommon **C**ore **S**tate **S**tandards
L.7.1.c: Place phrases and clauses within a sentence, recognizing and correcting misplaced and dangling modifiers.

Conventions

Mini-Lesson

Student Objectives

- Identify and correctly use the present, past and future tense of verbs. *(p. 518)*

The Simple Tenses

Use the present tense for actions that happen regularly or now. Use the past tense for actions that occurred in the past. Use the future tense for actions that will occur in the future. Discuss with students the different meanings, depending on the verb tense, of each of these sentences.

- *Anna reads every day.*
- *Anna read two books last week.*
- *Anna will read fifty books before the year is over.*

Display these sentences on the board. Have students write the correct verb to complete the sentence.

- *Next Tuesday, we (go, will go) to the museum.* (will go)
- *Yesterday, we (will go, went) to the ball game.* (went)

Tell students that using verb tenses correctly in their writing will help them accurately describe when events take place. For more practice with this skill, see page 537.

CCSS **Common Core State Standards**

L.7.1: Demonstrate command of the conventions of standard English grammar and usage when writing or speaking.

The Simple Tenses

Know the Rule

The tense of a verb tells when the action happens. The **present tense** indicates that something happens regularly or is true now. *(fly)* The **past tense** tells that something has happened in the past. The past tense is usually formed by adding *-ed* to the verb. *(call/called)* The past tense of some verbs has a different spelling. *(flew)* The **future tense** tells that something is going to happen. The future tense is formed with *will*. *(will fly)*

Practice the Rule

Number a sheet of paper 1–5. Write the verb in each sentence. Then identify the tense of the verb by writing **present tense, past tense,** or **future tense**.

1. Over six hundred species of birds nest in North America. nest–present tense
2. Not all birds migrate to warmer climates before winter. migrate–present tense
3. I will ask the guide at the nature preserve about these birds. will ask–future tense
4. Our bus to the nature preserve finally rumbled to a stop at the front gate. rumbled–past tense
5. On the way, my friends and I thought of questions for our guide. thought–past tense

Number your paper 6–10. Write the present-, past-, or future-tense form of the verb that correctly completes each sentence.

6. Last week in class, we _____ bird flight and migration. (study) studied
7. We heard about and _____ lots of interesting things about birds. (discover) discovered
8. For example, a bird's feathers _____ very little. (weigh) weigh
9. In the first part of our tour, we watched as a bird _____ seeds from the guide's hand. (eat) ate
10. Next Monday, we _____ the different habitats of birds. (explore) will explore

Progressive Verb Forms

Know the Rule

Progressive forms of verbs show continuing action. The **present-progressive** form of a verb consists of the helping verbs *am, is,* or *are* and the present participle of that verb. (*I am reading.*) The **past-progressive** form consists of the helping verb *was* or *were* and the present participle. (*They were reading.*) The **future-progressive** form consists of the helping verbs *will be* and the present participle. (*You will be reading.*)

Practice the Rule

Number a sheet of paper 1–5. Write the verb in each sentence, including its helping verb. Then identify the verb form by writing **present progressive, past progressive,** or **future progressive.**

1. Our class is studying different genres of fiction. is studying–present progressive
2. Joaquin is reading an English mystery novel. is reading–present progressive
3. I was considering a science fiction novel as my choice. was considering–past progressive
4. Two of my friends were searching the library for gothic horror stories. were searching–past progressive
5. My classmates and I will be presenting oral reports about our books next Wednesday. will be presenting–future progressive

Number your paper 6–10. Rewrite each sentence using the progressive form of the verb in parentheses.

6. I _____ information about the author of my book today in the library. (future progressive form of *research*) will be researching
7. Nicole _____ her oral presentation with a friend. (present progressive form of *practice*) is practicing
8. Our teacher _____ us on the content of our report as well as on our presentation. (future progressive form of *grade*) will be grading
9. Ashley _____ her book just before lunch. (past progressive form of *finish*) was finishing
10. Both David and Ana _____ on historical fiction books. (present progressive form of *report*) are reporting

Conventions

Mini-Lesson

Student Objectives

• Identify and correctly use progressive verb forms. (*p. 519*)

Progressive Verb Forms

Progressive forms of verbs show continuing action. The present progressive uses the helping verb *am, is,* or *are.* The past progressive uses the helping verb *was* or *were.* The future progressive uses *will be.* Display these sentences on the board. Have students complete the sentences using the progressive form of the verb in parentheses.

• *Eric and I _____ dance lessons. (present progressive, take)* (are taking)

• *Our instructor _____ us the flamenco. (past progressive, teach)* (was teaching)

• *I'm sure that we _____ many different dance steps. (future progressive, learn)* (will be learning)

Tell students that using progressive verb forms in their writing will help them more accurately identify when events are taking place. For more practice with this skill, see page 538.

CCSS Common Core State Standards
L.7.1: Demonstrate command of the conventions of standard English grammar and usage when writing or speaking.

Conventions

Mini-Lesson

Student Objectives

- Identify and correctly use emphatic verb forms. (p. 520)

Emphatic Verb Forms

Emphatic forms of the present tense and past tense show emphasis. Discuss with students the different meanings of the following sentences.

- *I want that book.*
- *I do want that book. (emphatic present tense; gives greater emphasis)*
- *I finished my work on time.*
- *I did finish my work on time. (emphatic past tense; gives greater emphasis)*

Display these sentences on the board. Have students change the verb to the emphatic verb form of the past tense.

- *I fed the cat and the dog.* (I **did feed** the cat and the dog.)
- *I gave my best during the race.* (I **did give** my best during the race.)

Tell students that using emphatic verb forms in their writing can help vary their sentence structure and add emphasis when needed. For more practice with this skill, see page 538.

CCSS **C**ommon **C**ore **S**tate **S**tandards

L.7.1: Demonstrate command of the conventions of standard English grammar and usage when writing or speaking.

Conventions Grammar, Usage & Mechanics

Emphatic Verb Forms

Know the Rule

> **Emphatic forms** of the present tense and the past tense show emphasis. These forms are made by using the present or past form of the verb *do* with the base form of a verb.
> **Examples:**
> I **do like** making some money during school vacations.
> Caitlyn **did refuse** the position in the school library.

Practice the Rule

Number a sheet of paper 1–5. Rewrite each sentence, changing the verb to the emphatic form of the present tense.

1. I work part-time at the bookstore during my spring vacation. do work
2. Kelly wants a job like that for herself this summer. does want
3. I think I'm old enough for a part-time job. do think
4. Yes, my parents agree with me about my getting a job. do agree
5. I appreciate your offer of work at the library. do appreciate

Number your paper 6–10. Rewrite each sentence, changing the verb to the emphatic form of the past tense.

6. My mother suggested the possibility of my working during summer vacation. did suggest
7. Yes, I accepted the job mowing Mrs. Dolan's lawn. did accept
8. I volunteered a few hours each weekend at a local park. did volunteer
9. Yes, I finished the assigned tasks. did finish
10. I anticipated having several hours of free time last weekend. did anticipate

Transitive Verbs and Intransitive Verbs

Know the Rule

Action verbs may or may not need an object to complete the action of the verb. An action verb that has an object is called a **transitive verb**. An action verb that does not have an object is called an **intransitive verb**. Many verbs can be either transitive or intransitive, depending on their use in a sentence.

Examples:
In 2005, a terrible natural disaster **occurred**. (intransitive verb)
We **researched** Hurricane Katrina on the library computers. (transitive verb)

Practice the Rule

Number a sheet of paper 1–10. Write the verb in each sentence. Then write whether the verb is transitive or intransitive. If the verb is transitive, write the direct object.

1. A powerful hurricane <u>battered</u> the city of New Orleans. battered–transitive–city
2. Huge waves <u>pounded</u> the walls that protected the city from floodwaters. pounded–transitive–walls
3. Eventually, the walls, called levees, <u>collapsed</u>. collapsed–intransitive
4. Floodwaters <u>rose</u> higher and higher in the city streets. rose–intransitive
5. Thousands of people <u>evacuated</u> their homes. evacuated–transitive–homes
6. Government officials and volunteers <u>rescued</u> stranded inhabitants. rescued–transitive–inhabitants
7. Thousands of college students <u>volunteered</u>. volunteered–intransitive
8. The high winds and flooding <u>caused</u> terrible damage throughout the city. caused–transitive–damage
9. In the years after the flood, parts of New Orleans have <u>recovered</u>. recovered–intransitive
10. People <u>repaired</u> the damaged streets and buildings. repaired–transitive–streets, buildings

Mini-Lesson

Student Objectives

• Identify transitive verbs and intransitive verbs. *(p. 521)*

Transitive Verbs and Intransitive Verbs

An action verb that has an object is a transitive verb. An action verb that does not have an object is an intransitive verb. If students have difficulty distinguishing transitive and intransitive verbs, suggest that they ask *whom?* or *what?* after the verb. If the answer is a noun or pronoun, the verb is transitive. Display these sentences on the board. Have students identify transitive verbs and their objects and intransitive verbs.

• *Lightning struck the plane.* (*struck:* transitive; *plane:* direct object)

• *The pilot flew the plane expertly.* (*flew:* transitive; *plane:* direct object)

• *The plane even arrived on time.* (*arrived:* intransitive)

Tell students that understanding transitive and intransitive verbs will enable them to write more complicated sentences and thereby add variety to their means of expression. For more practice with this skill, see page 538.

CCSS **Common Core State Standards**
L.7.1: Demonstrate command of the conventions of standard English grammar and usage when writing or speaking.

Conventions

Mini-Lesson

Student Objectives

• Identify and correctly use conjunctions. *(p. 522)*

Conjunctions

Display these sentences. Have students choose the correct conjunction and tell what kind it is.

• *Ron worked hard on the project, _____ he did not win a prize. (and, but)* (but: coordinating)

• *Wing did not enter the contest _____ he did not think he could win. (although, because)* (because: subordinating)

• *_____ Ramon had an original idea, he still did not win. (Because, Although)* (Although: subordinating)

• *Mario's execution was perfect, _____ he won first prize. (and, but)* (and: coordinating)

Tell students that using conjunctions in their writing can help them vary their sentence structure and clarify the relationships between clauses. Point out that using a coordinating conjunction to connect two independent clauses results in a compound sentence. Using a subordinating conjunction in a dependent clause to connect an idea to an independent clause results in a complex sentence. For more practice with this skill, see page 539.

CCSS **Common Core State Standards**

L.7.1: Demonstrate command of the conventions of standard English grammar and usage when writing or speaking. **L.7.1.b:** Choose among simple, compound, complex, and compound-complex sentences to signal differing relationships among ideas.

Conventions

Know the Rule

> **Coordinating conjunctions** (*and, but, or, so*) connect words or groups of words (including independent clauses) that are of equal importance in a sentence.
>
> **Subordinating conjunctions** (such as *although, because, since, if, after,* and *before*) show how one clause is related to another more important clause. Subordinating conjunctions are used at the beginning of adverb clauses.

Practice the Rule

On a separate sheet of paper, write the conjunction in each sentence and identify it as a coordinating conjunction or a subordinating conjunction.

1. Many sports have dishonest players, and baseball is no exception. coordinating conjunction
2. Although the 1919 World Series scandal happened long ago, it lives on. subordinating conjunction
3. Several Chicago players joined together to throw the World Series because they were dissatisfied with their low salaries. subordinating conjunction
4. The poorly paid players disliked the team's owner, but they also disliked the players making better salaries. coordinating conjunction
5. The players wanted more money, so they contacted local gangsters. coordinating conjunction

On a separate sheet of paper, choose the conjunction in parentheses that best completes the sentence.

6. The gangsters agreed to pay the players _____ they would lose the World Series. (if/although/but) if
7. The White Sox lost three of the first four games against the Cincinnati Reds, _____ the gangsters refused to pay the players any money. (if/or/but) but
8. _____ they had not been paid any money, the dishonest White Sox players decided that they would not throw the series. (Because/If/Although) Because
9. _____ Chicago won the next two games, the gangsters paid the players a visit. (Although/After/If) After
10. The gangsters scared the players into throwing the eighth game, _____ the Cincinnati Reds won the World Series. (but/and/since) and

More Conjunctions

Know the Rule

Correlative conjunctions always appear in pairs. They connect words or groups of words and provide more emphasis than coordinating conjunctions.

Examples:

Both bats **and** flying squirrels are mammals.

Neither bats **nor** flying squirrels have wings like those of birds.

Common Correlative Conjunctions

both...and	neither...nor	not only...but (also)
either...or	whether...or	

Practice the Rule

On a separate sheet of paper, write each sentence. Underline the correlative conjunctions in it.

1. A flying squirrel may be hunted at night by <u>either</u> owls <u>or</u> coyotes.
2. Its tail helps the flying squirrel <u>both</u> control its flight <u>and</u> stop before landing.
3. Active at night, bats spend the daylight hours <u>either</u> grooming <u>or</u> sleeping.
4. Bats are threatened by <u>both</u> disease <u>and</u> the presence of wind turbines.
5. We associate bats with <u>both</u> heroes, such as Batman, <u>and</u> villains, such as Dracula.
6. A hound is a type of dog that helps hunters <u>not only</u> track the prey being hunted, <u>but also</u> chase the prey.
7. There are many kinds of hounds, including <u>both</u> the beagle <u>and</u> the dachshund.
8. Most hunting hounds use <u>either</u> sight <u>or</u> scent to track prey.

On a separate sheet of paper, combine each pair of sentences by using the correlative conjunctions in parentheses that follow each pair.

9. Do you know whether the whippet is a hound or a spaniel?
   Do you know if the whippet is a hound? Do you know if the whippet is a spaniel? (whether...or)
10. Neither poodles nor border collies are classified as hounds.
    Poodles are not classified as hounds. Border collies are not classified as hounds. (neither...nor)

 **Conventions**

Mini-Lesson

Student Objectives

- Identify and correctly use correlative conjunctions. *(p. 523)*

More Conjunctions

Correlative conjunctions connect words or groups of words and provide more emphasis than coordinating conjunctions. Display these sentences on the board. Have students combine each pair of sentences by using the correlative conjunctions in parentheses.

- *Maria dances well. She is an excellent singer. (not only. . .but also)* (Maria not only dances well but also is an excellent singer.)

- *I will go to the game. I will go to finish my paper. (either. . .or)* (Either I will go to the game, or I will finish my paper.)

- *Jason doesn't sing well. Kim doesn't sing well. (neither. . .nor)* (Neither Jason nor Kim sings well.)

Tell students that using correlative conjunctions in their writing will help them make forceful and precise connections between words or groups of words. For more practice with this skill, see page 539.

CCSS **Common Core State Standards**

L.7.1: Demonstrate command of the conventions of standard English grammar and usage when writing or speaking.

Mini-Lesson

Student Objectives

• Identify and correctly use irregular verbs. *(p. 524)*

Irregular Verbs

Irregular verbs do not follow the same rules for forming past and past participle forms as regular verbs. The past and past participle forms of irregular verbs must be memorized. Display these sentences. Have students choose the correct past tense form of the irregular verb in parentheses.

• *I _____ some money to my friend, Miguel. (lend)* (lent)

• *Herman _____ his bicycle last week. (sell)* (sold)

• *I _____ Herman that he could probably get a better price. (tell)* (told)

• *Herman's buyer _____ for the bicycle with cash. (pay)* (paid)

• *I _____ that Herman should have waited for a better price. (think)* (thought)

Tell students that using irregular verbs correctly will help them avoid distracting and confusing errors in their writing. For more practice with this skill, see page 539.

CCSS **Common Core State Standards**

L.7.1: Demonstrate command of the conventions of standard English grammar and usage when writing or speaking.

Irregular Verbs

Know the Rule

The past and past participle of regular verbs are formed by adding *-ed* to the present form. (*climb, climbed, have climbed*) The past and past participle of **irregular verbs** are not formed by adding *-ed*. The best way to learn the past and past participle of irregular verbs is to memorize them. This chart shows the forms of a few irregular verbs.

Present	Past	Past Participle
do	did	(has, have) done
fly	flew	(has, have) flown
have	had	(has, have) had
ring	rang	(has, have) rung

Practice the Rule

Number a sheet of paper 1–5. Write each sentence using the correct form of the verb in parentheses.

1. I (have knowed/have known) about Amelia Earhart since reading about her last month.
2. She (flied/flew) by herself across the Atlantic Ocean in 1932.
3. No woman (had done/had did) that before her historic flight.
4. Earhart also (wrote/written) best-selling books about her adventures flying.
5. With each new accomplishment as a pilot, Earhart's fame (growed/grew).

Number your paper 6–10. Write each sentence using the past or past participle of the verb in parentheses.

6. In 1935, Earhart _____ more famous by flying from Hawaii to California. (become) became
7. In 1936, she _____ planning for a flight around the world. (begin) began
8. No woman had _____ around the world before. (fly) flown
9. Earhart and her navigator never _____ it around the world. (make) made
10. Sometime on July 2, 1937, their plane crashed and _____ in the ocean. (sink) sank

Subject-Verb Agreement

Know the Rule

The **subject** of a sentence and its **verb must agree in number**. Use a singular verb with a singular subject. Use a plural verb with a plural subject.

- A **collective noun,** such as *family, group, team,* or *flock,* names more than one person or thing acting together as one group. Collective nouns are almost always considered singular and require a singular verb.

  Example:
  My **family enjoys** hiking.

- Most **indefinite pronouns,** including *everyone, nobody, nothing,* and *anything,* are considered singular. These pronouns require a singular verb.

  Examples:
  Everybody is excited about the dance this Friday.

- A few indefinite pronouns, such as *many* and *several,* are considered plural.
  Several are going early to decorate the gym.

Practice the Rule

Number a sheet of paper 1–10. Write each sentence, using the correct form of the verb in parentheses. Then underline the simple subject.

1. <u>Nobody</u> (want/**wants**) to miss the homecoming football game this Friday night.
2. My <u>family</u> (look/**looks**) forward to the game every year.
3. <u>Nothing</u> (excite/**excites**) my father more than the thought of attending the game.
4. Of course, our school's <u>team</u> (expect/**expects**) to win the game.
5. The <u>crowd</u> at the homecoming game (**is**/are) always very noisy.
6. <u>Everyone</u> (attend/**attends**) expecting a close, exciting game.
7. Our <u>class</u> always (yell/**yells**) the loudest at the school pep rally on Friday afternoon.
8. A <u>group</u> of cheerleaders usually (lead/**leads**) us in cheers for the team.
9. <u>Several</u> from the high school often (**visit**/visits) the middle school for the pep rally.
10. For a few hours, <u>everything</u> related to schoolwork (are/**is**) happily forgotten.

 **Conventions**

Mini-Lesson

Student Objectives

- Understand and apply the rules of subject-verb agreement. (p. 525)

Subject-Verb Agreement

The subject of a sentence and its verb must agree in number. Remind students that the noun closest to the verb is not always the subject of the sentence. Display the following sentences. Have students identify the subject of the sentence and tell which verb agrees with each subject.

- *Pictures of the dancer (is, are) displayed at the local museum.* (Pictures, are)

- *Displays in the museum (includes, include) photographs of notable residents.* (Displays, include)

- *Exhibits spanning the century (graces, grace) the museum.* (Exhibits, grace)

- *My family (plans, plan) on visiting the museum soon.* (family, plans)

Tell students that using correct subject-verb agreement in their writing will help them avoid distracting and confusing grammatical errors. For more practice with this skill, see page 540.

CCSS **C**ommon **C**ore **S**tate **S**tandards

L.7.1: Demonstrate command of the conventions of standard English grammar and usage when writing or speaking.

Conventions

Mini-Lesson

Student Objectives

- Identify and use auxiliary verbs. *(p. 526)*

Auxiliary Verbs

An auxiliary verb works with the main verb for a variety of purposes. Some common auxiliary verbs are *could, should, might, may, did, is, will,* and *would.* Auxiliary verbs combined with the main verb form a verb phrase. Display these sentences. Have students find the verb phrases and the auxiliary verb in each verb phrase.

- *I have checked the location of the concert. (have checked: have)*

- *We can park in the public parking lot. (can park: can)*

- *We should ask Eva for directions. (should ask: should)*

- *We had planned this event for a long time. (had planned: had)*

Tell students that identifying and using auxiliary verbs can help them clarify and add complexity and variety to their writing. For more practice with this skill, see page 540.

CCSS **Common Core State Standards**
L.7.1: Demonstrate command of the conventions of standard English grammar and usage when writing or speaking.

Auxiliary Verbs

Know the Rule

An **auxiliary verb**, or **helping verb**, works with a main verb. Auxiliary verbs serve a variety of purposes. Some auxiliary verbs, such as *could, should, might,* and *may,* show how likely something is to happen. Other auxiliary verbs, such as *did, is, will,* and *would,* indicate the tense of the main verb. Sometimes other words can appear between the auxiliary verb and the main verb.

Examples:
Just about anything that produces some kind of sound **can serve** as a musical instrument.
A bluegrass musician **might** even **play** a pair of spoons during a song.

Practice the Rule

Number a sheet of paper 1–10. Write the auxiliary verb and the main verb in each sentence.

1. Knowing the characteristics of musical instruments should influence an aspiring musician's choice of instrument. should influence
2. One person may want an instrument with a soothing sound. may want
3. That person probably would avoid the electric guitar. would avoid
4. Someone with good rhythm might enjoy the drums. might enjoy
5. Which kind of stringed instrument would suit me best? would suit
6. Someone thinking about learning the harp should know about the instrument's large size. should know
7. A piano will require a large financial investment. will require
8. Is the flute always used in an orchestra? is used
9. Can you devote several hours each week to practicing an instrument? can devote
10. A person must consider many factors when choosing a musical instrument. must consider

Titles

Know the Rule

When writing, **underline** the titles of longer works, such as books, magazines, newspapers, and movies. If using a computer, use italics because such titles appear in italics in printed material. Use **quotation marks** around the titles of shorter works, such as songs, stories, and poems. Capitalize the first word and the last word in titles. Capitalize all other words except articles, short prepositions, and coordinating conjunctions. Also, capitalize short verbs, such as *is* and *are*.

Practice the Rule

Number a sheet of paper 1–10. Rewrite each sentence, punctuating and capitalizing each title correctly.

1. The famous poem the raven was written by the American author Edgar Allan Poe who lived in the first half of the nineteenth century. *"The Raven"*

2. Poe also wrote many well-known horror stories, including the masque of the red death and the fall of the house of usher. *"The Masque of the Red Death"* *"The Fall of the House of Usher."*

3. The 1962 horror movie premature burial was based on a story by Poe. *Premature Burial*

4. Poe's poem annabel lee is about the early death of a beautiful woman. *"Annabel Lee"*

5. Poe wrote only one novel, the narrative of arthur gordon pym of nantucket. *The Narrative of Arthur Gordon Pym of Nantucket*

6. Lois Lowry's novel number the stars takes place during World War II. *Number the Stars*

7. Folk singer Woody Guthrie wrote the song this land is your land. *"This Land Is Your Land."*

8. Don't you just love Billy Collins's poem introduction to poetry? *"Introduction to Poetry"?*

9. In sixth grade, I memorized the poem stopping by woods on a snowy evening. *"Stopping by Woods on a Snowy Evening."*

10. My little brother's favorite song is Hakuna Matata from The lion king. *"Hakuna Matata"* *The Lion King*

Conventions

Mini-Lesson

Student Objectives

- Capitalize and punctuate titles correctly. *(p. 527)*

Titles

Titles of longer works are underlined when they are written by hand or set in italics. Titles of shorter works are set in quotation marks. Capitalize the first and last word and all other words except articles and prepositions in titles. Display the following sentences. Have students rewrite each sentence, punctuating and capitalizing each title correctly.

- *My favorite book is Black beauty.* (My favorite book is *Black Beauty,* or My favorite book is Black Beauty.)

- *Our teacher told us to read the article, Building Bird feeders for the winter.* (Our teacher told us to read the article, "Building Bird Feeders for the Winter.")

Tell students that correctly capitalizing and punctuating titles of longer and shorter works in their writing will help them clarify what the titles refer to and avoid distracting and confusing grammatical errors. For more practice with this skill, see page 540.

CCSS **C**ommon **C**ore **S**tate **S**tandards

L.7.2: Demonstrate command of the conventions of standard English capitalization, punctuation, and spelling when writing.

Conventions

Mini-Lesson

Student Objectives

• Use commas correctly. *(p. 528)*

Commas

Use commas to separate nouns of direct address and to set off nonessential clauses. Also place a comma after a subordinating clause used at the beginning of a sentence. Display these sentences. Have students discuss and explain why commas do or do not need to be added.

- *If we each do our job the event will go well.* (If we each do our job, the event will go well: subordinating clause at beginning of sentence)

- *Mario are you going to bring the props?* (Mario, are you going to bring the props?: direct address)

- *Alonzo, who had won the contest last year, did not win this year.* (Correct as is, nonessential clause set off by commas)

Tell students that using commas correctly in their writing will help make the meaning of their sentences clearer. For more practice with this skill, see page 541.

CCSS **C**ommon **C**ore **S**tate **S**tandards
L.7.2: Demonstrate command of the conventions of standard English capitalization, punctuation, and spelling when writing.

Commas

Know the Rule

Commas tell a reader where to pause. Use a comma to separate a noun of direct address from the rest of a sentence. Place a comma after a subordinating clause when it is used at the beginning of a sentence. Set off nonessential, also called nonrestrictive, clauses with commas. A nonessential clause provides information that may be interesting but not necessary to the meaning of the sentence.

Examples:
Mr. Diaz, will we have any homework tonight?
If I've learned anything this year, it's that we have homework every night.
I was hoping that, **because of today's soccer tournament,** we would have a break from homework.

Practice the Rule

Number a sheet of paper 1–8. Write each sentence, adding commas where needed. After each sentence, write the reason for the comma.

1. Ms. Stewart, is soccer the most popular game in the world? direct address

2. People play soccer, which is sometimes called the world game, in almost every country in the world. nonessential clause

3. Although few points are scored during a game, soccer matches are consistently exciting. subordinating clause

4. The English professional soccer league, which is called the Premier League, scored an average 2.48 points per game in 2005. nonessential clause

5. Whereas the goalkeepers may use their hands to stop an attempted goal and to throw the ball back onto the field, the other players are not allowed to touch the ball with their hands or arms. subordinating clause

6. World Cup Soccer games have been held every four years since 1930, except 1942 and 1946. nonessential clause

7. When the World Cup games are on TV, people around the world gather to watch and cheer on their favorite teams. subordinating clause

8. Do you have any more questions, Anthony? direct address

More Commas

Know the Rule

Use a **comma** between coordinate adjectives that describe the same noun, but never place a comma between the final adjective and the noun itself. Coordinate adjectives are "equal" adjectives. Ask these questions to determine whether the adjectives are coordinate:
- Does the sentence make sense if the adjectives are reversed in order?
- Does the sentence make sense if the word *and* comes between the adjectives?

Examples:

The library is a gray stone building.

The chattering, noisy crowd of children burst through the doors.

Practice the Rule

Number a sheet of paper 1–10. Write each incorrect sentence, placing commas as necessary between coordinate adjectives. Write **Correct** if the sentence is correct as is.

1. Jake loves the old, musty smell of the town library.
2. Ms. McMichael is the new children's librarian. **Correct**
3. She told Jake that he would find longer, more interesting books in the young adult section.
4. Jake climbed the creaky wooden stairs to the second floor. **Correct**
5. The second floor was a whole new world for Jake. **Correct**
6. Jake entered a clean, spacious room.
7. A row of new desktop computers lined one wall. **Correct**
8. Mr. Gomes extended a friendly, warm welcome to Jake.
9. He pointed out a large, extensive collection of CDs and DVDs.
10. Jake selected a new, best-selling book to take home.

Mini-Lesson

Student Objectives

- Correctly use commas between coordinating adjectives. *(p. 529)*

More Commas

Adjectives are coordinate if they equally modify a noun. If you can reverse the order of the adjectives or add *and* between them, they are coordinate adjectives. Use a comma between coordinate adjectives that describe the same noun. Do not place a comma between the final adjective and the noun. Display the following sentences. Have students place commas as needed between the coordinate adjectives.

- *The group walked quietly down the dark damp hallway.* (The group walked quietly down the dark, damp hallway.)

- *The swift smooth and elegant flight of the bird took my breath away.* (The swift, smooth, and elegant flight of the bird took my breath away.)

Tell students that correctly using commas between coordinating adjectives in their writing will help make the meaning of their sentences clearer. For more practice with this skill, see page 541.

CCSS **C**ommon **C**ore **S**tate **S**tandards

L.7.2.a: Use a comma to separate coordinate adjectives. (e.g., *It was a fascinating, enjoyable movie* but not *He wore an old[,] green shirt*).

Mini-Lesson

Student Objectives

• Use semicolons and colons correctly. *(p. 530)*

Semicolons and Colons

Semicolons can be used instead of a comma and conjunction to separate independent clauses. A colon can be used to separate two independent clauses, to introduce a list, and to separate parts of references in a bibliography as well as hours or minutes in an expression of time. Display these sentences. Have students rewrite the sentences using semicolons and colons correctly.

• *The flight was smooth most of the passengers slept through the entire flight.* (The flight was smooth; most of the passengers slept through the entire flight.)

• *Be sure you pack the following hiking shoes, rain gear, and a camera.* (Be sure you pack the following: hiking shoes, rain gear, and a camera.)

Tell students that using semicolons and colons correctly in their writing will help make the meaning of their sentences clearer. For more practice with this skill, see page 541.

CCSS **Common Core State Standards**

L.7.2: Demonstrate command of the conventions of standard English capitalization, punctuation, and spelling when writing.

Conventions **Grammar, Usage & Mechanics**

Semicolons and Colons

Know the Rule

A **semicolon** (;) can be used instead of a comma and conjunction to separate the independent clauses in a compound sentence. A **colon** (:) can be used to separate two independent clauses when the second explains the first. Be sure to capitalize the first letter of the second sentence. A colon can also be used to introduce a list at the end of a sentence, to separate parts of references in a bibliography, and to separate hours and minutes in an expression of time.

Examples:

Science fiction books may be set in outer space**;** they may also take place in the distant future.

Our summer reading list includes the following books**:** *A Single Shard, A Year Down Yonder,* and *Lily's Crossing.*

The article on poetry appeared in *World Book Encyclopedia* 12**:**125–127.

Practice the Rule

Number your paper 1–8. Rewrite the sentences using semicolons and colons correctly.

1. Historical fiction requires that the reader know a little bit about the setting of the story; science fiction does not require this of the reader.

2. Science fiction stories are my favorite kind of stories; they are exciting and challenge my imagination as I read.

3. I can't meet you at the science museum until 4:30 P.M.

4. H.G. Wells is a science fiction author who lived over a hundred years ago; he wrote my favorite science fiction book, *The Time Machine.*

5. My favorite science fiction authors include the following: Frank Herbert, Ursula K. Le Guin, and William Gibson.

6. Ray Bradbury has published more than 500 titles: short stories, novels, plays, screenplays, television scripts, and verse.

7. "All Summer in a Day" is an often-read short story; it was published in 1954.

8. The original *Star Wars* movie will be shown at 7:00 P.M.

Brackets and Dashes

Know the Rule

Use **brackets** to set off an interruption to a direct quote.
Use **dashes** to show a sudden break in thought. A dash can also be used instead of the words, *in other words* and *that is* before an explanation.

Examples:
Today at Cooperstown—there's no better place to be today—five players were inducted into the Baseball Hall of Fame.
"I am honored by this [his induction into the Hall of Fame] and honored to be standing in such company," said the great left-handed pitcher.

Practice the Rule

Number a sheet of paper 1–8. Write each sentence, adding brackets or dashes where they are needed.

1. Hall of Fame Weekend that will be quite a celebration will be the last weekend in July this year.
2. "He the great pitcher Robin Roberts was one of the nicest guys I ever met," said his former teammate.
3. The famous Detroit Tigers announcer Ernie Harwell I can hear his voice in my imagination died in 2010.
4. "Sandy Koufax the superstar Los Angeles Dodger pitcher from the 1960s retired early," explained our coach, "because he had arthritis."
5. Hank Aaron the great homerun champion was inducted into the Hall of Fame in 1982.
6. In his speech, Aaron said, "They Jackie Robinson and Roy Campanella proved to the world that a man's ability is limited only by his lack of opportunity."
7. My dad's baseball card collection it must be worth thousands of dollars is kept locked in a drawer in his office.
8. Baseball America's pastime is a well-loved sport.

Conventions

Mini-Lesson

Student Objectives

- Use brackets and dashes correctly. *(p. 531)*

Brackets and Dashes

Use brackets to set off an interruption to a direct quote. Use dashes to show a sudden break in thought. Display these sentences. Have students rewrite the sentences, adding brackets or dashes where needed.

- *Cooking this is news to many people is pretty easy once you learn the basics.* (Cooking—this is news to many people—is pretty easy once you learn the basics.)

- *"The speaker Ron Godell mesmerized the crowd with his knowledge."* ("The speaker [Ron Godell] mesmerized the crowd with his knowledge.")

- *Cooks some of them excellent are often quite modest about their talents.* (Cooks—some of them excellent—are often quite modest about their talents.)

Tell students that using brackets and dashes correctly in their writing will help make the meaning of their sentences clearer. For more practice with this skill, see page 541.

CCSS **C**ommon **C**ore **S**tate **S**tandards
L.7.2: Demonstrate command of the conventions of standard English capitalization, punctuation, and spelling when writing.

More Practice

Compound Subjects and Compound Predicates

Write the compound subjects or the compound predicates in each sentence. Then write the conjunction that connects them.

1. (Coal) and (oil) are important energy sources around the world.
2. Does (West Virginia) or (Kentucky) provide most of America's coal?
3. The (sun) and (wind) are other potential energy sources.
4. Some environmentalists (prefer) and (promote) solar energy.
5. Solar panels (look) unattractive but (are) useful.

Direct Objects and Indirect Objects

Write the direct object in each sentence and label it **direct object**. If the sentence has an indirect object, write it and label it **indirect object**.

1. Our teacher gave the (class) a quiz this morning.
2. The test required an understanding of the American Revolution.
3. The second essay question gave (me) considerable trouble.
4. I collected the finished tests at the end of the period.
5. Mr. Erikson took the tests from me.

Predicate Nouns and Predicate Adjectives

Write the subject of the sentence. Then write the predicate noun or predicate adjective and label it either **predicate noun** or **predicate adjective**.

1. Ted Williams was a (superstar) for the Boston Red Sox from 1938–1960. predicate noun
2. He became the greatest (hitter) of his generation. predicate noun
3. Williams's final appearance as a player was (astonishing). predicate adjective
4. His last hit was a (home run) to deep center field in Boston's Fenway Park. predicate noun
5. Fenway Park is (well known) to baseball fans. predicate adjective

CCSS Common Core State Standards

L.7.1: Demonstrate command of the conventions of standard English grammar and usage when writing or speaking.

T532 **Appendix A: Grammar Practice**

More Practice

Kinds of Sentences

Write **declarative, interrogative, imperative,** or **exclamatory** to identify the type of each sentence.

1. Please point to Puerto Rico on the classroom map. imperative
2. What are the main crops grown in the fields of Puerto Rico? interrogative
3. Baseball, boxing, and volleyball are popular sports in Puerto Rico. declarative
4. The beaches of Puerto Rico are so beautiful! exclamatory
5. How far is Puerto Rico from Florida? interrogative

Dependent Clauses and Independent Clauses

Copy the sentences. Underline each dependent clause once and each independent clause twice.

1. Just after they first take office, presidents are usually very popular.
2. If America's economy is strong, most people will approve of the president's actions.
3. Public approval can quickly disappear if the public loses confidence.
4. When presidents become unpopular, they risk losing the next election.
5. A candidate will win an election if he or she connects with the voters.

Adjective Clauses

Copy the sentences. Underline the adjective clause in each sentence. Circle the noun or pronoun that each adjective clause describes.

1. Valerie volunteered to work one weekend at a city park that is four blocks from her apartment building.
2. Her mother, who also wanted to volunteer, accompanied Valerie.
3. Ms. Sanchez, who is a park official, was in charge of cleaning up.
4. Her crew, which worked very hard for two days, picked up the trash.
5. City residents appreciate having a park that is free of litter.

CCSS **C**ommon **C**ore **S**tate **S**tandards

L.7.1: Demonstrate command of the conventions of standard English grammar and usage when writing or speaking. **L.7.1.a:** Explain the function of phrases and clauses in general and their function in specific sentences. **L.7.1.c:** Place phrases and clauses within a sentence, recognizing and correcting misplaced and dangling modifiers. **L.7.2:** Demonstrate command of the conventions of standard English capitalization.

More Practice

Adverb Clauses

Copy the sentences. Underline the adverb clause in each sentence. Circle the verb, adjective, or adverb that the adverb clause tells about.

1. My uncle (goes) bird watching <u>whenever he has some spare time.</u>
2. He is always (hopeful) <u>that he will spy a rare or unusual bird.</u>
3. <u>Whenever he sees such a bird,</u> he (writes) about it in his journal.
4. He (keeps) a journal of his hikes <u>so that he can remember the birds.</u>
5. He (always) has his journal with him <u>unless he forgets it.</u>

Avoiding Run-on Sentences and Comma Splices

Correct sentences 1 and 2 by adding a comma and a conjunction. Correct sentences 3 and 4 with a semicolon. Correct sentence 5 by making two sentences. Possible responses.

1. People recycle bottles and cans , but there are other things to recycle.
2. Recycling is one solution to the problem , and repairing and reusing things that can be fixed is another.
3. Magazines and newspapers can be recycled ; computers and cell phones can be recycled as well.
4. Department stores throw away tons of clothes and shoes that are not sold , these stores could donate the clothes to charities.
5. After sporting events, some arenas donate left-over food . They they give it to homeless shelters.

Common Nouns and Proper Nouns

Copy each sentence. Circle each common noun. Underline each proper noun.

1. <u>Lake Erie</u> is (part) of a (group) of large freshwater (lakes) in eastern <u>North America</u>.
2. The five large (lakes) are collectively known as the <u>Great Lakes</u>.
3. During the (winter), the (lakes) cause heavy (snowfall) in (states) such as <u>Ohio</u> and <u>Michigan</u>.
4. Our (teacher), <u>Mr. Stevens</u>, was born in the (city) of <u>Rochester</u>, which is located on the (shore) of <u>Lake Ontario</u>.
5. A large (amusement park) in <u>Ohio</u> is right on <u>Lake Erie</u>.

CCSS **C**ommon **C**ore **S**tate **S**tandards

L.7.1.a: Explain the function of phrases and clauses in general and their function in specific sentences. **L.7.1.c:** Place phrases and clauses within a sentence, recognizing and correcting misplaced and dangling modifiers. **L.7.2:** Demonstrate command of the conventions of standard English capitalization.

More Practice

Singular Nouns and Plural Nouns

Write the plural form of each singular noun.

1. item items
2. city cities
3. knife knives
4. man men

5. notebook notebooks
6. life lives
7. train trains
8. house houses

Personal Pronouns

Write the personal pronoun in each sentence. Then write whether it is first person, second person, or third person. A sentence may have more than one personal pronoun.

1. Last week, we began studying about South America. first person
2. You made a list of the countries on that continent. second person
3. Jake told us that Liberia and Morocco were in South America. first person
4. He is wrong because they are both countries in Africa. third person
5. I can't wait until we start our unit on China. first person

Compound Personal Pronouns

Write the appropriate compound personal pronoun to refer to each underlined noun or pronoun.

1. I reminded _____ to exercise thirty minutes today. myself
2. Mr. Greene bought _____ a membership at a gym in our neighborhood. himself
3. Marie has asked _____ why she doesn't exercise more. herself
4. If people would force _____ to exercise more, they would be healthier. themselves
5. We have to be careful not to hurt _____ when we exercise. ourselves

CCSS **Common Core State Standards**
L.7.1: Demonstrate command of the conventions of standard English grammar and usage when writing or speaking. **L.7.2:** Demonstrate command of the conventions of standard English capitalization.

More Practice

Possessive Pronouns

Write the possessive pronoun in each sentence.

1. I was very nervous about giving my first oral report before the class. **my**
2. Maya had given hers about the early American colonies the day before. **hers**
3. Her oral report was extremely interesting and well organized. **Her**
4. After Maya's report, most of us were nervous about giving our reports. **our**
5. Ethan gave his report about John Adams, which was excellent. **his**

Relative Pronouns and Interrogative Pronouns

Write each sentence. Underline each relative pronoun. Circle each interrogative pronoun.

1. (Whom) do you consider the most important scientist of the last century?
2. Stephen Hawking, whose theories about stars are mind-boggling, has to be on the list.
3. (What) is Albert Einstein famous for having discovered?
4. Einstein is a famous mathematician who actually failed math one year in high school.
5. Can you believe that such a brilliant person could fail a math course?

Articles

Write each sentence, using the correct article in parentheses. Then underline the article **the** each time it appears and the word to which it refers.

1. The Greeks of ancient times were (a/(an)) amazing race of people.
2. The Parthenon is (a/(an)) example of their achievement in architecture.
3. Built as (a)/an) temple over two thousand years ago, the building is considered (a/(an)) enduring symbol of Greek civilization.
4. Located on (a/an) hill above the city of Athens, the ruins of the Parthenon are (a/(an)) important tourist attraction today.
5. ((The)/A) Greek islands would be (the/(a)) wonderful place to visit.

CCSS **Common Core State Standards**

L.7.1: Demonstrate command of the conventions of standard English grammar and usage when writing or speaking.

More Practice

Demonstrative Pronouns and Demonstrative Adjectives

Write the demonstrative adjective or demonstrative pronoun in each sentence. After each demonstrative adjective, write the noun that it describes. After each demonstrative pronoun, write the noun or pronoun it replaces.

1. This is the website on volcanoes the librarian told me about. **This, website**
2. These links lead to photographs and interesting data related to volcanoes. **These, links**
3. You can sit at that computer and log on to the same website. **that, computer**
4. This is the information on famous volcanoes that I used in my report. **This, information**
5. You can print out the information on those printers over there. **those, printers**

Prepositions

Write the prepositional phrase or phrases in each sentence.

1. Throughout history, gold has been a sign of wealth.
2. It is used in coins and expensive jewelry.
3. Artists applied gold to the surfaces of paintings during the Renaissance.
4. The presence of gold in the paintings made them very valuable.
5. Alchemists tried to make gold from many different kinds of common metals.

The Simple Tenses

Write the sentences. Use the present-, past-, or future-tense form of the verb that best completes each sentence.

1. In 1861, John Carlton _____ a patent for a small card people could mail without an envelope. (obtain) **obtained**
2. Today we _____ these small cards postcards. (call) **call**
3. Postcards _____ less to mail than letters. (cost) **cost**
4. Tomorrow I _____ a postcard from Los Angeles to my family. (send) **will send**
5. Maybe someday I _____ a postcard from someone. (receive) **will receive**

CCSS **Common Core State Standards**

L.7.1: Demonstrate command of the conventions of standard English grammar and usage when writing or speaking. **L.7.1.c:** Place phrases and clauses within a sentence, recognizing and correcting misplaced and dangling modifiers.

More Practice

Progressive Verb Forms

Write the verb in each sentence, including its helping verb. Then identify the verb form as present progressive, past progressive, or future progressive.

1. My brother and I <u>were reading</u> about the environment. past progressive
2. He <u>was concentrating</u> mainly on the environment in our city. past progressive
3. Air pollution <u>is becoming</u> a problem in our city. present progressive
4. My brother and I <u>will be planting</u> a tree on the roof of our building. future progressive
5. More people <u>are doing</u> things to improve the environment. present progressive

Emphatic Verb Forms

Write each sentence, changing the underlined verb to the emphatic form of the present tense or the past tense.

1. I <u>think</u> that our hockey team played very well yesterday. do think
2. The team <u>made</u> a few mistakes, though. did make
3. Coach Novak <u>admonished</u> several players. did admonish
4. Nevertheless, I'm sure the team <u>appreciates</u> the school's support. does appreciate
5. Everyone at school <u>enjoys</u> having a hockey team. does enjoy

Transitive Verbs and Intransitive Verbs

Write the verb in each sentence. Then write whether the verb is transitive or intransitive. If the verb is transitive, write the direct object.

1. The Mississippi River <u>originates</u> at Lake Itasca in Minnesota. intransitive
2. The waters of the river <u>flow</u> slowly to the Gulf of Mexico. intransitive
3. The river <u>transports</u> tons of sediment to the Gulf of Mexico. transitive–tons
4. From north to south, many famous bridges <u>span</u> the great river. transitive–river
5. Ships of all types carry cargo to cities along the river. transitive—cargo

CCSS **C**ommon **C**ore **S**tate **S**tandards
L.7.1: Demonstrate command of the conventions of standard English grammar and usage when writing or speaking.

More Practice

Conjunctions

Write the conjunction in each sentence and identify it as a coordinating conjunction or a subordinating conjunction.

subordinating conjunction
1. <u>Although</u> I was prepared to give my oral report, I was relieved that school was cancelled.

subordinating conjunction
2. Classes were cancelled <u>because</u> heavy snow had fallen during the night.

coordinating conjunction
3. I did the visuals, <u>and</u> my partner prepared the written report.

coordinating conjunction
4. We are both ready to give the report, <u>but</u> we're also a little nervous.

subordinating conjunction
5. Much to our surprise, everyone clapped <u>after</u> we gave our report!

More Conjunctions

Underline the correlative conjunctions in each sentence.

1. The novels of Mark Twain include <u>both</u> *The Prince and the Pauper* <u>and</u> *The Adventures of Tom Sawyer.*

2. Generally, readers find Twain's novel *The Adventures of Huckleberry Finn* <u>either</u> obnoxious <u>or</u> funny.

3. <u>Whether</u> people like Twain <u>or</u> hate him, they usually acknowledge that he is a major American author.

4. Twain wrote <u>not only</u> novels <u>but also</u> short stories.

5. I enjoyed reading <u>both</u> *The Adventures of Tom Sawyer* <u>and</u> *Life on the Mississippi.*

Irregular Verbs

Write the sentences. Use the correct form of the verb in parentheses.

1. Our class (has began/(has begun)) a lesson on the American Revolution.

2. Elena ((chose)/choosed) a book about George Washington.

3. Washington (leaded/(led)) the colonial forces against the British army.

4. I (have wrote/(have written)) a poem about the brave soldiers on both sides.

5. Vikram ((read)/readed) a book about the Marquis de Lafayette.

CCSS **C**ommon **C**ore **S**tate **S**tandards

L.7.1: Demonstrate command of the conventions of standard English grammar and usage when writing or speaking. **L.7.1.b:** Choose among simple, compound, complex, and compound-complex sentences to signal differing relationships among ideas.

More Practice

Subject-Verb Agreement

Write each sentence, using the correct form of the verb in parentheses. Then underline the simple subject.

1. <u>Everyone</u> (need/**needs**) to keep up with technological advancements.
2. New <u>products</u> (**appear**/appears) almost every month.
3. <u>Families</u> (**replace**/replaces) computers and cell phones all the time.
4. <u>People</u> (**spend**/spends) lots of money on electrical products.
5. Used electronic <u>devices</u> (**take**/takes) up space in landfills.

Auxiliary Verbs (Helping Verbs)

Write the sentences. Underline the auxiliary verb once and the main verb twice in each sentence.

1. <u>Can</u> you <u>repair</u> a leaky faucet?
2. Someone with some understanding of plumbing <u>could</u> <u>help</u> you.
3. Hiring a professional plumber <u>can</u> <u>cost</u> lots of money.
4. We all <u>should</u> <u>know</u> a little bit about home improvement.
5. <u>Do</u> you <u>have</u> a basic set of tools?

Titles If students use a computer, the underlined titles should be italic.

Write each sentence, punctuating and capitalizing each title correctly.

1. Released in 1981, raiders of the lost ark is a famous American adventure movie. <u>Raiders of the Lost Ark</u>
2. The first movie based on William Shakespeare's play romeo and juliet was made in 1936. <u>Romeo and Juliet</u>
3. Has Ambrose Bierce's famous short story an occurrence at owl creek bridge ever been turned into a movie? "An Occurrence at Owl Creek Bridge"
4. Lewis Carroll's poem jabberwocky is funny but uses lots of made-up words. "Jabberwocky"
5. Fairy tales by the Grimm brothers include cinderella and little red riding hood. "Cinderella" "Little Red Riding Hood"

CCSS **C**ommon **C**ore **S**tate **S**tandards

L.7.1: Demonstrate command of the conventions of standard English grammar and usage when writing or speaking. **L.7.2:** Demonstrate command of the conventions of standard English capitalization.

More Practice

Commas

Write each sentence, adding commas where needed.

1. Though Lin was only thirteen, she knew that she wanted to be an airline pilot.
2. Ms. Hall, can you tell us what education an airline pilot needs?
3. Learning to fly a plane, which requires hours of practice, can be expensive.
4. A student pilot has to take difficult, intensive classes.
5. Would you rather fly a jet, a propeller plane, or a helicopter?

Semicolons and Colons

Rewrite the sentences using semicolons and colons correctly.

1. The swim meet is scheduled to start at 1:30 this afternoon.
2. The competition should start on time; the predicted rain could, of course, delay the start.   *; or : The*
3. The teams competing include the following: Bayside's Sharks, Marengo's Fish, The Middletown Blue, and The Morgantown Streaks.
4. The short races are always exciting; the high diving competition usually follows these races.
5. All the events should be over by 5:00.

Brackets and Dashes

Write the sentences. Add brackets or dashes where they are needed. Hint: Use brackets when additional information is added to a direct quotation.

1. "I am honored by this award [the school literary prize], and I'm glad you liked my story," said Camilla.
2. The school literary prize—given every year for the best student writing—has become a prestigious award among students.
3. "I wish," added Camilla, "that I could share the prize with all of you [the other student writers]."
4. Next year's literary contest will include new categories—essay and blog—each of which will be awarded a prize.
5. The English teachers hope that everyone—and they do mean everyone—will enter the contest.

CCSS **C**ommon **C**ore **S**tate **S**tandards

L.7.2: Demonstrate command of the conventions of standard English capitalization. **L.7.2.a:** Use a comma to separate coordinate adjectives (e.g., *It was a fascinating, enjoyable movie* but not *He wore an old[,] green shirt*).

Transitions

Certain words and phrases can help make the meaning of your writing clearer. Below are lists of words and phrases that you can use to help readers understand more completely what you are trying to say.

Time Order

about	first	today	later
after	second	tomorrow	finally
at	to begin	until	then
before	yesterday	next	as soon as
during	meanwhile	soon	in the end

Cause and Effect

and so	as a result	because	besides
consequently	once	since	so
therefore			

Compare and Contrast

Compare:	also	as	both
	in the same way	like	likewise
	one way	similarly	
Contrast:	although	but	even though
	however	still	on the other hand
	otherwise	yet	

Words and phrases that can show location:

above	across	around	behind
below	beneath	beside	between
down	in back of	in front of	inside
near	next to	on top of	outside
over	under		

Words and phrases that can conclude or summarize:

finally	in conclusion	in the end	lastly
therefore	to conclude		

Appendix B
Rubrics

Mode-Specific Rubrics This section contains 4-, 5-, and 6-point rubrics that can be used with any piece of Narrative, Informative/Explanatory, Opinion/Argument, and Descriptive writing. Rubrics based on the six traits of writing can help students identify their writing goals and better understand the expectations of each writing assignment. Rubrics also provide valuable self-assessment for students during the revising process.

Narrative Writing Rubric

	4	3	2	1
Ideas	An engaging topic, experience, or series of events is supported by relevant details. Memorable descriptions develop the narrative. Carefully selected ideas completely satisfy the reader.	Most of the details are relevant and supportive. Descriptions are adequate. The ideas selected by the author frequently meet the needs of the reader.	The narrative is not supported by enough relevant details. Descriptions are inadequate. The ideas selected by the author sometimes meet the needs of the reader.	The topic is not clear. Details are unrelated to the topic.
Organization	The narrative has an engaging beginning and an ending that leaves the reader thinking or feeling. Events are logically and creatively sequenced. A variety of effective transition words, phrases, and clauses signifies shifts in the setting and plot.	The beginning and the conclusion are functional, but one may be stronger than the other. The sequence of events is logical, but may have a flaw or two. More or better transitions may be needed to guide the reader.	The beginning does not get the reader's attention, or the ending does not satisfy. Some events are out of order. Transitions are needed.	The writing is not organized into a beginning, middle, and ending.
Voice	The voice, mood, and tone are perfect for the purpose and audience. Dialogue, if used, is realistic and fits all the characters.	The voice, mood, and tone are appropriate in places, but inconsistent. Dialogue, if used, usually fits the characters.	The voice sounds disinterested. Mood and tone are weak. Dialogue, if used, is unrealistic or does not fit the characters.	Voice, mood, and tone are not established.
Word Choice	Clear and precise nouns and verbs consistently capture the imagery and action of the story. Descriptive language clearly conveys the experiences and events. Modifiers are strong.	Some nouns and verbs are strong, but others are weak. Descriptive language conveys most of the imagery, experiences, and events. Modifiers are satisfactory.	Many nouns and verbs do not capture the imagery or action of the story. The descriptive language is overly dependent on modifiers, and many of these are weak.	Words are overused, very weak, or incorrect. Descriptive language is not used.
Sentence Fluency	A variety of sentence structures and sentence beginnings makes the narrative flow smoothly. To read this paper aloud with inflection and feeling is effortless.	A few sentences share the same structures, lengths, or beginnings. The writing flows reasonably well. It is possible to read this writing aloud with inflection and feeling.	Many sentences have the same structures, lengths, or beginnings. The flow is robotic or rambling. It is difficult to read this writing aloud with inflection and feeling.	Sentences are incorrectly written or incomplete. The writing is difficult to follow.
Conventions	The narrative has been carefully edited. Grammar, usage, and mechanics are correct.	The narrative contains some minor errors that may distract the reader, but meaning remains clear.	The narrative contains many errors. Line-by-line editing in specific places is needed.	The writing has not been edited. Serious errors affect or alter the meaning.

Informative/Explanatory Writing Rubric

	4	3	2	1
Ideas	The topic is introduced clearly. It is developed and supported with relevant facts and concrete details. If included, quotations are relevant, accurate, and insightful. Carefully selected ideas completely answer the reader's main questions.	The topic is introduced adequately. Some facts, details, and quotations (if included) support the topic adequately. The reader's main questions are frequently answered.	The topic is introduced. Facts, details, and quotations (if included) do not develop and support the topic effectively. A few of the reader's questions are answered.	The topic is not clear. The topic is not supported by facts and details. The author did not think about what questions the reader might have.
Organization	The ideas, concepts, and information are organized into a strong introduction, body, and conclusion. Varied, appropriate, and unique transitions connect and clarify relationships among ideas.	The ideas, concepts, and information are organized into an introduction, body, and conclusion. More or better transitions may be needed.	An introduction, body, and conclusion are present. Some transitions may be inappropriate or incorrect.	The text is not organized into an introduction, body, and conclusion. It is hard or impossible to follow the ideas.
Voice	The writer's voice is appropriate for the purpose and audience. The tone is informative, respectful, and consistent.	The writer's voice is mostly appropriate for the purpose and audience. The tone is mostly informative and respectful, but may be too informal in some places.	The writer's voice is not very appropriate for the purpose or audience. The tone is inconsistent.	The writer's voice is very weak or absent. The tone is not established.
Word Choice	The language is exact and concise. Domain-specific vocabulary is used correctly and explained, as needed. Nouns and verbs are clear and precise, supported by a few carefully selected modifiers.	Some of the language is exact, but some is too general or vague. Some domain-specific vocabulary is used but not explained. Some nouns and verbs are weak, requiring too much help from modifiers. Modifiers are satisfactory.	Some language is confusing. Domain-specific vocabulary may be used incorrectly. Nouns and verbs lack clarity and precision. Too many or too few modifiers are used, and many of these are weak.	Many words are repeated or used incorrectly. Domain-specific vocabulary is not used.
Sentence Fluency	The sentences vary greatly in length and structure, adding style and interest. Almost all sentences begin differently. The text flows smoothly and is effortlessly read aloud with inflection.	Sentence length and structure vary somewhat, with some sentences adding style or interest. Some sentence beginnings are repeated. Parts of the text flow smoothly. The paper can be read aloud with inflection.	In many places, the writing does not flow smoothly because sentences are the same length or begin the same way. The paper is difficult to read aloud with inflection.	Sentences are incomplete or incorrect. The text does not flow smoothly.
Conventions	The text has been carefully edited. Grammar, usage, and mechanics are correct.	The text contains some minor errors that may distract the reader, but meaning remains clear.	Many errors are repeated. Line-by-line editing is needed. The errors interfere with meaning in some places.	The text has not been edited. Serious errors affect or alter the meaning.

Argument Writing Rubric

	4	3	2	1
Ideas	The writer's claim is stated clearly. Counterclaims are anticipated and addressed very well. Accurate reasons and evidence from reliable sources support the claim.	The writer's claim is stated adequately. The author may fail to anticipate or address one or more common counterclaims. One or two reasons or pieces of evidence may not be from reliable sources.	A claim is stated. Counterclaims are not anticipated or are not addressed well. There is little accurate support for the writer's claim.	The writer does not state a claim. Reasons and evidence are not provided.
Organization	The argument is organized logically, including a strong introduction. A compelling conclusion restates the thesis and includes a call to action. Clear and unique transitions clarify the relationships between the claim, reasons, supporting evidence, and counterclaims.	The argument is organized logically, including an introduction. The conclusion may not restate the thesis or may not include a call to action. More or better transitions may be needed to clarify the relationships between the claim, reasons, supporting evidence, and counterclaims.	The argument is not organized logically. The introduction or conclusion is missing (or problematic). Transitions are not appropriate or effective. Counterclaims are not addressed effectively.	The writing is not organized as an argument. The introduction and conclusion are missing. Transitions are not used. Counterclaims are not addressed.
Voice	The voice strongly supports the writer's purpose and consistently connects with the audience. A respectful, confident tone is maintained.	The voice mostly supports the writer's purpose. The tone is mostly respectful and confident, but may be too informal in some places.	The voice is fairly weak or passive throughout the piece and fails to connect with the audience. The tone is inconsistent.	The voice is flat or absent.
Word Choice	Compelling language conveys the writer's ideas and engages the reader. Nouns and verbs are clear and precise, supported by a few carefully selected modifiers.	Some of the language is compelling, but some is vague or ineffective. Some nouns and verbs are strong, but others are weak, requiring too much help from modifiers. Modifiers are satisfactory.	Much of the language is vague or ineffective. Nouns and verbs lack clarity or precision. Too many or too few modifiers are used, and many of these are weak.	The language is not compelling. Words are weak, negative, or used incorrectly.
Sentence Fluency	The sentences vary greatly in length and structure, adding style and interest. Almost all sentences begin differently. The text flows smoothly and is effortlessly read aloud with inflection.	The sentences vary somewhat, with some sentences adding style or interest. Some sentence beginnings are repeated. Parts of the text flow smoothly. The paper can be read aloud with inflection.	Sentence length and structure vary somewhat. Some sentences are the same length or begin the same way. The paper is difficult to read aloud with inflection.	In many places, the writing does not flow smoothly because sentences are not flow smoothly. The paper does not flow smoothly. Sentences are incomplete or incorrect. Sentence beginnings are repeated over and over again. The text does not flow smoothly.
Conventions	The writing has been carefully edited. Grammar, usage, and mechanics are correct.	The writing contains some minor errors that may distract the reader, but meaning remains clear.	Many errors are repeated. Line-by-line editing in specific places is needed. The errors interfere with meaning in some places.	The writing has not been edited. Serious errors affect or alter the meaning.

Strategies for Writers.

Descriptive Writing Rubric

	4	3	2	1
Ideas	The topic is focused and exactly the right size. Sensory details clearly develop, describe, and reveal the subject. Carefully chosen ideas help the reader to completely experience what is being described.	The topic may need to be more carefully focused. Some sensory details reveal the subject. The author's ideas sometimes help the reader experience what is being described.	The topic is not well focused. Too few sensory details reveal the subject. The ideas fail to consistently help the reader experience what is being described.	The topic is unfocused or unclear. Details are random or missing. The ideas do not support the reader's experience of the topic.
Organization	The description is organized logically and creatively, including an engaging introduction and a thoughtfully crafted conclusion. Varied and appropriate transitions clarify relationships between ideas.	The description is organized logically, including a functional introduction and conclusion. More or better transitions may be needed to clarify relationships between ideas.	The description is not well organized. The introduction or the conclusion is weak or missing. Transitions are weak or confusing. Some of the ideas are hard to follow.	The writing is not organized. The introduction and the conclusion are missing. Transitions are not used.
Voice	An authentic, clear voice conveys the writer's purpose and connects with the reader. The mood is perfect, and the tone conveys respect for the subject and the audience.	The voice connects with the reader in some places. The tone is appropriate but inconsistent. An appropriate mood is somewhat established.	The voice may convey purpose but does not connect with the reader. The mood and tone may not be appropriate.	The voice is weak or absent. Mood and tone are not established.
Word Choice	Precise, descriptive words (including nouns, verbs, and modifiers) bring the subject to life. Figurative language and comparisons create a clear, coherent picture.	Some words are precise and descriptive, but others are not. Some nouns and verbs may rely too heavily on modifiers for clarity. Figurative language and/ or comparisons sometimes create a clear picture.	Nouns and verbs lack precision and clarity. Too many or too few modifiers are used, and many of these are weak. Figurative language and/or comparisons do not create a clear picture.	Words are basic and very limited. Figurative language and comparisons are not used.
Sentence Fluency	A variety of sentences and/or lines adds interest and energy to the description. The writing flows very smoothly. Reading this aloud with inflection and feeling is effortless.	Some sentences and/or lines are varied and interesting. The writing flows smoothly some of the time. It can be read aloud with inflection and feeling.	Many sentences and/or lines are not varied or interesting. Most of the writing does not flow smoothly. It is difficult to read aloud with inflection or feeling.	Sentences and/or lines are incomplete or incorrect. The writing does not flow.
Conventions	The description has been carefully edited. Grammar, usage, and mechanics are correct.	The description contains some minor errors that may distract the reader, but meaning remains clear.	Many errors are repeated. Line-by-line editing in specific places is needed. Errors interfere with meaning in places.	The writing has not been edited. Serious errors affect or alter the meaning.

Narrative Writing Rubric

	5	4	3	2	1
Ideas	An engaging topic, experience, or series of events is supported by relevant details. Memorable descriptions develop the narrative. Carefully selected ideas completely satisfy the reader.	Most of the details are relevant and supportive. Most descriptions are memorable. Carefully selected ideas satisfy most of the reader's needs.	Some of the details may be unrelated or marginally relevant. Descriptions are adequate. The ideas selected by the author frequently meet the needs of the reader.	The narrative is not supported by enough relevant details. Descriptions are inadequate. The ideas selected by the author sometimes meet the needs of the reader.	The topic is not clear. Details are unrelated to the topic.
Organization	The narrative has an engaging beginning and an ending that leaves the reader thinking or feeling. Events are logically and creatively sequenced. A variety of effective transition words, phrases, and clauses signifies shifts in the setting and plot.	The narrative has an interesting beginning and satisfying ending. Events are logically sequenced. Most transitions are effective, especially as they signify shifts in the setting and plot.	The beginning and the conclusion are functional, but one may be stronger than the other. The sequence of events is logical, but may have a flaw or two. More or better transitions may be needed to guide the reader.	The beginning does not get the reader's attention, or the ending does not satisfy. Some events are out of order. Transitions are needed.	The writing is not organized into a beginning, middle, and ending.
Voice	The voice, mood, and tone are perfect for the purpose and audience. Dialogue, if used, is realistic and fits all the characters.	The voice, mood, and tone are appropriate. Dialogue, if used, is realistic and usually fits the characters well.	The voice, mood, and tone are appropriate in places, but inconsistent. Dialogue, if used, sometimes fits the characters.	The voice sounds disinterested. Mood and tone are weak. Dialogue, if used, is unrealistic or does not fit the characters.	Voice, mood, and tone are not established.
Word Choice	Clear and precise nouns and verbs consistently capture the imagery and action of the story. Descriptive language clearly conveys the experiences and events. Modifiers are strong.	Most of the nouns and verbs are clear, capturing the imagery and action of the story. Descriptive language conveys the experiences and events. Modifiers are strong.	Some nouns and verbs are strong, but others are weak. Descriptive language conveys most of the imagery, experiences, and events. Modifiers are satisfactory.	Many nouns and verbs do not capture the imagery or action of the story. The descriptive language is overly dependent on modifiers, and many of these are weak.	Words are overused, very weak, or incorrect. Descriptive language is not used.
Sentence Fluency	A variety of sentence structures and sentence beginnings makes the narrative flow smoothly. To read this paper aloud with inflection and feeling is effortless.	Most sentence structures and sentence beginnings are varied and flow well. Most of the sentences are well crafted. It is easy to read this writing aloud with inflection and feeling.	A few sentences share the same structures, lengths, or beginnings. The writing flows reasonably well. It is possible to read this writing aloud with inflection and feeling.	Many sentences have the same structures, lengths, or beginnings. The flow is robotic or rambling. It is difficult to read this writing aloud with inflection and feeling.	Sentences are incorrectly written or incomplete. The writing is difficult to follow.
Conventions	The narrative has been carefully edited. Grammar, usage, and mechanics are correct.	The narrative contains one or two minor errors that are easily corrected.	The narrative contains some minor errors that may distract the reader, but meaning remains clear.	The narrative contains many errors. Line-by-line editing in specific places is needed.	The writing has not been edited. Serious errors affect or alter the meaning.

Informative/Explanatory Writing Rubric

	5	4	3	2	1
Ideas	The topic is introduced clearly. It is developed and supported with relevant facts and concrete details. If included, quotations are relevant, accurate, and insightful. Carefully selected ideas completely answer the reader's main questions.	The topic is introduced well. Almost all the facts and details support the topic well. If included, quotations are relevant and accurate. Almost all of the reader's main questions are answered.	The topic is introduced adequately. Some facts, details, and quotations (if included) support the topic adequately. The reader's main questions are frequently answered.	The topic is introduced. Facts, details, and quotations (if included) do not develop and support the topic effectively. A few of the reader's questions are answered.	The topic is not clear. The topic is not supported by facts and details. The author did not think about what questions the reader might have.
Organization	The ideas, concepts, and information are organized into a strong introduction, body, and conclusion. Varied, appropriate, and unique transitions connect and clarify relationships among ideas.	The ideas, concepts, and information are organized into an introduction, body, and conclusion. Most transitions are appropriate and helpful.	The ideas, concepts, and information are organized into an introduction, body, and conclusion. More or better transitions may be needed.	An introduction, body, and conclusion are present. Some transitions may be inappropriate or incorrect.	The text is not organized into an introduction, body, and conclusion. It is hard or impossible to follow the ideas.
Voice	The writer's voice is appropriate for the purpose and audience. The tone is informative, respectful, and consistent.	The writer's voice is appropriate for the purpose and audience most of the time. The tone is almost always informative and respectful.	The writer's voice is mostly appropriate for the purpose and audience. The tone is mostly informative and respectful, but may be too informal in some places.	The writer's voice is not very appropriate for the purpose or audience. The tone is inconsistent.	The writer's voice is very weak or absent. The tone is not established.
Word Choice	The language is exact and concise. Domain-specific vocabulary is used correctly and explained, as needed. Nouns and verbs are clear and precise, supported by a few carefully selected modifiers.	Most of the language is exact and concise. Domain-specific vocabulary is used correctly and usually explained, as needed. Most nouns and verbs are clear and precise. Most modifiers are carefully selected.	Some of the language is exact, but some is too general or vague. Some domain-specific vocabulary is used but not explained. Some nouns and verbs are weak, requiring too much help from modifiers. Modifiers are satisfactory.	Some language is confusing. Domain-specific vocabulary may be used incorrectly. Nouns and verbs lack clarity and precision. Too many or too few modifiers are used, and many of these are weak.	Many words are repeated or used incorrectly. Domain-specific vocabulary is not used.
Sentence Fluency	The sentences vary greatly in length and structure, adding style and interest. Almost all sentences begin differently. The text flows smoothly and is effortlessly read aloud with inflection.	Most of the sentences vary in their beginnings, lengths, and structures. Several add style or interest. Most of the text flows smoothly and is easy to read aloud with inflection.	Sentence length and structure vary somewhat, with some sentences adding style or interest. Some sentence beginnings are repeated. Parts of the text flow smoothly. The paper can be read aloud with inflection.	In many places, the writing does not flow smoothly because sentences are the same length or begin the same way. The paper is difficult to read aloud with inflection.	Sentences are incomplete or incorrect. The text does not flow smoothly.
Conventions	The text has been carefully edited. Grammar, usage, and mechanics are correct.	The text contains one or two minor errors, but the meaning remains clear.	The text contains some minor errors that may distract the reader, but meaning remains clear.	Many errors are repeated. Line-by-line editing in specific places is needed. The errors interfere with meaning in some places.	The text has not been edited. Serious errors affect or alter the meaning.

Argument Writing Rubric

	5	4	3	2	1
Ideas	The writer's claim is stated clearly. Counterclaims are anticipated and addressed very well. Accurate reasons and evidence support the claim.	The writer's claim is stated clearly. Counterclaims are anticipated and addressed well. Most of the reasons and evidence are accurate and from reliable sources.	The writer's claim is stated adequately. The author may fail to anticipate or address one or more common counterclaims. One or two reasons or pieces of evidence may not be from reliable sources.	A claim is stated. Counterclaims are not anticipated or are not addressed well. There is little accurate support for the writer's claim.	The writer does not state a claim. Reasons and evidence are not provided.
Organization	The argument is organized logically, including a strong introduction. A compelling conclusion restates the thesis and includes a call to action. Clear and unique transitions clarify the relationships between the claim, reasons, supporting evidence, and counterclaims.	The argument is organized logically, including a good introduction. The conclusion restates the thesis and may include a call to action. Most transitions clarify the relationships between the claim, reasons, supporting evidence, and counterclaims.	The argument is organized logically, including an introduction. The conclusion may not restate the thesis or may not include a call to action. More or better transitions may be needed to clarify the relationships between the claim, reasons, supporting evidence, and counterclaims.	The argument is not organized logically. The introduction or conclusion is missing (or problematic). Transitions are not appropriate or effective. Counterclaims are not addressed effectively.	The writing is not organized as an argument. The introduction and conclusion are missing. Transitions are not used. Counterclaims are not addressed.
Voice	The voice strongly supports the writer's purpose and consistently connects with the audience. A respectful, confident tone is maintained.	The voice supports the writer's purpose and almost always connects with the audience. A respectful, confident tone is maintained.	The voice mostly supports the writer's purpose. The tone is mostly respectful and confident, but may be too informal in some places.	The voice is fairly weak or passive throughout the piece and fails to connect with the audience. The tone is inconsistent.	The voice is flat or absent.
Word Choice	Compelling language conveys the writer's ideas and engages the reader. Nouns and verbs are clear and precise, supported by a few carefully selected modifiers.	Most of the language is compelling. Nouns and verbs are mostly clear and precise. Most modifiers are carefully selected.	Some of the language is compelling, but some is vague or ineffective. Some nouns and verbs are strong, but others are weak, requiring too much help from modifiers. Modifiers are satisfactory.	Much of the language is vague or ineffective. Nouns and verbs lack clarity or precision. Too many or too few modifiers are used, and many of these are weak.	The language is not compelling. Words are weak, negative, or used incorrectly.
Sentence Fluency	The sentences vary greatly in length and structure, adding style and interest. Almost all sentences begin differently. The text flows smoothly and is effortlessly read aloud with inflection.	The sentences vary in length and structure, in their beginnings, lengths, and structures. Several add style or interest. Most of the text flows smoothly and is easy to read aloud with inflection.	Most of the sentences vary in their beginnings, lengths, and structures. Several add style or interest. Some sentence beginnings are repeated. Parts of the text flow smoothly. The paper can be read aloud with inflection.	Sentence length and structure vary somewhat, with some sentences adding style or interest. Some sentence beginnings are repeated. The writing does not flow smoothly because sentences are the same length or begin the same way. The paper is difficult to read aloud with inflection.	Sentences are incomplete or incorrect. Sentence beginnings are repeated over and over again. The text does not flow smoothly.
Conventions	The writing has been carefully edited. Grammar, usage, and mechanics are correct.	The writing contains one or two minor errors, but the meaning remains clear.	The writing contains some minor errors that may distract the reader, but meaning remains clear.	Many errors are repeated. Line-by-line editing in specific places is needed. The errors interfere with meaning in some places.	The writing has not been edited. Serious errors affect or alter the meaning.

Descriptive Writing Rubric

	5	4	3	2	1
Ideas	The topic is focused and exactly the right size. Sensory details clearly develop, describe, and reveal the subject. Carefully chosen ideas help the reader to completely experience what is being described.	The topic is focused and the right size. Many sensory details develop, describe, and reveal the subject. The ideas selected usually enable the reader to experience what is being described.	The topic may need to be more carefully focused. Some sensory details reveal the subject. The author's ideas sometimes help the reader experience what is being described.	The topic is not well focused. Too few sensory details reveal the subject. The ideas fail to consistently help the reader experience what is being described.	The topic is unfocused or unclear. Details are random or missing. The ideas do not support the reader's experience of the topic.
Organization	The description is organized logically and creatively, including an engaging introduction and a thoughtfully crafted conclusion. Varied and appropriate transitions clarify relationships between ideas.	The description is organized logically, including a strong introduction and a strong conclusion. Most of the transitions clarify relationships between ideas.	The description is organized logically, including a functional introduction and conclusion. More or better transitions may be needed to clarify relationships between ideas.	The description is not well organized. The introduction or the conclusion is weak or missing. Transitions are weak or confusing. Some of the ideas are hard to follow.	The writing is not organized. The introduction and the conclusion are missing. Transitions are not used.
Voice	An authentic, clear voice conveys the writer's purpose and connects with the reader. The mood is perfect, and the tone conveys respect for the subject and the audience.	The voice is clear and connects with the reader most of the time. The mood is appropriate, and the tone conveys respect for the subject and audience most of the time.	The voice connects with the reader in some places. The tone is appropriate but inconsistent. An appropriate mood is somewhat established.	The voice may convey purpose but does not connect with the reader. The mood and tone may not be appropriate.	The voice is weak or absent. Mood and tone are not established.
Word Choice	Precise, descriptive words (including nouns, verbs, and modifiers) bring the subject to life. Figurative language and comparisons create a clear, coherent picture.	Most words (including nouns, verbs, and modifiers) are precise and descriptive. Figurative language and comparisons create a clear, coherent picture most of the time.	Some words are precise and descriptive, but others are not. Some nouns and verbs may rely too heavily on modifiers for clarity. Figurative language and/or comparisons sometimes create a clear picture.	Nouns and verbs lack precision and clarity. Too many or too few modifiers are used, and many of these are weak. Figurative language and/or comparisons do not create a clear picture.	Words are basic and very limited. Figurative language and comparisons are not used.
Sentence Fluency	A variety of sentences and/or lines adds interest and energy to the description. The writing flows very smoothly. Reading this aloud with inflection and feeling is effortless.	Most sentences and/or lines are varied and interesting. The writing flows smoothly most of the time. It is easy to read aloud with inflection and feeling.	Some sentences and/or lines are varied and interesting. The writing flows smoothly some of the time. It can be read aloud with inflection and feeling.	Many sentences and/or lines are not varied or interesting. Most of the writing does not flow smoothly. It is difficult to read aloud with inflection or feeling.	Sentences and/or lines are incomplete or incorrect. The writing does not flow.
Conventions	The description has been carefully edited. Grammar, usage, and mechanics are correct.	The description contains one or two minor errors that are easily corrected. Meaning is clear.	The description contains some minor errors that may distract the reader, but meaning remains clear.	Many errors are repeated. Line-by-line editing in specific places is needed. Errors interfere with meaning in places.	The writing has not been edited. Serious errors affect or alter the meaning.

Narrative Writing Rubric

	6	5	4	3	2	1
Ideas	An engaging topic, experience, or series of events is supported by relevant details. Memorable descriptions develop the narrative. Carefully selected ideas completely satisfy the reader.	Most of the details are relevant and supportive. Most descriptions are memorable. Carefully selected ideas satisfy most of the reader's needs.	Some of the details may be unrelated or marginally supportive, but descriptions are adequate. The ideas selected by the author frequently meet the needs of the reader.	The narrative is not supported by enough relevant details. Many details are unrelated. The author did not consider the needs of the reader.	The topic may not be clear. Details are unrelated to the topic.	The topic is not clear. Details are unrelated to the topic.
Organization	The narrative has an engaging beginning and an ending that leaves the reader thinking or feeling. Events are logically and creatively sequenced. A variety of effective transition words, phrases, and clauses signifies shifts in the setting and plot.	The narrative has an interesting beginning and satisfying ending. Events are logically sequenced. Most transitions are effective, especially as they signify shifts in the setting and plot.	The beginning and the conclusion are functional, but one may be stronger than the other. The sequence of events is logical, but may have a flaw or two. More or better transitions may be needed to guide the reader.	The beginning does not get the reader's attention, or the ending does not satisfy. Some events are out of order. Transitions are needed.	The beginning and ending are weak. The sequence of events is seriously flawed. Transitions are not used.	The writing is not organized into a beginning, middle, and ending.
Voice	The voice, mood, and tone consistently capture the imagery and action of the story. Descriptive language clearly conveys the experiences and events. Modifiers are strong.	The voice, mood, and tone are appropriate. Dialogue, if used, is realistic and usually fits the characters well.	The voice, mood, and tone are appropriate in places, but inconsistent. Dialogue, if used, sometimes fits the characters.	The voice sounds disinterested. Mood and tone are weak. Dialogue, if used, is inappropriate for the audience. Dialogue, if used, is unrealistic.	The voice, mood, and tone are not established.	Voice, mood, and tone are not established.
Word Choice	Clear and precise nouns and verbs consistently capture the imagery and action of the story. Descriptive language clearly conveys the experiences and events. Modifiers are strong.	Most of the nouns and verbs are clear, capturing the imagery and action of the story. Descriptive language conveys the experiences and events well. The majority of the modifiers are strong.	Some nouns and verbs are strong, but others are weak. Descriptive language conveys most of the imagery, experiences, and events. Modifiers are satisfactory.	Many nouns and verbs do not capture the imagery or action of the story. The descriptive language is overly dependent on modifiers, and many of these are weak.	Words are not powerful or precise. Descriptive language is not used.	Words are overused, very weak, or incorrect.
Sentence Fluency	A variety of sentence structures and sentence beginnings makes the narrative flow smoothly. To read this paper aloud with inflection and feeling is effortless.	Most sentence structures and sentence beginnings are varied and flow well. Most of the sentences are well crafted. It is easy to read this writing aloud with inflection and feeling.	A few sentences share the same structures, lengths, or beginnings. The writing flows reasonably well. It is possible to read this writing aloud with inflection and feeling.	Many sentences have the same structures, lengths, or beginnings. The flow is robotic or rambling. It is difficult to read this writing aloud with inflection and feeling.	Sentences have little variation. The narrative does not flow well.	Sentences are incorrectly written or incomplete. The writing is difficult to follow.
Conventions	The narrative has been carefully edited. Grammar, usage, and mechanics are correct.	The narrative contains one or two minor errors that are easily corrected.	The narrative contains some minor errors that may distract the reader, but meaning remains clear.	The narrative contains many errors. Line-by-line editing in specific places is needed.	Serious errors affect or alter the meaning.	The writing has not been edited.

Strategies for Writers. Copyright © Zaner-Bloser, Inc. This page may be duplicated for classroom use.

Informative/Explanatory Writing Rubric

	6	5	4	3	2	1
Ideas	The topic is introduced clearly. It is developed and supported with relevant facts and concrete details. If included, quotations are relevant, accurate, and insightful. Carefully selected ideas completely answer the reader's main questions.	The topic is introduced well. Almost all the facts and details support the topic well. If included, quotations are relevant and accurate. Almost all of the reader's main questions are answered.	The topic is introduced adequately. Some facts, details, and quotations (if included) support the topic adequately. The reader's main questions are frequently answered.	The topic is introduced. Facts, details, and quotations (if included) do not develop and support the topic effectively. A few of the reader's questions are answered.	The topic is not introduced, or more than one topic is introduced. Details are not relevant. Facts are not included. The author did not think about what questions the reader might have.	The topic is not clear. The topic is not supported by facts and details.
Organization	The ideas, concepts, and information are organized into a strong introduction, body, and conclusion. Varied and unique transitions connect and clarify relationships among ideas.	The ideas, concepts, and information are organized into an introduction, body, and conclusion. Most transitions are appropriate and helpful.	The ideas, concepts, and information are organized into an introduction, body, and conclusion. More or better transitions may be needed.	An introduction, body, and conclusion are present. Some transitions may be inappropriate or incorrect.	The text is not well organized. The introduction and conclusion are weak or missing. Transitions are not used.	The text is not organized into an introduction, body, and conclusion. It is difficult to follow the ideas.
Voice	The writer's voice is appropriate for the purpose and audience. The tone is informative, respectful, and consistent.	The writer's voice is appropriate for the purpose and audience most of the time. The tone is almost always informative and respectful.	The writer's voice is mostly appropriate for the purpose and audience. The tone is mostly informative and respectful, but may be too informal in some places.	The writer's voice is not very appropriate for the purpose or audience. The tone is inconsistent.	The writer's voice is not appropriate. The tone is too informal.	The writer's voice is very weak or absent. The tone is not established.
Word Choice	The language is exact and concise. Domain-specific vocabulary is used correctly and explained, as needed. Nouns and verbs are clear and precise, supported by a few carefully selected modifiers.	Most of the language is exact and concise. Domain-specific vocabulary is used correctly and usually explained, as needed. Most nouns and verbs are clear and precise. Most modifiers are carefully selected.	Some of the language is exact, but some is too general or vague. Some domain-specific vocabulary is used but not explained. Some nouns and verbs are weak, requiring too much help from modifiers. Modifiers are satisfactory.	Some language is confusing. Domain-specific vocabulary may be used incorrectly. Nouns and verbs lack clarity and precision. Too many or too few modifiers are used, and many of these are weak.	The language is very basic and limited. Domain-specific vocabulary is used incorrectly. Nouns and verbs are vague, unclear, or confusing. Modifiers may be missing.	Many words are repeated or used incorrectly. Domain-specific vocabulary is not used.
Sentence Fluency	The sentences vary greatly in length and structure, adding style and interest. Almost all sentences begin differently. The text flows smoothly and is effortlessly read aloud with inflection.	Most of the sentences vary in their beginnings, lengths, and structures. Several add style or interest. Most of the text flows smoothly and is easy to read aloud with inflection.	Sentence length and structure vary somewhat, with some sentences adding style or interest. Some sentence beginnings are repeated. Parts of the text flow smoothly. The paper can be read aloud with inflection.	In many places, the writing does not flow smoothly because sentences are the same length or begin the same way. The paper is difficult to read aloud with inflection.	Most sentences are the same length and structure. Sentence beginnings are repeated over and over again. The flow is too robotic or rambling.	Sentences are incomplete or incorrect. The text does not flow smoothly.
Conventions	The text has been carefully edited. Grammar, usage, and mechanics are correct.	The text contains one or two minor errors, but the meaning remains clear.	The text contains some minor errors that may distract the reader, but meaning remains clear.	Many errors are repeated. Line-by-line editing in specific places is needed. The errors interfere with meaning in some places.	Serious errors affect or alter the meaning.	The text has not been edited.

Argument Writing Rubric

	6	5	4	3	2	1
Ideas	The writer's claim is stated clearly. Counterclaims are anticipated and addressed very well. Accurate reasons and evidence from reliable sources support the claim.	The writer's claim is stated adequately. The author may fail to anticipate or address one or more common counterclaims. One or two reasons or pieces of evidence may not be from reliable sources.	A claim is stated. Counterclaims are not anticipated or are not addressed well. Reasons and evidence are unrelated or inaccurate.	The writer's claim is not stated clearly. Counterclaims are not addressed as an argument.	The writer does not state a claim. Reasons and evidence are not provided.	
Organization	The argument is organized logically, including a strong introduction. A compelling conclusion restates the thesis and includes a call to action. Clear and unique transitions clarify the relationships between the claim, reasons, supporting evidence, and counterclaims.	The argument is organized logically, including a good introduction. The conclusion restates the thesis and may include a call to action. Most transitions clarify the relationships between the claim, reasons, supporting evidence, and counterclaims.	The argument is organized logically, including an introduction. The conclusion may not restate the thesis or may not include a call to action. More or better transitions may be needed to clarify the relationships between the claim, reasons, supporting evidence, and counterclaims.	The argument is not organized logically. The introduction and conclusion are not appropriate or effective. Counterclaims are not addressed.	The argument is not organized as an argument.	
Voice	The voice strongly supports the writer's purpose and consistently connects with the audience. A respectful, confident tone is maintained.	The voice supports the writer's purpose and almost always connects with the audience. A respectful, confident tone is maintained.	The voice mostly supports the writer's purpose. The tone is mostly respectful and confident, but may be too informal in some places.	The voice is fairly weak or passive throughout the piece and fails to connect with the audience. The tone is inconsistent.	The voice is weak or inappropriate for the purpose and audience. A respectful, confident tone is not established.	The voice is flat or absent.
Word Choice	Compelling language conveys the writer's ideas and engages the reader. Nouns and verbs are clear and precise, supported by a few carefully selected modifiers.	Most of the language is compelling. Nouns and verbs are mostly clear and precise. Most modifiers are carefully selected.	Some of the language is compelling, but some is vague or ineffective. Some nouns and verbs are strong, but others are weak, requiring too much help from modifiers. Modifiers are satisfactory.	Much of the language is vague or ineffective. Nouns and verbs lack clarity or precision. Too many or too few modifiers are used, and many of these are weak.	The language is not compelling. Many words are very basic. Nouns and verbs are vague, unclear, or confusing. Modifiers may be missing.	Words are weak, negative, or used incorrectly.
Sentence Fluency	The sentences vary greatly in length and structure, adding style and interest. Almost all sentences begin differently. The text flows smoothly and is effortless to read aloud with inflection.	Most of the sentences vary in their beginnings, lengths, and structures. Several add style and interest. Most of the text flows smoothly and is easy to read aloud with inflection.	Sentence length and structure vary somewhat, with some sentences adding style or interest. Some sentence beginnings are repeated. Parts of the text flow smoothly. The paper can be read aloud with inflection.	In many places, the writing does not flow smoothly because sentences are the same length or begin the same way. The paper is difficult to read aloud with inflection.	Most sentences are the same length and structure. Sentence beginnings are repeated over and over again. The flow is too robotic or rambling.	Sentences are incomplete or incorrect. The text does not flow smoothly.
Conventions	The writing has been carefully edited. Grammar, usage, and mechanics are correct.	The writing contains one or two minor errors, but the meaning remains clear.	The writing contains some minor errors that may distract the reader, but meaning remains clear.	Many errors are repeated. Line-by-line editing in specific places is needed. The errors interfere with meaning in some places.	Serious errors affect or alter the meaning.	The writing has not been edited.

Strategies for Writers.

Descriptive Writing Rubric

	6	5	4	3	2	1
Ideas	The topic is focused and exactly the right size. Sensory details clearly develop, describe, and reveal the subject. Carefully chosen ideas help the reader to completely experience what is being described.	The topic is focused and the right size. Many sensory details develop, describe, and reveal the subject. The ideas selected usually enable the reader to experience what is being described.	The topic may need to be more carefully focused. Some sensory details reveal the subject. The author's ideas sometimes help the reader experience what is being described.	The topic is not well focused. Too few sensory details reveal the subject. The ideas fail to consistently help the reader experience what is being described.	The topic is not focused. Details are scarce, or may relate to more than one subject. The ideas do not support the reader's experience of the topic.	The topic is unfocused or unclear. Details are random or missing.
Organization	The description is organized logically and creatively, including an engaging introduction and a thoughtfully crafted conclusion. Varied and appropriate transitions clarify relationships between ideas.	The description is organized logically, including a strong introduction and a strong conclusion. Most of the transitions clarify relationships between ideas.	The description is organized logically, including a functional introduction and conclusion. More or better transitions may be needed to clarify relationships between ideas.	The description is not well organized. The introduction or the conclusion is weak or missing. Transitions are weak or confusing. Some of the ideas are hard to follow.	The description is not organized. The introduction and the conclusion are missing. Transitions are incorrect or missing. The ideas are hard to follow.	The writing is not organized. Transitions are not used.
Voice	An authentic, clear voice conveys the writer's purpose and connects with the reader. The mood is perfect, and the tone conveys respect for the subject and the audience.	The voice is clear and connects with the reader most of the time. The mood is appropriate, and the tone conveys respect for the subject and audience most of the time.	The voice connects with the reader in some places. The tone is appropriate but inconsistent. An appropriate mood is somewhat established.	The voice may convey purpose but does not connect with the reader. The mood and tone may not be appropriate.	The voice does not convey purpose or connect with the reader. The mood and tone are inappropriate.	The voice is weak or absent. Mood and tone are not established.
Word Choice	Precise, descriptive words (including nouns, verbs, and modifiers) bring the subject to life. Figurative language and comparisons create a clear, coherent picture.	Most words (including nouns, verbs, and modifiers) are precise and descriptive. Figurative language and comparisons create a clear, coherent picture most of the time.	Some words are precise and descriptive, but others are not. Some nouns and verbs may rely too heavily on modifiers for clarity. Figurative language and/or comparisons sometimes create a clear picture.	Nouns and verbs lack precision and clarity. Too many or too few modifiers are used, and many of these are weak. Figurative language and/or comparisons do not create a clear picture.	Words are vague or confusing. Figurative language or comparisons are incomplete or missing.	Words are basic and very limited. Figurative language and comparisons are not used.
Sentence Fluency	A variety of sentences and/or lines adds interest and energy to the description. The writing flows very smoothly. Reading this aloud with inflection and feeling is effortless.	Most sentences and/or lines are varied and interesting. The writing flows smoothly most of the time. It is easy to read aloud with inflection and feeling.	Some sentences and/or lines are varied and interesting. The writing flows smoothly some of the time. It can be read aloud with inflection and feeling.	Many sentences and/or lines are not varied or interesting. Most of the writing does not flow smoothly. It is difficult to read aloud with inflection or feeling.	Sentences and/or lines are very basic, limited, or repetitive. The writing is predictable and dull.	Sentences and/or lines are incomplete or incorrect. The writing does not flow.
Conventions	The description has been carefully edited. Grammar, usage, and mechanics are correct.	The description contains one or two minor errors that are easily corrected. Meaning is clear.	The description contains some minor errors that may distract the reader, but meaning remains clear.	Many errors are repeated. Line-by-line editing in specific places is needed. Errors interfere with meaning in places.	Serious errors affect or alter the meaning.	The writing has not been edited.

Scope and Sequence

	Grade 6	Grade 7	Grade 8
Conferencing	Z14–Z15, T15, T17, T19, T41, T43, T45, T65, T67, T69, T89, T91, T93, T141, T143, T145, T165, T167, T169, T191, T193, T195, T215, T217, T219, T261, T265, T269, T289, T291, T293, T311, T313, T315, T333, T335, T337, T381, T383, T385, T403, T405, T407, T427, T429, T431, T449, T451, T453	Z14–Z15, T17, T19, T21, T41, T43, T45, T66, T70, T73, T95, T97, T99, T145, T147, T149, T170, T174, T178, T202, T205, T207, T227, T229, T231, T275, T277, T279, T297, T299, T301, T323, T325, T327, T347, T349, T351, T395, T397, T399, T417, T419, T421, T441, T444, T447, T467, T469, T471	Z14–Z15, T15, T17, T19, T37, T39, T41, T59, T61, T63, T85, T87, T133, T135, T137, T161, T166, T170, T193, T195, T198, T219, T221, T223, T267, T269, T271, T293, T296, T299, T319, T321, T323, T345, T347, T349, T395, T397, T399, T421, T425, T427, T447, T449, T451, T469, T471, T473
Differentiated Instruction	Z12–Z13, T13, T16, T24, T39, T42, T50, T63, T66, T74, T87, T90, T98, T112, T113, T118, T121, T137, T142, T150, T161, T166, T174, T187, T192, T200, T213, T216, T224, T232, T233, T235, T238, T239, T244, T245, T247, T266, T274, T287, T290, T298, T309, T312, T320, T331, T334, T342, T348, T349, T351, T354, T355, T360, T361, T363, T377, T382, T390, T401, T404, T412,	Z12–Z13, T15, T18, T26, T39, T41, T43, T50, T63, T78, T93, T96, T104, T114, T115, T117, T120, T121, T126, T127, T129, T143, T146, T154, T167, T184, T199, T204, T212, T225, T228, T236, T244, T245, T247, T250, T259, T273, T276, T295, T298, T306, T321, T324, T332, T345, T348, T356, T364, T365, T367, T370, T379, T380, T393, T396, T404, T415, T418, T426, T437, T452,	Z12–Z13, T13, T16, T24, T35, T38, T46, T57, T60, T68, T82, T86, T94, T102, T103, T105, T108, T109, T114, T115, T117, T131, T134, T142, T157, T176, T191, T194, T204, T217, T220, T228, T234, T235, T237, T240, T241, T246, T247, T263, T276, T294, T304, T317, T320, T328, T343, T346, T354, T362, T363, T365, T368, T369, T374, T375, T377, T393, T396, T404, T419, T432,

	Grade 6	Grade 7	Grade 8
Differentiated Instruction (cont.)			
	T425, T428, T436, T447, T450, T458, T464, T465, T467, T470, T471, T476, T477, T479, T579	T465, T468, T476, T482, T483, T485, T488, T497, T498	T445, T448, T456, T467, T470, T478, T484, T485, T487, T490, T491, T496, T497, T499
English Language Learners			
	Z13, T10, T11, T14, T18, T36, T37, T40, T44, T60, T61, T64, T68, T84, T85, T88, T92, T104, T105, T110, T111, T116, T117, T134, T135, T138, T139, T144, T158, T159, T162, T163, T168, T184, T185, T188, T189, T194, T210, T211, T214, T218, T230, T231, T235, T237, T242, T243, T258, T259, T262, T263, T268, T284, T285, T288, T292, T306, T307, T310, T314, T328, T329, T332, T336, T346, T347, T352, T353, T358, T359, T374, T375, T378, T379, T384, T398, T399, T402, T406, T422, T426, T430, T444, T445, T448, T452, T462, T463, T468, T469, T474, T475	Z13, T12, T13, T16, T20, T36, T37, T40, T44, T60, T61, T64, T65, T72, T90, T91, T94, T98, T112, T113, T118, T119, T124, T125, T140, T141, T144, T148, T164, T165, T168, T169, T176, T177, T196, T197, T200, T201, T206, T222, T223, T226, T230, T242, T243, T248, T249, T254, T255, T270, T271, T274, T278, T292, T293, T296, T300, T318, T319, T322, T326, T342, T343, T346, T350, T362, T363, T368, T374, T390, T391, T394, T398, T412, T413, T416, T420, T434, T435, T438, T439, T440, T445, T446, T447, T462, T463, T466, T470, T480, T481, T486, T487, T492, T493	T10, T11, T14, T18, T32, T33, T36, T40, T54, T55, T58, T62, T80, T81, T84, T88, T100, T101, T106, T107, T112, T113, T128, T129, T132, T136, T154, T155, T158, T159, T168, T169, T188, T189, T192, T196, T197, T214, T215, T218, T222, T232, T233, T238, T239, T244, T245, T260, T261, T264, T265, T270, T286, T287, T290, T291, T298, T314, T315, T318, T322, T340, T341, T344, T348, T360, T361, T366, T367, T372, T373, T390, T391, T394, T398, T416, T417, T420, T426, T442, T443, T446, T450, T464, T465, T468, T472, T482, T483, T488, T489, T494, T495

Scope and Sequence (continued)

Grammar, Usage, and Mechanics

	Grade 6	Grade 7	Grade 8
abbreviations/acronyms		T182	T529, T530, T541
action verbs	T96		T520, T538
active and passive voice	T341		T507, T534
adjective and adverb clauses		T474, T475, T506, T507, T533, T534	T511, T512, T535
adjectives	T199, T456, T485	T182, T450–T451, T503, T516, T529, T536	T454
adverbs	T457	T450–T451	T523, T539
apostrophes	T410	T143, T152	T476
appositives	T388	T282	T202
articles	T498	T450, T515, T536	
auxiliary verbs		T234, T526	T327, T540
brackets and dashes		T531, T541	
capitalization	T507	T76, T167, T170, T181, T182, T183	
colons	T512	T331, T530, T541	T430
comma splices	T22	T24, T508, T533	T66
commas	T49, T273, T510, T511	T24, T76, T153, T282, T475, T505, T528, T529, T541	T175, T455
comparative adjectives		T451	T454
complex sentences	T272	T103	T174, T509, T510, T535
compound personal pronouns		T512, T535	T274
compound sentences	T487	T15, T23, T102, T153, T330, T530	T174, T509, T510, T535
compound subjects and predicates			T275
compound words		T512	T527, T540

	Grade 6	Grade 7	Grade 8
Grammar, Usage, and Mechanics (cont.)			
conjunctions	T23	T24–T25, T102–T103, T522, T523, T539	T525, T540
demonstrative pronouns and adjectives		T516, T536	T519, T538
dependent and independent clauses		T505, T533	T508, T534
direct and indirect objects		T502, T532	T203
direct quotations	T48	T76	T44
double negatives		T304	T526, T540
frequently confused words	T411, T502	T355	T352–T353
future tense		T518, T536	
homophones	T318–T319	T354	
hyphens		T77	
indefinite pronouns	T73	T283	T93
infinitive phrases		T305	
initials	T508	T181, T182	
interjections	T499		
irregular verbs	T173, T340, T503	T235, T524, T538	T23
linking verbs	T96	T450, T503	T520, T538
negatives	T504		T526
nouns	T198, T199, T496	T182	T45, T478, T509, T510, T513, T516, T536, T537
parallel structure			T506, T534
parentheses		T77	T531
participial phrases			T504, T533, T541
personal pronouns	T72, T493	T21, T511, T512, T534	
possessive pronouns	T72, T492	T210, T513, T535	T517, T537

Scope and Sequence (continued)

Grammar, Usage, and Mechanics (cont.)	Grade 6	Grade 7	Grade 8
predicate nouns and adjectives	T389	T503, T532	T503, T533
prepositional phrases	T222–T223	T403	T226
prepositions		T403, T517, T536	T524, T539, T544
present perfect tense	T496		
pronoun antecedents	T296, T495	T210	T302
relative pronouns and adverbs	T297	T514, T535	T518, T537
run-on sentences	T22	T23, T24, T508, T533	T66
semicolons	T512	T330, T530, T541	T532, T542
sentence fragments	T22	T23, T24, T25	T66
subject and object pronouns	T172	T210, T211, T511, T512	T92, T303
subject and predicate	T22	T501, T532	T431
subject-verb agreement	T148, T505	T424–T425, T525, T538	T402–T403
superlative adjectives			T454
titles	T509	T183, T527, T540	T141
transitive and intransitive verbs		T521, T538	T522, T539
verb moods			T528, T541
verb tenses	T97, T434, T435, T496	T48, T49, T518, T519, T520, T536, T537, T538	T22, T326, T521, T538
verbals and verbal phrases	T149	T305, T402	T140, T227, T505, T514, T533, T536

Writing Modes and Genres			
Argument Essay	T278A–T299		T278A–T307
Argument Writing	T250A–T365	T262A–T381	T252–T379
Biographic Sketch/Biography	T76A–T101	T384A–T405	T48A–T71
Book Review/Report	T252A–T277		T122A–T145

	Grade 6	Grade 7	Grade 8
Writing Modes and Genres (cont.)			
Cause-and-Effect Report	T152A–T175	T134A–T155	
Descriptive Article	T416A–T437		
Descriptive Paragraph/Essay	T368A–T391	T428A–T455	T436A–T457
Descriptive Writing	T366A–T481	T382A–T499	T380A–T501
Editorial		T264A–T285	T254A–T277
E-Mail		T30A–T51	
Explanatory Essay	T204A–T227		T208A–T229
Eyewitness Account	T4A–T27		
Formal Proposal			T332A–T357
Geographic Description		T428A–T455	
Historical Episode	T28A–T53	T52A–T81	T26A–T47
How-To Essay			T180A–T207
Informative/Explanatory Writing	T124A–T249	T132A–T261	T120A–T251
Letters: Friendly, Business	T300A–T321	T286A–T309	T382A–T407
Literary Analysis		T336A–T359	
Memoir			T4A–T25
Narrative Writing	T2A–T123	T2A–T131	T2A–T119
Observation Report	T392A–T415	T406A–T427	T408A–T435
Personal Narrative		T4A–T29	
Play		T82A–T109	
Poem	T438A–T459	T456A–T477	T458A–T479
Problem-Solution Essay		T214A–T239	
Research Report	T176A–T203	T156A–T187	T146A–T179
Response to Literature	T252A–T277	T336A–T359	T122A–T145
Scientific Observation			T408A–T513
Short Story	T54A–T75		T72A–T97

Scope and Sequence (continued)

	Grade 6	Grade 7	Grade 8
Writing Modes and Genres (cont.)			
Speech	T322A–T343		T308A–T331
Summary	T126A–T151	T188A–T213	
Test Writing	T102A–T123, T228A–T249, T344A–T365, T460A–T481	T110A–T131, T240A–T261, T360A–T381, T478A–T499	T98A–T119, T230A–T251, T358A–T379, T480A–T501
Website Review		T310A–T335	
Graphic Organizers			
5 W's Chart	T15, T113	T17, T121	
Argument Map	T333	T297, T371	T319
Biography Map	T89		
Cause-and-Effect Chain	T165	T145	T421
Character Chart		T395	
Five-Senses Chart	T427		
Flow Chart			T345
Main-Idea Table		T41, T203	T395
Network Tree	T289, T355		
Observation Chart		T417, T489	
Order-of-Importance Organizer	T311		
Outline	T191	T171	T161, T219, T262, T369
Paragraph Organizer		T347	
Problem-Solution Frame		T227, T275	T267
Pro-and-Con Chart		T323	
Sequence Chain	T403		T193, T241
Spider Map	T139, T239, T380, T471		

	Grade 6	Grade 7	Grade 8
Graphic Organizers (cont.)			
Story Map/Frame	T41	T67, T95	T15, T37, T85, T109, T491
Storyboard	T65	T170	
Timeline			T59
Two-Column Chart			T133
Venn Diagram	T265		
Web	T215, T449	T441, T467	T447, T469
Listening and Speaking			
	T24, T50, T74, T98, T150, T174, T200, T224, T274, T320, T324, T390, T412, T436, T458	T26, T50, T104, T154, T184, T212, T236, T284, T306, T332, T356, T404, T426, T452, T476	T24, T46, T68, T94, T142, T176, T228, T276, T304, T328, T354, T404, T432, T456, T478
Publish & Presentation			
	T24, T50, T74, T98, T150, T174, T200, T224, T274, T298, T320, T324, T390, T412, T436, T458	T26, T50, T78, T104, T154, T184, T212, T236, T284, T306, T332, T356, T404, T426, T452, T476	T24, T46, T68, T94, T142, T176, T204, T228, T276, T304, T328, T354, T404, T432, T456, T478
Rubrics			
	Z10, T8–T13, T34–T39, T58–T63, T82–T87, T132–T137, T156, T161, T182–T187, T208, T213, T256–T261, T282–T287, T304–T309, T326–T331, T372–T377, T396–T401, T420–T425, T442–T447, T526–T529, T530–T533, T534–T537	Z10, T10–T15, T34–T39, T58–T63, T88–T93, T138–T143, T162–T167, T194–T199, T220–T225, T269–T273, T290–T295, T316–T321, T340–T345, T388–T393, T410–T415, T432–T437, T460–T465, T544–T547, T548–T551, T552–T555	Z10, T8–T13, T30–T35, T52–T57, T78–T83, T126–T131, T152–T157, T186–T191, T212–T217, T258–T263, T284–T289, T312–T317, T338–T343, T388–T393, T414–T419, T440–T445, T462–T467, T546–T549, T550–T553, T554–T557

Scope and Sequence (continued)

	Grade 6	Grade 7	Grade 8
Technology	Z7, T12, T25, T38, T51, T62, T75, T86, T99, T136, T151, T160, T175, T186, T201, T212, T225, T286, T299, T308, T321, T330, T343, T376, T391, T400, T413, T424, T437, T446, T459	Z7, T14, T27, T38, T51, T62, T79, T92, T105, T142, T155, T166, T185, T198, T213, T224, T237, T272, T285, T294, T307, T320, T333, T344, T357, T392, T405, T414, T427, T436, T453, T477	Z7, T12, T25, T34, T47, T56, T69, T82, T95, T130, T143, T156, T177, T190, T205, T216, T229, T262, T277, T288, T305, T316, T329, T342, T355, T392, T405, T418, T433, T444, T457, T466, T479
Text Exemplars	T4, T5, T28, T29, T54, T55, T76, T77, T102, T103, T126, T127, T152, T153, T176, T177, T204, T205, T228, T229, T252, T253, T278, T279, T300, T301, T322, T323, T344, T345, T368, T369, T392, T393, T416, T417, T438, T439, T460, T461	T4, T5, T30, T31, T52, T53, T82, T83, T110, T111, T134, T135, T156, T157, T188, T189, T214, T215, T240, T241, T264, T265, T286, T287, T310, T311, T336, T337, T360, T361, T384, T385, T406, T407, T428, T429, T456, T457, T478, T479	T4, T5, T26, T27, T48, T49, T72, T73, T98, T99, T122, T123, T146, T147, T180, T181, T208, T209, T230, T231, T254, T255, T278, T279, T308, T309, T332, T333, T358, T359, T382, T383, T408, T409, T436, T437, T458, T459, T480, T481
Traits	Z8, T6, T30, T56, T78, T104, T128, T154, T178, T206, T230, T254, T280, T302, T324, T346, T370, T394, T418, T440, T462	Z8, T6, T32, T54, T84, T112, T136, T158, T190, T216, T242, T266, T288, T312, T338, T362, T386, T408, T430, T458, T480	Z8, T6, T28, T50, T73, T100, T124, T148, T182, T210, T232, T256, T280, T310, T334, T359, T384, T410, T438, T460, T482

	Grade 6	Grade 7	Grade 8
Writing Across the Curriculum			
	Z17, T76A–T101, T204A–T227, T322A–T343, T438A–T459	Z17, T82A–T109, T214A–T239, T336A–T359, T428A–T455	Z17, T72A–T97, T208A–T229, T332A–T357, T458A–T479
Writing Process			
Prewrite	T14, T15, T40, T64, T65, T88, T89, T110–T115, T138–T141, T162–T165, T187–T191, T214, T215, T236–T241, T262–T265, T288, T289, T310, T311, T332, T333, T352–T357, T378–T381, T402, T403, T426, T427, T448, T449, T468–T473	T40, T41, T64–T67, T94, T95, T118–T123, T144, T145, T168–T171, T200–T203, T226, T227, T248–T253, T274, T275, T296, T297, T322, T323, T346, T347, T368–T373, T394, T395, T416, T417, T438–T441, T466, T467, T486–T491	T14, T15, T36, T37, T58, T59, T84, T85, T106–T111, T132, T133, T158–T163, T192, T193, T218, T219, T238–T243, T265–T267, T290–T293, T318, T319, T344, T345, T366–T371, T394, T395, T420, T421, T446, T447, T468, T469, T488–T493
Draft	T16–T17, T42–T43, T66–T67, T90–T91, T116–T117, T142–T143, T166–T167, T192–T193, T216–T217, T242–T243, T266–T267, T290–T291, T312–T313, T334–T335, T358, T359, T382–T383, T404–T405, T428–T429, T450–T451, T474–T475	T18–T19, T42–T43, T68–T71, T96–T97, T124–T125, T146–T147, T172–T175, T204–T205, T228–T229, T254–T255, T276–T277, T298–T299, T324–T325, T348–T349, T374–T375, T396–T397, T418–T419, T442–T445, T468–T469, T492–T493	T16–T17, T38–T39, T60–T61, T86–T87, T112–T113, T134, T135, T165–T167, T194–T195, T220–T221, T244–T245, T268–T269, T294–T297, T320–T321, T346–T347, T372–T373, T396–T397, T422–T425, T448–T449, T470–T471, T494, T495

Scope and Sequence (continued)

	Grade 6	Grade 7	Grade 8
Writing Process (cont.)			
Revise	T18–T20, T44–T46, T68–T70, T92–T94, T118–T120, T144, T146, T168–T170, T194–T196, T218–T220, T244–T246, T268, T270, T292–T294, T314, T316, T336–T338, T360–T362, T384–T386, T406–T408, T430–T432, T452–T454, T476–T478	T20–T22, T44–T46, T72–T74, T98–T100, T126–T128, T148–T150, T176–T180, T206–T208, T230–T232, T256–T258, T278–T280, T300–T302, T326–T328, T350–T352, T376–T378, T398–T400, T420–T422, T446–T448, T470–T472, T494–T496	T18–T20, T40–T42, T62–T64, T88–T90, T114–T116, T136–T138, T168–T172, T196–T200, T222–T224, T246–T248, T270–T272, T298–T300, T322–T324, T348–T350, T374–T376, T398–T400, T426–T428, T450–T452, T472–T474, T496–T498
Edit	T21, T47, T71, T95, T121–T122, T147, T171, T197, T221, T247–T248, T271, T295, T317, T339, T363–T364, T387, T409, T433, T455, T479–T480	T23, T47, T75, T101, T129–T130, T151, T181, T209, T233, T259–T260, T281, T303, T329, T353, T379–T380, T401, T423, T449, T473, T497–T498	T21, T43, T65, T91, T117–T118, T139, T173, T201, T225, T249–T250, T273, T301, T325, T351, T377–T378, T401, T429, T453, T475, T499–T500
Publish	T24, T50, T74, T98, T150, T174, T200, T224, T274, T298, T320, T342, T390, T412, T346, T458	T26, T50, T78, T104, T154, T184, T212, T236, T284, T306, T332, T356, T404, T426, T452, T476	T24, T46, T68, T94, T142, T176, T228, T276, T304, T328, T354, T404, T432, T456, T478

Index